C

7
IRISH PLAYS

SEVEN IRISH PLAYS

1946

1964

edited, with an introduction by

Goode

ROBERT HOGAN

///

UNIVERSITY OF MINNESOTA PRESS

Minneapolis

Library of Congress Catalog Card Number: 67-20594

PUBLISHED IN GREAT BRITAIN, INDIA, AND PAKISTAN BY THE OXFORD UNIVERSITY PRESS, LONDON, BOMBAY, AND KARACHI, AND IN CANADA BY THE COPP CLARK PUBLISHING CO. LIMITED, TORONTO

♣ TABLE OF CONTENTS ♣

7
IRISH PLAYS

IRISH PLAYS

♣ PULL BACK THE GREEN CURTAINS ♣

SEAN O'CASEY'S last long play was called *Behind the Green Curtains*, and that is also an apt phrase for the recent Irish drama. Devotees of the theater are well informed of the Beckett-Ionesco-Artaud theater of the absurd that emanates from Paris, they are aware of the late Bertolt Brecht's still magnificent Berliner Ensemble from East Germany, they know the exciting developments of the post-Osborne theatre in London, and they even know the latest innocuous developments in New York. But what has happened recently on the Irish stage seems for the rest of the world to have been played behind a green curtain that is impenetrably thick. Save for a stray explosion or two by Brendan Behan, little has been heard from Ireland in the last thirty or forty years. What was once with beautiful accuracy called the Irish dramatic renaissance is now apparently with Yeats in his grave.

But only apparently. In reality, the new drama of Ireland is as rich as drama being written anywhere else in the world. The reason so little has been heard of it is more a matter of theatrical economics than of dramatic merit. Probably something more than ninety per cent of the international repertoire of modern plays is drawn from the commercial stages of London, Paris, Berlin, and New York. A new play produced in Dublin or San Francisco or Sydney or Mexico City has about as much chance of gaining a lasting niche in that repertoire as a Fourth of July pageant produced by the local high school in Ozark, Alabama. This fact is deplorable and unhealthy, but it is also one of the facts of theatrical life.

This volume is an attempt to call attention to some dramatic writing that has been ignored by the major commercial stages of the world and

3

that is, therefore, largely unknown. The book is a selection of some of the best plays written in Ireland since the end of the Second World War. Only one of the authors represented here is much known outside of Ireland, and he, Bryan MacMahon, is known for his fiction rather than for his plays. Only three of the plays here have been previously published, and those only in Ireland in acting editions. Despite this record, all of these men are richly talented writers. One proof of that point is, I think, that this book would have suffered no diminution in quality had they been represented by other plays than these here. And, without meaning to disparage the work of these fine playwrights, I think that this book would also have suffered no diminution in quality had it contained plays by six other new Irish playwrights.

I am saying, in other words, that the new drama of Ireland is still vital. The Irish renaissance is not with Yeats in his grave, and O'Casey did not drop it into the Irish Sea as he crossed over to England in 1926, saying "Inishfallen, Fare Thee Well." Let us pull back the green curtains and see just how vital it has always been.

☘

Around the turn of the century there was a magnificent cultural explosion in the small, wet, green island directly west of England. For years and years before, this island, Ireland, had quietly exported its great writers to its sister isle to the east, and there they had promptly become some of the major adornments of English literature. But around 1900, after the great national traumas of the Famine and the Parnell debacle, Ireland was moving, this time inexorably, toward its national independence. There was a great ferment of national feeling, and it was to culminate in the Easter Rising of 1916.

Around 1900, however, that fervent nationalism took several forms. There was a purely political aspect of it, embodied both in Ireland's legal representatives to the English parliament and in the secret Irish Republican Brotherhood. There was an increased sense of national identity that appeared most lastingly and dramatically in the Gaelic League and the fine, quixotic struggle to revive the dying Irish language. And, finally, there was the suddenly awakened realization that Ireland had a great mythic past and a rich untapped present, both offering exciting new subjects for the Irish dramatist.

Such literary wild geese as Congreve, Farquhar, Goldsmith, Sheridan, and Wilde had adopted a basically English subject matter and English literary modes. In the last half of the nineteenth century, the prolific Dion Boucicault did turn to Ireland for the subject matter of about six plays. But the treatment of Irish problems in *The Colleen Bawn, Arrah-na-Pogue, The Shaughraun, The Amadan, The Rapparee*, and *The O'Dowd* was too rosily romantic, too Walt Disneyish, to be anything more than stirring or nostalgic entertainment for Irish emigrants in England and America.

It was really only with the formation of the Irish Literary Theatre by W. B. Yeats, Edward Martyn, and George Moore in the closing years of the century that Irish playwrights began to write in an Irish way about Ireland and for Ireland. Some of the first attempts — the Moore-Martyn *The Bending of the Bough*, for example — were little more than awkward imitations of an outmoded English stagecraft flavored with a mild dash of provincial Ibsenism. Some others, like Alice Milligan's *The Last Feast of the Fianna* or Douglas Hyde's *Casadh an tSúgáin* (later translated as *The Twisting of the Rope*) were definitely Irish but just as definitely slight.

After three seasons, Moore and Martyn dropped out of the movement, and the Irish Literary Theatre was disbanded. From its strong initiating impulse, though, arose the Irish National Theatre Society whose guiding spirits were ultimately Yeats, Lady Augusta Gregory, and, for too short a time, John Synge. The Society was fortunate in discovering a writer of genius like Synge and a prolific first-rate talent like Lady Gregory, and it also discovered fine realistic work in the powerful tragedies of young Padraic Colum and the popular comedies of William Boyle. It was equally fortunate in drawing to it a rarely talented group of young Irish actors, so that it no longer had to depend on players imported from England. Chief among these early actors were Frank and Willie Fay who became, respectively, the Abbey's first voice coach and its first real stage director. And also among the early members were such subsequently distinguished players as Sara Allgood, her sister Maire O'Neill, Dudley Digges, Mary Walker, and Arthur Sinclair. Even more important for the group's survival was the Englishwoman Miss Annie Horniman, a friend of Yeats, who gave the theater its first real home, the renovated old Mechanics Theatre in Abbey Street, and whose subsidy kept the theater alive during its difficult early years.

The world outside Ireland first became aware that something fresh and vigorous was stirring in the drama when the group journeyed to London for two performances on Saturday, May 2, 1903. But the Abbey drew its greatest publicity from the celebrated 1907 riots over Synge's masterpiece

5

The Playboy of the Western World. After this famous furor, the little theater was generally recognized as one of the first of the world.

Yet even now it is not quite realized outside of Ireland just how fine the early Abbey repertoire was. The literate world knows the work of Synge and Yeats and Lady Gregory (although to my mind it rather overvalues Yeats's plays and undervalues Lady Gregory's), but it hardly realizes that Padraic Colum's early writing culminated in one grim, *Lear*-like, realistic masterpiece, *Thomas Muskerry.* It probably does not yet realize how fine were the talents of those two young men from Cork, T. C. Murray and Lennox Robinson. Murray was a painstaking master of tragic structure whose best plays slowly but inevitably rise to a shattering conclusion. His *Autumn Fire,* to take but one example, does not suffer in the least from comparison with O'Neill's similar *Desire Under the Elms.* The urbane and prolific Lennox Robinson was closely associated with the Abbey for forty years, and he was to prove as deft in smiling comedy as he was probing in serious drama. Fifty years has not dimmed the effectiveness of his delightful comedy *The Whiteheaded Boy,* and his serious plays, like *The Lost Leader, The Big House,* and *Killycreggs in Twilight,* are still examples of realism at its intelligent best.

Finally among these early Abbey writers is one who may yet rank with Synge — that lonely genius George Fitzmaurice, all of whose works have even now not been produced or published. But in pieces like *The Dandy Dolls, The Magic Glasses, The Enchanted Land,* and *The Ointment Blue,* Fitzmaurice displayed a dialogue as ripe as Synge's, an imagination as inventively grotesque, and a thematic wryness uniquely his own. He wrote three times as many plays as did Synge, and, like Synge, he wrote masterpieces.

Fitzmaurice's last Abbey play appeared in 1923, shortly before the production of Sean O'Casey's first Abbey play, *The Shadow of a Gunman.* *The Gunman* is the fifth most performed in the theater's history, and it was followed a year later by the theater's second most performed play, O'Casey's *Juno and the Paycock.* Then, two years later, in 1926, O'Casey completed his Dublin trilogy with his early masterpiece and the theater's most performed play, *The Plough and the Stars.* These three plays made a profound impression. They treated with startling vividness an area of Dublin life, the slums, that had barely been touched upon before. At the same time, they contained some of the most hilarious comic scenes ever written for the Abbey and some of the most poignantly felt and bitterly moving tragedy. And, further, the abrupt juxtapositions of comedy and tragedy in the plays added a memorable dimension of savage and unforgettable irony.

Despite its subsequent popularity, the initial performances of *The Plough and the Stars* precipitated the Abbey's second major riots when a group of patriotic ladies, with the memory of 1916 fresh in their minds, led a protest against the play. Now that nationalist passions have cooled, even the Irish have seen the justness of what W. B. Yeats bellowed from the stage of the Abbey to the enraged audience:

You have disgraced yourselves again. Is this to be an ever-recurring celebration of the arrival of Irish genius? Synge first and then O'Casey. The news of the happenings of the last few minutes will go from country to country. Dublin has once more rocked the cradle of genius. From such a scene in this theatre went forth the fame of Synge. Equally the fame of O'Casey is born here tonight. This is his apotheosis.

Shortly after the riots, O'Casey left for England. Then in 1928, the Abbey refused his experimental play *The Silver Tassie*, and an acrimonious argument was waged in the public press. The effect of this rebuff was the further alienation of O'Casey from both Ireland and the Abbey.

To most people, the great days of the Irish drama ended when O'Casey left for England, and relatively little is known outside of Ireland of its still hardily flourishing drama. It is generally thought that the Abbey — with Synge and Lady Gregory and then Yeats dead, with Fitzmaurice neglected and O'Casey gone, with St. John Ervine devoting himself mainly to the English stage, and with Frank O'Connor being cashiered from the Abbey board — had sunk into a rut of imitative kitchen comedies modeled upon the broad early work of George Shiels. Still, even in the 1930's and 1940's, an occasional dramatist, such as Paul Vincent Carroll or Denis Johnston, would break through the green curtains to become known internationally. And still there was much estimable and memorable new work appearing only on Dublin's stages.

An idea of the best that was being written may be gathered from the contents of Curtis Canfield's indispensable anthology of 1936, *Plays of Changing Ireland*. Canfield included Yeats's *The Words Upon the Window-Pane*, George Shiels's *The New Gossoon*, Lennox Robinson's *Church Street*, and Rutherford Mayne's *Bridge Head*, all produced by the Abbey, as well as Denis Johnston's *The Old Lady Says "No!"*, Lord Longford's

Yahoo, Lady Longford's *Mr. Jiggins of Jigginstown*, and Mary Manning's *"Youth's the Season — ?"*, all produced by the Gate.

In the 1930's the Abbey was a bit overshadowed by the eclectic staging methods of the Dublin Gate Theatre, which was formed in 1928 by Hilton Edwards and Micheál Mac Liammóir. Yet the four Abbey plays in Canfield's collection show that the theater was still producing sound work. Yeats's play, although untypically in prose, is one of his strongest and most admired late pieces; Robinson's is a fascinating Pirandellian experiment with realism; Shiels's is a really adroit realistic comedy of Ulster; and Mayne's is still one of the most thoughtful examples of serious realism that the Abbey ever produced. Murray, Ervine, and Brinsley MacNamara still contributed an occasional fine piece to the Abbey, and the 1930's also saw the emergence of the brilliant and combative writing of Paul Vincent Carroll as well as the quiet and delicate work of Teresa Deevy. The theater hardly encouraged Miss Deevy as much as it should have; it foolishly rejected Carroll's fine *The White Steed* and ignored his later work including excellent pieces like *The Old Foolishness, Green Cars Go East*, and *The Devil Came from Dublin*. Still, it did produce such superb dramas as Miss Deevy's *Katie Roche* and Carroll's *Shadow and Substance*.

At the same time, the theater continued to produce the many plays of George Shiels, who was growing farther and farther away from the broad comedies which had first made his reputation. His later work like the long-running *The Rugged Path* and *The Passing Day* took on an increasing subtlety of technique and a disconcerting wryness of tone.

In these years, it is true, the Abbey produced some trivial work, but it still got a large number of excellent scripts. What really harmed its reputation was not its plays but its methods of production — a laxness of direction, a growing tendency to play for broad effects, and a lack of imagination that held it bound by the tightest confines of photographic realism. Some of the dourest plays of Shiels were twisted almost out of recognition by actors striving for every conceivable easy laugh. Sean O'Faolain noticed the same tendency when his highly literate comedy *She Had To Do Something* was, after a week on the Abbey stage, transformed into a broad farce.

The Gate Theatre appeared all the more impressive by contrast. Edwards and Mac Liammóir were firmly committed to the notion of doing plays, not in one particular style, but in whatever style the play itself demanded. The range of plays they chose from the world's dramatic literature went from *Faust* to *Back to Methuselah* and from *Oedipus Rex* to

Ten Nights in a Bar Room. The patrons of the Gate saw many dramatic modes, many styles of acting, and stage settings that ranged from a Moscow Art Theatre literalism to the most imaginative stylization. Edwards was a brilliant and painstaking director as well as a fine character actor; Mac Liammóir was a remarkable romantic actor as well as a superb designer of sets and costumes. The company contained many good players, the most famous later being perhaps James Mason, Orson Welles, Peggy Cummins, Geraldine Fitzgerald, and Cyril Cusack.

The Gate presented a well-rounded program from the dramatic literature of the world, and therefore staged fewer original Irish plays than did the Abbey. Still, it did stage new plays by such veteran Abbey writers as Colum, Robinson, MacNamara, and Murray; it did produce poetic plays by Yeats, Austin Clarke, and Donagh MacDonagh; and it even developed a small stable of its own writers, the most important of which were Denis Johnston, Mary Manning, Lord and Lady Longford, Maura Laverty, and Mac Liammóir himself.

Denis Johnston is one of the most intelligent of Irish playwrights; indeed, he is probably so intelligent that his best works — that dazzling expressionistic indictment of modern Ireland *The Old Lady Says "No!"* or those thoughtful pieces of straight realism like *The Moon in the Yellow River* and *The Scythe and the Sunset* — are probably too tough for the conventional stage. He is intelligent enough, however, to have learned a great deal about theatrical necessity; so such later works as his delightful farce *The Golden Cuckoo*, his brutal Swiftean tragedy *The Dreaming Dust*, and his provocative courtroom drama *Strange Occurrence on Ireland's Eye* are as playable as they are, at least among plays, profound.

Mary Manning was barely out of her teens when her first plays were done by the Gate and Mac Liammóir remarked that her "brain, nimble and observant as it was, could not yet keep pace with a tongue so caustic that even her native city . . . was a little in awe of her." That incisive perception and satiric wit were beautifully evident in *"Youth's the Season — ?"* which still comes near to being the most sophisticated and yet poignant study of young people to come out of modern Dublin.

Mac Liammóir has written a good deal for the stage, including adaptations, translations, and pageants, but his best work is his original blending of Gothic fantasy and drawing-room comedy in such charming pieces as *Ill Met by Moonlight* and *Where Stars Walk*. With such writers as these and David Sears and Maura Laverty and Robert Collis, the Gate, until at least about 1950, probably equaled the Abbey in the quality of its original

9

plays, and there can be no doubt that it surpassed the Abbey in the polish of its productions.

The most important offshoot of the Gate was Longford Productions. Edward Arthur Henry Pakenham, the sixth Earl of Longford, had been the financial savior of the Gate in its early days, and the theater had presented some of his plays and some by his wife, Christine. In 1936, Longford broke away from the Gate and organized his own company which thereafter divided the theater with Edwards and Mac Liammóir, each group taking the building for half a year. The Longford Company was not so brilliant a one as the Gate, but until Lord Longford's death, on February 4, 1961, the company reputably produced a large number of classic plays and English comedies that Dublin would hardly otherwise have seen.

The original plays the company produced were mainly those of Lord and Lady Longford. The most interesting of Longford's own plays is *Yahoo*, a version of the Swift story. In most ways, *Yahoo* does not measure up to Johnston's *The Dreaming Dust*, but the expressionistic conclusion is eminently theatrical. Lady Longford was a more prolific playwright and an extremely polished one. Her plays fall easily into three pigeonholes: adaptations of novels such as *Pride and Prejudice* and *The Absentee*, chronicle plays of Irish history, and gently satiric comedies of contemporary Irish life. The comedies are undoubtedly her forte, and in ones like *Mr. Jiggins of Jigginstown* and *The Hill of Quirke* she contrives to be deliciously accurate about the foibles of Irish life and yet, in a very un-Irish way, unmalicious. Really, Longford Productions would have justified itself had it produced no one but Lady Longford.

⚜

No laudatory paragraph is needed about the plays of W. B. Yeats, for enthusiastic academic critics have described him as "one of the most conscious craftsmen the theatre has ever known" and "one of its most successful artists." One of his plays is said to contain "one of the great *coups de théâtre* of the twentieth century" and another is described as "one of the most shattering experiences that the modern theatre has to offer." This seems to me exaggerated praise, as if the legitimate enthusiasm for his poetry had become a bit misplaced. Still, Yeats had an occasional success on the stage, and his forty years of experimentation with poetic drama might seem to have laid down a path for other poetic dramatists to follow.

Largely, however, neither other poets nor Yeats's own theater was converted to poetic drama. There have been few later practitioners of the verse play in Ireland, none that closely followed Yeats's example, and only one of great merit.

The best regarded, although not I think the best, Irish poetic dramatist since Yeats is Austin Clarke. Although he doubtless considers himself primarily a poet, Clarke probably qualifies as a man of letters, in the best sense of the term. He has written much poetry, a bookful of plays, several novels, and a large amount of literary journalism. Also, in 1940, Clarke and Robert Farren, a poet and verse dramatist and at present an Abbey director, founded the Dublin Verse Speaking Society which performed verse plays every week over Radio Éireann. From this group, Clarke then formed the Lyric Theatre Company which rented the Abbey for one or two weeks during the year to do a program of verse plays. Clarke kept this group together for several years and produced interesting verse plays by Gordon Bottomly, Laurence Binyon, T. Sturge Moore, T. S. Eliot, and Archibald MacLeish, as well as Irish plays by himself, Yeats, Donagh MacDonagh, and George Fitzmaurice.

Admittedly, Clarke did yeoman service for the drama in Dublin, but I am still no enthusiast for his own plays. His farces and comedies seem to lack much sense of what theatrical humor is. The poetic dialogue of all of his plays is technically adroit and often a fascinatingly intricate adaptation of some Gaelic device to English verse. Usually, though, Clarke's dialogue seems to me to function no better than the dialogue of *The Cocktail Party*, which may have some loose validity as poetry on the printed page, but which is indistinguishable from prose when spoken on the stage.

In justice to Clarke, I should admit, however, that his *The Plot Succeeds*, produced by the Lyric Theatre Company in February, 1950, really does succeed as an amusing farce. I should also admit that many critics regard his poetic dramas very highly.

Donagh MacDonagh's *Happy As Larry* is one of the best-known verse plays of recent years. Originally produced by Clarke's Lyric Theatre Company, it has also been seen in London and twice in New York, and has been included in a Penguin in company with verse plays by Eliot, Christopher Fry, and Charles Williams. MacDonagh is a Dublin district justice and the son of the 1916 poet Thomas MacDonagh. His other verse plays include *God's Gentry*, a ballad opera first produced by the Belfast Arts Theatre in August, 1951; *Lady Spider*, another dramatization of the Deirdre story; and *Step-in-the-Hollow*, a comedy produced by the Gate on March 11, 1957 and later published in a Penguin.

MacDonagh is a difficult playwright to discuss, for his verse varies considerably from play to play, not only in its quality but also in what he apparently wants it to do. The two published plays are comedies, and to my mind little more successful than the comedies of Clarke. The one offers a kind of mild fantasy, the other a kind of boisterous horseplay, and both seem remarkably loose as poetry — flat in diction and longwinded when they should be tightly witty. The two unpublished plays are better. The verse of the ballad opera about tinkers is not distinguished, but the songs lift the piece into considerable theatrical life. The Deirdre play is a more realistic rendering than other versions, but the plot is well built and the characters better drawn than what one has come to expect from a verse play. The language is simple, conversational, even sometimes colloquial. Though it occasionally sounds like prose, it sounds like good prose. Its poetic quality resides mainly in a frequent use of metaphor and image, but never enough metaphor and image to harm the basic muscularity of the language. The dialogue is less beautiful than that of the AE, Yeats, or Synge versions, but it probably would work better on the stage. Indeed, most of MacDonagh's verse, even in its limp moments, would probably be better stage speech than the poetry of Clarke.

Although it will be counted an eccentric view by fervent Yeatsians who have never heard of Padraic Fallon, I think that Fallon is the only verse dramatist of Ireland to have written a theatrical masterpiece. In fact, I think that he has written two. In this age of high-pressure advertising, when "excellent" means "not immoderately dull" and "stupendous" means "rather good," a critic should use terms like "masterpiece" with considerable reluctance. However, if the term fits the work of any recent Irish writer, it must definitely be assigned to the two best verse plays of Fallon.

Fallon is little known outside of Ireland, although a few of his poems usually turn up in anthologies of Irish verse. If his name is not, like Shelley's, writ in water, it is at least writ in that equally tenuous element, air, for all of his plays were written to be performed over Radio Éireann, and none has been published. According to Micheál Ó h Aodha who has directed many of them, Fallon's best plays are *Diarmuid and Grainne* and *The Vision of Mac Conglinne*. Probably neither could be staged unless in the simplest and most stylized fashion or in the most complicated and expensive. Yet neither way would do justice to the plays, for both are really wrought for the ear. It is not only that the words are alternately beautiful and cunningly witty, but also that even the visual spectacle of uncostumed actors speaking the lines on a bare stage would detract from the bold vistas the words alone conjure up in the imagination.

Both plays are drawn from Irish legend. *Diarmuid and Grainne* is basically a serious play, and *The Vision of Mac Conglinne*, which Clarke treated more pallidly in his *The Son of Learning*, is mainly a comedy. Both have been modernized, Freudianized, Jungianized, and, above all, Fallonized by an imaginative scope (*pace* to the Joyce industry) unique in Irish letters. It is not only that Fallon can rise to a vastness of scene and make his characters take on an elemental intensity, but also that the quality of the imagination is so various, so vivid, so fertile, and so fresh. The control of language is that of a virtuoso. Fallon can move from a tight formality to a supple simplicity: he can, for instance, move from a charming romantic lyric to a dazzling display of puns.

This description must sound like mere uncritical enthusiasm. It is not really, for there are things wrong with Fallon's plays — primarily their length. The two best are too long. Still, when his plays are measured against the best work of his better known colleagues, a judicious restraint is hard to maintain. And, although the pieces were written for radio, there is more drama in them than in ninety per cent of the grey, sapless, lifeless things that occasionally are heralded for a season or two as the advance guard of a renaissance of poetry in the drama.

♣

The chief Abbey playwright of the 1940's was Louis D'Alton, the son of an old Shakespearean actor and an actor himself as well as a director and producer and probably the most thoroughly professional playwright who had yet appeared in Ireland. Without striving for the heights or reaching for the depths of feeling, D'Alton's plays have an impressively uniform competence, and if that seem faint praise it is not meant to be. Although at bottom a realistic playwright, he successfully attempted comedy, tragedy, farce, fantasy, the historical portrait, and the Shavian discussion drama. Plays like *Lovers Meeting* and *The Money Doesn't Matter* are among the most successful revivals in recent Abbey history, and his engrossingly witty *This Other Eden* may take its place with Shaw's *John Bull's Other Island* and O'Casey's *Purple Dust* as a definitive dramatic statement about Anglo-Irish relations.

Since the end of the war, the Abbey has been under constant fire from critics, theater buffs, men of letters, and even just men in the street. Their main target has been the theater's managing director Ernest Blythe. Though it is true that Mr. Blythe has been a far from adventurous leader, he has points in his favor. At any rate, it seems fruitless to rehash here what will shortly be only an academic question for historians of the theater. It seems more important to note that the postwar Abbey, even under Mr. Blythe, has developed at least five first-rate talents and given intermittent encouragement to at least as many more.

On April 26, 1943, Michael J. Molloy's first Abbey play, *Old Road*, was produced. On February 11, 1946, Walter Macken was first represented at the Abbey with *Mungo's Mansion*. In March, 1949, Bryan Mac-Mahon's *The Bugle in the Blood* was first produced. In April, 1950, Seamus Byrne's *Design for a Headstone* was performed, and in January, 1954, John O'Donovan's first Abbey play, *The Half-Millionaire.*

These five men, appearing in little more than a decade, have each written at least two plays that will bear comparison with all but the best work of Synge, Fitzmaurice, and O'Casey himself. Indeed, it might be fairly said that the Abbey in the sixty-five years of its distinguished existence could hardly have boasted, at any one time, of another five men of equal excellence.

All of the five but Macken are represented and discussed later in this volume, but Macken himself strongly warrants a word here. He is not only a popular and powerful writer of fiction, but he is eminently a man of the theater. He served his apprenticeship in the Taibhdhearc, the Gaelic-speaking theatre of Galway, and in the nine years of his principal connection there he was responsible for directing perhaps two hundred plays. Besides directing, he is one of the better realistic actors in the country. He acted much in Galway and also a couple of seasons in Dublin with the Abbey. He got excellent notices on his New York appearances in Molloy's *The King of Friday's Men* and also as the father in his own strong, dour *Home Is the Hero*. His published plays include *Mungo's Mansion, Home Is the Hero* (Abbey, July 1952), *Vacant Possession*, and *Twilight of a Warrior* (Abbey, November 1955). His most recent work to be seen in Dublin was *The Voices of Doolin* produced by Cyril Cusack during the 1960 Theatre Festival.

His early plays are O'Casey-like accounts of life in the Galway slums. Although they never quite rise from melodrama into tragedy, they contain some broadly boisterous comedy, and the dialogue often has a vehement intensity. *Home Is the Hero* is a fine, if curiously sullen family play, but *Twilight of a Warrior* is one of the strongest dramatic comments upon recent Irish political history. His recent *Voices of Doolin* is a complex and agonized portrait of a drunkard that reconfirms one's impression that Macken has been moving steadily away from broad theatricality toward an ever-deepening delineation of character. He is a vigorous man, probably still at the height of his powers, and anything else that he writes should be worth close attention.

Among the better recent Abbey plays is John Murphy's very popular *The Country Boy*, which was produced on May 11, 1959 (the Group Theatre in Belfast had given the premiere of the play on April 7). The piece treats the old problems of emigration and rural marriages, and makes a fairly serious contrast of the Irish and American ways of life. Despite a somewhat stacked deck which makes America come off as a chrome-plated jungle that kills the spirit of man and Ireland appear rather like a Bord Failte travel poster, the play contains some telling satire, some probing characterization, and some excellent roles for actors. Although not, to my mind, quite up to the Abbey standards of Ervine, Robinson, and Rutherford Mayne, *The Country Boy* works well in the theater and is more thoughtful than most plays. Murphy is a Mayo man whose second play was rejected by the Abbey and who has since emigrated to Canada.

The most promising recent Abbey discovery is Tom Coffey, four of whose pieces the Abbey has presented in the last few years. *The Long Sorrow* is a workmanlike one-act about the I.R.A.'s occasional flurries along the border. *Anyone Could Rob a Bank* is a frequently revived farce, and *Stranger, Beware*, the best of the lot, is both an engrossing murder melodrama and a thoughtful comment upon village life in the more isolated areas of the West. *The Call*, which was produced on March 14, 1966, is "a comedy of family life in a small southwestern town." I have not yet read or seen it, but Coffey regards it as a rather thin piece.

His best plays to date are *Them*, first produced by Orion Productions in November, 1963, and *Gone Tomorrow*, which won the Irish Life Drama Award for 1965 and was then presented during the 1965 Theatre Festival. *Them* is a beautifully restrained yet intensely moving play about a twenty-one-year-old imbecile and his family's terrible problem of what to do with him. *Gone Tomorrow* is an effective coming-of-age story written in a considerably lower emotional key than *Them*. Its easy and simultaneous use of several different acting areas indicates that Coffey has liberated himself from the box set and can handle the freer realism of the best recent drama. Coffey is a fast and prolific writer and somewhat uneven. The unevenness is not in quality, for his plays usually do exactly what he wants them to. The problem is that he does not always want them to do very much. His best work, however, is exciting stuff.

The outlook for the Abbey appears brighter at this moment than it has for years. The new, excellently equipped theater in Abbey Street is finally, after the company's fifteen year exile in the Queen's, completed, and a large advisory board composed mainly of experienced theater people has been appointed, apparently to keep the directors from getting too stodgy. I, myself, in those moments when I can resist an Irish temptation to damn for the delight of damning, do not think that the Abbey was ever so totally bereft of good work as has been frequently charged. In the thirties, the forties, and the fifties, the theater has always found at least a few fine plays. Its past does not look, to a judicious view, at all bad, and its future looks immensely promising.

♣

Some of the better new playwrights have made their mark without much help from the Abbey, the Gate, the Theatre Festival, or the more adventurous commercial managements such as Orion, Gemini, or the now defunct Globe. Among these men must be included such well known names as Brendan Behan and John B. Keane, as well as some others unknown outside Ireland and insufficiently appreciated there. I have in mind particularly such disparate talents as Seamus de Burca, Gerard Healy, and Maurice Meldon.

Seamus de Burca is the Irish pen name of Jimmy Bourke, one of the seven sons of P. J. Bourke, a former manager of the Queen's and a writer of Boucicault-like melodramas, who founded what his sons have developed into a small theatrical empire. Despite such impressive relatives as his uncle Peadar Kearney, the author of the Irish national anthem, and his cousins the Behan brothers, de Burca has written under the shadow of old-fashioned Queen's melodrama. Certainly his own rousing adaptation of Kickham's novel *Knocknagow* helped to foster the notion that he too was a belated son of Boucicault. Actually, he has been a slow-developing writer, and his early plays written in the 1930's were largely imitative and negligible. Recently his work has been done by semi-professional groups at the Gate, and both *Limpid River* (first produced on June 11, 1956) and *The Howards* (first produced on February 16, 1959) are exceptionally fine realistic family plays. *The Howards* has a venomous ferocity to it, and Mrs. Howard is as strong a role for a middle-aged woman as has been written since Brinsley MacNamara's *Margaret Gillan*. *Limpid River* is an equally engrossing but more lovingly drawn portrait, this time of a lower-middle-class Dublin family in 1919. The piece has one of the best male character roles of recent years, that of a Queen's theater actor of the old school with a seedy appearance, a grand manner, a booming voice, and an infinite capacity for drink. De Burca is an uneven writer, but Dublin has yet to realize that his two best plays are consummate theater.

Gerard Healy, who died in London in 1963 while playing the Jesuit preacher in Hugh Leonard's Joyce adaptation *Stephen D*, was a stage manager with the Gate, an actor for the Abbey and Radio Éireann, and one of the founders of the short-lived Players' Theatre. He wrote only two plays, but both are excellent. *Thy Dear Father*, performed at the Abbey on August 30, 1943, is a realistic study of religious hysteria and a courageous indictment of hyper-piety. The psychological change in the main character is probably a bit more stage-real than psychologically plausible, but the play is deftly done, honest, and strong. His other play, *The Black Stranger*, was first put on by the Players' Theatre at the Opera House, Cork, on February 26, 1945. The play tells of the destruction of two families in 1846 and 1847, during the potato famine. Like *Thy Dear Father*, the play is simple, terse, without artifice. Although Healy's frightening subject helps him to gain his effect, the play is a powerful accomplishment that could hardly fail, given a halfway adequate performance, to disturb its audience deeply.

Though Maurice Meldon was only thirty-two when he died in a traffic accident in 1958, he was already regarded by many theatergoers as "the most exciting new voice in the Irish theatre." After his play *Song of the Parakeet* won a Radio Éireann competition in 1950, the Abbey accepted his *House under Green Shadows* and produced it for a week in February, 1951, and that play was chosen by a Dublin newspaper as the best of the year. The Abbey accepted but never produced his next piece, *The Halcyon Horseman*, and his last productions were by the 37 Theatre Club which performed his *Aisling* and his *The Purple Path to the Poppy Field*. His last play, *No Moon for the Hunter*, a version of the Diarmuid and Grainne story, was rejected by the Abbey.

Only three of Meldon's plays have been published. *House under Green Shadows* is the most conventional and has been much admired. Although it may play strongly, this story of the decay of a Big House reads like a rather overwritten and florid melodrama. *Aisling*, which means "The Vision," is an expressionistic treatment of recent Irish history, and in tone and technique is reminiscent of Johnston's *The Old Lady Says "No!"* Like Johnston's play, this excellent piece would not work well outside Ireland, for it requires a knowledge of Irish history and literature that most audiences do not have. Nevertheless, the play contains not only fine parodies, but also poignant situations involving characters that, even more than in Johnston, become humans rather than symbols. It is a wry and salutary comment. Still primarily of Irish interest, but probably more effective outside of Erin, is *The Purple Path to the Poppy Field*, a long one-act allegory castigating some of the more hidebound values of modern Ireland. The overt story is a simpler and less diffuse one than that of *Aisling*, and the snarling bitterness of its indictment is restrained by the formal wittiness of the parable.

J. P. Donleavy is no Irishman and his main work has been in fiction, but his lively and faithful adaptation of his novel *The Ginger Man* is worth mentioning for its own extravagantly theatrical merits and as the most recent example of clerical pressure on the theater. This bawdy account of Sebastian Dangerfield's puerile fury against his wife, his friends, Trinity College, Dublin, Ireland, and the world, was closed after only three nights in the Gaiety, Dublin, when Donleavy refused to make cuts recommended by the office of Archbishop McQuaid. The faults of the play are pretty much those of the novel, as well as those of Osborne's *Look Back in Anger*, of which it seems a randy Dublin version. In Donleavy as in Osborne, virile theatrical virtues more than compensate for thematic immaturity.

What introduction is needed for Brendan Behan? He was the noisiest and most newsworthy playwright of his day, and further testimony is hardly required either for his own exuberant personality or for the vivid theatricality of his two long plays. Yet two points might be made. First, as a man he was a great deal more than a comic, stage-Irish Dylan Thomas. Second, despite some of his slapdash later books like *Brendan Behan's New York* or the tape-recorded *Confessions of an Irish Rebel*, he was, in his two long plays, more than a slovenly genius with a great deal of luck and very little sense of form or style. *The Hostage* has, partly because of Behan's interruptions of the free-wheeling Joan Littlewood production, acquired the reputation as little more than a commedia dell' arte framework on which a talented director and actors could build up a piece of real theater. It has a perfectly adequate structure, and, although it seems thin on the page, it was not written for the page. *The Quare Fellow* does exist quite richly on the page; it is, as we shall see when Behan's reputation subsides into the past, a really written play, carefully built and distinguished.

☙

Even despite the Abbey's recent signs of vitality, the most potent theatrical force in Ireland at present is the Dublin Theatre Festival. During its two weeks' run every September, it generates more excitement, gets more publicity abroad, and, most important, calls forth the largest number of significant new plays from both new and established writers.

The brainchild of the theatrical entrepreneur Brendan Smith, the Festival grew out of a now defunct national celebration, the Tostal. The first Theatre Festival to be produced independently of the Tostal was that of 1958, which was a celebrated fiasco. The featured plays of that year were to have been the world premiere of O'Casey's brilliant comedy *The Drums of Father Ned*, the premiere of *Bloomsday*, a *Ulysses* adaptation by the Ulsterman Alan McClelland, and the presentation of three mime plays by Samuel Beckett. The archbishop of Dublin was asked to inaugurate the Festival with a mass, and when he refused some of the producers were thrown into a pious panic. *Bloomsday* was summarily dropped, Beckett withdrew his plays in sympathetic protest, and O'Casey was not too subtly pressured to withdraw his play. He withdrew it, although not at all subtly but with a typical explosion, and the upshot was that the first Theatre Festival was an ignominious miscarriage.

After this last twitch of puritanical timidity, the Festival made a tentative re-beginning in 1959, and from then on it has gone from strength to strength. Though it has produced some mediocre revivals and some uninspired musicals, it has given a stage to some of the most interesting work of established writers like Macken, Molloy, and Byrne; it has given a boost to young writers who had already begun to make a name elsewhere, men like Keane, Hugh Leonard, Tom Coffey, G. P. Gallivan, and Brian Friel; and it has fathered some fine plays by totally new people like James Douglas, James McKenna, Conor Farrington, Eugene McCabe, and Patrick Galvin.

There have been many criticisms of the Festival: it tries to do too much in too little time; there are not enough good actors to fill the casts of seventeen or eighteen plays; the choice of plays is slanted toward possible acceptance by the West End or Broadway; the Festival kills the drama for the rest of the year. Some of these points are well taken, and, of course, the Festival cannot create a total renaissance in two weeks' activity out of every fifty-two. Obviously the Festival's efforts need to be augmented during the rest of the year by the efforts of other companies. But the perhaps rejuvenated Abbey gives considerable hope of taking up some of the slack, and when its efforts are joined by the fine occasional productions of Phyllis Ryan, of the still active Mac Liammóir and Edwards, and of Liam Miller's little Lantern Theatre, the prospect seems hardly as bleak as it is generally painted. But the Festival itself, despite its limitations and failures, is a cultural godsend to the Irish theater.

The most frequently represented young playwright in the Festivals has been Hugh Leonard (the pseudonym of John Keyes Byrne); 1966 saw his seventh Festival production. Leonard is at present a television script writer for Granada for half the year, and this stint allows him to devote himself to stage plays for the rest of the time. His first long play, *The Big Birthday*, was put on by the Abbey in January, 1956, and in January, 1957, the Abbey did his *A Leap in the Dark*. In March, 1958, the Globe performed his *Madigan's Lock*. In 1961, Gemini produced his Irish adaptation of *Peer Gynt*, called *The Passion of Peter Ginty*, during the Festival, and for the 1962 Festival did his adaptation from Joyce, *Stephen D*. For the 1963 Festival, Gemini did his original psychological melodrama *The Poker Session*, as well as his adaptation from Joyce's *Dubliners*, called *Dublin One*. In August, 1964, Gemini produced his adaptation from Labiche's *Célimare* called *The Family Way*, and for the 1965 Festival did his adaptation of Flann O'Brien's novel *The Dalkey Archive* under the engaging title of *When the Saints Go Cycling In*. His *Mick and Mick* appeared in the 1966 Festival.

There is probably no more technically proficient young Irish playwright than Leonard. He is a professional in the best sense, and his plays have a smoothness, a deftness, and a polish that Dublin had probably not seen since the death of Louis D'Alton. His original plays may suffer slightly from his facility. The engrossing *Poker Session*, for instance, seems to promise more than a melodramatic twist of the plot at the end. His adaptations, however, are no less than brilliant, and the superb *Stephen D* might be taken as a model of the adaptor's craft.

G. P. Gallivan, who works for Trans World Airlines in Dublin, is best known for a trilogy of historical plays — *Decision at Easter* about the 1916 Rising, *Mourn the Ivy Leaf* about Parnell, and *The Stepping Stone* about Michael Collins. His first professional production was the Globe's presentation of *Decision at Easter* on March 16, 1959. He wrote the book for a musical about Henry Morgan, *Sir Buccaneer*, which appeared in the 1964 Festival, and his political parable *Campobasso* appeared in the 1965 Festival. Gallivan's historical plays are competent, but not immoderately exciting. His best work by far is an engrossing unproduced play called *A Beginning of Truth*. In it, he cuts more deeply into character and comments more fluently on contemporary Ireland than most of his younger colleagues. He was born in 1920, and has been a later starter than the other new playwrights, but with this excellent piece he may have hit his stride.

Among the other notable Festival efforts at least four single plays must be mentioned. In 1960, Alan Simpson produced the boisterous Dublin Teddy-boy musical *The Scatterin'* by the young sculptor James McKenna; 1961 was notable for an overlong but worthy Dublinization of Kafka's *The Trial*, called *the Temptation of Mr. O*, by the fine actor Cyril Cusack; the 1963 Festival saw the Gate production of Conor Farrington's *The Last P.M.*, a satirical fantasy greatly admired by Frank O'Connor; and the 1964 Festival saw the production of a powerful domestic tragedy called *The King of the Castle*. This was by Eugene McCabe, a new young writer, who won the 1963 Irish Life Drama Award with it.

Also in 1964 appeared the piece which has been so far the most successful Festival play abroad. This was the Gate's production of Brian Friel's *Philadelphia, Here I Come!*, which was later presented on Broadway by David Merrick and which in the New York Drama Critics' balloting lost out by only one vote to the *Marat/Sade* for the best play of the year award. Friel is an ex-schoolteacher from Derry who was already known for his excellent short stories, two volumes of which, *The Saucer of Larks* and *The Gold in the Sea*, have appeared. His earlier stage writing includes *The Francophile*, originally done by the Group Theatre in Belfast; *The Enemy Within*, a religious play performed by the Abbey, and *The Blind Mice*, done in Dublin by the Eblana. His latest play, *The Loves of Cass Maguire*, appeared briefly in New York in the fall of 1966.

Friel's only published play so far is *Philadelphia, Here I Come!*, and in it he uses the old O'Neill device of splitting a character into two parts and giving each part to a separate actor. What was often stiff in O'Neill is beautifully flexible in Friel's hands, and the public and private selves of young Gar O'Donnell, who is emigrating from his little Irish village, offer many moments of rare sadness and hilarity. If Friel never writes anything better than this, he has won his place in the history books.

☙

Before the twentieth century, Ulster, like southern Ireland, had no native drama. But in 1901, inspired by the dramatic activity in Dublin, some Belfast enthusiasts formed what eventually was known as the Ulster Literary Theatre. For a number of years, the group produced quite worthy plays, mostly short ones by Bulmer Hobson, Joseph Campbell, Richard

Rowley, and Lewis Purcell. It also produced the early work of Rutherford Mayne and, late in its existence, the early work of George Shiels.

In more recent years, the organization that best carried on the tradition of the Ulster Literary Theatre was the Group Theatre, which was organized in the early 1940's by Gerald Morrow, Harold Goldblatt, Joseph Tomelty, and others. Its most popular pieces were Tomelty's comedy *Right Again, Barnum* and Shiels's comedy *Borderwine*, both of which ran for fifteen weeks. In 1958, after some rocky times, the Group seemed rejuvenated with the appointment of a new board of directors and a new artistic director, Jim Ellis. Several good new plays were announced for production, including Friel's *The Francophile*, Jack Loudan's *Trouble in the Square*, John Murphy's *The Country Boy*, and Sam Thompson's *Over the Bridge*.

Unfortunately, the Group came to grief about *Over the Bridge*, which was already in rehearsal when the directors decided to withdraw it, fearing that its touchy subject, the relations between Presbyterian and Catholic dock workers, would be too inflammatory. The fiery Thompson bitterly fought this "banning" of his play, and managed to get it on independently, produced by Ellis and with Tomelty in the cast. It was a striking success in Belfast, enthusiastically received in Dublin, and well reviewed in London. The various resignations occasioned by the dispute, however, signalled the beginning of the end for the Group Theatre; unfortunately the end came just when the organization seemed on the verge of excellence.

There have been two other notable Belfast theaters. The first to appear after the Group was the Belfast Arts Theatre formed in 1947 by Hubert Wilmot, a brother of one of the Abbey directors. In its early years, the Arts mounted an impressive selection of modern plays whose range and variety could challenge that of Dublin's Gate. The company played Ibsen, Chekhov, Wilde, Pirandello, Evreinov, Capek, Claudel, Cocteau, Eliot, O'Neill, Rice, Miller, Fry, and many others. They did fewer new plays than the Gate, though, and only one new Irish play, Donagh MacDonagh's *God's Gentry*. Still, for several years a Belfastman might have got a fair knowledge of the modern drama by attending the Arts. Then, after a few years, the quality of plays began to decline, and the company leaned more to commercial fare like Coward, Rattigan, and Van Druten. In the last few years, the standards have sunk even lower, to Agatha Christie mysteries, Brian Rix farces, and the Belfast farces of Sam Cree. The Arts is now a self-supporting group with a handsome and comfortable new theater. Its productions are competent, but it has entered on a placid middle age and seems interested in drama only as entertainment rather than as art.

At the opposite extreme is the Lyric Players Theatre, founded in 1951 by Mrs. Mary O'Malley as "a medium for poetic drama." I have not seen enough of their productions to judge of their habitual competence. What I have seen I thought not altogether up to professional standards. Still, the company is the only one ever to work its way through all of Yeats's plays, and it has also produced poetic pieces by Clarke, MacDonagh, Robert Farren, and Valentine Iremonger. It has tried Aristophanes, Euripides, Shakespeare, Jonson, Milton, Ibsen's *Peer Gynt*, Lorca, Eliot, Fry, and Dylan Thomas. It has done such demanding plays as O'Casey's *The Silver Tassie* and Mary Manning's adaptation of *Finnegans Wake*, entitled *The Voices of Shem*. It has also put on several new Irish prose plays by Keane, Gallivan, and James Plunkett. Although it has not yet drawn a group of writers to it, the Lyric Players have traveled through the masterpieces of world drama.

The group has spawned several healthy offshoots — a drama school, a children's theater, a literary magazine called *Threshold*, a shop for selling Irish handicrafts, an art gallery, and an academy of music. In June, 1965, the cornerstone of a new theater building was laid. All in all, it is a gallant, admirable, and thoroughgoing cultural offensive.

The best modern playwrights of Ulster are Rutherford Mayne, St. John Ervine, George Shiels, Joseph Tomelty, Sam Thompson, and Brian Friel. Mayne and Shiels became notably familiar, however, for their connection with the Abbey, and Ervine for his connection with the theater of London and of New York. More recently, Friel also, by the London and New York success of *Philadelphia, Here I Come!*, seems likely to make his mark on the world stage rather than the Belfast one.

Tomelty and Thompson are less well known but nevertheless interesting writers. Tomelty was born on March 12, 1911, and his early Ulster comedies were produced by Ulster Radio and by the Group Theatre. In 1951, with Tyrone Guthrie and Alan McClelland, Tomelty formed a company to present Shiels's *The Passing Day* in London. He is a fine character actor, and was noticed during the run of the play by David Lean, the film director. Since then he has appeared in about thirty films and many television shows. He is a prolific writer and has published a couple of novels in addition to his dramas. The best of his recent plays are the domestic tragedy *The End House*, produced in 1944 by the Group and by the Abbey; *All Soul's Night*, produced in 1948 by the Group and in 1949 by the Ab-

23

bey; and *Is the Priest at Home?*, produced by the Group and the Abbey in 1954. A serious automobile accident interfered with his writing for several years, but recently he has turned out several scripts, such as *To Have a Little House* and *The Sensitive Man*, which, although yet unpublished and unproduced, are both intriguing experiments in realism.

His early comedies may be too deeply rooted in Belfast life to survive transplanting, but they have a fine racy banter of dialogue. *The End House* is a Belfast domestic tragicomedy that, like so many Irish plays, seems a variation on *Juno and the Paycock* and suffers from the fact. *All Soul's Night*, a tragedy of the North Ireland fishermen, is strongly reminiscent of *Riders to the Sea*, and is a powerful though in comparison with Synge's masterpiece a sluggish and predictable tragedy. *Is the Priest at Home?* is a wry comic defense of the Irish parish priest, who, according to the thesis of the play, is more of a slave to his parishioners than a tyrant over them. So far at least, Tomelty's work ranks him with Robinson and Shiels and D'Alton rather than with O'Casey and Synge and Fitzmaurice.

The most stirring new Ulster writer was the ship painter Sam Thompson, who was born on May 21, 1916, and who died of a heart attack on February 1, 1965. His first play, *Brush in Hand*, was broadcast over the Ulster BBC in 1956. The success of it and several other radio plays led him to write his first stage play, the controversial *Over the Bridge* whose tribulations have already been mentioned. His second stage play was *The Evangelist*, a study of the rabble-rousing kind of preacher. It was produced in 1963 by Louis Elliman in Dublin and Belfast. In June, 1964, Thompson was the unsuccessful Labour candidate for the Belfast parliament. His final play, *Cemented With Love*, was posthumously televised. In his last years, he did some acting in Ireland and England.

None of Thompson's plays is as yet published, and they are very hard to come by. I have succeeded in tracking down only *Over the Bridge*, which is a straightforward realistic play with a large cast. Although it would be powerful anywhere, its strength would be somewhat lessened in a community with less religious tension than Belfast. Still and all, few Northern writers have had the courage to attack such a subject, and Thompson's death as he was only just finding himself was a severe loss to the Ulster and to the Irish theater.

☘

In my possibly biased view, the Shakespeare of the Irish drama is Sean O'Casey. Yet he was not, as Shakespeare was not, one single towering mountain in the middle of a vast plain. His pre-eminence was always and still is challenged by a host of writers of talent and even of genius. This fact is what makes the continuing Irish renaissance such a rich and fascinating period.

In recent years, critics like David Krause and Ronald Ayling have been making the point that O'Casey's pre-eminence rests upon a great deal more than three early tragicomic masterpieces. I shall not belabor the point here again, for the many successful recent productions of O'Casey's later work have proved it far better than any critic could. Even the Irish seem to be slowly and grudgingly admitting the fact. The fine one-act *The Hall of Healing* was recently seen at the Abbey, and Gemini has recently produced *The Drums of Father Ned* at the Olympia.

Yet for the record, let the statement be made again, if not the case argued. When O'Casey went to England in 1926, he did not leave his genius behind in the North Circular Road. His first efforts in England, like *The Silver Tassie* and *Within the Gates* and *The Star Turns Red*, were attempts, often brilliant and sometimes floundering, to hammer out a new dramatic style. Slowly, he found that style, and the neopastoral tragedies, comedies and what we shall have to call for want of a better word triumphs of his later years are a magnificent culmination of his genius. Plays like *Purple Dust, Cock-a-Doodle Dandy, The Bishop's Bonfire, The Drums of Father Ned, Time to Go*, and *Figuro in the Night* all speak to Ireland with a voice of immediacy and to the whole world with the lasting voice of greatness.

♣

What distinguishes the older Irish drama from the new is largely, I think, the new writer's sense of belonging to the world rather than just to Ireland. As Dominic Behan irreverently put it in *Posterity Be Damned*, "Mother Ireland, Get off my back." The Irish problem is no longer one of Ireland versus England, but of Ireland as a harassed member of the community of nations, having to cope with all of the anxieties and crises that the rest of us do. No island — to paraphrase John Donne — is an island anymore. Ireland's Frank Aiken was a distinguished servant of the UN, and Irish troops served in Katanga. Ireland, like the rest of us, is afflicted with economic problems and with labor disputes. The skyline of Dublin is now dotted with television antennas, and automobiles are pushing the bicycles off the streets. The acrid simplicities of Bob Dylan drip from the juke boxes of the O'Connell Street snackeries, and you can buy Mod fashions in Capel as well as in Grafton Street. Ireland is more aware of the modern world, more a part of the modern world, than it ever was before.

All of this has an effect on the Irish dramatist. The earlier dramatists were usually realistic in manner and (pun intended) parochial in theme. A few attempted to combat the realistic manner. Indeed, Yeats founded the Abbey as a theater basically for poetic and lyric drama. That, of course, was not what it became, and, although Yeats continued to the end of his career to write experimental and poetic plays, he finally wound up wanting a drawing-room theater for a few friends — a fact which some modern critics seem to regard as a triumph. Fitzmaurice tilted against realism and suffered forty years of neglect. O'Casey did manage to hammer out an inimitable unrealistic style and Samuel Beckett an imitable one, but neither of them even tried to do it in Dublin. Excellent though the classic Irish drama was, it stayed firmly planted inside the box set.

Realism has also been the basic manner of modern drama in the Western world. But the last thirty years have seen so much experiment in Europe and America that the quality of the realistic manner has subtly changed. The experiments of Pirandello, Capek, O'Neill, Rice, and Brecht have left their mark, and so for that matter has musical comedy. It is not so much that modern audiences can now take in *Waiting for Godot* without blinking in bafflement as that they can look at *Death of a Salesman* or *A Man for All Seasons* as basically realistic plays. The realism of these plays is a considerably freer realism, though, than that which was practiced by John Galsworthy and Somerset Maugham. It dispenses with a box set, and it ranges through space as through time. This quality the younger Irish dramatists have assimilated. We see it in Leonard, in Douglas, in Coffey, in Friel, and, of course, in O'Casey, who will probably always be one of the younger Irish dramatists. And though there is nothing intrinsically wrong with fourth-wall realism, free realism can only liberate the young playwright from sterile imitation of his theatrical heritage.

The themes of the older Irish plays were usually, in a descending scale of importance, either for or against money, land, the made marriage, patriotism and hero worship, social climbing, emigration, and the clergy. We still find these themes, but we find them translated into terms of individual anguish rather than seen as uniquely national problems. Or, if they are national, the angle is different from that of Shiels or T. C. Murray.

To take one example, Shiels's Abbey play *The Fort Field* of 1942 posed the situation of a fairy ring which government engineers wanted to plow under for an airstrip. The government at first was loudly opposed by the superstitious villagers, but the play shows how the villagers overcame their superstitions and finally helped to destroy the fairy ring, thoroughly delighted to be making a lot of money by their efforts. This view in itself is quite an advance on the mist-that-does-be-on-the-bog attitude of the earlier Celtic Twilight. However, about twenty-five years after Shiels's play, James Douglas used the same situation in his television play *The Hollow Field*. His theme and attitude, though, were quite different. His engineer did not conquer the villagers' superstition, and left the fairy ring surrounded by an ugly barbed wire fence to preserve "one of Ireland's untouchables." Unlike Shiels, Douglas allows no simple solution. He sees a wryer vision of only partial accomplishment and even of symbolic failure. Moreover, his play makes an individual statement that Shiels's social document does not. In Shiels, the village as a whole wins through. In Douglas, the engineer does not make a human contact with the girl who loves him, but goes off alone to exile in France in brooding anguish.

I do not use the Douglas play to suggest that the essence of the new drama in Ireland or anywhere else is a dour view of a seedy Samuel Beckett character alone in his ashcan or talking only to his tape recorder. And I certainly do not mean that the essence of the new drama is necessarily dour. It is, however, a greater consciousness of individuality apart from a particular society. This does not mean that the new drama of Ireland cannot be Irish. Friel's Gar O'Donnell is firmly set in as Irish a situation as can be, and so are Leonard's Stephen Dedalus, and Douglas's Harry Hopkins, and Keane's Hiker Lacey. But at the same time, each character is alone in himself. No island is an island, but also no man is a society.

The one quality that most carries over from the earlier Irish drama to the new, and the one quality that is most indigenously Irish is — how shall I phrase it? — livingness, perhaps. A spontaneity, a verve, an immediacy, a sense of richness and fullness. Often in the older drama it appeared in the dialogue — Synge's, Lady Gregory's, O'Casey's. Often it appeared in the quality of the imagination — wildly flamboyant, richly grotesque, as in Fitzmaurice, in Synge, even in — I am not totally biased — Yeats. And it appears, this quality, in various ways in the best plays of the new writers. It appears in the sense of loss and the melancholy of Molloy, in the color and vital traditionalism of MacMahon, in the searing immediacy of what Byrne has to say, in the lusty defiance with which O'Donovan's Chief Justice greets certain defeat, in Keane's abruptness and sensuality.

No, the Irish dramatic renaissance is definitely not with Yeats in his grave. Indeed, perhaps it was never with Yeats at all.

♣ *MICHAEL MOLLOY* ♣

MICHAEL MOLLOY'S masterpiece, *The King of Friday's Men*, despite
Walter Macken heading the cast, had a poor Broadway production in
1951, and closed after four performances. Molloy is otherwise hardly
known outside Ireland, but, even in a national drama noted for producing
superb playwrights, he stands up well as a chief candidate for the mantle
worn by Synge, Fitzmaurice, and O'Casey. When his first plays were produced, Dublin journalistic critics heralded him as the new Synge. But he is
a slow and painstaking writer, who often requires a year or more to complete a play, and journalistic memories are short. Still, for once, the jour-
nalists were right. In subject matter, treatment, and the quality of his dialogue, Molloy is the most Syngean of all Irish dramatists — including, I
think, Synge himself.

The reason is that Synge, for all his genius, was an Anglo-Irishman
looking at the real Ireland from the outside. As he wrote in the preface to
The Playboy, "I got more aid than any learning could have given me from
a chink in the floor of the old Wicklow house where I was staying, that let
me hear what was being said by the servant girls in the kitchen." Molloy
got his aid from being in the kitchen itself.

Michael Joseph Molloy was born on March 3, 1917, the fifth of eight
children, in Milltown, County Galway. His father managed a shop and his
mother was a national schoolteacher. He himself went to a seminary for
four years but had to drop out because of illness. He now lives on a farm
of thirty-six acres just outside Milltown and next to the farm on which he
was born. Although a shy and diffident man, he is closer to his material,

29

the Irish countryside, than almost any other Irish dramatist except John B. Keane, who acknowledges his influence.

Molloy's plays include *Old Road*, first produced at the Abbey on April 26, 1943; *The Visiting House*, produced at the Abbey on November 18, 1946; *The King of Friday's Men*, produced at the Abbey on October 18, 1948; *The Wood of the Whispering*, produced at the Abbey on January 26, 1953; the one-act *The Paddy Pedlar* which the Abbey produced on September 5, 1953; *The Will and the Way*, which the Abbey produced on September 5, 1955; *Daughter from over the Water*, which was given its first professional production by Siobhan McKenna at the Gaiety, Dublin, on April 13, 1964; *The Wooing of Duvesa*, which the Abbey produced in September during the 1964 Theatre Festival; and *The Bitter Pill*, a one-act produced so far only by amateurs.

Molloy's plays are either rich re-creations of life in the West or equally rich historical plays. Even his contemporary plays, however, hark back to a stabler Ireland whose customs and manners have had time over the centuries to mature. This Ireland, as he well realizes, is a fading Ireland, and his plays mournfully dramatize the tension between the two worlds. The economic pressures of the modern world are depopulating the West, and those few people who remain inhabit a more mobile world. Their horizon is no longer limited to a few miles; their automobiles can take them into Galway for a film on the nights they are not at home watching *Gunsmoke* on television. Plays like *Old Road* and *The Wood of the Whispering*, even more memorably than O'Casey's fantasy *Figuro in the Night*, document this civilization dying for lack of youth, for inability to make a living or to marry. Conversely, a play like *Daughter from over the Water* shows the debasing effect of the modern world upon a girl who has emigrated to London.

Molloy's chief artistic problem is that his material is dying out on him. The Visiting House upon which our play is based is now a ruin down the road from where he lives. The day of the Visiting House was over fifteen or twenty years ago. The society can no longer support it, and perhaps does not need it. Molloy's plays, then, have lots of old people in them as well as old customs. *The Will and the Way*, for instance, shows really what will be one of the last amateur performances of an old-time patriotic melodrama. One other way in which Molloy has combatted his dying material is to return to the past in historical plays like *The King of Friday's Men* and *The Wooing of Duvesa*. But both of these and his contemporary plays are among the saddest ever written by an Irishman, and that perhaps is their chief claim to Irishness.

They contain a deal more than this pervasive and beautiful melancholy. Although many of his people are gently sex-haunted, he has also written scenes of ferocious activity. He is not afraid of a monumental stage fight, as when Bartley Dowd, the bullyman of Tyrawley, takes on all of Caesar French's press gang in *The King of Friday's Men*. And though they are basically gentle plays, they contain moments of devastating grotesquerie. For instance, there is that show-stopping moment in *The Paddy Pedlar* when the exhausted rag of a pedlar, who has been carrying his mother's body around in a sack, is freed from his bonds, and whips out his knife:

PEDLAR: Hullabaloo! Hullabaloo! (*Twice he leaps into the air with that hiss of savage joy; drawing back the knife each time as if to charge at Ooshla. But instead he leaps again, and cries aloud in triumph*) Now Mama! Timmy has his knife! Timmy has his knife! No one'll dare harm you no more!

And finally Molloy's dialogue must be mentioned. It does not have the thick, rolling, rhythmic periods of Synge. It is not encrusted with wit, pun, allusion, and alliteration as is O'Casey's late dialogue. It does not contain quite the fancy of Fitzmaurice. But it does have almost everything else, including that quality, often lacking in Synge and O'Casey, of easiness for the actors to speak and the audience to understand. I have probably over-used the word "richness" in connection with Molloy, but readers of *The Visiting House* will find in its dialogue an abundance of that richness for which the Irish drama in its great moments has always been noted, and which has been too little heard on the modern stage.

The Visiting House

A LIGHT COMEDY IN THREE ACTS

BROC HEAVEY, merryman and master of the Visiting House

MARY HEAVEY, daughter of the Visiting House

TIM CORRY, newcomer to the Visiting House

MURT KING, ganger of the Visiting House

MICKLE CONLON, the Man of Learning

VERB TO BE, the Man of Education

KATE, the Scoffer

BEEZIE, the Woman of Gifts

IGOE, a farmer

JULIA, an unwilling spinster

THE HAWS and THE GIRLS, rank and file of the Visiting House

Act I

The scene is in Broc Heavey's Visiting House on the outskirts of a crowded peasant village near the Galway-Mayo border, at nightfall of an autumn evening. Visiting Houses were those institutions that kept Irish folklore alive for a thousand years and left it with one of the greatest folklore libraries on paper and tape of any country in the world; this is one of the last of the Visiting Houses. It has the usual old-fashioned farmhouse kitchen. The fireplace is in the left-hand wall (left from the point of view of one facing the audience); the dresser is against the right-hand wall. The window is in the middle of the back wall; the door is on the right of it; on the left of it is a rough home made form four or five feet long. The table is between the center of the kitchen and the dresser. There is a chair on the far side of the fire from the audience and on the near side a little low stool. Another couple of chairs are drawn up to the table. The kitchen looks neat and moderately prosperous.

© Copyright 1967 by Michael Molloy. Address inquiries concerning performance or translation rights to Robert Hogan, Proscenium Press, Box 561, Dixon, California 95620. The play was first produced at the Abbey Theatre on November 18, 1946, directed by Michael J. Dolan, with settings by Alicia Sweetman.

Mickle, the Man of Learning, is seated at the fire on the chair. He is a bony old warrior, shriveled with age, but indomitable. He wears a long-tailed frieze coat, literally green with age, except about the sleeves where it has been extensively patched in many colors; also old corduroy trousers, bound tightly with thongs at the ankles and below the knees. Mickle is a man of many and abruptly changing moods; senile and wandering at one moment; at the next a thunderous-voiced, fiery-eyed and magnificent veteran; in another moment again grave, gentle and pathetic. Mickle in disputation is a sight worth seeing as, with his hat hitched up on the back of his head, he slashes at the floor with his stick to emphasize various points and roars at his opponent with a voice of astonishing power. On his legs he is very different, for his legs are his weakest section, and, as he totters from place to place, with every step an adventure, he looks an infinitely aged man. Before speaking, Mickle must sit down or grip something for support.

MICKLE (*chuckling to himself over the fire*): Aha, asthore . . . asthore . . . aha, aha, asthore . . . (*crooning to himself*)

> I haven't come shabby, as soon you will see,
> I'm willing to call and to pay;
> So be easy and free when you're drinking with me;
> I'm a man you don't meet every day.
> So be easy and free when you're drinking with me;
> I'm a man you don't meet every day.

(*Chuckling to himself softly.*) Aha, asthore, asthore, asthore.
The kitchen door is wide open, and through it can be seen a stranger dismounting from his bicycle. He leaves bicycle against the wall of the house, and comes to the door. He is about twenty-five years of age, with the sturdy build and strong facial bones of the hardy son of the soil. He is an able, intelligent, cheerfully imperturbable fellow, cool and reposeful rather than boisterous, slow rather than impetuous in speech. A connoisseur of conversation, like many of his type, he prefers to listen and relish rather than do most of the talking himself. A keen sense of humor is his outstanding trait, and through it he can be most easily aroused to enthusiasm. He wears a cap, a collar and tie, and his Sunday clothes generally. Standing in the doorway, he has a good look round; then he studies the old man for a few moments. Mickle is still chuckling over the fire, his chin upon his stick.

TIM (*genially*): Would you be Mickle Conlon?

MICKLE (*absently, without turning*): The very wan, asthore.

TIM: Is this Broc Heavey's Visiting House, Mickle?

MICKLE (*dreamily*): 'Tis, asthore, Broc's Visiting House. Why wouldn't it, asthore?

TIM: I'm right, so; my journey is done.

He comes in, throws cap on table, stoops to take pins out of his trouser cuffs.

33

MICKLE (*suddenly rousing and turning on Tim with the utmost fury*): Tell me here; out with the truth directly: are you wan of the Haws?

TIM (*amused*): Not me, Mickle.

MICKLE (*fiercely*): You are that wan of the Haws!

TIM: No, Mickle, I'm a black stranger. You never seen me before.

MICKLE: Well, if I didn't, I'll see you now. (*Still thundering.*) Sit down there by the brink of the table, till I draw to you. And if I see you're no stranger, but only wan of the Haws, your life'll be taken away directly.

He clambers slowly to his feet and sets out.

TIM (*chuckling*): That's fair enough, Mickle.

He sits at the table, removes the cycling pins at his leisure, and watches the progress of the old man. Mickle at length arrives at Tim's right hand, leaves his stick against the table, and, by leaning with both hands on the table, is no longer obliged to concentrate on his legs. He peers into Tim's face.

TIM: I amn't wan of the Haws, Mickle.

MICKLE (*mild now, and grave*): You are not, asthore . . . The way it is I have no sight in this eye at all, asthore, and the sight is spreading in the other eye, too. The Haws know well, and they're up to all tricks; they are, asthore.

TIM: I'm wan Corry from Kilduff — six strong miles.

MICKLE: I didn't go that far with a long time, asthore. This many a year I'm like the robin: I stop near the house: I do, asthore.

His eyes seem fixed dimly on some far distance.

TIM: I hear you're on the hammer of a hundherd, Mickle.

MICKLE: They could get no account of my age, asthore; but they have it reckoned up that I'm two years to the good of ninety.

TIM: You'll never feel making the five score, so?

MICKLE (*shaking his head*): I will not, asthore; the age is too big, asthore; the age will put me to death soon, asthore. And 'twould be the best thing, for if I stopped longer in the world I'd be a queer oul' specimen. I would, asthore.

TIM: Where's Broc and the daughter?

MICKLE: Broc is up the land fencing, and herself is gone two miles there a-back to the shop, buying her commands, and my commands too.

TIM: Why, Mickle? Have you nowan in your own home?

MICKLE (*gravely*): Not wan, asthore. I'm my own cook, slut, and butler; I am, asthore.

He takes his stick, totters back to his chair again. Tim has time to go to the door and look out.

TIM (*looking down*): Ye have a great regiment of houses in this village, Mickle. (*Comes back to table, sits down again.*) Do many come visiting to this house, Mickle?

MICKLE (*vigorously*): Directly, Corry, I'll give you the particular account of that . . . (*He settles himself in chair, grips stick, slashes at floor a few times, working up to his best full-throated style.*) Every night, Corry, the neighbors from the village; the oul' people that understand something, and the young gang we baptized the Haws, because they understand nothing. From the villages around wans'll be coming round the back end of the year, when there's a good stretch in the nights; and that time, too, an odd wan from a good way off, foreigners the same as yourself, that heard good account of us.

TIM: They tell me this Visiting House has no equal for sport.

MICKLE: Then they told you what was true. Broc isn't greatly up in the learning and stories that was going in the Visiting Houses before now. But Broc is the best merryman that rose up in all my time; and there's sport and wit here as good as ever I seen.

TIM: He behaved a great man to keep the Visiting House so numerous and good.

A merry stave of song is heard outside. Mickle straightens intently.

MICKLE: That's her! That's my best friend in the world! With every five steps she must give out a storm of song.

Enter the daughter of the Visiting House, lilting something about having been a moonshiner for many a year. Nineteen years of age, she can be as lighthearted and lively as any of her age, but she finds the world too wonderful a place to take it altogether frivolously, so her most characteristic mood is one of brisk, busy, almost rapt gravity, such as might be found in a doll-attending young lady of six or so. Her spontaneity is striking; the words tumble up unchecked, uncensored; speech, expression, and gesture register as clearly as day every movement of thought and feeling; you can see her think. She is wholly free from sentimentality or coquetry. In her humorous moments she is comradely and unaffected; but Tim judges her to be most amusing when she is most serious. She is dressed in her best, and carries her purchases in a black canvas bag.

MARY (*round-eyed*): Tim!

TIM (*cheerfully*): How is yourself?

His attitude toward her throughout is a blend of affection and amusement.

MARY (*running to him delighted*): Is it visiting you came?

TIM: The very thing.

MICKLE (*thundering*): Have you my commands?

MARY (*to Mickle*): Here they're to you. (*Gives him items, Mickle, with his "Aha, asthore," chuckling rapturously.*) Your tea and half pound of sugar and a pound of beef, and 'tisn't wan ounce of tobacco this time, but two — a full half quarter!

She runs off merrily to dresser, and empties remaining items upon it.

35

MICKLE (*loudly*): Now, Corry, isn't she my best friend in the world? (*To Mary.*) When you die, asthore, there'll be a thunderstorm and lightning, a volcano, a whirlwind, and an earthquake; there will, asthore!

Mary throws her beret on the dresser, runs back to Tim and kneels beside him.

MARY (*triumphantly*): And now, Tim! So at long last you're believing this Visiting House is worth traveling seven miles to!

TIM (*smiling*): 'Tisn't that altogether.

MARY: And what brought you up, so?

TIM: So as myself and yourself could have a conversation. Will he be off soon?

MARY: In a couple of minutes, when he has his commands run over.

TIM: There's no hurry.

He glances at Mickle, who has turned away from them and is chuckling over his "commands."

MARY (*lowering her voice*): Tim, don't let on to father or the old people about you and me courting.

TIM (*smiling*): Did they get no wrinkle of that at all yet?

MARY: Not them. They never heard tell of you any more than myself did till I met you at the dances in Thooraree Hall. And what they don't know won't trouble them.

TIM: There's no fear of the Haws to tell?

MARY: Not them. I have a great hand with the Haws.

TIM: Good yourself.

MARY (*suddenly*): Tim! (*She jumps up, her eyes sparkling.*) Before Mickle goes we'll play a small trick on him. Wait till you see. Mickle!

MICKLE (*cutting tobacco*): What's it, asthore?

MARY: Here's wan that has great education. I'll bet you have no question hard enough to stumble this wan.

MICKLE (*turning grimly*): I'll bet a dog I'll stumble him. Wait first till I make safe my commands.

He piles same into his large colored handkerchief, ties the four corners together.

MARY: Now we'll have the value! (*She pulls form from wall, sets it between Tim and Mickle.*) Have you memory, Tim, of the wan the government sent around with the dictaphone picking out the stories and songs in the Irish tongue that were going in the Visiting Houses before now?

TIM: To be sure, I remember him.

MARY: Well, Mickle was very near two months giving lessons to that wan, and ever since he's full sure nowan has learning as good as him. Ssh!

MICKLE (*facing round, stick gripped across his knees in his best fighting attitude*): Corry, do you reckon you have great education?

36

TIM (*with a grin*): The best, Mickle.

MICKLE: Well, I never got a day's education, or went a day in my life to school. I have only the learning that was handed down from the generations in the Visiting Houses before now. Do you still reckon you have the best education, Corry?

TIM: Away better, Mickle.

MICKLE (*growling darkly to himself*): All right, Corry, all right, all right, all right . . . (*He slashes the floor with stick a few times, working himself up, then straightening fiercely.*) Who were the giants and unbelievers of olden times, that believed in no religion but strength and reckoned they could conquer the whole world in strength?

TIM: I give in; I'm ignorant of them, Mickle.

MICKLE (*scornfully*): Did you never hear tell in all your schooling of Finn and Ossian and Goll McMorna, and Conawn and Oscar, and Diarmuid Donn? And their seven regiments, every member giants too, and unbelievers, and all putting in their time at sharpening their weapons, making corpses of heroes, and putting it all down in history? With all your education, you're ignorant of them, Corry!

TIM: No lie, Mickle. I was ignorant of them.

MICKLE (*pressing home the attack*): When Ossian, after three hundred years in Tir-Na-N-Og, tripped home, and found his equals, the giants, dead and gone, and Ireland populated with dwarfeens of ordinary men the same as now, what ways of living did he get, Corry?

TIM: Mickle, I'm in doubt you don't know that yourself.

MARY: Wait till you see.

MICKLE: Ossian was that big, Corry, as they didn't know was he a man at all, so they gave him a beast's work — drawing stones.

MARY (*who is enjoying all this*): Now Tim, can you match him for learning?

MICKLE: Wan last chance I'll give you, Corry. When Ossian the unbeliever arg'd with St. Patrick about Heaven and Hell, and God's mercy and God's rights, and all other politics about God, what then, Corry, were the two points Ossian had greatly against God?

TIM: If you have them, Mickle, I'll give in I'm on the beaten hand.

MICKLE: I can give you the first point, Corry. "If the Fenians knew in time," said Ossian, "that your God was so naygerly as He'd condemn the whole world for the loss of wan apple, we'd send him free to Heaven seven muleloads of apples, so as He'd spare the world."

MARY (*chuckling*): Wasn't that a great point, Tim?

MICKLE (*not heeding the interruption*): And I can give you the second point, Corry. "Look at the blackbird," said Ossian, "he don't go near Mass or priest, and look at how prosperous he is! He can build his house, and live as good as the best . . ." Now, who has the best learning, Corry?

TIM: I give in, Mickle. You have the best learning.

MICKLE: From Dublin, and Galway, and all over, Corry, they come to me for learning. All their lives they spent in schools and college, still and all, they knew nothing: and I never went a day to school; still look at how I know everything — every single thing, Corry!

MARY: Isn't it the truth, Tim?

TIM: Mickle, there's nowan can come up to you.

Victory assured, Mickle turns his back on them, chuckling to himself.

MICKLE: Education, asthore . . . and after it all ye know nothing!

He pockets his groceries and rises.

TIM (*chuckling*): Well, that's wan good oul' character ye have here.

MARY: Amn't I telling you evermore, Tim, we have the finest of characters drawing to us?

She rises, takes off her topcoat, hangs it behind door, and puts on her apron.

MICKLE (*leaning on chair*): I must make my ground off home now with my commands, asthore, but I'll be back to ye soon, when the Visiting House will be on the border of gathering in . . . I will, asthore. (*Sets out.*)

MARY (*coming back to form*): Mickle is away the best storyteller around here. (*Regretfully.*) Isn't it a pity he has to die?

TIM: 'Tis the same up our side. The stories is leaving the country.

MARY (*gravely*): Look at that! (*Briskly.*) And now, Tim, you and me can have a conversation. Sit over here anear me on the form.

TIM (*cheerfully*): Right! (*Sits beside her, takes out a packet of cigarettes.*)

MARY (*suddenly and gravely*): Though now, Tim, you have the chair well warmed, so maybe you'd sooner stop in it?

TIM (*smiling*): It won't take me long to warm this, too. (*Offers her a cigarette.*)

MARY: Thanks, Tim. And now is it a news you have for me?

TIM: 'Tis, and a good news. D'ye remember me telling you how I'm discontented with Ireland these late years?

MARY (*gravely*): Many's the time you told me that, Tim.

TIM: I was happy enough before now when we were living in Mountain. Then there was thirty houses of us crashed together the same as this village, and every kitchen flooded out with young and old, and the finest of sport in the Visiting Houses every night in it. But since the Land Commission shifted some of us to new holdings in Kilduff, I'm discontented with Ireland.

MARY: But Tim, ye have more land, and better land, in Kilduff than ye had in Mountain.

TIM: Still and all, the houses are too far apart for the old people to go visiting, and there's no right sport or Visiting House without them.

MARY (*gravely*): No lie, Tim. Some Land Commission villages do be awful scattered and lonesome. But how do you know would you have any better sport in Manchester?

TIM: They tell me so, whatever. Every night there in the pubs, playing darts, and cardplaying for drinks, and back in the smoking room singing songs, with pianos chorusing the songs, and all fun, man.

MARY: But, Tim, 'tis a year and more since you wrote to your cousin the ganger in Manchester, so, likely he'll never get a place for you when he didn't before now.

TIM (*producing letter*): That come today. He has the job got for me at last.

MARY (*dismayed*): Tim! You're going from me!

TIM (*cheerfully*): I'm to go over and start work five weeks from today.

MARY: Oh dear! . . . Tim, this is an awful tragic!

TIM (*playfully*): Why would it?

MARY: Why wouldn't it? Don't you know well 'tis a thorny pillow for me to lose you, even if we're courting only a couple of months itself?

TIM: You'll soon get another fellow to bring you from the halls. You'll not be long idle.

MARY (*dubiously*): I know, Tim; but will I get wan even half as nice as you? That's the question.

TIM (*cheerfully*): I was reckoning up there was only wan plan that'd make me contented with Ireland.

MARY: What's that, Tim?

TIM: Ye have a good and lively village here, by all accounts. So if you and me married I'd be well content to settle here.

MARY (*stunned*): Me to bring you in here!

TIM: Why not? I'd bring in the four-hundred-pound legacy the aunt left me. Your oul' lad'd be getting a fair bargain, considering ye haven't a big holding of land.

MARY (*alarmed*): But, Tim, if we married in here, don't you see what would happen? Within a year the first screecher'd be born for us, and then the village'd come visiting here no more.

TIM (*whistling*): Right enough! I overlooked that. They don't like coming where the cradle is in the corner.

MARY: Nowan'll come visiting where the cradle is in the corner, and the whole village, father and all'd go visiting in Mickle's any more after that.

TIM: But what harm? Sure, Mickle's is only across the road, you might say. Couldn't you come visiting there every night yourself, too?

MARY (*amazed*): Tim! You're talking wild. Don't you understand? The minute the first screecher'd be born to us, I could go visiting no more. I'd be jailed up by myself here every night minding screechers.

TIM: You're not ready to surrender to marriage yet, so?

MARY: No, nor for many a year. I don't know how I'll surrender to marriage at all ever when I'll think how 'twill lose me all the sport I enjoyed here evermore.

TIM: Well, wance a man takes the habit of England, he don't come back, so you and me'll not cross each other's tracks again.

MARY (*despondently*): That's sure, Tim, and did you ever see anything like how Mickle's words is coming in?

TIM: Why? What did he say?

MARY: He sez if I got too great to any of ye before I was ready for marriage I'd suffer long and suffer sad for it — and now look at how his words is coming in!

She goes to fire, poking it together while he watches her, cheerful as ever.

TIM: In a few months, when you get word that I'm married beyond — you'll soon forget me.

MARY (*turning suddenly, tongs in hand*): Tim!

TIM: What's it?

MARY: With your four hundred pounds couldn't you get some other girl around here that'd be heir to a holding of land? Then you'd have the sport of the world visiting here every night, and we'd have you for a neighbor.

TIM (*chuckling*): Well, that might be something better than never to see wan another again!

MARY: To be sure it would, Tim.

TIM: Still and all, wance I can't anchor yourself I'm more inclined for Manchester.

MARY: Because why? Because you're not understanding there's better sport here than ever you'd have in England.

TIM: So you say. I'll see for myself tonight, whatever.

MARY: That's what you'll do, Tim. Study our Visiting House greatly, and see would you be happy to live anear it, and I'll be thinking out wan that'll have land, and house, and outhouses and all.

TIM: Right! But say no word to her till I give you leave. For 'twill take a whipping great Visiting House to wean me from my trial of England.

MARY: Ssh! That's the voice of father's footstep!

They look in the direction of the door. Enter the Merryman and Master of the Visiting House. He is a long, lean, hardy, loose-limbed, middle-aged man; features keen, complexion dark, eyes strikingly lively, face mobile and expressive. Like most Visiting House veterans, Broc is an excellent talker, better than most is he an original phrase-maker, an improviser, and master of repartee. An unbroken fifteen-minute solo narrative, whether humorous or serious, comes quite naturally from Broc. The narrative once under way, his gift takes possession of him, and the audience is forgotten; pause, emphasis, repetition, gesture (in the use of his hands he is a master). In fact, every trick of narration is applied with effortless and unconscious skill. As will appear, he is virtually a professional actor, his stage this Visiting House, where he has given nightly performances for many years. In disposition he is normally mild and genial; keen and enthusiastic where his Visiting House performances are concerned, fiery and implacable whenever they are endangered. In style, Broc, this representative of the Visiting House's latest (and final) phase, might be described as an actor of the naturalistic school; as distinct from that full-blooded Shakespearean Mickle, survivor of the Visiting House's more heroic days. He walks in slowly, without looking to left or right. In one hand he carries a bill hook. He is smoking a pipe, the shank of which is broken and not two inches long; his brows are contracted, his eyes fixed in concentration. He leaves the bill hook against the wall, then goes into room on right.

MARY (*jumping up*): And the ducks, the devils, have to be put in yet! (*She runs past him, then turns suddenly.*) Tim, don't open your mouth only when he'll speak to you. Whenever his brains is working composing sport and plots for the night, he's better pleased wan not to speak to him.

She runs out. Broc comes from room, still smoking, still thinking. He carries a form. This he leaves against back wall, under window. He is continuing on his way toward room door on left, when he notices Tim.

BROC (*genially, but a trifle absently*): Good evening, sir.

The "sir" is jocular and a habitual form of address with Broc.

TIM: Good evening.

BROC: Did you come far?

TIM: Kilduff . . . stronger than six mile.

BROC (*smiling*): Far enough, sir, far enough.

He wanders on into the room, returns with a chair, which he places on the far side of the fire. He takes chairs from table and places them also in this wide semicircle of seats facing fire. All this journeying is done in leisurely fashion, with odd pauses; Broc's mobile face changing from frowns, as he grapples with difficulties, to smiles and triumphant finger-crackings as he solves them. In short, the artist in the throes of composition, an impressive sight when the artist is wholly unaffected and unselfconscious, as in this case. Tim watches every move intrigued and amused. Finally Broc comes to the table.

BROC (*looking down at table*): Card-playing ye have mostly up your country?

TIM: That's it. Card-playing.

BROC: The card-playing was bound to capture your Visiting Houses wance the people got too educated to heed th' oul' storytellers with their giants and magic spells.

TIM: Still, the card-playing never captured your Visiting House.

BROC (*glowing*): Never, sir, and I'll tell you why: every day while I'm working in the fields, digging or weeding, putting down a crop or lifting it, my brain is working too, composing a rousing night's sport for them. For every night I have a new plot composed that the youth'd prefer before any card-playing. That's the way to defeat the card-playing: that's the way, sir.

TIM: All tell me you have the brains of the world for sport.

Broc moves table to back wall on right of door. He comes back to center, quenches and begins to clean out his pipe.

BROC: Last night two characters from Creevagh, two great wits — in their own opinions — come visiting; and we had the sport of the world stirring up storms between them and the old professors of my Academy. Before they went, I threw them a bait that'll be sure to draw them again tonight. So the chief plots for tonight, sir, 'll be against the two wits from Creevagh.

He takes Tim's cap from the table, hangs it on the wall near the dresser. Mary runs in, carrying some eggs in her apron.

MARY: Father, did he tell you about the plot we made against Mickle? (*She puts eggs in a bowl on the dresser.*) I let on Tim Corry here had great education, and at once Mickle threw down the gage on him.

BROC: Too simple. Ye didn't squeeze that plot good enough . . . A great deal a better plot could be composed in that line. (*Snapping his fingers in sudden excitement.*) Wait a minute! (*He hurries to the door.*) Verb To Be is fastening the latch of his door; we'll just have time to outline it. (*Coming back eagerly.*) Corry, are you any good of a character? Could you play a part?

TIM (*cheerfully*): I'll do the best I can for ye.

BROC: Good! Mary, bring forward that stick of lead pencil and the notebook you do be taking down Beezie's songs in.

She runs into bedroom. He turns to Tim again.

BROC: Corry, could you play the part of a fellow from the government the same as the folklore collector they sent some years ago looking for the old songs and stories that were going in the Visiting Houses long ago?

TIM: I have a fair good memory of that fella's carry-on. He come many a night to our village.

BROC: Good! It'll be easy for you, so. (*He takes a chair, planks it beside dresser.*) You'll want to sit far away over here, for they'll have their spyglasses set watching what you're writing down.

TIM (*coming over*): I'll talk simple the same as the last fella. I couldn't act a swell so good.

BROC: As simple as you like, sir.

He goes for a second chair. Mary returns with notebook and pencil, and gives them to Tim.

MARY: This end, Tim, the leaves is vacant.

BROC: Girl, go down to Mickle, and tell him there's a professor here that wants him directly. (*To Tim.*) We must finish this plot quick before the two wits from Creevagh come and take all our time.

He places second chair near Tim so that the person sitting on it would have his back to kitchen door. Mary has run to the door, and is looking toward the village.

MARY: Here's Verb To Be coming, and I can hear the Haws collecting below at Julia's.

BROC: Tell the Haws about the plot, so as they'll not come in noisy; and tell Murt to stop down the road and watch out for the two wits from Creevagh.

MARY: I will.

She disappears. Broc goes to door, watching approach of Verb To Be.

BROC: Let you be writing away hard and fast, and say as less as you can. There's a great jealousy in the line of learning between Mickle and Verb To Be, and that's what this plot'll blaze up. . . . Ssh! (*He comes in hurriedly, sits on chair near Tim, with his back to the door. Then loudly —*) Have you that much wrote down, sir?

TIM: I have. Go ahead.

Enter Verb To Be, the Man of Education. He is over seventy, but does not look more than sixty. A stocky, erect figure, with impressive forehead, large, grave, steady eyes, and full black beard streaked with grey. He wears an old bowler hat and black clothes, very worn and patched, but buttoned neatly about him. Verb To Be cannot help being aware that he is the most learned man in the neighborhood; nevertheless (and greatly to his credit) there is nothing haughty about him. He is merely dignified and grave. His speech is slow, Verb To Be weighing his words carefully. His voice is deep and musical, his articulation perfect. In sum, a simple soul and a gullible and, as such, highly prized in this Visiting House. He halts, seeing Tim writing and Broc narrating. He stands at corner of table, looking on gravely, while neither pretends to notice his arrival.

BROC (*in his best style*): "Have ye any other female in the house?" sez the Prince. "No," sez the oul' raps of stepsisters, "we have only wan dwarfeen of a drudge." "Send her out, whatever," sez he; so Cinderella come out and put on the shoe, and he swept her off with him on the horse. When they were passing her mother's grave the invisible voice rose up again:

> Backwards peep, backwards peep.
> There is NO blood upon the shoe.

43

It fits so nice, and she behind,
She IS the bride for you.

When the Prince heard that, he said no word, only hooked her off to the palace, put improved clothes on her, and married her, and they had family.

BROC (*rising*): And now sir, while you're writing down that wan, I'll cross the road for a man that could whip oul' Harry Stotle himself for learning. (*He turns, sees Verb To Be.*) Here he is, sir! The very man I was telling you about!

VERB TO BE (*fixing his great, sagelike eyes upon Tim*): Sir, goodday.

TIM: Goodday.

Verb To Be makes his way with dignity, sits on end of stool nearest Tim. Broc is standing further back, halfway between them.

BROC: Here's a man, sir, that has shelves in his brain for all branches of learning.

TIM: Have you learning?

VERB TO BE: Sir, my schooling was as follows: I went five years to Kelly, the Bishop McHale schoolmaster, teaching in Roche's barn. Then, sir, the National Schools came into the district, and I finished my schooling with them.

BROC: On slates they were doing the sums that time, sir, and Verb To Be done what wasn't equaled before or since. He done a sum so long it took three slates.

TIM: He did! Is that so?

VERB TO BE: Sir, three slates is correct.

BROC: Was it any wonder the master reckoned Verb To Be'd make a bank manager if he stopped in school two years more?

TIM: A bank manager! Did he say that?

VERB TO BE: Yes, sir; in two years, he said. But in the second year I was obliged to go to England harvesting, so I was unable to attend the examination for bank managers.

BROC: Every sentence Verb To Be read in his life he has memory of it. He's the man for you.

VERB TO BE: Sir, are you looking for learning?

TIM: I am. The government sent me.

VERB TO BE: Sir, I am at your disposal.

BROC (*slyly*): As for Mickle, sir, you needn't believe him. He has not the best learning.

VERB TO BE (*starting*): Sir, did Conlon tell you he had learning?

TIM: He did.

VERB TO BE (*vigorously*): Sir, the truth is that Conlon's education was entirely neglected. He is so ignorant, sir, that he thinks the old superstitions and legends of the Visiting Houses were true learning.

BROC (*to Verb To Be*): And d'ye know what he tells me about them Visiting House tales and histories the last fellow was collecting?

VERB TO BE: What?

BROC: It appears the government examined them greatly since, and weighed them up very strict, and found out at last they were only all rubbish and lies.

VERB TO BE (*rising*): Sir, is that correct?

TIM: 'Tis.

VERB TO BE (*urgently*): Sir, don't stir from here till I bring Conlon before you. If you tell him how his learning is proved to be rubbish, I'll give you free every lesson I have.

He sets out for the door. As he does so, voices and laughter are heard outside. Mary appears first.

MARY: Ssh! Go easy, let ye. (*She comes in smiling.*) Here's the Haws in to ye!

They file in past her, with lurking grins and sidelong looks at the stranger. They sit along the back wall, some on the form, more on the table. Between men and girls, they should number nearly a dozen (the minimum four men and two or three girls) between sixteen and thirty and of widely varying intelligence and liveliness. There is some giggling and whispering, but in the main they concentrate on the drama being enacted before them. One of the girls is Julia, whom we will describe later . . . Verb To Be and Broc have paid not the slightest attention to this routine entry of the Haws. Broc leaves his chair, crosses to right of Tim, stands with his back to the dresser.

VERB TO BE (*en route to the door*): Is there any sign of Conlon?

MARY (*at the door, smiling*): Here he is to ye!

VERB TO BE (*to Tim, urgently*): Sir, tell him now how his learning was proved to be rubbish. Put the truth standing.

BROC (*with mock gravity*): Verb To Be, I doubt we should spare him that. Nowan likes to be told he's ignorant.

VERB TO BE: Isn't he telling us for years that we're ignorant? Did he spare us? Sir, it is your duty to tell him and bring back his humility.

MARY: Here he is!

Mary sits down by the table as Mickle enters. Verb To Be returns to his seat. Mickle reaches corner of table, leans upon it, glares dimly around.

MICKLE: Tell me this directly. Is Corry here yet, or is he at large?

BROC: He is not at large, Mickle. He's here, and going strong.

MICKLE: Well, soon he'll be going weak. Corry, you have great education. How did Finn's mother get her death the time herself and Finn were hid-

45

ing in the woods from a gang that was watching to kill them, the same as you'd be watching a hare?

TIM: I doubt that's unknown, Mickle.

MICKLE: 'Tis not unknown, Corry. This day they ventured out to a hurling and who met them but the gang! As quick as wink, Finn rose her up on his shoulders and made off through the woods, with the gang full pelt at his heels. All the way the brambles were hitting her, and he was going at such a swift that the brambles soon had her worn away. So when he brought her safe from them at last, there wasn't a pick left only her two shin bones . . . That's how Finn's mother met her death, Corry; and you didn't know that?

TIM: I was ignorant of that, Mickle.

MICKLE: Me and you, Corry, and the rest rubbish of ye (*glaring around*) could sit down with four millionaires, and the millionaires'd give all their heed to me, and none to ye, because ye know nothing, and I know all.

He sits on chair which Broc has vacated, and is thus seated with his back to the door, halfway between Verb To Be and Tim.

VERB TO BE (*breathing hard*): Now, sir, you see why that man's absence is dear to me, and his presence painful. Sir, he is so ignorant that he is ignorant of his ignorance!

BROC: Sir, did you tell Mickle yet that you were from the government?

TIM: Not yet. He said he'd be back again.

MARY (*jumping up from table*): I'll tell him now. (*Runs to Mickle.*) Mickle, do you know who Mr. Corry is?

MICKLE (*wandering*): No, asthore. He gave me the particular account of himself, but I have all lost again. I'm suffering lately from loss of memory, asthore.

MARY: He's looking for lessons for the government, the same as the fellow that was around before.

MICKLE (*livening up instantly*): Is that so? Are you from the government, Mr. Corry?

TIM: That's so. I'm looking for learning.

MICKLE (*slashing at floor grimly*): Well, mind, Corry, what I have to say. You'll get no lesson from me till you promise me higher pay than the last vagabone of ye. Only wan half gill of whiskey he gave me, and two half quarters of tobaccy, for three fortnight's lessons in the cream of the learning of Ireland.

VERB TO BE: Conlon, how do you know yet will your lesson suit him at all?

MICKLE: Is it my lessons not to suit? Didn't the last wan say there wasn't my equal in Ireland for learning and brightness?

BROC (*hastily*): Easy now let ye; ye're putting astray Mr. Corry's time. (*To Tim.*) Well, sir, barring the few pieces I gave you, about poor oul' Whang the Miller and Cinderella and how the Pied Piper played the trick, the divil a much more learning I can command; but here's a true genuine Professor. . . . Now, Verb To Be, out with your full complement of learning.

He crosses to behind Verb To Be.

MICKLE (*scornfully*): Go ahead, Verb To Be. Let Corry hear your rubbish.

VERB TO BE (*ignoring Mickle*): Sir, to give my full complement of learning would take too long; but I'll give you a few main heads.

TIM: That'll do. (*Prepares to write.*)

VERB TO BE: Sir, I can give you "The Sayings of Poor Richard" and "The Principles of Politeness." I can give you the Spaniards Christopher Columbus and Don Quixton, and the English Robinson Crusoe, Dick Turpin, Black Bess, and Queen Bess. I can give you speeches by Robert Emmet and other patriots in the ty-ranny times; and I can skirmish through the speech against Warren Hastings. I can give you poems by the composers Scott and Robert Burns, and Tom Moore, and "The Isles of Greece" by the chief composer of the world: Lord Byron. Would that much do you, sir, for a commencement?

TIM: It will — if it all come out of books.

VERB TO BE (*with a triumphant side glance at Mickle*): Sir, like all true learning, it derived from books.

BROC: Good man, Verb To Be! (*Subdued applause from the Haws.*) And now, sir, you have no business asking this lot (*indicating the Haws*). All the learning they have is how to draw the cork out of a bottle. Mickle is the next you should test now. (*Loudly.*) Mickle, he wants to hear your litany of learning.

MICKLE (*grimly*): All right; all right; all right! (*Slashes grimly at floor, working himself up, then speaks loudly.*) Corry, I'm as blind as a piper, and I can see none. Have you your two ears laid well back, and all ready for my litany of learning?

TIM: To be sure, Mickle.

MICKLE: I can give you the particular account of the giants and unbelievers of olden times; Finn that killed Awlawn, Son of the Wonder; Diarmuid Donn that the women of Ireland were after like the sheep after the green grass in March; Oscar that took his flail with him to Hell and leathered as black as the crane all the divils in it, when the Fenians wouldn't give in to God and were sent to Hell at last; Ossian that gave in to God and is to this day a saint in all the prayerbooks; Goll McMorna, a hardy chuck that done great actions too; and Conawn that hadn't a rib of hair between himself and the sky.

BROC and HAWS: Good man, Mickle; good Mickle, etc. Mickle for it!

MICKLE: I can give you the particular account of the Gobawn Saor, the castle

47

builder, that invented stonework — the wan trade the world couldn't improve on in a thousand years since. I can give you the Bolgadhawn that preferred the sound of the potatoes boiling to the angels singing in Heaven. I can give you St. Brigid that saved the life of Our Saviour when King Herod's men come after Him with guns and all other convayniences for killing; St. Columcille that prophesied when Ireland'd be in danger; St. Patrick that never cut his hair or beard out of humility and because pride is the greatest sin in the world. . . . I can narrate to you oul' King James that withdrew back the Irish army at the battle of the Boyne for fear they'd make a widow of his daughter; I can narrate to you Dean Swift, that had the worst-conducted wife and the smartest servant boy in the ring of Ireland. I can give you Shawn-a-Sagarth from Ballintubber, that had five pound to get from the government for every priest he'd kill in the ty-ranny times. . . . I can give you songs in the Irish tongue by Raftery, a special composer that was gifted by God, and songs by Cormac Dall, the composer that'd tell no lie. I can read you the Blakes and the Bodkins that were landlords over this parish before now, with every oul' moll and bully in the county like merrymen in and out to them. I can give you the three men that are standing this night in the pits of Hell — Gorman the Bailiff, and Dennehy the Bailiff, and Bailiff Hynes. I can give you the man that freed us out from all bailiffs and landlords at last — Michael Davitt from Straide (*taking off his hat*), may Heaven be his rest! . . . Have you enough, Corry, or do you want another litany more?

TIM: That much'll do for a while, Mickle.

BROC: Isn't that great learning, sir? And 'tisn't wan litany more he could give, but twenty litanies more.

VERB TO BE: Sir, ask him where it derived from.

TIM: Did it come out of books, Mickle?

MICKLE (*with scorn*): Not wan jot or tittle of it! The same as all right learning, it was handed down in the Visiting Houses before now.

VERB TO BE: Now, sir, do your duty. Put the truth standing.

BROC (*rising*): I'll tell you, Mickle. It appears the government are gone to the bad since the last fellow was around. They reckon now no learning is true but booklearning.

MICKLE: Corry, do you and the government venture to say that my learning isn't true and perfect learning?

VERB TO BE (*to Tim*): Sir, do your duty. Put the truth standing.

TIM: The government discovered lately, Mickle, that the learning of the Visiting Houses was only all lies.

MICKLE (*fiercely*): My learning only lies! Corry, if the government say that, they should be flung out as rotten as dogs!

VERB TO BE: Conlon, how dare you say that about a government that hasn't its equal in the world for brightness?

MICKLE (*rounding upon Verb To Be furiously*): Verb To Be, you're like the goat — all noise and no wool. What do you know about brightness?

VERB TO BE: Conlon, I know more than you, that couldn't read your name over a door.

MICKLE: Verb To Be, if there was a law brought out condemning ignorant men, you'd be the first man in Ireland to be hung.

VERB TO BE (*jumping up*): Well here, Conlon. (*Tosses his hat on the floor between them, points to it.*) From there; from the earth to the sky, I'll bet I can argue with you on anything.

MICKLE: All right; all right; all right! When Ossian seen the Fenians in Hell and asked God to ease them out of their situation, and spill water on them, what offer did God make?

VERB TO BE: Conlon, there was never such a person as Ossian. He's a legend.

MICKLE: That's an upright lie. Isn't he a saint down in all the prayerbooks? Are the prayerbooks liars?

VERB TO BE: He's only a legend. His name is not down in the prayerbooks.

MICKLE (*to the company*): D'ye hear him? He's an unbeliever! He's turning Communist!

BROC (*rising*): Wait, men; ye have a collegian here. Let him judge between ye.

VERB TO BE: I agree to that.

MICKLE: All right. Corry, was there giants in Ireland long ago, awful rude men that reckoned they could conquer the whole world in strength?

BROC (*moving quickly to where Verb To Be cannot see him*): Now, sir, which is right? (*Points to Mickle.*)

TIM: Mickle is right.

MICKLE: Now, Verb To Be, you liary vagabone! Now who has the best learning?

BROC: Good man, Mickle!

THE HAWS: Good Conlon! . . . He caps all! . . . Hi for Mickle! . . . He's your domino for you!

MARY: Good yourself, Mickle.

Verb To Be has been stunned for a moment, and stands looking dumbly from Mickle to Tim. Then he takes up his hat and turns to Tim.

VERB TO BE (*restraining himself*): Sir, since you say that, you are either an uneducated man or a fool. Whether or which, sir, I bid you goodday.

He puts on his hat and sets out for the door.

MICKLE: He's off! He's on the beaten hand!

VERB TO BE (*turning*): Conlon, I am not on the beaten hand. But I'm disgusted!

MICKLE: You're disgusted because you must give in I have the best learning.

VERB TO BE (*coming back again*): Conlon, what learning have you? Can you write a copperplate hand the same as me? Have you Euclid and surveying, the same as me? Have you the capitals of Europe? Have you the Verbal Distinctions? Have you the English and Irish Vulgarisms? Can you explain cascade? Can you explain baboon? Can you spell Antitrinitarian, the same as me?

MICKLE: Sure, that's not learning! Sure that's only education! What did I want with that rubbish when I could get the finest of learning in the Visiting Houses without it?

VERB TO BE: Conlon, your ignorance is insurmountable. I'll say no more. Men, I bid ye goodday. (*Turns to go.*)

BROC (*urgently*): Verb To Be, remember this. Whichever of ye quits first has the day lost. Any road, that's what people'll say.

Verb To Be pauses irresolutely.

MICKLE: And, Corry, that question was the easiest I have. If I put him the question that stumbled a rank of schoolmasters wan year at the Sports, he was wiped out directly.

BROC (*urgently, to the still hesitating Verb To Be*): If you quit, they'll have it you lost.

Verb To Be comes back slowly to his place, looks around.

VERB TO BE: Very well, men. I'm taking the field against him again. (*Grimly.*) And this time, Conlon, I'll argue with you till your teeth fall out.

Sits down and faces Mickle.

MICKLE: All right, Verb To Be. Answer this question. What is the most difference between these times and the olden times?

VERB TO BE: In these times, Ireland has no ice and is populated with Irish; in olden times, in the Icy Age, Ireland was covered with ice and populated with Eskimoes.

MICKLE: Verb To Be, that is not the most difference.

VERB TO BE: And what's the most difference?

MICKLE: In these times, there's nothing talking only mankind; in olden times, everything was talking — animals and birds, and serpents, the dead, and all sorts from the next world, skulls and graves and everything.

Murt crashes through the doorway. He is a powerful, black, gloomy giant of a fellow; not listlessly gloomy, but vigorously and restlessly, a veritable smouldering volcano of a man. His eyes are dark and wild; his voice is so powerful that even his conversational tones amount almost to a shout. He is in his late thirties.

MURT (*roaring*): Broc, the two wits is landed!

Sensation. Mickle and Verb To Be are forgotten.

BROC (*jumping up*): Are you sure 'tis them?

MURT (*pointing*): 'Tis very like their images, Broc.

MARY (*running to the door*): Surely and truly it is their images!
Broc goes for his hat.

BROC (*putting on hat*): Has Kenny the otter trap, can you see?

MARY: He's carrying something.

MURT (*roaring*): An otter trap it is, for the wide world!

BROC: We have them fooled, so! They're believing there's an otter in it. Mr. Corry, wait for me, you.

Broc goes into room on right. Immediately discipline relaxes, and the Haws rush for the window and door.

THE HAWS: 'Tis them, all right! . . . Look at Kenny stepping down, and him lame! . . . We could study them better from across the road. . . . Outside, let ye!

In a moment they are swarming out.

MURT (*wrathfully*): Go easy, will ye. If they hear ye laughing, they'll tumble to it that we're fooling them . . . Easy, I tell ye!

Murt follows them out. Mickle, chuckling to himself, is already on the way. Verb To Be comes to Tim gravely.

VERB TO BE: Sir, it would be convenient if you could postpone further lessons till we see this joke played.

TIM: Go ahead. There's no hurry.

VERB TO BE: Sir, you're a gentleman. One gentleman can always know another.

Thus, impressively, Verb To Be makes his exit. Tim hides notebook in dresser, goes to fire, and lights a cigarette. Murt strides in, gives Tim one of his quick, wild stares.

MURT (*shouting as if the man were two fields away*): Hallo, there!

TIM: Hallo!

But Murt has already turned his back upon him. He sits on table, looking out door moodily.

TIM: This is a dang good Visiting House ye have here.

MURT (*turning suddenly and powerfully*): Your woman tells me you're for Manchester, Corry.

TIM: Next month. Will she miss me?

MURT: Certainly. (*With Murt it is cert-ain-ly; not one mighty word, but three.*) But never mind her; do what's best for yourself. Every wan in Ireland must look after himself, and let God look after all . . . Isn't that the way to say it, Corry?

TIM (*with a grin, for he knows Murt of old*): That's the way to say it.

MURT: Certainly, Corry. (*Coming downstage.*) And that's the way I say it to me own woman I'm great to eleven years. Ye're acquainted, Corry?

He sits on form.

TIM: I met her with the rest of ye at the dances.

MURT (*powerfully*): My oul' lad won't give me leave to marry for ten year more; I sez: "And by that time you'll be starved out, and the age'll be beginning to look on you. Never mind waiting for me," I sez. "Marry the first you can get," I sez. . . . Wasn't it the way to say it, Corry?

TIM: 'Twas, but why won't he give you leave to marry?

MURT: I'm time enough, he sez. Time enough! — and I on the borders of thirty-seven year! (*He jumps up so fiercely as to knock over the form, goes back to table, glances back darkly.*) This I'm going to tell you, Corry. Weren't for the while's sport we have here at night, I was long since disgusted with the world. (*He returns to looking out the door again.*)

TIM: Is Julia not inclined to look for another wan?

MURT: If she were itself, Corry, 'twouldn't be easy to get wan that'd suit her.

TIM: How is that?

MURT: He'd want to be master of a few hundred pound to restock the land. Her oul' lad drank everything living off the land before he died at last — my curse forever on him!

Broc enters carrying blanket, which he folds across chair at the fire.

BROC: Corry, I'll be as busy as a nailer till this plot is over, and so will Murt here, and herself must mind the house till Beezie comes. Murt, get somewan that'll direct him to the lake, and make him the wiser of everything.

MURT (*powerfully*): Certainly. (*Goes.*)

BROC (*folding blanket*): Every night, Corry, a new plot and every plot to have a new clue; that's the way to throng a Visiting House; that's the way, sir.

TIM: At this rate I'll come every night pleasuring with ye.

BROC: You're welcome, Corry, for you'd be an apt boy at playing parts for us. You played the inspector very nice.

TIM (*delighted*): D'ye reckon so?

BROC: In playing a part the main thing is to be cool and not to laugh. (*Goes to the door, then turns suddenly with an air of secrecy.*) Corry, is that daughter of mine gone out?

TIM: She is.

BROC: Good! (*Comes in looking serious.*) Tell me here; do you see her middling often at Thooraree Hall?

TIM: To be sure I see her in it, with the rest of the gang from this village.

BROC: D'ye know the fellow she's courting in it?

TIM: Wait till I see do I. (*Pretends to think.*) Well, I'll tell you what; the next night at the Hall I'll find out for you.

BROC: Find out whether they're courting strong, and what kind he is. I want to know all for a reason I have.

TIM: Why? Did you hear anything against him?

BROC (*bitterly*): I have plenty heard against him from the Haws. It appears he's the very class of fella I fair hate, so if I can help it, he'll never put his ring on her, or his name on my ass cart. (*Sets out for door again.*)
Enter Murt.

MURT: Here, Corry; me own woman.

BROC (*briskly to Murt*): And now, sir, you and me'll want to be making tracks.

MURT (*rehearsing as they go*): The minute I hear the dive of the stone in the water I'm to shout — "The otter! That's him!" (*Exit Broc and Murt.*)
Julia comes in. She is thirty or more, thin, dark, sallow, her clothes rather shabby. She is placid and good-humored, living only for the day; nothing can really excite or worry her. Her voice is deep and slow.

JULIA (*smiling*): We're soon enough going yet, Corry.
She sits on form against back wall.

TIM (*vigorously*): Well, the divil in Hell choke the same Haws! (*Striding to the door.*) Where are they till I catch up and slay them?

JULIA: Why? What did they do on you?

TIM: Do on me! They have every lie worse than another told to Broc about me! They have my character broken with him!

JULIA (*smiling*): Not them, Corry, they never said thing about you at all. They told him 'twas a fella from Kiltevna she was courting.

TIM (*coming in*): A fella from Kiltevna! What did they go spinning him that lie for?

JULIA: What else but teasing him? Broc was evermore dreading and fore-telling that she'd surely fall for some fella with nothing only good looks, with no wit in him, and no belief in sport, a sourface that'd want only talk about the crops and the fairs in the Visiting House.

TIM (*chuckling*): Be heggins: the very kind that'd balk all sport in a Visiting House!

JULIA: Before she was a month going to the dances the Haws in divilment told him she was gone daft after that very class of fella from Kiltevna.

TIM: So that's it!
He sits beside her on the form.

TIM (*ruefully*): Well, Broc can spare himself worrying. She's as hardy against marriage as ever I seen.

JULIA: You stand no chance, Corry, unless you first coax Broc to your side.

TIM: Is it Broc? What could he do with her?

JULIA: He's very able. He might compose some plan that'd coax her mind round to marriage.

TIM (*chuckling*): Right enough! That fellow is as cute as a pet fox. But how could I win him to my side?

JULIA: Come visiting every night a while first, and prove yourself lively and able in all plots the kind he likes in his Visiting House. Then you could tell him you have a wish for her.

TIM (*with enthusiasm*): No lie; he might help me with her then — if 'twas only to keep out that dry skin from Kiltevna!

JULIA: Very apt he would, Corry.

TIM: All right, be heggins, my plan is made. I'll be here every night, and play my best in all plots. Then at last I'll tell him of the wish I have for her and the four hundred pound I have to sweeten it.

JULIA: 'Tis better than her own plan of marrying you to some other girl around with a farm.

TIM (*chuckling*): To humor her I said I'd consider that; but not me. All *I'm* watching is a chance to wheedle herself.

JULIA: Here 'she is!

Song is heard outside. Mary runs in with an armful of turf.

MARY (*triumphantly*): Now, Tim, you vexer! Now wouldn't the sport here delight you?

TIM: After tonight I'm believing all ever you told me about this Visiting House.

MARY (*delighted*): And Tim, now you'll be happy to settle around this country?

TIM: Before I'd make up my mind about that I'd want to come visiting a week or two more.

MARY: The very thing you'll do, Tim.

She throws down turf on the hearth. Behind her back, Tim and Julia exchange meaning glances.

JULIA (*rising*): The very thing. And now the plot should be due. I'll see is there any sign. (*She goes.*)

MARY (*turning to him urgently*): Tim, I'm after exploring the whole parish in my mind, and there's only wan around with a farm that'd be nice enough for you.

TIM (*humorously*): What harm? Wan is enough for me.

MARY: This one is a few years older than you all right; but no matter; she's a nice kind talker, as gentle as a baby, and she hasn't a single wan in the house with her only God Almighty.

TIM: Who is she?

MARY: Her that's gone out that door — Julia!

TIM: Julia! Murt's woman!

MARY: He can't marry her, Tim, because he has no money to restock her land. You have, so you'd just suit her.

TIM (*alarmed*): What, man! That fellow is cracked about her. He'd go for my throat like a dog.

MARY: Not him, Tim. Isn't he every day of the year telling her to get some-wan when himself can do nothing for her?

TIM: Well, in a couple of weeks' time when I have Murt reckoned up I'll maybe see you're right.

MARY: You will see, Tim, and in the meantime you'll want to be weaning your mind away from me, and setting it at Julia instead.

TIM: Right enough.

MARY: And you mustn't be home from the dances with me any more, Tim.

TIM (*hastily*): Oh, murther! Why so?

MARY: For that'd keep your mind thinking of me.

TIM: Well, I'll tell you what'd be better again. Me to be home with you, and all the way you can be telling me all the bad points you have and all the good points Julia has. That's what'll soon change my mind.

MARY: D'ye reckon so, Tim?

TIM: What, man, I'm sure so.

MARY: All right so, you can be home with me from the dances; but no kiss; for any more that'd be awful bad for you.

TIM: Or a better plan again, if you were to kiss me very clumsy and rough, for then I'd like you less every time.

MARY (*dubious*): Tim, I never would be able to manage that plan clever enough. No kiss at all'd be away safer for you.

TIM: Not it! And d'ye know another way you could help me?

MARY: How, Tim?

TIM: If you'd reckon up all the good points of marriage, and be telling them out to me, 'twould make me more greedy for marrying Julia.

MARY: Tim, that'd be a good plan.

Julia runs in.

JULIA: Corry, the shouting is started! The plot is going forward!

TIM (*jumping up*): Then we'll want to be gathering our legs out of here!

JULIA: Keep close to me.

She runs out.

TIM (*turning at door*): Don't forget; be reckoning up the good points of mar-riage for me.

MARY: I'll be at it every day as often as I have toes.

TIM (*grinning*): Do, and maybe 'twill soon win your own mind around to marriage.

MARY (*hastily*): No, no, Tim! Not for many a year yet.

TIM (*laughing*): We'll see, whatever.

Julia's voice is heard calling "Corry! Corry!"

TIM: I'm coming. (*Runs out.*)

MARY: The vexer! He's still planning to capture meself! . . .

She produces cigarette-end from a secret pocket, and crosses to fire.

MARY (*shaking her head regretfully*): Badly I behaved to get so great to him when I wasn't ready for marriage. (*Quick curtain.*)

Act II

The scene is the same, and the time is after dark a week later. The stage is in darkness, apart from a little light from the fire. Three men are seated near the fire, while a fourth is barely discernible as he stands upright, facing the audience, in the darkest part of the stage. Suddenly this man's face is dimly illuminated by a strange red glow which gives it a distorted and unearthly appearance. It remains thus for several seconds.

BROC (*seated near fire*): What's your thinking about that, Corry?

TIM (*at fire*): 'Tis most surprising. How do ye bring it about?

BROC: 'Tis as simple as simple. Set a bicycle lamp under your jacket lapels, and shoot a dash of light through colored paper onto your face.

TIM: Coogan played his part well last night. He acted so afraid that I was nearly believing he did see a ghost.

The ghost face disappears, and its owner goes into bedroom.

BROC: I planned with Coogan to say that so as their brains'd be nicely softened up for tonight's ghost plot.

TIM: Mocking is catching. We're all right if some real ghost doesn't appear out of jealousy.

Paddy comes out of room carrying the kitchen lamp.

BROC (*going to door*): Now I'll show you where you're to appear.

TIM: Just what I'm panting to know.

Broc and Paddy go out. Tim rises, goes to dresser. Murt remains seated at fire poking it with the tongs with gloomy ferocity.

TIM: Murt, go easy with that fire, or you'll not leave a spark in it. . . . I promised I'd set the rat trap for her.

He gets an old rat trap from under the dresser, also some bacon and a knife from the dresser, and sets to work at the table, baiting and setting the trap.

MURT (*turning wildly and suddenly, tongs in hand*): Corry, what do you reckon brought the dark cloud over Ireland first?

TIM: Some reckon 'twas after the famine times, when the runaway matches gave over, and the matchmaking come in.

MURT (*fiercely emphasizing his points with the tongs on the floor*): Whatever the reason, Corry, the dark cloud is over us. The people is turning quare. And the cats is turning quare. Rabbits is all they want — they won't look at a rat, Corry!

56

TIM (*smiling*) : Only for the rat traps we were lost, man.

Murt rises, then, tongs in hand, advances upon Tim slowly and grimly, as if he were about to brain him. But instead he nearly splits the table with a blow.

MURT: Eleven years I'm great to Julia; still he'll not give me leave to marry for ten year more. Isn't that man deserving of strychnine, Corry?

TIM: His way of thinking is too strong in this country, whatever.

MURT (*powerfully*): I'll tell you how it'll be, Corry; there'll be no marriage for me ever.

TIM: Right enough, when a fellow has only a small holding of land the women won't marry him unless he's young.

MURT: Certainly, Corry. And I have only a small holding, and I'll not get leave to marry young, so there'll be no marriage ever for me.

TIM: There's many a wan in your case.

MURT: Certainly. And if we marry in spite of them, they'll will the farm to someone else and leave us without the breadth of our backs of anything living.

TIM: That's sure. The will is their rifle evermore.

His fury largely expended, Murt returns to fire bitterly, sits down once more.

MURT (*darkly*): This I'm going to tell you, Corry. Weren't for the while's sport we have here at night I'd be many a time tempted to shave and cut my throat.

Broc enters briskly, carrying axe and a crosscut.

BROC: Now let ye study these a while. They're to relieve us from the two worst dangers to tonight's plot. What would ye say the dangers are?

TIM: This, I'd reckon: if th' oul' people wance suspicion either ourselves or the Haws — the plot is no more.

BROC: That's it. So we'll let on to th' oul' people I asked the Haws to come visiting early, and cut a lock of firewood for me. Sooner than do a bit of work, the Haws'll not come here at all tonight. Instead they'll set off for Dowd's for a night's card-playing, and they'll take care the whole vil-lage'll see them going. That'll put the Haws out of suspicion.

MURT (*powerfully*): Certainly.

TIM: Good yourself!

BROC: Myself'll be raging mad over the Haws to fail me, and when th' oul' people see me without a word for a dog, and cross enough to bite a croc-odile's sting, they'll not suspicion me either. So the plot'll be safe.

TIM: There's no banging of you.

BROC (*sternly*): And mind, Murt, when yourself and the Haws sneak back by the bog to share in the plot, keep a deadly eye on the Haws. The first wan that's noisy, draw his blood.

Broc hurries out with axe and crosscut.

MURT: The Haws have no choice but to obey me. They have a row on for Thooraree Hall Sunday night, and they stand no chance without me.

TIM: You should leave them to fight their own battles.

MURT: But, Corry, they aren't fit. There isn't wan of them man enough to beat a carpet. How could I see my own village lose all rows as rotten as pears?

Broc strides in.

BROC (*to Murt*): Hurry on, sir. Gather up the Haws. Gather them up.

MURT: Certainly.

Murt goes out. Broc gets himself a drink from the dresser.

BROC (*jug in hand*): Fresh buttermilk . . . Maybe yourself'd take a few pours?

TIM: Be heggins, I will take a couple.

BROC: As many pours as you like, sir.

Leaves jug and mug before Tim and goes to the fire to drink his own.

TIM (*pouring out*): If this plot knocks as many laughs out of me as last night's, I'll be well thirsty.

BROC (*becoming grave*): Now, Corry, tell me: did you inquire at last night's dance about this boyo from Kiltevna that she's great to?

TIM: He is just the kind the Haws made out he was; goodlooking but a dry skin with no wit in him and no belief in sport. When duskus comes itself and he has to stop working he'll go to the Visiting House, and he don't want any conversation in it only the last fair and the next fair, the prospects of the crops, and the prospects of the hens.

BROC: My blood runs cold to think of his like settling here. (*He rises and begins to walk up and down, greatly perturbed.*) He'd quench the Visiting House in the run of a week.

TIM (*slyly*): 'Tis a pity she ever got great to such a wan. And herself so nice she could have any lad going into Thooraree.

Broc stops pacing suddenly and takes a long look at Tim, who pretends not to notice.

BROC (*suddenly*): Well, now, Corry, wance you said as much I'll tell you my plan for splitting herself and the boyo from Kiltevna.

TIM: What's that?

BROC: I'm a good while watching out for a right able, lively lad, wan that'd delight in plots and sport, and, as soon as I get him, I'll do the best I can to make a match with him, and shoulder out this sourface from Kiltevna.

TIM: You'll want to get wan she'll like.

BROC: That's the first point. Well, I'm remarking every night how the minute you come in the door her two eyes soften with joy, so I'm in doubt she has a wish for you.

TIM (*as if incredulous*): For me, is it?

BROC: For you, Corry. And have you any wish for her?

TIM (*as if reluctant*): Well, there's nothing like the truth, so I might as well give it to you — there isn't a girl going into Thooraree Hall I'd prefer before her.

BROC (*immensely relieved and delighted*): Corry, 'tis as good as a glass of whiskey to me to hear that. (*Sternly again — fanatically almost.*) But mind you, the fellow I want for her isn't a middling character, able only for simple parts in simple plots the same as the Haws. What I'm looking for is a right able character fit for the hardest parts in hard plots. All the week I gave you only simple parts till you'd have practice got; but to-night I'm testing you right with a hard part. If you play tonight's part good, I'll help you all roads to win marriage from her.

TIM: All right. Every trick that's in me I'll set working, and pass the test.

A clatter of tinware is heard outside.

BROC: Here's herself! (*With a wink.*) Keep your tongue in your pocket now about all I told you.

He hurries out in the best of humor. Tim chuckles, rubs his hands with great satisfaction, crosses to fire with his mug of milk. Mary comes in with a can of milk and a tin or mug, which she brings to the table.

MARY (*in good humor*): Have you the rat trap ready, Tim?

TIM: Ready and deadly, man. Tomorrow there'll be a rat short in the world.

MARY: Good yourself. I'll set it at the foot of the bed. (*She transfers trap to the dresser, and comes over to him, looking very grave.*) And now, Tim, there's a thing I must give you good fighting over. (*She sits beside him.*)

TIM (*cheerfully*): What's it?

MARY: You're a week visiting here and delighted with the sport in it. Then why don't you at once ask Murt would he mind Julia to marry you? What are you delaying for?

TIM: What, man? I couldn't propose for her till first I have my mind cooled away from you, and warmed up toward herself.

MARY: You're at that work a week, Tim, and by now you should have it done. Is it not thriving with you, or what?

TIM (*with a worried air*): There's no good denying it, 'tisn't thriving with me at all.

MARY (*dismayed*): Tim, this is an awful lamentable thing. And d'ye think why is it failing you?

TIM (*with mock seriousness*): 'Tis failing me because you had me too far dazzled, and too long. 'Twould be as easy to set a gander hatching as 'twould be to banish you from my head now.

MARY: You had no right ever to get so fond of me when I wasn't ready for marriage.

TIM: The way that happened I never felt till you had me dazzled.

MARY (*regretfully*): Wan thing is sure, I had no right to let you with me from the dance last night. That's only bad for you. 'Tis only making us have twice more wish for each other.

TIM (*cunningly*): Not it. For on the road home didn't you make known to me all the good points Julia has and all the flaws you have: hot-tempered and the like?

MARY: Well, Tim, it's the truth; I have temper. A person wouldn't be long sticking a pin in me until I'd shout "Stop!"

TIM: When I have them flaws reckoned up a while they'll banish you from my head at last.

MARY: No lie, we'll suffer sad for a while. Last night at the dance I couldn't see any lad I'd have nature for like I have for you.

TIM (*pouncing*): My belief is, it must be allotted for us pair to marry, and if we don't, we'll have bad luck.

MARY: Good luck or bad, Tim, I couldn't marry for many a year on account 'twould lose me the Visiting House.

TIM: Well, what about this plan? Us to wed, and I'd take turn about at minding whatever'd be born for us. So each of us could go visiting every second night.

MARY: But you're only a man. What would you know about minding screechers?

TIM: What do you know yourself?

MARY: Nothing, God forgive me! Still and all, on account I'm a woman I'd learn, but you never would.

TIM: What trouble is in it except leave the tongs across the pram for fear they'd fall out?

MARY (*jumping up in alarm*): Tim! I'm away from my right mind!

TIM: Why so?

MARY: Talking of marriage when I amn't ready for it for many a year yet. (*Reproachfully.*) You vexer, you're only putting me off about Julia, till you manage some ways to get around myself!

TIM (*with an air of injured innocence*): What, man, not me! I only want time to get great to Julia, and haven't I a long month yet for asking her?

MARY: You have not a month, Tim. For if Murt takes it anyways bad, Julia won't join you. Then we'll have to rummage the country for another girl for you.

TIM (*reassuringly*): My four hundred pounds'll easy get wan.

MARY: That's where you're wrong, Tim. Girls with a farm are scarce enough, and you're that hard pleased we might take weeks looking for wan you'd like well enough. My mind is made up. Tonight I'll tell Murt that you're proposing for Julia.

And off with her to the dresser.

TIM (*alarmed*): Not tonight whatever. He's in awful trouble altogether to-night.

MARY: Sure he's in the same trouble at the start of every night. But the night's sport'll soon put him at the height of his glee, and that'll be our time to ask him.

TIM (*urgently*): No matter what time you ask that lad, you'll draw down bother. That's as sure as you're a foot high.

MARY (*confidently*): Wait till you see how clever I'll manage him. Ssh! (*Listens.*) They're coming. Tim, keep the ghost talk going, you, for the first while. I have to strain the milk.

She brings can, jugs, and strainer to table and is now in the best of humor.

TIM: I'll hold it for you.

Holds strainer over jugs while she pours out. Verb To Be and Beezie enter. Beezie is a slow-moving but fresh old lady, dressed in her workaday long black skirt reaching to her ankles, and a black shawl. On occasions she can be lively and humorous, but more usually she is meditative, credulous, and even a little mysterious. She stands in doorway, looking down road in opposite direction to village.

VERB TO BE (*with his accustomed dignity*): I wish ye well.

He sits on form, lights his pipe.

TIM (*heartily*): How are ye?

BEEZIE (*very seriously, coming up to Tim*): Tell me, here: did ye see any-thing at the bridgeen and you going home last night?

TIM: The divil a thing; or tonight when I was coming; and I kept a sharp watch out the two times.

BEEZIE: Throth, Coogan seen thing in it last night whatever.

MARY (*as if skeptical*): Beezie, I doubt Coogan was only humbugging us.

BEEZIE: Why would he? Wasn't he shaking in his boots with the 'fraid? And wasn't there wans seen at that bridgeen ever?

TIM: He was afeard all right. He wouldn't go home that way again only my-self was with him.

VERB TO BE: In the faction fighting times, several were killed there; and they were seen from time to time. That's positive.

Mary finishes operations at dresser, and goes into the room. Beezie is still at door, watching the neighborhood of the bridge.

TIM (*shaking his head*): I don't know; I'm in doubt them tales were all only lies and imagination. I reckon nowan from the next world ever come back at all.

VERB TO BE (*somewhat severely*): Young man, you think that because your reading was neglected. If you read more — if you read the Christmas number of *Ireland's Own*, you'd know better.

TIM: Well, maybe they were appearing in times past; but you'd hear of nothing lately.

VERB TO BE: There's this much in what you say. According as priests and Masses are getting more numerous, a lot are freed from their penances and such ones are no longer appearing.

BEEZIE (*coming in*): Well, that's where the two of ye are wrong. Members of the next world are as plentiful as ever they were.

She sits on form at end near fire.

TIM: How is it they aren't seen, so?

BEEZIE: Because nowan could see them ever, except wan that'd be gifted; and 'tis the gifted persons that are getting scarce.

TIM: Did you know anywan to be gifted?

BEEZIE (*complacently*): Throth I did. All our family were gifted. From the two sides we had it.

TIM: You had!

VERB TO BE (*to Beezie*): Narrate to him about what you met at Tully's lone bush not two months ago.

BEEZIE (*impressively*): I was crossing the bog by myself wan night, and just at the lone bush I was made afeard.

TIM: What did you see?

BEEZIE (*gravely*): Nothing.

TIM: Something you heard, so?

BEEZIE: No; I didn't hear anything either.

TIM: And how did you know there was anything in it at all, so?

BEEZIE (*staring*): What kind of talk is that? Don't you know there must be something in it when I was made afeard?

Broc appears in door, carrying crosscut and axe, and looking very stern.

BROC: I asked the Haws to come and cut a lock of firewood for me. Did you see them anywhere?

BEEZIE: They're gone across the bog to Dowd's playing for a pig's head. They told me to tell you.

BROC (*fiercely*): What pig's head? I didn't hear of anywan to kill a pig.

BEEZIE: I didn't either.

VERB TO BE: There was none killed to my knowing.

BROC (*furious*): All right. After tonight the Haws have full stripes and promotions got to the rank of blackguards.

He almost flings axe and crosscut into corner in his fury.

TIM (*to Broc*): Broc, d'ye reckon the pig's head is only a lie, and an excuse to dodge the work?

BROC: Certainly so; but all right. I'll even up matters with the Haws.

BEEZIE: They should be ashamed of their story.

VERB TO BE: That is a case of ingratitude.

BROC (*still savage*): It's a wonder ye wouldn't wake up the fire a piece itself. (*Pokes it.*) It appears everything is to be left to me in this house.

The trio exchange glances, and at this stage Verb To Be decides to pour oil on troubled waters.

VERB TO BE: Have you a bright plot composed for tonight, Broc?

BROC: No plots tonight. I'm away from the laughing country altogether tonight. (*He strides out fiercely.*)

BEEZIE: He's awful vexed. Did you see him shuffling his teeth with vexation?

Mickle appears in doorway, peering toward bridge likewise.

MICKLE: My eyes is stimless; I have no business looking. (*Loudly.*) Did ye remark thing at the bridgeen tonight?

BEEZIE: Nothing yet whatever, Mickle.

He comes in slowly to his chair, left of table and about middle of kitchen. Mary comes from room with some knitting; she sets to work at table.

MARY (*drawing her*): D'ye know, Beezie? I reckon 'twas only bog lights Coogan seen.

BEEZIE: Why would it? Didn't he reckon there was a face in it, too? Wasn't it that put his heart in his mouth altogether?

MARY: But you were out looking within five minutes, and there was nothing to be seen. If there was thing in it at all, it couldn't be vanished away that quick.

BEEZIE: Why couldn't it? Aren't them wans coming and going like the bad weather?

TIM: Mickle, did anywan you ever knew come back from the next world?

MICKLE: Didn't I know th' oul' fortuneteller, Biddy the Tosser, that lived in a nook drawing to Cosslough?

TIM: Did she come back?

MICKLE: Biddy got the loan of a scissor from a neighbor, and before she returned it, wan day the fever thawed down on top of her, and soon delved Biddy into her grave. The neighbor searched high up and low down for the scissor, but if she lit the house she couldn't find it till Biddy came back in the midnight, and told her where 'twas hid away. . . . I seen Biddy above wance, when she was living.

BEEZIE (*pensively*): In the next world they're very strict all right. If there was anything you forgot to give back, or to do, they'll make you come back, and settle up about it.

TIM: Verb To Be, have you any case?

VERB TO BE (*impressively*): Young man, not only have I cases, but I can prove them to you moreover.

TIM: Good, yourself.

VERB TO BE: In former times, a couple in Dublin were in doubt whether there was a next world or no. They promised whichever'd die first'd come back

63

and tell the other. He died first, and that night he appeared, and told her all.

MARY: Verb To Be, maybe 'twas to dream it she did.

VERB TO BE: It was not, for he left her a proof. He put his hand on her wrist; her wrist blackened and withered up, and she hadn't the use of it again till the day she died. . . . That case happened without a doubt. I read it in a book — in *Our Boys*.

MICKLE: Verb To Be, for wance in your days you have the truth. Anywan that promises to come back must come back, and I'll give ye more foundation for that in a while's time.

Meanwhile, he gets out his tobacco and pipe.

TIM: But all them cases happened years and years ago. You wouldn't hear of anything at all appearing lately?

BEEZIE: What are you saying? 'Tisn't two years since a girl from Creeveeshal died, and was seen in the midnight on the side of the road, down on her two knees, and talk about crying! — She's draw the birds out of their eggs with her crying.

MICKLE: Matt behaved a bad man that night. He had right to ask her trouble.

BEEZIE: Sure he was too mad with the 'fraid. He broke into the nearest house, and wouldn't leave that again till break of day in the morning.

TIM: So nowan knows what was her trouble.

VERB TO BE: Likely she was lonesome and homesick, and they let her back to this world for a visit.

MICKLE: That was why they gave young Daly leave to come back, whatever.

MARY: Tell Tim about that case, Mickle.

MICKLE: They gave him leave to come visiting every night for a month, but he wasn't allowed to be in conversation with anywan, only a few words the first night, when he told them his business. Any more after that they'd not be long in bed till they'd hear his chair draw up to the fire — till his month was expired, and he was heard no more from that out.

During this last narrative, Kate enters. A usual Visiting House entry, inasmuch as none takes the slightest notice. . . . She is a raw-boned Amazon of middle age, very blunt of speech and manner.

KATE (*disgusted*): By cramp! Are ye at this rubbish of ghost's talk again? Didn't I tell ye I can't stand that?

BEEZIE (*indignantly*): What are you saying? Because you saw nothing yourself, do you think nowan ever saw anything?

KATE: Nowan ever saw anything, except wans that were boozed or suffering from imagination. (*Confidently.*) Amn't I right, Corry?

She sits beside Beezie.

TIM: I don't know, be heggins. Verb To Be read cases in books.

KATE: And what's to stop books from being liary? Sure paper can't refuse ink. Give over this rubbish and tell me, Corry, have you any newses?

Almost immediately after Kate's entry, Broc appears stealthily outside. By the audience he can be seen signaling in direction of the bridge. Finally, he sets his face in a very grim expression once more, and steps through doorway with an armful of turf.

BROC (*looking out*): Corry, if I had seven miles to cycle the same as you, I'd be making tracks.

TIM: D'ye reckon 'twill rain?

BROC: 'Twill, and dash great rain. All day long the hills is crushing nearer.

TIM: I'll be making a start so. (*Rises.*)

Broc brings turf down to the fire. Tim is putting on his cap and topcoat at the dresser.

TIM: Anyroad, I have pains in my bones all day, and I'm doubting 'tis the invoice of the 'flu. (*Turns to Beezie.*) Beezie, if you come a few steps of the road I'll give you them two verses you were short in "Shawn Tracy."

BEEZIE (*delighted*): Did you trace them? (*Rising.*)

TIM: I did. They have that song greatly off in our country.

BEEZIE (*following him out*): I'll be as thankful to you as the daylight. I'm with two years looking for the finish of that song.

TIM: Goodnight to ye all. (*He goes out.*)

ALL: Goodnight! . . . Safe home! . . . Good luck! . . .

Beezie stands at door looking out. Broc has fixed up fire, sits on stool with back to wall, turned toward audience and away from the others. He is still in a very bitter mood — except when he grins broadly behind a sheltering hand.

VERB TO BE (*to Beezie*): Is there anything visible yet?

BEEZIE: No, but I'll not pass the bridgeen whatever. (*She goes.*)

VERB TO BE: Likely it was only bog lights Coogan saw.

MICKLE (*abruptly, in slashing style*): When my grandfather was rising up, Captain Dillon was landlord in Gortmore, and he was a bad actor. He seized the cow on a poor widow, and her children reduced down and died for want of milk, so she went on her two knees, and cursed him with every curse she had. The curses weren't slow in working. Before the year was out, the War came in at Killala, the Captain went down and the French swept the head off him at Castlebar. All right; 'twasn't long after that till the servant girl was going dying and the Captain's widow made her promise to come back, and tell how her man fared. The girl was fourteen years dead before she came back. "I had to travel the whole world to catch him," she said. "His penance for seizing the cow is to go through the world evermore with a small stick, hitting every piece of cow dung on

65

the way." So that's what has most of them rambling. 'Tis doing penance for some sin they are.

KATE: Mickle, didn't I tell you to give over that rubbish of talk?

MICKLE (*thundering*): Kate Duggan, there's only this wan flaw in you: you're as ignorant as a cartload of clogs.

Tim comes in laughing heartily.

TIM: Did you ever hear the equal of this? Beezie reckons she sees him!

KATE: What's that?

MICKLE: Is it wan from the next world?

MARY: Is it the wan Coogan saw?

She is feigning alarm, and throughout the "plot" this well-trained daughter of the visiting house will play her part with skill.

TIM: She reckons so.

VERB TO BE: Where is he situated?

TIM: At the bridgeen. We weren't ten yards from it when he landed there — so she reckons.

MARY: And did you see him, Tim?

TIM: The divil a thing at all I could see. I doubt her eyes are dazzled or something.

MARY: Here she is.

Beezie appears in doorway, very thoughtful, and completely unhurried and untroubled. She stands looking raptly down the road and nodding to herself from time to time.

KATE (*disgusted*): Come in out of that, you daft oul' fool.

MARY: What can you see, Beezie?

No reply. Beezie does not even hear the question.

TIM: She reckons she could see it all the ways up to the door there, but curse the thing I could see. (*Looks out window.*)

KATE: Beezie!

VERB TO BE: It could be a case of hallucinations. They are very numerous in females.

Beezie comes upstage slowly at last.

BEEZIE (*briefly and somewhat absently*): There's a member of the next world on guard at the bridgeen.

She stands deep in thought in the middle of the stage.

VERB TO BE: What is his occupation?

BEEZIE: Nothing, only looking this side greatly and drawing an odd awful sigh.

MICKLE (*sternly*): Did you not ask him his trouble?

BEEZIE (*apologetically*): I didn't, Mickle — I didn't altogether like the looks of him.

66

MICKLE: Well, go back directly and ask him. 'Tis something he forgot to do, or to give back when he was in this world.

Having thus solved the problem to his own satisfaction, Mickle dismisses the subject from his mind, crosses to the fire, pipe in hand, and for some time to come is solely occupied with the work of lighting same.

BEEZIE: I have no occasion to ask him now. I have a plan made that'll ease him out of all trouble, it doesn't matter what it is.

She sits at table, takes purse from her bosom, counts out some silver therefrom.

MARY: I must look. (*Runs to door.*) Beezie, I can see nowan at the bridgeen.

TIM: And myself could see nothing.

BEEZIE (*vigorously*): I'm telling ye evermore only a gifted wan can see them. At last ye have the proofs of it. (*To Mary.*) Come here, girl.

MARY: What's it?

BEEZIE: I want you to go on a message for me.

MARY (*horrified*): Is it to ask him his troubles?

BEEZIE (*impatiently*): How could he hear your voice when you're not gifted? Whatever else ye'll do let ye talk sense.

Broc suddenly comes to life and strides to door, all, particularly Beezie, watching him intently.

TIM: Can you see thing?

Broc comes up to Beezie sternly.

BROC: Woman, is it out for humbugging the people you are?

BEEZIE (*mildly*): Broc, 'tis a great wonder you can't see him, for on your mother's side there was a gift walking, too.

BROC (*grimly*): There's nothing in it, woman — 'tis some image that traveled down to your eyes from your brains. (*And he goes back to his stool.*)

TIM: That's it, to be sure. Well, I'll be making off. Goodnight to ye.

KATE, ETC.: Goodnight, Corry.

MARY: Goodnight, and be sure to come tomorrow night again.

TIM: I will. (*He disappears.*)

BEEZIE: Mary, run up to the priest and ask him to read a Mass for the poor fellow. No matter what trouble his ghost is in, the Mass is the surest thing to free him out again.

MARY: Beezie, before we do anything, we should make sure is he in it first. (*She runs over to Verb To Be.*) Verb To Be, you're an educated man and couldn't be led astray. Let you take a look.

VERB TO BE (*grandly*): Well, I'll do what I can for ye. (*Rises.*)

MARY: Good yourself. Whatever you'll say'll settle it.

KATE: Verb To Be, you're as daft as Beezie.

VERB TO BE: Candidately, I'd say it's a case of hallucinations . . . (*Arrives in doorway, gasps.*) God bless me!

MARY: He sees something!

BEEZIE (*complacently*): What did I tell ye?

Verb To Be pushes back his hat, wipes his forehead, stares, blinks, stares again.

KATE: He's as bad as Beezie. No lie: There's no fool like th' oul' fool!

Verb To Be comes in unsteadily.

MARY: What did you see?

VERB TO BE (*to himself*): It couldn't be! God save us all!

He goes back to have another look, is staggered again, gasps "God save us!"

BEEZIE: Verb To Be, don't stop long there. If that wan gives you a blast of his eyes, you mightn't be the better of it.

Verb To Be looks at her startled, comes in, and sets out for the dresser.

MARY: What did you see?

But Verb To Be is busy pouring out a drink of milk for himself at the dresser.

BEEZIE (*to Verb To Be*): You could have a dash in you all right. Your mother seen the Headless Coach one time. Mary, didn't I tell you to be going to the priest?

MARY: But if a ghost is in it itself, how do ye know he's in need of a Mass? Maybe he's in Heaven already.

VERB TO BE (*vehemently*): Girl, he is not in Heaven. By the looks of him he's far from it.

BROC (*swings round fiercely*): Verb To Be, are you starting out now to humbug the people?

VERB TO BE: Broc, he is in it; and the image of a murderer's ghost that was pictured in *Our Boys*.

BROC: Rubbish! There's nothing in it.

KATE: Now you're talking.

MARY (*runs to Kate*): Kate, two of us seen him; and three couldn't. Let you look now and yours'll be the last word.

BEEZIE (*with infinite scorn*): Is it that wan to see him! When nowan belonging to her saw anything since the foundation of the world.

KATE: Because my people walked the roads sober and sensible, not the same as yours.

MARY: Go on, Kate. Sure it won't kill you to look.

KATE: All right, I'll go to the door. (*Rises.*) And straight from there, by cramp, to some house where there's sensible talk. (*She strides out, jumps instantly.*) Be the Blessed Book!

MARY: Do you see anything?

VERB TO BE: She sees him!

Kate bolts into kitchen after one look.

KATE (*wildly*): Beezie and Verb To Be and Mickle . . . . the curse of my

68

heart on ye! I told ye to give over talking of them. I told ye it do rouse them up. Now ye have us all in jeopardy!

BEEZIE (*rising in her wrath*): Are you trying to make out you're gifted? When nowan belonging to you ever saw anything!

KATE: That's a lie. They seen lights and many a thing, only I never believed them before now.

VERB TO BE: Stop let ye: this is no time for skirmishing. If somebody doesn't ask him his trouble he'll draw to the first light he sees, and there it is! (*Pointing to lamp.*)

MARY (*frightened*): Oh, dear!

BEEZIE (*calmly*): How could I forget that? Put out the lamp.

Kate has already arrived at the lamp when Broc jumps up.

BROC (*sternly*): Come away from that lamp.

KATE: Broc, he's in it, I tell you.

BROC (*grimly*): Promise or no promise, no member of the next world can come back, and I can prove it to ye. D'ye remember the night long ago I had the variance with oul' Paddy Kelly?

BEEZIE: Why wouldn't we?

BROC: And ye remember all the oaths he took that night that he'd come back from the dead and burn me? And how well he never did after?

VERB TO BE: How that was: Paddy had you accused in the wrong, so they wouldn't let him back.

BROC: If anywan at all could come back, 'twould fail them to hold Paddy. He'd break down all doors to get back, and burn me.

The door is flung open, and Tim enters breathlessly, topcoat torn open, cap awry.

TIM: Beezie, you had the truth. There is something that isn't right at the bridgeen.

MARY: What did you see?

TIM: Nothing: but Murt's mare sees something — the pair of us are after wrestling her till we're torn to pieces, but no good: she'll not pass the bridgeen.

KATE: Now, Broc! Is the mare suffering from imagination?

BROC (*gravely*): There's thing in it so. (*Rising in sudden alarm.*) And d'ye know who it was? 'Tis oul' Paddy Kelly coming back to burn me at last. It's Paddy, I tell ye!

TIM: We're safe here any road, for it appears he's the far side of the bridgeen, and they aren't allowed to cross over running water.

VERB TO BE: We overlooked that.

BEEZIE (*nodding*): They reckon that rule was passed in the next world all right.

BROC: But we don't know was it passed against them all; and we must make sure of that point. (*Takes up lamp.*) Open the door, Beezie, and see is he in it yet.

Tim opens door, Broc steps out holding aloft the lamp. Beezie follows him out.

KATE (*alarmed*): What kind of work is that? Drawing him on us.

BROC: I want to see will the light draw him across the bridgeen.

BEEZIE (*excited*): He's stirring! And looking at us greatly.

MARY: Father, give over, let ye.

BEEZIE: By the stick! He's vanished away altogether!

KATE: He is!

BROC: The lamp banished him. Some of them can't abide light at all. That's the finish of him. (*Carries lamp back to table.*)

KATE (*going to door to Beezie*): Now is our chance to escape from this end of the village.

She looks toward bridge too, and in another moment both Beezie and herself nearly jump out of their shoes.

BEEZIE: He's appearing again!

KATE: He's this side of the bridgeen!

BEEZIE: He's shooting straight for us!

KATE: In everywan, and close the door!

BROC (*turning down light*): Close the door, Corry; cover up the window, girl.

Tim bolts door, Mary holds topcoat to window.

KATE (*moaning*): My heart's blood'll give in. My heart's blood'll give in.

She sits on stool at fire, wraps her apron around her head.

BEEZIE (*impatiently*): What kind of talk is that? What can he do but tell us his trouble and ask us to set it right?

BROC: Let ye stand your ground; ye're safe. I'm running for my life for fear it might be Paddy Kelly.

He opens kitchen door and runs out. Mary quickly closes and bolts it again.

MICKLE (*thundering*): What are ye quenching the light for? What conjuring have ye?

VERB TO BE: We never harmed him when he was on earth, so he can't harm us now. I read that regulation in *Ireland's Own*.

He sits on form. Beezie is already there, and most of the company is now huddled about the fire. Mickle has risen and is leaning upon back of chair.

MICKLE: Will ye answer me up? What have ye the lamp blew for?

BEEZIE: Because there's a member of the next world about to burst in on top of us.

MICKLE (*furious*): That the breadth of a hen's eye of luck may never come anear ye! Ye never asked him his trouble yet!

BEEZIE: He'll be here any minute now, and then you can ask him yourself.

MICKLE: I'll ask him directly. Corry, open that door. (*He moves to center.*)

MARY (*running to door*): Ye will not. I don't want that wan in our house.

VERB TO BE: Keep it fast closed, girl. It's easier to let his kind in than to put them out again.

The torchlight now begins to shine dimly through window. Tim has been watching for this.

TIM: Beezie, take a peep out of the window you, and see will he pass.

This draws attention to light outside window.

BEEZIE (*jumping up*): Look! He's landed.

TIM (*looking*): I don't see anything.

VERB TO BE: 'Tis him!

The light passes the window slowly, and a moment later a knocking at the door begins; a slow, even-paced, cold-blooded, sinister knocking.

KATE (*terrified*): Quick, Mickle, before he breaks in on us.

TIM: Speak up, Mickle!

VERB TO BE: Hurry, man, before the door goes down!

MICKLE (*powerfully*): Who's that abroadside? (*No reply.*) Who's that abroadside? . . . Answer up, I tell you. (*Still no reply, the knocking continuing meanwhile.*)

BEEZIE: Them don't hear or answer till the third time. Go ahead again, Mickle.

MICKLE: Who's that abroadside?

The knocking stops abruptly. There is a pause.

THE VOICE (*a deep, steady, unemotional monotone*): I killed Risteard Oge O'Cullinane a hundred years ago.

BEEZIE (*to Verb To Be*): The like was killed at the bridgeen all right.

MICKLE: Was it that sin has you rambling?

THE VOICE: My sentence is to stop in the world till the Judgment Day.

BEEZIE (*nodding*): The same as wan me grandfather met.

MICKLE: And what are you looking for now?

THE VOICE: Peace and shelter between four walls and a roof.

MICKLE: And can't you get that up the country; some empty house where you'll not be annoying anywan?

THE VOICE: I'm not allowed into any house unless a living person directs me.

MICKLE: And nowan ever directed you in the hundred years you're rambling the world?

THE VOICE: I can appear only one week in fifty years.

MICKLE: All right, I'll soon reckon up a shelter for you.

MARY: Oul' Thady's house is idle.

KATE: Stop, girl. D'ye want him planted in the middle of the village on us?

MICKLE: Would they give you leave to lodge in the Chapel?

THE VOICE: Yes. Will I go in there?

VERB TO BE (*urgently*): Man alive, there's another of his kind lodging there already.

MICKLE: I'll make him the wiser of that. (*Loudly.*) There's another of ye lodging there already. D'ye mind that?

THE VOICE: No. I know him. He lodges in the belfry.

MICKLE: That's the wan. He was without shelter the same as yourself till a fellow from Carrymac directed him.

THE VOICE: On fine nights can I take a canter through the countryside pleasuring?

MICKLE: And tell me here. What pleasuring can your kind have?

THE VOICE: Watching, and knocking frights out of members of the living.

MICKLE: How could you do that when you can only appear every fifty years?

THE VOICE: In my true image only once every fifty years; in the image of a black dog on any dark night.

VERB TO BE (*rising in alarm*): A black dog! The very thing that followed me the night of Thady's wake! God save me! I let fly a couple of stones at him that night!

BEEZIE: I told you you'd suffer yet for that.

MICKLE: We have a lad here that pelted stones at you wan night. (*Verb To Be jumps up with a cry of "Conlon," but Mickle goes ahead unheeding*) Are you to punish him before his dying day?

THE VOICE (*sternly*): Did he throw the stones defying me? Or did he throw them because he was frightened?

VERB TO BE: Because I was frightened! Tell him quick, man!

MICKLE (*furious*): And before now you had us tired telling how you weren't afeard at all that night!

VERB TO BE: I give in, 'twas lies I told ye. I was as white as a miller that night. (*Desperate.*) Tell him quick, will you?

MICKLE (*thundering*): Well, Verb To Be, 'twould serve you right if he paralyzed you to the ground.

VERB TO BE (*desperate*): He has me betrayed! I'm done! (*Runs toward door, calls out.*) Sir, 'twas frightened I was that night.

THE VOICE (*very menacing*): Did he throw the stones defying me?

BEEZIE (*sharply*): Verb To Be, don't you know well he can only hear Mickle, the first person that spoke to him?

VERB TO BE (*despairingly*): I'm done! He'll not say a single word to save me! (*He runs over to corner of dresser.*)

Three fierce knocks upon the door silence them all.

THE VOICE (*terribly*): Twice I asked, and no answer. So he must be guilty, and I must punish.

The door latch begins to rattle violently, and the door and whole house to shake under powerful blows.

MARY (*jumping up*): He's breaking in. I'm for under the bed. (*She runs into bedroom.*)

TIM: Now he'll give us all the dog's knock! (*He dives under table.*)

KATE (*wailing*): He will! He'll do away with us all now. (*She huddles against the wall.*)

BEEZIE (*grave, but calm*): Not us; only Verb To Be. (*To latter, reflectively.*) A short prayer now is the likeliest you'll have time to finish.

VERB TO BE (*kneeling against a chair, weakly and sadly*): Goodbye to ye. I forgive every wan — even Conlon.

He buries his face in his hand and awaits the end. Mickle sets out for the door, the bombardment continuing unabated.

TIM (*shouting*): Verb To Be, you should go out to him, and not have him destroying the door.

KATE: Verb To Be, go on out, and don't be drawing destruction on us all.

Crash follows crash upon the door, but Mickle has arrived there by now.

MICKLE: Yourself abroadside!

THE VOICE (*fiercely*): Did he throw the stones defying me?

MICKLE: He did not, asthore. 'Twas how he lost the head with the 'fraid, and didn't know what he was at.

THE VOICE (*after a pause, back to the old deep monotone*): They have let me off punishing him.

MICKLE: All right, asthore; and wance you say that I'll give you free leave to go rambling up and down your choice places, on fine nights.

THE VOICE: Can I go now to the Chapel?

MICKLE: Before you go, asthore, tell me this; did you hear when am I to join ye? (*No reply.*) D'ye hear me, asthore. How soon am I to join ye?

THE VOICE (*low*): Can I go now? I should go now.

BEEZIE: Mickle, he can't answer you that. They aren't allowed to mention anything only their own troubles and business.

MICKLE: It appears so. (*Loudly.*) All right, asthore, go ahead to the Chapel, and good luck till they free you out at last, and flock you with us all the Judgment Day.

A moment later the light passes the window and disappears.

BEEZIE, KATE, VERB TO BE: He's gone! He's off! He's vanished away!

Beezie hurries to the door and looks out. Tim raises the lamp.

MICKLE: Ye should never let a chance astray of doing a good turn to his kind. We might be in the same fixes ourselves for long enough before we come to God at last. (*He comes back to his chair.*)

KATE: Is he gone, Beezie?

BEEZIE: I can't see trace or tidings of him.

73

KATE (*bounding up*): I'll be the first with the news to the village. (*She runs out and off.*)

BEEZIE (*grimly*): You'll not be first to every house, whatever.

VERB TO BE (*hastening out*): Let you do the houses on the left, and I'll take the houses on the right. (*They go.*)

MICKLE: I must give the particular account to oul' Honor D'Arcy. She's learning to die the same as myself, and tidings from the next world is the most she likes to hear. (*Sets out.*) Yes, asthore.

Mickle goes. Mary turns to Tim triumphantly.

MARY: Tim, how did you like that plot?

TIM: 'Tis happy for ye; 'tis happy for ye. Ye don't know how happy 'tis for ye to have such sport every night.

He sits down on the form, takes out cigarettes.

MARY: Any more, Kate'll not be so smart jeering at every news of wan from the next world. (*She looks out door.*) Tim, here's Murt — and he laughing till you could shove a turf basket down his throat.

TIM: Laughing, is it? And a while ago he was fit to chew iron!

MARY: The plot has his trouble vanished now, the same as I said it would. (*Running in.*) Now's our chance to ask him about Julia.

TIM: Do not. It'll only draw down bother.

MARY: Ssh! Leave him to me. I'm the wan knows how to manage him.

She makes a pretense of being busy at the dresser. Thunderous laughter is heard outside, and in a moment Murt comes in, wildly hilarious.

MURT (*roaring as usual*): He is! He is! Curse the lie in it. (*Coming up to Tim.*) Corry, isn't Broc the brightest composer from here to the Shannon shore?

TIM: His match isn't in it, man.

MURT: Corry, he's the greatest show in the world for tricks, he is! Curse the lie in it! (*Chuckling ferociously he goes into room, brings out form, which he leaves against back wall for the Haws as in Act I.*)

MURT (*chuckling again*): There's no lie in it. Curse the lie in it! (*He takes up table.*)

MARY (*quickly*): Murt, I was just telling Tim about how your father wouldn't give you leave to marry Julia for ten years yet — making out you were time enough.

Instantly the merriment dies out of Murt's face. He looks at her grimly a moment, then puts the table against the back wall, and sits on the edge of it.

MURT (*darkly*): This I'm going to tell you, Corry, about our country. If every oul' lad in it was hung that deserved to be hung, Ireland's hangman would be a millionaire.

MARY: And I was telling him how hard it is on Julia managing the farm by herself, without stock or crops and she many a time taking side-leps with the hunger.

MURT (*powerfully*): Sure that's none of my doing. Didn't I give her liberty to marry the first wan she could get that'd have a good capital?

Now thoroughly roused, he strides downstage.

MARY: That's what I was telling him, too.

MURT (*off again*): I sez to her, Corry: "Everywan in Ireland," I sez, "must look after herself, and let God look after all. Never mind waiting for me," I sez. "Marry the first you can get, before you're starved out, and the age begins to look on you." Wasn't that the way to say it, Corry?

TIM: That was the way to say it.

MURT: Certainly, Corry, and if wan proposed for her, could I say wan word against him? 'Twould take the sheet off my coffin if I done the like.

He sits on chair.

MARY (*quickly*): Well, Murt, here's Tim that has four hundred pounds. Wouldn't he suit her grandly?

Murt is stunned for a few moments.

MURT: Corry, if you married her this evening, what could I do, only say "God send ye luck!"

He sits down in desolation.

MARY: Tim, what did I tell you?

MURT (*suddenly*): But maybe she wouldn't be willing. (*To Tim.*) Did you ask her yet?

MARY: He didn't, but mesel' did.

MURT (*staring*): And was it you introduced the match?

MARY: 'Twas.

MURT (*white with fury*): Hell and the divil! Hell and the divil! (*He is up, flinging the chair backward to the floor.*) Woman, only I don't like to disobey my religion, I'd take, and drown you in a boghole.

MARY (*dumbfounded*): What's wrong with you?

MURT: Look at her, Corry; Doctor Crippen the murderer was decent anear her. She went behind my back to rob me of a woman I'm great to eleven years!

MARY: Wasn't I only helping her to carry out your advice?

MURT: What other advice could I give her, when myself could do nothing for her? But did I ever say 'twould please me to lose her?

MARY: And don't you like to see her get what's best for her?

MURT (*thundering*): Everywan in Ireland must look after himself, and let God look after all. 'Tis my business to keep her as long as I can; and Corry's business to get a wife where he can, and her business to get a husband where she can, but you that had no business in it at all, that went behind my back to rob me of my wan comfort in the world! . . . By that oath there (*indicating his palm*), you'll have your children reared before 'll cross this threshold again. (*Sets out for door.*)

TIM (*hastily following him*): Murt, I was never considering Julia. I was only teasing my own girl here.

MURT: That's your business, Corry, I have nothing against you. (*Turning on Mary again.*) Doctor Crippen! Doctor Crippen! Doctor Crippen!

MARY: Murt, give me wan minute. (*She runs and clutches him.*)

MURT: Doctor Crippen! I have only wan thing to give you — my curse, and the curse of the Nine Blind McDonalds down on you! (*He thrusts her away, and goes off roaring "Doctor Crippen!"*)

MARY (*at door*): Murt, come back; Murt. (*Indignantly.*) Tim, isn't that the vexer? Did you ever see such a vexer?

TIM (*urgently*): Straightaway we must set out and pacify him, or your father'll be fit to be tied.

MARY (*alarmed*): Right enough. And did you hear the oath he took to come visiting no more, and the vexer has such awful awful principles.

Enter three of the Haws, alarmed and bewildered.

PADDY (*to Mary*): What did you do on Murt?

MICKY: He's calling you from a tinker to a tailor.

MATT: He wants us to come to Dowd's card-playing house, and come visiting here no more.

MARY (*stunned*): He do!

TIM: This is the worst yet!

Murt strides in; thrusting Haws out of his way, he comes to middle of kitchen, turns, and sweeps up his hand, pointing to door.

MURT (*to Haws*): Here — out!

PADDY: Why, Murt?

MICKY: What's wrong?

MURT: Out, I tell ye.

MATT: But what's up?

MURT: All right so wait here, and the next time ye're in trouble at the dance halls, don't come crushing around me . . . (*Sets out for door.*) Doctor Crippen! (*This for Mary who attempts vainly to intercept him. He is off again, roaring "Doctor Crippen."*)

PADDY (*disgusted*): "Here out!" You couldn't say less to an ass.

MARY: Never mind him, let ye.

MICKY: But we have a row on for Thooraree Hall on Sunday night.

MATT: And we stand no chance without him.

PADDY: Come on, lads. (*And off they go.*)

MARY (*to last of them*): Mick, let ye do your best to pacify him.

MICKY: We will, directly he slackens down a piece. (*Goes.*)

Mary runs to door, pauses.

TIM: They stand no chance. Nowan stands any chance only Julia. Run down to her.

Mary is already at the door, when she stops, and her face grows graver still.

MARY: To her I'm going; but, Tim, Julia'll not swing him either wance he has that oath took. He has such awful principles.

TIM: If Murt and the Haws come no more, the Visiting House'll be greatly injured.

Very grave, he goes to form, sits down.

MARY: And, Tim, there's a worse tragic in it. Julia'll not marry you now, wance Murt took it so bad. And there's no other wan around with a place that'd be anyways nice so as I could let you go to her.

TIM: I never will forgive myself. To go injuring the finest Visiting House that ever I was a customer of!

MARY: And, Tim, how will I be? With you in Manchester and the Haws every night in Dowd's and myself there in the corner threw without a single wan of my own generation. I'll marry and keep you, Tim, before I suffer lonesomeness the equal of that.

A laugh is heard outside. Tim jumps.

TIM: Your father! That's him!

MARY (*jumping up*): Keep him till I see can Julia do anything. (*Meeting Broc at door.*) Father, I'm going meeting the Haws.

BROC (*genially*): God bless you.

She goes. He comes in, smoking pipe, relaxed and in the best of humor. He goes to dresser, gets from there a mug and a spoon and, this done, at last turns to Tim.

BROC: Tonight, Corry, you played a middling hard part as nice as I could ask to see. You have your examination passed. You'll do.

TIM (*delighted*): I'm good enough, you reckon?

BROC (*glowing*): In the run of a few months, when I'd have you fully trained and grounded up in plots, you'd be a king character.

TIM: Well, I must go to England next month unless you help me to win marriage from her.

BROC: We must plan that up and down. You're the son-in-law that'd suit me. (*Noticing and taking up the knocked over chair.*) I see ye had Murt here again.

He comes over to fire with mug and spoon.

TIM: And I'd bring in a few hundred pounds I got of a legacy.

BROC (*nodding*): Good again, sir; for money is sweet, too . . . (*Returning to the larger prospect.*) And man alive, if I had you playing with me here, the Visiting House'd be thronged for many a year, it didn't matter if Mickle died, or if the divil sent radio sets to the village with every news from here to hell.

77

TIM: Wan job I'll be able for myself, and that's weaning her away from the fella from Kiltevna.

BROC (*eagerly*): Corry, do you reckon you'll be able to shoulder him out?

TIM: In wan fortnight I'll have it done. But getting her to surrender to marriage'll be the hardest.

BROC: That's so. . . . Well now, any more let you be here a good while before myself and the visiting house come in, and keep at her, wheedling and coaxing her till you have her fatigued out. And that's when myself'll come under her with a plan that'll bring her to the ground as nice as ever you seen.

TIM: If you do, I'll be as thankful as six men.

BROC: Right, sir, and if you'll see what's delaying the Haws, I'll be running a few plans over in my brains.

TIM: Right . . . I'll see. (*Goes.*)

BROC (*absently*): God bless you, sir: God bless you. (*Thrusts supper aside, begins to think hard.*) That might soften her. . . . No sir, no, no, no. . . . That'd be something better. . . . Gallant, sir, gallant. (*Slapping his knee.*) That'll bring her down, that'll bring her down! (*He turns to his supper.*)

Act III

The scene is the same, the time a month later. The visiting house is in session. Broc is there, back to the wall, smoking his pipe and looking serious and abstracted. Beezie and Verb To Be are on form; Kate on chair towards center. Mickle's chair is unoccupied, he not having arrived yet. Mary is seated at table making the merest pretense at knitting. She seems depressed and troubled. The visiting house is in one of its quieter moods, perhaps because Tim is expected for the last time. Verb To Be, taking advantage of the lull, is treating the company to some items from his jackdaw's hoard of extraordinary information.

VERB TO BE (*almost beaming*): And did I ever tell ye the two witty sallies the composer Tom Moore had one day with the composer Robert Burns?

KATE: No.

VERB TO BE: Robert Burns was sweeping the street when Moore came the way and rhymed:

> "You silly loon,
> Leave down thy broom
> And let a body pass thee by."

Said Burns back:

> "You silly ass,
> Why can't you pass
> Between yonder wall and I?"

Weren't these two good sallies?

BEEZIE: They were, in troth.

KATE: By cramp, you'd reckon a composer'd knock out a better living than road-sweeping.

BROC (*dogmatically*): A composer always lives poor and dies poor. He doesn't mind. He knows if he was rich he couldn't compose about sorrows and poverty and the troubles of the world. A rich man can never be a composer.

BEEZIE: The composers that stepped out around here saw hard times whatever. They reckon Raftery and oul' Cormac Dall were many a time growing hairs on their legs with the hunger.

VERB TO BE: And here's an additional fact. A composer always lets his hair grow long.

KATE: Why so?

VERB TO BE: Because a composer doesn't mind what his head or his face looks like. All he cares about is his brains.

Mickle comes in, spoiling for fight.

MICKLE: Did the Prabaire come in yet?

BROC: Not yet, Mickle.

MICKLE (*loudly*): The Prabaire gave that tale the wrong telling last night.

KATE: The Prabaire! . . . a man that's tired dead and buried a score of years!

BROC (*somberly*): Mickle has no memory of that any more. The cogs of his brain are worn, and they're slipping.

BEEZIE (*chuckling*): Musha, God be with the Prabaire's time when storytelling was the go every night in the Visiting House. That's when we had the sport.

By now, Mickle is seated in his usual chair, middle of the kitchen, and ready for action.

MICKLE: The Prabaire gave it the wrong telling last night.

KATE: What tale was that, Mickle?

MICKLE: I'll soon tell ye, and I'll give ye the true telling. The Gobawn and his son were after building the highest castle in the world beyond in England; and directly the tyranny drop had to come out in the English. "We'll put the Gobawn into eternity now," they said. "Then he'll not be able to build a higher castle for any other country." The Gobawn and the son were working on top of the walls, so straight down went the English, and pulled away the scaffolding, and left the pair above with no ways of coming down. They were there a month till the hunger and cold had them looking in the Gate at St. Peter, when this day a simpleton was passing by, and they told him the awful fixes they were in. "Can't ye come down the way ye went up?" said the simpleton. At wance the pair set into it knocking the walls, and when the English saw that, they knew they were bested, so they put back the scaffolding and freed them out again.

BEEZIE (*nodding*): That was it. And where had the Prabaire the wrong grip on it?

MICKLE: The Prabaire made out 'twas in Scotland it happened; and he was as liary as the telephone in that point. What happened in Scotland the Gobawn's son made the mistake with the steeple.

VERB TO BE (*aside to Kate*): All ridiculous — legendary!

MICKLE (*overhearing*): Verb To Be, are you making out that isn't the truth?

VERB TO BE: How often did I tell you the Gobawn Saor is unknown in the history of Ireland?

MICKLE (*in a fury*): Well, Verb To Be, there's chaff and rubbish in every stack, but there isn't as much as wan handful sound in you.

VERB TO BE (*hat off — the battle signal*): Conlon, are you underestimating me again?

MICKLE: I'm saying you're as ignorant as a tinker's dog.

BEEZIE: Easy, let ye!

VERB TO BE (*on his feet*): Who's ignorant? You that can't answer the simplest questions we had off in first class at school! You that can't answer "What is a lie"? or even "What is a woman"?

MICKLE (*scornfully*): All right, I'm on the beaten hand. I don't know what is a woman. What is she, you?

VERB TO BE: She's man's useful companion, not the slave of his passion, his sharer in prosperity, and his friend in adversity . . . What we could answer in the first class at school.

KATE: Good, Verb To Be.

MICKLE: All right, now answer this — Why can no woman keep a secret?

VERB TO BE: That question is ridiculous.

MICKLE: 'Tis not ridiculous. How could she keep a secret when she has no apple in her throat?

Tim appears in the doorway, looking amused at the familiar sounds of conflict.

BEEZIE: Now ye're on level terms, and let ye leave it so.

BROC (*jumping up delighted*): Here he's landed!

MARY (*spinning round*): Tim! (*Then, controlling herself, she sits down again.*)

KATE: By cramp! . . . himself!

TIM: Goodmorrow to ye.

Takes off coat and hangs it beside dresser.

BEEZIE: We thought you mustn't be coming at all tonight.

TIM: What, man. I wouldn't go off without leaving ye farewell.

MICKLE: You're for Manchester in the morning, Corry?

TIM: For Manchester, Mickle.

Kate has transferred to beside Verb To Be, and Tim takes the chair.

MICKLE: That's where you'll win riches, asthore. Myself saved sixteen pounds in it when we were building the ship canal. (*Takes out his pipe.*)

TIM: What's the best news since about Murt?

VERB TO BE: The best news is bad. Five o'clock he got up this evening.

TIM: Five o'clock! And four o'clock yesterday! He's going worse every day.

KATE: His thinking now is that, for all the gain or thanks he'll get for his day's work, he's as well off to stop in bed.

BEEZIE: Wance them lads see there'll be no marriage for them, they do generally always let the farm go to rack.

TIM: That's so, but I never seen wan to give up all work so sudden as Murt.

BROC (*dogmatically*): Wance himself and the Haws started visiting in Dowd's card-playing house every night, that was bound to happen. There's no laugh in Dowd's to brighten him up, so the thinking soon captured him altogether.

TIM: How d'ye reckon it'll come out at finish?

KATE: They reckon oul' Murt'll have to give in, and give him leave to marry Julia, for no threats'll make Murt go back to work this time.

Julia runs in excitedly.

JULIA: Broc, Igoe is after finding out about last night's plot against him, and he's coming down to put you in jeopardy.

All are startled except Broc.

KATE: By cramp!

VERB TO BE: God bless me!

BEEZIE: Worra, worra, worra!

TIM: By heggins!

BROC (*sharply*): Who told him?

JULIA: Oul' Dockeray come home drunk from the Pension and blundered it out to him.

BROC (*going to door*): How near is he drew?

JULIA: He's only starting his tea yet. He'll not be coming till that's over.

BROC: 'Tis all right so. By the time he comes I'll have another plot composed that'll drive him off again (*to crowd*). Ye'd better shift till all is ready.

He comes down to center of stage, still smoking and thinking hard.

BEEZIE (*rising*): Come across to my place, let ye.

KATE: By cramp, we'd be safer in it.

VERB TO BE: Broc, if you want my help in the plot, I'll be at your disposal.

MICKLE: Broc, give Igoe a good dressing. Too peevish that wan is.

All are hurrying out, except Tim and Mary, who is putting away her knitting.

TIM: Will you want me?

BROC: I will, stop, you.

Mary goes into bedroom with knitting.

TIM: How will you defeat Igoe?

BROC: The best play always is to come under them lads at wance with a new plot before they get time to attack you for the last wan. . . . (*He paces about, thinking hard, stops suddenly, grimly.*) Right you are, sir, that'll settle Igoe; that'll settle him.

Gets cork from dresser, burns one end of it at fire. Mary comes from room.

BROC (*vigorously*): Girl, go out to the barn, and bring in a couple of sheaves of straw.

She, without a word, goes out.

BROC (*vigorously*): Now, sir, I'll be going out readying the plot, and let you pitch into her again. Tell her again you'll surely marry somewan in England and not come back to her.

TIM: I gave here a wrinkle of that last night, and 'twas poison to her.

BROC (*triumphantly*): And she's in and out all day since with eyes like a sick pup. I'm telling you, man, sooner than chance losing you for good she'll give in to marriage now.

TIM: If I had another week I might swing her, but I have only this last night.

BROC: I'm telling you, you have her at the church door. Wan more shove and she's in. (*He demonstrates the action humorously with his boot.*)

TIM: I'll do my best, whatever.

BROC: Do, and in a while's time mysel'll come back, and throw a couple of more bullets into her.

Mary comes in with straw.

BROC: Throw it there, girl. (*Indicating floor at back wall, left of window.*) And here, Corry (*giving him cork*), disguise your face something like the night you acted the traveling showman — only no whisker.

TIM: Right.

BROC: I'll get you some clothes that'll suit, and then explain the plot. (*Goes.*)

MARY: You'll want the mirror, Tim. (*Gets up.*)

TIM: Good yourself. (*Sits at table. She sets mirror in front of him, propping it against a jug.*) They reckon Murt's oul' fella'll have to give in and let him marry Julia.

MARY (*absently*): Very apt, Tim.

TIM: Then Murt'll be in such glee he'll forgive you, and come visiting with the Haws again.

MARY: If I wasn't sure of that, d'ye think I'd let you go to England for a couple of years itself? (*She is doing something at dresser.*)

TIM (*dabbing cork on his eyebrows*): In two years to the day I'll be back to you — unless wan beyond tempts me and I marry her instead (*slyly*).

MARY (*turning round agitated*): Tim! Why do you say the like again? Didn't I tell you I'd marry you in two years?

TIM (*with his skillful simulation of seriousness*): Well, I don't know whether 'tis how the wans beyond are nicer than ye, or what, but the lads from my country don't be six months in it till they're married.

MARY: But, Tim, you'd know nothing about them foreigners; and they'd watch well to hide all flaws till you'd have them wed. How would you be if you got wan so lazy that she'd have her skirts worn sitting down, or wan so stingy that she wouldn't hang the kettle for fear it'd wear the fire, or wan so bad-tempered that she wouldn't leave a plate in the dresser but she'd fly at you.

TIM: They reckon the two worst things for a man are a nagging wife and a dripping roof.

MARY (*vigorously*): And I don't smoke much cigarettes — there'd be no fear of me to rob you; but the wans beyond wouldn't be happy unless they were smoking enough to blind an airplane. So you'll behave a bad man for yourself if you don't wait for me.

TIM (*as if impressed*): You could be right.

MARY: And anywan can tell you I don't lag from hard work from the time I quit the bed in the morning until the Visiting House come in at night.

TIM (*teasing*): Still you'll be getting a good age from now on, and they reckon the younger the chicken the sweeter the pickin'.

MARY: But sure at my age a girl is too young to know her own mind right, or know whether she'd sooner be good or bad.

TIM: D'ye reckon so?

MARY: I'm sure so. And I'll tell you another point about me. The best up girl is wan reared in a Visiting House because she has everywan's stories and everywan's songs and sayings. Isn't that so?

TIM: That's sure.

MARY: 'Tis for your own good I'm telling you all, Tim. On account I'm heir to the farm I can get wan any time; I have only to do that (*crooking her finger*), but on account we're so great I'd like you'd get the wan that'd suit you best.

TIM (*emphatically*): Sure I know well there's none of them can come up to you; but (*slyly dubious again*) there's whiles when a fellow reckons 'twould be ease to his bones to be married; and if a nice wan come the way at such a time she could easy spread a net for him.

MARY (*alarmed*): Oh, dear! . . . (*Considers.*) Tim, your only plan is to keep out of harm's way. Don't go to the dances or Irish Clubs or anywhere girls are apt to be. Instead, let you every night go drinking.

TIM: But if I do that, I'll have all spent up.

MARY: That doesn't matter, Tim. If you haven't a penny itself, I'll marry you behind father's back, then he'll have to let you in.

Broc strides in, carrying topcoat, hat, and muffler, all of good quality and new.

BROC: Here you are: Tarpey's clothes. Put them on, before you do any more.

TIM: Good, yourself. (*Puts them on.*)

BROC: Girl, make a bed there for him.

She proceeds to make up a straw bed on the floor.

BROC (*to Tim*): When Igoe comes in, you'll be lying there as drunk as a stick — by the way.

He takes table, and transfers it to back wall and to right of door.

TIM (*grinning*): Good, again.

BROC (*briskly, sitting on table*): And now, sir, there's thing I want to ask you. (*Nudging Tim.*) Have you any notion at all of coming back to Ireland again?

TIM: Likely I will, unless I'd chance to marry somewan beyond.

He sits on table beside Broc. Both pretend not to notice Mary's anxious interest in this turn of the conversation.

BROC: You'd have no business coming back here. In a few year this Visiting House'll be no more.

MARY (*alarmed*): Father, what kind of talk is that?

BROC: 'Tis true talk. Story-telling was threw out of the Visiting Houses in my time because the gang rising up had education, and were no longer believing in stories of giants and animals talking and the like. In a few years, when the present set of oul' people die out, all plots and wit'll be threw aside the same way too.

TIM: D'ye reckon so?

BROC: I'm sure so! The next gang that's rising up here'll have no belief in any sport, only dances and cards and company-keeping.

MARY (*indignant*): Well, father, you vexer! And before now you made out when our brains'd soften with age, we'd be comical characters, too, and as good as the present set of oul' people.

BROC (*scornfully*): Ye as good as them! Have ye stories by the hundherd in the two tongues, the same as Mickle? Have ye songs by the hundherd in the two tongues, the same as Beezie? Have ye hundherds of lessons and fictions off the same as Verb To Be? Have ye anything in the wide world only how to read the paper and add and subtract? (*Vigorously.*) And now, girl, in place of giving out rubbish, off with you to the turn of the road and see is there any sign of Igoe.

She looks at them a moment, stunned, then goes out. Broc chuckles triumphantly.

BROC: She's bleeding fast. A couple of bullets more and she's stretched down dead. (*He goes to fire, pokes it up.*)

TIM (*thoughtfully*): D'ye reckon all right the loss of the oul' people'll perish the Visiting House?

BROC (*very serious now*): 'Twill injure it sore, but 'twon't perish it, because God is good, and He'll never leave the village without a few fools. Only wan thing'll perish the Visiting House.

TIM: What's that?

BROC (*grave in turn*): Every year since I first got memory, things is getting dearer, and the people having to dress more stylish too, so every year 'twas getting harder to knock a living out of the land. You could make a better living on ten acres some years ago than you could now on twenty, and better than they'll make on fifty acres in time to come.

TIM: So the village'll die out unless the Land Commission scatter ye down Roscommon way where ye'll have more land. Wance they scatter, and quench the village, the Visiting House'll be no more.

BROC: That's so, but (*brightening up*) we could have a score of years' good sport here before that comes to pass.

MARY (*running in breathlessly*): Father, here's Murt looking like he was dragged backwards through a bush.

Murt enters, wilder looking than ever. He wears topcoat and cap, and carries some more clothes in a sack.

MURT (*powerfully*): Goodbye Broc Heavey, goodbye Corry; goodbye and good luck to everywan — barring Doctor Crippen (*with a fierce look at Mary*).

BROC: Did your father turn you out?

MURT: As soon as I got up a while ago, he sez: "Will you get up bright and early tomorrow, and set into it digging the spuds?" "What business have I?" I sez. "For all the gain or thanks I'll get, amn't I as well off to stop in bed?" "Get a bag," he sez: "Get a bag," he sez. "You can't live here any more."

TIM: Be heggins!

MARY: Oh, dear!

BROC (*grimly*): What did you say?

MURT: "All right," I sez, and readied up. "Which side are you heading?" he sez. "Up the country," I sez. "Good luck," he sez. "Good luck," I sez. (*Swinging bag across shoulder again.*) Goodbye to ye now.

BROC (*rising*): Man alive, won't you put the night over you here? The loft bed is idle.

MURT: I will not. Tonight I'm drawing for Thooraree.

TIM: Well, wait till we see can Broc pacify your oul' lad.

MURT: I will not. Myself and the oul' lad is finished up. Good luck to ye all, barring Doctor Crippen. My curse for ever on Doctor Crippen. (*Goes.*)

MARY: Father, is it only to frighten him oul' Murt is?

TIM: He's hardly bad enough to turn out his own son.

BROC: Throth he is, and well bad enough, and if I went up to pacify him, to bang the door in my face is all he'd do.

MARY (*dismayed*): Oh, dear! (*She runs to door, looks after Murt, then suddenly the other way.*) Father! Here's some of the Haws coming.

BROC (*fiercely, as he goes to door*): They are!

MARY: Wance Murt is gone they're not afeard now to come visiting here any more.

BROC (*grimly*): Well, if they come in here they'll go out as quick again. (*Goes to hearth, takes up tongs, stands ready.*)

TIM: Are you letting them back?

BROC: Is it let in a gang that's perish all plots with laughs and carry-ons when Murt isn't here to command them?

Three or four of the Haws come crowding in, all excited.

THE HAWS: Did ye hear? Murt is gone on the random! Oul' Murt turned on him dog-rough at last! He's gone up the country!

BROC (*fiercely*): Outside the door with ye!

THE HAWS (*bewildered*): Why so? What's wrong? What did we do?

BROC: Your master is gone, and I'll have ye no more, gigglers and tomfools that'd spoil all plots on me.

MICKY: Command us yourself any more, Broc.

PADDY: That's what you'll do.

BROC: How could I be watching ye, and carrying out plots at the same time? I couldn't, and I'll not try. Outside, I tell ye.

MARY: But, father, they'll soon be getting older and wiser.

BROC (*fiercely*): Fools can never grow wise. Are you going before I put sparks flying out of your heels! (*Takes live coal in tongs.*)

THE HAWS: But, Broc . . . Wan minute . . .

BROC: All right, if ye won't, all right. (*Swings back tongs for the throw.*)

THE HAWS (*storming out*): We're off! . . . Oh, hell! Let me out . . . Cripes, lads, quick!

BROC (*at door, roaring after them*): And if ye venture in here again, I'll break your necks out the door. (*Comes in fuming, and throws tongs on hearth.*)

MARY: Well, Tim, sure he isn't acting right? To go banishing the Haws, and leaving me any more without wan of my own generation.

BROC (*grimly*): I have no pity for you at all. 'Twas you drove out Murt, and pulled the gable out of my Visiting House. (*Coming forward.*) Here, Corry, the plot is ready. I'll bring up Beezie, and let you be stretched down there drunk to the world.

MARY: But, father — (*But Broc is gone.*) Tim, did you ever see such a vexer?

TIM: He's upset over Murt. In a couple of days when he calms down a piece he'll let the Haws back again, likely.

He sits down on straw bed, with his back to the end of the form.

MARY: He never will, for when father scents anywan to be a danger to his visiting house, he's at wance a cross and awful man.

TIM: He went against them very hard right enough.

MARY: The Haws are as noisy as tinkers, so he never will let them back again . . . (*Awestruck.*) Oh, Tim, d'ye know what it is? (*She sits at end of form nearest him.*)

TIM: No.

MARY (*gravely*): I have no choice now but to surrender to marriage.

TIM (*chuckling*): How d'ye make that out?

MARY: Sure, how could I live and have no company here, neither yourself or the Haws — nothing but oul' specimens. Oh, dear! I never thought I'd have to give in to marriage so soon. . . .

TIM (*returning to the attack*): Well, I have marriage in the head a fair while, and it all weighed up and, mind you, I come across a few good points in it.

MARY (*interested*): Tell me, Tim: what good points?

TIM (*mischievously*): Well, wance we marry we can court together as often as we like, and as long as we like.

MARY (*smiling to herself at this*): Sure myself thought of that point.

TIM: And isn't it a good point?

MARY (*still smiling*): Why wouldn't it? (*Gravely.*) And another great point has just dawned on me in that line.

TIM: What's that?

MARY: Before now I'd very near lose the life when I'd hear a rat grinding under the bed; but any more when I have you with me I'll not mind greatly. Are you afeard of them, Tim?

TIM: Not me.

MARY: Well, then, any night a rat is in it you'll sleep the outside wan in the bed.

TIM: Right. I can sleep sound any side.

MARY: Look at that! But (*anxiously*) tell me this, Tim: would you want a clean shirt every week?

TIM: Well, I'd like it. Why?

MARY: Because there's some lads going, and you'd have to knock them down and strip them, before they'd surrender their shirts for you to wash.

TIM: In the line of clothes I like to have myself nicely picked together for Sunday.

MARY: And you're every day as shaved as a bishop. Not like some you don't be going around with a face like a rusty can. And tell me this: when you have drink in a day of a fair or thing, how do you go?

TIM: I set into it singing, and sing every song I have.

MARY (*pleased*): That's great. I'd only enjoy that. Anything so long as it wouldn't set you at loggerheads. No lie, Tim, you have wonderful great points.

Broc enters, still very grim-looking. He barely glances at the pair, goes to fire.

BROC (*briefly*): Beezie is coming. Then I'll read ye the plot.

MARY: Father, I'm going joining Tim here.

BROC (*as if surprised*): Is it marrying him?

TIM: The very thing.

BROC: Well, of all the surprises! But all right; the day ye marry I'll let the Haws back again, and he can be ganger over them.

MARY (*delighted*): Tim, d'ye hear that? The Visiting House'll be full wance more.

TIM: Good! The full of the kitchen; that's what we all like.

Off stage Murt is heard roaring "Broc! Broc!"

MARY: Murt!

TIM: Be heggins!

BROC: Back again!

MURT (*swinging in excitedly*): Broc! . . . th' oul' lad gave in. He's giving me leave to marry her.

BROC: He pursued you?

MURT: While I was leaving farewell up and down the village, he cut across the bog and was before me overside the bridgeen. "Go home, you fool," he sez. "I will not," I sez. "You and me is finished up," I sez. "Go home," he sez, "you fool, and marry your woman-fool, and let ye make ten fools more." "I will," I sez, "and I'll dig the spuds for you tomorrow, too . . ."

At this point, Broc springs almost tigerishly to the middle of the floor.

BROC (*vigorously*): Stop, man. Corry, strip again and hide away the straw. Now I have Murt and the Haws, and a better way of playing this plot.

He brushes past Murt and goes out.

TIM: Right. (*Jumps up, strips off coat, hat, muffler, etc.*)

MURT (*rumbling*): Does Broc think I'll come visiting again under the wan roof with Doctor Crippen?

MARY: But, Murt, only I vexed you and set your teeth, your father'd never give in.

MURT (*impressed*): 'Tis the truth. . . . (*Fierce again.*) But 'twas the dirty turn you had in the head to do!

TIM: Not her; she only blundered a piece. Man alive, you have the grandest girl in the world going in to you wan of these days, and that's no time for having ructions with your neighbors.

MURT: But, Corry, didn't you see the oath I took (*indicating his palm*) to visit here no more?

TIM: What, man! That oath was only all spite and vengeance. 'Twas a sin for you to take it, and 'twould be a worse sin for you to keep it.

MURT: You reckon so! Still I'll come here no more till she promises to avoid doing wrong any more if she can.

MARY: I will, Murt; surely and truly I will.

MURT: All right; so long as you keep to that I'll come visiting and I'll give you Doctor Crippen no more. (*Goes.*)

TIM (*clearing away straw*): That's Murt settled. Now you can be happy in earnest.

She makes no reply, but sits on form near fire looking very grave. He looks at her in surprise, then starts.

TIM: Be heggins! Right enough! Now your pals are back to you, and you have no occasion to marry!

MARY (*anxiously*): But, Tim, after we had all settled up, you'll be awful vexed to me if I put you off again.

TIM (*after consideration, cheerfully*): I will not be vexed to you, and I'll tell you why. (*Throws bundle of straw in corner.*) The hurry I was in before I was afeard you'd get great to some other fellow at the dances before I'd be three months in Manchester, but I have more trust in you now.

MARY: Tim, I will not forget you. And let you keep far away from the dances and wherever girls'd be. Spend every night in the pubs, and you'll be safe.

TIM (*slyly*): There's thing I must tell you about that. In England the girls are in the pubs every night as good as the men.

MARY: Oh, dear! You're safe nowhere in England so!

Enter Beezie in great humor.

BEEZIE: Now ye'll see a good plot played!

MARY (*jumping up*): Are the Haws coming?

BEEZIE: The whole caper of them!

Mary collects the straw in a bundle, and carries it into the bedroom. Beezie sits on Mickle's chair. Tim takes the mirror from the dresser, and wipes the cork off his face.

TIM: Beezie, have you a chief part in this plot?

BEEZIE: Throth, I have. Any hard plot that's going forward he makes sure to elect me.

TIM: Here they come! (*He hurries into the bedroom with the mirror. Broc comes in, hurriedly puts on the coat, hat, and muffler Tim has taken off. Murt and the Haws swarm in, Murt directing operations sternly as ever.*)

MURT: Hurry, let ye. He's drew near. The form, quick.

THE HAWS: We'll not lag. Watch the door, you. I seen him, lads! He's frothing at the mouth all over!

*Two bring the second form from the room, and leave it against back wall.
The others, under Murt's personal supervision, transfer table to under window, about a foot from the back wall and so outside the form. They take the
second form and place it along and outside the table. This is hardly done
when the Girls rush in.*

MURT: Whereabouts is he?

JULIA: Just dawning over the top of the hill.

THE GIRLS: He has the road lit with curses. He's cursing before him. Quick,
let ye.

*They stand behind the table. The Haws take up positions along the table.
Murt parades the line haranguing them all.*

MURT (*sternly*): Let ye all watch to be well conducted, and keep your faces
very strict whenever he'll look at ye. Anywan that laughs at the wrong
time'll be put out for the night!

BROC (*coming over*): Quick now, and make a rank around me.

*He curls up on the table. The Haws sit on the edges so as to screen him from
view. Murt covers the end near the door, standing up as if about to go out.*

BROC: Remember you're not to throw me out till the second time. Go ahead,
Beezie. (*He ducks down out of sight.*)

BEEZIE: I'll give him "Slashing Tom Keogh." He likes that wan greatly.

*Beezie sings with great spirit the following, to which the Haws beat time
with their feet, usually joining in for the words "Slashing Tom Keogh" when
they occur at the end of a verse.*

> "Mary, asthore, oh, where did you go?"
>   "Ah, mother, acushla, you might like to know,
> I was out in the Creggs, and I met with Tom Keogh.
> And he gave me some plums from the trees of Moynoe."

> "Ah, Mary asthore, you are but eighteen,
>   To be out in the Creggs with that idle dalteen,
> If your father he hears it, we'll be all in a show,
> He'll pull all the plum trees that grow in Moynoe."

*During the singing, Tim and Mary return from the rooms. Tim, his face re-
stored to its normal color, sits on Broc's stool on opposite side of fire from
Beezie. Mary sits beside Beezie near fire. She looks troubled. As the second
verse ends, Igoe bounds into kitchen. He is a little bouncing demon of a man,
middle-aged, his life spent in lightning transitions from furious rages to blazing enthusiasms; lack of strength and stature have made his rages ludicrous
rather than dangerous, but the torrents of defamatory invective in which they
culminate are feared by all.*

IGOE (*roaring, fists aloft for battle*): D'ye forget that I'm a son of Bideen
D'Arcy, that stunned a Black and Tan with her churn dash? (*Sees Broc
is absent.*) Where is he?

MURT (*looking out door*): He's due back whatever.

IGOE: Where did he go?

MURT: Down the road with the black bottle, dosing somewan's cow likely.

IGOE (*grimly*): I'll wait — if 'twas a week. I have a rib to break in Heavey. (*He sits with his back to the dresser.*)

BEEZIE: What did he do on you?

IGOE (*grimly*): Beezie Durkan, never mind you. Look after your own business, and you'll get more than enough to do.

MURT: Beezie, go ahead with the song whatever.

BEEZIE: What business have I, when ye won't give me silence?

IGOE (*keenly interested*): Beezie, were you singing a song?

BEEZIE: I was giving them "Slashing Tom Keogh."

IGOE (*delighted*): Beezie! Wan of the best ballads that come out of Ireland! (*Furious.*) And they wouldn't give it a hearing! (*Jumping up and roaring at the Haws.*) Silence, ye sons of Irish hags! (*Down again.*) God spare you the health, Beezie!

BEEZIE: I'll set off again where ye broke in on me.

IGOE: Anywhere at all.

BEEZIE:

> "Ah, mother asthore, if I am but eighteen,
> You married my father, and he but sixteen;
> He was not able to plow or to sow,
> Or to drill the Sinn Feiners like Slashing Tom Keogh."

IGOE (*uproariously*): Good, Beezie!

BEEZIE:

> "Arrah, Mary asthore, there's a Peeler in town,
> Who gets a fine haul every month from the Crown,
> He'll drive all Sinn Feiners to Ballinasloe;
> That's the man for you Mary, not Slashing Tom Keogh."
>
> "Ah, mother asthore, talk of Peelers no more —"

BROC (*in a changed and drunken voice*): Hi, there! Hi, there! How can a man sleep? Give over that noise, I say. (*But he remains out of sight behind the backs of the Haws.*)

MURT: Stop your mouth there.

THE HAWS: Give over there . . . Stop that . . . Conduct yourself there. Quiet, will you?

IGOE (*on his feet, furious*): Who is he?

MURT: Some straggler of a stranger that was sleeping here when we came in.

THE HAWS: Nowan knows who he is. He's awful boozed whatever. It's coming out his eyes, man.

IGOE (*to Mary*): Girl, who is he?

MARY: I don't know either; I was abroadside milking. Father only was here.

IGOE: It makes no matter who he is. If he's badly conducted again, ye're to leave him abroad on the road with the dog.

MURT: We will in throth. Beezie, go ahead.

BEEZIE: "Ah, mother asthore, talk of Peelers no more;
When Ireland is free they'll get the back door,
With lock, stock, and barrel to the regions below;
Then, up the Sinn Feiners and Slashing Tom Keogh!"

BROC: Hi, there! You've roused me again. . . . Stop that noise there!

IGOE (*bounding up furiously*): Put him out. Bring him out and kill him against the ground.

MURT and HAWS: Out with him! No more chances for you. We must shift you this time. We'll decorate your face for you!

THE GIRLS: Ye'll have him killed. Easy, let ye. Ye'll have the life and senses and all knocked out of him.

The Haws carry him out with a great show of ferocity, Igoe exhorting them bloodthirstily from the rear. The girls swarm out after them.

IGOE: Punish him well. Don't spare your shoe leather. Make a parable of him.

He is about to follow them out when Beezie calls him.

BEEZIE: Igoe, Igoe, come here a minute.

IGOE (*coming back impatiently*): What's it? Hurry on, woman.

BEEZIE: I'm in doubt about the second-last verse, the first commencement of it. You had that song off greatly.

IGOE: The second-last . . .

"Since you've vexed me at all, pull out your oul' purse,
And give me my fortune for better or worse.
If the priest is in town before the cockcrow,
I'll be rolled in the blankets with Slashing Tom Keogh."

BEEZIE: That's it!

Broc appears in the doorway. He has taken off overcoat and hat and carries a black bottle.

BROC (*in consternation*): Am I gone wrong in the head? Or is it the Haws are mad? Who's that they're kicking hell's delight out of down the road?

IGOE: He's deserving of it. He wouldn't give Beezie silence.

BROC: D'ye know that fellow is the new civic guard, coming from a day's boozing in his civility clothes?

BEEZIE: Be the powers!

TIM: By heggins!

IGOE (*hoarsely*): Broc, we'll be put in jail till our bones rot.

BEEZIE: Throth, you will, Igoe. You commanded them.

BROC (*vigorously*): Your wan chance is to take a fly off through the bog to your own house. We'll make out you were a tramp, and we couldn't say who you were.

IGOE: Broc, let ye swear to that with all the oaths ye have. I'll pray for ye, and make it up for ye. (*Goes to door.*)

BROC: Run for your life. I'll do me best to pacify the guard.

IGOE: Give him costs for more drinks, I'll pay ye again.

BROC: Right! Run, you divil.

IGOE: I'm off (*desperately*). Save me now from bread and water, and I'll be good to ye while ye live. (*Disappears.*)

BROC (*after him*): Through the bog, and let nowan see you. (*Comes in smiling.*) That's the way, Corry, to pacify them lads. The other plot is cleared out of his head, and we're as great as ever. And now I must wind up this plot. I have the first glimpse got of a brand new wan that'll put another while of the world over us. (*Goes.*)

TIM: He has his full team back. He's a young man again. He's so happy.

BEEZIE (*setting out*): I must tell them how clever we managed Igoe.

TIM: Do. You're the best wan can put skin on the tale.

She goes. Tim and Mary are alone again. He looks at her and smiles. She has looked on at the plot apathetically. She sits on form with her back to the table. He sits beside her.

TIM: Didn't you enjoy that plot?

MARY: How could I, Tim, when I hadn't the heart to enjoy anything?

TIM (*kindly*): Well, I'll give you the truth at last. There's no fear in the wide earthly world of me to join anywan beyond. 'Twas your oul' lad put me up to frightening you with that tale.

MARY: But, Tim, I'm understanding now that nowan can be certain sure about that. No matter what you'd promise about not falling for the girls beyond, still and all I'd be at the pinch of death with anxiety.

TIM: Please yourself. Whatever you do will suit me.

MARY (*drawing nearer*): And I have an awful habit took lately of enjoying your company here every night. Wance you're gone I'll be too lonesome to enjoy the sport here any more, and I'll be too lonesome to enjoy the dances moreover.

TIM (*cheerfully*): Please yourself, so.

MARY: Mickle told me I'd suffer long and suffer sad, if I got too great to any of ye before I was ready for marriage, and now his words is come in.

She sits on form. Mickle appears in doorway, leans on corner of table.

MICKLE: Girl, is Corry at large?

TIM: Not me, Mickle. I'm here.

MICKLE: You're going tripping to England in the morning, Corry?

TIM: Very apt, Mickle.

MICKLE: All right, asthore. Before you leave us you'll maybe do thing for me. (*Makes his way to chair.*)

TIM: Anything in reason, Mickle, anything I can. (*He glances at Mary, who is in a brown study, ignoring Mickle and the subsequent proceedings.*)

MICKLE: This winter, Corry, I'll stop drawing my breath, and go out of the world, and all is ready only wan thing.

TIM: What's that, Mickle?

MICKLE: The coffin is paid for, and a good wan, too, that I'll not wear my elbows through in many a day. An iron cross a yard high is made with the blacksmith, made and paid for. Money is laid by for Masses and for a half barrel of porter for the wake. But there's wan thing short yet. Wan half barrel'd make a good enough wake for ordinary rubbish, the same as ye that have only education. But 'tisn't enough for me, the last man in Ireland that has learning, and the history of giants and olden times.

TIM: No lie, Mickle, we were disgraced forever, if you were waked with less than two half barrels.

MICKLE: Myself, Corry, hasn't as much money left as'd sound like that (*shaking his closed hand*); but you're the master of four hundred pounds, and reckoned a ready and a decent man. Would you give me the costs for a second half barrel, Corry?

TIM: Straight out I'll give it to you, and welcome. (*Takes out purse.*)

MICKLE: Give it to herself, asthore. She keeps all for me.

TIM: Right, Mickle. (*He crosses to beside Mary, gives her money.*)

MICKLE: Do, asthore, and directly my pipe is kindled I'll give you advices that'll pay you twice over for your decency. (*Kneels on hearth, lighting his pipe.*)

TIM (*to Mary*): There you are, that'll buy it.

MARY: Tim, a while ago when we were reckoning up about marriage, d'ye remember all the great points we dragged up in the run of a few minutes?

TIM: We did that, and I'll tell you another great point. When you're a while looking at the prime oul' characters, the same as Mickle, dying out wan after another, it leaves you very lonesome and there's only wan remedy for that lonesomeness — to marry, and start a young gang of your own.

MARY: They reckon so; and anyway I haven't two choices now. I couldn't let you go from me any more, Tim.

TIM (*cheerfully*): Whatever day you like, so, and the sooner the better. You'll see we'll be like larks we'll be so happy.

MARY (*smiling suddenly*): And d'ye know, Tim, there's wan good point about screechers. They do be as innocent as lambeens. You'd shake to pieces laughing at how comic they are. So I won't be away from all sport if I can't go visiting itself. (*Julia appears breathlessly.*)

JULIA: Here ye are! D'ye know ye're missing the sport of the world?

TIM (*jumping up*): We are!

MARY (*up likewise*): Is the plot flashing away again?

JULIA: Igoe went ahiding in his bed, clothes and boots on him and all and the false civic guard is cross-questioning him through the window.

MARY: Tim! (*She runs out, Julia following her.*)

TIM (*at their heels*): Wait for me, ye divils! (*They disappear.*)

Mickle is filling his pipe and crooning away to himself. At last he is ready.

MICKLE (*turning*): And now, Corry, wance you behaved such a decent man, I'll give you good advices that'll stand to you well when you're going dying, the same as me now. Your first plan, then, asthore, 'll be to coax the Mother of God, for she has a great hand with Our Saviour, and anything she wants she has only to ask Him. Wan single falling out! — that was all they had in all their time together on earth, and there wasn't much to that; there was not, asthore. They were going the road this day, asthore, and they seen a fellow that was someway crippled, and out of his proper shape. "Son," she sez, "you made a poor job of that wan" — she didn't think of herself; she did not, asthore. Our Saviour said no word till dusk-us, then, "Mother," he said, "in place of you and Me stopping in the wan lodging house tonight, I'll stop in the first house on the right, and you in the first house on the left." So they did, asthore, and she went in, and found a corpse laid overboard on the kitchen table, and snuff and tobaccy, and a gross of pipes and all ready for the wake, asthore. So, the same as everywan had to do before your time, she took a pipe and said, "The Lord have mercy on the dead!" and she smoked away there in honor of the dead; but not a single person come in to the wake, asthore, and she was by herself with the corpse till the morning. That was the penance Our Saviour put on her, so He must be middling vexed to her that day, all right. But that finished that, and 'twas the only falling out they had ever, asthore. Anything she wants she has only to ask Him, so keep her on your side, and when your tenure of time is up 'tis she'll have your bed dressed in Heaven and the finest of welcomes before you. (*Wandering.*) That's sure, asthore, that's sure, asthore . . . (*Suddenly and sternly.*) Corry, did you let that advice to you? (*Thundering.*) Corry, answer up and don't be disorderly. Corry! (*Finally he pokes out his stick, finds the form empty, and smiles.*) He's at large; he is, asthore. (*Turns back to fire cheerfully.*) No matter; now you'll have two half barrels, and the finest wake since the time of the gentlemen; now you can die away for yourself, asthore. . . . (*Gravely.*) For the first while right enough you'll be lonesome for the village; and lonesome for the Visiting House, too. (*Nodding.*) You will, in throth, asthore . . . But wance you have the lonesomeness and your Purgatory over, you'll be all right; (*in great humor*) you'll be as snug as a lamb in a shed; you will, asthore . . . asthore . .

♣ SEAMUS BYRNE ♣

THE most striking quality about the work of Seamus Byrne is its intensity of statement. His plots are intricate, his dialogue has a nervous immediacy, and he can delineate character consummately. But the most lasting impression one gains from his work is that it was written by a man with a great deal to say and with an urgent necessity to say it.

Although he looks much younger, Byrne was born in Dublin on December 27, 1904. He attended the National University, where in 1927 he received his LL. B. He was for nine years a solicitor in Leitrim, but then became involved in politics and was jailed for illegal radio transmissions for the I.R.A. in 1940. In jail he went on a hunger strike of twenty-one days, after which he was released, having served nine months of his two-year sentence. He is now a consultant for two law firms.

On April 8, 1950, the Abbey produced his *Design for a Headstone*, which was sufficiently outspoken to alarm both the left and the right. On its sixth night, Maria Duce, an ultra-right wing Catholic organization, staged a demonstration in the theater: protests were shouted, an attempted assault was made on Byrne, and several young men dashed down the aisle shouting, in refutation of a remark in the play, "Maritain was wrong!" Police were brought in on the next night; the demonstration, lacking popular support, dwindled away; and the play had a successful six weeks' run.

Byrne's other plays include *Innocent Bystander*, a study of embezzling solicitors in a provincial town, which the Abbey produced in November, 1951. The script of his third play, *A Hawk in the Handsaw*, which was a collaboration with the actress-producer Shelagh Richards and a study of a review comedian's desire to play *Hamlet*, has unfortunately been lost. His most recent play, *Little City*, went through several revisions during the years it waited for a producer who would not flinch from the subject of abortion. Finally produced in the 1962 Theatre Festival, it proved a strong but grim play. Its several minor plots may not be well enough developed to hold their own with the abortion plot, but the several stories suggest that Byrne's purpose was to indict more than enforced abortions. He was really attacking the hypocritical respectability that so thinly covers a variety of ignominious motives in a little city like Dublin.

Design for a Headstone by its subject matter begs for a comparison with that later, more famous prison play, Brendan Behan's *The Quare Fellow*. Probably Byrne's play bears the same relation to Behan's as Denis Johnston's 1916 play *The Scythe and the Sunset* does to O'Casey's 1916 play *The Plough and the Stars*. The superb Behan and O'Casey plays have proved their potency on the stage, and both basically exist as emotional attacks on, respectively, capital punishment and war. The Byrne and Johnston plays have their own effective emotional power, but both make a more complex statement about their subjects. Both contain intricate, exceptionally well-dramatized but nevertheless intellectual debates.

I yield to none in my admiration for the O'Casey and Behan masterpieces, but I suspect that plays like Johnston's and Byrne's are more adult and, in the best of all possible worlds, better. Behan and O'Casey make the traditional theatrical appeal to our feelings; Byrne and Johnston speak also to our brains.

What Byrne says in this play is valuable in itself, and it is also courageous. This is one of the rare Irish plays that coldly analyzes the motives and practices of the Church in Ireland, and the analysis is both accurate and unemotional. The priest here is no O'Caseyan boob or tyrant, but a literate spokesman for his point of view. Even more interesting is that Byrne has opposed the priest's view with force and clarity. I do not mean that Byrne the man has necessarily opposed the Church's view. He has, however, given a spirited opposition to one of his characters, and in providing a real debate he has found the real stuff of drama.

The play is not only more complex in statement than Behan's, but it is also more complex in technique. Byrne has more characters than Behan, and he develops them more. All of this makes his play more demanding for an audience, though in the long run it may make the play more meaningful and moving.

If there be notable faults in the work, they probably lie in the plotting. The old-fashioned device of the letter is rather artificial, and the jailbreak at the end, while exciting theater, tends to obscure the main theme. However, there is so much of excellence in the play, so much thickly drawn characterization, humor, tension, and, especially, meaning, that the faults weigh lightly indeed.

Design for a Headstone

Political Prisoners	Prison Warders
CONOR EGAN	PAT GERAGHTY
AIDAN O'LEARY	MOUTH PHELAN
KEVIN SHIELDS	CHARLES GRIMES
TOMMY MC GOVERN	PRINCIPAL WARDER
JIM O'SHEA	Criminal Prisoners
RUCTIONS MC GOWAN	JAKEY
BILL DUNNE	MUSCLES ROGAN
JOE FITZPATRICK	BUTCHER HEALY
MICHEÁL BREATHNACH	BAYER
P. J. CORRIGAN	Prison chaplain, FATHER MAGUIRE
O'SULLIVAN	MRS. EGAN

Other prisoners, warders, etc.

Act I

The time is before 1950, in the triple cell; that is, two cells made into one by the removal of dividing wall. A number of prisoners are wearing their own clothes, varying from slovenly to neat. Aidan and Kevin are playing chess, watched by Corrigan and O'Sullivan, who are irritated by the slow progress of the game and the long intervals between moves. Two others are playing draughts, a relatively fast game, and noisy. Another is embroidering crossed flags on a piece of linen set up on the legs of an upended table, as frame. Ructions and O'Shea are playing a game of rings. Tommy is hammering out a silver ring on a tapered stick, with the bolt from a stool as hammer. Micheál is teaching an Irish class at a blackboard. Jakey, the only prisoner in prison uniform of dark grey with two-inch black stripes, carries a slop pail, and is cleaning up lazily with a mop.

100

RUCTIONS (*about to throw*): What do I want?

O'SHEA: Seven for game. May grass grow in every cell in the jail before you get it.

RUCTIONS: In the bag, comrade. Sa mhala, sta se. (*Throws successfully.*) How much is that you owe me?

O'SHEA (*mock ruefully*): Me four good-looking Gold Flake cigarettes! The devil looks after his own.

RUCTIONS (*picks up ring*): You'd be better employed over there at your Irish class, instead of squandering your substance gambling.

O'SHEA: Here! Doubles or quits! Round the clock?

RUCTIONS (*to Tommy*): Well Tommy, how's it coming?

Tommy removes ring from stick for Ructions to try on; he takes pull from cigarette, and parks it on edge of form, which he bestrides. Jakey, hovering, darts forward expectantly and Tommy gives Jakey the butt.

JAKEY: Thanks, oul' skin; I was gummin'.

O'SHEA: Damn nice job, that ring!

RUCTIONS: A Victorian shilling: the stuff is in it.

Aidan moves a chessman. O'Sullivan sighs wearily, changes feet and exchanges glances with Corrigan.

CORRIGAN (*wearily*): Won't be long now! White to move and mate in two.

O'SULLIVAN: If she's that long mating, when will she spawn?

CORRIGAN: Bring out your queen, man — bring out your queen!

AIDAN (*resentfully*): Please! Besides, what are you waiting for? You can't use chessmen to play draughts.

O'SULLIVAN: Why not? What harm is in it?

CORRIGAN (*supports*): The other board is engaged.

AIDAN (*rigidly*): That's the rule.

O'Sullivan and Corrigan exchange aggrieved glances.

MICHEÁL (*calls class to attention*): Sibhse dilig! (*From blackboard.*) Cailleadh e, ar seisean. Cailleadh, aneadh? Bhuel, arsa mo dhuine leis an mbadoir, dha mba thu, ni rachadh me isteach mbad go deo arist (*singsong fashion*) rachadh me, ni rachadh me, an rachadh me, nach rachadh me, adeirmse go rachadh me, adeirmse nach rachadh me.

RUCTIONS (*aloud in opposition*): On raconte que lorsque ce vaillant amiral quitta son père pour prendre la mer pour la première fois, ce lui-ci l'exhorta à se bien conduire, en ajoutant qu'il esperait vivre assez longtemps pour le voir capitaine. Capitaine! repondit l'enfant: si je ne pensais pas arriver a être amiral, je ne partirais certainment pas.

JAKEY: Yours is a very different class of Irish from his.

RUCTIONS: Yes, Jakey; his is about a boatman; but mine! — mine is about an admiral!

Jakey nods with elaborate comprehension.

O'SHEA: Will you do me one, Tommy? When that's finished?

RUCTIONS: You need a Victorian shilling.

O'SHEA (*produces spoon from pocket*): I've got a spoon — with a handle on it!

TOMMY (*admiringly*): A handle, eh! Must be the last one in the jail! Right! Leave it with me.

O'SULLIVAN (*to Corrigan*): Why doesn't he huff him, for not taking the queen?

CORRIGAN: There's no huffing in chess, lug! And no crowning either.

O'SULLIVAN: Uncrowned king, eh? A good republican game!

Aidan puts hand to chessman, hesitant about move.

O'SULLIVAN (*mock warning*): Ah, ah!

AIDAN: What do *you* think I ought to do with it?

O'SULLIVAN: Do with what?

AIDAN (*exasperated*): This — my bishop.

O'SULLIVAN: I'd love to tell you!

RUCTIONS (*shouts*): Stick him up your jersey!

Those around laugh; Aidan affects not to hear.

O'SULLIVAN (*moves away to Corrigan*): Come on!

CORRIGAN (*moving in disgust*): Oh, Mother Ireland, get off me back!

RUCTIONS (*provocatively*): Chess in this jail is as much an instrument of oppression as wealth is outside it.

Aidan continues to ignore Ructions.

CORRIGAN (*to Tommy*): Are you going to engrave it — the ring?

RUCTIONS: My initials, and a design: a knight rampant on a draughts board. I was going to have a mitre; but I'm allergic to bishops.

Aidan reacts, but is silent.

MICHEÁL (*from blackboard*): Eistigidh, eistigidh uilig! Sibse thall, sibhse! Abairt a' lae, abairt a' lae.

RUCTIONS: That's a phrase a day, Jakey.

MICHEÁL: An imreocaidh tu cluiche ciseach? Imreocaidh. Ni imreocaidh. (*Calls.*) Anois. An imreocaidh tu . . . (*They all repeat each phrase after him.*) Cluiche ciseach. . . . Imreocaidh. Ni imreocaidh. . . . (*Translates.*) Will you play a game of basketball? I will play. I will not play. (*Dismisses class.*) Deanfaidh sin.

The Irish class breaks up. Micheál is stopped by Ructions.

RUCTIONS: How'd you say: Will you play a game of chess?

MICHEÁL: An imreocaidh tu cluiche fithohille?

RUCTIONS: I must remember that.

O'SHEA: Come on, Ructions! Round the clock — doubles or quits?

RUCTIONS (*derisively, throws rings*): An imreocaidh tu cluiche round the clock? (*Throws.*) I will play. (*Throws.*) I will not play.

MICHEÁL (*stung*): It might interest you to know that the warriors of ancient Ireland were *all* chess players.

RUCTIONS: It'd interest me a damned sight more to know if the chess players of modern Ireland were all warriors.

AIDAN (*rises to bait*): What do you mean?

RUCTIONS: There are only two boards in this place, and either will do to play draughts. One is reserved for the six who play chess — the gentlemen — and one is shared by a hundred men, the proletariat, who play draughts.

AIDAN: There's one for chess, one for draughts.

RUCTIONS: Well, I'll play draughts with either — yes, and I'll play draughts with chessmen, too — and the warrior who wants to stop me had better be quick on his feet.

AIDAN: Indeed?

O'SHEA: Take it easy, Ructions.

RUCTIONS (*ignores restraint*): By God, he'd better! I'll reason with the bastard first — and then I'll give him a belt in the snot.

Ructions and Aidan face one another threateningly. Dunne, acting as spotter, comes to cell door.

DUNNE: Aidan! Geraghty — he's on the wing.

Aidan nods acknowledgment. O'Shea draws Ructions to game to stop altercation.

O'SHEA (*tenders cigarettes to Ructions*): Four. Isn't that what I owe you?

RUCTIONS: That's all right. Keep them.

O'SHEA: Well, take two then.

Aidan and Kevin are whispering together excitedly.

RUCTIONS: Give them to the convict, there.

Jakey turns around in instant indignation.

O'SHEA: With the compliments of Ructions McGowan.

Jakey, despite indignation, accepts cigarettes and puts them inside the open breast of his shirt.

JAKEY (*to Ructions, bellicose*): You're makin' a big mistake, Mister — a bloody big mistake. I'm no convict, so I'm not. I'm an untried prisoner, on remand, the same as youse.

O'SHEA: What are you doing in the uniform?

JAKEY: On remand, the same as youse politicals. I should be out on bail, by rights, which I would be, too, only for the friggin' rawsers has their knife in me, and opposed bail. Them fellas is bad news — and always was!

O'SHEA: Why aren't you wearing your own clothes?

JAKEY: And get me good suit destroyed, is it? Put in the day in the wood yard, is it, when I could be gettin' a smoke off youse politicals, by takin' the job as Wardsman? Ay, and a bit o' gur thrown in. (*Sound of metal triangle being beaten on the circle.*) D'ye hear that? The triangle on the circle! Out goes all the bank clerks — the gentry wearin' their own clothes — out to get shaggin' welts on their hands choppin' blocks for the bastards. Aw, but Jakey is too hairy for that!

RUCTIONS: I'm sorry, Jakey. I thought —

JAKEY: See what thought did? Some people think too much. Youse politicals seem to think yez are God almighty, and that no one is innocent, barrin' yerselves.

RUCTIONS: Have a smoke: I'm sorry.

JAKEY (*puts cigarette in shirt*): I'll plank it for after.

RUCTIONS: What are you in for?

JAKEY: I'm in on a mistake: that's what.

O'SHEA (*jocosely*): Whose mistake? Yours or theirs?

Chorus of laughter.

JAKEY: Oh, yez can laugh. But I did me bit, me oul' segotia: don't forget that. I'm none o' yer peacetime soldiers. Jakey was in the thick of it, right up to the split. Yez know the rest: internecine strife, brother's hand turned against brother. But no more fightin' for Jakey! It's wan thing to bate the lard out o' the foreigner; but when it comes to civil war, it couldn't be good nor lucky.

O'SHEA (*bantering*): Ireland is yours for the taking, Jakey.

JAKEY: If I'd've knew as much then as I do now, I'd have lookin' for a pension. Ay, and gettin' it too; 'cos I couldn't be denied it. Oh, but the heroes got their whack, and Jakey gets sweet damn-all. And why? Because I'm too proud to stick out me hand, when the pensions is being gev out, that's why. I fought for Ireland, and not a pension.

RUCTIONS: What are you in for now?

JAKEY: Nothin': I told ye.

RUCTIONS: What are you charged with?

JAKEY: It's all a mistake. I'm charged with knockin' off and receivin' an article of clothin' or furniture, knowin' it to have been knocked off.

O'SHEA: Article of clothing or furniture — what the hell is that.

JAKEY: Legal. That's the legal for travelin' rug. The way it was, I found this rug. Found it in a car park.

RUCTIONS (*cynically*): Oh!

JAKEY: Bloody grand rug, it was, too. Worth a couple o' bar. Up comes this bloody big rawser, and tries to make out I'm stealin' it. A right get! But I'll get him up in our cully before he's very much older: He won't know what hit him: he'll think it was a concrete mixer, or a belt in the clock from the hand o' God. And I on me way to put in the advertisement.

RUCTIONS: What advertisement?

JAKEY: In the lost and found. So as the owner would know his rug wasn't lost; but that I had it safe, and was mindin' it for him. What else could I do, until I knew the proper person to give it back to? Just shows ye! I'd 've gettin' as much thanks for bloody well stickin' to it. (*Resigned.*) No matter! Th' oul' rug would only be on me conscience.

DUNNE (*from doorway*) : Here he comes!

Aidan and Kevin alert and rise when Warder Geraghty enters with basket containing papers and parcels on his arm. He looks at Aidan, then at crowded cell, embarrassed by number present; he sights Jakey.

GERAGHTY (*roars*) : Jakey!

JAKEY: Yes, Mr. G., I'm nearly finished.

GERAGHTY: What the hell are ye doin' here?

JAKEY: Givin' the place a bit of a clean up for these men.

GERAGHTY: Looks like a battlefield! How many cigarettes did ye clean up this morning?

JAKEY: Who? Me? I have as much on me, now, as — as ye have yerself.

Prisoners crowd about Geraghty expectantly for parcels.

O'SHEA: Papers, Pat?

RUCTIONS: Anything for me, Pat?

CORRIGAN: What about my razor blades, Pat?

GERAGHTY (*fussed*) : All in good time. Everything here! I'm doin' the exercise yard first — these parcels is all in order.

AIDAN (*to Geraghty, peremptorily*) : Well?

GERAGHTY (*uneasily*): I'm not sure, Mr. O'Leary — I think I might have somethin' here — in the bottom o' the basket. I'll look in, on me way back. (*To Jakey.*) And, you, get to hell out o' here! That place below is a common disgrace for want of a good do-out.

JAKEY: Right, Mr. G.! No sooner said!

Exit Geraghty, followed by prisoners interested in parcels.

AIDAN (*to Kevin*): Looks bad!

Kevin shrugs noncommittally; they resume chess.

JAKEY (*comments on Geraghty*) : A proper snakin' Jeese! A street angel to youse, o' course; but if ye worked under him in the bastardin' kitchen, you'd soon know to the differ.

RUCTIONS: Pat is all right.

JAKEY: O' course he's all right; sure, they're *all* all right, if it comes to that: as long as I'm comin' to this joint, I never met one that wasn't all right — only — don't ask them for anythin'.

O'SHEA: The man has to do his duty.

JAKEY: Duty! Hump that for a yarn! I remember hearin' one o' yer own — speakin', he was of a Sunday mornin' at the corner of Cathal Brugha Street, "Since when," says yer man, "since when have Irishmen subscribed to the fallacious doctrine that a man's duty is what he's paid for?"

Chorus of amused applause.

O'SHEA: Good for you, Jakey!

MICHEÁL: Mo seacht ngradh thu! Go mairidh thu!

JAKEY: That's a quare wan for the books! (*Exit Jakey.*)

RUCTIONS: *He* wasn't born with a silver spoon in his mouth.

O'SHEA: But he wasn't long getting his hands on one.

AIDAN (*authoritatively*): I want you all to clear out of here before Geraghty comes back. Except Tommy.

General chorus: "Righto." Exeunt Corrigan and O'Sullivan. Aidan resumes seat. Tommy holds up ring for Ructions' approval.

RUCTIONS: Grand! You're a craftsman, Tommy.

TOMMY: I could do a design, there, extend it out to the sides, there, and taper it off in Celtic interlace. Well?

RUCTIONS: I want you to do me a dragon. (*To O'Shea.*) Give me that Brian O'Higgins card.

O'Shea gives Christmas card of vivid green, blue, orange.

RUCTIONS: See that? Could you do that dragon?

TOMMY: Yes — I think I could do that.

RUCTIONS: Wrap the tail round him a few times — interlace it, if you like — and finish it up with his tail in his mouth.

O'SHEA (*amused*): His tail in his gob, eh?

RUCTIONS: And stick in a bit of green for an eye. Well?

TOMMY: I can do that.

O'SHEA: Is this dragon trying to choke himself?

RUCTIONS (*denunciatory*): He is the symbol of passive resistance — the sufferer unto death — the Christ-like worm who never turns — the monster consuming his own tissue.

O'SHEA (*uncomprehending levity*): Oh, Mother Ireland, get off my back!

RUCTIONS: Symbol of the hunger striker, who turns his violence against himself — whose mortal wound is self-inflicted — the warrior who raises his axe, only to cleave his own skull.

AIDAN (*furious*): You —! You —! Terence McSwiney! Thomas Ashe! Jack McNeila and Tony D'Arcy! Condemn *them*? Are these the men symbolized by your — by your obscenity? Tommy! You're not to do that, do you hear? I say, you're not to!

TOMMY: Aidan, I don't think Ructions meant —

AIDAN: That's an order. Give me that ring!

RUCTIONS: That's my property.

AIDAN (*takes ring*): In the absence of Conor Egan I'm acting O.C. I'll produce it at a court martial, and they can decide what to do.

RUCTIONS: On what charge?

AIDAN: It will be news to the executive to hear that you share the view of the bishops that hunger strike is suicide.

RUCTIONS: It will be news to the bishops too — to say nothing of it being news to me.

O'SHEA: He didn't say that, Aidan: what he meant was —

RUCTIONS: Let him fire ahead with his heresy hunt. Let him call his Inquisition. Maybe Mister Adjutant Aidan O'Leary will find he has more in common with the bishops of Ireland than I have.

TOMMY: He didn't say it was suicide.

AIDAN: He implied it.

RUCTIONS: If I didn't say it, I say it now: but I may mean that which John Mitchell defended, rather than that with which Tone was maligned.

AIDAN: That's for a court martial to find.

RUCTIONS: A silk weaver may use words more loosely than a bishop — even technical terms of doctrine — more loosely than yourself, with a brother on the Maynooth mission to China.

O'SHEA: Cut it out, Ructions.

RUCTIONS: Protecting the oldest civilization in the world from the infiltration of social justice.

TOMMY: That's enough. That'll do Ructions.

RUCTIONS: Hawking the mystical body of Christ around the world on a salary and commission basis.

AIDAN (*barely restraining himself*): I warn you!

RUCTIONS: No, I've no brother on the Maynooth mission to China! but to liquidate the gombeen class, I'd gladly join in a mission — the Chinese mission to Maynooth.

AIDAN: The executive can deal with you! You decry the country's language, scoff at its culture, its religion; malign its martyrs and heroes: ridicule the whole basis of national outlook and army morale. Why you ever joined the army — God alone knows.

RUCTIONS: To fight!

AIDAN: The court can decide whether your views are consonant with your continued membership.

RUCTIONS: You better know what my views are: that the state is built on violence — and only ousted by greater violence — the Church pronounces as lawful the government which can maintain order — thereby rationalizing the greater potential of violence. As for hunger strike, and passive stuff, the psychology is lousy!

AIDAN: The new O.C. can deal with it — when he's elected.

RUCTIONS: Elected, eh? Open ballot or Roman rota?

AIDAN: Conor Egan will be replaced by open ballot.

RUCTIONS: Come on, O'Shea, let's get to hell out of here.

Exeunt Ructions and O'Shea; enter Dunne.

DUNNE: I know you'll say it's impossible; but I think Conor Egan's back — I could swear I saw him being brought in and taken down to the base.

AIDAN: Conor? The O.C.? Nonsense! He couldn't be. Conor's convicted this morning; and convicted men go to Arbour Hill — to military detention.

DUNNE: Well, I've my doubts — I could almost swear —

AIDAN: Only untried prisoners are kept here in the remand section: you know that — or you ought to.

DUNNE: If it wasn't Conor, it was his dead spitting image.

AIDAN (*exasperated*): If he's convicted, he's gone to the Hill: there's no doubt about that.

DUNNE: He has a double, so.

Exit Dunne. Tommy examines O'Shea's spoon.

AIDAN: I wish to God it *was* Conor.

KEVIN: Yes. We could do with him — now.

AIDAN: Tommy! Have you the funds handy?

Tommy nods, resumes study of spoon as O'Sullivan enters.

O'SULLIVAN: Tommy, will ye do that now? The letter to me missus?

Despite irritating effect on Aidan, Tommy takes letter to be answered.

TOMMY (*pencil in hand*): Later. Tell me what to say. Dearest Mary? Darling Mary? What's the usual?

O'SULLIVAN: Tell her send in me heavy boots — my God, will ye look at these!

TOMMY: Yes, yes. Well? What else?

O'SULLIVAN: My God! this place is terrible hard on boots.

AIDAN (*patience gives out*): Tommy!

TOMMY: We'll go down to my cell; it's quieter there.

Exeunt Tommy and O'Sullivan. After long pause enter Geraghty: after a quick look around he hands letter to Aidan, goes back to door. Aidan reads, and nods significantly to Kevin.

AIDAN (*to Geraghty*): You read this?

GERAGHTY: No; but I know the contents.

AIDAN (*coldly abrupt*): How?

GERAGHTY: Wasn't I there and he writin' it?

KEVIN: Where?

GERAGHTY: The rat trap — in the snug — where anyone might have seen me.

KEVIN: Who was it?

GERAGHTY: Mrs. Conor Egan brought me there: *she* said to call him George — she introduced me. Who or what he really was, I don't know, but you'd never think, to look at him — what I mean is, he was only a small butt of a man, hardly in it, ye might say.

AIDAN: Was Conor's wife there all the time?

GERAGHTY: For the most part. Long enough to know what it was all about.

KEVIN: What? What the hell was *she* doing there?

GERAGHTY: It wasn't my place to order her out; that was up to yer man George. Too damn long she was there — for my likin'!

KEVIN (*increasingly alarmed*): Why do you say that?

GERAGHTY: She started creatin' — about the danger her husband was in. Why should he have to lead the escape? Why this and why the other? And all the time the ears cocked on the bartender, standin' within a long spit, and he listening goodo, pretendin' to wipe the table.

KEVIN (*tensely*): Well?

GERAGHTY: I was half expectin' —

KEVIN: Yes?

GERAGHTY: To see a bloody hole wiped through the table.

KEVIN: Damn the table! What did she say?

GERAGHTY: Her Conor and her Conor, and all to that. And all she wouldn't do! "Shush," says I to yer woman. Well! She flew at me. And the big wild eyes of her borin' me through! Y'd think it was *me* was after appointin' her husband O.C. But George didn't put much pass on her. Just soothed her down, then sent her below to give us the bend from across the street, if it was all right for us to clear out. He said she was just *hysterical*.

KEVIN (*purposefully casual*): What did you have to drink?

GERAGHTY: Whiskey, I called for; but, I leave it to God, it wasn't whiskey; sulfulious acid! take the paint off a door!

KEVIN (*trap question*): What did *he* drink?

GERAGHTY: Damn the drop!

KEVIN (*quickly alert*): Nothing?

GERAGHTY: Never as much as — wait, though, he did — now I come to think of it, he bought a grapefruit — if ye call that a drink. Ay, "Grapefruit for G, George," says he.

Aidan and Kevin exchange glances. Kevin takes letter and examines paper.

KEVIN (*to Aidan*): Fire ahead!

AIDAN (*to Geraghty*): Well?

GERAGHTY: It's all bloody fine and large talkin', but I've my wife and kids to remember; and this could be a serious thing. A bit of a note, or a letter to post, is all very well, once in a way: that's neither here nor there: but — them yokes! — revolvers! — Where would I be? Eight of them! Eight! Am I mad or what? Sure, I must be!

AIDAN: They'd be invaluable! — of course you'd receive recognition.

GERAGHTY: Too bloody true, I would! Well, I'm just the very boy that doesn't want — *recognition*!

AIDAN: I mean you'd be paid.

GERAGHTY: There's a gap to be plugged with every penny; but — well, money wouldn't pay me: that's the plain way of puttin' it.

Kevin holds paper up to window, finds watermark, comes across.

KEVIN: The rat trap, you said?

GERAGHTY (*defensively*): Yes — why?

KEVIN: Mrs. Conor Egan?

GERAGHTY: 'Course! Your O.C.'s wife; why?

KEVIN (*displays paper*): She supplied the paper?

GERAGHTY: No. I did. I had some with me — in case, like.

KEVIN: Where did you get it?

GERAGHTY: The paper?

KEVIN: Yes.

GERAGHTY: It's — eh — it's a bit of prison stuff: they do have it in the office.

KEVIN: Yes? Well?

GERAGHTY: I do swipe a bit, now and then. Off and on, like, for the kids' schoolin' — pens, paper, suchlike — rubbers — sure, it'd cost ye a bloody mint!

KEVIN (*hands paper to Aidan*): Watermark.

GERAGHTY (*indignantly*): Now, if youse two think — there's nothin' hookey about me — and if ye don't like to trust me — well — ye can do the other thing.

AIDAN (*hastily*): We do, Pat, we do.

GERAGHTY: Well, if ye don't, and this man doesn't seem to —

KEVIN (*cold distaste*): All right! We trust you.

GERAGHTY: Might be better for me if ye didn't. Taking me life in me hands!

KEVIN: So long as you *know* that!

GERAGHTY (*bellicose*): Know what?

KEVIN: That you *are* taking your life in your hands — and the lives of *other* men too.

GERAGHTY: And amn't I stakin' me life, amn't I? Stakin' me bloody job — never mind stakin' me life!

KEVIN: Then you *have* decided?

GERAGHTY: I didn't say that. Decidin' is *one* thing.

KEVIN: But doing, another. (*Impatient.*) How much?

GERAGHTY (*uneasily, looks out doorway*): The chief should be on his rounds now; and if I was to be seen here —

AIDAN (*shouts impatiently*): How much? How much per gun?

GERAGHTY (*frightened*): God! D'ye want to bring them in on top of us, man?

Geraghty goes to door, and almost collides with Jakey, who enters with dixie in hand: both silent, long pause.

GERAGHTY (*explodes in anger and fright*): Where the hell are ye goin'? What's that ye have? What are ye doin'?

JAKEY (*perplexed by attack*): Just an oul' dixie, Mr. G. I was lookin' to see if I could see ye — to see would it be all right for me to slip down to the kitchen — to get a drop of chah — give meself a bit of a scrape — and have meself lookin' decent — I done them lavaterries lovely.

GERAGHTY (*partly reassured*): Go on, then! But if the chief gets you in the kitchen — remember! — ye got no permission from me.

JAKEY (*to all*): Hard to beat th' oul' drop of scald, whah! And what I don't drink I can shave with. (*Salutes as he exits.*) One off! (*Exit Jakey.*)

GERAGHTY: Did he — did he tape anythin', would you say?

AIDAN: *His* mind is on the tea.

KEVIN: I don't know.

GERAGHTY: Sow a nest in yer ear, he would. (*To Aidan.*) My God! You're the terrible man. Never say a thing like that again. (*To Kevin.*) Stand over there, you that has a head on yer shoulders, near the door, like a good man.

Kevin takes up position at doorway.

AIDAN: Well, now that that's all settled —

GERAGHTY (*interrupts*): A word, if ye please: then *you* can talk. Not to make two bites of a cherry, I have them all. Now, speak up!

AIDAN: You have? You mean — ?

GERAGHTY: The whole lot! Planked! Eight of them! Where I can lay me hands on them. Only to get them in. Have ye me? Eight! And the stuff as well. Any God's amount of it!

AIDAN: God, that's wonderful!

GERAGHTY: Only nothin' is to take place before Thursday: that's my half day. It wouldn't suit me for anythin' to happen, and me on duty. I'm only on this wing temporary, while oul' Gallagher is on leave. I'll be back in the kitchen from Friday, so — any day after that.

AIDAN: Yes, yes. And when would you be able to —

GERAGHTY: That's the bogey. Two at a time. Them yokes is bulky. Two after dinner; two this evening; and tomorrow is Wednesday, two in the mornin'. That makes six. After that, I'm on visits duty; so it's shut shop — napoo! What more d'ye need? Isn't six buckets?

AIDAN: We need the eight.

GERAGHTY: Yez are bunched, so. I'm not stickin' me neck out — any more than it's out already.

AIDAN: But you must see, Pat — now, look, Pat! —

GERAGHTY: Never mind Patting me. It's all Pat with yez, now. Pat here and Pat there; but it'll be easy talkin' to Pat if Pat comes a cropper, arse over tip, between the whole bloody lot of ye. What about me? How much am I gettin'?

KEVIN: For eight?

GERAGHTY: For six — take it or leave it.

Aidan and Kevin exchange glances.

KEVIN (*compromise*) : For six, then — and two on a visit.

GERAGHTY: How? Two on a visit?

KEVIN: See Conor Egan's wife again and —

GERAGHTY: What! Mrs. Egan! I'd as lief not see that woman again. I'm tellin' ye now — mark my words — she's bad news: she has as much use for me, as the devil has for holy water.

KEVIN: See her again. Tell her to send in George to me — tomorrow, at three, on a visit. *You*, arrange to be on the visit, and hand over the guns to me then.

AIDAN: Yes, of course. In the visitor's room.

GERAGHTY: Yez must take me for a right hawk! — and where was *I*, if *you* were searched, coming off the visit?

KEVIN: Then, don't hand them to me there: give them to me here — when you bring me back.

GERAGHTY (*after pause*): Might work! Like as not! This will put years on me. Bloody glad when it's all over. (*Decides.*) Right! Six — and two on a visit — providin' I manage to see Mrs. Egan. I only hope to God I'm doin' the right thing. (*Puts out hand to Aidan.*) Come on, then! Give!

AIDAN: Twenty.

GERAGHTY: What!

AIDAN: The letter said you agreed for the —

GERAGHTY: Forty quid and don't vex me!

Aidan looks at Kevin, who nods. Geraghty sees nod.

GERAGHTY: And ten more for me risk in havin' to see Mrs. Egan again, makin' in all fifty.

KEVIN: Okay; but no more! Twenty-five now, and the balance when —

GERAGHTY: Fifty down! On the nail! Them things is like the Ten Commandments; if ye're caught with one, ye're guilty of all.

Aidan consents with Kevin by glance; goes to cell door; calls.

AIDAN: Tommy!

Geraghty busies himself with basket, produces journal.

GERAGHTY (*reads*) : Whose name is that? Show-sam MacJilly — somethin'.

AIDAN: Seosamh Mac Giolla Phadraig — Joe Fitz. The architects' journal. Leave it here for him.

GERAGHTY: A son of poor oul' Turlough, what? — that was shot above in the Cornmarket in 1922? I remember well.

Enter Tommy, who, after confab with Aidan and Kevin, gives money to Aidan, whilst Geraghty elaborately studies journal. Aidan pays Geraghty, who pockets the money, uncounted, puts journal on bed, and walks quickly from cell. Exit Geraghty.

KEVIN (*to Tommy, after pause*): Better transfer the rest of the funds — in case.

TOMMY: Yes, I was thinking. Joe Fitz's album would do the trick. His autograph album; the one he calls his roll of honor. The cover is packed with cotton wool.

AIDAN: Right!

KEVIN: The section leaders: I'll round them up, shall I?

AIDAN: Very good! And report back — both!

Exeunt Tommy and Kevin. Aidan, alone, ponders his problem, and somewhat wearily goes over to bed, on which he relaxes, full length. Enter Conor Egan, medium height, neatly dressed in poorish clothes: he is somewhat older than most of the others: of an age with Tommy. He is easy in manner, rather informal: his natural humility has prevented him from becoming stiff or regimental in contrast to Aidan or Kevin. Aidan rises.

AIDAN: Conor! Dunne said you were in the base — but — I couldn't believe it. What happened?

CONOR: I'll tell you that later, Aidan. Geraghty? Did you see him?

AIDAN (*uneasily*): We gave him fifty pounds. Why?

CONOR: Good!

AIDAN: I'm very relieved to hear you say so: we didn't know what to think: he said he met George, that your wife brought him.

CONOR: Kathleen. Yes, that's right: she did.

AIDAN: How do *you* know? Did you see her?

CONOR: They let me have a few minutes with her — after the conviction.

AIDAN: Then you were convicted? (*Puzzled.*) Well, then, how — what did you get?

CONOR: Two years — hard. To be served here — in the criminal section.

AIDAN: The criminal section?

CONOR (*smilingly*): The sentence not to take effect — if I enter into a recognizance — to break my army connection.

AIDAN: The curs! So that's the game. To abolish political treatment.

CONOR: Yes, that's the game. The court adjourned until Thursday — to let me think it over. (*Grimly.*) I've thought it over.

AIDAN: Yes?

CONOR: I'm going on hunger strike — against criminal status.

AIDAN: But Conor, the escape? We're getting eight revolvers.

CONOR: I'm not going with you.

AIDAN (*disappointed*): Oh, Conor!

CONOR: Of course, I'll give you a hand with it. But I'm not going — I can't.

AIDAN (*walks, pauses, incisively guesses*): It's your wife Kathleen? Isn't it?

CONOR: Yes, in a way. Though not really. How did you know?

AIDAN: Geraghty told us. He said she was — well, upset.

CONOR: She didn't want me to lead the escape. She — she wasn't herself —

she's expecting a baby — she pressed me very hard — to drop the escape idea.

AIDAN: And you promised?

CONOR (*firmly*): No. I didn't. I'm rather sorry now I didn't.

AIDAN: Geraghty said she threatened — did she?

CONOR: I suppose you *could* call it a threat — not that I really think she would — I don't think it for a moment; but I never saw her like that before — in some way, at breaking point: and she *might* see Burke, as she threatened.

AIDAN: Who's Burke?

CONOR: The danger is she might say too much, to get the fellow to stop it.

AIDAN (*outburst*): What fellow, to stop what?

CONOR: Burke — her brother-in-law: he's in the guards — a sergeant.

AIDAN (*appalled*): Oh! Does she know you're thinking of hunger strike?

CONOR: No. I couldn't tell her that, then.

AIDAN: Had she known that she mightn't have asked for the promise.

CONOR: I didn't promise.

AIDAN: She might have preferred the escape to the certain death of hunger strike.

CONOR (*resentment against wife*): I didn't give her the choice.

AIDAN: Choice? Then it was a choice?

CONOR: No, no, no, no: my decision on hunger strike has nothing to do with Kathleen's attitude: it's not just an alternative — I'd have done it anyway. This threat of criminal status — we've got to meet that, at the start, and hunger strike met it before.

AIDAN: Of course, Conor, I believe you. But why *didn't* you tell her you had hunger strike in mind?

CONOR: Oh, I was — I was too damned furious.

AIDAN: Furious? Furious at what?

CONOR: At — why, at her threat, of course.

AIDAN: Although you didn't think she'd carry it out?

CONOR (*vehemently*): No, I didn't: I don't now!

AIDAN (*doubtful*): I see — Conor, surely fury is another aspect of fear?

CONOR (*angry at questioning*): Another aspect, be damned! There's no aspect — no fear! — fear of what? — an idle threat?

AIDAN (*doubtful*): All right. And your fury? — that plays *no part* in your hunger-strike decision? I hope I'm not being hurtful in making this suggestion: that your motives *might* be mixed.

CONOR (*wearily controls tendency to anger*): They're not, they're not. If I doubted Kathleen seriously, I *would* have promised. Why not? I wasn't going on the escape. My decision was made.

AIDAN: Well, then — why not promise?

CONOR (*impatiently*): I told you — because I was angry.

114

Aidan remains worriedly unconvinced.

CONOR (*rises decisively*) : Where's Kevin — and Tommy?

AIDAN: Rounding up the section leaders.

CONOR: Right! I'd better see them — and get this job in hand. Come on! We'll see them together, and work out the details.

As they are about to leave enter Warder Grimes.

GRIMES: Father Maguire — to see O'Leary.

AIDAN: Who?

GRIMES: The chaplain — he's waiting at your cell — hurry up!

AIDAN (*to Conor*): I'd better see him.

CONOR: I'll go ahead. (*Exit Conor.*)

AIDAN: I'll see him here.

Grimes, about to remonstrate, remembers he is dealing with a political prisoner, leaves. Returns with Father Maguire, a priest in early middle age.

GRIMES: Father Maguire.

AIDAN (*civilly*) : Goodday, Father.

MAGUIRE (*rather kindly approach*) : Ah, O'Leary — you wanted to see me?

AIDAN: I wanted to see you, Father, about your sermon on Sunday last — on secret societies — and about this. (*Produces printed leaflet.*)

MAGUIRE: Yes. Well?

AIDAN (*re leaflet*): The pastoral letter of 'twenty-two — a document almost twenty years old. You have been handing these out to the men — you and the other two confessors. Further, you asked them, in the confessional, if they were members of an illegal organization — and if they were prepared to sever their connection with —

MAGUIRE (*meeting challenge*): Yes, yes, I have, I have. And required them to cease membership of a secret society, as I am bound to do. And, in a number of cases, I withheld absolution. Well?

AIDAN: Withheld in every single case! Because you couldn't break them.

MAGUIRE: What is the purpose of this discussion? The state holds power under God; and an act of rebellion is sin. It is my bounden duty to point that out; and bullying won't prevent me.

AIDAN (*provocatively*) : Is it your duty to *create* sin?

MAGUIRE: If you have chosen this occasion merely to be offensive, there's no point in continuing.

AIDAN: Isn't the word "bullying" offensive? Or do you regard yourself as entitled to more courtesy than you extend?

MAGUIRE (*restrains anger*) : Very well, I withdraw the word. Now what is it you want?

AIDAN: Most of the men are Catholic. Far from wishing to be offensive, you have been selected as the one priest with whom discussion is possible.

MAGUIRE (*unappreciatively*) : Thanks.

115

AIDAN: The army is not a secret society, as defined by the Church.

MAGUIRE (*irritably*): Isn't it secret? Isn't it oath-bound?

AIDAN: No man gives a blank check on his conscience: therefore it is not secret, within the Church's definition.

MAGUIRE: It is — as I understand it.

AIDAN: And this term "the lawful government": you must know as well as I — indeed, far better! — that the basis of the state is not so easily disposed of.

MAGUIRE: The government has been elected by the people.

AIDAN: So was the Spanish government, which Franco overturned.

MAGUIRE: That election was invalid.

AIDAN: Yet, Maritain, the ablest Thomist in Europe, pronounced it a lawful government. So, you would absolve Franco; and, presumably, Maritain would withhold.

MAGUIRE: I should act according to my lights.

AIDAN: For a priest to meet so complex a problem with the oversimplification "that the government has been elected by the people," why! it's merely an impertinence.

MAGUIRE (*reasonable approach*): Let's be sensible, man. Do you expect a simple sermon, given in a prison chapel, to deal with the complexities of moral philosophy? Our Blessed Lord Himself said: "Render unto Caesar the things which are Caesar's." What could be more simple?

AIDAN: Maritain wrote a treatise on the scope of civil authority: *he* called it "The Things Which Are *Not* Caesar's." What could be more complex?

MAGUIRE: Young man, take care that your ability to read — and, as you think, to understand Maritain, is not the guise of spiritual pride. "I will not serve," cried Lucifer.

AIDAN: If spiritual pride be my damnation, it will have been erected as a barrier against the rubbish masquerading as Catholic doctrine. The word of God has been mangled between the teeth of His bishops. Yet, I have kept faith in the Church. I claim it as her triumph that she survives all opposition; and as a sign of her divinity, that she even survives the devoted efforts of her ministers.

MAGUIRE (*stung*): Thank you.

AIDAN (*tears leaflet*): A political tract, disguised as a pastoral letter.

MAGUIRE: I am acting under my bishop's guidance.

AIDAN: We look for a priest of God, not a bishop's employee. (*Turns away regretfully.*) Oh, I'm sorry to speak like this —

MAGUIRE (*affected by visible sincerity*): I think I understand. At all events, I believe you — I mean, that you are sincere — that you do believe what you say.

AIDAN (*desperately*): Father, something must be done. Must be! There are

116

some who don't care much — some, who *seem* not to care at all. And there are *some* who are glad to see the inadequacy of the Catholic Church to meet the situation in which these men are placed. But mostly these are simple men who would be eased by the confession and communion which is part of their ordinary lives outside, as much a part of them as home. My God! Can you not see that we are literally crying out to you — men — boys. (*Produces letter, reads.*) My mother. She says, "Aidan, darling, don't forget, next Friday is the first Friday. I offer up my communion for you, every single week."

About to continue, breaks off emotionally overcome, and turning back toward Maguire, Aidan sits on bed.

MAGUIRE (*gently*): O'Leary! O'Leary, son! — Come and see me tomorrow. Will you? Will you come, O'Leary? (*Aidan nods head.*) Good lad! Do come! We — we'll try to be *adequate* to the situation — together.

AIDAN (*forced composure*): Goodbye, Father, I'll come. And thanks.

Exit Maguire. Jakey at cell door, with bucket and brush, looks back for pursuers, produces from inside shirt front a pound lump of butter, dumps it in bucket, and throws brush in on top of it.

JAKEY: A bit o' butther — I see ye had his nibs with ye — the man o' God, whah? (*Takes journal.*) Be all right to tear a sheet outa this?

AIDAN: Not that! (*Gives newspaper.*) Here!

JAKEY (*starts to wrap butter*): Anythin' at all to keep it clean. (*Smells bucket.*) God knows what was in that last. It wasn't butther, anyway. (*Notices blackboard.*) Be all right to plank it here, till the bastardin' screw gets off the wing? (*Puts butter behind board.*)

AIDAN: It's cleaner than the bucket, at all events.

JAKEY: Ye needn't say a word to that oul' bucket. The newspaper men used to say, in the troubled times, that an umbrella was as good as a passport: get ye through any cordon. That's the beauty o' that oul' bucket: where ye like, when ye fancy, in this kip, only to have it with ye. — Were ye duckin' Mass, or what? (*Aidan's expression is indignant denial.*) I thought when I seen Father Maguire, like — I'm a Catlic meself, too — only I'm down as Church of Ireland.

AIDAN (*rather shocked*): Oh! Is that wise?

JAKEY: Doesn't it come to the wan thing in the finish — barrin' the Protestants doesn't believe in the saints? Aren't we all sons of Adam? Seed and breed of a gardener, humped out o' the job for stealin' apples?

AIDAN: And why Church of Ireland?

JAKEY: It's yer only dart if ye want a bit of a sleep of a Sunday mornin' — imagine them not believin' in saints! Not even Saint Anthony! 'Cos, fair play, it's bloody miraculous the way that man can find a thing when he puts his mind to it. Nothin' he can't find! (*Sighs.*) All the same, I wouldn't be where I am, if he hadn't've findin' that bloody rug! (*Picks up journal.*) Institute of Arch-i-tects.

Enter Fitzpatrick with Tommy, who hands autograph album to Aidan.

TOMMY: That's it. Fine cover!

FITZ: It was my father's: he had it in 'twenty-two. (*Points.*) Erskine Childers' signature. (*Turning pages.*) Cathal Brugha — O'Connell Street. Thomas Ashe. McSwiney. Both on hunger strike. Rory O'Connor, executed. Paddy McGrath: Tony D'Arcy: Jack Mac: they're all dead.

AIDAN: Like me to do something in it?

FITZ (*hesitant*): No, well — I'd rather not — they're all dead.

AIDAN (*to Tommy*): Righto. (*Exit Aidan.*)

TOMMY (*takes album to Fitz*): I'll give it to you later.

JAKEY (*to Fitz, apropos journal*): This your book? Are ye in the buildin'?

FITZ: I'm studying architecture.

Enter Ructions with Micheál, and draws design on blackboard showing alarm clock with leads from terminals to battery and dump.

JAKEY: Churches and chapels?

FITZ: Houses, theaters, even jails.

JAKEY: This is not a bad oul' post — as a jail, I mean.

FITZ: A thing of beauty — but — a joy forever? — Why is it called the triple cell? It's two cells, let in together: there's the crossbeam.

JAKEY: 'Cos it sleeps three. You can't have two prisoners together, that's the rule.

FITZ: Why not?

JAKEY: Ask me barney. (*Sees Grimes pass cell, rushes to door to watch his progress down wing.*)

RUCTIONS (*to Micheál*): There's your alarm clock, back view; there's your terminals; there's your battery; your dump. And there's your leads. From there, to there, to there; that's your full circuit. See?

Jakey, having checked Grimes' progress, rushes to blackboard, retrieves butter, dumps in bucket, and gets his brush.

JAKEY: Excuse me!

RUCTIONS (*rearranging board*): Ignorant sod! (*Exit Jakey. Ructions continues lecture.*) Now, to close your circuit. That's the gap. The winder is extended: a bit of metal will do. The alarm goes off for whatever time you've set it. When it does, the winder revolves — touches the metal, closing the circuit — and, whoops! — up she goes!

MICHEÁL: Very neat!

Enter Conor with Kevin and Aidan. Immediately all rush to welcome Conor. Fitz hovers around, idolatrous.

RUCTIONS: Conor!

MICHEÁL: By all that's holy!

TOMMY: Aren't you going to Arbour Hill?

CONOR (*grimly*): No, I'm not. I'm sentenced to two years — here, in the criminal section.

TOMMY: You mean — with the lags — the criminals?

MICHEÁL: But you must get political treatment — military detention.

RUCTIONS: They can't just chuck you in with a lot of housebreakers, abortionists, sex perverts, scum.

CONOR: They can! That's going to be the fate of every political prisoner from now on.

MICHEÁL: Political treatment was won very many years ago — by hunger strike: do they think we'll let it go easily as that?

TOMMY: But how are you here in D wing — with the remands?

CONOR: Aidan will tell you all about that. My sentence doesn't come into effect till Thursday.

RUCTIONS: Thursday! That's the day I go down. Probably get the same sentence.

CONOR: In the meanwhile I want you lads to organize resistance.

MICHEÁL: By God! We'll resist it.

RUCTIONS: They've a bloody long way to go before they get me to accept criminal status.

FITZ: They can't make you a criminal, Conor. They can't! They can't! — What are you going to do?

CONOR (*quietly, wearily*): Political treatment was won — a long time ago — by hunger strike.

FITZ (*awed*): Hunger strike! And, Conor — are — are you — going to — ?

CONOR (*smilingly*): I'm going to talk to the men, Fitz, when *you* get them for me.

Fitz backs away, awed, toward exit. Exit Fitz.

CONOR: There's no other weapon, lads. I am. I'm going on hunger strike. (*General gasp of horror.*)

MICHEÁL: It's — it's damnable.

TOMMY (*quietly, steps forward*): I'm with you, Conor, if you want me.

Micheál finding outlet for indignation, steps beside Tommy, stands at attention, calls out.

MICHEÁL: Volunteers!

Aidan and Kevin step into line. Only Ructions stands apart.

RUCTIONS: No, Conor, I won't. I won't do a hunger strike. (*Replying to unspoken charge.*) And it's not that I'm afraid.

CONOR (*smilingly*): That's all right, Ructions. No, lads, no. Thanks, but no. Hunger strike is a one-man job. The general resistance will have to take another form.

The file of volunteers breaks alignment.

119

RUCTIONS (*to Conor*): I'm next to be convicted, I know. On Thursday next, with you, I'll probably be convicted. But I'll never do a hunger strike — not even if I'm ordered.

CONOR: No man has ever been ordered: no man ever will be. It has nothing to do with physique or courage: it's just something you can or can't do.

RUCTIONS: I got in hot water already today about my opinions on hunger strike. I little thought, at the time, there was one in the offing.

MICHEÁL: They both got a bit hot: that's all.

RUCTIONS: And Aidan said something about court martial.

CONOR: All right, Ructions. Don't worry too much about all that.

RUCTIONS: All the same, Conor, I'd as soon do a hunger strike, myself, as see you do one. The bastards!

CONOR: You'll have your own job. And no light one!

Enter Fitz, followed by all the men, so that cell is full, and crowd overflows out into the wing. Excited hubbub: "Two years!" "Criminals," "Lags," "Political treatment," "Hunger strike." Fitz gets autograph album, and, in a whisper, negotiates with Conor for his autograph. Kevin submits list of names to Conor.

AIDAN: Order, men! Order! Attention! (*When they come to attention.*) Stand easy. I think you know the position, men: your O.C., Conor Egan, has been sentenced to serve a term of two years as a common criminal, here in this prison.

Chorus of growls, interruptions: "Let them try it, Conor."

Please! No interruptions. In the last thirty years lives have been given on this issue — political treatment for political prisoners. Those lives were not given in vain: political treatment was won.

Fitz presents pen and open autograph album to Conor.

A new effort is now being made to break that practice, to present your leader, your O.C., to the people of Ireland as a criminal. That effort must be defeated. The principle must be fought for again. Fought for and won. What is entailed? It may be that lives will be lost — on hunger strike. It may be that we shall win without the loss of one. (*Conor signs album.*) But of this be sure: win we must, or know to our everlasting shame that ours was the generation that suffered the loss of a principle that was purchased at a great price and assured to us in blood. (*Changes from platform technique to practical routine.*) The form of resistance will be non-cooperative. Those convicted will do no work, accept no orders, wear no prison clothing; do nothing in fact implying acceptance of criminal status. You may expect to be given solitary confinement. It is no great price to pay for success. No man is asked to do more — no man expected to do less. The Conors — Conors — (*Conor attracts Aidan's attention, and whispers.*) Your O.C. will say a few words to you.

120

Conor rises amidst cheers. His speech differs from Aidan's cold formality in that he talks to the men as equals, with a rather diffident friendliness.

CONOR: All right, lads. I'm not going to talk about hunger strike. But something that concerns all of you — I'll talk about solitary instead. Tommy, there, knows a great deal more about it than I do: that's where he learnt to make rings. But *some* of you may find what *I* have to say helpful. Solitary *can* be undermining, over a long period. No books, no papers. Sometimes, not even a rosary beads. Yes, you can do a lot of things with a beads, besides just pray. Fiddle with them — feel them — get to recognize, by touch alone, a flaw in a single bead. Four white walls to four black walls, changing to four white walls again. Dreary enough! Play tricks with the light that streams down from the cell window — project an image onto the wall, and wait for the shadowy bars to form again against the white. Trace the veins in the back of your hand. Or study, for the millionth time, the Venetian red door, unsmiling as a sulky child. Yes, it *can* be undermining; but it need not be, at all. Set out for a walk from your home place, as I often did, in my mind's eye; though I never got very far on the walk, for I stopped and chatted with people I knew, and with people I didn't even like; for I really didn't know them at all till I met them again — in solitary. And those — the ones I thought I knew well — met them again — knew them afresh — my father — and my mother. No. Solitary need not be a loss: it wasn't for me: nor will it be for you. Some of you will think this strange — but when I heard of this new threat — solitary! — again! — something leapt inside me, that was very like a welcome. That's all, lads — except, good luck!

General move to disband. Aidan calls from list of names.

AIDAN: The following will remain behind. Tommy McGovern.

TOMMY (*steps forward*): Annseo.

AIDAN: O'Shea, Breathnach, McGowan, Fitzpatrick, Dunne. (*All step into position, saying "Annseo" except Ructions.*) Ructions McGowan.

RUCTIONS (*steps into position*): Annseo.

AIDAN: The rest may leave. (*Exeunt men.*)

Aidan, Kevin, and Conor confer.

O'SHEA: Since when was Fitz made a section leader?

RUCTIONS: Old school tie! We skinners hang together!

AIDAN: Dunne! Take the door. (*Dunne keeps watch.*) Operation escape. Not today. Possibly tomorrow, approximately three o'clock, afternoon. The team is O'Shea, Breathnach, McGowan, Fitzpatrick, Kevin, Tommy, and myself.

CONOR: That's only seven.

KEVIN (*drawing diagram on blackboard*): The eighth gun goes to George.

AIDAN: Each section leader engaged will hand over to a deputy, who is to

121

maintain order in the section until the operation is concluded. The order in which escapes take place will be controlled by Kevin, who is in sole charge. Kevin, take over.

KEVIN (*explains diagram*): That's the circle. Four wings: A, B, C, and D. That's the passage from the circle, visitor's room, offices. That's the courtyard, main gate, and there's the wicket. That's the drive to the main road, and there the warders' houses. There are eight guns, disposed thus: Two there, visitor's room, George and I. Two on the circle, Aidan and Fitz. One on each wing, O'Shea on A, Ructions on B, Micheál on C, and Tommy, D. I meet George at three in the visitor's room; he takes Geraghty prisoner, across the passage to the office. While George holds the office, I come back and get the warder on the circle gate. Ructions, from B, can see me approach: he signals Aidan and Fitz. Aidan and Fitz take the circle. Tommy must be ready at D to take custody of the prisoners: every man rounds up his own wing, and hands them over to Tommy: and no man enters the courtyard until we've all our prisoners.

O'SHEA: What about the 'phone? Who cut it?

KEVIN: Nobody. Later I'll come to that: Tommy will be taking incoming calls; and he'll have to 'phone for a taxi.

RUCTIONS: A taxi! Begod, you're doing it in style!

KEVIN: It's too risky for any of us to cross the city in broad daylight.

Sound of disturbance outside: Dunne looks in.

AIDAN: They say there are five squad cars outside.

DUNNE (*unperturbed*): Another batch, I suppose.

KEVIN: Each wing has special difficulties from the point of rounding up warders. A has the bathhouse and the workshop. B opens onto the hospital.

DUNNE (*looks in again*): I think it's a raid. Hundreds of guards massed outside, and five squad cars as well.

KEVIN: C has an exit to the wood yard: so has A. D is easy. Now, we'll take A. That's you, O'Shea. You've the workshop at the far end.

DUNNE (*looks in again, a crowd behind him*): It is, it is. It's a raid! It's a raid!

CONOR: Looks like they've got onto something.

AIDAN: But they couldn't have — they couldn't — (*Sudden disquiet.*) Conor — you don't think — ? You don't think it could — ?

CONOR: What?

AIDAN: The threat — you remember? You wouldn't promise —

CONOR (*insistent confidence*): Kathleen? No, no, no, no. You can take that as certain.

KEVIN: Shall we fight it out, Conor?

CONOR (*exhilarated*): It will give the men exercise — keep them fit. Every man take his cell door off its hinges! Get tools, bed legs, anything as a weapon! And don't let yourselves be locked up without a fight.

The crowds immediately rush off: sounds of breaking doors, stools, etc. Exeunt Aidan, Conor, O'Shea, Ructions, Micheál, and Tommy snatching up Fitz's album on way.

FITZ (*to Kevin*) : The door off its hinges? How?

KEVIN (*erases diagram from blackboard*) : I thought you were an architect. What the hell have you got a Bible for?

Kevin inserts Bible in doorjamb, and leans heavily against door, until hinges give.

FITZ (*astonished, then amused*) : Oh! I see now.

Fitz goes to help Kevin with door, as slow curtain.

Act II

A few days later in the kitchen, an octagonal room, big, the walls continuing in triangular panels to apex of ceiling, bell-tent shape. Steamers, boilers, a few large tables, shelving with army-pattern food containers (dixies) on them. An exit to a passage and an exit to the back kitchen. Prisoners, some hangdog, some cheerful, leave the kitchen, carrying their jackets, Geraghty hurrying them on their way. Some lean against tables, finishing meals from dixie tops, replace their spoons in their pockets as they leave. Geraghty, slovenly in appearance, cap back off forehead, impatient for them to leave. Jakey, more of a kitchen manager than a prisoner, checks steamers to see if they are empty. Conor and Ructions, wearing their own clothes, sit idly by, watching entire proceedings. As the curtain goes up Jakey enters with muslin bag containing cheese in the process of being made: he has bag on stick which he puts across a boiler to dry out the cheese.

JAKEY (*explains action*) : A bit o' cheese that I'm makin'. This is me chance to get it dried out while these is at their dinner. (*Exit Jakey to back kitchen.*)

Sound of triangle being beaten on the circle.

GERAGHTY (*roars at prisoners*) : Come on, you lads! Up to your cells! Are yez goin' to be there all day or what? (*To Butcher, eating, leaning on table.*) Hi, you Butcher! On yer mark!

The roar has little effect: prisoners take their time about leaving. Butcher continues eating. A few more prisoners pass through from back kitchen to passage. Enter Jakey.

JAKEY: Hi, Butcher! have you no home to go to? Ye're fillin' that bloody big belly o' yours the whole mornin'. Stew, no less! Wouldn't be mapped, outside, for more than bread and tea.

123

Butcher, disdainfully, goes to the trouble of scraping the last bit out of the dixie top.

JAKEY (*handing Butcher a dixie*): Here, take that up to Bill out o' the tailor's. Tell him he's all set — only I want them smokes today — today, tell him — it's urgent.

BUTCHER: All set for what?

JAKEY: He'll know. Will ye take yer shaggin' thumb out o' the man's dinner?

Licking offending thumb, exit Butcher by passage. Exit Jakey with dixies to store. Geraghty comes over to Conor and Ructions.

GERAGHTY (*pleasantly, to Conor*): Two years? Was that what you got this morning?

CONOR: Yes.

GERAGHTY (*to Ructions*): And you? The same?

RUCTIONS: Two years: criminal section.

GERAGHTY (*discreet mixture sympathetic indignation*): Holy God tonight.

RUCTIONS (*businesslike*): Are our lads back in D1 yet, or are they still in solitary?

GERAGHTY: Ye should've seen the wing after them! All the doors off the hinges. The deserted village wasn't in it! But they got in a flock of carpenters: so your lads is sure to be back soon. I wouldn't say but this evening, after dinner.

RUCTIONS: Good!

CONOR: Were *you* questioned after the raid?

GERAGHTY: No, I wasn't actually questioned — but I'm in doubt they got on to something.

RUCTIONS (*dismisses Geraghty's fear*): Not at all! (*To Conor.*) Routine raid: that's all it was.

CONOR (*to reassure Geraghty*): Yes, I think so. Purely routine!

Geraghty looks from one to the other suspiciously.

RUCTIONS (*confidently*): We can get on with the job, so?

GERAGHTY (*nervously*): The job? Ye — ye mean?

RUCTIONS: The breakout. The escape. When can we have a chat?

GERAGHTY (*backs away, frighted*): Not now! Later! (*Enter Jakey. Geraghty attacks Jakey roughly.*) The cut o' the place! a battlefield and the visitin' committee comin' today!

JAKEY: Buckingham Palace won't be in it by the time me and these two gets through.

Conor and Ructions alert at Jakey's reference to them. Enter Muscles, who hangs around in background, waiting. Jakey takes dixie from steamer, smells with relish.

JAKEY (*to Geraghty*): Are ye havin' a bit? 'Course ye' are! Hair on yer chest! Are ye havin' the stew? Or the call? — both! The stew as well.

GERAGHTY: Would ye like Muscles to stay down and give ye a hand?

JAKEY (*after contemptuous glance at Muscles, a small weedy man*): A hand to what?

Muscles suffers the insult in resentful silence.

RUCTIONS: We're not working, Conor and I.

JAKEY: I know yez are not. Don't I know? Two of yez not workin': and one o' yez not eatin'! Noncooperation! So what? Th' oul' shack'll stand up.

RUCTIONS (*looks at Muscles*): If you like we can go to our cells.

MUSCLES (*eagerly*): I can stay down, Jakey? Me?

JAKEY (*contempt*): You! Standin' there the livelong mornin', one hand as long as another!

MUSCLES: That's — if ye like.

JAKEY (*abusive, mimics*): "If ye like." Well, Jakey doesn't humpin' like — is that good enough? (*To Ructions.*) Youse two, stay where yez are!

GERAGHTY (*seriously*): No matter how the cat jumps, I want that back kitchen done out — before the visitin' committee comes — and I want no lick and a promise — I want it scrubbed — have ye got me?

JAKEY: It'll be done — and done proper!

GERAGHTY: I want no half sheet from the department when the committee puts in their report.

JAKEY: Ye'll get no half sheet after me! Ye never got one — now did ye? Or anythin' ever I done? No, nor ye won't. Work! There's not enough work in th' oul' back kitchen to keep me from broodin' on me sorrows.

MUSCLES (*appeals*): Jakey! (*Jakey ignores him, and leaves dixie in store for Geraghty, addressing him as he exits to store.*)

JAKEY (*to Geraghty*): Leave off frettin' and have yer bit o' dinner.

GERAGHTY: Right! (*Geraghty exits to store.*)

Jakey returns from store.

MUSCLES (*appeals*): Jakey!

JAKEY: Hump off, you! (*To Ructions.*) Keep out o' the store, and let Pat have his bit in peace. He's sensitive, d'ye know? (*To Muscles, contemptuously.*) When I look at you — words fail me.

Muscles wriggles self-consciously under the insult.

MUSCLES (*cravenly*): Give us one o' them dinners then.

Jakey goes to back kitchen.

MUSCLES (*calls in to store*): He has nine dinners beyond in the steamer. (*Geraghty appears not to hear. Calls in to back kitchen.*) Will ye, Jakey?

JAKEY (*enters from back kitchen*): Will-ye was a bad fella.

MUSCLES (*sudden fury, to Geraghty in store*): Nine! That's where the prisoners' rations is goin'! Nine dinners for one man! Quare oul' justice!

JAKEY (*unaffected by exposure*): If I had ninety-nine, your good-lookin'

125

belly will still be innocent of any crime. Ay, and nine hundred and ninety-nine: and hump the begrudgers after! D'ye see now?

Enter Geraghty.

GERAGHTY (*expels Muscles*): Come on, now! On yer mark! (*Exit Geraghty to store.*)

MUSCLES (*going toward exit*): Amn't I workin' the same as him? Fish o' one and flesh of another!

JAKEY: Workin'! Sure, no one here does any work except the poor bloody juveniles. And maybe the governor. But sure, he's paid. (*To Muscles.*) Go on! before I call the police.

MUSCLES (*leaving*): Ye bloody robber!

JAKEY (*provocatively*): Empty belly has a clear conscience. (*Exit Muscles.*) (*Comments chattily.*) Classic bloody man, Muscles. Always neckin' for somethin' off ye. If it's not a smoke, it's the lend of a flicker. Ye can't go into the lavatory but he's in on the bloody top of ye — for the butt — the very time ye might be short. Not but what he's all right, if he had it him-self — ah, but sure then, he never has! (*Hands dixie to Ructions.*) Get that down ye! Then ye can talk!

RUCTIONS (*accepts*): Looks good.

JAKEY (*gives Ructions spoon from pocket*): Ye want not to forget to bring down yer own spoon in future. (*Second dixie to Ructions.*) And call-cannon.

RUCTIONS (*hesitates*): Is there enough?

JAKEY (*points steamer*): And the steamer packed to the roof! Sure, we're laughin', man. And a few more to have in bed in the oul' cell. Put another dollop o' butther in that, and ye needn't call the queen yer aunt, plenty more where that came from. (*Offers dixie to Conor.*) Oh, I should've askin' you first seein' as you're O.C. and not him.

Conor refuses with a smile.

JAKEY: 'Course ye will! Sure ye won't say No to a bit o' gur the like o' that? And celery too — if ye have the fancy.

CONOR: No, thanks.

Ructions looks at Conor, then starts to eat his own. Enter Geraghty.

JAKEY (*to Geraghty entering*): Yes, Mr. G, don't go off, now, and forget to leave us out the bit of tea and sugar.

GERAGHTY: Okay! Fat chance I have of forgettin'!

Enter Warder Grimes, from passage exit.

GRIMES (*inquires of Geraghty*): Egan?

GERAGHTY (*regimental before another warder*): Egan!

GRIMES (*to Conor, who looks up*): Governor!

CONOR (*to Ructions*): That's it: now we'll see. (*Prepares to leave.*)

126

JAKEY (*reminded, in sudden alarm*): My Jase! The governor's dinner! It never went up, I clean forgot. That bloody Muscles — arguin' the toss!

GERAGHTY (*unperturbed*): Is there anythin' left?

JAKEY: I'll scrape up somethin'. Where's his plate? Look at it there, before me eyes! (*Takes enamel plate.*) If it was a dog it'd bite me. (*To Grimes.*) Where's he now? In his room?

GRIMES: No. He's out in the front office. Come on, Egan: the governor is waiting!

RUCTIONS: Luck, Conor!

Exeunt Conor and Grimes.

GERAGHTY (*reminded, goes to store*): Oh, tea and sugar. (*Exit Geraghty.*)

JAKEY (*from his private store of dinners, picks pieces of meat and potatoes to put on plate. As he selects*): He's not gettin' that! (*Eats a scrap.*) Here's a bit of fat! That it may choke the bastard!

RUCTIONS (*incredulously*): The governor doesn't eat that?

JAKEY: Eat that, is it! The man would resign from the job first.

RUCTIONS: Would that matter?

JAKEY: Matter? It matters this matter; the day the governor leaves this kip, I'm goin' — d'ye hear? — I'm marchin' out in a body. (*Points plate.*) That's only a sample. I plonk it in his room: the governor doesn't even be there; he's only there in the mornin'.

RUCTIONS (*intrigued*): Who eats it?

JAKEY: Sometimes the wardsman on the circle, when he'd be doin' out the room — sometimes the governor's dog; it all depends who gets there first. Though, fair play! I often seen the oul' dog smell it, and then leave it for the wardsman. (*Exit Jakey.*)

RUCTIONS (*calls peremptorily*): Pat!

Geraghty enters, uneasy and unsure of himself.

GERAGHTY (*gives packet cigarettes to Ructions*): You'll be wantin' these. Remember, ye didn't get them from me. (*Avoiding issue.*) You're Egan's friend. Why don't you give the man an advice? What's he want hunger strikin' for? Everything here, to yer own hand. Many a one up in the shops would give his eyes for a job down here. Eat, drink, and follow the band!

RUCTIONS: When do you plan to contact our lads in D1?

GERAGHTY: Mother o' God how can I? I tell ye I couldn't pull a pound.

RUCTIONS (*adamant*): When and how are you going to get the stuff up to them?

GERAGHTY: Ye mean — the guns? Ye know bloody well they're watchin' me. I tell ye they're keepin' a tab on me — waitin' for me to make the move — God in Heaven! Ye don't expect me!

RUCTIONS (*unsympathetic*): Wind up?

GERAGHTY (*self-pity*): Sorry day for me I ever got into handigrips with ye. If it had to be the same again, I'd think the twice, I can tell you that. Me on the jump all the time — not knowin' where or when!

RUCTIONS: It's no more dangerous now than when you agreed to do it; that raid was just a coincidence.

GERAGHTY: Coincidence me backside! I seen too many coincidences.

RUCTIONS: That's all it was.

GERAGHTY: Coincidences butther no parsnips for a man with a wife and seven kids. You're goin' beyond the beyonds!

RUCTIONS: There isn't a single danger to you — except the one.

GERAGHTY (*apprehensively*): Danger?

RUCTIONS (*grimly*): Our lads.

GERAGHTY (*fright*): You mean — ?

RUCTIONS: Maybe it *wasn't* a coincidence — perhaps an informer!

GERAGHTY (*panics at impact of a fear half anticipated*): I knew that's what ye'd think: I knew it in me heart and soul — I swear to God it wasn't me — before God! — that I may drop! (*Inspired by panic.*) How do you know it wasn't George? — the bloody runt — couldn't it be him as well as me? — him and his bloody grapefruit! — I never seen a pioneer yet that wasn't a bastard in his heart.

RUCTIONS (*smiling irony*): Of course! George! That's who it was ! We never even thought of him. (*Advances on Geraghty in sudden anger, raising fist.*) You scut of hell!

GERAGHTY (*retreats cravenly before Ructions*): Now listen Ructions — Mister McGowan — listen to me, now — listen a minute; you're a sensible man — and a decent man — and I'm not sayin' it *was* George — I'm only sayin' it could've been — and so it could — as well as me. For the matter o' that, what's to stop it being Mrs. Egan?

RUCTIONS (*contempt*): Mrs. Egan! Of course! She and George — hand in glove — pioneers together!

GERAGHTY: I'm not sayin' that at all — I'm only sayin' it could have been.

RUCTIONS (*thunderous*): And it could have been Pat Geraghty — getting paid at both ends.

GERAGHTY: Merciful God! Who says that? Who says it? Who? D'yez think I'm a bloody out-and-out . . . (*Shies at word.*)

RUCTIONS: Informer?

GERAGHTY: Look, I swear — I swear — I swear to God —

RUCTIONS (*calms him*): I believe you. (*Geraghty seems eased.*) But I'm only one. (*Geraghty takes fright again. Businesslike.*) Go through with it; get in the revolvers; that clears the air and answers any suggestions.

GERAGHTY: How can I? Answer me that! How am I going to as much as see them, never mind give them the — things?

RUCTIONS: Give them to me.

GERAGHTY: To you? Here? Here in the kitchen? — with me in charge? Give them to you and get them got! Get them got on you down here! Jeese, tonight are you mad or what?

RUCTIONS: We'll get them up to the lads — one by one — up with the grub — up on the trays — in the dixies.

GERAGHTY: Now, look! Look here, like a good man!

RUCTIONS (*turns away*): Please yourself.

GERAGHTY: Now, look! I swear to God.

RUCTIONS (*washing hands of it*): You haven't got to convince me! I think you're the soul of honor!

Sounds off stop further talk. Enter Jakey with a piece of blazing sheet, which he lets drop on table to burn out.

JAKEY: Conor's not back? (*Without answer.*) Bloody grand bit o' tinder this. Somebody's sheet! The lad on the furnace gave it to me — for nothin' — only a can o' milk. (*To Geraghty's reaction.*) Ye needn't fret — if we're short, itself, there's always the tap. (*Puts piece tinder in polish box: then to Ructions.*) D'ye want a bit?

RUCTIONS: What's it for?

JAKEY: Tinder. Have ye ne'er a flicker? I'll get ye one. The boxer has one — up on the looms — he doesn't smoke; but he'd go to hell after a bit o' scented soap. (*Gives Ructions piece.*) Here's a bit. Come in handy.

GERAGHTY: Don't leave that stuff around here, gettin' me in trouble.

Jakey conceals balance in one of a line of disused dixies on shelf, Ructions noting with interest.

JAKEY (*at shelf*): One of these oul' dixies. I wonder what could be keepin' Conor? They wouldn't be lettin' him out, whah?

RUCTIONS (*refers dixies*): Are these not used?

JAKEY (*hands one to Ructions*): Bunched, the most o' them! Leakin'. Your best dart — the both o' yez — is to put in a petition.

RUCTIONS (*displays dixie to Geraghty*): Handy size! Would hold — a large object!

Geraghty swallows hard, anticipating further trouble.

JAKEY: Sure, everyone puts a petition in: the most they can do is say No. Sixteen I had in, from time to time. Always the same oul' three and four pence. Soldier on! The humpin' law must take its course. But youse two! Certainties! Six months off for the askin'. (*To Geraghty.*) Are ye goin' to yer dinner, Mr. G? Or are ye waitin' till Conor comes back?

GERAGHTY (*depressed*): Time enough.

JAKEY (*gets dinner from steamer*): Whether or which, I'll be havin' me own. (*To Ructions.*) Well — what about the petition?

RUCTIONS: No, Jakey — I don't think so.

JAKEY (*shakes head*): Too proud, whah? Too proud to bend the head. It's easy seein' youse haven't to care — there's no one to look to you for anythin'; *youse* haven't to think o' the home front.

RUCTIONS: I'm not married, if that's what you mean.

JAKEY: I was thinkin' as much.

RUCTIONS: Are you?

JAKEY: The way it is, I am, and I'm not. As the fella says: I am — a bit! (*Sits on table, a thumb in direction of Geraghty.*) Yer man there has a houseful.

GERAGHTY (*depressed*): Too true, I have!

JAKEY (*sits on table to eat*): Time was when the I.R.A. was good gas. No better! Fightin' for freedom, on the run, flyin' columns, and all to that. When you and I were seventeen. But that was a revolution. Ye had the Countess, and Maud Gonne — and Dev sittin' up in the oul' Ford, and she goin' goodo round the town, the same as it might be a motorcar. But sure, that was a hundred year ago! Things is very different now. People is too hard put to live: hard set to get the bit to put in their mouth at all, with everything two prices; they haven't the time to be fightin' for freedom, careering about the place, romancin' about a republic. I'm tellin' yez now, yez missed the bus: yez missed the bus. Them days is gone.

RUCTIONS: The fight goes on, until it is won.

JAKEY: The fight may go on, as you say; but the revolution is over. (*To Geraghty.*) Isn't that the sacred truth, Mr. G?

Geraghty, absorbed in his own troubles, makes no reply.

JAKEY: As for hunger strikin', it's played out! (*Nostalgic.*) I remember one that was forcible fed. Ay, and walked a new pair of boots off me feet, follyin' the crowds to the city hall, where the man was laid out, for all to view — all down the quays, trudgin' me way, with the bloody tears streamin' down from me eyes. Lyin' in state, he was. Ay, and kissed the corpse — a man I didn't know from Adam, till I met him there that mornin'; I disremember what was his name: it was done out lovely on the breastplate in Irish letters. Some said it was made of gold. Rosary on top o' rosary, for th' eternal repose o' the man's soul. Prayin' and prayin'. But it wasn't prayin', I was. Eggin' God on, I was — to nail the bastard that forcible fed him. Eggin' Him on! — I nearly threatened. And lookit me now! Get it, no matter how you get it: it's got to be got! Get it, no matter how you get it: it's got to be got! As for goin' to another man's funeral! He's not mapped! I'm put to the pin o' me collar, to keep meself from goin' to me own.

Enter Warder Phelan with Bayer, an elderly Jew, central European, miserably apprehensive, in strange surroundings, with a poor knowledge of English, carrying a dixie. Jakey is unwelcoming in the extreme.

JAKEY: Jase! Will ye look what the cat brung in! Came up overnight, like a mushroom! I hope ye brought your welcome with ye.

PHELAN (*to Geraghty*): You'll have to fix this man up.

JAKEY (*anticipates*): He got no dinner? He shaggin' did. And as for the stew, it is full o' meat when it left here.

PHELAN (*to Geraghty*): The poor old fellow got nothing to eat.

Geraghty with a gesture, leaves responsibility to Jakey.

JAKEY: The customer is always right; but what's that danglin' there in his left hand?

PHELAN: He can't eat it: he's a Jew.

JAKEY: A Jewman, whah! (*Mock welcome.*) The hard man! How are ye doin'? (*To others.*) Sure, I know him well. (*Banters Jew.*) Didn't I often lend you money?

BAYER (*alarmed, at a loss to understand*): Money?

JAKEY (*banters*): And now ye came to pay me back? Well, ye didn't come a day too soon; for I haven't as much as a jingle.

PHELAN (*to Jakey*): The man doesn't know what you're saying.

BAYER (*with difficulty*): Yes, yes I understand — when he will speak English.

PHELAN: He comes from a place called Latvia: in on a currency charge, he is.

JAKEY: Sure, that nearly makes him a Christian! they're all in on that, now. Cardinals, archbishops, and all. Laffia? And where's that? The back o' beyant, I suppose. Ay, and what ails him that he can't eat?

PHELAN (*impatiently*): He's a Jew, didn't I tell you?

JAKEY: And hasn't a Jewman a pair o' teeth in his head, the same as a Christian?

PHELAN: He can't eat it; it has to be kosher: it has to be special cooked.

JAKEY: Special cooked! And what do you expect me to give him? a blood transfusion?

GERAGHTY (*intervenes*): He should see the doctor and get an order: that goes on the diet sheet: vegetables, a loaf of bread, hot or cold milk, an ounce of cheese or jam, maybe once or twice in the week.

JAKEY (*uncompliant*): I've no milk. Can't he do with a porridge? And see the doctor in the mornin'? I'll give him a bit o' jam, as well; but he'll get no bread — we're short of bread.

PHELAN: Porridge, is that the best you can do?

JAKEY: Won't that do ye, Von Shilly? Porridge and a bit o' jam?

BAYER (*uncomprehending*): I'm Jewish! Jewish! You understand?

JAKEY (*gets cold porridge*): Ay, well, if things is the way you think they are, you'll get your reward in the next life. In the meanwhile, this oul' porridge will keep ye goin'. (*Exits store for jam.*) Stay there till I get ye the bit o' jam.

RUCTIONS: Why not heat the porridge for him?

PHELAN: It's past my dinner hour already.

GERAGHTY: I'll give it a warm while he's weighing the jam.

Geraghty takes dixie of porridge and floats it on top of the boiler. Jakey puts spoonful of jam from jam pot on a dirty square inch of paper, weighs it on a faulty scales. Enter principal warder. Geraghty and Phelan come to attention: Jakey smartens up: Bayer is more lost than ever. Only Ructions remains indifferent.

PRINCIPAL: Mr. Geraghty!

GERAGHTY (*smartly*): Sir!

PRINCIPAL: Have Conor Egan's dinner sent up. Take it to the medical orderly. And see that it's regulation weight — you may have to make an affidavit.

GERAGHTY: Very good, sir! At once, sir!

PRINCIPAL: What's this other man doing here?

PHELAN: Special dinner, sir! A Jew, sir!

PRINCIPAL: Oh! (*To Geraghty.*) Well?

GERAGHTY: Everything in order, sir?

PRINCIPAL (*to Jakey*): Take it up now! Jump to it!

JAKEY: Yessir, yessir.

Exit principal warder.

JAKEY (*indignant comment*): A right get! The Maryboro' touch! (*To Geraghty*). Will I give Conor one o' me own specials?

GERAGHTY: Ye will not! Ye heard what he said: the regulation dinner. I'll have to swear an affidavit.

RUCTIONS (*puzzled*): What do you make of all that?

GERAGHTY: There I leave you.

JAKEY (*gives square of jam to Bayer, taking dixie from him*): Give us a look at that oul' dinner o' yours. (*Shows Geraghty.*) Looks all right.

GERAGHTY: What's the regulation weight? Where's the card? There *was* a card. Is it four ounces or two with potatoes?

JAKEY (*unperturbed*): If there was a card, I never seen it.

GERAGHTY (*fussed*): I have to take me solemn oath! Is it four ounces or is it three?

JAKEY (*holds out dixie for inspection*): I'll swear there's a good four ounces in that. Three, anyway.

GERAGHTY: You'll swear! What'll I swear? No card! No weights! And even if I had the both, th' oul' balance is not workin'.

JAKEY (*defends*): That scales is all right. (*Demonstrates.*) Works goodo, it does — only give it a tip o' your finger.

GERAGHTY: And what bread? Six with soup, four with stew — ah, give the man an eight ounce, he's a long fast before him.

JAKEY: Sweet God! Hunger strike!

GERAGHTY: Now, take it to the medical orderly?

JAKEY: The nark is on!

RUCTIONS: What's the medical orderly for?

JAKEY (*conscience-stricken*): I should've heatin' it in the steamer. But, sure, what's the good when he won't eat it? (*Suddenly realizes.*) Forcible feed him! That's what the medical orderly's for. Gettin' it down through the tube into the man's stomach. (*Displays eight-ounce loaf.*) How are they goin' to get *that* through a tube? Answer me that! A loaf of bread! Can't be done! Or, could they?

PHELAN (*amateur medical bombast*): Extraordinary what they can do now, compared with what they usedn't to be able to even try and do.

JAKEY (*impressed, puzzled*): Do they upend th' oul' dixie and pour it down through the nozzle?

PHELAN (*medical bombast*): They have ways. Hypodermic, and so on. Sure, look at penicillin, for instance. Some says medical science is only in its infancy.

JAKEY: What was the longest ever was done of a hunger strike?

PHELAN: A black man, I think, holds the record.

JAKEY: A black, whah?

GERAGHTY: The lord mayor of Cork, Terence McSwiney, went all of sixty-two days — Lord have mercy on him.

Geraghty and Phelan lift caps in respect.

JAKEY (*toward exit, meditatively*): Sixty-two! Gas if yer man went sixty-three! (*Toward exit, stops again.*) This is a very historical moment that we're in now. (*Dramatically.*) There's this man's last dinner — there, in th' oul' dixie in me hand. In a minute or two, I'll be handin' him that — his last meal — in this life. Imagine the way that I'll feel — when he takes it — in his right hand — and my hand, drops to me side — like that. And, in years to come. (*Breaks off disappointed.*) Sure, maybe, he mightn't die at all! (*Exit Jakey.*)

GERAGHTY (*comments*): Classic man, the same Jakey! The place doesn't be the same at all, when he goes out. Not that he stays out very long. Just stretch his legs and get a breath of fresh air.

PHELAN: Come on, Bayer. (*Toward boiler.*) Give us the porridge.

GERAGHTY (*inspects boiler*): Gone to the bottom! Sank like a stone! That dixie must've been leakin'.

RUCTIONS (*takes colcannon from Jakey's store in steamer, for Bayer. Gives Bayer*): Here!

GERAGHTY: Hey, what'll Jakey say?

PHELAN (*to Bayer*): C'mon then. Take it up with you!

GERAGHTY (*points stool*): He will not: he'll eat it there. Get me in the shaggin' row!

Bayer sits and eats ravenously.

PHELAN (*resentfully to Geraghty*): Have *I* no dinner to go to? (*Sits on edge of table, looks at Bayer.*) Not disclosing American assets! Says to the judge, it wasn't him — it was his brother!

GERAGHTY: Nothin' miraculous about that. Jew or Gentile — it's always the brother — we know that. It's a common disgrace to have an educated man like that out in the woodyard choppin' blocks.

RUCTIONS: Couldn't you fix him up inside?

GERAGHTY (*hastily*): He wouldn't be any use down here. (*To Phelan.*) A wardsman's job?

PHELAN: No — Wait though — I could — I could fix him up in a wardsman's job — now, I bethink me — in D1 — your lads is back there after dinner.

RUCTIONS (*alive*): Oh!

GERAGHTY (*suspicious of Ructions' intent*): Dirty oul' job for a man like that! Carryin' slops and the like.

RUCTIONS (*to Bayer*): Monsieur le garde va vous donner autre chose à faire, au lieu de couper les buches: ça vous plait?

BAYER: Mais oui! J'en serais enchanté.

RUCTIONS: He says, himself, he would be enchanted. He much prefers slops to blocks.

PHELAN: Right, then! I'll fix him up. (*To Bayer.*) Come on, you!

Exeunt Phelan and Bayer.

RUCTIONS (*grimly pleasant*): Well, Pat? What are you thinking of?

GERAGHTY: No; but what are *you* thinkin' of?

RUCTIONS (*admits unspoken charge*): That's right, Pat. That Jew! There's nothing to stop him. Two at a time, Pat. The first lot after dinner today.

GERAGHTY: Sufferin' God! — you don't realize — if you'd as much as a hap'-orth o' sense —

RUCTIONS: Two, Pat! Either that — or —

GERAGHTY: Or what?

RUCTIONS: Even I wouldn't believe you.

GERAGHTY: But, listen, man, listen —

Approach of Jakey ends conversation. Enter Jakey.

JAKEY: They're all up there — governor, Conor, doctor and all — clustered together like Brown's cows. Chawin' the rag — but very polite. The medical orderly baulked me proper, so that I couldn't get next or near — not within a long spit: so I couldn't make out a word was said. (*To Geraghty.*) Will I go for Muscles? Then you could pack up.

GERAGHTY: Ye were as well to have him first as last!

JAKEY (*at exit, sights new arrival*): Talk of the devil!

GERAGHTY: Who? Muscles?

Enter Conor, who reports to Ructions. Geraghty and Jakey listening avidly, with unconcealed interest.

RUCTIONS: Conor! (*Anxiously.*) Well?

CONOR (*with all the weariness of a well-known routine*): Just a formal business. The doctor gave me some good advice, that hunger strike was bad for the health. The orderly formally offered me food — equally formally, I refused it, the governor said my privileges would be suspended — but that I could declare the strike off up to three o'clock.

JAKEY (*extremely disappointed*): Not even a clockin' match!

GERAGHTY (*equally disappointed*): Ah, I better hook it.

CONOR (*to Geraghty*): Could you let me have a drop of ink?

GERAGHTY: Ink? To be sure! (*To Jakey.*) Ye'll get ink in the store.

JAKEY (*as Geraghty goes to exit*): Ye're not forgettin' what-ye-know? Are ye carryin'?

GERAGHTY (*with bad grace gives small piece of plug tobacco*): Here! Will that do? That's all I have.

JAKEY (*ungraciously*): Hardtack! It'll have to, I s'pose.

GERAGHTY (*at exit*): And have the place lookin' decent. (*Exit Geraghty.*)

JAKEY: Didn't bloody break himself!

CONOR (*quiet anxiety*): I'd like to get my letter done.

JAKEY (*goes to store*): Right! And I'll wet the drop o' chah.

Exit Jakey.

CONOR (*sets stool at table*): I want to get it done quickly: I think that's what the governor meant about "privileges suspended" — in case I wanted to write to — anyone — before three o'clock.

RUCTIONS: Your wife?

CONOR (*in difficulty*): I — I have to write her — something.

RUCTIONS: Then you haven't — ?

CONOR: No — I'm hoping she might half — know —

Jakey returns with ink, gives it to Conor, who sets about letter.

JAKEY (*to Ructions*): How do you spell "industrious"? I have it in me petition.

RUCTIONS: I-n-d-u-s-t-r-i-o-u-s.

JAKEY: And "sole support." How do you spell that?

RUCTIONS: S-o-l-e s-u-p-p-o-r-t.

JAKEY: S-o-l-e? Ye're sure?

RUCTIONS: Yes. S-o-l-e.

JAKEY (*unconvincingly*): I think I have the both right. Or have I? That bloody Muscles!

Jakey, with razor blade, shaves and chops plug tobacco, adds tobacco dust, and rolls cigarette, while Ructions watches him, and Conor struggles with letter.

RUCTIONS (*to Conor*): Jakey's married.

JAKEY: Not exactly. Sort of engaged. I have a child.

RUCTIONS: Why can't you marry?

JAKEY: I've a terrible dread of doin' anythin' final. I'd trust no woman — except me mother. (*To Conor, for confirmation.*) Isn't that right, general? Queer cattle, they are — say one thing, and mean another.

CONOR (*with significance*): I trust my wife completely: when she says a thing, she means it.

JAKEY (*by way of excuse*): Ay, well, my woman's a Protestant. How can I marry her — and she holdin' with divorce, and all? Strikin' at the very roots of family life!

RUCTIONS (*re Jakey's cigarette paper*): Is that toilet paper?

JAKEY: Yes.

RUCTIONS: I didn't know there was any here.

JAKEY: Very scarce and hard to get! On account of it's handy for rollin' one. I'll give ye a pull in a minute.

Ructions gives Jakey a real cigarette.

JAKEY (*diagnoses origin of cigarette*): Pat, what? Die at the tail of a political, he would. Tells me he has nine. An oul' screw for your life!

Jakey operates flicker, that is, he rubs razor blade against flint embedded in wood, directing sparks to tinder in box. Ructions lights from tinder: gives cigarette to Conor who holds it abstractedly, unable to write letter.

JAKEY (*notices Conor's malaise*): One thing I hate is to write a letter. (*Ructions, aware of obviously interrupting Conor, tries to discourage Jakey by showing no interest.*) Though mind ye I like gettin' them. A good one is as good as an oul' book. Ah, no: books is better. Charles Dickens, Peter Cheyney, Edgar Wallace, all in the library here! Some o' them very hard readin'! If I'd've knew, back in school, I was goin' to spend so much o' me time in this joint, I'd've lookin' after me education. (*Extinguishes butt.*) Th' oul' back kitchen! (*Exit Jakey.*)

CONOR (*rises, after staring hopelessly at letter for a moment*): God! I don't know what to tell her. She must know, in her heart of hearts, that I've got to do this — I've got to —

RUCTIONS: Conor, I spoke to Geraghty: I'm sure we'll get him to function.

CONOR: You don't like hunger strike — do you, Ructions?

RUCTIONS: This is something we can do. Do, Conor! — not suffer. Fight, Conor — shoot our way out — not just present them with a martyr — a gift on a silver salver — a body on a marble slab.

CONOR: Ructions, we've been through all this.

RUCTIONS: I've got a line, a wardsman — an old Jew — I got him a feed — he was here with Phelan. Phelan, it was, who told me that our lads were back today. This is something really worthwhile — something really practical. Two guns after dinner. Two, today, I told him.

CONOR (*impressed*): What? Did he say he'd bring them in?

RUCTIONS: I frightened the gizzard out of him. Just one word, "informer."

CONOR: Informer! But he didn't — he isn't —

RUCTIONS (*impatiently*): I know, but he panicked completely. Said it was George — that it must have been George. Anyone! Anyone on earth! But *he* wasn't an informer. (*Laughingly.*) Why, he even mentioned your wife. Said it was Mrs. Egan.

CONOR (*perturbed*): Kathleen! (*Turns to letter, then looks up.*) What made him think it was Kathleen?

RUCTIONS: He didn't *think* it — he just *said* it.

CONOR: If he didn't think it, why did he say it?

RUCTIONS: He lost his nerve: that's all it was. Besides, he didn't say it was she: he only said it could have been.

CONOR: "Could have been"? It couldn't have been. Had he any grounds — the smallest — even for suspicion?

RUCTIONS: Of course not —

CONOR: Well then? Surely if there were any grounds I should have known. I saw my wife that very morning.

RUCTIONS: Of course, Conor, you'd have known.

CONOR (*dual meaning, deflated*): Yes — I *should* have known —

RUCTIONS: It wasn't that way at all: he was casting around for someone to blame: he didn't know what to say: he was bitched, bewildered by the charge. Damn fool: he even thinks I'm going to use the Jew.

CONOR: Aren't you?

RUCTIONS: Lord, no. The man can't put a foot under him in any language except French. I used him to sound Geraghty: I may use him as a decoy. But Jakey's the man. Jakey and his special dinners. Jakey and his colcannon, loaded with onions and butter. Loaded, Conor, do you hear? Loaded, to give eight men a meal fit for freemen. That's the answer, Jakey!

Jakey brings Ructions mug of tea.

JAKEY: Did I hear me name mentioned? Or was it just me oul' conscience? (*Hands tea.*) I just want to scour this oul' table down. (*Exit Jakey to back kitchen.*)

CONOR: Go very easy. Don't say too much.

RUCTIONS: I'm only going to sound him.

Re-enter Jakey.

JAKEY: I thrun a bucketful over it — it'll have to scour itself down. (*As Conor makes fresh effort at letter, Jakey seats himself on writing table, to drink tea.*) Very peaceable in here, all the same? (*Glances at Conor.*)

Still and all, a china would rather be at home: isn't that strange? Life is very sweet.

RUCTIONS (*offers cigarette*): Like one?

JAKEY (*takes and puts inside shirtfront*): Takin' all yours, I am.

RUCTIONS: How do you manage for cigarettes?

JAKEY: If I was on me oath, I couldn't tell ye where me next one is comin' from. God is good — but ye wouldn't want to rely on Him for every little morsel. I have me steadies — regular customers — so I'm not stuck.

RUCTIONS: Customers?

JAKEY: Ay, for me specials. Me special dinners. Without them, I was sunk. Bill in the tailor's — good for four: the boxer, on the looms — then, there's casuals — passin' trade — so, between hoppin' and trottin' — fellows with petitions in.

RUCTIONS: Petitions?

JAKEY: Some, when they have a petition in, gives up smokin' as well — a kind of Act of Mortification. Some says novenas.

RUCTIONS: You haven't much faith in prayer?

JAKEY: As much as the next! But I'm not like some of the gougers here — tryin' to rope in the Holy Ghost on a housebreak, by prayin' for an inspiration.

RUCTIONS (*tentatively*): I wonder — if we could get some cigarettes down — now that our fellows are back in D1?

JAKEY (*alert*): Back? Are ye sure they're back?

RUCTIONS: Phelan said so.

JAKEY: Mouth Phelan? He ought to know.

RUCTIONS: And the Jew is there as wardsman.

JAKEY: Von Shilly, wardsman in D1! And your butties back! Holy Saint Patrick! You're laughin' man! Sure, that's as good as money. Hundreds of thousands of cigarettes, only to put your hand on them. Hey, but — will they part, whah? They wouldn't give ye the back o' the hand — now, that yez are — *where* yez are?

RUCTIONS: O'Shea would help. I'm sure he would. O'Shea is all right.

JAKEY: O'Shea, whah?

CONOR: And O'Leary, Aidan O'Leary. He's O.C. I think O'Leary would be better.

JAKEY (*memorizes*): Aidan O'Leary and O'Shea. Touch the both up! Who knows? — maybe draw double the ration! Send up a couple o' dinners, first — just to soften them up.

CONOR: That seems a good idea.

RUCTIONS (*to Jakey*): Then it can be done?

JAKEY: Done? It's as good as done, already. Only give them a couple o' days first. Starve them out. Then, up she comes. Two dinners. Bacon and cabbage — swimmin' in butther — the full o' two shaggin' dixies! Then we'll see who has the smokes: they'll be comin' in on every post. Looksee, neighbor, they'll come all right — if it was only for shame's sake. (*Expansiveness of potential wealth.*) Here, give us one o' them cigarettes.

Ructions gives cigarettes: Jakey is smoking when Bayer appears in kitchen, timorous, hesitant, bucket in hand.

JAKEY (*alarmed at quiet entry*): Sufferin' Jay! Ye put the heart crossways in me breast, Von Shilly. Come on in! We're all friends here. Th' oul' ticker's bad. What's that ye have in yer hand?

BAYER (*advances with paper*): The officer — he says for me to —

JAKEY (*takes paper*): The officer, whah? Ye mean the screw? Dekko that! Drop o' tea? Like a mouthful? There's me own, and have a gargle. (*Bayer takes appreciatively and drinks.*) "Memorandum for Diet Sheet. Forty-seven for D1." (*To Ructions.*) Your lads. Ay, well, they're all welcome. (*To Bayer.*) How long are ye doin'? Twelve?

BAYER: No, no, no, no. Six months.

JAKEY: Six? It's only a sleep. Hump the begrudgers!

BAYER (*befogged*): Begrudgers? I am innocent.

JAKEY: Ye needn't tell me! Same as me!

BAYER: No, no, no, no. I did no crime.

JAKEY: Same as me! No crime! — D'ye know what I'm goin' to tell ye, Von Shilly? I asked men that I know, here — men ye could trust to tell the truth — asked them straight as man to man — did they do it, or did they not? D'ye know what? — this is no lie — there isn't six guilty men in the whole bloody prison.

BAYER (*protests*): My brother. He is belonging the money. He is not here. He is in New York.

JAKEY: Ay, well, if I was your innocent brother, that's where I'd be too. — There's no use having two innocent men doin' time for the *one* job.

Bayer returns mug.

JAKEY: Another mouthful?

BAYER: Hot water, please.

JAKEY: Too strong, what? Good complaint.

BAYER (*points bucket*): In him — for washing.

JAKEY (*takes bucket to refill from back kitchen*): Oh, to wash out your cell. Right.

In Jakey's absence, Bayer studies surroundings, hopefully apprehensively, locates, by sense of smell, food in steamers; and moves over to savor the odors; moves back into position before return of Jakey. Bayer takes bucket, the weight of which almost topples him into the bucket; he struggles to carry it across kitchen.

JAKEY (*calls after him*): Ye, you-with-all-the-money! (*Bayer turns.*) Ye better call a taxi! (*Jakey goes to help him.*) Here, I'll give ye a hand as far as the circle: ye're on yer tod from there, to manage as best you can.

Jakey carries bucket with ease. Exeunt Jakey and Bayer.

RUCTIONS: Now, Conor! What about it? Doesn't it look good?

CONOR (*unresponsive*): Perhaps, too good! I'm uneasy.

RUCTIONS (*impatient*): Uneasy? What the hell about?

CONOR (*serious*): Suppose it wasn't a routine raid? Suppose — that they *were* tipped off — an informer.

RUCTIONS (*discounts possibility*): How? By whom? Well? George was the only one outside: it wasn't George.

CONOR (*slowly*): No — not George.

Conor thinks a moment, looks at Ructions, then averts eyes.

RUCTIONS (*impatiently*): Well?

Conor is too immersed in thought to realize that Ructions is awaiting answer.

RUCTIONS (*impatiently*): Who?

CONOR (*recalled*): What? Oh, sorry! (*Effort at composure.*) And three inside: O'Leary, Kevin, and myself.

RUCTIONS (*impatiently downright*): It wasn't Kevin: it wasn't you.

CONOR: You've omitted one.

RUCTIONS (*genuinely puzzled*): What? Did I? (*Recollects.*) Oh, yes. I omitted to mention your wife. She was outside.

Conor feels almost slapped in the face.

CONOR: Yes — she was. — I was going to say — O'Leary.

RUCTIONS (*defensively*): The omission wasn't deliberate — it just means —

CONOR (*forcing pace*): Just means what? — that he might be guilty?

RUCTIONS (*defensively*): Not necessarily. Could equally mean I took his innocence for granted. — In the very same way as —

CONOR: As what?

RUCTIONS (*shortly*): Nothing. — I don't pretend to like O'Leary — not many of us do. He's not one of us, whatever he is. Not a tradesman — not a farmer — what is he? — not a working man. A rebel against his own class? Bourgeois outcast, of some kind — making common cause with republicans?

CONOR: Bourgeois? I suppose he is: his father has a hardware shop — a big man in a small town: he wouldn't have Aidan home after he left Maynooth — yes, he was kicked out — he disputed the infallibility of the bishops — he couldn't equate might with right, nor accept, what they called, the lawful state.

RUCTIONS: I'm sorry about that — but he isn't one of us.

CONOR: Nor was Pearse. Nor McDonagh. O'Leary hasn't the backslapping touch which enables a leader to lose his cause, survive the loss, and prosper.

RUCTIONS: I don't want his Catholic Ireland — nor his hierarchical society — and all that Thomas Aquinas stuff.

CONOR: O'Leary's fight is for natural justice.

RUCTIONS (*derisive*): Of course!

CONOR: An O'Leary in nineteen twenty-two might have made the difference when the split came and the rush for spoils. Some lingered in the ranks — some lingered only long enough to repent their loyalty — and scampered after treason. Our Pearses and McDonaghs were dead. Our Plunketts, Ceannts, O'Rahillys. Our Connollys. All gone! An O'Leary might have helped.

RUCTIONS: You lingered a little yourself, Conor. And for so much longer. Why?

CONOR (*reflectively*): I didn't know. It wasn't that things were clear-cut — or the issues well defined — I was only an ignorant kid then. I think it was just a feeling. Republic was a magic word.

RUCTIONS: A shibboleth, meaning the Island of Saints and Scholars? Where the meek should inherit the means of production? Heaven was yours for the taking — and not just a businessman's ramp? Republic must be given a meaning the Jakeys understand. The vision of God is not enough. Pie in the sky tomorrow won't do — it must be edible, here and now. That's what sold the Christian faith — what put it on the map!

CONOR: No. It was nothing that could be consumed. It was something — a value — that could be perceived by something other than the senses. A value transcending life itself — something that couldn't be crucified — transcending, even, the infamous gibbet.

RUCTIONS: Live, horse, and you'll get grass, in the pasture land of paradise. But Karl Marx preached it, here and now. The Christian churches have had their chance — wasted their talents. Not until Marx came, like a thief in the night, did Mother Church bestir herself, then she made a belated effort to stage a deathbed repentance. Her deathbed was one of labor — she brought forth a mouse — Rerum Novarum — like a rabbit out of a hat. What the hell *are* you fighting for?

CONOR (*slowly*): Perhaps I'm not fighting *for* at all. Perhaps I'm just fighting *against*.

RUCTIONS: The stage Irishman come to life! — ag'in the government, is that all?

CONOR: Resisting. Resisting every pressure that tends to make man a thing: for that, to me, is the great sin.

RUCTIONS (*rises, remembering hunger strike*): And is that what you're going to? (*Suddenly appalled.*) Conor, you can't! You mustn't! You can't do a hunger strike for that! To die! — for a thing as formless — as shapeless — a will o' the wisp — a nothing! Conor, get out of this blasted place! Get

out! Get out into the clear air! Jail gets a man in a queer way. Apathy —
then tension — a frenzy to break the inertness of things by attempting the
impossible. Get out! Take charge of the escape. Contact O'Shea. Or
O'Leary. Both. Please, Conor! and lead the escape yourself.

CONOR (*after long pause*) : I haven't written her three lines.

*Ructions walks away, abandoning the effort. Enter Jakey, rolling down shirt-
sleeves.*

JAKEY: I'm done! Master Pat will be all smiles, now. Until the visitin' committee's gone. Then it's the back o' me hand again, for another month.
(*To Conor.*) Ye never got yer letter done? (*Without answer.*) No matter! Bad news travels fast. (*To Ructions.*) And Pat give you them cigarettes?

RUCTIONS: Yes. Why?

JAKEY: 'Cos he's a bastard, that's the why, and all his seed and breed. Not
a solitary one for me, the man that's keepin' him in his job. Hardtack
is good enough for Jakey. Keepin' the tally on bread for him! Doin' the
diet sheet, and all! Ignorant as the tail o' me shirt! 'Course he'll promise!
Quick to promise, slow to perform! Him and his seven shaggin' kids!
Where would they be, if it wasn't for me? Keepin' them! Cheese and
butther goin' out o' here, hand over fist, goodo! All good nourishin' food!
Prisoners' rations into the bargain. The man should be prosecuted.

Enter Phelan with batch of official envelopes.

PHELAN (*fussily*): Mr. Geraghty not back yet? The visitin' committee's on
their rounds. Where in thunder is he?

JAKEY (*easy insolence*): Up in Nelly's room. Like as not, he's in Foley's
snug, pourin' his dinner down his gullet.

PHELAN (*hands envelope to Jakey*). For you!

JAKEY (*recognizes envelope*): Petitions, whah? Same oul' story! "Soldier on!
The law must take its course."

PHELAN: They're headin' for the hospital now; and, as sure as eggs, it's the
kitchen after. (*Gives newspaper to Ructions from inside his tunic.*) You
might like that. Remember! Ye didn't get it from me.

RUCTIONS: Thanks.

PHELAN (*leaving, fussed*): Where am I going to get this man?

JAKEY: Foley's. Slip over for a gargle: I'll tell the committee to folly yez up.
(*Exit Phelan.*) (*Starts to read letter.*) "I am instructed be the minister —"
(*Astonished.*) Me seventeenth petition; and they gave me a month off!
What's comin' over them at all? They must've gettin' the wind up — in
case they might lose me custom.

RUCTIONS (*alarmed*): A month. When are you going out?

JAKEY (*consults letter*): "The twenty-first inst." When is that?

RUCTIONS (*sighs relief*): Three weeks.

JAKEY (*new plans*): Three! I'll be out in time for Leopardstown. Give us a look at that paper, till I see if it gives the runners. (*Ructions is unfolding paper.*) Hey, that's a stop press, that is! (*Ructions, inspired, glances at paper, slowly turns to Conor, who is still immersed in his letter.*)

RUCTIONS (*horrified*): Oh, Christ! George! It's George!

JAKEY: And who's George, when he's at home?

CONOR (*alarmed*): George? What about him?

Ructions cannot answer.

CONOR (*rises*): He's killed — ? Dead?

Ructions confirms by nod.

JAKEY (*interest awakened*): Give us a lamp at that: who's George?

RUCTIONS (*to Conor*): Yes, they got him — they got him, all right —

CONOR: You mean, he's —

RUCTIONS (*offering paper*): His body was found — on the Silver Strand — in Wicklow — riddled with bullets —

CONOR (*horrified whisper, involuntarily makes sign of the cross, ignoring proffered paper*): George — George — Lord have mercy —

JAKEY (*takes up paper*): Dekko that! Dekko that paper!

Ructions turns away. Conor lowers head and recoils from sight when he finds himself looking at his letter.

JAKEY (*reading quotes*): "The Silver Strand." Isn't that Wickelah? (*In default of answer.*) 'Tis so Wickelah. (*Reads slowly.*) ". . . the deceased was found — half buried in sand — at a point some distance from the highway. Several bullets had entered the body — lacerating the left lung." (*His own comment.*) The lung is a very vital spot! (*Continues to read.*) ". . . it has not yet been ascertained how many . . ." (*Reads silently. Exaggerated horror.*) My Jase! They riddled him! Made a cullender o' the man's body, and then thrun him there to rot — the same as he might be a dog! (*Jakey searches and fails to find continuation of column. Disgust with paucity of report.*) Well that's the dear three-halfpence worth! (*Finds continuation.*) Wait, though, there's more! ". . . a card was attached about the neck o' the dead man — with the word — the word — (*Breaks off, looks up from paper.*) Aw, shag him. And shag him again! They didn't give him half enough! An informer!

RUCTIONS (*coldly menacing*): He wasn't an informer!

JAKEY (*easily*): Not makin' a liar of ye: it says here —

RUCTIONS (*thunderous*): He wasn't an informer.

JAKEY: I'm only sayin' —

RUCTIONS (*roars*): He wasn't!

Ructions' roar silences Jakey.

CONOR (*coldly*): What does it say? Read it!

Conor stays Ructions with a signal.

JAKEY (*reads*): "A card was attached about the neck of the dead man, with the word 'Spy' inscribed thereon, in black — " in block — the print is bad — in black or block letters.

No comment from Conor or Ructions.

JAKEY (*spits vindictively*): The melt!

Ructions, unable to contain anger, rushes at Jakey. Conor intervenes to release Jakey, who drops to the ground.

CONOR: Let him go! Do you hear? Let him go!

RUCTIONS (*construing Conor's worried expression*): Conor! you don't believe that George — ?

CONOR (*agonized*): Oh, I don't know what to believe.

RUCTIONS (*horror*): Conor!

CONOR (*hated admission*): Anything — is possible.

RUCTIONS (*horror*): A *horrible* thing to say!

CONOR: More horrible to think: cuts through an image in your mind, so that the picture falls away.

Ructions and Conor avoid each other's glances. Jakey has watched passage between them, now interpolates, after pause.

JAKEY (*extreme cynicism, almost whispered*): Ye might live in a man's pocket, and, still and all, ye'd never know. But when he's caught, ye bloody know ye knew, all the time.

Ructions, about to round viciously on Jakey, is stopped by Conor's outburst.

CONOR: No, no, no, no! I couldn't — I couldn't believe it of George. — I'd sooner believe it of my wife! George never!

RUCTIONS (*relieved, impulsively*): I'm *glad* to hear you say that.

Enter Geraghty, agitated, wearing greatcoat.

GERAGHTY (*roughly to Jakey*): What the hell are *you* doin' there?

JAKEY (*studied impertinence*): Can't ye see what I'm doin'? Workin'!

GERAGHTY (*peremptorily*): Get the hand cart out! We've to get the linen.

JAKEY (*lazily*): If a fella had an oul' fag now, he'd have plenty o' time to smoke it, if he had it.

GERAGHTY (*roughly*): D'ye hear what I said? On yer mark!

JAKEY (*confident refusal*): There's two prisoners on that hand cart: that's the rule: one to push, one to pull.

GERAGHTY: Rule or no rule. You're well able to pull it. The visitin' committee's here.

JAKEY (*unimpressed, comes over to Geraghty*): I s'pose ye're wearin' th' oul' topcoat to hide the porter stains on yer tunic? Able or not, that's the rule: there's *three* prisoners here.

GERAGHTY (*exasperated*): Them two is noncooperatin'.

JAKEY: Ye can tell that to the committee. And if you don't, I will, when I'm asked for me explanations.

144

GERAGHTY (*effort to browbeat*): Now, looksee, Jakey! Don't start anythin'!

JAKEY: I'm startin' nothin' I can't finish. I'll give a proper, exact account — the ins and outs of the whole carry-on — what goes out o' the joint and what comes in — and all the whys and wherefores.

GERAGHTY (*declines issue*): Maybe th' oul' hand cart is a bit heavy.

JAKEY (*follows up advantage*): Did ye think o' me cigarettes?

GERAGHTY: Yer what? (*Changes tone.*) Oh, yer cigarettes — oh, yes. I have them here for ye. Five? Will that do?

JAKEY (*takes them ungraciously*): I s'pose it will have to. (*Cigarettes inside shirt.*) Did ye say for me to get Muscles to help with the cart?

GERAGHTY: Muscles? Oh, Muscles! 'Course! Get him down, like a good lad. (*Face-saving effort at severity.*) And don't be there till ye're back! D'ye hear?

JAKEY: Right Mr. G! One off! (*Exit Jakey.*)

GERAGHTY (*comment on Jakey*): Diabolical bastard! (*Fumbles keys.*) I'd better unlock the hand cart.

RUCTIONS (*delays Geraghty, on way to exit*): Did you bring them?

GERAGHTY (*aggressive bluff*): No, I didn't bring them: I didn't get half a chance, man.

RUCTIONS (*deflated*): Oh!

GERAGHTY (*stresses caution*): I'm tellin' ye, Jakey knows somethin'; he's no daw! Guess eggs where he seen shells. With his five cigarettes.

RUCTIONS: He knows you gave me cigarettes: there's nothing to panic about in that.

CONOR (*quiet intervention*): And he knows that George was murdered.

GERAGHTY (*stiffens with fright; splutters questions*): How? How does he know that? Who told him? Who? (*Breaks off.*) So yez know! Yes — it's — it's true —

CONOR: And you knew! Why didn't you tell us?

GERAGHTY: I was going to — I swear I was — but I couldn't — I didn't get the chance — how could I? I only heard it meself, this minute, and comin' out o' the pub. I swear to God! — and then I thought — I — I — I don't know what I thought.

CONOR (*severely*): You should have told us!

GERAGHTY (*outburst*): God, have yez no heart at all? D'ye realize that it might have been me — a man with seven childer — what in the name o' the good God ever possessed me to get into tangles with youse crowd? Me, that always kept meself decent! Yourselves and yer bloody fifty! Sure, it burnt a hole in me pocket, before I'd anythin' paid for. And now look at the trouble I'm in! (*Anxiously to Ructions.*) Supposin' that chap talked! (*Ructions is incredulous.*) Well, he could have, couldn't he? (*Increasing panic.*) Supposin' he mentioned names! The cowardly bastard!

145

(*Ructions springs up in attack: Geraghty backs away, caught between Ructions and Conor. Withdrawal.*) Ah, but he wouldn't, I don't think. Poor chap, Lord have mercy on him. I'm sure he kept his mouth shut. Would ye say he would, or what?

CONOR (*cold distaste*): He didn't talk! And he can't now.

GERAGHTY: Not that I think he would, for a moment! A good chap — a chap that wouldn't — that wouldn't talk!

In the pause which follows, Enter Jakey: he studies Geraghty's distress, then speaks with forced unawareness.

JAKEY: Mouth Phelan's on the circle: he's openin' up Muscles.

GERAGHTY (*mutters*): . . . unlock this oul' hand cart. (*Exit Geraghty.*)

JAKEY (*refers Geraghty*): What ails yer man? (*Without answer.*) He's maggotty!

RUCTIONS (*denial in question form*): He's not drunk?

JAKEY (*superior wisdom*): He might as well be as the way he is: he's half canned, now! And the bulge in his pocket — did ye see that? (*Diagnosis.*) He's carryin' the bottle!

RUCTIONS: Yes, I saw that.

Enter Muscles: coat on arm, eagerly.

JAKEY (*to Muscles*): Pat's on it again.

MUSCLES (*simulated interest*): Is he? (*Eagerly.*) Am I wantin'?

JAKEY: Ay. To pull the hand cart.

MUSCLES (*vanished enthusiasm*): Oh!

JAKEY (*decisively*): I push — you pull.

MUSCLES: Meanin' that you'll have a good lean up against the back of the hand cart.

JAKEY: Either that, or shag up to the shops and nurse a good-lookin' mail bag! — Did ye get them offa the boxer?

Geraghty appears at doorway.

MUSCLES (*thumbs downwards*): Down the field! Can't pay! I told him you said you'd clock him.

JAKEY (*indignant*): Ye told him *I* said? What the hell made ye say that?

MUSCLES (*contempt*): Six foot four! I'd sink him in a dry spit!

GERAGHTY: Come on, you two! On yer mark! It's close on three o'clock.

JAKEY (*leaving, to Ructions*): Keep an eye to that steamer; and let no one touch that grub.

Exeunt Geraghty, Jakey, Muscles.

CONOR: Three o'clock!

RUCTIONS: He had them! — he had them! — he had them with him. You heard what Jakey said? That was the bulge in his pocket.

CONOR (*quietly*): Ructions, old man — it wouldn't make any difference.

RUCTIONS (*insistent*): I know he had them — then lost his nerve, when he heard the news about George.

CONOR (*quietly*): He had no guns: he'll bring no guns: there'll be no escape.

RUCTIONS: Conor, stay! Stay and lead it.

CONOR: If there were — I should stay; not to lead it — but to stop it!

RUCTIONS: Stop it! Are you mad?

CONOR: Until we know beyond a doubt who informed, and caused the raid. (*With relief.*) However, he'll bring no guns; and you can't escape on promises — I'm going on.

RUCTIONS (*desperate plea*): Conor, it's suicide — suicide!

Enter Father Maguire and Phelan, in time to hear Ructions.

MAGUIRE (*gravely*): Yes, Egan — I'm afraid it is — suicide.

RUCTIONS (*resentfully*): If we happen to use the same word, we don't share the same meaning.

PHELAN (*rebukes*): That's Father Maguire you're speaking to.

RUCTIONS: What should I do? Fall down on my face? Kiss the hem of his garment?

MAGUIRE (*ignores Ructions, to Conor*): You must not compass your own death. To abstain from food is a positive act, as much as to cut your own throat.

RUCTIONS (*angry*): Hunger strike is not suicide.

MAGUIRE (*generally, debatable*): I do not say it *is* suicide; but *a* hunger strike may be. (*To Conor.*) I had intended to see you in the privacy of your own cell, to ask you to consider the gravity of your action.

CONOR (*quietly*): Yes, Father, I understand. (*To Ructions.*) Ructions, old man, I'm going, now —

RUCTIONS (*furiously to Maguire*): Did Christ accept criminal status? Did *He* knuckle down to Caesar — and disclaim the title of Son of Man? Did He? Or did He compass his own death? Was the crucifixion suicide?

PHELAN (*aghast*): Ye might be struck dead in yer tracks for that!

RUCTIONS (*furiously derisive*): Strike, man of God! Smite me! Wither me where I stand!

CONOR (*intervenes*): Ructions, don't! For God's sake, don't — don't say any more. I'm going, now. I must go. Goodbye, Ructions — goodbye, old man. (*Shakes hands with Ructions, pats his shoulder.*) Everything will be all right. (*Confidently assures.*) You'll see. (*To Phelan, demands.*) I want to see the governor, first. (*To Maguire.*) Father — I — I —

MAGUIRE: I'll follow you, Egan, if I may.

Exeunt Conor and Phelan.

MAGUIRE (*long pause, compassionately*): If you're a Catholic, or ever were, I'm sorry to find you in this plight. Truly sorry! — somewhat guilty. (*Ap-*

peals.) We, who should have sustained you — who should have helped you through it all — tell me, McGowan, tell me, what have we done?

RUCTIONS (*contempt*): Bunk!

MAGUIRE: Build Utopia, if you will! The Church will rejoice. And when it crashes down — rebuild! But lofty towers or a heap of rubble, it still remains the vale of tears.

RUCTIONS: I've no use for all that — pap!

MAGUIRE: No use for wisdom? Nor for the breast which for two thousand years has nurtured civilization?

RUCTIONS: Suckled a brood of slaves — on poison!

MAGUIRE (*angrily*): Yours is the generation that cannot stomach the bitterness of truth. You must be fed on sweets, and comforts. State-aided, cosseted, insured! The human lot is strong red meat, for which you have no palate. Wiser than the children of light! Salt of the earth! Blessed, indeed! Insanely blessed — in that you do not *want* the pap, which is your greatest need! (*Controls anger: toward objective.*) May I come and see you?

RUCTIONS (*challenge, rather than invitation*): Sure! Come! (*Provocative.*) One of us might be the gainer. (*Hostile.*) Besides, I shall want to know about Conor.

MAGUIRE: Conor? (*Remembers.*) Oh, Egan, yes.

RUCTIONS: And your effort to convince him that his fight for truth is a mortal sin.

MAGUIRE: I shall tell him the facts, dispassionately: that is my sacred, bounden duty. Hunger strike contains all the elements — the material elements — of suicide.

Sounds of prisoners resuming work after dinner; the kitchen gradually fills up.

RUCTIONS: The end may justify the means.

MAGUIRE: No, no. Sin is an act of will. The object of volition is not only the end in view but also the means chosen.

A few prisoners stand nearby, openly listening in.

RUCTIONS (*angrily*): More subtleties! More snares! Church and state, moving, hand in hand, to crush the soul of a single man — because he rose up from his knees — because he struggled to his feet, and dared to raise his eyes to the light! And this you call your sacred, bounden duty. Toward whom, toward what? Toward God or man? Is this the tribute due to Caesar by Holy Mother Church — or the Scarlet Whore of Babylon giving the beast his money's worth?

Gasp of astonishment from prisoners. Maguire closes his eyes, wincing. There is a titter from a prisoner and Maguire wheels suddenly to leave. Exit Maguire.

PRISONER (*on Maguire's exit, derisively*): One off!

148

ANOTHER: Scarlet whore o' where, did he say? Dubbelin? Who's she?

BUTCHER: Some oul' bag from Fenian Street.

Ructions walks away, unaware that Butcher is already at the steamer, surveying the food. The prisoners form in small groups about any one prisoner with a cigarette butt; the flickers are operated, and the butts lighted.

PRISONER: Ay, soldier, where's Pat?

Ructions doesn't answer. A prisoner picks up Conor's unfinished letter, seats himself on stool, and starts to read it. From the groups come the Comments on the stew.

COMMENTS: Such a shaggin' stew! More meat in an egg! Maybe it's meat ye want! It's game ball, if ye dip yer bread! My bit o' meat turned out to be a bubble! Someone forgot to pull the chain!

In a group, someone pulls too long on a butt.

PRISONER (*abuse*): Ye've the guts shagged out of it! Ye've made it a shaggin' waistcoat!

PRISONER (*sees Butcher at steamer*): Hey, Butcher, come out o' that!

General chorus of "Hey Butcher!"

RUCTIONS (*to Butcher, taking dixie*): Put that back.

BUTCHER (*blusters*): Who says?

RUCTIONS: Put it back!

BUTCHER (*fluster*): Will you make me? You and who else with ye? Ay, where d'ye bury yer dead?

Chorus of derision from prisoners, trying to start a fight. "Hey, that man's a Republican soldier: that man'd plug ye!" "Good oul' Butch! Let him have it!" "Give him the good oul' one-two!" "Hit Butch and ye hit the ground!" "Give the man a square deal! Give the man a square meal!" Ructions takes dixie from unresisting Butcher, and replaces it in steamer. Butcher slinks off to back kitchen with derisive calls after him: "Pull up yer socks, yer nose is bleedin'." And "Ye big, empty bag!" Enter Jakey, laden with white coats and cloths. Jakey snatches Conor's letter from prisoner, and reads it.

JAKEY (*having read*): The flamin' bitch! His own wife! And Burke! Burke — the bloody rawser! (*To prisoner who has read, giving coat.*) Take one o' these, and shag off out o' here! (*Announces.*) Come on, youse! Get into yer bloody nightshirts!

Prisoners extinguish butts and don coats of all sizes.

JAKEY (*to Ructions*): The visitin' committee's on the job!

Enter Geraghty, followed by Muscles, carrying more linen. The tempo of activity speeds up: prisoners collect trays, cover tables with white cloth, cover butter with muslin, push buckets out of sight, sweep floor, shine steamer, etc., to produce a façade of order and cleanliness. Geraghty, fussed, alternates pleas with threats. Geraghty hangs up greatcoat.

GERAGHTY: C'm lads! On yer mark! The place is a battlefield. There'll be tea for all of you after, and a loaf per man, well butthered. (*To Butcher.*) Sufferin' God, where are ye goin'? Go back to where ye came from!

Ructions, having seen greatcoat hung up, takes two of the disused dixies down from shelf, moves over to coat.

JAKEY (*to Ructions*) : Are ye wearin' a white coat?

RUCTIONS: No!

Geraghty moves over between Ructions and Jakey, to shield Ructions.

GERAGHTY (*to Jakey*) : He's not cooperatin'.

JAKEY (*to Ructions*) : Well, will you check the numbers when I call out the diet sheet?

RUCTIONS (*at pocket of Geraghty's greatcoat*) : Oh, go to hell!

Geraghty pushes Jakey away, and urges others on with: "Come on, lads!" "Now, lads!" Ructions removes two revolvers from the pockets, puts them in the dixies, and places on top of shelf of unused dixies. Enter Phelan. In the midst of all the confusion, stands to attention, and announces:

PHELAN (*loudly*) : VISITORS!

Act III

SCENE 1

A month later in the waiting room, which has white walls and is constructed on the same lines as a cell, but with a fireplace, counter table, and chairs. Warder Phelan is on duty: he gets a blue form to complete a visiting request for Mrs. Kathleen Egan.

PHELAN (*complaint*) : At this hour of the morning! Visiting hours is two to four; and we're workin' shorthanded. Howsoever, I'll fill up the form, and send it up. I can do no more. Who, did ye say, ye wanted to see?

MRS. EGAN (*overawed*) : My husband — Conor.

PHELAN (*impatiently*) : Look ma'am! We've five hundred men in there — with a fair sprinkling of Conors: have ye any particular preference, or is it a matter of indifference, providing the name is Conor?

MRS. EGAN (*hastily*) : Conor, my husband. Conor Egan. Conor Patrick Egan.

PHELAN (*as he goes to fill in the name*) : Egan? Is that the man — would that be the chap on hunger strike? (*Mrs. Egan nods. Phelan repents roughness.*) Sit, down, there, ma'am. I'm sorry for taking ye up short. You're — uh — the widow — I mean you're the said Conor Egan's wife?

MRS. EGAN: Yes, I'm his wife.

Enter Jakey, in his own clothes, carrying basket on arm.

PHELAN (*good-humored jibe*): So you're back again? You're hardly out a week.

JAKEY (*gloomily*): A week today. — Remember that petition? If I hadn't've puttin' in that, I'd be goin' out tomorrow, instead of comin' in today. — I'm in two minds will I go to the bother o' changin' me oul' clothes. I got a sickener o' this place.

PHELAN (*genuinely surprised*): Why? What's wrong with it?

JAKEY (*disapproval*): Down the banks! Even the kitchen! — and it won't be the same, at all, without poor Pat.

PHELAN (*enlightened*): Geraghty? (*Lifts cap reverently.*) Poor Pat Geraghty! A decent man — if ever there was!

JAKEY (*admitting nothing*): Whether he was or not. (*Pointed.*) If someone had to be polished off — there was lots of other oul' screws, far better entitled.

Phelan is inclined to take it as a personal remark.

JAKEY (*abruptly*): Any parcels for D wing?

PHELAN: I'll be taking them up, meself, in a minute. (*Gives Jakey a cigarette.*) Here! While ye're waiting, give that oul' fire a rake-out, and get her going. (*Jakey goes to fireplace: Phelan turns to complete form. Reads.*) "Conor Patrick Egan." Right, ma'am! I'll 'phone them up now, to look into your case, and see what can be done. (*Exit Phelan.*)

Jakey has caught name; but Phelan has left door open. The phone call is heard being put through, and the door is then closed from the outside.

JAKEY (*he has closed the door*): Shows very nice feeling! He wouldn't want to hear what we're sayin'. (*Lowers voice.*) Mrs. Egan, whah? Conor's wife? I was thinkin' as much.

MRS. EGAN (*notes Jakey's unprepossessing appearance*): Do — do you know Conor?

JAKEY: Know him, is it? Why wouldn't I? Didn't the two of us soldier together? (*Mrs. Egan not reassured.*) 'Course, I'm not a captain, or anythin'. Just an ordinary five eighths — not very long attached.

MRS. EGAN (*apology for doubt in her face*): Oh, I see.

JAKEY: Conor and me is pack, all right! I seen him, not very long ago, the very *day* he went on it.

MRS. EGAN (*suddenly affected*): Thirty days, it is! Oh, God! Thirty days since he touched food!

JAKEY: Thirty? Is it that long? Ye wouldn't feel the time goin' in! (*Mrs. Egan's face shows her hurt. Consoles.*) He'll be all right, Mrs. Egan. They'll *have* to — they'll *have* to release him. There's great public feeling outside — the people is gettin' up about it. Sure the picture houses is near broke! Empty they are! Not a sinner goin' in!

MRS. EGAN (*hardly daring to hope*): Is — is that true?

151

JAKEY (*amends*): Well — very small queues.

MRS. EGAN: How — how did *you* get out?

JAKEY: Me? Me term was up. Ah, but, sure, then they got me again, on another job: so I'm back.

Phelan looks in. Mrs. Egan immediately rises.

PHELAN: They're getting the chief: they'll ring me back.

JAKEY (*at fire*): These oul' sticks is wet.

Exit Phelan.

JAKEY: Talkin' o' which, did *you* ever get that letter?

MRS. EGAN (*interest aroused*): Letter? What letter? From Conor?

JAKEY (*reads her face*): Ye didn't, whah? I was thinkin' as much.

MRS. EGAN: Every day I wrote him. Every day since I knew. But he never replied. Are you sure he wrote. Are you sure?

JAKEY: I wish I was as sure of Heaven. He give it to this certain party — a warder — to post for him outside. I warned him against the shag — (*corrects*) — the warder; but he wouldn't be said or led by me — he give it!

MRS. EGAN (*infinite relief*): He wrote! He wrote! Nothing else matters: thank God for that. You can't know what that means to me, Mr. —

JAKEY (*supplies word*): Jakey — for short.

MRS. EGAN: Mr. Jakey.

JAKEY (*meaningly*): Maybe ye were just as well that our letter went astray. — Conor wasn't too pleased with the way things went, over the sendin' in o' them yokes — the guns, I mean.

MRS. EGAN (*distraught*): I know. I know: but you don't understand. Why should Conor risk his life? Why should he have to lead the escape? Hasn't he done enough — since 1918?

JAKEY: No later than yesterday mornin', me missus put the selfsame question: "Why must it always be you?" says she, "if the house fell *you* pushed it." — The day Conor writ that letter — will I ever forget? — just the two of us there in the kitchen — and I lend Conor me fountain pen — and when he had it finished and done, he reads it over and turns to me. "Jakey," says he, "it's a sad thing — a very sad thing — when a man's wife —" (*Breaks off.*)

MRS. EGAN (*agonized*): When a man's wife what? What did he say? Tell me! What?

JAKEY: He left it at that — said no more — not another syllable out o' his mouth. — Then handed me the letter, and I knew that the thing that was troublin' him was — how you could ever bring yerself — to do the thing ye did.

MRS. EGAN (*impassioned*): I didn't! I didn't! Oh, Conor, I never did! I wanted to — yes — times out of number — but, I couldn't — I never did.

JAKEY (*apprehensively*): Sh-sh-sh, like a good woman: you'll have that fella in on top of us, wantin' to know what doesn't concern him. (*Mrs. Egan makes effort to regain control. Puzzled by denial.*) Ye didn't, whah? — Tell me! What made ye even want to?

MRS. EGAN: Leitrim we lived in, when we were married. In a middling backward place: nearly *too* quiet, you might say, with Conor away organizing. Seldom it took him away from home — until after the baby was born: then seldom became often. Not that he stayed away long! He didn't. I knew he'd be back soon; but, if I did, I knew, too, that soon he'd be away again. — Queer! the things that come into your mind when you're striving to think of nothing at all. Soon! I thought: he'll be back soon — if he ever comes back at all. Down on my knees at the kitchen fire — and asked God to help them. To help them with the organizing — to give them the freedom they wanted — all that they craved, at their own sweet will — but to let me have my home.

JAKEY (*surface sympathy*): That's the way o' the world, ma'am. — Conor mentioned another china — was there someone by the name o' Burke?

MRS. EGAN (*surprised*): Sergeant Burke? Charley?

JAKEY (*fastens on it victoriously*): Sergeant Charley! The very man!

MRS. EGAN (*perturbed*): Did Conor — ? What did Conor say?

JAKEY: I disremember the exact words; but unless I'm greatly astray, Conor wouldn't have breakin' his heart if Sergeant Charley, and not George, was found on the Silver Strand that mornin' with a bullet in his gizzard.

MRS. EGAN: George? You think that — that that's why George was shot?

JAKEY (*roughly*): They never gave the chap the gun for speakin' out of his turn!

MRS. EGAN (*frantic*): The police shot him — the specials. They did! They did! It had nothing to do with the guns! It wasn't — it wasn't an execution.

JAKEY (*pursues relentlessly*): So be! Well listen, lady! Was Pat Geraghty an execution?

MRS. EGAN (*a trapped witness*): Geraghty? The — the warder — ?

JAKEY (*roughly, incredulous*): And the Silver Strand, a coinstance, whah? The specials again? For why? For breakin' the by-laws, I suppose, by sunbathin' on the Strand — at two o'clock in the mornin'?

MRS. EGAN (*frantic*): He tricked them — got money from them — fifty or a hundred pounds — he did — he did! — and after he had promised —

JAKEY (*interrupts roughly*): There's hair on that! — The man was never employed for his honesty. (*Walks away a few steps; suddenly wheels.*) There's a man walkin' the streets now, with a cheery nod — and a smile for all — and plenty o' money in his pocket — blood money — the price o' two — Sergeant buckaleero Charley! — yer lovely brother-in-law!

MRS. EGAN (*rises*): He didn't: he didn't! Charley Burke is a decent man: he

153

helped me: and that's all he did. He helped me to stop the escape. But he gave no names. I know he didn't. He wrote he didn't.

JAKEY (*unbelief*): Swore, whah? Well, you know yer own know; and I know mine; but, I'm tellin' you, Mrs. Egan — there's swearin' and swearin' in it!

MRS. EGAN: But Charley's my own brother-in-law — my sister's husband — he didn't — he couldn't —

JAKEY (*skeptic*): Brother-in-law! Brother-in-law, me gearcase! I have one! *I* know — as for stoppin' a man escapin' — yer best dart is shoot him!

MRS. EGAN: Charley didn't want anyone shot. They'd be met, he said, when they tried to escape, and escorted back to the prison.

JAKEY (*alive*): Met where?

MRS. EGAN: Post a squad outside, he said, in the warders' houses, and wait for them there.

JAKEY (*impressed*): A sitdown raid, whah! in the warders' houses!

MRS. EGAN (*appeals*): Charley's a very good man: he wouldn't want anyone shot.

JAKEY (*reflectively*): A sitdown raid! (*Complete change of front.*) Excuse me makin' the mistake. The man's your brother-in-law; you're the best judge yerself. (*Detects noise outside.*) Sh-sh-sh. Walls have ears.

Jakey resumes reading newspaper, and is engrossed when Phelan enters. Mrs. Egan rises immediately.

MRS. EGAN: Well? Can I see him now?

PHELAN (*official casualness*): Ye're as wise now as I am meself. The chief will see you: that's all I know.

MRS. EGAN: But I must see him, I must! Mrs. Fitzpatrick said I could: she said she'd arrange it.

PHELAN (*surprised*): Mrs. Fitzpatrick? Ye mean Mrs. Turlough Fitzpatrick, her husband was shot in the Cornmarket in the ruskey in 'twenty-two?

MRS. EGAN: Yes. Her son is in here. She said there was no difficulty, that she'd 'phone the minister.

PHELAN: Of course, if *she* said it! — There again — Mrs. Fitz is one thing — and the minister another! The chief is sendin' down for ye: that's all I know. (*Exiting, to Jakey.*) What are *you* doing? Crosswords?

JAKEY (*unperturbed*): It's a poor jail that can't afford *two* gentlemen. Clock-watchin', like yerself.

Exit Phelan. Mrs. Egan immediately produces letter from handbag and thrusts it toward Jakey.

MRS. EGAN: See Conor! Give him that! In case I'm not let to see him. That'll explain everything.

JAKEY (*alarmed*): I'm not in touch with Conor.

MRS. EGAN (*presses*): Give it to Aidan O'Leary, then: he'll get it to Conor. Please! Please!

JAKEY (*backs away*): A letter? Aw, no! Jakey's no halk!

MRS. EGAN (*frantic*): Oh, you must! You're Conor's friend. I swear to you, he's killing himself. Oh God! you don't know Conor at all: he's hard: he's hard: he's doing this to punish me: that's all it is — to punish me —

Mrs. Egan advances toward Jakey as she speaks: he retreats, then suddenly advances to meet her, threateningly.

JAKEY (*threat from fright*): Another inch, and I'll clock ye one! I'm tellin' ye, now! Ye betther not — or before God! — I'll crease ye!

Mrs. Egan halts, breaks down in tears, retreats. Jakey, now thoroughly ashamed of his cowardice, recovers from fright and speaks gently to her — yet carefully keeps a safe distance.

JAKEY: It's not that ye haven't me sympathy — I'm sorry for ye, Mrs. Egan. And I'd do it too — with a heart and a half! — so I would — only — well — you know yerself the way it is: too much shootin' goin' on — all very well, once in a way; but who's to say who'll be the next? (*Uneasy shrug.*) I can tell ye, I'm the happy man to be in out o' the rain!

MRS. EGAN (*lifts her head, distraught*): Dear God! What *will* I do?

JAKEY (*sympathy*): See the priest. That's yer best dart! Father Maguire: and get *him* to speak to Conor.

MRS. EGAN (*some slight hope*): Father Maguire? And where will I — ?

JAKEY: Ask for him when ye see the chief: he'll put you right.

Enter Phelan. Mrs. Egan's back is toward him, the counter table between her and Jakey. As Phelan speaks, she puts letter on counter table, under pile of blue forms, catching Jakey's eye as she does so. Jakey involuntarily makes move to stop her, restrains himself in presence of Phelan, and remains uneasily conscious of existence of letter to the end of the scene.

PHELAN (*briskly*): Now, ma'am. This man will take ye to the chief.

MRS. EGAN (*hopefully*): Then — then — ?

PHELAN (*avoids discussion*): He'll tell you all.

MRS. EGAN (*addresses Phelan, obliquely addressing Jakey, with excessive gratitude. Phelan, puzzled. Jakey shiftily uneasy*): Thank you! Thank you *very* much! I'll *never* forget *your* kindness — never — !

Exit Mrs. Egan. Sounds of escort warder.

PHELAN (*to Jakey, taken aback by gratitude*): Very nice little woman! (*Almost an accusation against Jakey.*) Very civil and polite!

Jakey just nods admission. Phelan moves over to arrange forms on table: Jakey galvanizes to stop him finding letter.

JAKEY (*suddenly*): Give us one o' your cigarettes.

PHELAN (*leaves forms to give cigarette, unwillingly*): Ah, very! But her man is not going out of here — until he goes out in a box!

Sound of gate bell ringing, long and hard.

PHELAN (*bets on diagnosis*): Hear that holy hullabaloo? Mrs. Fitz, for a dollar! Herself and the daughter — in and out of here, all day. Not because her son is in here! But to know — if you don't mind! — Conor Egan's condition. — The nearer that man gets to his death, the more and the more thicker, they cluster round — like flies in a knacker's yard! — (*Quotes.*) "Lovers of freedom, throughout the civilized world — *and* England — we demand this man's release." (*Disgusted comment.*) What they want is a funeral!

Again Phelan goes to forms. Again Jakey hastily improvises delaying tactics.

JAKEY: He could be only skin and bone, by now?

PHELAN (*ponderous understatement*): He's far from well! — Has himself to thank! — he wouldn't take the liquid paraffin. (*Gate bell rings again, furiously.*) She can wait! (*Resumes discourse.*) Said they were trying to give him food — then, the next thing, that the veins in his hand were tampered with — ay, and left it on the doctor! — said that their proper color was blue, and that now they were colored Venetian red. — 'Course, that mightn't be gospel: that's what the medical orderly said.

JAKEY: De-delusions, whah?

PHELAN (*weightily*): In one word — delusions! (*Pontificates.*) Ye see, the waste matter, in the body, goes, what they call, toxic: then, the next thing is, the poor brain — the mind, d'ye see? — the brain is a very delicate thing.

Gate bell, as Phelan speaks again.

PHELAN (*ominously*): I don't want to put a nail in his coffin: but I'd be very much surprised — ! (*Leaves sentence unfinished. Reconstructs diagnosis of bell.*) Y'know, *that* might be old Riordan: he's due to take over the gate. Are ye coming with me to D1?

JAKEY: Be all right to go by reception? I think I might change me oul' clothes.

PHELAN: Right! Wait till ye see the puss on Riordan when he has to light his own fire. (*Exit Phelan.*)

Jakey, after quandary of doubt, plunges, takes letter from table, puts inside shirt. Exit Jakey, exaggeratedly casual.

SCENE 2

Later the same day in the triple cell, as in Act I. Chess, draughts, rings, embroidered flags in progress. Enter Kevin.

KEVIN: Now lads! Please!

All file out except Kevin, Micheál, O'Shea, Tommy, Fitz, and Dunne, who takes over the door duty. Kevin draws the escape diagram on blackboard, with the ease of regular performance: nobody shows much interest in what has become a tiresome routine. Dunne pulls door to from outside, having sprung lock to prevent slamming. O'Shea rolls a cigarette laboriously.

KEVIN (*begins lecture*): As you know, the guns are disposed thus (*points diagram*): A — O'Shea: D — Tommy: C — Micheál: Aidan and I on the circle. And whoever is in Ructions' place will have to look after B.

O'SHEA: There are only four of us here.

KEVIN: Aidan has gone to the governor's office: he cannot be very long.

O'SHEA: We have this lecture now four times a week; when are we getting the guns?

KEVIN: You'll know that in good time.

TOMMY (*lying on bed, sympathizes with O'Shea*): Kevin, it does seem a waste of time — except that it helps to keep up morale.

O'Shea, somewhat provocatively, absorbs himself in the rolling of his cigarette.

KEVIN: When Aidan and I take the circle, Tommy will have to be ready. O'Shea! What am I saying? O'Shea!

O'SHEA (*absorbed in cigarette, says off by rote*): "When Aidan and I take the circle, Tommy will have to be ready at D to take custody of the prisoners: I'll open the circle gate, hand over the warder to Aidan, who will hand him to Tommy at D." We know — we know all that — but when is it all going to happen?

KEVIN: I'm in charge of this operation: if you'd rather not listen — you know what to do.

O'SHEA: I don't mind listening, Kevin: but, look! it amounts to this. Give me the chalk! (*Rises, takes chalk, and proceeds to demonstrate lecture. At blackboard.*) If you like, I'll give you the whole lecture. "That's A wing, that's B, that's C, that's D, the circle, the passage, the courtyard, the gate: that's the drive from the gate to the main road; and they're the warders' houses." (*The warders' houses are illustrated heavily on board by thick white line, with impatient stroke of the flat of the chalk.*) I've got to hate those warders' houses! I see warders' houses, in my sleep! If I'd my way, I'd blow those warders' houses to hell — and replace them all with bell tents!

KEVIN (*takes chalk*): All right! In future — to please Jim O'Shea — they're the warders' bell tents. Where was I?

Sounds of fuss outside. Dunne resisting someone's entry. Dunne sticks in his head.

DUNNE: It's Jakey! I told him he couldn't come in.

KEVIN (*irritably*): He can't. — Wait! — Let him in.

Enter Jakey hastily: scans place for bucket.

JAKEY: 'Scuse me! It's the bucket: th' oul' chief is on the circle, and I have to have me alibi to work me passage to the kitchen.

Kevin notices Jakey's evident interest in diagram and stands in the way to obscure view.

JAKEY: What is it? A sunburst? Or the flag o' the Japanese?

KEVIN (*rudely*): Shorthand. Means mind your own business.

JAKEY (*reproved*): Oh!

Jakey takes the bucket, and is leaving, when Kevin detains him.

KEVIN: You went out on petition, recently?

JAKEY: Yeh. Why?

KEVIN: Always go out on petition?

JAKEY: In all me puff — never before! 'Twas what ye might call — a novelty.

KEVIN (*studies Jakey's face*): You were only out for a week?

JAKEY: Short and sweet, like an ass's gallop.

KEVIN (*still studying*): Was it worth your while? For a week?

Jakey picks up innuendo and is uneasy.

JAKEY: I near got meself married — if that's what you mean by worth me while.

KEVIN (*pursues*): What did you think I meant?

JAKEY (*resentfully*): It's all alick-alike to me what ye meant — as the devil says to the collier.

Exit Jakey: Kevin stands watching exit and hesitates a moment before continuing lecture.

KEVIN (*resuming lecture*): Where was I?

Dunne looks in again, having shown out Jakey.

DUNNE (*announces*): The O.C.

Aidan enters, halts inside door: ominous pause.

AIDAN: Yes. He's dead.

General gasp of "Conor." Dunne comes in, closes door over.

TOMMY: Conor — dead?

AIDAN: Something over an hour ago.

TOMMY (*low voice*): I never thought they'd let him die.

MICHEÁL: I did: but I thought he'd go longer than thirty days.

AIDAN: The only consolation is he won: Conor won!

TOMMY: Thank God for that! Poor old Conor won — too late!

KEVIN: You're sure? He won political treatment?

AIDAN: The governor didn't use the term political treatment — he said that Ructions was coming back, to D1 — what else can it mean?

KEVIN: Did you ask him what it meant?

AIDAN: Yes. He couldn't say more than that. He couldn't even show me a memo — he said the department of justice had phoned him — and he was prepared to act on that — to transfer Ructions here.

O'SHEA: He's not giving much away, is he?

AIDAN: The governor? Oh, he was decent enough. Pretty rotten job! I expect, really, he's not supposed to tell me anything, at all.

AIDAN: He said we could have the prison chapel — if I liked to arrange it with Father Maguire.

TOMMY: A Mass?

AIDAN: I think we should.

MICHEÁL: Oh Lord yes, we should. We'd have to do that.

TOMMY: First George! Then Conor! (*Association.*) Can't be many more left, now, out of the 'twenty-two crowd.

O'SHEA: How well they didn't give in — until they were sure he would die!

MICHEÁL: Lord, yes. They took their pound of flesh.

FITZ: The same as they did with my father: let him bleed to death — and then claimed they tried to staunch his wounds. It all came out at the inquest. (*Question at large, unanswered.*) I suppose there'll be an inquest?

TOMMY (*worried*): It all strikes me as very queer.

KEVIN: How do you mean — queer?

TOMMY: To let him die — and *then* admit his claim was right.

MICHEÁL (*heatedly*): They'd do the same again tomorrow — if they thought they'd get you! They hate the old crowd!

General chorus of "Of course!"

AIDAN: I suppose I'd better make an announcement to the men?

DUNNE: Shall I get them in?

Enter Ructions. O'Shea, Micheál, and Tommy go to welcome Ructions. Kevin and Aidan rather less cordial. Fitz reciprocates standing hostility. Dunne friendly.

O'SHEA: Ructions, by the holy smoke!

MICHEÁL: What way are ye at all?

TOMMY: Glad to see you back!

AIDAN (*formal*): So am I, McGowan.

RUCTIONS: Thanks — everybody — I'm glad to *be* back.

DUNNE: It'll do the men good to see your ugly mug again. (*To Aidan.*) Get them in now?

Aidan nods, and exit Dunne.

AIDAN (*to Ructions*): You know about Conor? (*Ructions nods.*) Of course, it's terrible — but wonderful that he won.

RUCTIONS: Did he? The governor didn't say that to me.

AIDAN: Nothing about political treatment?

RUCTIONS: Nothing! My sentence is suspended. I asked him for how long. He couldn't even tell me that. Just — suspended. So, for all I know I go back again tomorrow.

KEVIN: We'll know in a few days: they don't want to lose face by giving in to-day.

RUCTIONS: I think it's a move designed to confuse us — to make us think the fight is won — then, when things die down a bit — it's on again. Criminal status, as before.

TOMMY: I'm inclined to agree with Ructions.

KEVIN (*testily*): They won't give a formal admission today — the very day of Conor's death.

AIDAN: We must clear this. I'll see the governor again, and demand a formal admission.

RUCTIONS: I've demanded it — already.

KEVIN: *You* demanded it — already?

RUCTIONS: Why not?

FITZ: I thought Aidan was O.C.

O'SHEA (*unable to support Ructions*): That's true, Ructions — he is.

RUCTIONS: I know. Of those on remand. Conor and I are convicted men — were, I should say — for I'm the survivor. It's my right — and my duty — to carry on our fight.

KEVIN (*hostile*): Your fight?

AIDAN (*reasonably*): I don't want to quarrel, now, McGowan: but don't take me as agreeing. We can't let Conor's death go without an answer.

RUCTIONS (*points diagram*): There's your answer: the escape; and bring it off today. I suppose you're fixing final details.

AIDAN: Today?

RUCTIONS: Today is the day for it!

KEVIN: Details? And what about the guns?

RUCTIONS: I know the place pretty well, by now: six should be sufficient.

KEVIN (*irritably*): Six what, in the name of God?

RUCTIONS (*quotes*): Six what? (*To Aidan.*) I sent you three guns: did you get them? (*Wheels to O'Shea.*) And you three. Yes, you, O'Shea. (*Ructions is met by blank expressions. Enter Dunne. Sounds of crowd off, excitably.*) I sent them by Jakey. God almighty! You mean to say — ? The damned rat! (*Quickly.*) Where's Bayer? The Jew? Von Shilly?

KEVIN: Would he have them?

RUCTIONS: He might know something.

DUNNE: The Jew is somewhere on the wing. But Jakey himself is in the jail.

RUCTIONS: No, he went out some time ago.

KEVIN: He was here a few minutes ago.

RUCTIONS: Back! Good! (*Leaving.*) Well, then, I'll see him and —

KEVIN (*peremptorily*): Wait! (*Thoughtfully.*) That scamp Jakey was wardsman here at the time of the raid. (*To Tommy.*) Remember? He butted in the day we closed with Geraghty in the very middle of the deal.

TOMMY: That's so: he did. ·

KEVIN: And again, today! With the same pretext — a dixie or a bucket. (*All are impressed with the suspicion.*) What does it all add up to?

RUCTIONS (*irritably*): Nothing! Sweet damn-all!

KEVIN: No? Why didn't he give us the guns, then?

FITZ (*in support of Kevin*): There must be *some* reason.

RUCTIONS: If Jakey had a reason, *you* wouldn't understand it. Some petty resentment or other. Lags are queer. (*In face of general disbelief, to Tommy.*) Jakey's all right, I tell you: if he weren't they'd have had me long ago.

KEVIN: Perhaps it isn't you they want: just the guns they failed to get on the raid.

TOMMY: If it was Jakey who gave us away — Geraghty was — a mistake!

RUCTIONS (*indignant horror*): Mistake! What a word for murder!

KEVIN (*reproof*): Not murder! It was an execution.

RUCTIONS (*appalled*): Then — it *was* — our lads! I thought it was the specials. My God! Do you realize that he brought them in — Geraghty! — gave me six guns?

KEVIN (*defensively*): We're not responsible for decisions made outside in HQ.

RUCTIONS: And George? What about George? (*In default of reply.*) Well? Was he — ? Was he — ? (*Nobody answers.*) I see — another mistake!

KEVIN (*low voice, guiltily defensive*): HQ.

RUCTIONS (*attacks Kevin*): And *now*, your teeth are sunk in Jakey — with two mistakes to your credit!

KEVIN (*equally heated*): No one said it was Jakey: he's under suspicion, that's all — because of his own behavior.

RUCTIONS (*after long pause, decisively*): Right! If Jakey produces the guns, will you make the escape today?

KEVIN (*considers, hesitates, turns to Aidan*): Well, Aidan?

AIDAN: I'm with McGowan on that: today *is* the day!

KEVIN (*irritably*): Suppose it's a trap — and this pimp has been sent back in, to set it?

RUCTIONS (*impatiently*): It's not a trap.

KEVIN: It could be. They might decide that the best thing was to arrange our escape for us.

RUCTIONS: Nonsense!

KEVIN (*grimly*): And sit down at the gate to meet us!

RUCTIONS (*provocative in exasperation*): Escape is either a routine lecture — a lot of chitchat to pass the time — or else it's something you're going to try. Well? Which? Which is it?

KEVIN (*stung*): Very good! We'll try. Today! (*Resentfully.*) But remember,

outside ourselves, no one knows of this attempt: no one! — except Jakey
— if he gives us the guns.

RUCTIONS: Well?

KEVIN (*threat*): If it goes wrong — !

RUCTIONS: It won't go wrong.

KEVIN: If it does — it goes wrong for Jakey!

RUCTIONS: A test case, eh? Very good! (*Goes to diagram; to Kevin.*) Look!
This plan of yours. It was much too complicated. There's the circle.
When A, B, C, and D are fed, the warders all parade there, on the circle.
You haven't to round them up, at all, from the workshop, the wood yard,
or anywhere else. They round themselves up. There they are! Strike then!

KEVIN (*pleased*): They do? That makes it more than possible. We've got to
delay in D wing to have A, B, and C fed before D is locked up.

RUCTIONS: Can you take over from here? Or is there anything else? I want
to see this Jew.

KEVIN (*taking over*): That's all right. I have it.

Exit Ructions. Sounds of welcome from men outside.

TOMMY: Delay, eh? A game of basketball — in the exercise yard.

MICHEÁL (*enthusiastically*): Cluiche ciseach! deanfaidh sin! Deanfaidh sin
cuis!

KEVIN: Keep it going as long as they can — delay coming in for dinner — (*at
diagram*) Aidan and I from this end: O'Shea and Micheál from A and
C — Tommy on D, with Fitz as before all converging on the circle. — Now
let's go over this once more —

AIDAN: Kevin! No. The men.

KEVIN: Later, then, below in my cell.

*Aidan nods to Dunne; the crowd of men are in. Kevin carelessly erases dia-
gram, leaving the white mark of the warders' houses. Excited whispers of
men abate.*

AIDAN (*addresses assembled men*): You probably know already why you
have been summoned. Conor Egan is dead. Whilst the world's statesmen
prate of freedoms, for which they must live, and the people must die —
whilst God himself is in the headlines, and divine justice is acclaimed as
the war aim of opposing nations — in the criminal section of a remote
prison, the real fight for freedom goes on, the weight of it borne by one
man. Conor Egan, a farmer's son, takes up the universal burden, marked
with the stigma of criminal, bears that burden, to the death. You will remember Thomas Ashe's words: "Let me carry Thy Cross for Ireland,
Lord." Once again, an Irishman has taken up that precious burden. Go
ndeanaidh Dia trocaire ar a anam.

Enter Ructions.

AIDAN (*afterthought, as he walks away*): I am arranging with the chaplain to have Mass celebrated in the chapel here for the repose of Conor Egan's soul.

RUCTIONS (*calls aloud*): For men must work, women weep, and soldiers must pray! Are these the orders of the day?

TOMMY: Ructions, old man —

RUCTIONS (*shouts*): Do we ask the Church that struck him down to raise that hand again, in benediction — and crown the murder with a blessing?

FITZ: Shut up! you damned half-baked atheist!

RUCTIONS: Half-baked, eh? I forgot you liked your heretics burnt!

AIDAN (*anxious to avoid scene, dismisses men*): You may dismiss.

The men are scattering when Micheál halts them with an announcement.

MICHEÁL: Momeidin, le'n bhur dtoil, momeidin! Cuirfear na ranganna Gaedhilge ar ath lo — go ceann tamaillin: forgrochair dhibh ce'n uair thoiseocas siad. (*Translates.*) The Irish classes are suspended for the present — the re-opening date will be announced. (*Again men are disbanding.*) Momeidin eile! Abairt a' lae! Abairt a' lae! Tabhairfaidh me ceann dhibh. I'll give you the Abairt a' lae, the daily phrase now. (*Writes on board.*) "I nDil Chuimhne." (*Pronounces.*) I nDil Cuimhne, I nDil Cuimhne.

All repeat: "I nDil Cuimhne."

MICHEÁL: Abair aris e — chuile dhuine!

Roar in unison: "I nDil Cuimhne." A voice: "What does it mean?"

MICHEÁL: In loving memory. (*Adds words on board.*) Concubhair Mhic Aodhain. (*Calls out.*) I nDil Cuimhne Concubhair Mhic Aodhain.

Again the men are disbanding when Ructions stays them.

RUCTIONS (*calls out, as Micheál did*): Momeidin! Tabhairfaidh *mise* ceann dibh! (*At blackboard, chalk in hand.*) Abairt a' lae! A phrase a day! A phrase for a year and a day! A phrase from Voltaire. "When the last King is strangled with the gut of the last priest" — then let my epitaph be written! (*There is an attempt by one or two of the crowd to attack Ructions: the attackers are restrained by the others, Ructions, now in sheer fury, draws a crude headstone about Micheál's words on the blackboard. As he draws.*) Design for a headstone! Here lie the bodies of Conor Egan, of Christ, and of Turlough Fitzpatrick. Three fabulous heroes — distant myths — breakers of the seal of the tomb — who were buried securely in ritual.

Most of the men leave.

AIDAN (*not unsympathetically*): McGowan, take it easy! — After all, Conor survives.

RUCTIONS (*bitterly, throwing down chalk*): In autograph albums!

Fitz rushes out: Micheál follows.

KEVIN (*list in hand, to Ructions*): Did you see the Jew?

163

RUCTIONS: He's getting Jakey. The stuff is here in the wing, he doesn't know where, but it is.

KEVIN (*to Aidan*): There isn't much time: we're going below to my cell. That's the list. With McGowan back, we're seven, unless we drop Fitzpatrick.

RUCTIONS: I told you I'm carrying on the fight: you needn't drop Fitzpatrick: I'm staying to do a hunger strike.

AIDAN (*to Kevin*): I'll see the governor now. (*To Ructions.*) It's for me to decide who stays — if there's any staying to be done. Staying is a one-man job!

RUCTIONS (*challenge*): Agreed!

Exit Kevin.

O'SHEA: Are you coming, Ructions?

RUCTIONS: No, Jim!

Exit O'Shea. Tommy comes over to put hand on Ructions' shoulder.

TOMMY: Well, Ruc?

RUCTIONS: Well, Tommy?

TOMMY: Anything — I could do.

RUCTIONS: No, thanks. (*Afterthought.*) You might get me back my ring?

TOMMY: All right, I will. (*Exit Tommy.*)

Ructions is left with Aidan, who, about to leave, stops at door, turns, and in an effort to be friendly addresses Ructions.

AIDAN: Your ring? The one with the dragon?

RUCTIONS (*unresponsive*): Yes.

AIDAN: The self-consuming monster, symbolizing the hunger striker! Why do you want to stay, now?

RUCTIONS: I'll answer that question by asking another. — Did (*blurts it out*) did Conor break the strike?

AIDAN: Break — ? You mean — did — ?

RUCTIONS: Yes, that's what I mean: did he take food before he died?

AIDAN (*angry response*): How dare you make the — (*Change of front.*) Why do you ask that? Who told you? Well, who?

RUCTIONS (*grimly*): The governor. (*Accuses.*) Didn't he tell you?

AIDAN (*distressed admission*): Yes — he — (*uncritical loyalty*). But I didn't believe him. I don't now. It's a lie! Conor didn't!

RUCTIONS (*grimly sardonic*): No!

AIDAN (*fearfully*): Why do you say No like that? Why? That No means Yes.

RUCTIONS: Because Maguire might have put on the pressure.

AIDAN: Father Maguire? What kind of — pressure?

RUCTIONS: The kind that would break Conor — or you — refusal of absolution.

Aidan turns away, an agonized admission of the possibility.

RUCTIONS (*after pause, squaring up to meet trouble*): That's why I want to stay!

AIDAN (*low voice*): — I'll see the governor, now: I'll — I'll thrash it out with him.

Exit Aidan. After pause enter Bayer.

BAYER (*reporting*): He comes. Presque immediatement!

Ructions nods acknowledgment. Bayer, anxious to show some work, takes duster and wipes board, carefully avoiding to wipe either warders' houses or "abairt a' lae." The operation gets on Ructions' nerves.

RUCTIONS (*shouts*): Wipe it! Wipe it! Wipe the bloody thing off! (*Bayer fails to understand.*) Ecrasez ça! Ecrasez l'infame! (*Shout diminishes to a cry of pain.*) Wipe it! Wipe it! Wipe it!

BAYER (*recognizes*): Ah, Voltaire? Vous l'avez lu?

Enter Jakey, with bucket, in time to overhear Ructions; Phelan follows.

JAKEY (*takes duster from Bayer*): Don't ye hear what the shaggin' man says — wipe it! (*Jakey wipes at one stroke, leaving portion of headstone, and warders' houses intact. To Ructions.*) How's the body? (*To Bayer.*) Shag off you, Von Shilly! Ye dyin'-looking parlormaid!

PHELAN (*sternly to Bayer*): Come along!

BAYER (*mystified*): But — where — where — ?

PHELAN (*roughly*): Never mind where!

JAKEY: The wood yard — that's the where!

BAYER (*leaving, distressed*): The wood yard?

JAKEY (*busy show of activity*): No wonder the governor sent for me, with th' oul' kip goin' to rack and ruin. The cut o' the place! As Pat used to say — a battlefield! (*To Phelan.*) Ye'll get no half sheet after me.

PHELAN (*to Ructions*): Poor Egan! Somethin' cruel! What that man must have went through! Even the doctors — the specialists — they don't know the half of it! (*In default of response, resignedly.*) Ah, well! (*To Bayer.*) Come on, you!

Exeunt Phelan and Bayer.

JAKEY (*to Ructions*): I have them — articles — for ye below. (*Reply to glance.*) On top o' the cisterns — one on each.

RUCTIONS: Good! I was worried. (*Accusation.*) You bypassed O'Leary and O'Shea. Why?

JAKEY: O'Leary doesn't like me. Besides, I knew I'd be back soon: I didn't want to miss the gas. — I'd a terrible job to get back at all, so I had. That bloody Muscles!

RUCTIONS: He let you down?

JAKEY (*sentence begins disappointed tone, ends vindictively*): The last thing I expected! — though I wasn't a bit surprised. — Leave it to the bloody

165

Protestant! Gets into the box — takes the Book — and *then* tells the bloody truth! — Near gets me acquitted! And I in a sweat to get back!

RUCTIONS: Wasn't he right to tell the truth?

JAKEY (*understandingly*): That might happen to any man to get himself out of the trouble! Of course! Could happen to a bishop! — But, Holy God! to tell the truth after givin' me his sacred word!

RUCTIONS (*anxiously*): You're sure those things are all right?

JAKEY: 'Course! Rolled up snug, they are, in oiled rags: six rounds in each.

RUCTIONS (*after pause, devitalized*): I'm worried.

JAKEY: I can see that.

RUCTIONS: About you!

JAKEY: Me?

RUCTIONS: What brought you back? On my account? To give me the stuff?

JAKEY (*hesitant*): Well — yes — as a matter of fact.

RUCTIONS: Straight. Was there any other reason?

JAKEY (*reluctantly*): Well, between you *and* the missus, Maisie: She was at me again. All the time! About gettin' married. That's what brung me out, in the first place. To test the ground — see how she was shapin'. But I knew I'd have to come back — to get out of harm's way.

Enter Kevin.

RUCTIONS (*assures Kevin about Jakey*): I think it's all right.

KEVIN (*Unbelieving*): I hope so. (*To Jakey.*) Sixteen convictions? Is that right? And only once out on petition?

JAKEY (*truculent*): Seventeen, if ye want to know — countin' the next. (*Indignant.*) If you're smellin' out an informer, ye needn't point the finger at me. Ructions, there, will tell ye: that's not *my* form!

RUCTIONS: Kevin! Jakey helped me to conceal them.

JAKEY (*hastily*): Easy on, there! Not so fast! Jakey concealed nothin'! No, nor mixed nor meddled with nothin'. — As for who gave yez away, youse know yer own know; and I know mine. A shut mouth catches no flies and I'll be the wiser, after!

RUCTIONS (*to Jakey*): Shut up, you damned fool! Landing yourself into trouble. (*To Kevin.*) There's no evidence against him.

JAKEY (*abuses Kevin*): No. No more nor there was against Pat — and that much was *too* much! But I can and will prove me innocence, if and when I have to. Not that I want to bring out the dirt! But many's the man that hit the ground for want o' speakin' up!

KEVIN (*provocatively*): Speak up, then! Bring out the dirt!

RUCTIONS (*intervenes*): Wait, Kevin! Wait! (*To Jakey.*) Slip down and bring me up one.

JAKEY (*innocently*): One what?

RUCTIONS (*angry shout*): Go on! Do as I tell you!

Exit Jakey, sulkily.

KEVIN: What's that going to prove?

RUCTIONS: That he's done his job?

KEVIN: What does he mean bring out the dirt?

RUCTIONS (*impatiently*): I'll find out what he means: he'll tell you nothing: you're hostile.

KEVIN: Suppose he's walking us into it.

RUCTIONS (*emphatic*): He's not.

KEVIN (*threat*): If anything does go wrong —

RUCTIONS: It won't go wrong — it's cut and dried.

KEVIN (*grimly*): If it does — we've got a hostage.

RUCTIONS (*glance after Jakey*): You mean — Ja — ?

KEVIN (*grimly*): This plan of yours simplifies things: we've decided to work with five — and leave a gun — for the hostage.

RUCTIONS: Kevin, it's not like you to let yourself get on edge, like this.

KEVIN (*uncompromising*): Maybe! — The hostage job will go by ballot.

Exit Kevin. After pause enter Maguire.

MAGUIRE: Aidan O'Leary here?

Ructions alerts at voice: but does not look around to answer. Maguire comes in, looks about for himself, hesitates about addressing Ructions, and is about to leave when Ructions stands in his path.

RUCTIONS (*grimly*): Did you give Conor absolution?

Maguire changes mind about speaking: he will not answer in that form.

RUCTIONS (*thunderous*): Did you?

MAGUIRE: I cannot answer that question: at least, I *will* not, in that form.

RUCTIONS (*sneering appreciation*): The seal of the Confessional! Does that cover a three-cornered chat, in the sanctuary of a prison kitchen? — (*Insistent.*) Well? Did you? Answer me! Did you give him absolution?

Maguire maintains a resolute silence.

RUCTIONS (*suddenly miserable*): Did he — did he break the strike?

MAGUIRE (*unwillingly, with a degree of sympathy*): He took food — yes.

RUCTIONS (*revived antagonism*): Under pressure from you! (*Walks away, utterly miserable.*) God! he lost!

MAGUIRE (*utter sincerity*): I rejoice in Egan's victory — in that he achieved the immortality, which is the proper birthright of the soul.

RUCTIONS (*approaches angrily*): Victory! My God, I could kill you for that word. Victory! I could! And I will! I will d'you hear? (*Cold, low-voiced determination.*) I'll wait for you!

MAGUIRE (*unafraid, gently*): I hope not, for both our sakes.

Jakey has entered in middle of it.

MAGUIRE: Ah, Jakey! Where's O'Leary? Aidan O'Leary?

167

JAKEY: O'Leary, Father? He might be out in the exercise yard — will I see, Father?

MAGUIRE (*leaving*): I'll see, myself, thank you. (*Afterthought.*) Don't forget Sunday morning, Jakey: Mass is more than a duty: it's a very, very great privilege. (*Exit Maguire.*)

JAKEY (*comments*): Privilege, whah? Special reserved for men that can't refuse it! — But yer man forgets that six o'clock of a Sunday mornin' is very near Saturday night! (*Gun from bucket.*) Here! See is she all right.

Ructions unrolls oiled rag, looks at gun, looks at door, Maguire in mind.

JAKEY (*part thought-reading*): Ye're in bad form, whah? Conor, whah? I s'pose the man o' God told ye? (*Sighs.*) I could've tellin' ye meself.

RUCTIONS: Why didn't you?

Ructions cleans and polishes gun with oiled rag, almost with affection.

JAKEY (*doubtfully*): Well, now — after the way ye took it about George, like: ye went very near to jump on me corpse for readin' ye the bit out o' the paper! — You're a very hard man to tell anythin' to. — Mouth Phelan it was told me. But I didn't altogether believe him. I would've sayin' that the thing that'd most be on a man's mind, after thirty days, would be a good feed: But Mouth said, no! — brandy! (*Ructions continues cleaning gun, absorbed, so that Jakey finds it difficult to broach Mrs. Egan subject.*) Did I tell ye I seen Con's wife? Early, that was, at the gate. Cut up! Ye wouldn't give tuppence for her: though she must've been good-lookin' in her day. — Said it was all on her account, that he done it!

RUCTIONS (*laconic*): A woman!

JAKEY (*warming to it*): Give out he done it to punish her! On account of she had a brother-in-law, a sergeant in the rawsers. And told me to tell O'Leary.

RUCTIONS (*his attention not wholly caught*): Rubbish! Fantastic!

JAKEY: All the same — s'posin' it was true — that the sergeant-in-law got wind o' the word, and let it slip —

RUCTIONS (*impatiently*): Wind of what word?

JAKEY: Like — the time o' the raid —

RUCTIONS (*throws down oiled rag on bed*): Oh, shut up! — I want to think.

JAKEY (*abandons effort*): Right!

RUCTIONS (*after deliberation*): Jakey, I think you're entitled to know — you're under suspicion, as a tout.

JAKEY (*worried*): A man with half an eye could see that from that Kevin fella's puss. (*Touch of panic.*) That's why I'd like ye to see O'Leary. See him, Ructions, and tell him! Tell him that ye know, for a fact . . .

RUCTIONS (*unresponsive*): And what *do* I know — for a fact?

JAKEY (*aggrieved*): That's all me thanks! (*Fright.*) See him, Ructions! See him now!

RUCTIONS (*unsympathetic*): In a sweat, eh? There's nothing against you — you fool! — except what you say, yourself. What *did* you mean bring out the dirt? (*No reply.*) Well, what?

Ructions still holding gun, has it, unwittingly, pointed at Jakey.

JAKEY (*hesitant*): God, ye're a terrible hard man to tell anythin' to. And that bloody yoke in yer hand doesn't make ye any the easier!

RUCTIONS (*lowers gun*): Fire ahead! (*Presses.*) Well, what?

JAKEY (*hesitant*): I told ye before — Mrs. Egan — Conor's wife — and this china Burke, the sergeant.

RUCTIONS: You know Burke?

JAKEY: Know him! Every dog goin' the road knows Burke!

RUCTIONS: What of him?

JAKEY: He told her there'd be a squad outside, a sitdown raid, in the warders' houses, just at the gate, to meet you.

RUCTIONS (*attention caught*): A sitdown? (*Puzzled.*) How could *he* know about the escape?

JAKEY: *She* told him, I tell ye — she gave it away — it was her that split, in the first go-off: not that chap, George or poor oul' Pat. (*This penetrates to Ructions, slowly: he rises, gun in hand, in a slow rage; Jakey panics and fumbles in his clothes as he backs away.*) She did: she did: I swear she did! The woman told me: she told me herself: she did: she did: it's all writ down here in the letter: ye can read it with yer own two eyes.

RUCTIONS (*advances in cold rage*): Show me the letter — (*as Jakey fumbles*) — if ye haven't lost it!

JAKEY (*fumbles with and fails*): I could've sworn I — it's gone! Gone with the wind! (*Panics.*) I must've losin' it — droppin' it in reception, and I changin' out o' me good clothes. (*Sees Ructions advance.*) I swear — I swear —

Ructions grips Jakey by the throat.

RUCTIONS: I've a damned good mind to let them plug you — or plug you myself, you dirty scum!

JAKEY: Ructions, don't! For God's sake, don't! Don't, Ructions!

RUCTIONS (*throws Jakey to ground*): You'd like us to shoot Burke? You rotten degenerate! Even when truth is on your side, you must plaster it with a string of lies, and produce something fantastic! (*Points gun at Jakey.*) It's a lie, isn't it? Say it is! Say it's a damned lie! By God! I'll spread your guts around!

Jakey, terror-stricken, cannot speak: he nods his head vigorously.

RUCTIONS (*shouts*): Say it! Do you hear? Say it!

JAKEY (*pants*): Yes, Ructions — a lie, yes — it is, it is — yes, yes, fan-fan-fantastic!

RUCTIONS (*stands back from him*): Get up! (*As Jakey slowly rises, Ruc-*

tions says with emotion.) If you take my advice — you'll keep your dirty, slanderous tongue off Conor Egan's widow.

Enter Dunne, good-humoredly.

DUNNE (*to Ructions*): Kevin. He wants you. Now! (*Levity.*) He's holding a raffle.

RUCTIONS (*to Dunne*): All right! I'm coming. (*Exit Dunne. Ructions turns at doorway, contemptuously yet considerately speaks to Jakey.*) I'll speak to O'Leary.

JAKEY (*subdued, grateful*): Thanks.

Exit Ructions, gun in belt. Jakey is fingering his hurt throat, when enter Muscles, very unsure of his welcome, dressed in his own clothes, several sizes too large for him.

JAKEY (*surprised*): Muscles! What happened?

MUSCLES (*laconic*): Them fieldglasses! They were got!

JAKEY: Yer good glasses! Got! Weren't them yer own? Ye told me ye found them!

MUSCLES (*contempt*): Found them!

JAKEY (*abuse*): Ye have to tell something fantastic. It's never the truth: and't never the lie. If ye'd only stick to one or th' other: it's tellin' the both that chokes ye.

MUSCLES (*retaliates*): You'll catch it hot and heavy when me sister Maisey sees ye.

JAKEY (*annoyed*): Ye're always Maiseyin' out o' ye! — What for?

MUSCLES: For jewkin' out o' the marriage.

JAKEY: Queer thing! When a man has to come in here for a bit o' peace. (*Attacks.*) You're the nice brother-in-law, blew the gaff I was innocent!

MUSCLES (*astonished*): Me! Blew the gaff? Aw, no, Jakey! That I may stiffen! She asked me. I swore you were solid guilty!

JAKEY (*appeased, retracts*): Did ye? Fair enough!

MUSCLES (*after pause, pleads*): Is it worth me while changin' me oul' clothes? (*Jakey makes no answer.*) Is it? Jakey? Worth me while?

JAKEY (*roughly*): And put in yer day here scratchin' yerself!

MUSCLES (*indignant*): Who? Scratchin' hisself?

JAKEY: Even itchy, ye're too lazy!

MUSCLES (*produces packet cigarettes*): Is it, Jakey?

JAKEY (*sees cigarettes*): Go on then and change yer oul' duds.

Muscles gives Jakey cigarette and light: lights butt for himself.

JAKEY (*takes a welcome smoke*): I'd be glad to be back in th' oul' kitchen, where nobody promises ye nothin': but ye get a bit o' whatever is goin'. (*As Muscles is leaving.*) Better leave them dossies with me.

Muscles parts with cigarettes unwillingly. Exit Muscles. Enter Ructions and Aidan, urgent tempo.

170

RUCTIONS (*to Jakey*): Get those articles down now. (*To Aidan.*) Where?

AIDAN: Kevin's cell.

RUCTIONS (*to Jakey*): Take them to cell number thirteen. Quickly!

JAKEY: I'll do no such thing! You can collect them from me, down below.

RUCTIONS: Right! Hurry! And wait till I come.

Exit Jakey.

RUCTIONS (*unusually gentle*): O'Leary, hadn't you better let me do this strike?

AIDAN (*distressed, puzzled*): I can't understand why Conor broke it — broke it! — and then died.

RUCTIONS: Because the Reverend Strikebreaker advised him it was mortal sin — dinned it into him, day after day.

AIDAN (*insistent*): It isn't: it isn't! It can't be that.

RUCTIONS: Take the escape, O'Leary: and let me carry on.

AIDAN (*resolute*): McGowan, I've told you: I mean it: you go — I stay!

Enter Dunne, elatedly reports to Aidan, handing him slip of paper.

DUNNE: Reporting as a result of ballot. I drew hostage. (*Relaxes from attention.*) I take it that means I'm coming on the escape team?

AIDAN (*in difficulty*): No, Dunne. I'm — I'm afraid it doesn't. — Kevin will tell you your duties: he will also give you a gun.

DUNNE (*disappointed*): Oh!

AIDAN: There's — there's a job!

DUNNE (*resumes disciplined behavior*): Very good! (*Exit Dunne.*)

Enter Maguire, almost colliding with Dunne's exit.

MAGUIRE (*sees O'Leary*): Ah, O'Leary — here you are! I've been looking for you.

Maguire pulls up short at Aidan's obvious distress, and Ructions' unconcealed hostility.

AIDAN (*hesitant*): Father, I — I want to ask you something —

RUCTIONS (*puts question for him, crudely*): Did you break Conor off the strike?

MAGUIRE: — I did my duty toward Egan.

RUCTIONS: Didn't you set yourself out to break him?

MAGUIRE (*slowly*): Not to break him — to make him!

RUCTIONS: Didn't you tell him it was suicide? Tell him, in my own presence? In the kitchen?

MAGUIRE: I told him it could be.

RUCTIONS (*bitterly*): You sowed the ground with a crop that flowered when the blood supply to his brain failed — choking the facts — obscuring the truth — splitting his simple objective into a thousand fragments. (*To Aidan.*) That's your incipient bishop! Infallible — and mistaken! (*After

171

pause, to Maguire.) After that, it was simple! (*Appeals to O'Leary.*)
O'Leary, I put it to you: how can *you* do a hunger strike? How?

MAGUIRE (*appalled*): A hunger strike? Another?

AIDAN (*resolute*): I can! I will!

Jakey is at door.

JAKEY (*impatiently*): I can't wait all day: I've to lug down that dixie tray.

RUCTIONS: I'm coming.

Exit Ructions, Jakey collects tray, and seeing opportunity to clear his personal position through Maguire, he returns.

JAKEY: Excuse me, Father. I seen Mrs. Egan this mornin', below in the waitin' room: and she wanted to see you badly urgent.

MAGUIRE (*compassionately*): Yes, yes, I saw her.

JAKEY (*greatly concerned*): I hope she told ye the whole ins and outs — it's very important for all concerned — you see the way it is —

MAGUIRE: Yes, yes, poor creature: she was with me for some time.

JAKEY: I was thinkin', Father — if you told Mr. O'Leary —

MAGUIRE (*interrupts*): Quite right! It might avert tragedy.

JAKEY (*personal emphasis*): That's right, Father — a tragedy!

MAGUIRE (*dismisses Jakey*): You may leave all that to me, Jakey. And, thank you, Jakey.

JAKEY (*leaving emphatically*): No. Father — thank *you*! Thank you very much, Father! (*Exit Jakey.*)

MAGUIRE (*to Aidan*): This can't be true: another strike?

AIDAN: It is true. Either McGowan or I. And I defy you to say it is suicide.

MAGUIRE (*appeals*): O'Leary, after what has happened isn't this insane?

AIDAN (*defiantly angry*): Is it? Is it suicide?

MAGUIRE (*appeals*): I say to you, as I said to Egan: consider the end in view: consider the means chosen; consider them well: for sin may lurk in either.

AIDAN (*angry, approaches*): Did you say to Mrs. Egan that her husband's death was suicide?

MAGUIRE (*quiet bombshell*): No, O'Leary. She said it to me.

AIDAN (*stunned*): She — ?

MAGUIRE: She told me that it would be. I saw her husband afterwards.

AIDAN (*at a loss*): She told — you — ?

MAGUIRE: She used the word. She told me that, and much besides, and when I saw Egan, I questioned him.

AIDAN (*fearful to answer*): And when — you questioned — ?

MAGUIRE (*declining direct answer, turns away*): I later heard his confession.

AIDAN (*desperately*): And then — did he — did he?

MAGUIRE: You must think what you like. I cannot answer any question. — It may console you to know, that I both believe and hope that he died in the state of grace — thanks be to the good God!

172

AIDAN (*outburst*): Con's death wasn't suicide — it's a slander — a filthy slander! I know! I know! I know!

MAGUIRE (*gentleness giving place to tone of rebuke*): Don't shout at me! I have been gentle with this other boy — this foolish lad McGowan. I may not be so with you! His mind is a rubbish heap, packed with snippets from the popular press. He has glanced at the outlines of everything, and finished up in a maze. But *his* grievances are just — are real — so real that they choke his mind with anger, and terrible indignation. So blind with anger, he cannot see the wood for the trees, nor the vision of God for the golden bough. So angry that he cannot hear. He cannot hear, for he will not listen. He hates us all. Hates us, because we failed him. But he is not indifferent: in that lies his salvation. If we failed him — there's something we *have* to give — something we withheld: if there is *something* — then, he believes. (*Quietly.*) McGowan's anger will subside — oh, yes, it will — in God's good time — then we can help him remake his soul. — And God's good time may be quite soon — sooner than any of us think — an elemental situation.

AIDAN: What do you mean by an elemental situation?

MAGUIRE: When a man faces death — he discerns his real motives.

AIDAN (*shocked*): You mean — hunger strike?

MAGUIRE: It well may be.

AIDAN (*walks away, in bitter anger*): And that's *all* it means to you!

MAGUIRE (*philosophic perspective, not unsympathetic*): What *more* should it mean? (*Challenge.*) What *is* this summum bonum which is not the attainment of God?

AIDAN (*studied taunt*): Sounding brass and tinkling cymbal! (*Tirade, after pause.*) If McGowan's mind is a rubbish heap, it is you who neglected to teach him — neglected to build on the vacant lot. You who starved him spiritually! The food on which he might have thriven was deemed too strong for his consumption. Truth, you held, was a dangerous thing: it might lead to excess: and since excess was sin, truth must be doled in short measure!

MAGUIRE: You yourself once thought of priesthood?

AIDAN (*sore spot*): What if I did?

MAGUIRE: And now? Anti-cleric?

AIDAN (*with bite*): Every serious Catholic is! Must be!

MAGUIRE (*diffidently*): My son, would you not try again?

AIDAN (*scouts idea, turning away*): No, no, no, no — (*Turns back again, aggressively.*) — But make no mistake! — I'm nursing no broken chalice!

MAGUIRE (*intrigued*): Broken chalice?

AIDAN: The symbol is James Joyce's.

MAGUIRE (*detects an affinity*): Ah, yes, of course! — Poor Joyce! — He too — thought of priesthood?

AIDAN (*defensive*): What if he did?

MAGUIRE (*disarmingly*): Nothing! Nothing whatever! (*Long pause.*) Saint Thomas's definition of pride: you remember? The inordinate desire to excel.

AIDAN: Aquinas! Yes. Why?

MAGUIRE (*quietly*): Saint Thomas, I prefer to call him. — Pride does not easily yield. Indeed, it seldom repents. Especially pride frustrated. It is a match for any situation — even the elemental.

AIDAN: What is this? (*Rises.*) What are you trying to suggest?

MAGUIRE: Pride pursues the noblest ideal — pursues the good — relentlessly — inordinately — turns to the good that perishes from the good that perishes not!

AIDAN (*in rage*): Strikebreaker! You are! Get out! Get out!

MAGUIRE (*quietly*): I have finished. (*Sighs wearily, goes to exit, halts, and turns.*) If you bait and spring a trap for your soul — *you* will effect your release? Thou *shalt* not tempt the Lord thy God! (*Exit Maguire.*)

Aidan reflects, aghast at the possible truth of Maguire's suggestion: he stands shocked: suddenly he is roused from inertia by the sound of triangle on the circle. Enter Ructions and Kevin, the latter with two guns and autograph album.

KEVIN (*reports to Aidan*): All in position. O'Shea on A, with Micheál on C. A little bit worried about Fitz: but Tommy will give him a hand from D. A wing is finished and locked up. Juvenile wing must be nearly done. Then it's up to take the circle. Which of you is it to be, with me?

RUCTIONS: Aidan goes. I stay.

Kevin looks to Aidan for decision: Aidan is silent.

JAKEY (*sticks in his head and calls*): Mouth Phelan is comin' down the wing. D'ye hear, Ructions — he's on me heels!

Exit Jakey. Ructions takes the gun from Kevin, goes to door and leans casually against it, waiting for Phelan, whom Ructions now sees in passage. Kevin leaves autograph album on bed.

RUCTIONS (*calls Phelan*): Hey, Phelan, listen — tell me this —

PHELAN (*fussily*): Can't now — The chief is on the circle.

RUCTIONS: What did Conor have to eat when he came off the strike?

PHELAN (*unable to resist temptation to air medical knowledge*): Eat! Sure, the stomach couldn't take any food, man.

RUCTIONS (*humility of ignorance*): Couldn't it?

Phelan moves in, speaking: Kevin moves in between Phelan and door.

PHELAN: The most he could get was peptonized milk and a thimbleful of brandy.

KEVIN (*exits past Phelan, moving Phelan further inside cell*): Excuse me! (*Exit Kevin.*)

RUCTIONS (*looks out to check position*): Brandy? Why brandy?

PHELAN (*full conversational stride*): To maintain the cardiac action — th' oul' ticker, ye know! Ye see, the way it is —

RUCTIONS (*peremptory*): Take off your coat!

PHELAN: Me coat? me — me — (*Sees gun in Ructions' hand.*) God-tonight-and-tomorrow — (*Makes automatic sign of cross.*)

RUCTIONS (*removes Phelan's cap*): And your cap.

Aidan, in position behind Phelan, helps him take off coat, and puts it on himself, Ructions whistles, and enter Dunne and Corrigan, armed with stool legs.

RUCTIONS (*to Dunne*): Across the wing, Bill! to thirteen. (*To Phelan.*) I hope you're not superstitious. (*Dunne and Corrigan get Phelan between them.*) Spring the lock, Corrigan: and stay with him till it's over.

Exeunt Dunne, Corrigan, and Phelan. Ructions looks out into passage, then turns to Aidan.

RUCTIONS (*to Aidan*): Okay! It's clear. Kevin's waiting.

Aidan has adjusted cap and coat: he is quiet and perhaps ashamed: he holds out hand for handshake, Ructions, after moment's hesitation, puts gun in Aidan's hand.

RUCTIONS: That's yours. Good luck!

Exit Aidan. After pause, Ructions goes to door to watch operation: he tenses, watching them converge on circle. A shout from the exercise yard at first frightens him, then he smiles, recollecting the Cluiche Ciseach. Lights cigarette and stands on bed to watch progress of Cluiche Ciseach. Enter Jakey, hurriedly, stops at door to keep in touch with events without himself being seen.

JAKEY (*excited commentary*): Right as the mail! Goin', goodo, they are! 'Clare to me God, a sight for sore eyes.

RUCTIONS (*comes to door*): So far so good. There's the gate to the passage yet — then the front office — that's no fun! — and then — then the main gate! (*To Jakey.*) Who's on it? Old Riordan?

JAKEY: He was this mornin': I'd say he'd be terrible quick to get out o' harm's way. Sure, they're laughin' man — they're laughin'. Nothin' to stop them. Away on a hack!

RUCTIONS (*soberly, going to window again*): Easy — if you say it quick.

JAKEY (*anxious*): I only hope Mrs. Egan was wrong — and there's no one there to meet them. (*Proposes.*) I'll grease up to D3 — get a rare oul' view from there — from the road up to the main gate.

RUCTIONS (*sternly*): Stay where you are.

JAKEY (*presses*): Ye can see down past the warders' houses.

RUCTIONS (*adamant*): Stay! We don't want to distract them with any unnecessary movement.

JAKEY (*resignedly*): Right ye be! (*Anxious.*) If she was right aself — ah, but sure she couldn't be: is it to pay men good money, and have them on their backsides, sittin' down there for a month? (*A cheer from the basketball players.*) D'ye hear them Clife Ciseachs?

RUCTIONS: Who?

JAKEY: Them Clife Ciseachs, or whatever ye call them — them fellas playin' basketball? (*Indignantly.*) Sure ye wouldn't hear a volley o' shots with that unholy row! (*Ructions laughs. Jakey looks out again, interestedly. Reports.*) They have the lot — the whole bunch — all together, like Brown's cows — and the chief himself, in the middle! I wonder would he ask me now, where am I goin' with the bucket! Strange when ye see a pale-faced man, that used to have such a good color! — They're lockin' them up! 'Clare to me God! And they're goin' in too, meek as Moses. (*Ructions comes over to verify: then jumps up again on the bed straining to get a view from the window.*) And th' oul' chief! In he goes, like any oul' lag! It's a wonder they wouldn't give him a prod, and when he resists, plug him! They might prod in vain! No hair on him! He's not goin' to lose his life. No, but, maybe he'll lose his job! (*Disappointed.*) They might only dock his pension. (*Hand to heart.*) Me heart's goin' like the hammers o' hell! (*Assigns reason.*) When the time comes, every man's a patriot. (*Proof.*) Nothin' 'd suit me betther now, only go down with a gun in me mitt and blow the head offa th' oul' chief. (*Tapering.*) More than the half o' them in now! The warders in the cells, and the prisoners outside. As good as a pantomime! (*To Ructions enthusiastically.*) Ructions, you should've goin'. Ye still could — go on, man! — now is yer chance — the ball at yer foot — and the two o' them is on the circle still. Mrs. Egan was crazy.

RUCTIONS: I'm staying.

JAKEY: Is it? — I suppose it is — another hunger strike? (*Ructions does not answer: Jakey comes over from door.*) Ye know yer own business best — but take care now! — I'm tellin' ye, as a friend, mind ye — take care, would ye bite off more than ye can chew.

Enter Muscles, alarmed.

JAKEY (*roughly*): Where d'ye think you're goin'?

MUSCLES: Hey, Jakey, there's somethin' up!

JAKEY (*flattening*): The sky's up: that's what's up!

MUSCLES: I jewked out when I heard all the commotion.

JAKEY (*discounts*): What commotion? There was *no* commotion.

MUSCLES (*rapid tempo*): All the commotion, and all the screws was on parade, like they were knockin' off for dinner — so I jewked in again, for fear I'd be seen – then, after a bit, jewked out again: there wasn't a single warder there! Not a sight or light o' the one o' them! Only a few politicals, standin' round, and slammin' doors: ye'd think they were after buyin' the joint!

JAKEY: Ye jewked in and ye jewked out! I told ye to clean them lavaterries and stay there till I called ye. Didn't I? Well, go back and do them.

MUSCLES (*protests*): I done them. (*Admiringly.*) I done them lovely!

JAKEY (*exasperated*): Well, then go back and *dirty* them, and *then* clean them again!

Exit Muscles.

JAKEY (*looks out*): They're gone! Not a sinner there! Will I slip up to D3 now? Can see the main gate from there.

RUCTIONS (*quietly*): Right! Let me know when the first leaves.

JAKEY (*jubilant*): I will so! (*About to leave, finds letter in pocket. Turns.*) If it was a dog, it'd bite me! – the letter! – stickin' in the linin', it was – Mrs. Conor's letter. (*Hands to Ructions.*) Ye can be havin' a read of it. (*Goes towards exit.*)

RUCTIONS: Wait! (*Opens letter.*)

JAKEY (*impatiently*): Ye'll have me late: they'll be gone.

RUCTIONS (*appalled at letter*): So it was Conor's wife! It was she! Gave it way! – brought on the raid! – and – Oh, God! – poor Conor!

JAKEY (*resentfully*): Nothin' about poor Jakey: blamin' me in the wrong.

RUCTIONS: I knew you weren't guilty.

JAKEY (*unappeased*): Quare way of treatin' an innocent man! Stick a gun in his kisser, after fellin' him to the ground! Still and all, might be worse! I got to me feet again: them other two stayed where they fell.

RUCTIONS (*angry*): George! – And Geraghty! Yes, by God! she *should* be – she *should* be executed.

JAKEY (*disagrees*): Should she, though? Sergeant Charley'd get my vote. All that poor woman done was try and save what she lost – her man.

RUCTIONS (*reconsiders*): Yes. Suppress it. Say nothing about that letter to anyone, d'you hear?

JAKEY: Sing dumb? I'm game!

RUCTIONS: I want your *oath*.

JAKEY (*resolute*): Oath? I'll go further; I'll gi' ye me word of honor. (*As Ructions is about to pocket letter.*) Ye seen where she said about the squad – waitin'?

RUCTIONS (*paces, considering: then dismisses possibility*): There'll be no squad: if they thought we had got the guns in, they'd have raided us again.

JAKEY (*doubtful agreement*): I s'pose. All the same – better that *I* keep that letter: it's me only proof – outside of Father Maguire.

RUCTIONS (*dismisses suggestion*): And lose it again? You need no proof: I'll destroy it.

JAKEY (*accepts overriding*): So be! (*Jocose.*) But, just in case — don't destroy Father Maguire. (*Recalled to escape.*) I better skip, or I'll miss it all.

Exit Jakey. Ructions pockets letter; slight pause, and Aidan enters. Ructions' back is turned, and Aidan is divesting himself of warder's coat and cap when Ructions sees him.

RUCTIONS: Well?

AIDAN: We've a clear path. Straight through the passages. The uniform was invaluable: got me across the courtyard: we're holding the main gate now. Tommy 'phoned: there should be a car waiting. (*Significantly.*) Kevin is on the circle — waiting. (*Meaning does not penetrate.*) Go on!

RUCTIONS: What?

AIDAN (*severely*): Go on, I said! Get out!

RUCTIONS: But — but — I'm not going — I'm staying.

AIDAN (*angry*): You're taking orders! You're going!

RUCTIONS (*angry*): I'm staying!

AIDAN: You're in action — taking orders. (*Ructions shakes head in refusal. Aidan raises gun.*) I swear, McGowan, I will! That's the penalty. Thirty seconds!

Ructions, about to speak, changes mind and stands waiting.

AIDAN (*lowering gun, softens tone to an appeal*): It's mine, McGowan. It's my job. *You* know that.

RUCTIONS (*all hostility gone*): All right, Aidan. Perhaps — it is. (*Extends hand.*) Good luck!

AIDAN (*changes gun to left hand for handshake*): Thanks. (*Hands gun to Ructions.*) Yours, Ructions — and Tommy has your ring.

Aidan turns his back on Ructions, who exits, at a run. After a pause, enter Muscles, whose eye, from the moment of entry, fastens on warder's coat. Aidan stands on bed to see escape.

MUSCLES (*palpable excuse*): Ye didn't see Jakey about?

AIDAN (*coldly*): He's not here.

MUSCLES: No. — He must be — somewhere else?

AIDAN: Yes.

MUSCLES (*delays*): Mr. O'Leary — ye wouldn't happen to have an oul' smoke — like — would ye?

AIDAN: I don't smoke.

MUSCLES (*accepts verdict*): No. (*Hope springs eternal.*) A bit of dust would do — or even a bit o' hard tack.

Aidan does not answer. Machinegun fire in distance.

MUSCLES: I wonder who owns th' oul' coat, whah? (*No answer.*) It's like a warder's coat. (*No answer.*) Some oul' screw! Ye'd think a screw'd know better than to leave his topcoat hangin' round? God knows what's in them pockets: money, maybe! Or tobacco. Deserves to have it took, he does! Askin' for it, that's what he is! (*Picks up coat. Fingers it.*) Nice bit o' stuff that's in it too!

AIDAN (*turns round*): Put it down, and get out!

MUSCLES: What harm am I doin'? I'm not goin' to run away with it, am I?

AIDAN (*advances*): Get out!

MUSCLES (*retreating, pointedly*): Might be safer with me than where it is. (*Exit Muscles.*)

Another burst of machinegun fire. After long pause, enter Jakey, running, and calling out: "Ructions, Ructions!" He pulls up short, when he comes into cell and sees Aidan.

JAKEY: Ructions, Ructions! (*Sees Aidan.*) Oh, it's you — Mr. O'Leary. (*Nonplussed.*) You're not — you're not — Ructions.

AIDAN: Who?

JAKEY: Th' other chap — McGowan — Ructions —

AIDAN: He's not here.

JAKEY: No. (*Drops head despondently.*) It — it doesn't matter — a whole lot — now.

Jakey stands there despondently. Aidan, though his attention is caught, remains impassive, impersonal.

JAKEY (*lifts head*): I seen the taxi at the gate —

AIDAN (*alive*): Yes?

JAKEY: And the squad car pullin' across the road, right in the middle, to block it —

AIDAN: What!

JAKEY (*graphic*): Round with the taxi behind her — and up onto the path — the squad car hadn't time to reverse — then a burst o' machinegun fire — from the warders' houses — they must've been lyin' in ambush there. Down off the path with her, onto the road — but whoever was in her must've been riddled — and on she careered down the length o' the drive, and away with her round the corner.

AIDAN (*tensed*): And McGowan? Ructions?

JAKEY (*on verge of tears*): That's what I came down to see — was it him, at all — he missed th' oul' taxi — they wouldn't wait — and he started to run like the hammers o' hell, tryin' to catch up — he was wastin' his time! — then the second burst come — he hit the ground a unmerciful bang — like a bellyflop on wather. He never moved. It was him, all right. It was Ructions.

Cheers from basketball players mingle with the hammering on the cell doors by captive warders.

JAKEY: D'ye hear them now, tryin' to get out? Th' oul' screws. They'll bring the bloody house down. I better go, before the ruckey really starts. (*Afterthought.*) And Mr. O'Leary if anyone asks ye — ye didn't see me, high-up or low-down. All I know is, I was below — me and Muscles — givin' them a good do-out. (*Passes Aidan to get bucket.*) 'Scuse me!

Jakey picks up bucket, and faces Aidan, so that Jakey's back is to the doorway when Dunne enters with gun, followed by O'Sullivan and Corrigan.

JAKEY (*to Aidan*): If I'd've stayin' out and gettin' married, this mightn't've happened. Isn't that strange?

AIDAN (*coldly, looking at Dunne*): We know!

JAKEY (*misses implication, turning to leave*): One off!

DUNNE: Come along, Jakey!

JAKEY: What's — ? (*Panics, drops bucket, to Aidan.*) The letter? The letter! Did Ructions give ye the letter?

Dunne covers Jakey with gun. O'Sullivan and Corrigan start to drag Jakey from cell.

JAKEY (*screams to Aidan*): The letter! The letter! (*Screams throughout operation of removal from cell and from passage, when he has been dragged off. Exit Jakey.*) Father Maguire! Father Maguire! Father Maguire knows about the letter — he knows — he knows — he knows — (*Jakey's screams continue until he is out of earshot.*)

DUNNE (*to Aidan*): What letter? What does he mean Father Maguire knows about the letter?

AIDAN (*coldly resolute*): To gain time. You haven't much time to give him; but give him whatever you can — to make his peace with God.

Exit Dunne, gun in hand. Aidan walks toward window. The sounds of basketball players are louder, almost jubilant, mingled with the hammering on cell doors. Aidan picks up from bed autograph album, looks at it, deliberating. The sound of a single shot is heard. Aidan finds fountain pen and signs autograph album. After long pause, enter Dunne, gun held limply, he seems dazed by the accomplished act, almost panicked.

AIDAN (*sights Dunne*): The cistern? The cistern? You didn't put it back? (*Dunne is too dazed to reply. He shakes his head.*) Damnation! (*Aidan takes oiled rag from bed, takes gun, wipes fingerprints in rag, rolls gun in rag. Nodding direction of bed.*) Pick it up! (*Dunne picks up warder's coat, and holds it up.*) Higher, damn you, higher! (*Dunne holds higher to facilitate access to pocket, Aidan rams the wrapped gun into pocket, and throws coat on bed. Points far side of chess table.*) There! Sit down! (*Dunne listlessly does as bidden. Aidan sits opposite him.*) Move! Go on, move! Make a move — any move! (*Dunne is immobile, paralyzed. Aidan moves a chessman. More gently, to encourage him.*) Now! Go on! It's easy! (*Dunne, with an effort, succeeds in making a move. Aidan, as though pondering next move.*) We'll play this out to a finish.

Sound of triangle on circle, being beaten incessantly, in alarm, the jail resounding to the din. The curtain comes down very slowly.

♣ *BRYAN MacMAHON* ♣

LISTOWEL in County Kerry is a quiet, rather out-of-the-way, little market town, but it has made an inordinately large and important contribution to modern Irish letters. From it came that strange genius George Fitzmaurice, the popular novelist Maurice Walsh who is well known for his story *The Quiet Man*, and, as we shall see, one of the most exciting of the young dramatists, John B. Keane. From it also came Bryan Mac-Mahon the author of *Song of the Anvil*.

In the United States, which he occasionally visits to lecture in universities, MacMahon is known for his fiction. His first collection of short stories, *The Lion Tamer and Other Stories* of 1949, went through three printings in its first two months. His other books include *Children of the Rainbow* of 1952, *The Red Petticoat* of 1955, a children's story, *Jack O'Moora and the King of Ireland's Son*, and in 1967 *The Honey Spike*, a novel based on his play of the same name.

He was born in 1909. His mother was a schoolteacher, and he himself, despite his lecturing jaunts to Harvard or the Iowa Writers Workshop, has taught in the primary school at Listowel for thirty-five years. For ten years, until it became too demanding, he also ran a bookshop in Listowel. He founded the Listowel Drama Group which existed for seventeen years before splitting into two separate groups. His first playwriting was done to give the society some easy farces to play.

A couple of these early pieces have been published pseudonymously, but they are unimportant, conventional work. His first serious play was a *Juno*-like family tragedy, *The Bugle in the Blood*, which the Abbey did in March, 1949. Although a little dated now, the play has some splendid

O'Caseyan effects from MacMahon's use of song and poetry and of comedy and tragedy abruptly juxtaposed. Some of the characters, particularly the comic ones, are a bit broader than life, but the fire-breathing patriot of a mother could be a devastating role in the hands of a good actress.

Song of the Anvil, MacMahon's second Abbey play, is a much more individual piece and reflects the author's interest in folklore and fantasy. Although it is deeply rooted in the daily life of the west of Ireland and deeply engrossing just as a story, it exists also as an almost allegorical comment about how a basic Irish need for a bit of color in one's life can only be satisfied by a fusion of the traditional and the modern. There seem to be four chief forces in the play: there is the classic story-telling of Ireland, exemplified by Ulick Madigan; there is the force of pagan superstition, exemplified by that semi-sinister wizard Darby Jer O'Shea; there is the Christian force, embodied in the initially ineffectual and drunken Father O'Priest McHugh; and there is the force of youth and the modern world, embodied in the Irish-American girl Ellenrose Schneider. MacMahon's meaning is pointed strongly by the ending, when Ulick is absolved from the bonds of the past to marry Ellenrose and when Father O'Priest, taking Ulick's place, fuses Christianity and Irish tradition in a new biblical Irish wonder tale about a man named Christy Love.

The theatrical values of the play are easily apparent. The play fuses humor, fantasy, satire, and melodrama; its characterization is dramatically droll and yet more than superficially theatrical; and finally it offers a grand opportunity for purely theatrical effects in the use of costumes, dancers, singers, and musicians. It is an original and exciting play, and good enough to hold its own with the similar pastoral fantasies of O'Casey.

One of the play's few rivals is MacMahon's last, *The Honey Spike*, which was first put on at the Abbey on May 22, 1961. This play reflects MacMahon's intimate knowledge of tinker life and lore, and, like Brecht's *Mother Courage*, is one of the few plays to adapt the picaresque structure of the novel. The play tells of a young tinker and his wife who race across Ireland in their cart, from the Giant's Causeway in the north to a hospital, the Honey Spike of the title, in South Kerry. The scenes along the way — at the Border, at Lough Derg, at Killorglin on the Gathering Day of Puck Fair — show us significant Irish types and give us a meaningful cross section of modern Ireland. But in Breda and Martin Claffey, the two young tinkers, MacMahon creates more than significant types; he creates two real and memorable individuals. Breda's anguish when Martin deserts her at Puck Fair and Martin's own agonized speech at Breda's death are two of the saddest and finest scenes in the modern Irish drama. But like *Song of the Anvil*, the play is not all sadness. Woven into it are riddles, ballads, spectacle, fights, a great deal of humorous observation, and a pervasive tension. The only recent work that greatly resembles it in subject or in quality is Faulkner's novel *As I Lay Dying*. And certainly readers of *Song of the Anvil* will not think it exaggerated when I say that *The Honey Spike* may take a very respectable position among the world's great journey literature.

Song of the Anvil

GARRETT GOWA FITZGERALD, a farrier and blacksmith

DEBORAH FITZGERALD, his wife

ULICK MADIGAN, a neighbor

DARBY JER O'SHEA, a small farmer

ELLENROSE SCHNEIDER, niece of Deborah Fitzgerald

MICK-TWIN O'DONNELL, a small farmer

PADDY-TWIN O'DONNELL, his twin brother

KITSY CARTY, a spinster from the neighborhood

FATHER "O'PRIEST" MC HUGH, a priest in retirement

WALTER CUNNINGHAM, a newspaper reporter

Various neighbors of the glen, including strawboys, a melodeon player, a bone tapper, and musicians playing the tin whistle, flute, fiddle, chanter, accordion, and bodhran.

Act I

A summer's evening in the interior of a forge in the coastal valley of Glensharoon, in the Barony of Iveragh, County Kerry. The walls are of cut cliffstone and, though begrimed, gleam with a ferrous or sulphur stain. Midway in the left wall is the semicircular doorway with doors which may be closed in halves. From the doorway a slight ramp descends to the floor. The hearth is right center stage, and the great bellows is to the right of it. The anvil is in front of the hearth. From the main doorway a slightly raised passage runs right around the forge and to the back of a pillar of masonry supporting the roof. Midway in the right wall a step gives access, via a "linney" (leanto) or porch to the dwellinghouse. Left of the hearth is a block which is used as a seat. Downstage from the main doorway is a window of iron latticework with two shutters opening inwards. Beneath the window is a worn log which serves as a stool. Before curtain-rise the ding-dong-diddero of the anvil is heard. Vaguely it beats to the rhythm of "Kryle na Ceardchan" ("The Curse of the

SONG OF THE ANVIL

Forge"), a traditional curse which is rung with a hammer on the anvil. This rhythm will recur, in different forms, throughout the play. As the curtain rises, the smith — Garrett Gowa Fitzgerald — a huge man, of a simple but fierce nature, is seen finishing the dressing of a horseshoe. Ulick Madigan, a young man of twenty-two or twenty-three, his back turned to the forge, his head bent, is blowing on the bellows. Although at intervals we catch glimpses of his profile we do not see his face fully until later in the play. For a few moments the smith continues to work, then taking the horseshoe in the tongs, he plunges it into the trough which is inset on the front of the hearth. He casts the cooled horseshoe to the floor.

GARRETT G.: Horseshoes, by hell! Aye, and the horse to wear them all but skedaddled from the glen. (*Beats time reminiscently on the anvil.*) There's a song of joy and sorrow that'll shortly not be heard again. Wait, Ulick lad, I'll wipe the anvil clean for you. (*He wipes the anvil with his apron.*) Madigan, sit there a while on your anvil throne.

Ulick, groping backwards, sits on the anvil with his shoes on the anvil block and his back to the audience.

GARRETT G.: Day almost down. The sun will soon be quenching in the sea. This forge — a place that saw diversion in its time — now moves to silence and the dark. Ulick! Ulick, is something wrong by you? Has someone sniggered in a pub in Tanavalla town about the fancies and the tales you tell to make us feel we're not a dying breed in Glensharoon? If that's the case, by God! they'll feel the force of Garrett Gowa's right arm.

Ulick does not reply.

GARRETT G.: Ulick, are you not listening with your ears?

Ulick does not reply.

GARRETT G.: Sweet angels' King! I should have known. I saw you just like this before, the time you made us catch a thousand butterflies and let them off inside the empty chapel, to praise, you said, the Lord our God with flutterings. Ulick, you'll listen now? Life is before you, son. Your gifted parents, rest their souls, are dead and gone. Look! Sell your farm to the O'Donnell twins, and ramble out across the sea to where your people are. With brains like yours, there's chances going abegging there.

Ulick does not reply.

GARRETT G.: What holds you here? The sea, the mountains, or the moon's pull? That, or your cursed shelf of books. I warn you that if dreams gain the upper hand inside your head, you'll finish shivering like Father-O'-the-Priest.

Ulick does not reply.

GARRETT G.: All right, *avic*, all right. Walk off upon your variegated road. God in His heaven knows we need commodities like dreams. This glen, that once was thronged with life, is draining fast. We look to you for

187

whims to light our barren lives and keep us all from going raving mad. You'd better make this dream the champion dream of all your life and, as you're at it, lock the whim inside the glen. There's plenty scoffers down in Tanavalla town and maybe traitors nearer home as well . . . But what's the use of my advising you and you not even listening with your ears? There are times I'd like to lift my hand and belt you with a foolish blow across the ear.

Garrett Gowa raises his hand over Ulick's head. Ulick glances up, calmly and authoritatively. The hand drops.

GARRETT G.: This glen is dying, man, I say! Soon Darby Jer with all his superstitions will be our King and then we're surely given to darkness at the last.

Darby Jer O'Shea has entered from the doorway to the road. He is a tall, erect man in the seventies. He is a man of bizarre dignity, dressed in black and wears a wild, black hat. His trouser legs are caught with bicycle clips (though he never rides a bicycle). He wears brown boots, and carries a thumbstick 50 inches high (that is, a peeled stick with a little fork at the top). On occasion he lapses from aloof dignity into unexpected malevolence.

DARBY JER: Welcome or welcome not, I say that Darby Jer is here! (*To Garrett.*) You'd better bid her stop her gallop up at once. She's chasing me from post to pillar all this day.

GARRETT G.: Who had the courage to go chasing Darby Jer O'Shea?

DARBY JER: Her that Brigid, sister to your wife, bred by the queer German narra-back in the queer town of Hartford, Conn. in the U.S.A.

GARRETT G. (*laughs*): You pestered Ellenrose's mother in the days gone by, and you a cranky fellow facing forty then and she a lass with ribbons swinging from her poll. (*Mockingly.*) How does the girl go pestering you at all?

DARBY JER: With questions!

GARRETT G.: Why don't you dart into the Gaelic tongue and pretend that you're dull of what she's asking you?

DARBY JER: I did that same — but she has the Irish learned from her ma!

GARRETT G. (*laughs*): Only a month the girl is here, and yet she's brought a touch of life and wonder into a house, a house that lacks a hound, a cat, or child. Questions will neither kill nor cure.

DARBY JER: There's certain questions can both kill and cure. "And what do you know," she says, "of charms and spells"?

GARRETT G.: She asked a prime authority on subjects such as these.

DARBY JER: What do you signify by that remark?

GARRETT G.: Nothing. Let that hare sit — you hear?

DARBY JER: I'll let the hare sit, if I like. And if I don't . . . (*Seeing Ulick.*) Him! Him beyond! Is he not listening with his ears?

GARRETT G.: He's not. He's belted off to dream this hour or more.

Darby Jer walks all round Ulick, examining him closely.

GARRETT G.: Tell me now, Darby Jer, all capers set aside, would winking at a woman put a stir on him?

DARBY JER (*indignant*): You're out for mockin' me again, I see! Do you begrudge me to come visitin' here?

GARRETT G.: Neither myself nor Deborah, my wife, begrudge you fire and roof, providing only that you . . .

DARBY JER: That I what?

GARRETT G.: For God's good sake, I ask you not to work that other stuff. Wait! For certain I saw a stir in him.

DARBY JER: What's in his brain will out at last and bull the living world. (*Glancing at the linney door.*) Well, by the king and nine of spades, that one is fastened on my track again.

Darby Jer returns, apprehensively, to a seat on the raised passage, upstage, left. Enter Ellenrose Schneider, an American girl of nineteen or so. Her appearance suggests that she is strident — yet in manner she is restrained and sincere.

ELLENROSE: Hi, Uncle Garrett! Hi there, Darby Jer! Hi, Ulick! (*Pause.*) Ulick, hi!

GARRETT G.: No use in calling him!

ELLENROSE: Why not?

GARRETT G.: He isn't listening with his ears, that's all.

ELLENROSE (*walking all round Ulick*): Say! Is Ulick in a daze or does he get the falling fits like Father O'? Or is he just another candidate who won't be happy till he's in the crazy bin?

GARRETT G.: His body's here. His mind has moved away.

ELLENROSE: For folks who claim they don't believe in leprechauns, you've got some mighty odd ideas in Glensharoon. Is he aware what's going on around him in the forge?

GARRETT G.: He's idled off into a most important dream. When he's awake he'll order us what's right to do.

ELLENROSE: It's all so strange and new to me, and yet it's kind of known to me as well. (*Laughs.*)

GARRETT G.: That God send us laughter's cause! Time now to rinse my hands and features of the sweat of the day.

Garrett Gowa goes out the doorway leading to the linney. As Ellenrose moves cautiously around Ulick, she is watched covertly by Darby Jer.

ELLENROSE: How come a thing can be strange and yet familiar, too? Ulick! Say, Ulick Madigan! . . . It's true; he isn't listening with his ears at all. Darby! I'll tell you why I laughed a while ago.

DARBY JER: No need to tell!

189

ELLENROSE: Well, tell I will! Yesterday, as I was on the mountainside, helping to spread the peat for the O'Donnell twins, I saw a huge flat stone
stuck deep into the clay. It was on that long patch of grass, above the sea,
below the old Martello Tower. I had the keenest urge to set that stone
upon its side and roll it down the hill into the waves. I tried to raise it but
I had no luck. I hollered out to Paddy-Twin and Mick but deaf as two
bats they were, that pair! I tugged and tugged until at last I raised the
stone; and you know something, Darby Jer O'Shea? Beneath that rock
there was a mighty clan — believe it or believe it not — a mighty clan . . .
of yellow ants.

Ulick straightens his back and listens intently.

DARBY JER: Ants, is it?

ELLENROSE: That's what they were — ants. And they were milling about, just
like a subway crowd. I nearly had conniption fits watching them move to
and fro. Some clutched white bundles larger than themselves. They
seemed to answer to a code, or tribal law. And, Darby Jer, if I tell you
what I thought of as I watched those ants as they were crawling there,
you won't tell Uncle Garrett, will you?

DARBY JER: There's no informer in my seed or breed!

ELLENROSE: They reminded me of you-all here, struggling to stick together
in this glen.

DARBY JER (*with a cackling laugh*): Of us?

ELLENROSE: Don't get angry, Darby Jer!

DARBY JER: The living spit and stamp of us, you say?

ELLENROSE: Now, look! I didn't say that just to be smart!

*Ulick comes stiffly off the anvil, partly showing his profile as he does so, and
stands with his hand on the beakhorn.*

ELLENROSE: Hey! Darby Jer! Has Ulick finally come to?

DARBY JER (*cackling*): Small yalla articles that creep around the stones; our
brand and image, that's what they are indeed, running with bags and little bundles. (*Cackles.*)

ELLENROSE: I thought he was awake, but no! (*To Darby Jer.*) Don't take me
wrong; I wouldn't for a minute think of mocking people who're my very
own.

DARBY JER: Racing like hares with all their gathered gets (*cackles*).

GARRETT G. (*entering, drying face and hands with towel*): Hey, Darby Jer!
We've had our bellyful of cackling from your mouth.

DARBY JER: I tell you, larded farrier, if you refer to Darby Jer again in peevish sentiments like that, by all the knowledge I possess, I'll . . .

*Ulick moans, walks dreamily to the bellows house and, shielding his face
from view, leans against the handle of the bellows as if in pain. There is a si-*

lence as Darby Jer, Garrett Gowa, and Ellenrose watch him. Ellenrose turns
away and sits on the step to linney doorway.

    Mick-Twin and Paddy-Twin O'Donnell back into forge from the road-
way. They are indicating something in the sky. Mick-Twin is large and slob-
bish; Paddy-Twin is small and alert. Both are dressed in similar clothes, but
Mick-Twin wears an old, dark beret and Paddy-Twin a faded red one. They
wear turned-down Wellingtons. Being twins, they move as an odd unit; at
times, however, they show in odd ways their differing individualities.

PADDY-TWIN: God's gospel! After sixty years they're back again. Look!
    Strain your eyes there, Mick-my-Twin, and see them black against the
    evening light.

MICK-TWIN: I see them now, as plain as naked day. Paddy, my lovely twin,
    'twas you that saw them first. "Glory to God!" you said, "the eagles are
    back again!"

PADDY-TWIN: The Golden Eagles are back! There they go, raging, tearing,
    sweeping clean across the sky.

DARBY JER: The eagles back? For years I dreamed that this would come to
    pass. Out of my road, ye griping pair of twins!

During the following, the twins do a complicated series of steps, designed
ostensibly to give Darby Jer access to the doorway, but in reality meant to
delay his exit.

PADDY-TWIN: Watch their vagaries and gymnastics now. Look! They cut a
    scythe of light above the yellow west.

MICK-TWIN: O, God of Glory, may You be praised forever!

DARBY JER: Out of my road, ye tramps! Back, I say! and let me view the
    wonder of the yellow birds.

PADDY-TWIN (*to Darby Jer*): What awkward fooling have you, man?

MICK-TWIN: Pick up your legs!

PADDY-TWIN: Nailed to the ground he is, and miracles aloft.

MICK-TWIN: Hurry, you clown, or they'll skedaddle and be seen no more!

DARBY JER: Gangway, I say, or else I'll blast and curse the pair of ye.

PADDY-TWIN: Yourself you're leggin'! Look, you're free!

MICK-TWIN: Hurry! Be quick and catch the eagles in the sky.

As Darby Jer rushes out, the twins fall on one another's shoulders, laughing.

MICK-TWIN: Paddy, my lovely Twin, that God spare your brain.

PADDY-TWIN: 'Tis I've the mind, and you the body, boy.

MICK-TWIN: He swallowed the story to his navel down.

ELLENROSE: Are there no eagles there?

PADDY-TWIN: The only eagle there is an old seagull hunting carrion under
    Foylenanean. (*Suddenly serious.*) That's payment for our Irish grey —
    she dead in calf.

MICK-TWIN: And payment, too, for all his superstitious murmurings on May Eve.

PADDY-TWIN: Our bonavs dead! Our pigsty drenched with blood.

MICK-TWIN: Our corn lodged! Our potatoes blackened in the pit.

PADDY-TWIN: And him, and none but him, the fault of all.

GARRETT G.: You'll pay for this, O'Donnell Twins. Take my advice and out the kitchen way with ye.

MICK-TWIN (*overbravely*): We'll stand our ground. I'm not a bit in dread of him.

PADDY-TWIN: That's what we'll do. (*Laughing.*) Glory to God! The eagles and they back again.

MICK-TWIN: They raging, sweeping, tearing clean across the sky!

As Darby Jer re-enters the forge, the twins, who have been rejoicing, suddenly assume poses of innocence. Darby Jer halts three times on his way to his seat at the side of the hearth.

DARBY JER (*pause*): *Me*, that hates misered farmers with their snotty handkerchiefs of fields. *Ye* that are courting Kitsy Carty for five and twenty Shroves and tossing coins to see who'll bed her down in wedlock at the last. *Me* that if I gripped that hammer west the forge, I'd ring a cursing Kryle to melt your breed for seven generations yet to come. Gu'long, ye halves of cross-got miserable men!

GARRETT G.: Clap down a foot on it, I say! I'll countenance no squabbling in my forge. (*Ulick moans.*) Wait, Ulick lad!

Garrett Gowa turns to guide Ulick back to his seat on the anvil.

PADDY-TWIN (*realizing for the first time that Ulick is in dream*): I own to God! Is he long there?

GARRETT G.: This hour and more.

MICK-TWIN: Is he not listening with his ears?

GARRETT G.: He's not!

PADDY-TWIN: You got no clue to what revolves within his head?

GARRETT G.: No sign at all!

PADDY-TWIN: By the bright orphans out of Antioch, this time for sure he'll alter mind and body of the glen.

ELLENROSE: I think the glen is lovely as it is.

PADDY-TWIN: 'Tis easy for you talk. But you've never seen its winter face in full.

ELLENROSE: Well, what I've seen I've liked. It's just as my mom described to me many times. I seemed to know each rock and cliff before I even laid eyes on it. A little change in all your attitudes — a little change in Ulick's attitude as well — that's what you need . . . no more!

PADDY-TWIN: That's fine-feathered chat, my German-Yankee girl. Tell me — you've found it lately, Garrett Gowa?

GARRETT G.: For a long time I've felt it, son. But then the thought refused to take its shape in words, until last Sunday night — out in the morning hours, Debby, my wife, awoke from sleep . . .

Deborah has entered from the kitchen.

GARRETT G. (*coming close to Deborah*): Debby, my darling, hang me a liar if I stray from truth. "We're old," I said to her; "Our stories all concern the dead." She took a fit of sobbing, did my wife.

DEBORAH: I'm fit to take a fit of sobbing now again when I see Ulick Madigan and he not listening with his ears. (*To Ellenrose.*) All this is strange to you, a girl; the young that should be walking, paired, in fuchsia-bright boreens, all drifted off in daft and idle dreams.

ELLENROSE: I'm really very happy here, Aunt Deborah.

DEBORAH: I hope so, child. We do our best. (*To twins.*) God bless ye, Twins. And how's the courtin' getting on with ye?

PADDY-TWIN: We're glad you drew that subject down.

MICK-TWIN: We're puzzled and no mistake.

DEBORAH: And are ye now?

PADDY-TWIN: We are, indeed. As well you know, 'tis I'm all brains and Mick-my-Twin's all meat and muscle. Do you consider that the holy Pope of Rome would let us marry Kitsy Carty as a single man seeing we're twins and came together at a single birth?

MICK-TWIN: There's our hobble in a dozen words.

DEBORAH: Ye're burly boyos, no mistake. Do ye ever take Kitsy in your reckoning?

PADDY-TWIN: Now that you come to mention it, she's like a wandering cow this week or more.

MICK-TWIN: What can be itching her at all, at all?

DEBORAH (*laughing*): Keep pondering on that riddle, let ye, men, and when ye least expect an answer, it might come.

Exit Deborah to kitchen, via linney.

PADDY-TWIN: Garrett! Do you suppose the hour is right to whistle up the boys and girls are gathered at the bridge? They're ravening wild to hear what *he* will say.

GARRETT G.: Wait for a while until he yawns three times. Ever and always that's his signal. Wait! Praise be to God! There goes the first long yawn. Look! isn't he the pattern of a leopard cat, testing the power of his four lovely bones?

The others react in murmured amazement at Ulick's yawn. When Ulick is at his most rigid, Father O'Priest McHugh, a retired priest, enters from the roadway. He is dressed in shabby, dusty, clerical clothes and is collarless. He carries a string of mushrooms. Tired, neurotic, and wan as he is, he is not eccentric.

193

FATHER O'P.: Alpha, Beta, Gamma, Delta . . . ! In bomb-scarred Coventry, I used to dream of finding these. Epsilon, Zeta, Eta, Theta. So Master Ulick's spinning his crazy web again. Take a poor priest's advice and hold whatever comes a secret in this glen. Strangers! I want no strangers here, to patronize a raveled clergyman, with "Where's his mission?", "What's he doing here?" . . . Twins! regarding Father Crofts, the parish priest, you have your lesson off by rote?

PADDY-TWIN: The minute that we clap our eyes on the black motor from the parochial house . . .

MICK-TWIN: Rounding the rock that's on the pass above, we're to come racin' to inform you right away.

FATHER O'P.: Inform, you said? That word gave Ulick Madigan a dart.

GARRETT G.: Inform's a word that has a history of blood.

PADDY-TWIN: It tells of a bitter tale of horseshoes on a naked breast.

MICK-TWIN: As sure as I have hopes to see the Son of Man, that word will not be used by me again.

FATHER O'P.: Is Darby mute of malice, or by act of God? Wait! You and I are brothers, Darby Jer, brothers in age and bitterness; brothers as well because we somehow stretch beyond what's here. (*Holding up the mushrooms to Ellenrose.*) You'll roast me one, or two, or three of these?

ELLENROSE: As many as you like.

FATHER O'P.: I'll strip each mushroom of its skin; then as each cup is roasted to a T, I'll add one tiny pinch of salt. Then, raising it aloft like this, I'll say . . .

His raised hands must have suggested to Father O'Priest the raising of the paten at the offertory of the Mass, for he stops abruptly and glares around.

FATHER O'P. (*intensely*): Stop gaping at my hands, let ye, and you the most of all there, Darby Jer.

Father O'Priest goes quickly into linney. Ellenrose follows.

DARBY JER: Ireland was always crucified by farmers' sons. Dressed up in regimental black they are and muttering Latin underneath their teeth for fear the commonality 'd know what they'd to say.

GARRETT G. (*laughing*): Darby the Dumb to talk again! That's the finest miracle since Moses was a barefoot boy.

The twins join in the laughter.

DARBY JER: To hell with each and every one of ye! To the bright bells of . . .

As Darby Jer turns to go out the doorway he strikes against Kitsy Carty, a spinster in her late thirties. Kitsy is an odd mixture of sadness, cuteness, humor, with a dash of ecstasy.

DARBY JER (*to Kitsy*): Maybe you're out for legging, and for fooling me the same as these?

KITSY: Ah, Darby Jer! You're a true cross between a cuckoo and a pointer dog. (*To the others.*) The word's abroad. How goes it with himself? The buckos are waiting anxious at the bridge.

GARRETT G.: Kitsy, stay here and give the signal when the time is ripe.

KITSY (*glancing at the twins*): I hope this scheme will put a stir in some of ye I'll leave without a name.

DARBY JER (*near doorway*): Then, Kitsy Carty, you're the right romantic ape! What hope of generation have you here? Or here? (*Points to twins.*) I'll have a certain cause of laughter in all that.

Exit Darby Jer, laughing heartily.

KITSY (*at window, right*): 'Tis mortal quiet in the world, in sure. (*Looks around, sighs.*) The time that Ulick led the Italian terrazzo workingman all the ways up the road from Tanavalla town to put a stir on twenty women in this glen . . .

GARRETT G. (*laughing*): The time he met the blackie sailor on the slip, and told Old Nell he was her brother back from sea . . .

PADDY-TWIN: The time he found the Chinese banknotes floated in . . . Those were the days! He'll make those days come back again.

MICK-TWIN: I own to God he will!

KITSY (*exalted*): What will it be, will come to follow on his dream? I know! As sure as all the stars that stand above our skulls, a vision it will be!

ALL: What vision?

KITSY (*exalted*): There was the time the Doolin girl in Cappaheigue witnessed the Virgin and the Blessed Baby caught in the tealeaves of her breakfast cup. Life I'd surrender with a smile tonight if 'twas a vision Ulick ordered me to see.

GARRETT G.: 'Tis only cracked, cantankerous women believe that. A vision, faith! And have poor Father O' in shining balls of sweat for fear 'twould reach the ears of Father Crofts. Kitsy! I warn you now — I'll have no visions emanating from my forge.

KITSY (*still entranced*): I know! I know! Combing her amber hair she'll be, out by the crag of Donaleen and there a man will grab her at the crack o' day and drag her home and wed her true and breed a dozen webtoed screechers, got in love between the man and merry maid.

GARRETT G.: A calf with seven legs might even show his snout again.

PADDY-TWIN: Aye! or a boy be born with antlers like a deer.

GARRETT G.: Or an Alsatian bitch throw litter off an otter dog . . .

MICK-TWIN: Fine times ahead!

KITSY (*looking at Ulick*): Look, now, the grand attentive set of him!

PADDY-TWIN: You'd take your oath he heard every syllable we spoke.

GARRETT G.: Sssh! I'd say 'tis close to waking he is now. (*To Kitsy.*) What giggling have you, girl?

KITSY (*dreamily*): It just walked over me!

GARRETT G.: And what was that?

KITSY (*whispering, laughing*): Temptation! (*All react; loudly.*) Temptation for to push him from his anvil throne.

PADDY-TWIN: Do no such thing!

MICK-TWIN: Wake him that's dreaming there, and, for a God's own fact, our twenty years of courtin' are no more.

KITSY: And I still say I'll belt him in the shoulder blades and send him kicking into the bellows mouth. Stand back!

GARRETT G.: Look, Kitsy, look! There goes the second yawn.

Ulick yawns.

KITSY: Praise be to God! That was a most ferocious yawn. I'll run and tell the lads at once.

GARRETT G.: Wait! That's not a patch on what's to come!

Darby Jer has stolen in from the roadway.

DARBY JER: I came to rest my bones, no more. Let ye go on with what queer capers ye do have. I'll blind my eyes to what's occurring in the forge.

GARRETT G.: Be off at once, I say!

DARBY JER: You'll turn me out?

GARRETT G.: I'll turn you out! You did your worst the day you stood on Gobna-Trá, and cursed a currach moving out to Donal's Rock. And then poor Sean, my sister's son, came floating with the tide. Be off at once, I say!

DARBY JER: I'll go my road, my head cocked up for height, and that I may be scourged if I cast shadow on your floor again. (*Turning to speak plaintively.*) What do ye want to do with me at all? Cast me upon the mountains like the lepers long ago? (*Pleadingly.*) Can I come back when he's awake itself?

GARRETT G. (*relenting*): All right! . . . Come back! Hold on there now! What's that you're hiding in your coat?

Catches Darby Jer and swings him round.

DARBY JER: Nothing at all!

GARRETT G.: And what have you been muttering to yourself beside that trough of mine since early day?

DARBY JER: 'Twas Mary Peggy had the toothache pain. She asked me say the charm to Aolites, standing a soldier at Jerusalem's gate.

KITSY: Rummage his person quick, you fool of fools.

GARRETT G.: What have you there, I say again?

Garrett Gowa snatches at the low inner pocket of Darby's overcoat and after a little struggle finds a bottle of blackish water.

DARBY JER: 'Tis holy water, only 'tis stale a while.

KITSY: I'd not believe his dying gospel oath!

GARRETT G.: It's water from my trough he has! I have it now — forgewater is a solvent remedy for curing aches in teeth. But aches, like rats, must find another home. If my jaw aches within the week, you wretch, I'll comb your skull with pritchell or with rake.

Garrett Gowa flings the bottle against the hearth where it breaks. Ulick yawns prodigiously. All cry out with delight.

PADDY-TWIN: Look! There it goes! The final yawn of all.

KITSY: I'll run and tell the lads at once.

Kitsy rushes toward doorway leading to road.

PADDY-TWIN: Hold there awhile! Come here, let ye! Don't raise your voices overloud. (*They gather round.*) Why don't we hold the first of glory for ourselves, and let the others scratch themselves, or enter in the end of all delights?

MICK-TWIN: Aye — we can dole it out to them in dribs and drabs.

All clamor in agreement.

PADDY-TWIN: Garrett! He's mortal quiet in himself. You're certain that he's roused at last?

GARRETT G.: He's wide awake for sure.

PADDY-TWIN: Who'll dare to ask him now what tale or plot or mimicry he has in store for us?

KITSY: Whoever asks, let him be sure put in a spar for me to have the plot well spiced with things of love.

DARBY JER: For me, ask what's beyond! Or what's beyond beyond!

GARRETT G.: Fall silent all! I'll put the question to him straightaway. (*Goes behind the anvil and faces Ulick.*) Ulick, would you be listening with your ears?

There is no reply.

GARRETT G. (*loudly*): Ulick Madigan, from Upper Gloshnanooneenmawn, I ask again — are you now listening with your ears?

Ulick's head revolves very slowly on his shoulders.

ULICK: I am!

All break into cries of delight and gratitude.

GARRETT G.: Ulick, my treasure and my pride! Tell us what wonder have you in store for us?

ULICK (*sly*): In store for ye, is it?

KITSY: Ulick, my heart, don't forget to hide something in the whim for me.

PADDY-TWIN: It's coaxiorum that she's hinting at, so that she'll draw the men. Put blood in it instead, I tell you, man.

GARRETT G.: Put fire and flame in it.

PADDY-TWIN: Or, best of all, what's there right real before our eyes, to dress it up in glory clothes, we knowing all from head to heel, yet pretending to ourselves we know damn-all. Eh, Ulick, son?

ULICK (*laughing*): You're daft as coots. A little nap I took, no more, just what a foal takes for a while in a field of aftergrass. Give me a fag, some one of ye, at once!

They rival each other to offer Ulick a cigarette, and to light it for him. Ulick walks to the lattice window in the right-hand wall. The red-gold of sunset strikes his face.

ULICK: Day almost down. The western ocean thronged with gold. I think I'll take a ramble on the cliffs. 'Twill serve to clear my head. Good luck to ye!

GARRETT G. (*coming between Ulick and the doorway*): Do no such thing!

PADDY-TWIN: Spill out your thoughts or, by the Man Above, 'twill be the worse for you.

MICK-TWIN: And I'm no fool when my temper's up.

Ulick laughs loudly.

KITSY: Ah, turn him loose, if that's his will, for where's the good in spancel-ling a dream? For long I've felt it in my flesh he's lost his dreaming trade. 'Tis casting spittle in the face of God to start complaining now. Farewell to wonder! — that's my slogan for the balance of my days.

GARRETT G.: That's female chat! We're males and not so easy pacified as you.

PADDY-TWIN: Swinging to anger we are now.

MICK-TWIN: You can say that again, my brother.

KITSY: Ever and always you are clumsy fools of men. You're all for fists and red-hot brands itself. But I'm for wheedling secrets out of him instead. (*Wheedling.*) Ulick, my snow-white child . . .

ULICK (*breaking into laughter*): Kitsy, you're gay, damn gay! But, wait! Be-fore I cogitate upon the matter highest in my head, something I often meant to ask you to your face — Kitsy, with you, what way is life?

KITSY: The blind could read my litany of grief, the dumb recite it, and the deaf could hear it, too. My mother old, she like an iron tyrant in the bed. The rest all wandered off or sunk beneath the clay. The fearful leap of forty years before me now and I must jump it with no partner to my hip. Life is a curséd drag on women such as me. (*Rounding on the twins.*) And these curmudgeons here, with ne'er a wanton maggot underneath their hides to drive them, lusting, to the glebe where I, a woman, live. (*In bitter mimicry.*) "Kitsy, with you, what way is life?"

ULICK: Twins, before I walk away — or stay, with ye, what way is life?

PADDY-TWIN: Grey out!

MICK-TWIN: Grey, out and out!

PADDY-TWIN: If I start out to lift a rock has slithered from a gap, I have to yell for Mick-my-Twin to lend a hand.

MICK-TWIN: And me, God help me, I'm illiterate. So, if a scrap of writing comes my road, I have to say: "Where are my glasses?" until my brother's home to read it for me.

ULICK: Hey, Darby Jer, what way is life with you?

DARBY JER: It's life, you said? Life? I've seen my share of that commodity. I've worked the charm of the maggot's knot on a dying calf and ripped his tangled gut. I've set four hay ropes pouring milk like paps. The black books opened, aye and closed again, that, too, I've seen. I've also felt the scourge of having a young maid laugh and mock and jeer at what I had to say to her. Regarding what is left to me of life, I'm wild to see a wonder once again. If you have such a thing then stop your chat and spit it out upon the ground.

ULICK: And you there, Gowa! With you, what way is life?

Garrett Gowa is at the anvil. He has begun quietly to tap the Kryle in mute anguish. Hearing it, Darby Jer stiffens. Garrett stops beating the Kryle to reply to Ulick.

GARRETT G.: No child to grace my forge, and no kind nephew since my sister's son was lost alobstering. Always within my heart is low, now that the German-Yankee girl will soon go back across the sea, ever and always I keep thinking of a midnight forty years ago, the night my father's father led me here and told me of life and death and landlords' wrongs and taught me how to ring the anvil curse.

Garrett Gowa begins to ring the "Kryle" or curse, on the anvil. The sound has an odd effect on Darby Jer. He begins to declaim in an old-world chant.

DARBY JER (*chanting*):

I saw Death of a morning early,
And he spoke to me in a voice right surly.
"Where," says he, "in the Glen does the landlord dwell?"

"I came," says he, "for to melt his seeding,
And I came," says he, "for to blast his breeding,
And I came," says he, "for to drag him down to hell."

ALL EXCEPT ULICK:

Then welcome, Death, in the morning early,
And welcome, too, to your voice so surly,
And we'll show you now . . .

ULICK (*shouting, laughing*): As daft as coots ye are, I say. Hey, Darby Jer! You'd need to stop that curséd Kryle and turn to something with the sun on it. (*Moving toward the door, halting.*) Still, all in all, it looks as if ye're ripe . . .

GARRETT G.: Barring it goes against the law of God, we're ripe for anything you say.

DARBY JER: And that itself for me, providing only that it stirs the dust.

ULICK (*returning*): I hope ye don't expect a tale or feat from me. Ye're making out a little mound of earth to be the size of Brandon Hill itself.

All have turned away disconsolately.

199

GARRETT G.: We'll beg no more!

KITSY: No more we'll beg!

PADDY-TWIN: No more!

MICK-TWIN: No more!

DARBY JER: No more!

ULICK: By that same token 'twas at Mount Brandon's foot, this whim occurred to me. (*All are tempted to turn.*) Wait! Lost and found within my mind it is, like seabirds flying in the sunset light. (*All have turned and have now come close behind him.*) At times I see the seabirds' painted evening gold; at times again I . . . (*Ulick turns quickly on his heel.*) What gaping have ye? Have I two heads on me, or what?

KITSY: The single head alone!

PADDY-TWIN: And it our hope of resurrection yet to come.

ULICK: Just like a bunch of sucky-calves you follow me. (*Reminiscently.*) Where did I have this whim? Out on the mountain flank it was. The day was close. I lay upon the humpy ground. On the far line of sky the Skelligs Rock was wavering in the heat. Level with the sod, I placed my ear. And then . . .

GARRETT G.: Yes?

PADDY-TWIN: Yes?

MICK-TWIN: Yes?

KITSY: Yes, Ulick, yes?

ULICK: There on the clay, upon a tiny hill, I saw a golden army marshaling.

A short silence. Unseen by the others, Father O'Priest has stolen in from the kitchen. From this point, until the end of Act I, a faint golden light begins, very gradually, to suffuse the scene. This light, for which the sunset offers excuse, waxes and wanes with the belief and disbelief of the players in the fantasy of the Golden Folk. The light rarely shines on Darby Jer, and does not shine at all on Father O'Priest.

KITSY: Men?

ULICK: Not men!

PADDY-TWIN: What, so?

ULICK: These were far cleverer than the cleverest men.

ALL: Oh!

ULICK: I watched them close. Six legs each soldier had. Each was three bodies mated up in one. Their capers were so accurate, so wise, they seemed possessed of beauty and of worth. I tell ye, men and women of this glen, better than us of Christian life they were by far.

FATHER O'P. (*sarcastically*): I wish ye'd stick to something safe, something like geligniting fish. (*Angrily.*) I told ye a thousand times, I want no peering at this glen. Is there a way by which I can keep tag on ye? Wait! (*He goes to kitchen door.*) Ellenrose! Here, Ellenrose!

Ellenrose enters.

ELLENROSE: Yes, Father, what's it now?

FATHER O'P.: Look well about the forge, then tell me what you see.

ELLENROSE: Well, just an ordinary group of friends, I guess. My relatives and their old neighbors, too.

FATHER O'P.: There's more to it than that!

ELLENROSE: Father McHugh, I don't know what you mean.

Father O'Priest is close to Ellenrose. They make, as it were, a single point. Ulick makes a second point, and Darby Jer a third. Between these points lies a rough triangle.

FATHER O'P.: Here is the omnipresent square of Irish life.

ELLENROSE: I still don't get what you are driving at.

FATHER O'P.: Four angles to a square. Here, in the pagan angle, sits old Darby Jer — observe his rancorous Druidic eyes. Here's Ulick, manning well the classic nook, abandoned as it is to arabesque of dream. And here, God help me in my hour of need, I stand to man the Christian corner of the square.

ELLENROSE (*tolerantly*): All well and good, but . . . See! You've only got three angles in your square.

Ellenrose has now moved so that the crude square is evidenced.

FATHER O'P.: You are the fourth.

ELLENROSE: I?

FATHER O'P.: Yes, you! The pagan, the Greek, the Galilean — you.

ELLENROSE: And which faction do I represent?

FATHER O'P.: You stand for youth, and that which follows on the first of prime.

Ellenrose and Ulick are staring at each other.

FATHER O'P. (*whispering*): You hear me, girl? Or can it be that you're not listening with your ears?

ELLENROSE (*remotely*): I hear you, Father. Yes.

A pause.

GARRETT G.: Father! Your sister Moll is in the haggard west screening her eyes against the sunset light. God love you and all else to that . . . Hike off! Don't cause your sister pain.

PADDY-TWIN: We wouldn't cross you for the world and all but if you'd only take it in your head to ramble off, as true as God, I'd say an aspiration for your nerves and head.

MICK-TWIN: And me! I'd even say a Memorare for your poor old soul. So ramble off at once.

Ulick and Ellenrose are still staring at one another.

KITSY: Why should he ramble off, I say. Sweet Father O', what you have called to light between the boy and girl that's standing there might be a riddle to these dullard men but to the likes of me it's clear as clearest day. What say you, Ellenrose, my heart? Do I speak true?

Ellenrose does not reply. Suddenly she turns away.

KITSY: All of a sudden you're different, child!

ELLENROSE (*brightly*): Oh, I'm not different! No, I'm still the same. Say! You all have got the willies in this glen. Father, what are we doing, anyway? We're only breaking up their little game. Come on, let's go, and let them have their ball.

FATHER O'P.: Gogai o gog, where shall I make my nest? If I make it in the heather it will die in the bad weather. Gogai o gog, where shall I make my nest?

Ellenrose and Father O'Priest go out by the doorway to the road.

PADDY-TWIN (*angrily*): The dream is broken now!

GARRETT G.: Smashed into flitters by a shattered priest.

DARBY JER: 'Tis not the first prime bubble that his equals caught and broke.

PADDY-TWIN: He was short-taken to talk and act like that. And, Kitsy Carty, so were you short-taken too; you with your gab of mysteries and love.

KITSY: My mysteries and love! I tell ye straight that I'm equipped to read where others see a blank white page. Ulick, a mhic mo chroi istigh, be ready now; throw your mind back to where it roamed before the cracked and lovely priest kindled a fire that I've no need to name. Throw your mind back, I say again.

ULICK (*angrily*): 'Tis gone, I tell you, woman! Gone!

KITSY: Not gone at all, my love; just set aside; the others, waiting at the bridge below, they're all agog to hear the news. You'll not . . .

ULICK: Race to the bridge and tell them anything you wish. Tell them 'twas but a bully-ball of wind I had. (*He turns in anguish.*)

KITSY (*wheedling still*): Cast your mind back, son of my very side. You told us here that, out upon the mountainside, you saw an amber army cleverer than Christian folk. What happened then?

ULICK (*remotely*): What happened then? Garrett! You are my distant relative and friend.

GARRETT G.: What is it, son?

ULICK: At times I wander in and out of what is true. These others, here and at the bridge — while I'm asleep-awake like that, do they begin to mock and scoff at me?

GARRETT G. (*to others*): I dare the single one of ye to mock at him, for if ye do I'll brand ye with a horseshoe when 'tis red as those that went before me branded Milo the landgrabber in days gone by.

KITSY: Ulick!

ULICK: No more, you hear! No more!

KITSY: One tiny taste to quench my thirst. For me, your gossip, that's not overmuch to ask. These grand battalions that you chanced upon — you spoke with them, maybe?

GARRETT G.: Maybe 'twas them that first conversed with him.

PADDY-TWIN: And whispered secrets worth a shower of gold.

MICK-TWIN: Secrets of life and death.

KITSY: Secrets of love and birth.

DARBY JER: They taught him wonder curses, that I'd swear. (*Loudly.*) You hear me, Ulick, in your faraway?

ULICK: I hear you, Darby Jer.

Deborah enters the forge, from the kitchen. The others, with spread fingers, warn her not to interrupt.

ULICK (*brightly*): Re-entering my brain box now it is for sure. Clearer than is the moon upon a night of May, I see the dream — but, what's the use? Ripeness has ebbed from you again.

KITSY: Never more ripe than now!

GARRETT G.: We swear 'tis true!

KITSY: O, God above! with us the life of dream alone is right. Without it, what are we but daft and wrong? Let you grow gabby, Ulick, son, else doctors will view us one by one and in the end we'll all be dragged away. My lovely boy! Go back a piece upon your road of thought. (*Prompts.*) "Out on the mountainside . . . the day," you said, "was close."

ULICK: The day was close. Apass the Spaniard's Grave upwards I walked, traveling the Camel's Path to the Cairn above. There, by the pleasant green beneath the tower, I stretched myself. Awake-asleep I was. And there below my face, among the stems, I saw the soldiers wearing uniforms of gold.

GARRETT G.: Of gold, you say?

ULICK: Of honey gold . . . Drilling they were, in wonderful parade. Spying my face, the soldiers scurried underground. I called to mind the magnifying glass young Blakeney keeps for kindling fires — 'twas hid high in a hole within the tower walls. I called to mind as well the spade ye twin O'Donnells use for stripping peat. I found the glass, I grabbed the spade, and with a downward thrust of steel I cut the little hill in two — there was a mighty city bare.

KITSY: A city underground?

DEBORAH: Those were the very words he spoke!

ULICK: I placed the glass above a crowded city street. Tradesmen and gardeners, merchants and dairymen, saddlers and shepherds, too, all racing off. There, too, were females, clutching little babes in arms and then the soldiers formed their broken ranks and fought the shaft that ripped their capital. Kneeling, I watched them scurry to and fro.

MICK-TWIN: A fool like me could learn a power from people such as these . . .

GARRETT G.: This whim will blind the stars!

PADDY-TWIN: 'Twill quench the glory of the moon.

KITSY: This is the common thing dressed up in glory clothes.

DEBORAH: Go easy, daughters and sons of fools, or do ye want the tale to dart away?

KITSY: God love the females with the babes in arms! What then?

ULICK: I watched and watched and watched, and if I were to talk from now until the Judgment Hour, I couldn't tell the half of all their cleverness. What Mick the Twin said there a while ago is right: even a fool could learn a power from people such as these — we could grow wise, and beautiful and strange.

ALL (*whispering*): Wise and beautiful and strange!

DARBY JER (*explosively*): Ah! to the devil damn with all of this! Does he imagine that we're double, treble goms? His Golden Folk to hell and miles beyond! There on the humpy ground below the tower he saw a miserable multitude of creeping, lousy . . .

KITSY (*advancing, with her nails up*): We know! We know! We know! I'll tear the very eyeballs from your face if you shoot out that viper's tongue again. Ah! God be praised, in days to come we five will boast we had the first of it!

PADDY-TWIN: We have the first of it, in sure!

MICK-TWIN: 'Twill fill our heads for years and years.

GARRETT G.: Kitsy! I near forgot. Now is the time to summon those who're waiting at the bridge below.

KITSY: I'll let a yell at them at once.

Kitsy opens the door to roadway and calls out.

KITSY: Oho! So that's the way with ye, is it? Ye were impatient and ye ganged around the door! Come in, let ye! Don't crush or I'll be sure to puck ye on the heads.

Two men and two women jostle inside the doorway.

KITSY: Enough of ye, I say! Get back! The rest can listen from abroad.

DARBY JER: Aye! Listen from abroad they will indeed, to lies and trumpery. I tell ye, idiots and seed of idiots, too, if ye're to listen to his tale, ye're nothing but a flock of mountain sheep.

All solemnly imitate the bleating of sheep so as to annoy the old man. At the same time they advance as a unit upon him.

ALL: Baa — a — a — a — a . . . (*Darby Jer backs, step by step.*)

DARBY JER (*halting, then advancing upon his foes*): How dare ye baa at me like that! I, that have powers beyond the swing of mortal man. Gu'long, ye clutch of turkeys fattening for the board!

ALL (*solemnly, as again they advance*): Gobble . . . obble . . . obble.
(*Again Darby Jer backs away.*)

DARBY JER (*halting suddenly*): The cheek of ye to gobble at my neck again.
(*Advancing on them.*) Ye're nothing but a fleet of ignorant, ill-bred geese!

ALL (*solemnly, as again they advance*): Hiss . . . iss . . . iss . . .

All hiss Darby Jer to the doorway leading to the road, where he halts and draws himself to his full height.

DARBY JER: Stand back! (*They stand. Again Darby Jer advances.*) Aye! sheep and turkey cocks and geese itself ye have become, and shortly ye'll become what crawls upon the clay. I know where Sergeant Clever found his clue. He found it on the Yankee girl's mouth, and there 'twill end in lips on lips again. Before that day, cut off my ear if he don't make this glen the mocking stock of Ireland all. Cut off my ear if this adventure doesn't end with the reek of human flesh within this forge. Cut off my ear again, I say . . .

DEBORAH: Neighbors! We've heard our fill.

KITSY: More than our fill, I say! Hey, turn to dogs, the pack of ye and bark this son of Satan from the forge.

All swirl about and bark at Darby Jer, who, step by step, is driven out on the roadway. As the door slams behind him, all laugh heartily.

GARRETT G.: The jealous duffer! No one will shed a tear that he has gone. Now for as fine a fancy as ever walked on Ireland's ground.

All break into excited comment.

PADDY-TWIN: Hush all your tongues! Greater than comets in the sky this is! — articles we've walked upon a thousand times lifted by him and given a sovereign twist.

MICK-TWIN (*to newcomers*): If ye kept guessing till the break of day, ye'd never guess what Ulick perched upon.

DEBORAH: Good news for women in it, too.

KITSY: Babies in arms, they crowing in a city bright with sun.

GARRETT G.: Tradesmen! Dressed in the finest yellow cloth!

PADDY-TWIN: Put listening ears on ye! Let not a syllable be lost as Ulick tells ye of the Golden Folk.

All whisper the words "Golden Folk" in a broken rhythm, faintly reminiscent of the beat of the Kryle. Ulick has sprung to the stool-log beneath the latticed window in the left hand wall of the forge. As he turns to speak, the faces of the people are burnished with the golden light of the sunset striking through the window behind him.

ULICK: There is a wonder city underground and in it live a people dressed in gold. They are more numerous than the stars above. They are far wiser than the wisest men, and in this golden city underneath the clay . . .

Curtain falls slowly, while Ulick is still speaking.

Act II

The forge, Sunday morning, a month later. The characters are now dressed in Sunday clothes. One or two straw suits hang on the walls of the forge. Darby Jer cautiously enters the empty forge from the roadway and shuts the door behind him. As he moves across the stage, he pauses, now and again, to peer here and there. Halting, he addresses the anvil.

DARBY JER: You and your Golden Folk! (*Strikes the anvil with his thumb-stick, laughs.*) Brigades of ants, as clever as Christians! Was there ever such a daft concoction? And these stumps of fools, they now believe they're Yella Men themselves! And where are all the Yella Men today? They're down in the Sunday chapel, with their beaks apart, gaping and listening to the "farmer's son." I've something here that'll set a hound among the hares. (*Takes a white egg from his pocket and holds it up on the palm of his hand; to the egg.*) You're weak, but you have power to back you. (*He takes out a second egg.*) And here's your twin brother. 'Twas ye that spilled a currach on its flank. 'Twas ye that tore a priest apart with shivers and nerves. 'Twas ye that caused O'Donnells' cow to drop her life. And, now, I'll set ye to tame the Golden Folk. My father always said ye should be planted high and in an unlikely place. I think I've found the spot — a place they'd never think of trying if they were thinking from now to the crack of doom.

Darby Jer moves toward doorway to linney, and, mounting a box, prepares to place the eggs in the hole in the wall. As he does so, Ellenrose enters quickly from the kitchen. Darby Jer replaces the eggs in his pocket.

ELLENROSE (*turning and seeing Darby Jer*): Say! What were *you* doing? (*Mockingly.*) So you don't feel like telling me? Okay! Somehow I'd say that Uncle Garrett will be angry to find you slingeing here in his forge instead of attending Sunday Mass. Here, Darby, I'll make a deal with you! You tell me about the Gaelic poets of old and I won't say a word about your antics here. You won't? Okay! . . . Hi, Uncle Garrett! Hi!

DARBY JER: No! Don't call him! I'll tell you anything you want to know.

ELLENROSE: Okay! First tell me about Owen Roe O'Sullivan, the poet.

DARBY JER: He was a thundering tramp and scamp!

ELLENROSE: What did he do?

DARBY JER (*a little embarrassed*): What did he do? He "sang a song" with young women here and there.

ELLENROSE (*mockingly*): No great harm in that! Maybe duets are out of fashion these days, but if they want to sing them, let them go right ahead.

DARBY JER: You're on the wrong track. I'll tell you how it was, girl — he took those women "off their roads."

206

ELLENROSE (*mockingly*): Gave them a bum steer! Hmm! It could be he didn't know the countryside.

DARBY JER: What's that you're saying? He knew this country from one end to the other. It was just, as regards women, he was . . . he was . . . kind of . . .

ELLENROSE (*laughing*): Well — I think I've got your meaning at last. And if you aren't the cutest and the corniest guy! Here you are, Darby Jer, the last of Ireland's medicinemen, living in a glen where folk believe they're ants, and yet you balk at the simple facts of life. Well! Well! Now, flex your vocal cords and stand over there! I'm waiting to hear you sing the song my mother said she'd stand in the snow to hear you sing. Come on — the song of love and sorrow, Darby Jer, or else I'll yell and call my uncle.

DARBY JER: My throat is raw. My two tonsils are the size of . . .

ELLENROSE: Of eggs? Sing, Darby Jer, the love and sorrow song. I'll look away. But I *must* hear that song.

At last, Darby Jer begins to sing, quaveringly at first, but gathering the remnants of old passion as the song proceeds.

DARBY JER (*singing*):

> 'Tis my bitter sorrow that by tomorrow
> I go not out to my true love's bower,
> Where the stream that's running spills clearest honey
> And, in winter time, see! the branch in flower!
> No frost, no snowing, no red wind blowing
> By the bright abode of my secret queen,
> But her body moving with the salmon's beauty
> And her hair as bright as the corn, when green.

As Darby Jer sings, he sheds the darkness of his nature. The song tells of an old love that is the cause of his sorrow. As the old man continues to sing, Ellenrose draws nearer to him, as if in understanding. When the song has ended, there is an odd silence that bridges the years between them. Of a sudden Darby Jer, who has been standing with his head bent, reverts to harshness.

DARBY JER: You're out for mocking me, the same as them that went before you mocked me long ago!

ELLENROSE: No, Darby Jer, I'm not out for mocking you at all.

DARBY JER: If you don't let me alone, I'll curse the love that's ripening in your heart and turn it dry as seagrass that's spread on the stones.

ELLENROSE: No, Darby Jer, I don't make fun of you. It's just that your song hurts me as much as it hurts you. I guess we're both mixed up . . .

Deborah enters from the linney, Ellenrose goes out by the same door.

DEBORAH: I'd say you're thronging that girl's head with bawdiness and lies. And dodging the Holy Sacrifice as well! You'll not be harbored here,

Darby Jer. Ulick is on the anvil now. He and the Golden Folk will drag you to the ground.

DARBY JER: I don't take pattern from the vermin underfoot.

DEBORAH: You take your pattern from worse than that. And you know well we don't believe the other thing. It's just an old pastime we have, to color the rocks and the sea and the sky.

DARBY JER: The biggest fool walking Ireland's ground could see that you believe.

DEBORAH (*weakly*): No! It's all a game.

DARBY JER: It's no game at all!

DEBORAH: A game! A game, I say! We never kissed the ace of hearts at consecration time like you, so that you'd never lose a game of cards.

DARBY JER: You play a deadlier game than me. But watch for the flaw and weakness of the glen. Like me, ye're mortal afraid of being mocked. "Whoever informs upon the Golden Folk, I'll brand his breast!" Those are the words of Garrett Gowa, the man with whom you've spent your bitter years.

DEBORAH: Our years were bitter only since poor Sean was drowned. You know that well! That was the morning you were seen muttering on Gob-na-Trá. And you, you talk of laughingstocks, a man who went foolish in your middle years on a girl who had barely cast her confirmation veil.

DARBY JER: That gave ye prime diversion! But I know ye all! One whisper in a pub in Tanavalla town and all your world comes tumbling. On Sundays ye quake till Father Crofts has gone away. An angler with his fist of twigs; a walking student from Japan; even a peddler selling cloth — all sorts of strangers can set ye quaking in your shoes.

Paddy-Twin and Mick-Twin back onto the stage through the doorway to the road. Both are looking out through the doorway. In his buttonhole each wears a large horse daisy, obviously picked on the roadside as they were returning from Mass.

PADDY-TWIN: There was a stranger at the Mass.

MICK-TWIN: And he was bearded like a tramp.

PADDY-TWIN: The chapel stirred as he walked up the aisle.

MICK-TWIN: Right to the very top he went and in he goes to Hanley's pew.

DARBY JER: What did I say? Strangers can set ye quaking in your shoes.

DEBORAH: This stranger signifies nothing.

PADDY-TWIN: That's right, Deborah. He signifies nothing at all. We've often had old tramps here before.

MICK-TWIN (*gleefully*): Whether he was a tramp or not, I've news that'll stir your hearts! Listen, the lot of ye! I prayed at Mass.

DEBORAH: You did?

MICK-TWIN: I did! And my mind, I . . . I think, is fixed. By hell, I tell ye now, I intend to marry Kitsy by the first of Shrove.

DEBORAH (*sarcastically*): Be careful, child! Don't do anything in a hurry!

PADDY-TWIN: Ulick himself and his talk about the Golden Folk stirred him up. Myself and Mick, we thought that one of us should wed. So we asked ourselves in whom the heat was working the strongest.

MICK-TWIN: And as a test, we took to raising rocks above our heads.

DEBORAH: That was a wonderful test!

MICK-TWIN: I raised a rock as big as Beenastoompa Hill.

DEBORAH: You did?

MICK-TWIN: I did; but when we started asking riddles of one another, he answered them all. Then I argued that 'twas he should marry instead of me.

DEBORAH: And what did Paddy say?

MICK-TWIN (*sighs*): Women, he said, were odd and strange and queer; he said they'd often jilt a scholar and wed a fool.

PADDY-TWIN: That's what I say again. At Mass I told him pray. "Today you're young," I whispered, "but soon you'll be old and, maybe, wear a beard."

MICK-TWIN: And then we saw the Sign from God! At that same second the tramp wearing the beard walked up the Chapel aisle.

DEBORAH: Did Ulick see this stranger?

PADDY-TWIN: He did, indeed! At Gospel time he swung his face like this, and I could read his one blazing eye which was asking: "What brought *him* here?" You there, Darby Jer! If I was you, I'd fetter up my hand for fear 'twould scribble out a note, signed, maybe, by "A Moonlighter" or "A Friend."

Enter Garrett Gowa, also from the roadway. He is dressed in Sunday brown and wears a bright tie, obviously a present from a relative in the United States. He also wears a watchchain with a football medal swinging from it.

PADDY-TWIN: You saw the tramp?

GARRETT G.: I saw the stranger, but I'd take my oath that he's not tramp.

MICK-TWIN: He has a beard as dirty as the hob.

GARRETT G.: Nowadays the world is biting its tail. The learned and the rich are dressed in black beards and rags (*looking at twins*) while the ignorant go round in shining blue. (*To Mick-Twin, who is at the window.*) What are you looking at?

MICK-TWIN: I'm watching for Father Crofts, the parish priest.

GARRETT G.: What business have you of him?

MICK-TWIN: Come the first of Shrove, I intend to marry Kitsy.

GARRETT G.: Shrove is a long way off.

MICK-TWIN: I know! But I'd rather get the letter of freedom now, for fear that later on I'd back — like Mickey Michael's mule.

GARRETT G.: Watch your brother, Paddy-Twin, when he starts chatting with the parish priest.

PADDY-TWIN: I'll watch him.

GARRETT G.: Darby Jer, you'd better make no ins and outs on the stranger. Another thing! I grudge the shelter of my roof to those who'd rather have it than the House of God.

Darby Jer stamps fiercely toward the door to the roadway and, with a malevolent under-breath remark in Gaelic, strides out.

DEBORAH: How often have I asked you not to cross that fella's road? Do you want us melted from the face of the earth?

GARRETT G.: Some day I'll break him into . . .

DEBORAH: 'Tis he'll break you! These latter days he's working charms with eggs again. The Man Below can work in curious ways and Darby Jer may twist the Golden whim to suit his own ends, unless poor Father O' can stand against his power. "Strike down the honest man," my mother used to say, "but be sure to kiss the rogue!"

PADDY-TWIN: Only he's afraid of Ulick, he'd likely split upon the . . . what ye know!

GARRETT G.: I'm not so sure. Darby hates informers to the core.

MICK-TWIN: And I'm a fool as well as the rest of ye for I'm sorry now that I made fun of him. A man facing for his marriage bed, like me, should watch his p's and q's.

PADDY-TWIN (*at door, sarcastically*): He might deprive you of your manhood, Mick-Twin, and leave you unfit for lifting rocks.

MICK-TWIN: That's true! (*To Paddy-Twin.*) What are you looking at?

PADDY-TWIN: Father Crofts — he's over there in a dining room — God bless his appetite — with a baby's dribbler around his neck. He's eating the schoolmissus out of house and home. And there's the stranger, sauntering toward the pier. O, Lord on high! He's talking to Darby Jer. And now he's asking him questions.

MICK-TWIN: Talk on, my twin!

PADDY-TWIN: There's Father O'Priest, he's up there skulking on the hill. He's reddening his pipe. I can see the puffs of smoke. He won't show his face till he's sure that Father Crofts is gone.

GARRETT G.: That hill is tinder-dry. I hope he doesn't set it on fire.

MICK-TWIN: Hey! Watch for the parish priest! I'm thinking about that letter of freedom I have to get. I must ask you one question, Garrett Gowa. The night I'm wed to Kitsy, will you release the suits of straw we used at Mick the mouse's wedding?

GARRETT G.: I won't!

MICK-TWIN: You won't?

GARRETT G.: I won't! They're for the Golden Folk alone.

PADDY-TWIN: Hold on a while! Father O' is standing up. And now he's slipping down the Clash. Likely as not he'll enter by the back door.

MICK-TWIN: Keep watching!

PADDY-TWIN: Ha, ha! The stranger's parting ways with Darby Jer. O, merciful! He's spotted Father O' behind the beehive cell. I declare to . . . He's gone to have a word . . . or two, with Father O'.

GARRETT G. (*surly*): A word or two. Aye, or maybe three or four!

DEBORAH: I bet the priest will be clever enough to put him off.

PADDY-TWIN: You're right, begod! He *has* put him off. And now the stranger's heading for the schoolmissus's. There he goes up the steps! There he's in! Will Father Crofts tell all he knows?

GARRETT G.: The parish priest knows nothing about what's going on here. Else he'd have given us all a dart in his sermon while ago.

DEBORAH: That's true, God knows! Well, Golden Folk or not, men must be fed. Garrett, don't ramble off with yourself. The dinner will soon be ready. (*At door to linney.*) Is that you, Kitsy? Here! Into the forge with you and keep an eye on the men.

Kitsy enters from the linney and Deborah whispers.

DEBORAH (*whispering*): You're lookin' lovely, girl! The news is good?

KITSY: 'Tis good indeed, I hope! And, Debbie Fitz, I'm not the one to forget your kindness.

Deborah goes out via the linney. Kitsy sits on the step just inside the door. She has a satisfied look on her face.

PADDY-TWIN: Here, watch the stranger, Mick-my-Twin. (*To Kitsy.*) My brother told you all?

KITSY: As we were coming out from Mass, he told me all.

PADDY-TWIN: That's fair enough! He's watching for the parish priest.

KITSY: I know!

PADDY-TWIN: Now that you're down for marrying *us*, there's a couple of questions I must ask. Do you give in to feeding infants out of tins?

KITSY: 'Tis false to nature. And I disagree.

PADDY-TWIN: Good girl, begod! And, tell me, are you in dread of having twins?

KITSY: I'm not a whack in dread of having twins.

PADDY-TWIN: I hope your body is as brave as your tongue. Let me tell you that twins as big as us would wear you to the bone. Another thing! I hear my grandmother to say that generations back, triplets were in our line. What do you say to that?

KITSY (*simply*): That was the message that my Maker gave me when he put me into life. If three or four or five — or six itself — came at a single birth,

211

I'd clap my hands up to the moon, and say: "Welcome be the holy will of God!"

PADDY-TWIN (*shaking hands with her*): You're fit to join us, Kitsy girl. So, set your mind at ease, we'll be good heads to you, never fear.

MICK-TWIN: Here's Ulick now!

Ulick enters from the roadway.

ULICK (*abruptly, harshly*): And who was here?

GARRETT G.: Darby and my wife, Deborah, and Ellenrose, too, I'd say, and those you see before you.

ULICK: Was no one else here?

All murmur "No!"

ULICK (*to Mick-Twin*): You! Have you made up your mind?

MICK-TWIN: God help me, I have!

ULICK: Did you have your chat with Father Crofts?

MICK-TWIN: When Father Crofts is finished talking to the stranger, I'll have my chat with him.

ULICK (*to Mick-Twin*): Keep watching out! (*To Paddy-Twin.*) And you! Come here! You know the Lenihan lass who lives at the other side of the river?

PADDY-TWIN: Is it the one with the bandy legs, who walks like this?

ULICK: Bandy or straight, I sent her word to join up the Golden Folk. And, maybe, she'll join with you as well.

PADDY-TWIN: Ulick asthore, I'm a poor pattern of a man. I have it now! Let my brother Mick manage both the women. And . . . I'll rock the pair of cradles when the children come.

KITSY: What's that you say, you jasper! You that stole into life like a wren on an eagle's back!

PADDY-TWIN: That Lenihan lassie — if she was left alone with me, I'd melt out of my standing like soft candle grease.

KITSY: 'Tis the likes of you and your cowardly tribe has Ireland in the hobble that she's in. 'Tis you, and all the mean, misbegotten . . .

GARRETT G.: Clap down a foot on it! (*To Paddy-Twin.*) When you joined the Golden Folk you promised that, no matter what *he* said, you'd obey.

PADDY-TWIN: The Golden Folk, is it? And, if it came to that, what do I give a rambling damn about the Golden Folk?

All wheel with a gasp. Paddy-Twin is suddenly aghast at what he has said.

PADDY-TWIN: Maybe I spoke hasty-like! Maybe I . . .

GARRETT G. (*going after him, step by step*): 'Tis true for Kitsy. You came into life like a wren on an eagle's back. Now we've a chance to raise this glen from death to life, to have this forge thronged with men dressed in golden straw. And "What do I care about the Golden Folk?" you say. (*Catches Paddy-Twin by the lapels.*) Listen, you get! You'll marry if *he* tells you so. Take care that you don't turn sour and babble tales in strangers' ears, for if you do I'll set a horseshoe in that fire and there'll be ne'er a horse waiting in the forge. You hear?

Paddy-Twin goes limp. Garrett Gowa flings him away. Recovering, Paddy-Twin scuttles behind the anvil. Enter Father O'Priest from kitchen. His clerical suit and collar are more presentable than on weekdays.

FATHER O'P. (*Reciting, remotely*):

> And up and down the people go
> Gazing where the lilies blow
> Round an Island there below —
> The Island of Shalott . . .

Father O'Priest goes to doorway to road, stands well back from it, raises himself on tiptoe, and looks out.

FATHER O'P.: Mick-Twin, you'll be sure to tell me when that parish priest of yours has gone. The less he sees of unkempt clergymen, the better for his peace of mind.

MICK-TWIN: Aye! I'll do that!

Ulick nods to Garrett Gowa.

GARRETT G.: Father!

FATHER O'P.: What is it? Speak up!

GARRETT G.: The laddo with the beard! You had a chat with him?

FATHER O'P.: He asked me if I were the parish priest. I told him I was not. He has a motorcar behind the rocks of Boscabell.

GARRETT G.: He has? And these fools here thought he was a tramp because he had a beard.

FATHER O'P.: Don't say you weren't warned. He means no good for all of us.

Enter Deborah from the linney.

DEBORAH: Father, you raced through the kitchen very quick. Look! I've a peal salmon that I've boiled all in a piece. When I set him out on the willow dish he'll be a beauty. Stay and eat a bite of dinner with us. Kitsy will tell your sister Moll, as she is going home, not to expect you.

FATHER O'P.: I'm tempted! Yes, for once, to be just as good as Father Crofts, I'll stay.

MICK-TWIN: Hey! Your man is at the door and he's chatting with the parish priest. The schoolmissus — look at her there behind with her ears well cocked. And Darby Jer is there — he's the dead spit of an old pointer dog. "Goodbye! Goodbye!" — that's what they're saying. The beardy fellow's looking around him. He's walking a few steps. By hell! but here he comes!

ULICK (*taking control*): You, Father O', sit down there in Darby's place. And Paddy, sit next to your twin and watch him for idle talk. Debby, you near Kitsy there. All ready now?

GARRETT G.: Be on your guard! Watch every word you speak.

ULICK: If things get out of hand, pretend you're stupid or insane. At your ease, all of you!

Ulick is on the anvil. His back is turned and he has adopted his pose of listlessness. After a little pause, Walter Cunningham appears in the doorway by the road. He is a newspaper reporter in his early twenties. He wears a short slightly soiled white raincoat, beneath which is a brightly colored pullover. He has a black, arty beard.

WALTER: I hope I'm not intruding! May I come in?

GARRETT G. (*with false heartiness*): Come in, young man.

WALTER: Thank you! Yes, thanks indeed. Well, it's . . . first-class weather for the time of year. And, may I say it, I like your lovely countryside.

GARRETT G.: It's not so bad.

An awkward silence.

GARRETT G.: You'll be a canvasser for electric light?

WALTER (*smiling*): No! I'm not a canvasser for electric light!

PADDY-TWIN: He had a chat with the parish priest. So you can be sure he's a merchant going around selling holy breads, or colza oil, or altar wine.

WALTER: Good heavens, no!

MICK-TWIN: I was looking at the river this morning and the sea trout are runnin' like fair hell. Mister, the Blue and Silver minnow is the daddy of all lures that murders sea trout here.

WALTER: I'm not an angler, either!

GARRETT G.: There's mention made that the coastguard station is to be patched up and turned into a Gaelic school. Sir, our Gaelic is rusty, but if we thought that there would be a college here . . .

Walter shakes his head laughingly.

DEBORAH: A Hogan lady 'twas, a third cousin of my own, that died in Buffalo in the U.S.A. and left a sum of money unclaimed. You'll likely be a lawyer's clerk?

Walter shakes his head laughingly.

FATHER O'P. (*sharply*): Have sense, the lot of ye! He could be interested in a score of things. He could be interested in algae or in souterrains, in ocean currents or even in the folk art of the final primitives.

PADDY-TWIN: That's right! Or he could be collecting the razor shells that are found east in Letteree.

MICK-TWIN: Aye! Or perhaps he'd like to follow the Kerry beagles when they go tonguing after hares on the hills.

WALTER: I could be interested in any or all of these. Yes! . . . Why, I could even be an entomologist. (*Father O'Priest alone reacts.*) But then, I'll tell you the truth. I'm interested in people, only.

ALL (*in a whisper of amazement*): It's people that he likes.

GARRETT G.: We're slow-witted people here. In all our talk we didn't even catch your name.

WALTER: The name is Cunningham — Walter Cunningham.

KITSY (*a little amazed and pleased*): Sir, it's men and women you like?

WALTER: That's right!

KITSY: Why are you so fond of them?

WALTER: That's not so easy to explain. People are various. They're wonderful. They're . . .

PADDY-TWIN: What makes them wonderful?

WALTER: It could be their odd, bizarre, almost insane ideas.

GARRETT G. (*heavily*): I see! Will you be stopping long within the glen?

WALTER: I've been in Tanavalla a week today. How long I stay — that depends on what I find.

GARRETT G.: And what you're looking for, have you found it yet?

WALTER: It's hard to say. This much I'll say . . . (*He pauses and glances around the forge.*) Here in your glen I've found a people who are completely alive. It's as if your faces were colored by a sunset light. Why, even the little child I met upon the road . . .

DEBORAH: Children can be notorious liars when they like!

WALTER: Not this one, I assure you! (*Pause.*) You'll excuse me. I have the sense, somehow, that I'm intruding. This young man here! (*Indicating Ulick.*)

MICK-TWIN: When he's like that, he doesn't count at all.

WALTER: No?

MICK-TWIN: He hasn't heard one single word we said. We look to him for whims and notions and things like that.

WALTER: What notions?

MICK-TWIN: Yes, he has the strangest notions underneath the stars. For more than twenty years me and my brother were harmlessly courting Kitsy who's there beyond. And then one night, brave Ulick told a story, and after he'd done (*claps his hands*) honest to God, I couldn't catch a woman quick enough.

WALTER: He told a tale?

MICK-TWIN (*delightedly*): He told a gala story fit to blind the moon. And, more than that, he . . .

Ulick slides off the anvil and goes to the bellows house.

PADDY-TWIN (*suddenly catching his brother by the sleeve and putting him behind him*): Sir! excuse me — my brother is a class of fool. God save our souls — we're twins. Body alone was issued him and brains was given to me at birth. The biggest of the pair will wed. That's all! There's no mystery in that, is there?

WALTER (*pregnantly*): Of course not! It's all as clear as glass.

Ulick is now resting on the handle of the bellows. Walter moves to the hearth and takes up a hammer.

WALTER: As I came here, in a wayside forge across the bay, I met a smith. Just as I called, he blew his top — something about a farm that was boycotted. I heard him beat an angry rhythm out — like this!

Walter taps the Kryle. Darby Jer enters from the roadway.

DARBY JER (*chanting, in time to the Kryle*):

> "I came," says he, "for to melt his seeding,
> And I came," says he, "for to blast his breeding,
> And I came," says he, "for to drag him down to Hell."
> Then welcome, Death, in the morning early,
> And welcome, too, to your voice so surly,
> And I'll show you now . . .

Ellenrose, wearing an apron, enters from kitchen. She looks mildly at Darby Jer, who ceases to chant.

ELLENROSE (*to Deborah*): The salmon isn't cooked yet. I think I'll let it boil a little longer.

Ellenrose stares at the stranger. There is a moment of awkwardness. Ulick begins, almost imperceptibly, to blow the bellows on the dead fire.

WALTER: I can plainly see that I'm intruding . . .

ELLENROSE: The motorcar behind the rocks — it's yours?

WALTER: It's mine. And it's quite nice to ride in. It's smooth and fast. Say! Would you like to try a run in her?

The tempo of the bellows has increased.

ELLENROSE: Ooo! I'd love to! Yes!

WALTER: You would?

ELLENROSE: Sure! Just say the word!

WALTER: You bet! I'm saying the word right now! Where would you like to go?

ELLENROSE: Oh, anyplace at all, as long as it's away from here. How would you like to run me to the top of Maam Pass and back again? Say! I'd love to see the Spanish trawlers and the Blasket Islands far away. That view always reminds me of the shore of my own New England.

WALTER: Come on!

ELLENROSE (*returning to remove her apron*): Aunt Debby! Kitsy! We'll be back before you've missed us. One word! (*Meaningly.*) With overcooking don't let that salmon spoil.

Both whisk out onto the roadway. The labored rocking of the bellows is like the breathing of an angry animal.

KITSY: Oh, blessed hour! That was the courting speed! And me! To think that I wasted twenty years of life hung on an old meathook swinging between yes and no . . . I could let down my hair and cry to think of all the love-ly love I've missed.

FATHER O'P. (*looking after the pair*):

> From the bank and from the river
> He flashed into the crystal mirror.
> "Tirra-lirra," by the river,
> Sang Sir Launcelot."

(*Pauses at doorway to road.*) You're listening, all of you? Before I was ordained, I used to lie awake, night after night. The vow of chastity it was. I thought it hard for a man to swap an earthly manhood for an eternal manhood gotten of the loins (*barely audible*) of Christ. And you here in this glen — you have surrendered both — you fools! (*Pause.*)

> Out flew the web and floated wide,
> The mirror cracked from side to side:
> "I am half-sick of shadows," cried
> The Lady of Shalott.

Exit Father O'Priest to the kitchen.

MICK-TWIN (*looking out window and turning to shout*): My soul to the eighty-nine devils and back again! There's Father Crofts and he's sitting into his car. What'll I do at all? I own to God, he's starting her up. It's miles too late now to ask him if I'm free to wed Kitsy Carty.

DEBORAH: 'Tis no such thing, too late! Race off at once, you circus clown!

KITSY: Race off, I say, or by the Man that's in Heaven, I'll crush your ugly skull!

MICK-TWIN: Paddy, you're lighter on your pins than I am. Race off and catch the parish priest.

PADDY-TWIN: Faith, I will not! He might only marry me instead of you.

DEBORAH: You pandy-belly! Race off, I say!

MICK-TWIN: By Moses, I will! (*Runs. Stops.*) I wonder will he charge me much to give me the Latin letter saying that I'm free?

KITSY (*screaming*): If you don't race off this mortal second, I'll run my ten talons down your face.

MICK-TWIN: Stand back! Give me a run at it! I'm off! (*Stops at doorway, turns.*) Oh hell! I've left my silver in the pocket of my other pants. Wait! I'll ask him to put it down against me in the book until my cow calves.

KITSY: O, Lord on high, the priest is gone! And he's taken my hope of gener-ation in his track. (*To Mick-Twin.*) I'll stretch you dead!

PADDY-TWIN (*to Mick-Twin*): Clear for the door. Your life's in jeopardy.

Grabbing an iron, Kitsy chases Mick-Twin out of the forge. Paddy-Twin races after both. Deborah goes to the door and glances after the three, then turns to sit on the log beneath the latticed window.

ULICK (*explosively, to Garrett Gowa*): And you!

217

GARRETT G.: And me?

ULICK: And you! To let her off with strangers in a stranger's car!

GARRETT G.: Why didn't you stop her, man?

ULICK: Why should I, and you her uncle standing deaf and dumb beside me?

DEBORAH (*meaningly*): If 'twas a thing we thought you'd like to have her stopped . . .

ULICK (*flaring*): Who said I did?

DEBORAH: Calm yourself! As soon as she comes back, we'll tell her off for running away with strangers.

ULICK: Pretend I've said no word, you hear?

GARRETT G.: We hear!

DEBORAH: We hear and understand!

ULICK (*to Darby Jer*): And you! You had a chat with the stranger down there at the pier. What were ye talking about?

DARBY JER: I'm under no obligation to tell *you* that!

ULICK: Whether you are or not, we'll shortly see.

DARBY JER: How will you see, bantam cock?

ULICK: By calling to your mind what was done to Milo the Emergency long ago.

DARBY JER: I know that better than yourself.

ULICK: Then read your bloody book again. He was strapped to a fi'-barred gate in this forge. His breast was bared, a horseshoe was reddened in that fire, and the grandfather of Garrett Gowa . . .

DARBY JER: I know what happened, no mistake. For I was there. I'm not in dread of iron when 'tis reddened in a fire and I'm not in dread of Captain Death either. But of this one thing I am afraid — to be branded as a spy, so that my kin would light with shame if my name were said.

GARRETT G.: What were ye talking about at the pier?

DARBY JER: We were talking of one William Shakespeare who poached a salmon and ran away. We spoke, too, of the day that Colmcille foretold would come when a fine marriageable girl strolling through empty Ireland would cry: "Mamma, today I saw a man!" And the stranger came close enough to your Golden Folk when he declared that when a spider builds his web he really builds a great suspension bridge.

GARRETT G. (*at door*): He came close to the bone on that. I can see the car shining above on the Maam.

DEBORAH: The pair are chatting and looking at the view. Wait! They're settling into the car now.

GARRETT G.: Here comes the car-een, and it flashing like a ball of fire.

DEBORAH (*signing to Garrett Gowa*): He looks a likely kind of lad.

GARRETT G. (*understanding*): A likely lad, indeed.

DARBY JER: In one hand's turn, he'd maybe crucify us all.

DEBORAH: I'd swear he has the world of songs.

GARRETT G.: We'd need lodgers like him in this place . . .

Deborah and Garrett Gowa have been making vague signs to Darby Jer to indicate that they wish to nettle Ulick.

DARBY JER: I'll hold to my own judgment. (*Suddenly appreciating the situation.*) But, still and all, he seems a clever boy, one that is fit to sit on that anvil there and . . .

ULICK (*nettled and shouting*): The pair of God's pigheads, you and you! How long would he be dreaming up the Golden Folk?

GARRETT G.: We'll grant you that!

ULICK: You'll grant me more than that before this week is out!

DEBORAH (*smilingly*): Ulick, you're a little slow where women are concerned, but, just the same, you're the prince of all. . . . Mother o' mercy, I forgot! The salmon will be spoiled!

Deborah rushes to kitchen through linney.

ULICK: We'll follow Deborah.

GARRETT G.: Aye, and at the same time we'll keep an eye through the window.

ULICK: The minute the car stops, go out and chat with him. If he comes into the forge, I'll talk with him alone. That way, I'll search his mind.

GARRETT G.: And you, Darby! You'd better be going! And make no hurry to come back, either!

Exit Garrett Gowa and Ulick to the kitchen through the linney. Darby Jer who has been pretending to leave by the door to roadway, now returns.

DARBY JER: If *she* comes here, he'll chat with *her* alone — that's what he means. "Off with you, Darby Jer!" he says. I never got a chance till now to do what I came here to do. "And make no hurry to come back!" he says to me . . .

Darby Jer quickly goes to the door right and, standing on the box, hides the eggs in the hole in the wall.

DARBY JER (*to the eggs*): There, brothers! Do your very best to cause disturbance in the forge.

Hearing Ellenrose whistling a lively version of " 'Tis My Bitter Sorrow," Darby Jer scuttles down and hides himself at the back of the chimney. Enter Ellenrose from the roadway.

ELLENROSE (*bursting in*): Say! (*Finding no one before her.*) What do you know! There's no one here! (*Curtseying to the anvil.*) Your Royal Highness, would you be listening with your ears? (*Looks out.*) Uh huh! And there's Uncle Garrett talking to the stranger. I see! (*Reminiscently.*) Yes, Mr. Cunningham, those are the Skelligs Rocks. That's the Cow and Calf. The way you looked down at the anthill was too plain. It's obvious to me that you're inquiring about the Golden Folk.

Enter Father O'Priest from the kitchen.

FATHER O'P.: Quick, while the smith is out there chatting on the road.

ELLENROSE: Father!

FATHER O'P.: What is it?

ELLENROSE: I'm not sure that, by giving you this, I'm doing the right thing. Uncle Garrett would . . .

FATHER O'P.: Be quick, I tell you! (*His fingers indicate a little whiskey in a glass.*) This little much is all I want — no more! I tell you that it stirs my heart.

ELLENROSE: Father, I . . .

FATHER O'P.: What is it, girl? Speak up! I see! You wish to humble me. You wish me to beg on bended knees. Is that it?

ELLENROSE: No, Father . . . no!

FATHER O'P.: I've hinted at it many times, but now I give you my priestly word — this little much is all I ever take. It's just . . . it's just . . . In temperament, you see, I cannot, must not, dare not, go too low, for when I take this little much I'm suddenly taut and trim and brave. And today, now, as I speak to you, I'm far below the safety line. Without it, I'll go reeling, tottering, falling round the forge. Now that you've humbled me, be quick!

ELLENROSE: Forgive me, Father! Yes, I'll be quick. I'll get it from the room above. It's mine, you know. I bought it in Tanavalla. I'll dole it out to you in what my Papa called "der arm shot."

Exit Ellenrose to kitchen.

FATHER O'P.: Below the safety line! (*Speaking to seat of hearth where Darby usually sits.*) Darby, some day we'll meet head on — you with your eggs and parceled meat; me with my torn Ritual in my hands, and when we meet . . .

Enter Ellenrose.

ELLENROSE: Quick Father! In with you! It's on the shelf in the linney. And be sure to hide the glass!

Father O'Priest goes out quickly, drinks the whiskey, and returns to the forge.

FATHER O'P.: Exactly right! God bless! It's a foretaste of the heavens up above. Good girl! I saw you and the stranger standing together on the Maam. The pair of you, together, standing there . . .

As the priest moves away, Ellenrose shows agitation in her movements.

ELLENROSE: Father!

FATHER O'P. (*sharply*): What's that? What's that, I say?

ELLENROSE: You trusted me. I'll trust you in return. Father . . . ! (*A pause.*) Ulick . . . Ulick disturbs me very much. I . . .

FATHER O'P.: Do you think I'm blind and deaf? I know!

ELLENROSE: All he can think of is his Golden Folk. He can't even see me with his eyes. And these folk here, by degrees I begin to feel their hunger for the wild colored life. There's a battle going on inside me, Father. I feel myself torn in two. My dad — God rest him — he was practical. Bavarian and dour. Mother, she's Irish and a peasant, and the strange thing is that she's forever talking of White Horses and May Eve, of grace and canticles. While he's . . . Father, I couldn't tell this to another soul besides yourself but now I have to tell you that I'm going right through hell. Please . . . please advise me what I'm to do?

FATHER O'P.: Not even a whiskey drop is ever for itself!

ELLENROSE: Please, Father . . . please!

FATHER O'P.: One always pays! I know the formula. First it's charity, then confidence, emotional blackmail, and last of all the begging bowl stretched out to catch advice.

ELLENROSE: I'm sorry, Father!

FATHER O'P.: I know it well. It's "Scapegoat priest, take my sack of troubles and be off!" I'm sick of it, you hear?

ELLENROSE: Oh, please forget I ever said a word.

FATHER O'P.: Sick to the heart of it! You asked advice? Then take it now! And grip it close! Don't sour with age, like Darby Jer — or me! Hold fast to what you love. (*Shouting.*) You hear me, girl. And never again trouble me for advice.

Father O'Priest moves quickly offstage to kitchen. Enter Kitsy quickly from roadway.

KITSY (*ecstatic*): 'Twas God that did it, Ellenrose! Right at the gable of Sean Bawn's a duck hopped up, and whir! there he was fettered in the radiator of the priest's car. Father Crofts got out, his head a pure ball of fire with rage. I saw my chance and I took it like a man. I shelled Mick the Twin with rocks and stones until he hopped to ask the priest for the letter saying he was free. Thanks be to all the gorgeous saints of Italy and Spain. Thanks be to Finian Leper and to Finian the Crookèd. Thanks be to each and every martyr ever lost his blood . . .

Paddy-Twin has just come in the doorway from the road and has a stare of disaster in his eyes.

PADDY-TWIN: Kitsy!

KITSY: What is it, Paddy-Twin?

PADDY-TWIN: Your goose is cooked!

KITSY: What's that you say?

PADDY-TWIN: The priest's new suit was destroyed with feathers and blood. My twin took one gawk at his face, then shut his mouth, took to his heels, and ran.

KITSY: He ran?

PADDY-TWIN: He legged it like a deer. If you grab iron, girl, I'll help you get revenge.

KITSY (*smiling with an odd dignity*): 'Tis as well for me to sing my grief as to cry it now. Paddy, I'll chase your twin no more. Soon I'll compose my face and I'll walk abroad, and I'll hold my head high as any decent woman should.

PADDY-TWIN: Kitsy! You've changed! You've changed greatly. All of a sudden I see you as a kind of noble queen. (*He takes up a weapon from the hearth.*) By the King of all the angels, for leaving this fine woman in the lurch, I'll pound my brother on the skull until he oozes out his brains.

Paddy-Twin rushes out the doorway to the road.

KITSY (*moving toward doorway to road*): Aye, that's the way with life — one day it's black and another day it's white. God bless you, Ellenrose, I'm jealous of you — you're so fine and young and I'm . . . If what we know comes knocking at your door, run out and answer — that's a fool's advice! Remember, girl, what I'm saying to you. Time races like a hare from fire.

Meanwhile Ulick has come just inside the linney doorway. Kitsy looks wistfully from him to Ellenrose, then back again. She turns and moves out to the roadway with the dignity of the acceptance of her fate. There is an odd silence. Ulick moves restlessly here and there, all the while watching the road.

ULICK (*abruptly*): Yourself and the stranger . . . !

ELLENROSE: Yes!

ULICK: What did ye have to say to one another up there at the Maam?

ELLENROSE: You reckon you've the right to know?

ULICK: What did ye have to say?

ELLENROSE: We spoke of reality and human beings, things that would hardly interest you.

ULICK: Did he make any mention of the . . . ?

ELLENROSE: He made no mention of your precious ants at all.

ULICK (*angrily*): Don't call them that!

ELLENROSE: Yes! I see! (*Thoughtfully.*) Maybe it's not a masquerade. Ulick, listen to me carefully. I think your mind at this moment is balanced on a blade. Here there is brilliance; there, there is something terrible and dark. Why don't you quit the game? Why don't you open your eyes? Yes, certainly, see what's in the faraway. But also see (*meaningly*) what's close beside you right here in the forge.

ULICK: Do you think I don't see what's here beside me in the forge? I too heard Kitsy say: "Time races like a hare from fire!" It runs for me as well as for you. And look! Of their own accord my arms are rising up to . . .

ELLENROSE: To?

ULICK: To clasp you close! (*They embrace.*) I love you, Ellenrose. I've

222

loved you since you first walked into this forge. Whatever comes to pass, you must trust me . . . Look! The stranger's coming here. Off with you now. I'll talk with him alone.

With a final embrace, Ellenrose rushes to the kitchen. Enter Walter Cunningham from the roadway.

WALTER (*more authoritative now*): You are Ulick Madigan?

ULICK: Yes!

WALTER: There's no one here to hear what I've to say to you?

ULICK: No!

WALTER: This letter of yours! (*Ulick starts . . . a pause.*) It made its way to me. This story that you tell — is it true?

ULICK: It's not!

WALTER: It's not?

ULICK: It's lies!

WALTER: I see!

ULICK: It's lies, I tell you; a tangled bag of lies!

WALTER: You wrote the letter?

ULICK: I wrote it as a sort of joke — a lie.

WALTER: There must be more to it than that?

ULICK: There's no more to it than that!

WALTER: Look! If you wish this affair to stay a prank, or a joke, or a lie as you call it, that's fine. Newspapers are used to all sorts of cranks. But for my own personal satisfaction, I'd like to hear a little more about what's going on here in the glen.

ULICK: I can't explain!

WALTER: Yes, you can!

ULICK: I tell you that I can't. It's just that I have a craze for coloring life — that's all!

WALTER: I see!

ULICK (*angrily*): You see? How could the likes of you see? To you this place is picturesque. To me it's daft and desolate. And it's dying fast. Once, out of the struggle for the land, came storytellers, dancers, poets, men who made fiddle music fit to stir the stars. But they are all dead — all dead, I tell you, man. The young people — they have all gone across the sea. We were alone and moving toward our end. And then, when all seemed lost, one winter's night, we held a trial all night long until the crack of dawn to find a man who'd tell a flamin' variegated lie . . .

WALTER: You won?

ULICK: I won! And do you know what 'twas like? 'Twas like as if the voice of God was roaring from my blood. Ever since then, for me, gannet and gull, lizard and eel, even the tongs and kettle on the hob, must speak and act like Christian men.

WALTER: I think I see! And how did this latest fancy of yours begin?

ULICK: Something the girl said.

WALTER: The American girl?

ULICK: Yes! She said something about a stone she stirred up there on the mountain, and when the stone was raised (*dreamily*) there were the Golden Folk.

WALTER: These others — do they believe they're what you say?

ULICK: In times of fierce emotion, yes — they all believe, except, of course, the broken priest and Darby Jer.

WALTER: What about the girl?

ULICK: In her, her mother's blood will tell. Then she's certain to believe.

WALTER: One question more — do you yourself believe?

ULICK (*thoughtfully*): Do I believe? I've never faced that before. It's as if a thing that's said and said again can at last wear the groove that is belief. Belief, at times, can be a game of cards that's played to certain rules.

WALTER: So this is all a game?

ULICK (*angrily*): Don't twist my words!

WALTER: I'm sorry! One other point — why, in your letter, did you betray these people, and then, when I've come here, go back on what you said?

ULICK (*catching Walter by lapels of coat, shouting*): Betray? Who has betrayed?

WALTER: You! By your letter you betrayed!

ULICK (*releasing Walter*): You fool! I wrote that letter that these here might live. They hold two things as crimes beyond repair — to be laughed at and to be betrayed.

WALTER: And you've committed both! You asked that they be laughed at in the newspapers. You asked that they be betrayed.

ULICK: I did it only that the shock might spring them back to life.

WALTER: In that you ran a risk.

ULICK (*anguished*): I ran the risk of life and death. And now, when all is set, I find that I'm weak and drawn aside.

WALTER: By love, is it?

ULICK: No! No! . . . I've changed my mind again! Print everything. Take pictures here. Scald me alive — by name. Build up a tale of witchcraft in a Kerry glen that'll make us the laughingstock of Ireland and of foreign lands. You understand?

WALTER: I think I do! And out of it will come . . . ?

ULICK: Out of it will come beauty full as a Mass that's sung. Women and men at nature's war and peace. I know you think me daft. But I'm in the sanity that goes before the final craze. You'll do exactly as I say?

WALTER: I'll do it — yes! But I'll do it in my own time and way.

ULICK: Good! Out with you now, before I change my mind once again. Wait!

I'll leave the forge first. You follow me in your car. Where the two rocks are standing by the road I'll wait, and there I'll tell you all. You understand?

WALTER: I understand!

Ulick goes to the roadway. Moving about the forge, Walter looks curiously here and there. After a short time, Walter goes quickly out to the roadway. When he has gone Darby Jer, cackling, emerges from his hiding place in the bellows house. As he moves, quickly but cautiously, to the doorway to the road, Deborah enters the forge by the doorway from the kitchen.

DEBORAH: You're mighty happy for a Sunday, Darby Jer.

DARBY JER (*recovering from a start*): Now that you come to mention it, I am!

DEBORAH: And why are you so happy, Darby Jer?

DARBY JER: Nothing much, except . . .

DEBORAH: Except?

DARBY JER: Except a sack of secrets spilled out upon the ground and the idiots of Ireland gathered into one glen. And then a holy boyo tippling at the barley juice, a foreign slip in love, a woman jilted too, and strangers with beards — they having bailiff's heads. And there — I near forgot! — Judas Iscariot and he walking Ireland's ground again.

Chuckling, Darby Jer moves out doorway that leads to road. Deborah's face is troubled as she watches him go.

Act III

Night a few days later at the forge. Before curtain-up, the sound of the hammer is heard beating on the anvil to the rhythm of the Kryle. On curtain-rise, Garrett Gowa is seen finishing the making of an iron gate which measures approximately seven feet by four and a half feet and which has a large V pattern rising from about the latch to end in heel angles of the gate. The gate is now spread flat on hearth and anvil. On the hearth the fire licks lazily. Overhead a Tilley lamp is lighting. Ulick is standing, looking through the latticed window, left stage. The moonlight is faint on his face. Darby Jer is sitting to the left of the hearth, Garrett Gowa hums the Kryle rhythm which is now lively and gay.

GARRETT G.: Stir yourself there, Darby Jer! Come here and hold the gate. Rise from your seat, I say. Grip the end of it. Hurry! I want this forge ready before the Golden Folk arrive.

Reluctantly, Darby Jer rises and holds the end of the gate. Humming, Garrett Gowa hammers on the rivets.

GARRETT G.: Eh, Ulick! Are you listening with your ears?

ULICK: I am!

GARRETT G.: Good man! 'Tis a while since you had need to walk out at random in that strange desert of your mind. The Golden Folk! (*Laughs.*) They to be underneath our brogues for generations back and we to be pure dark of they being there at all. By the red nose of Moses, this is a fancy and no mistake! Do you know what you did, Ulick? You took the blindfold from our eyes and made us see. Tell me, are you listening to me at all?

ULICK: I am!

GARRETT G.: Here's a word of warning from an old friend, so be sure to heed it. Our appetite for marvels must be nourished, so, whatever you do, don't falter in the coining of diversion for us. Our heads are in this and so are our hearts. I hope to hell our souls are not locked in it as well . . . Hold up the gate — do you hear me, Darby Jer?

Humming, the smith finishes the clenching of the rivets, then places the hammer on the hearth. Darby Jer sits on his seat once more.

GARRETT G.: There now, Jack Meehan of Paurkeen, this gate will keep your cows from straying into crops and . . . Whisht! Hold! . . . I thought I heard . . .

Music of melodeon, playing the Kryle tune, and the clack of bones tapping the Kryle rhythm is heard in the distance.

GARRETT G.: Yes! Yes! I'm right! 'Tis them! The Golden Folk are coming here for the Dance of Gold. (*To Darby Jer.*) Be quick, you pooka! Up! (*Music.*) Grip the gate I tell you and take it out of this!

Garrett Gowa and Darby Jer upend the gate and place it against the wall backstage left.

GARRETT G.: We're just in time! Aye, here they come!

ULICK (*turning, transfigured a little*): I'll lower the lamp a bit now. That way, the moonlight will shine upon the dance.

Ulick lowers the lamp. Garrett Gowa takes a hammer and with it beats time on the anvil. The licking of the fire throws erratic gold on the walls and ceiling of the forge. Straw-clad figures of men and women enter. They are chatting and dancing slowly, spasmodically and grotesquely, in time to the Kryle rhythm, played on melodeon and rib bones. The dancing gathers momentum. The scene is lighted by the flame of the fire and the moonlight through the doorway and window. Presently the dance grows faster, and the dancers begin to chant:

> Now we're the Golden Folk,
> Loyal and olden folk,
> Now we're the Golden Folk indeed!
> Heart's blood and rainbow's glory,

226

Green grass an' flamin' story,
Now we're the Golden Folk indeed!

(*Higher and still more weird.*)

Now we're the Golden Folk,
Powerful and glowing folk,
Now we're the Golden Folk indeed!

Mad sea and wind a-blowing,
Red iron when it's glowing,
Now we're the Golden Folk indeed!

The dance has now become devilishly fast and fully alive. The cries and movements are wildness itself. Meanwhile, Ellenrose has entered from the doorway left. She moves haltingly on the edge of the dancers. She appears taken by a series of emotions, among them revulsion, curiosity, and racial remembrance. She moves swiftly here and there as if seeking someone to whom she can impart important news. Then she moves tentatively but gradually with growing confidence into the dance. Deborah has appeared in doorway right from kitchen and linney. Music and chanting rise to a crescendo. At last the dancing and the music weaken to a weird slowness. One by one the dancers move off until only the straw-clad bone-tapper is left, still tapping time. He revolves a few times, then makes a snakelike gesture with the bones, mock-striking at Garrett Gowa and Darby Jer. Then, still tapping, he moves off after the others. The music dies away in the distance. Onstage are Ellenrose, Garrett Gowa, Ulick, Darby Jer, and Deborah. Ellenrose looks around fearfully, hesitates, indicates surrender to racial remembrance, then goes out quickly by the doorway to the road. Deborah swiftly follows her to the doorway, where she stands.

DEBORAH: The girl! (*Pause.*) The girl, I tell ye! When she came in at the middle of the dance there was a stare in her eyes. She looked as if she had bitter news to tell us. Aye! and though she danced for a while with the rest of them, look how she skeltered from the forge. I'd swear she's gone racing across the strand to look for Father O'.

GARRETT G.: She danced, did she? That same is good. It proves that her blood is telling in the heel of all.

Garrett Gowa raises the lamp.

DEBORAH: Her blood is telling. Yes — I'm with you there! But danger's telling also. And, unless I'm mistaken, deep in her eyes I spotted something else.

GARRETT G.: Women are moody bits of stuff. And 'tis well known that ye go by opposites rather than go walking side by side. When we had sorrow nothing under God's sky would suit ye but to go seeking joy. Now that we've joy, ye're seeking sorrow back again.

Deborah stands for a moment or two by the doorway to the road, then goes out thoughtfully to the roadway left. Paddy-Twin, Mick-Twin, and Kitsy rush in from the roadway. Laughingly they pull sops of straw from their heads and shoulders.

PADDY-TWIN: Ulick! You're the king of all the world! Here, man, up with you and mount your anvil throne.

He leads Ulick to the anvil.

KITSY: Life has some sort of a smell and taste to it at last. Tell me, neighbors, am I talking truth?

PADDY-TWIN: By hell, but you are! Lately me and this awkward twin of mine are poxed with luck. Why — our cows are giving torrents of rich milk.

MICK-TWIN: And our sheep, every one of them is mud fat, and hanging with good wool.

KITSY: The same with us! This year the spuds are living balls of flour.

GARRETT G.: The Golden Folk have brought me joy just as it's brought it to the rest of ye. Work making gates has piled up on me. The horse can scratch himself. Good days have come again, eh, Darby Jer? And that reminds me! You worked your share of shabby rogueries and failed. What have you to say to that?

DARBY JER (*mildly*): Easy to speak my share! Ye'll chant and prance and ply your asses' bones. Aye! ye'll go on and on until an informer spits venom on the ground and then ye'll turn on one another's flesh like cannibals.

GARRETT G.: Informer, is it? Is that the word you said?

DARBY JER: That's the very word I said.

PADDY-TWIN: I know you! You've something up your cuff. Talk out your twisted mind.

DARBY JER (*still mild*): I know my know! Take caution, lest in the middle of your famous jollity, ye breed a spy of silk.

GARRETT G.: A spy, is it?

DARBY JER: That's the very thing I said. For spy's a word with plenty blood in it. And what's more, I want to tell ye that red-hot iron and the Kryle are in it, too. Take caution lest ye breed a spy who'll set all this country rocking like a rocking chair with one long loud guffaw at ye — my Yalla Men indeed!

GARRETT G.: There's meat in what the old serpent says, so stitch up your lips. You hear me, all of you?

ALL: We hear you!

GARRETT G.: If any stranger asks ye anything about . . . (*He moves toward the twins . . . angrily.*) This fellow who came smelling around here after Mass last Sunday, now that I come to think of it, he spoke with each of you — alone . . . No! No! (*To Darby Jer.*) Back to your barrel, you old badger. Now I spot your plan. What you want to do is to set us at one another's throats.

228

DARBY JER: I'll bide my hour and see. Time's an almanac that will prove me right.

Enter Deborah from the road. She stands in the doorway, looking out; then, closing the door behind her, she comes fully into the forge.

DEBORAH: I looked for her east and west. I thought I saw her shadow racing against the breaking waves. And then I heard the voice of Father O'. He's poorly again. I heard him chanting loudly on the farthest shore.

KITSY: They'll both be back. Tell me, Garrett Gowa . . .

DEBORAH: Kitsy! (*Pause.*) Kitsy, I say! You read the girl's eyes?

KITSY (*evasive*): Whose eyes? (*Louder.*) Whose eyes?

DEBORAH: I know by your antics that, like myself, you read her eyes.

KITSY: What ails you, woman, in the name of God?

DEBORAH: No need to answer that, for you're a woman just the same as myself. (*Looking at Ulick.*) Are *you* too jealous to tell us about the joy you saw in the girl's two eyes? (*Looking at Darby Jer.*) Or are *you* in dread to tell us about the sorrow you saw there, too?

KITSY (*evasively*): I saw nothing in God's good world, except a lassie getting all of a sudden flustered of a yellow night. It could be one of a thousand things was eating her. Tell on, let ye, about the Golden Folk.

DEBORAH: Kitsy!

KITSY: Ah! hush your "Kitsy," Deborah Fitzgerald.

DEBORAH: All that I'm asking you is to . . .

KITSY: I want no more of it! Here we are as happy as the days are long till bloody-you come fretting with your old lonely fiddle face. You saw the moon and calves with hats and mushrooms come alive, and pigs standing on two legs and smoking clay pipes — that's what you saw!

GARRETT G.: Enough of it! Now, what ye're requesting me this while back — I'll let ye question Ulick about the Golden Folk.

Eager cries as the others press round.

GARRETT G.: Be easy, blast ye, or I'll scorch one of your polls. I'll allow ye draw what's sufficient for a week and no more! Paddy-Twin is first!

PADDY-TWIN: Ulick, my brainy boy, tell me what ranks and divisions have the Golden Folk?

ULICK (*withdrawn*): What's that?

GARRETT G.: He asked you: What ranks and divisions have the Golden Folk?

ULICK (*waking up somewhat and gaining in exaltation as the scene goes on; again the yellow light fills and ebbs with belief and disbelief*): The same as us. Only they have a better ordering, I'd say.

PADDY-TWIN: Have they smallholding farmers, the same as we have here?

ULICK: They have, indeed.

MICK-TWIN: They haven't suckling calves?

ULICK: They have! And they keep green insect cows in stalls.

229

PADDY-TWIN: Well, glory-o! And do they milk these mannikins of cows?

ULICK: Of course they do! But 'tis only fools like us that pull the paps. The Golden Folk strip their cows of honeydew by stroking them and singing an old wonder tune so that they yield their udders full.

KITSY: And have they an army made of men that can curse and swear? And have they barracks and bugle calls and all to that?

ULICK: Aye! They've soldiers and sergeants, and they've officers as well. They battle strangers with their powerful jaws. Each of the Golden Folk is made in three little bits and each bitteen, if it is cut off, can battle on its own.

Cries of astonishment.

GARRETT G.: 'Tis my turn now! Once at Tanavalla, I saw a traveler, naked to his waist — a powerful fellow — hoisting balls of steel above his head. The likes of him, would he be found among the Golden Folk?

ULICK: He would, faith! Some of them can balance mighty leaves over their heads. It's just the same as if me or you could lift the rock of Cloch-na-Rón and fire it down into the sea to block up the Spaniard's Gap.

Cries of astonishment.

PADDY-TWIN: Hold on! I've a rattler here that's certain to stagger him. Have they a public house, like Paka's beyond; a place with big red barrels in it full to brim with porter?

MICK-TWIN: He'll never riddle that!

GARRETT G.: By my mortal oath, he'll try his best.

ULICK: They pump one of their own with honeydew. He swells to the size of a grape. To us that's equal to a whale stranded.

PADDY-TWIN: And does he burst when he's pumped up like that, the same as a warble fly that's full of blood?

ULICK: He doesn't burst. He stays alive and well, this barrel boy. His comrades raise him up and up and they tell him to grip the rafters with his two front legs. And then . . . the light falls sideways in amber through the living cask of wine.

GARRETT G.: I own to hell! Compared with that what are scabby, mangy human beings but common trash.

PADDY-TWIN: They're trash indeed! As for me — d'ye know what? I feel as if I was born again.

MICK-TWIN: And me!

KITSY: And me!

GARRETT G.: And me!

DEBORAH: And me as well as the rest of ye!

DARBY JER: Oho! the born again! Was ever such a flock of donkeys gathered together in one place before. I'll put one question, Ulickeen, and no more!

These famous Golden Folk of yours — how do they bring their own into the world again?

KITSY: That's a proper question! And it's put in proper words.

DEBORAH: True enough! It's something that concerns us all.

PADDY-TWIN: It's the first of life.

MICK-TWIN: Out with the answer, Ulick — if you're able for it.

GARRETT G.: You'll get an answer, never fear!

DARBY JER (*sarcastically*): I'll get an answer and no mistake. I will indeed. Eh, Ulick! Are you turned deaf and dumb? Is it like a stallion or like a ram they mate? Or maybe 'tis like a cock salmon when November's in the door to us. Tell us how they breed, your famous Yellow Men.

ULICK (*lamely*): High in the sky, they mate . . .

DARBY JER: You're a convicted liar, picked and painted! In all your meanderings of words I heard you making no mention at all of their having wings.

ULICK (*shouting*): Then, hear it now! (*Withdrawn.*) There comes a day when certain of the Golden Folk sprout wings. These are the males; then in the good city underground, unheralded, there walks a winged queen . . .

Ellenrose, apprehensive, yet moving quietly appears at the doorway to road. Kitsy sees her. As yet Ulick does not.

KITSY (*whispering to Ulick*): Tell on, my treasure. Time races like a hare from fire.

ULICK: High in the sky, she flies — the queen. The chieftains follow her to the highest spires of air. And there with one she selects from among the princely ones . . .

Ulick now sees Ellenrose. All hang tensely as if suddenly aware of a deep feeling between Ulick and the girl. Ulick turns away. His mood alters to one of angry embarrassment.

DEBORAH: Yes, Ulick, son!

KITSY: Yes, Ulick, son!

ULICK: She mates! And then she drops to earth. She sheds her wings. She digs a shelter. She drags a stone on top of her. She lays her eggs and hatches them to life. Thus there is born a new generation of the Golden Folk.

Ulick swings round on his anvil seat. Ellenrose, nervous and undecided, moves across the stage. As she turns at the doorway to the kitchen there is, in the forge, a moment of tense, silent apprehension. Deborah is concerned. The girl goes out.

DARBY JER (*laughing scornfully*): A queen aloft, in the highest spires of air. I own to hell, ye doting fools, maybe ye give credit to this tale.

GARRETT G.: You're jealous, you switcher!

KITSY: If Darby had thought this tale of glory out, we'd never hear the end of his cleverness.

GARRETT G.: This has a better skin than any trick of his.

PADDY-TWIN: That's true! Him and his dark enquiries by improper means after what's lost and what's hidden and what's to come.

MICK-TWIN: 'Tis scalded like an old lobster he should be!

All except Deborah have begun almost imperceptibly to encircle Darby Jer.

GARRETT G.: Wait! Maybe he has a second question to put to Ulick?

DARBY JER: I have! I've a query that's the prince of all, and if he answers this, then, by my blood and bone, Darby Jer will surrender.

GARRETT G.: What's laming you?

PADDY-TWIN: Ulick is standing here to answer anything you ask.

DARBY JER: I'll ask my question so. (*To Ulick.*) These Golden buckos of yours, they who go breeding for themselves in the high spires of the air, they who outstrip us poor humans in the cleverness of the mind, have they a Man Above; have they a Man Below?

Father O'Priest has entered by the doorway to the road. He has heard Darby Jer's question. He pauses. Seeing the priest, Ulick makes no reply. Father O'Priest walks slowly across the floor to the linney doorway. One by one the speakers quickly leave their places to address him.

KITSY (*concernedly*): Father!

FATHER O'P.: What is it?

KITSY: There's something wrong with you! It's the first time ever you've come in here and you not chanting an old rhyme. I'd say that you and the girl are leagued against us. You want to . . . (*Intimate.*) Father!

FATHER O'P.: What is it, woman?

KITSY (*intimate*): In God's name, don't break the colored bubble of our dream. If you do, my chance of full womanhood is gone. You understand?

Father O'Priest nods knowingly.

DEBORAH (*intimate*): Father, the way it is with me, I'm at the gateway out to forty-three and maybe this whim would set an infant upon my floor. You understand?

Father O'Priest nods knowingly.

PADDY-TWIN (*intimate*): Father, me and my brother, our minds for the first time in our lives are switching a certain way. Don't drive them back — you understand?

Father O'Priest nods knowingly.

MICK-TWIN (*intimate*): Father, I'm as awkward as a basketful of brogues (*pathetically*) but in this wonder thing, I . . . I . . . . you understand?

FATHER O'P.: I understand . . . I understand you all. No, I'll not break this

232

dream of yours. I, too, was born in this glen. May God direct me what to do!

Ellenrose appears at doorway to kitchen.

FATHER O'P.: Ah, Ellenrose, so there you are at last. You failed to get my message from the town. I see! And now the trembling in my bones begins again. I see! I leave you here to do the other thing. (*Goes quickly to doorway of kitchen. Stops.*) Ulick, I'd say they have allegiance to the Man Above! Yes, vaguely it may be, but . . . God bless you, Darby Jer.

Exit Father O'Priest. A moment's awkward silence.

PADDY-TWIN: It's just as good he was afraid to tell us what he knew!

MICK-TWIN: You'd say 'twas printed on his face?

PADDY-TWIN: Plain as a pikestaff it was printed on his face. (*Indicating Ellenrose.*) It's printed as plain as a pikestaff on *her* face as well.

DEBORAH: Let her alone! I'll not have her dragged into this!

Garrett Gowa has advanced on Ellenrose.

KITSY: Garrett, I warn you! What the girl knows — let it lie asleep.

DEBORAH: There's nothing printed on her face.

GARRETT G.: What is it, girl? Tell out what you know.

KITSY: She knows nothing! I tell you that she knows nothing at all.

GARRETT G.: You hear me, girl! Tell what you know.

Ellenrose moves quickly to Deborah's side.

ELLENROSE (*agitated*): Aunt Deborah, we might as well have it over and done with. Today I cycled across the Maam and down into Tanavalla town. Your names are in the newspaper and Ulick's is given as leader. "A Glen Goes Crazy!" — that's what the headlines in the newspapers say. "The people think they're ants: they dress as ants." And Father Crofts — he's as furious as can be. I think that I can still hear the Tanavalla people hooting at me — they jeered me out of town. If I were you, I wouldn't . . . I guess you had to know. It's just too bad I had to be the one to tell you. Well, that's it all. I've told you everything. If I were you . . .

Ellenrose gestures vaguely. Then, halting at the doorway to look back in sadness, she goes quickly to the kitchen. Silence.

DEBORAH: I trusted this cursed dream!

KITSY: You think you were alone?

PADDY-TWIN: Aye, no mistake! Tanavalla will rock with guffaws.

MICK-TWIN: The way I feel, I'm fit to murder someone.

DARBY JER: Maybe you're all listening with your ears now. He's right among ye — the spy of silk.

GARRETT G.: The stranger who came here on Sunday — who talked with him alone?

DARBY JER: I'll tell you who spoke with him — the spy of silk!

233

GARRETT G.: Hush up your tongue! Who was talking with him — I ask ye again?

ULICK: I had a chat with him here. I thought we were alone.

GARRETT G.: That signifies nothing. Talk out — the rest of ye!

PADDY-TWIN: I saw Father O' talking to the beardy lad. They were right beside the beehive cell.

GARRETT G.: A priest is trained to guard his words. Who else?

KITSY: Don't forget that Ellenrose and him were together on the Maam!

ULICK: She gave me her word that she didn't mention the Golden Folk.

DEBORAH: And ye, the Twins — I seem to remember the smiles and scrapes and bows ye had for him.

PADDY-TWIN: I'd cut that throat from ear to ear before I'd sell the pass.

KITSY: You watched your brother, did you?

MICK-TWIN: He watched me like a hawk, and that's God's gospel truth.

PADDY-TWIN: Tell me, Deborah — before he went away, you had a couple of words in private with him, had you not?

DEBORAH: I tried to chat with him, but 'twas no use. He was in a hurry to be off.

MICK-TWIN (*looking at Kitsy*): Wait! Kitsy and him! Last Friday in town . . .

GARRETT G.: Kitsy and him, is it?

KITSY: On Friday last in the town of Tanavalla, he stood me halves of wine in Barron's pub and then put me a few questions by the ways no harm. But I let on I only had the Gaelic good and English bad. So, after a while, he gave up. And as you're at it, Garrett Gowa, you might as well trot out *your* alibi.

GARRETT G.: He got nothing out of me, that I swear to you. I also swear by the Kryle that if I lay hands upon the spy, I'll brand him with red iron . . . Wait! (*Looking at Darby Jer.*) There's one man here that spoke with him alone — the very first, too — and we never called his name yet.

PADDY-TWIN: I keep thinking — did the papers mention *his* name?

MICK-TWIN: I have him spotted!

KITSY: And, believe me, women aren't shortsighted no more than men.

GARRETT G.: The man we're referring to is you — Darby Jer O'Shea!

DARBY JER (*laughing uneasily*): Who, me? Me, by hell! and even if I *was* the spy I'd scorn to turn informer — on myself. Be on your road! I'll not confirm what ye allege. What's more, I'll not deny it, either.

GARRETT G.: You'd better do one or other quick!

MICK-TWIN: Before my fingers would ramble round your neck.

KITSY: He has havoc made and no mistake.

DEBORAH: Poor Sean! — I can see his corpse now and it floating on the roaring tide.

GARRETT G. (*advancing on Darby Jer, who retreats*): You had a race of it, you old fox. But now you're done. 'Tis you yourself's the spy of silk!
The others, too, are closing in on Darby Jer.
DARBY JER: Who, me? Stand out, let ye!
They falter.
DARBY JER: Stand out! You ding-a-dong whose dadda did a share of coining in this forge. Ye chancey twins: a pair who broke the seal of life before the lawful time. And you, Kitsy, you might like to know that there's a sup of daftness in your blood. If ye lay one finger on my fur I'll bestow a gift on ye that'll melt ye like snow. (*They retreat a little.*) I knew the Yellow lads'd heel; I knew damn well that they'd fly like rats cornered in barley stooks on a harvest day. I knew that once I'd . . .
Paddy-Twin who has moved into position behind Darby Jer now pounces on the old man and pins his arms.
PADDY-TWIN: Quick, Mick-my-Twin.
MICK-TWIN: Hold on! I'm coming to your aid.
Mick-Twin begins to throttle Darby Jer.
DARBY JER (*shouting*): He'll do for me! He'll do for me! Release my throat and I'll point out the spy. Release my throat and I'll . . . point out the . . . spy!
GARRETT G.: Here! That's enough! Ye can release him now!
MICK-TWIN (*smiling as he half releases Darby Jer*): I have it gauged how much an old-age pensioner like that can take before he's guzzled dead. (*Angrily.*) But if he doesn't shout out what he knows at once, I'll . . .
DARBY JER: I'll say my say!
GARRETT G.: Do it — smart and lively!
DARBY JER (*gasping*): I said I'll say my say!
PADDY-TWIN: We're waiting for you to talk.
DARBY JER: The way it is with me my mind is darting here and there like a fish, thinking as how my lips will tell ye what I know and still maybe not tell ye at all. (*The others lose patience.*) I have it! Let the lot of ye line up. Line up, let ye, and close your eyes. And then, so that in years to come it can't be said that I informed, I'll move behind ye with my eyes closed and I'll . . . kiss the spy.
GARRETT G.: Your antics be damned, man!
PADDY-TWIN: 'Tis hard to have patience with the likes of him!
MICK-TWIN: Look! My fingers are beginning to twitch. If he doesn't talk, I'll . . .
ULICK: Do what he tells you!
GARRETT G.: But, Ulick . . .
ULICK: Do what he tells you, all of you. And do it quick!
Grumbling, all make a line, with Ulick at the end, right.

DARBY JER (*with his back turned*): Are ye all in one file? Are all your eyes closed? If that's the way it is with ye I'll start out to find what I will find.

Darby Jer, his eyes half closed, moves in and out through the file. Now and then he pauses to peer venomously forward.

DARBY JER: From place to place! From place to place! From place to place! (*Reaching Ulick.*) And now I'll kiss the informer on his face.

As he embraces Ulick all the others open their eyes and break into laughter.

PADDY-TWIN: He's kissed Ulick!

MICK-TWIN: I own to God on high!

DEBORAH: He's kissed the man who made the dream for us!

KITSY: Was there ever known such treachery before?

GARRETT G.: He's as crooked as a dog's hind leg.

MICK-TWIN: Someone had better give me leave to catch him by the neck.

Garrett G. places a horseshoe on the fire, blows on the bellows, and heaps coals on the mounting flames.

GARRETT G.: Pen him in there. The last man was marked here was Milo the Emergency in eighty-eight. Close in now, Mick-the-Twin!

DARBY JER: No — no! No — no! No — no!

GARRETT G.: Grip him well, I tell you man!

There is a struggle.

ULICK: Wait! Let him go free!

GARRETT G.: Ulick! No one will dare to stop me now!

ULICK: Let him go, I say! Yes . . . . let him go!

GARRETT G.: Let him go, is it? The get who tried to nail every one of us to the cross!

PADDY-TWIN: And put the mark of a traitor on your people!

MICK-TWIN: This beat the blast. I'll . . . .

ULICK: You will not! All of you be listening with your ears. (*Pause.*) His kiss was true!

Silence.

ULICK: You've heard what I said. Have I to parse and spell it for the gang of ye. I told the stranger that you believed you were ants. Make what you like of it — you hear?

GARRETT G.: This is your word?

ULICK: It's my word — in God!

Silence.

DEBORAH (*softly*): Why did you do it, Ulick my love?

KITSY (*less softly*): Why did you do it, Ulickeen?

PADDY-TWIN (*a little louder*): Why did you do it, Ulick, comrade of us all?

MICK-TWIN: Why did you do it, Ulick O and O?

ULICK: That ye might live, ye fools!

DARBY JER (*slowly*): That ye might die, he means — the spy of silk!

In a silence of shock Ulick crouches over the anvil, with his back turned to the others. Garrett Gowa adjusts the iron in the fire and blows menacingly on the bellows. Paddy-Twin is close behind Ulick. He glances at Garrett Gowa who nods approval. Paddy-Twin leaps on Ulick and holds him firmly. Ulick struggles fiercely but Mick-Twin comes to his brother's aid and together they grasp Ulick. In the struggle Ulick's jacket has come off. Garrett Gowa and Paddy-Twin then stand the upended gate before the hearth. Ulick is strapped to it, his arms extended as if he were on a cross. The V pattern on the iron-work of the gate adds to the illusion of crucifixion. Garrett Gowa resumes blowing on the bellows. Mick-Twin mounts guard over Ulick. Ellenrose enters from the linney.

ELLENROSE: Listen, you men! I've seen strange lights moving above on the hill. (*She sees Ulick bound upon the gate.*) In the name of heaven, what are you doing here? There's something strange and frightening on your faces; something I've never seen before.

PADDY-TWIN: It's a thing of nothing, girl! Go back into the house.

ELLENROSE: My lord! You're going to maim him or to kill him! It's branded on your faces. It's as clear as day.

PADDY-TWIN: The big world has its laws.

MICK-TWIN: We have our laws, too.

DARBY JER: Be off now! And shut your eyes to what you've witnessed here.

ELLENROSE: Every one of you — you're on the verge of madness! Aunt Deborah, don't you realize what they're going to do? For the love of God I ask you to tell them stop!

Deborah does not reply.

ELLENROSE: Have you gone stark crazy, all of you? O, Kitsy dear, you're the woman who can talk of nothing but love. Look, now . . .

KITSY (*bitterly*): Your head is addled! Besides, 'twas you that ripened up the idea of the Golden Folk. 'Twas you, not me, he meant when he was talking about the queen among the chieftains in the sky. And if there's harm done, you'll have to answer to God for it.

ELLENROSE: My Lord in Heaven, no!

DARBY JER: Finish this foolish chat of love. (*Goes to window right and opening it a little peers out.*) I tell ye that all Ireland is rocking like a rocking chair with jeers at ye. Brand him, I say, and turn him loose. Your fathers didn't cringe and whine before a whiff of roasted flesh. Mark him, I say again!

Garrett Gowa prepares to take the horseshoe in the tongs.

ELLENROSE: Wait, Uncle Garrett. You, Aunt Debbie, too! Please, by the love between you both, don't do this thing. Twins, no please, don't turn away. And, Kitsy, remember that you're just another woman like myself. And you, too, Darby Jer. One dear to me was also dear to you. I love

237

him. I love him dearly. So for God's dear sake, don't do this thing, I beg and beg of you.

They do not relent. Garrett Gowa prepares to take horseshoe from fire.

ELLENROSE: I might have known! You're peasants to the core. Black peasants without hearts or minds or souls. Gott in Himmel! Habt Ihr Keine Herzen Gar Keine Sinn? That Christ Who died on a cross may scald ye in the depths of Hell. Listen, each of you! Listen, I say! For what you're doing now I'll swear you to the chair. If it's the last thing I do I'll see that each and every one of you is . . .

Paddy-Twin, now behind Ellenrose, obeying a nod from Garrett Gowa now pounces on Ellenrose and grips her arms.

ELLENROSE: Let me go, you half-a-man! Let me go free!

ULICK (*struggling*): When I get loose, I'll spill your belly on the ground!

DARBY JER: Now is the time to mark him!

ELLENROSE: Let me go!

ULICK: I'll walk the gallows high for you!

DARBY JER: Give me the brand, you cowardly lot of gets!

GARRETT G. (*pitching Darby Jer aside*): Out of my way at once!

Garrett Gowa takes the horseshoe in the tongs, places it on anvil, and hammers the pritchell into the red iron. Raising it up, he advances on Ulick.

GARRETT G.: I'll do what I set out to do!

Mick-Twin, catching the buttonholes of the collar band of Ulick's shirt in each hand, with a swift movement tears it from his breast. Ulick tenses himself. On the log stool Deborah and Kitsy clutch each other. Father O'Priest enters the forge from the kitchen. He is recovering from a mild nervous fit. All turn to watch him.

ELLENROSE: Father! Father O'Priest McHugh!

Mick-Twin places his palm across her mouth.

PADDY-TWIN: You might as well be talking to the wall.

FATHER O'P.: . . . Ducks on a pond . . . Grass bank beyond . . . Blue sky of spring . . . White clouds on the wing . . .

ELLENROSE (*her mouth free again*): Father! They're branding Ulick on the breast . . .

FATHER O'P.: . . . is ever for itself . . . always pays . . . scapegoat priest, accept my sins and go . . .

DARBY JER (*looking at the priest*): To think that all these years I was in dread of *that*! (*To Garrett.*) Here! In, I say, and let the iron kiss the flesh!

As Garrett Gowa moves in to brand Ulick, Ellenrose screams. Garrett Gowa halts.

FATHER O'P. (*recovering somewhat — to Garrett*): What? You're at that hell's own game again?

Garrett Gowa hesitates.

FATHER O'P. (*to Paddy-Twin*): Let that girl go before I beat you with my fist. Out of my road, Garrett Gowa!

Garrett moves a little aside and hesitates.

DARBY JER: "Out of my road!" he says when speaking to people of the whining sort. I'm waiting now to hear him say it to *me*!

FATHER O'P. (*with a little more strength*): Out of my road, I tell you, Darby Jer. I say it, not in my own, but in Another's Name. (*Darby Jer stands firm.*) You're tougher than I thought. A moment now! . . . Quick, Ellenrose! The ritual is there in the hole in the wall. It will give me something . . . something to set against Darby Jer's eggs and meat.

Ellenrose runs to get the ritual. She takes one of the eggs out of the hole, looks at it, and then replaces it. She finds the ritual and hands it to Father O'Priest who fumbles it open.

DARBY JER: With me now it's neither eggs nor meat but that which lies halfway between the egg and meat. Listen, let ye! My in calf heifer lost what she should hold. I'll plant what she lost on the land of him who falters. And I'll give my bond that he'll melt away like snow. There! Let him read his book and conquer that!

FATHER O'P. (*raising his right hand and speaking quaveringly*): In nomine Patris . . .

DARBY JER (*jeering*): He's apt to fall, I tell ye! Watch him close!

FATHER O'P. (*falteringly*): Et Filii . . .

The ritual falls out of his trembling hands. The priest staggers and almost falls to the ground.

DARBY JER: I told you he was apt to fall! I told you that he'd totter in the end after I'd said my say. Now maybe ye'll believe . . .

Darby Jer stands triumphant over the priest. Meanwhile, Ellenrose, recalling the significance of the eggs, has returned and taken them out of the hole in the wall. She walks slowly forward holding the eggs on her palm. All shrink away, then look at Darby Jer. Father O'Priest by a supreme effort gathers himself and raises his right hand.

FATHER O'P.: Et Spiritus Sancti . . .

The priest totters against the anvil and falls to one knee. Ellenrose walks to the door of the road which Kitsy opens for her. She flings the eggs into the night and returns, eyeing Darby Jer as she does so. Garrett Gowa flings the horseshoe on the hearth. All advance menacingly on Darby Jer. Suddenly the "Boo!" of a boycott horn, followed by mocking laughter, is heard through the open doorway. The sound of the horn and the mocking laughter has an odd effect on those within. Paddy-Twin rushes to doorway to road. Mick-Twin follows.

PADDY-TWIN: It's them from Tanavalla! And they're laughing at the Golden Folk!

MICK-TWIN: They're in the heather all around us.

Again the quiet mockery of the horn is followed by the sound of mocking laughter.

PADDY-TWIN (*slamming door and barring it*): They'll mock us till we draw the last breath.

MICK-TWIN: They're not the only ones will do that!

Faintly, the horn, the laughter.

DARBY JER: Here! What's a blow or curse among friends. This is leppin' life at last! Free Ulick out, let ye.

GARRETT G.: Free Ulick out, for he's the man will loose us from this hobble.

Mick-Twin cuts the bonds with a hoof knife and then helps Ulick quickly to place the gate against the wall of the forge, backstage left.

ULICK: Take weapons, let ye now!

DARBY JER: That's the very chat we want to hear!

GARRETT G.: I'll take this sledge.

PADDY-TWIN: This hammer will suit me fine.

MICK-TWIN: And I've a bar of steel.

DARBY JER: Here's a stout stick that has cracked many a skull before.

ULICK: Kitsy, after I have counted three, open the door. Here's one! Here's two! . . .

FATHER O'P.: Wait! (*All murmur.*) That road will end in taking human life.

GARRETT G.: If you've a better plan, then spit it out!

FATHER O'P.: Yes, I've a plan. First, put your weapons down. You hear me! Put your weapons down, I say!

Grudgingly, all lay down their weapons.

FATHER O'P.: This is my plan. The heather and the white grass above on the hillside are powder dry! (*He takes a shovelful of red coals from the hearth.*) I'll fling the coals of fire among them and that will rout them out.

DEBORAH (*delightedly*): And at the same time we'll let go one mad screech.

KITSY: They'll race like hares when they see the flames.

DARBY JER: The priest, the fire, and the women's screech — the plan is good, and if it wins, by hell! I give ye my word that I'll switch a Christian. Here Ulick, raise your voice and give us the signal to be off.

ULICK: Here's one! Here's two! . . .

DARBY JER: Here's bloody three, and up the Golden Folk!

Kitsy opens the door. Father O'Priest rushes out. The women screech. As the priest scatters the fire, the flames spring up. Excepting Ulick and Ellenrose, all have rushed outside.

KITSY: There's a fine present from Glensharoon!

DEBORAH: Quick, my buckos, or the flames will scorch your corduroys!

PADDY-TWIN: Watch that lad leppin' up the hill!

MICK-TWIN: There's one that's racing at his best.

GARRETT G.: Tell that to Tanavalla town!

DARBY JER: Up Glensharoon!

Cheers offstage. In the forge Ulick is putting on his jacket as if preparatory to going out. Conscious of the presence of Ellenrose he turns. After a pause he moves toward her. Both embrace.

DARBY JER (*returning, laughing*): That was a noble piece of sport! That was as fine a piece of entertainment as ever in all my life I . . .

Seeing the two in a close embrace, Darby Jer turns sadly aside to face the wall downstage left. Ulick and Ellenrose turn understandingly. Ellenrose walks a step toward the old man. The others return, laughing and speaking ad lib. Father O'Priest is last to appear. The old remoteness is in his eyes.

GARRETT G. (*laughing*): Hey, Darby Jer! Say something to the "farmer's son."

DARBY JER: I will! For all his nerves and shivers, he played the part of a true man. Beyond that, I'm not prepared to go.

All laugh.

GARRETT G.: What I was thinking to myself (*looking at Father O'Priest*), he looks a finished king. If Ulick gives permission, I think 'tis he should sit on the anvil.

ULICK: God knows, I'm tired of making dreams for ye. Yes, the priest is the man best entitled to be there.

PADDY-TWIN: Look how he saved us all from shedding blood.

MICK-TWIN: He has proved that he has a gallant head for plans.

All approve.

FATHER O'P.: No-no! Not me! Have anyone but me!

KITSY: Why not? You have double power — as man and as priest!

DEBORAH: And you'll make a double king as well.

FATHER O'P.: I won't, I tell you! I won't, I say!

GARRETT G.: Here, calm yourself! Sit down here on the anvil when you're bid. Look! I've rubbed it clean.

MICK-TWIN (*menacingly*): You'd better be heeding what Garrett Gowa has said to you.

Looking like a man at bay, Father O'Priest half sits, half leans, against the anvil. There is an uneasy silence. It is as if in imagination all are pacing round the priest. Vague signals are made to Garrett Gowa indicating that he should act as spokesman.

GARRETT G.: Father, are you listening to me with your ears?

FATHER O'P.: I am!

GARRETT G.: We wish you joy of where you are. But what we're thinking, and it's our opinion, it's the way you should . . . (*Stops.*)

DARBY JER (*to Garrett Gowa*): You're an old stammerer to the last. (*To Father O'Priest.*) I'll say their say for these clumsy goms. Aye! 'tis likely that you saved us from the charge of murder. But then, come to consider it, a courthouse is an airy place. There's fine colored swearing there and gala lads dressed up in gowns and in wigs. But I tell you that you did something else and no mistake. You made us as tame as geldings or bullocks. Cut cats we are now. For them, as well as for me, the Golden Folk was sport. But let you look and see the way we are situated now.

GARRETT G.: Aye! let him look. The horse's day is down and so is mine.

PADDY-TWIN: As for the sea, herring's an old tale our fathers told us long ago.

MICK-TWIN: Dead right you are in that.

DEBORAH: I sitting by my fire alone and the curlews crying like lost children in the sky.

KITSY: Me, too! I'll never sing the "Dandlin' Song" to one is born of my flesh.

GARRETT G.: Ulick, talk up, and give the judgment for us all.

ULICK: I've nothing to say beyond what I've already said a hundred times. Where life outside is hard, the inside life must make up for it and blaze in many hues. (*Indicating Father O'Priest.*) The rest is something this priest must think about.

DARBY JER: It's something he must think about — you can take your Gospel oath on that! We're dead, I tell you, Father O'Priest. Now, tell me, can you spring us back to life again.

FATHER O'P.: I know you! I know you — generation, seed, and stock. When I say my Mass at the Consecration you creep into the empty church to watch me like so many hungry hawks hoping that maybe I'll drop the chalice from these hands so that you'll race abroad and make a parish gossip of the fall. I'm tired and ill, but you — all of you — you're wonder-crazed. In God's name, I ask you — let me alone!

Father O'Priest relapses into a kind of half sleep.

PADDY-TWIN (*in a low voice*): We have a right to what we're asking of him. (*Murmurs of assent.*) I wonder what it's like for a common man like me to squeeze my hands tight about a priest of God?

FATHER O'P.: You'd grip me, is it, Twin?

PADDY-TWIN: Aye, I'd do that and more than that; the way I'm feeling now, I could as likely take your sacred life.

FATHER O'P.: I see! I see and also, I think, I understand! If that's the way, I'll have to try. You'll do exactly as I say?

ALL: We'll do exactly as you say!

FATHER O'P.: The little scrap of wisdom I can teach you is this: A place with children is like a well, and a place without children is a stagnant pool. Those among you who are ripe should, with God's blessing, mate and breed. So stand now, let ye, in proper pairs. Those who are past their prime or who are set apart should call to mind and cherish that which went before. Do as I say!

A moment of indecision, then Garrett Gowa takes his wife Deborah by the hand. Mick-Twin looks from Kitsy to his brother Paddy-Twin. He advances towards Kitsy but Paddy-Twin moves before him to take Kitsy's hand in his. She accepts him smilingly. Paddy-Twin with his left hand then catches his brother Mick-Twin. After a pause Ulick comes forward and takes Ellenrose by the hand. Darby Jer turns away to face the wall.

ELLENROSE: Darby! Please, Darby Jer, don't turn away from us. We don't want you to do that. So please listen to what I'm saying to you. While we are here, my mother — she's Bridget Schneider now but once she was Brigid Bawn O'Neill of this glen — sits by herself in her room in Hartford, Connecticut. No, she's not young any more, I guess. She's crippled: her sight has gone too. Say, Darby Jer, why don't you close your eyes and for the sake of that love which once was in your heart, pretend you're back over the years again and in your prime. Tell me now, young Darby Jer, can't you see Brigid Bawn O'Neill as she was when she was a girl. Can't you see her walk up that hill outside, open the door, come in, and stand right here in the middle of the forge? Eh, Darby Jer O'Shea?

DARBY JER (*turning, his eyes closed*): I'm back! You hear? I'm back over the years. And I'm in my prime again. And Brigid Bawn O'Neill . . . I hear her step coming up the hill. She's at the door, I tell ye. I see her body fill the forge with light. I see her stand in the middle of the floor. Thanks be to Christ, I've lived to see this hour!

GARRETT G. (*explosively*): All this to hell! (*To Father O'Priest.*) Is this the only wonder that you can give us?

All murmur approval.

FATHER O'P.: I've given you all I have. There is no more to give.

GARRETT G.: You'll not escape us by whining.

FATHER O'P.: What do you want of me?

DEBORAH: I'll tell you! We want stories and tales.

KITSY: We want accounts of women of beauty and they tied to wheels!

PADDY-TWIN: Swords of sharpness and giants, too!

MICK-TWIN: Shoes of swiftness that race on the hills!

ELLENROSE: Cloaks of darkness that make the wearers disappear!

GARRETT G.: We want horses with hooves of bronze, they racing on a lake, blood spilled on the ground, and planets overthrown.

The voices mingle in importunate demand.

FATHER O'P. (*shouting*): I've none of these! I've none of these at all!
All fall ominously silent.

DARBY JER: He's whipped like an old cripple and no mistake about it either. What can this cowardly priest set against the wonder of my Kryle? That anvil there, it ringing underneath the blows of seven blood relatives. And all of us . . . (*Chanting.*)

Death passed me by in the morning early
He passed me by with his voice so surly
And I saw him walk in the glen where the landlords dwell.

OTHERS (*chanting*):

And it's good, say we, that he'll melt their seeding;
And it's better still that he'll blast their breeding;
But it's best of all that he'll drag them down to Hell!

FATHER O'P. (*loudly*): No more of it! You hear! No more of it, I say! (*Silence.*) I'm a poor storyteller. Ye know that well. Ye know, too, that I left this glen when I was a boy and bound myself to another trade. But still, whether from fear or call of blood to blood, I'll do my best to be your wonder boy. (*Intimate.*) Send me a story, God! Send me some class of a fable that I once had in the rag bag of my brain. (*With the secret joy of remembrance.*) Wait! Wait, I tell ye! In England I used to tell a power of tales about a wandering Man called . . . Christy Love. Ah, but doubtless you've heard all those stories before?

PADDY-TWIN: Christy Love? We never heard a word of him!

MICK-TWIN: We've heard some tales about the Tricky Smith.

GARRETT G.: And we had lots of tales concerning Aristotle, the wise man who lived in Greece.

DEBORAH: We had the Legend of the Glass Mountain.

KITSY: And lovely Gráinne and she flying on a boar.

DARBY JER: The Fianna tales — we had them, too.

GARRETT G.: And we had the great yarn of Dick the Fool who kissed the windmill for a cross. But, as far as my memory goes, we never had a tale about this Christy Love.

All babble with excitement.

GARRETT G.: One voice, one tale!

Overhead, the lamp fails a little. As Garrett Gowa looks up, the lamplight takes up again.

GARRETT G.: While yet there's lamplight over our heads, I want silence to fall upon the forge.

A little muttering, easing down to silence. As the story following proceeds, the lamplight gradually falters and is replaced by the golden glow of the heather fire reflected on the open door and leaking through the slightly opened lattice window, left stage. Drawn in by the prospect of a story, others of the Golden Folk appear at the doorway to the road. These include the melodeon player and three girls.

FATHER O'P.: Once upon a time there was a man called Christy Love. He was a country tradesman and he had a soft heart. He worked away and then one day He had his seven 'nuffs of work, and so He said to His Mother: "Give Me your blessing, Mother, and I'll be off!" And off he rambled to find . . . a lot of things. He kept apples and nuts for the children He met. (*Looking at Ulick and Ellenrose.*) And if he saw a couple that were courting fair, "God bless ye, couple courting fair!" — that's what Christy Love'd say. After a time He changed and grew a pointed beard and then the people saw He was a Someone Far Beyond for He could do strange things that no one else had done before Him . . .

GARRETT G. (*whispering*): This story's shaping well!

PADDY-TWIN (*whispering*): Say that again, my son!

DEBORAH (*whispering*): His Mother's blessings on His head.

KITSY (*whispering*): His blessing on the couples courting, too!

DARBY JER (*whispering — fiercely*): Shut up your mouths! Tell us what happened after that?

FATHER O'P.: The things that Christy Love could do, 'tis only a printed fool would call them tricks. They were strange doings that were never seen before and, likely, never will be seen again. On fair day or market day the country people, who were just like us — they flocked about Him because they knew He was a wonder man. (*Pause.*) This day He rambled into a village and went down along the street. Twelve cronies of His were with Him. They were listening to His talk. A funeral goes by and then, touching a woman's shawl, "Who's dead?" He asks. "A grand young man, a widow's only son," was the answer He got. Then as Christy Love was turning to walk away, He heard the mother cry. Talking to one who was near: "Go to the funeral's head," He said, "and tell it to halt." The man ran off. The bearers stopped. Then someone raised the shout: "It's Christy Love!"

The others react in muted wonder.

KITSY (*whispering*): A grand young man was dead!

DEBORAH (*whispering*): He heard the mother's cry, did Christy Love.

FATHER O'P.: The people make a lane. He draws near. He sees the rust that's about the dead man's lips, and what He smells is clay. He crouches down. He takes the dead man's hand in His. He says: "Get up now, Sonny, and go home!" Then there is a flow of blood into the yellow cheeks. The body stirs. Again He says: "Get up now, Sonny, and go home!" The eyelids lift. The boy sits up. He sees the crowd. He sees his mother's face. He looks into the eyes of . . . Christy Love.

Father O'Priest is now limp against the anvil.

DARBY JER (*whispering*): I know the Man!

GARRETT G. (*whispering*): And so do I. (*Making a vague sign of the cross.*)
But I have never seen His face like this before.

Barely audible murmur of the others.

ULICK (*with the fierceness of suppressed joy*): Let no one name Him or I'll
cut him to the heart. In time to be this tale will ripen in our minds. Now
. . . Now we're the Golden Folk indeed.

DARBY JER (*singing, with a quavering joy*):

> Now we're the Golden Folk,
> Loyal and olden folk,
> Now we're the Golden Folk indeed!

OTHERS (*singing*):

> Heart's blood and rainbow's glory,
> Green grass and flaming story,
> Now we're the Golden Folk indeed!

ALL:

> Now we're the Golden Folk,
> Powerful and glowing folk,
> Now we're the Golden Folk indeed!
>
> Bright sea and wind a-blowing,
> Red iron and it glowing,
> Now we're the Golden Folk indeed!

*Through the open doorway is seen the glow of the heather fire, reflected
faintly above the sea. The lamp burns still lower. The smith beats out the
time on the anvil. In their exaltation the people weave in and out until their
movements revert to those of the slow "set" dance already danced in the
forge. The dance leaps to sudden life. This time, however, there is new joy
and glory to it. Dancing, the people sing and cry with joy and clap their
hands. The bone-tapper, wearing his straw costume, enters the forge, and,
tapping as he moves here and there on the outskirts of the dance, adds to the
mood of wholesome exaltation. Before the final slow curtain, Father O'Priest
moves across the stage to the long window set in the right hand wall. The
eyes of Darby Jer follow him as he moves away. As the priest throws open
the shutters, first his face and breast, then the forms of the other dancers,
turn red-gold in the light reflected from the burning hills. Slow curtain.*

♣ *JOHN O'DONOVAN* ♣

JOHN O'DONOVAN is a nonsmoker, a teetotaler, a vegetarian, and a writer of highly provocative comic plays. If this makes him sound like a modern edition of Bernard Shaw, I might also mention that he has written a book on Shaw, a play on Shaw, and wears a beard with a reddish tinge. The chief difference between him and Shaw is that O'Donovan could never be accused of writing sexless plays about unemotional characters. If anything, his plays tend to be — in a fashion not hitherto notably connected with the Irish drama — a bit on the ribald side. For instance, the opening of one hilarious unpublished and untitled play goes like this:

SPRATT: Morning Mr. Kilgarriff. What's the Prime Minister doing?
KILGARRIFF: Masturbating.

O'Donovan was born on January 29, 1921, in Dublin. He attended the Synge Street Christian Brothers School, and after a series of jobs in Dublin and Belfast drifted into journalism from which he finally resigned to go into freelance radio and television writing and broadcasting. He did a great deal of apprentice playwriting, and after several rejections his *Half-Millionaire* was accepted by the Abbey and ran for two weeks in 1954. In 1957, his farce about relations between Ulster and Eire, *The Less We Are Together*, ran for four months at the Abbey, but his next play, *The Change of Mind*, ran for only five weeks. One of his best plays, *The Shaws of Synge Street*, did even worse, running for only a week. And his last play at the Abbey, *Copperfaced Jack*, was, he felt, so botched that he determined to submit no more plays to the theater while Ernest Blythe remained in command. Fortunately, however, O'Donovan and the Abbey later buried

247

the shillelagh, and a new O'Donovan production, entitled *A Dean Swift Programme*, is in the offing.

The Less We Are Together is a very funny satirical farce somewhat reminiscent of Shaw's *The Apple Cart* but less substantial and, despite its high spirits and originality, probably not for export. *The Shaws of Synge Street* dramatizes some of the material that O'Donovan used in his book about Vandaleur Lee, *Shaw and the Charlatan Genius*. It is an exceptionally engrossing family play with perhaps half a dozen really challenging roles in it. Its theme seems to be the basic lust that smoulders beneath the Victorian respectability of most of the characters. Its form, because of its twisting strands of plot and its effectively grotesque juxtapositions of the sad and the funny, is tragicomic. And its final scene, the breakup of the family as Mrs. Shaw goes off to England, is as moving a final curtain as one might hope for.

Copperfaced Jack is best described in O'Donovan's own words:

My rebel is, as you've divined, a fictional variation of Emmet, of whom I am not at all an admirer. Adventurers who proclaim a rebellion and sign themselves President of the new republic command neither my respect nor my admiration especially when they scuttle off up a back street when the going gets hot and then whinge to their serving-maid "It wasn't *my* fault, it wasn't." (Emmet did this.) Jack himself is a notional portrait of John Scott, first Earl of Clonmell, Lord Chief Justice of the King's Bench, who died of gluttony and drunkenness on the very day that the Rebellion of 1798 (Wolfe Tone's) broke out. On the face of it, his career was that of an unmitigated scoundrel, but I happened to read extracts from his diary and found that he had a clear-sighted view of his own character and behaviour which kept him making attempts to reform himself until almost the day of his death. His great ability (he pulled himself up by his own bootstraps) and his ironic self-portraiture attracted me to him; and although I cannot document every trait I give him I believe I have re-created him quite faithfully.

Although there is much to admire in the play, especially the ripe raciness of the dialogue, what most commands attention and respect and delight is the magnificent creation of the Lord Chief Justice. One is reminded of two other Johns — Silver and Falstaff — for not only is the character drawn with a fine, swinging gusto, but he is also that stage rarity, a character containing contradictions. Jack demands great acting, but even on the page we can see that here is a figure to place beside Captain Jack Boyle as one of the memorable creations of the Irish stage.

The untitled play I quoted from at the beginning of this note deserves a word here. It is a randy, sardonic, Swiftean view of human nature that is as funny in its incidents as it is ghastly in its implications. The first act shows how modern society by its reckless folly destroys itself in an atomic explosion. Act II — yes, there is an Act II — shows how the few remaining people, given a chance to begin again, commence immediately to build up a new society precisely on the same old, irresponsible, savage lines as before. The Dublin theater has never seen a play, not even O'Donovan's own *The Less We Are Together*, as blackly funny or as Swifteanly bawdy. Unless the Dublin theater changes even more radically than it has, it is not likely to see one, either. And that would be a very considerable pity.

Copperfaced Jack

"Thus I stand, a public character, alone."— diary of Lord Clonmell

JOHN SCOTT, first Earl of Clonmell, Lord Chief Justice of the King's Bench in Ireland
ARTHUR WOLFE, attorney-general
FRANCIS HIGGINS, an informer
PETER SHANKS, JACK KEHOE, MICHAEL MAHON, TOM DOYLE, rebels
ELIZABETH SHANKS, a widow

MARY NEALE, engaged to Peter Shanks
MASTER PALMER, a physician
JACK FENNESSY, a carpenter
BRIAN BORROO, a convict
VIOLA, ROSALIND, BESSIE, whores
GALVIN, a hangman
GOVERNOR of Newgate Jail
MILLIGAN, Clonmell's attendant

Turnkeys, a chaplain, prisoners, soldiers

Act I

SCENE 1

A shabby room in a Dublin back street in May 1798. By the light of a candle stuck in a bottle two men are sitting at a rickety table. They are Jack Kehoe, middle-aged and shabby, and Michael Mahon, ten years younger, but with scantier hair. Both are poorly dressed and look as if they haven't had a bath since birth. Tom Doyle, a palefaced lad of eighteen, bursts in.

KEHOE (*whipping his feet off the table in alarm, then relaxing*): My God, I thought it was somebody. (*Puts up feet again.*)

DOYLE: Where's the General?

MAHON: Gone out to the jakes.

DOYLE: Have I missed anything?

© Copyright 1967 by John O'Donovan. Address inquiries concerning performance or translation rights to Robert Hogan, Proscenium Press, Box 561, Dixon, California 95620. The play was first performed at the Abbey Theatre, Dublin, on February 25, 1963, directed by Ria Mooney, with settings by Thomas MacAnna.

KEHOE: Naw.

MAHON: He has formed his government. You're in it.

DOYLE (*almost awed*): Me?! Then he really does like me. And trusts me.

MAHON: You're the secretary of state for — wait now till I think.

KEHOE (*picking his teeth*): Jasus, don't ask me. I'm chancellor of the exchequer, that's all I know.

MAHON: Secretary of State for Home Affairs — I'm nearly sure that's what it is.

DOYLE (*disappointed*): Oh . . . I was hoping I'd be — no matter.

KEHOE: D'ye think ye'll be able for the work, son?

DOYLE (*in a gust of fury*): By God, if you don't leave me alone I'll kill you.

Doyle has come near to Kehoe's feet, which are still propped up on the table. Kehoe nonchalantly raises a foot, props it against Doyle's chest, and pushes him. He staggers back and falls over a chair.

MAHON: Will youse pair stop —

DOYLE (*scrambling up*): I'll kill him for that. I'll kill him.

Doyle rushes at Kehoe again, and again Kehoe nonchalantly foots him backwards. This time Doyle staggers into the arms of Peter Shanks who has just entered. Shanks is young, slender, good-looking, grave, humorless. His movements are quick and nervous — indeed almost everything about him is quick. But although quick to lose his temper (and indeed to lose his head) he appears calm, because anger in him takes the form of pale cold resentment. He has to be goaded for a long time before he displays the more usual signs of anger. He tends to adopt oratorical poses; a favorite is the putting of one hand on his breast, the other behind his back, à la Napoleon.

MAHON (*jerking his thumb toward the unperturbed Kehoe*): He begun it, General.

SHANKS (*raising his hand*): Desist! I command you — desist.

MAHON: It was him begun it.

SHANKS: I want no recriminations. Sit down.

Mahon and Doyle sit. Kehoe doesn't remove his feet from the table. Shanks remains standing in his Napoleonic pose.

SHANKS: I will say no more about this unseemly episode. H'm. You were late for the meeting, Captain Doyle.

DOYLE: I'm sorry, General. I had to put heels on three pairs of shoes before the master would let me go.

KEHOE: I told Tom — Captain Doyle — about his new job.

DOYLE: I'm very grateful to you, General, for giving me the chance to show what I can do. It's the first chance I've ever got, General. And I won't ever let you down — never!

SHANKS: I hope that my trust in you will not prove to be misplaced.

KEHOE: So do we all, so do we all.

DOYLE (*springing up*): There, he's at me again. I'll choke him.

Mahon tries to pull Doyle down.

SHANKS (*looking at the floor*): Desist. I said desist.

A doorbell rings in the distance.

SHANKS: See who it is, Colonel Kehoe.

KEHOE: Send the Secretary of State for Home Affairs as he's on his feet.

SHANKS: I've given an order.

KEHOE: Well, give it to Tom Doyle.

SHANKS (*sharply*): Major Mahon.

Mahon rises.

SHANKS: The door.

MAHON: Well now after all, General, you did tell Jack Kehoe to —

SHANKS: Major Mahon, the door.

Doorbell rings again.

DOYLE: It's all right, General, I'll go.

SHANKS: Resume your seat, Captain. I've given Major Mahon an order.

MAHON: But surely it's the junior officer's job to —

SHANKS: My orders are not matters for discussion.

KEHOE: If one of youse fellows doesn't move a leg, he'll have to go and answer it himself.

No one makes a move.

DOYLE: Let *me* go, General.

SHANKS: No, Captain. (*With much dignity.*) I shall go myself. (*Goes.*)

DOYLE (*to Mahon*): Why didn't you go when he told you?

MAHON: He told him first, didn't he?

KEHOE (*spitting on floor*): Here's one chancellor of the exchequer who's not going to run messages like a whore's footman.

DOYLE: He thinks he's going to rise me again but he won't.

KEHOE: Secretary of State for Home Affairs and he wouldn't know whether you'd eat a home affair or wear it going to Mass of a Sunday.

DOYLE (*rushing at Kehoe*): Declare to God, I'll crucify him.

Kehoe pushes him back with his foot. When Doyle falls this time he lies still and moans.

DOYLE: Me back — oh my God me back.

MAHON (*kneeling beside Doyle and glaring at Kehoe*): Now look what you've done. (*Helps Doyle up.*)

DOYLE: Me back — me back — me back.

MAHON: Are you hurted, lad?

DOYLE (*alarmed*): I've cut meself. I'm bleeding. I can feel the blood running down me leg.

KEHOE: Are ye sure it's blood is running down your leg?

MAHON: It's the mercy of God you didn't kill yourself.

KEHOE: Well, he always wanted to die for Ireland, didn't he?

DOYLE (*feebly*): I'll rub the sneer off that fellow's face.

MAHON: Here — let's have a look at you.

Mahon begins to unfasten Doyle's belt. He lowers his trousers.

DOYLE (*wincing*): Oooh — go aisy, go aisy.

MAHON: Lean forward at bit. (*Takes candle and lifts tail of Doyle's shirt.*)

KEHOE: Don't set fire to him now whatever you do.

MAHON: You've cut yourself all right.

Shanks and Francis Higgins appear at the door.

SHANKS: What in heaven's name — ! (*Turns away in disgust.*)

KEHOE: Good day to you, Mr. Higgins.

SHANKS: Captain Doyle, be so kind as to cover yourself.

KEHOE: Yes, the view from over there must be fierce.

SHANKS (*still turned away*): Major Mahon, Captain Doyle: I require your explanation.

DOYLE (*straightening painfully*): I fell and hurt meself.

SHANKS (*immediately all sympathy*): Hurt yourself? Oh — he's bleeding.

MAHON: Just lean over the table, Tom, and I'll bathe it with a sup of water.

Mahon goes to one side, pours water from a jug into a dish, and splashes it on Doyle's wound. Meanwhile Higgins and Shanks have come forward. Higgins is a dark, blue-chinned, stocky man. One would imagine that no sensible man would trust him an inch.

HIGGINS: I'm afraid I can only remain for a few moments. But I had to come to find out if we are any nearer the day of liberty, when our country shall be free and prosperous under your wise and enlightened leadership?

SHANKS: Very near it now.

HIGGINS: And how is the glorious army of the revolution?

KEHOE: Couldn't be worse. All officers and no soldiers.

SHANKS: When the hour strikes the soldiers will be there. My country will not fail me.

HIGGINS: And how about the list of public enemies who are to be executed, General? How's that coming on?

DOYLE (*raising his head*): Joseph Byrne. He's on *my* list.

HIGGINS: Who is this enemy of our beloved country?

DOYLE: The bootmaker in Thomas Street. The man I work for.

HIGGINS: Joseph Byrne . . . Thomas Street. Good. I'll take a note of him. How about Mr. Wolfe?

KEHOE: Who's he when he's at home?

HIGGINS: Mr. Wolfe is the attorney-general.

KEHOE: Stick him on the list if you want him. *My* man is Copperfaced Jack.

HIGGINS: Splendid.

KEHOE: He had me uncle and me two cousins strung up for stealing one mangy sheep.

SHANKS: It's not because of your uncle and your cousins that the lord chief justice is on the list, Colonel Kehoe, but because he has betrayed his great office. He has swindled widows and orphans, accepted bribes, perverted the course of justice, disgraced the bench (*darkly*) and defiled unprotected women.

HIGGINS: Hanging would be too good for him, gentlemen.

KEHOE: Wait'll I get me hands around his fat throat . . .

HIGGINS: That's my brave comrade . . . good! (*Writing.*) For assassination . . . execution I should say . . . the lord chief justice. And let's put down Mr. Wolfe the attorney-general as well, shall we?

KEHOE: You can put down anyone you like.

SHANKS (*drawing Higgins aside*): These, Mr. Higgins, are the instruments I must use to tear the tyrant's hand from my country's throat. But believe me (*places hand on Higgins' arm*) they shall be replaced with worthier instruments at the first opportunity.

HIGGINS: When you call on me to serve you, General, you shall not call in vain.

Impulsively Shanks grasps Higgins' hand. There is a loud hammering on the outer door and a voice cries "Open in the name of the King."

KEHOE (*jumping up*): Jasus, we're caught.

Kehoe snatches the candle from the table and extinguishes it. The door is battered in and in the darkness a gleam of light shows the figures of armed soldiers rushing in. Shouts and confusion.

SCENE 2

The lord chief justice's room at the Four Courts, Dublin. A huge crimson velvet curtain with a gold fringe hangs in folds at the back; at right is a window curtained in a darker hue, at left a glowing fireplace, the light from which flickers on the huddled figure of the lord chief justice in his chair. He is in a dressing gown, and without his full-bottomed wig. His face, a mass of reddish purple flesh, shows the man who had been dangerously overfeeding and overdrinking all his life. Although enormously fat, he doesn't look in the least comical. Years of deference from subordinates and toadies have turned him into a bigger bully than he is by nature. But he is saved from complete insufferability by humor and by a genuine capacity for self-criticism. His wig, robe, and chain of office, are draped on a lay figure, right. There is a table on which are quill pens and an ink bottle, papers, books, a decanter of brandy, and glasses. A cupboard at the far left, a door right. Milligan enters with a lighted candelabrum, which he places on the table.

JUSTICE: Have I slept long, Milligan?

MILLIGAN: Only half an hour, m'lud.

JUSTICE: It's dark.

MILLIGAN: I drew the curtains, m'lud, so as not to have the sunlight disturb you.

JUSTICE: The looking glass.

Milligan gives him a hand mirror.

JUSTICE (*with a grimace*): God! Milligan, have you ever been able to look at yourself without hatred, loathing?

MILLIGAN: I wouldn't say I had any feelings in the matter, m'lud.

JUSTICE: Then you admire yourself — ?

He rises. Milligan helps him to dress.

JUSTICE: Did I ever tell you how I tried to sell my soul to the Devil?

MILLIGAN: It is one of your favorite stories, m'lud.

JUSTICE: I was only twelve or thirteen at the time. I wanted to go to London to see all the sights. The desire was purely instinctive. Nobody had talked to me about London. I cannot have read about it, for there were no books in my father's house . . . that I can remember. But this longing for London . . . it was extraordinary. It obsessed me. Now you or any ordinary person would have got there by simply running away from home.

MILLIGAN: Will you have the under-waistcoat?

JUSTICE: No. Oh very well. Yes, you would have simply run away from home. But I didn't. It never occurred to me. I have always done things the hard way. I remember a schoolmaster saying to me, "Name three flowers." Now you, like any normal human being, would have said wallflowers, buttercups, and daisies. But I had to think hard. "Antirrhinums." "Go on," said the schoolmaster. "Ah . . . chrysanthemums." "Go on," said the schoolmaster. But I couldn't remember a third flower.

MILLIGAN: The other arm, m'lud.

JUSTICE: So in order to get to London I decided that the first step was to sell my soul to the Devil. My soul for the fare to London and a little spending money . . . ten guineas. Ten guineas, Milligan. (*Turns and stares at Milligan.*) My God, how I have always undervalued myself. Not for a kingdom. Not for perpetual youth. Or good looks. Or women. Just the fare to London and a little pocket money. That's the sort of humility life in a poor country plants in you. The Devil didn't buy of course. I sat on the edge of my bed waiting for him. I opened the windows for him. I lighted a huge fire in the grate to encourage him. I thought he might have left the money in the old jug on the dresser where my mother kept the family fortune of three and sixpence – but no. Have you ever offered your soul to the Devil, Milligan?

MILLIGAN: I am perfectly satisfied with my situation in life, m'lud.

JUSTICE: Oh Thou who wert crucified to win eternal bliss for Milligan, the just man made perfect, look on Thy handiwork and be glad.

Milligan puts the wig on him.

JUSTICE: Four treason cases today, I think.

MILLIGAN: Yes, m'lud.

JUSTICE: Convey to the prisoners that Copperfaced Jack is in a merciful mood this morning. If they expedite matters by pleading guilty without more ado, the sentences will be light.

The lord chief justice swings around, his crimson robe spreading out behind him. He paces slowly toward the curtains, which are drawn up on either side as he approaches. The judicial seat, canopied in red and emblazoned with the royal arms of England, is revealed bathed in light while everything else grows dark. He climbs into his seat. There is a hushed murmur. At the right, a thin, wan beam picks out the dock; Doyle climbs into it.

DOYLE (*hoarsely*): Guilty, my lord.

Doyle stands back and is replaced by Kehoe.

KEHOE: Guilty, my lord.

Kehoe is replaced by Mahon.

MAHON: Guilty, my lord.

Mahon is replaced by Peter Shanks.

SHANKS: Not guilty.

JUSTICE: Speak up, man, speak up. Don't mumble.

SHANKS (*involuntarily straightening himself*): Not guilty.

JUSTICE (*threatening*): What did you say?

SHANKS: Not guilty. And I do not recognize the competence of this court to try me.

JUSTICE: Nevertheless it will try you.

SHANKS: I do not expect justice from Copperfaced Jack.

JUSTICE: Who's he?

SHANKS: A swindler. A thief. A lickspittle. A murderer. A fornicator in a fancy dress.

JUSTICE: "A fornicator in a fancy dress." I like the rhythm of that. Say it again for me.

SHANKS (*angry*): A man who filched the property of defenseless and innocent widows and orphans –

JUSTICE: "Defenseless and innocent!" Why do platitudes and patriotism always go together? So you plead not guilty?

SHANKS: I plead nothing.

A dark figure emerges from the shadows behind the dock and strikes Peter across the mouth.

JUSTICE (*pounding the desk, bellowing*): How dare you strike the prisoner! Turning my court into a beargarden! Let that man be taken away and whipped from the precinct of this court to the Tholsel and back again! (*Leans back and breathes deeply.*) Are you conducting your own defense, Mr. Shanks?

SHANKS: No lawyer shall speak for me. I shall speak for myself when the time comes.

JUSTICE: That time *has* come. The cornered rat can now fight for its life.

SHANKS: Dispense with your mummery. Have me hanged and be done with it. I do not fear to die for my country.

JUSTICE (*leaning back*): "Dispense with your mummery." No, Mr. Shanks, that will not do. "The fornicator in the —" how's this your phrase ran? "The fornicator in the —" Well, whatever it was it was good. It had a fine ring to it. There was feeling behind it, genuine human feeling. But "Abandon your mummery" — no, that wasn't it. "Dispense with your mummery." Pwa! Try again, Mr. Shanks.

SHANKS: Buffoon.

JUSTICE: Aren't we all, Mr. Shanks, each in his own way?

SHANKS: I shall take no further part in these scandalous proceedings. Henceforth I shall hold my peace.

JUSTICE (*throwing back his head and guffawing*): Henceforth he shall hold his peace!

SHANKS: The laughter of fools is like the crackling of thorns under a pot.

JUSTICE (*leaning forward, interested*): Oh — you are a Protestant: you have read the Bible. I had assumed you were a Papist.

SHANKS (*accusing him*): Atheist.

JUSTICE: Atheist? Me? Not at all. A devout believer. (*Leaning forward.*) Do you know, I once tried to sell my soul to the Devil?

SHANKS: Not tried. Succeeded.

JUSTICE: Good good good good. You keep your wits about you. But then you're young, Peter, young. Once upon a time I was young like you —

SHANKS: Who talks platitudes now?

JUSTICE: But you shall never be old and copperfaced like me.

SHANKS: Nor old and villainous. Nor old and dishonest.

JUSTICE: Peter, we've all been dishonest since we stopped walking on four legs and started walking on two. (*Leans back.*) Well, you didn't hold your peace for very long, did you? Never mind. Yet in a little while and you shall hold your peace for ever and for aye.

SHANKS: So shall you.

JUSTICE: It is cruel of you to remind me. You have had only twenty years to realize what you're leaving. I've had sixty. My pain is treble yours. (*In a kind tone.*) Guilty, Peter, guilty — ?

SHANKS: If it will facilitate you, I have done all your minions say I have done.

JUSTICE: Minions. Oh dear. Your father was either a schoolmaster or a minor poet. Or perhaps both. Let all the accused stand before me.

Doyle, Mahon, Kehoe take their place beside Shanks.

JUSTICE: You have admitted your guilt of one of the most heinous crimes it is possible to commit, a crime against every man, woman and child in this country. You have tried, by plotting rebellion, to disrupt the established order of things. You have incited men who are ordinarily peaceable and lawabiding to acts of violence and bloodshed.

SHANKS: To win freedom for our native land.

JUSTICE: Your object was to seize into your own obscure hands the power of government and the privileges which go with it. Who desires rebellion? Only the rebellious, who are at bottom the envious. It is no bad thing to strive to improve one's lot. On such ambition depends all human progress. It is open to any man who desires to rise in this world, to overcome the difficulties in his way. In some cases those difficulties are greater than in others. The accident of birth may place some of us halfway up to the summit of human society. But even those who are at the foot of the hill can climb all the way if they have the will and the energy.

SHANKS: Are you talking about yourself, Copperfaced Jack?

JUSTICE (*to Shanks with contempt*): The rebel is one who tries to reach the summit by using the strength and energy of others. He deludes fools into clearing the path for him. "Fight, my gallant fellow countrymen," he cries, "to free our beloved country by overthrowing the tyrant." Meaning, "Fight, my gullible fellow countrymen to make me — ME — your new master. To carry ME from a backstreet cellar to the palace of kings. Signed, Yours Faithlessly, the President of the New Republic."

SHANKS: He is prepared to shed his own blood to the last drop.

JUSTICE: The prize is worth the gamble. The pickpocket, the sheepstealer, the forger all risk their lives, but not with the damnable righteousness of the thief who is out to steal a whole country. There have been times when, sitting in the judgment seat, I would have said to some petty criminal, were I not bound by the law, "Go forth a free man. Your offense was no more than a trick of fate, a momentary lapse, which can be forgiven by men of good will." But when there stand before me men who have tried to deceive the credulous multitude with promises of the millennium, of an earthly paradise, then the act of duty becomes an act of pleasure. Every man may gamble with what belongs to him, even with his life. But let no man gamble with my life, my property, in the name of anything, least of all in the name of patriotism, or of liberty, equality, and fraternity. Nature gives us no liberty, Mr. Shanks; she laughs at our notions of equality, and she has set merciful bounds to fraternity. Most brothers dislike one another. (*Sotto voce.*) I don't like mine anyway. (*Aloud.*) O ye millions, I do not embrace ye, and I beg ye shall make no move to embrace me.

SHANKS: Few will want to do that, Copperfaced Jack.

JUSTICE: That is the gibe of a young man or a little man. In your case there will not be time enough left for you to show whether you were young or little.

SHANKS: Dulce et decorum est pro patria mori.

JUSTICE (*flinging an accusing finger at him*): A schoolmaster! Your father *was* a schoolmaster.

SHANKS: He was not.

JUSTICE: Perhaps not in the eyes of the world, Peter, but in the eyes of God — yes.

SHANKS: And in the eyes of Copperfaced Jack who thinks he's God.

JUSTICE (*groaning*): Oh these mechanical smart answers . . . I suppose I perpetrated them too when I was your age. Listen, Mr. Shanks. You do not give your life for your country by embroiling it in blood, turmoil, destruction, rapine, murder, robbery, and then getting your villainous neck strangled in a string. The true patriot is the man who, dying in his own bed, full of years and toil, can say, "I leave my country the richer by one new house I have built, one waste acre I have reclaimed, one new tree I have planted, even one new picture I have painted or poem I have written, be they good or bad. No blood has been wantonly shed by me. I have been the cause of no widow's tears, and no man is the poorer through any dealing with me." That is the true patriot.

SHANKS (*to the other accused*): What a windbag.

The lord chief justice snaps his fingers and Milligan climbs up to him and places the black cap on his head. Commotion in the dock. They all speak together.

DOYLE: Mercy, my lord — mercy! We were promised mercy if we pleaded guilty.

JUSTICE: What mercy would you have had on others if your rebellion had succeeded?

MAHON: I was misled, my lord. I wish to confess and to help the authorities in every way I can, in exchange for the chance to make a fresh start. I have information which will be of value to His Majesty's government.

KEHOE: He isn't the only one who has information, my lord.

JUSTICE: The only information I want I have — that my name was at the head of the list of those you were plotting to assassinate.

DOYLE: Not me, my lord, not me — him. He put your name down — I didn't. Mercy — mercy — I was promised mercy. I am innocent. I was led astray

259

— let me live — oh my lord, my lord, mercy — as you are a Christian gentleman — mercy.

KEHOE: Spare me, my lord. I have a wife and family — send me to jail for as long as you like, but not the rope — not the rope.

MAHON: We were told we'd get off if we pleaded guilty. The lousy lawyers have tricked us.

The lord chief justice silences the commotion with a blow of his fist on the desk.

JUSTICE: Mr. President of the New Republic, behold your ministry of all the talents.

Peter Shanks has moved apart, and stands cold and proud, his arms folded across his chest.

JUSTICE: Thomas Doyle, Michael Mahon, John Kehoe, Peter Shanks, you have pleaded guilty to the horrible crime of high treason against the person and lawful power of his sacred majesty. The sentence of the court is that you be taken hence to the place of public execution, and that you there be hanged by the neck until you are dead, after which your head shall be cut from your body and your body quartered and exposed in a public place for one calendar month. And may the Lord have mercy on your souls.

He waits expectantly, but no chaplain appears to say Amen. He leans over the side of his chair and shouts "Jenkins!" There is a flurry of curtains, and a fat and oily clergyman appears from behind the judicial seat. He unctuously turns up his eyes to the ceiling, so that the whites are startlingly visible, joins his hands and intones the word "Amen." With an oily glance at the men in the dock he stretches his right hand toward them in a sanctimonious benison, and withdraws. Immediately pandemonium breaks out in the dock. The three men begin howling and shouting at once. Dark figures come out of the shadows and drag the men away. Milligan creeps up to the lord chief justice and speaks to him in a low tone. The lord chief justice nods and Milligan creeps away again. Presently, a girl climbs into the dock, the very picture of terror. She can hardly be more than sixteen. She is very poorly dressed, and her long dark hair falls untidily around her shoulders. Her right hand clutches her dress nervously across her bosom. The lord chief justice gazes at her for some time before he speaks.

JUSTICE: Mary Neale, you stand where you are because you have associated with the scoundrels who stood in that dock before you. What have you to say for yourself?

MARY (*whispering*): Your honor — I — I —

JUSTICE (*thundering*): Speak up, child, speak up.

Mary goes white, her eyes close, she sways.

JUSTICE: Is the girl not represented by counsel? (*Silence.*) Very likely not.

She doesn't look as if she has the money to pay them. Have her brought
to my chambers after the court adjourns.

The shadowy figures seize Mary and take her away. The lord chief justice
shuffles papers on his desk, rapidly scrawls his signature on a few of them,
and then throws down the pen wearily.

JUSTICE: The court is adjourned until one o'clock.

The justice rises and descends with slow dignity; the curtains close over be-
hind him. The lights go up again in his room. He stands awaiting Milligan's
aid in unrobing. Milligan comes in carrying the lord chief justice's papers,
which he places on the table. While the lord chief justice pulls off his wig Mil-
ligan pours his brandy. He takes the brandy and hands the chain to Milligan,
who drapes it around the lay figure.

JUSTICE: An amusing young blackguard, Peter Shanks. Every bit as con-
ceited as you, Milligan. What a very humble man I am. Never once did I
dream of taking a short cut to greatness by leading a rebellion.

MILLIGAN: That young fellow will get to the top of a different tree from your
lordship.

JUSTICE: Don't gibe, Milligan. I hate people who gibe at the misfortunate. I
hate bullies.

Milligan's grip on the judge's robe as he takes it off, express his loathing of
his employer.

JUSTICE (*facing Milligan*): Besides, Milligan, I am not at the top of the tree.
I am not lord chancellor.

MILLIGAN: Not yet, m'lud.

JUSTICE: Not ever, Milligan. I was passed over in favor of a young whipper-
snapper, Milligan, although I licked all the right arses. I licked them,
he kicked them, I am where I am, he is where he is. I have always been
too humble, Milligan, too humble. (*Holds out his glass to be filled. Milli-*
gan fills it.) Milligan.

MILLIGAN: M'lud?

JUSTICE (*gently taking Milligan by the cravat and slowly shaking him*):
Whose arse are the young fellows licking now since they've stopped licking mine?

MILLIGAN: I have noticed, m'lud, that much attention is being paid to Mr.
Wolfe, the attorney-general.

A gust of fury sweeps through the lord chief justice. He flings Milligan away
from him. Milligan lies where he falls.

JUSTICE: Get up, man, get up.

But Milligan appears to be hurt. The lord chief justice rushes remorsefully to
him.

JUSTICE: Are you hurt, Anthony? I didn't mean to hurt you. (*He helps him*
to rise.)

MILLIGAN: It's all right, m'lud. (*Rubs his leg.*)

JUSTICE: Forgive me forgive me. I do not mean to hurt people, I do not mean to do it. I do it and I — you're all right, aren't you? Here. Drink this. (*Hands him his own glass of brandy.*)

MILLIGAN: Thank you no, m'lud.

JUSTICE: Go on, man, go on.

MILLIGAN: Really no, m'lud.

JUSTICE: You have not forgiven me, Anthony. I have lost another friend.

MILLIGAN: I'm all right now, m'lud.

JUSTICE: Are you sure? I'll fetch the physician?

MILLIGAN: No need, m'lud.

JUSTICE (*putting both hands on Milligan's shoulders*): I'm sorry. You have forgiven me — ?

MILLIGAN: There is nothing to forgive, m'lud. It was an accident.

JUSTICE (*flinging away*): Oh Milligan, you disgust me with your hypocritical lies. It was not an accident. It was deliberate. (*Turns to him.*) Damages, Milligan, damages. I shall pay you — well, a guinea. When your wages fall due next quarter, remind me. One guinea. (*Cheerful again.*) So it's Mr. Wolfe the attorney-general, eh? They see the hand of death on me? (*Sighs.*) Oh what would I not give to be Peter Shanks!

MILLIGAN: A condemned felon, m'lud?

JUSTICE: A young man, Milligan: young, young, young, YOUNG.

MILLIGAN: The hangman will soon make him as old as the earth, m'lud.

JUSTICE: Oh he could buy back his life quite easily. A few words of information, a pinch of incense on the altar of the false gods, and another fifty years of life are his. Another fifty years, Milligan. And here am I with life leaving me and I leaving life. (*With gathering ferocity.*) It took me fifty-nine years to become what I am now, and everything is being snatched from my hand. I could even bear to give up the chain of office but (*a note of anguish*) not my rose gardens and my trees, and my lovely house at Blackrock. Soon it'll all be someone else's. (*Almost snarling.*) Don't tell me it's the common lot: I've had enough platitudes for one day. (*The anguish grips him again.*) Then every little pain and ache — wondering if this is the beginning of the end. The first clutch of death. (*He rages in silence for a few moments, then the mood changes suddenly; a note of semihysterical merriment enters his voice.*) And there's that damned young fool throwing away his life like an empty bottle. Oh why doesn't the Devil exist, Milligan, so that I could sell him my soul for that young fool's fifty years of life? (*Throws himself wearily into his chair.*) Did I ever tell you, Milligan, about the time I tried to sell my soul to the Devil?

MILLIGAN: It is one of your favorite stories, m'lud.

JUSTICE (*sits, and leans back with closed eyes and joined hands*) : I was only twelve or thirteen at the time. I wanted to go to London to see all the sights. The desire was purely instinctive.

MILLIGAN (*offering him brandy*): May I venture to remind your lordship that you wished to see the female prisoner privately?

JUSTICE: What female prisoner?

MILLIGAN: Mary Neale, m'lud. The young female who is charged with aiding and abetting the rebels.

JUSTICE: Have her sent in.

The lord chief justice puts on his bob-wig, arranges the folds of his dressing gown more becomingly around him, and seats himself in his armchair in an imposing attitude. Milligan returns with two turnkeys who bring Mary into the room. The three men bow and withdraw, leaving Mary standing nervously in front of the lord chief justice. He looks at her silently; she trembles.

JUSTICE: Well, child, what have you to say for yourself?

MARY: I don't know, your honor.

JUSTICE: You're not a rebel, Mary, are you?

MARY: Oh no, your honor.

JUSTICE: It's not enough to say "Oh no, your honor," whilst you stand in danger of the rope going around your neck.

MARY (*whispering*) : Have mercy on me, your honor.

JUSTICE: What was the nature of your association with those rebels?

MARY: I don't understand, your honor.

JUSTICE: Come, child. You did associate with them?

MARY: Tom Doyle is my cousin, your honor. I have been going to his house ever since I was a little girl.

JUSTICE: You knew he was a rebel?

MARY: I swear before almighty God, your honor — no.

JUSTICE: How am I to believe you?

MARY: I'm telling the truth, your honor — on my oath I am.

JUSTICE: You wouldn't be here, my child, if you hadn't said and done things which no loyal citizen should say or do. How old are you?

MARY: Sixteen, your honor.

JUSTICE: Very young to be hanged, my child. But when I was a young man girls of twelve and thirteen were hanged for stealing a ribbon.

MARY (*sobbing*) : But I've done nothing, your honor — nothing.

JUSTICE (*fiercely*): You must have done or you wouldn't be here. (*Subsides.*) However, I don't believe that you are as dangerous a rebel as they say. The question is though, what view will the jury take? (*He walks slowly to the window, Mary looking after him fearfully.*) In certain circumstances I might be able to keep your case from the jury. (*Without looking around.*) Do you understand me, child?

263

MARY (*looking up*): Do you mean you could get me off?

JUSTICE: If I thought you were sincerely repentant —

MARY: But I've done nothing, your honor.

JUSTICE: Sincerely repentant — then I might have set you free. (*Turns and looks at her.*)

MARY (*she raises her eyes to his; a hint of insolence creeps into her voice*): What do you want me to do?

JUSTICE (*taking her by the chin*): What do I want you to do? Answer the question yourself, my child.

MARY (*a touch more insolent*): I wouldn't know how to answer your honor.

JUSTICE (*fierce*): Answer the question.

MARY (*intimidated*): I don't know what your honor wants.

JUSTICE: Answer the question. (*She is silent. He grips her hair, but not roughly, and forces her to look at him.*) I know what is in your mind, your pure clean unsullied mind. That you must open your gates for me to enter in. (*She begins to whimper.*) Oh Thou who wast crucified to redeem the souls of young pious virgins, look upon Thy handiwork and be glad. (*Pushes her away and goes to his chair.*) Every dog and devil in the town has had you. (*She bows her head and cries piteously.*) That is the truth, eh? Every dog and devil. (*He stares at her and shifts uncomfortably.*) Oh — does it matter? It mattered to me when I was your age, but that was because I was a child-man and did not know what women are. (*Goes over and puts arm around her shoulder.*) That was the time when I could look into a face like yours — but only from a distance: I was too humble to draw near. I could see in such a face only beauty, purity, chastity, and innocence — all without any taint of the chamber of horrors that lay behind my own face. (*Gently grips her hair and twists her face up to his.*) But now I know that the horrors behind this (*raps his forehead*) are nothing to the horrors behind that (*raps her forehead*). Eh? (*Puts his face close to hers.*) You would devour me, my dear, if I let you — eh? Sixteen and sixty. I have often been devoured, my dear, by sweet innocent buds of girlhood like yourself . . . when I was thirty-three, when I was thirty-eight, when I was forty, and forty-four, and even when I was fifty-six. There isn't much left to devour now — but still enough to tempt you. (*He puts his lips to hers. She does not shrink.*)

MARY (*whispering*): Are you telling me you love me?

JUSTICE (*staring hard at her*): I think you *are* a virgin. (*She nods.*) You are only a child. (*She puts her hand timidly on his breast.*) Only a child. (*Tenderly.*) Are your father and mother alive? (*She nods.*) I feel sorry for you — for all that you will have to suffer in this world — you're so young, and youth is a time of torment and suffering. I remember, my dear. (*Suddenly he stops, glances at her hand on his breast, then at her face.*

He walks over to his chair. She follows him. He laughs up at her.) My God: thirty-three . . . and thirty-eight . . . and forty . . . and forty-four . . . and fifty-six . . . and now fifty-nine. Go away, my dear, I am too old to bear any more pain. (*He slumps in his chair, his head bent. She looks at him uncertainly. He glances up.*) I said go away. No more pain. (*His head sinks again. She tiptoes to the door. When he hears her turn the handle he jerks upright.*) Where are you going?

MARY (*startled*): You told me to go away.

JUSTICE (*rising*): You are a prisoner. You have broken the law of the land and must pay the penalty. Nevertheless, you shall be set free. As far as your virtue is concerned you will leave this room as you came into it. (*Mary shows no reaction.*) I have a reputation for being severe. But it seems to me that I have always been more inclined to mercy than the judges who are reputed kind. But I cannot set you free without more ado. That would be to do you an injury, my child. Your reckless words and deeds must not go unpunished —

MARY: But I did nothing, your honor, I did nothing.

JUSTICE: To let them go unpunished would encourage you to repeat them. And the next time the judge might not be kind and merciful. You shall be whipped.

MARY (*terrified*): Send me to the jail instead.

JUSTICE (*angry*): I save you from being hanged and still you're not satisfied.

MARY: Oh not that . . . please not that — I couldn't bear it — before all those crowds of people — and they jeering and laughing at me. And the horrible man who whips you — oh please, your honor, not that. Send me to the jail — although I did nothing.

JUSTICE (*turning away*): You can be whipped or hanged. Please yourself.

MARY (*catching at his dressing gown*): Please — and I'll say a prayer for your honor night and morning for the rest of my life — I swear it. If you only knew how they laugh and jeer when the clothes are pulled off your back and — the disgrace, the disgrace.

JUSTICE (*with a sigh*): God forgive me for being a silly foolish old man. (*As if exasperated.*) You shall be whipped in private with nobody to see you. Does that satisfy you? (*She hangs her head and says nothing. He flings away angrily.*) This is preposterous. The lord chief justice bandying terms with a presumptuous little bitch from the streets. You shall stand trial. You shall be hanged — and may I be damned through all eternity if ever I surrender again to an impulse of kindliness.

MARY (*a whisper*): I accept whatever your honor says.

JUSTICE: Do you, by God? I am much obliged to you. You're quite sure that you do not expect the lord chief justice to whip you with his own hand?

MARY (*with a quick look at him, which shows her understanding of his intention*): Whatever your honor wishes.

JUSTICE (*stalking back to his chair and flinging himself into it angrily*): I am a fool. I should have let the law take its course with you. Get out of my sight. (*Mary does not move.*) Get out of my sight.

MARY (*a whisper*): I will let your honor do whatever you please.

The lord chief justice appears to be thinking deeply for a moment. Mary watches him closely, but he does not look at her.

JUSTICE: You will find a Bible on the table. (*Mary goes to the table.*) Take it in your right hand and kneel down and say after me: I swear before almighty God.

MARY (*kneeling*): I swear before almighty God.

JUSTICE: That I will never again utter any word.

MARY: That I will never again utter any word. Are you going to do it now?

JUSTICE: Or perform any action.

MARY: Are you going to —

JUSTICE: Or perform any action.

MARY: Or perform . . . (*she cannot find utterance*).

JUSTICE (*putting his hand on her shoulder*): Oh all right. Don't get into a state. Get up get up. (*She rises. He clasps her paternally.*) There there. Listen. You promise never to have anything to do with rebels again — ? (*Mary nods.*) Then there's an end to it. You shall be whipped and set free. (*Takes Bible from her and puts it on table.*) Now go into that room over there and prepare to receive your punishment.

She goes into the inner room. He quietly locks the public door, pours himself brandy and tosses it back. He goes to the cupboard and takes out a bundle of twigs. He makes more than one attempt to follow Mary into the room before he finally goes. The lights dim. After some time the lord chief justice stumbles out of the room, flings away the bundle of twigs, and sinks on the floor where he writhes and then lies still for a moment. The light gradually returns to the room. He drags himself up heavily. He looks ghastly. He searches for the bundle of twigs, finds it and flings it in the fire. He keeps mumbling to himself as he prowls restlessly around the room, stopping only to drink more brandy.

JUSTICE: Oh John Scott, John Scott, why do you do these things? You fool. You're mad, John Scott. You're an animal. Fifty-nine years old and you still do these vile things. Hateful. Vile. Bestial. Why why why why? What drives you to do them? And she knew — she knew you had been maneuvering her into letting you do it. Christ have mercy on me. She knew she knew she knew. They all know. People aren't fools. Those girls talk. They do — they must. (*Goes over to inner door, glaring.*) I hate you hate you hate you. You little whingeing bitch. (*Turns away.*) There must be other men in the world like you too, John Scott. (*Listens.*) Sobbing and whimpering and whingeing in there, you hateful little slut. (*In anguish.*) Oh you knew you knew you knew you knew. (*Opens door, speaks calmly.*) Come out to me. Come along.

Mary comes out. She is sobbing and holding her torn dress up on her shoulder. He takes her in his arms.

JUSTICE: Don't cry. For God's sake don't cry. I had to do it. You did wrong, you had to be punished. There there. (*Looks at her shoulders.*) It'll all be healed up by the time you're twice married.

MARY (*approaching hysterics*): I want my mother. I want my mother. Oh mother mother mother mother . . .

JUSTICE (*shaking her*): Quiet. Now come. Pull yourself together. It wasn't all that bad.

MARY (*her voice rising*): Get my mother, get my mother, get — get — get —

JUSTICE (*shaking her violently*): Hold your tongue.

A loud knock at the door.

JUSTICE (*pushing her toward the door*): Get in there and keep quiet. Don't disgrace yourself before other people.

He closes door after her. He makes sure the bundle of twigs has been consumed in the fire before he unlocks other door. Milligan enters.

MILLIGAN: Are you all right, m'lud?

JUSTICE (*in complete command of himself*): What do you mean, Milligan?

MILLIGAN: I was knocking at the door for a long time, but your lordship didn't seem to hear. (*Looks curiously around the room.*) Where is she? The female prisoner, m'lud?

JUSTICE: In the other room. She has given me most valuable information about these rebel dogs — but keep that to yourself. (*Suddenly.*) What are you staring at me like that for?

MILLIGAN: Staring — oh m'lud — I didn't realize —

JUSTICE (*furiously*): Am I growing two heads? And what were you sniffing and spying around the door for? (*Pounding the table.*) I will not be spied upon, d'you hear?

The lord chief justice suddenly clutches at his chest with a gasp of pain. Milligan watches him impassively. The spasm passes, but the justice, badly shaken, is obliged to totter to his chair, breathing heavily and with difficulty.

MILLIGAN: The attorney-general begs a moment's interview with your lordship concerning the female prisoner.

JUSTICE (*flaring up*): What concern is it of his what I say or do with the female prisoner? (*Subsiding.*) Oh, send him in.

Milligan goes to the door, bows the attorney-general in, then withdraws, shutting the door. The attorney-general, Arthur Wolfe, is a well-preserved fifty, elegant in figure and dress, quiet and calm.

267

WOLFE (*with a slight bow*): I have to apologize for being a little late for the trial this morning, but your lordship certainly dispatched those rascals very quickly. Now, about this girl —

JUSTICE: It was stupid to send a girl like that for trial.

WOLFE (*stiffly*): I understand you didn't deign to hear any evidence. We have enough to hang her.

JUSTICE: I believe you. When I was attorney-general I could always produce enough evidence to hang any man, woman or child in the kingdom ten times over.

WOLFE (*drawing himself up*): Chief justice, I —

JUSTICE: Give me any two lines in your handwriting, Mr. Attorney-General, and I'll put the rope around your own neck with them.

WOLFE: I take your point, chief justice, but this girl —

JUSTICE: Especially those confidential letters you send to the viceroy about me. (*Wolfe looks up startled. The lord chief justice grins.*) How do I know you write letters condemning my handling of certain trials?

WOLFE (*much confused*): Anything that I have said to his excellency —

JUSTICE: My dear Arthur, I wrote the same kind of letters when I was attorney-general. And when you are lord chief justice, the attorney-general will stab you in the back too. It's the way of the world. Now then, sit down and tell me what's the latest gossip about Copperfaced Jack.

WOLFE: Who's he?

JUSTICE: The brandy is beside you. (*Wolfe shakes his head. He sits.*) Well, what are they saying about Copperfaced Jack? What poor innocent widow is he alleged to have defrauded now? What (*there is a fraction of a second's hesitation*) what new vices has he plunged into?

WOLFE: I do not know the gentleman. And from what you say I'm rather glad I don't.

JUSTICE (*jovially*): Come come, confidence for confidence. Tell me the latest gossip about Copperfaced Jack and I'll tell you the latest gossip about yourself.

WOLFE: I never pay the slightest attention to the gossip about you.

JUSTICE: So there is gossip?

WOLFE: Is there a man in public life, chief justice, about whom there *isn't* any?

JUSTICE: You may speak freely. It will amuse me.

WOLFE (*smiling*): Well, what everyone says about you these days is that — well . . .

JUSTICE: Yes?

WOLFE: The thing is too foolish to repeat.

JUSTICE (*chilling*): I have asked you a question, Mr. Attorney-General. You will be good enough to reply.

WOLFE (*quickly coming to heel*): They say there's no hope of promotion for the next forty years, as your lordship is clearly determined to live to be a hundred.

JUSTICE (*scowling*): I see.

WOLFE: About the female prisoner.

JUSTICE: I am discharging her.

WOLFE: Chief justice, you can't. The evidence —

JUSTICE: Farcical, my dear Arthur, farcical. (*Pulls the bellrope by the fireplace.*)

WOLFE: There are eleven witnesses, absolutely unanimous.

JUSTICE: Oh Arthur, never have eleven witnesses absolutely unanimous, it shows they've been drilled too well. Have a few discrepancies — just as would occur if they were telling the truth.

WOLFE: I understand you have interviewed the girl privately?

JUSTICE: She is in the other room writing a full account of her knowledge of the rebels.

WOLFE: That's curious. She says she can neither read nor write.

JUSTICE: She did not so inform me.

Milligan comes in.

JUSTICE: I am going back into court, Milligan.

MILLIGAN: Yes, m'lud.

JUSTICE (*to Wolfe*): You will, I take it, be in time for *this* sitting?

WOLFE: I intend to be.

Milligan escorts the attorney-general out, closing the door. The lord chief justice clenches and unclenches his fists and babbles to himself again.

JUSTICE: Oh they're talking about you, John Scott, they know all about you. They're sniggering in corners about you. (*He beats his fists on his temples, writhing and shriveling before his own self-contempt.*) You fool, you fool, you fool, you fool.

Milligan enters with a letter on a salver.

JUSTICE (*calm*): Read it to me, Milligan.

MILLIGAN: I am informed it is confidential, m'lud.

The lord chief justice opens and reads letter. He throws it on the table carelessly.

JUSTICE: Milligan, how often have I told you that letters from the wives or mothers of prisoners are not to be brought to me?

MILLIGAN: M'lud, I did not know who it came from. It was handed to me by a servant.

JUSTICE: Was it not worth your while to enquire whose servant he was?

MILLIGAN: I'm sorry, m'lud.

JUSTICE: In this case you needn't be. I haven't seen the lady for thirty years — no, forty years. My first love, Milligan. Oh Eliza Eliza Eliza Eliza.

Bring her in. No wait. Get a turnkey to come and take the female prisoner away.

*Milligan goes. The lord chief justice opens the inner door and beckons Mary
out. He looks at her kindly and strokes her hair.*

JUSTICE: Well — ?

MARY (*rubbing her shoulder: a hint of insolence in her voice again*): You
hurt me.

JUSTICE (*jovial*): It hasn't taken you long to recover.

MARY: Do you do that to other girls?

JUSTICE: Of course not.

MARY: I have a feeling you do. You seem to have a lot of practice.

JUSTICE: Don't be insolent.

MARY: I want to go.

JUSTICE: Take care the rope isn't put around your neck.

MARY (*a touch of vixen*): You said I could go free.

JUSTICE: The attorney-general wants to hang you.

MARY (*angry*): You said I could go free. Aren't you supposed to be the judge?

JUSTICE: You're not afraid of me any longer?

MARY (*peevish*): You hurt me — deliberately.

*The lord chief justice puts his hand on her shoulder. She shakes him off. He
seems amused.*

MARY: Now let me go.

JUSTICE: No. I may change my mind about what is best to do to you.

MARY: I'll tell everybody about you. I'll tell them the sort of man you are.

JUSTICE (*furious*): I'll swing you, by God. With my own hands I'll swing
you.

MARY (*backing away*): Don't touch me. (*Her voice rises.*) Don't touch me.

JUSTICE (*with hatred*): You are beneath contempt. (*Recovers himself
quickly.*) A man loses his magic for a woman the moment he condescends
to be kind to her.

MARY (*peevish again*): Well you hurt me, so you did. You're cruel. That's
what you are: cruel. (*Turns away, mumbling.*) Treating me like that.
Don't you know a gentleman is not supposed to hurt a lady? What sort
of a mother had you got?

JUSTICE (*going to her, smiling*): I can't help liking you, my dear. (*She
makes no move when he puts his arm around her.*) I suppose I liked you
the moment I saw you. And I hate to think that when you go I shan't see
you again.

MARY (*muttering*): Pity about you. (*Pulls away the dress and shows him her
shoulder.*) Look at that.

JUSTICE: I shall kiss it and make it better. (*She will not let him.*) You forget
I have saved you from being hanged.

MARY (*almost putting out her tongue at him*): You couldn't have me hanged because I didn't do anything.

JUSTICE: I am tempted to let you devour me. (*Sighs.*) A man never learns, you know.

Milligan knocks and opens the door. He pauses. The turnkey is behind him.

JUSTICE: It was very wrong of you to tell me you could write, my child. However, I have taken good note of what you told me, and shall bear it in mind when you come before me in court. Milligan, have her brought back to court. (*Milligan beckons the turnkey in.*) Do not thank me, my child. It will be enough to lead a good and virtuous life from now on. If you remember me in your prayers, I shall feel well rewarded for what I have done for you.

The turnkey bows clumsily to the lord chief justice, and leads Mary off by the arm. The lord chief justice beckons Milligan to his side.

JUSTICE (*whispering*): Nobody — absolutely nobody — is to be let speak with her, either in court or when she leaves court.

MILLIGAN: Yes, m'lud. Mistress Shanks is outside, m'lud.

JUSTICE: I must put on my armor first.

Milligan helps him out of his dressing gown and into his red robe, chain, and wig.

JUSTICE: She will have put on her best gown for me, Milligan. I too must try to make an impression. (*Sits. Milligan arranges his robe in graceful folds.*) I wish it were six feet longer, Milligan, and that the color were purple. (*Sits.*) Cover my legs. Legs destroy dignity. The Romans knew that — hence the toga. Nobody can take King George the Third seriously as long as he keeps his legs so much in evidence. If he covered his legs like the Pope he could go as mad as he liked and nobody would notice. (*Milligan stands back to admire his handiwork.*) Well — ?

MILLIGAN: The chain, m'lud . . .

JUSTICE (*adjusting it*): Like so? (*Milligan nods.*) Admit the public. (*Leans back.*) I sometimes think that in a previous existence I was the Emperor Claudius, the most endearing of the Caesars.

Milligan has opened the door for Eliza Shanks. The lord chief justice makes no move: he seems lost in thought.

MILLIGAN: Mistress Shanks, m'lud.

The lord chief justice slowly turns his head. Eliza, already nervous, bursts into tears.

JUSTICE: You desired to see me, madam?

Eliza's distress increases. It has its inevitable effect upon the lord chief justice. He becomes uncomfortable, then jumps up and sweeps over to her.

JUSTICE (*taking her hand*): There there, you mustn't cry.

ELIZA: Mercy, my lord, mercy for my poor misfortunate son.

The lord chief justice motions Milligan to leave the room. He does so. The lord chief justice places a chair for her. Late middle age finds Eliza run to flesh. She hasn't really helped herself by dressing youthfully and touching up her complexion.

JUSTICE (*kissing her hand*): Well well, after all these years . . .

ELIZA: I know I take a great liberty, my lord — it is presumptuous of me — you have become such a very great man in the world since we last met.

JUSTICE: I remain the man I always was.

ELIZA: Peter is innocent, my lord.

JUSTICE: He confessed his guilt. I did what I could to save him from himself — even though I didn't know he was your son. The matter has now passed out of my hands.

ELIZA: I know that one little word from you —

JUSTICE: It is not quite as simple as that, my dear.

ELIZA (*pulling out her handkerchief*): You mean you won't help me —

JUSTICE: Eliza, I will help you all I can. (*Sits.*)

ELIZA: You are a great man —

JUSTICE: The law is greater than I.

ELIZA: You won't let them kill him on me — an innocent boy. I warned him not to listen to those people —

JUSTICE: What people?

ELIZA: Twice and three times his age, they are. Men who could buy and sell you — the real leaders of the rebellion — and walking round as free as the air under your very nose, while my Peter is where he is. Why don't you hang *them*, instead of young boys who haven't had time to grow up into sense? What sense had you got when you were his age, John Scott?

JUSTICE: You of all people may well ask that.

ELIZA: You were foolish and hot-headed — I don't mean any disrespect, my lord, but there was no harm in you. You were a fine open generous lad like Peter. I could show you the letters you wrote me —

JUSTICE (*sitting up*): Letters?!

ELIZA: All these years I have kept them. I hadn't the heart to throw them away, even when I married Shanks. I still read them, my lord.

JUSTICE: Put the past in the fire, Eliza.

ELIZA: Oh no, John Scott, I couldn't do that. I mean no disrespect — you are a great man now, but I still think of you as John Scott who — who used to say he was in love with me — I mean no disrespect, my lord.

JUSTICE: Letters? Um.

ELIZA: No man ever sent me letters like yours. You said you would gladly give your life for me —

JUSTICE: I meant it at the time.

ELIZA (*pathetic*): You were twenty, my lord, and you said you would gladly

give your life for me. You begged me for a tress of my hair, and said it
would inspire you all your life.

JUSTICE: Did I say that? It doesn't sound like me. I am not in the least sentimental.

ELIZA: But I never asked you for anything. Even when my husband died and
there was all that trouble over the property.

JUSTICE: I would have helped you had I known you were in trouble. What
you ask of me now is impossible. He has confessed his guilt in open court.
The law must take its course.

ELIZA: He is all I have —

JUSTICE: The country is on the brink of rebellion. The government has to
act with a hand of iron.

ELIZA: You said you would do anything for me —

JUSTICE: Damnation, you keep harping on what *I* said. What did *you* say?
What sort of a dance did *you* lead me in the days of my infatuation?

ELIZA: It was not my doing, my lord, that you were turned away from our
house. My father —

JUSTICE: Your father! Did your father lure me into believing that you loved
me?

ELIZA: My lord, I was perfectly sincere —

JUSTICE: Sincere! You made a fool of me. You ogled and languished and
simpered and pressed my hand under your cloak in church and I thought
I was beloved.

ELIZA: You were, my lord, you were.

JUSTICE: While all the time you were sniggering with your friends over my
letters —

ELIZA (*hotly*): I never showed as much as one line —

JUSTICE: You lie, madam. Flossie MacDonald was able to tell me what was
in them.

ELIZA: Flossie MacDonald! My God, you wouldn't want to believe the time
of day from that bitch.

JUSTICE: Your best friend.

ELIZA: Never.

JUSTICE: She told me it was you always led the merry girlish laughter at my
red pimply face, with my hands hanging out of the coat that was three
sizes too small for me.

ELIZA: Lies lies lies lies, all lies.

JUSTICE: It was you who joked about my uncle's cast-off shoes upon my feet.

ELIZA: Lies lies lies. I wanted to marry you.

JUSTICE: What?! Boozy Bolger the bailiff's lovely daughter marry the can-
dlemaker's ugly son! What a fool I was to aspire to such greatness. (*Vicious.*) But what were *you* to lead me on when you knew that the whole

thing was eternally impossible? I know what I call such women (*drives one hand into the other*) and I have had the whores whipped from one end of the town to the other.

ELIZA (*sobbing*): I loved you.

JUSTICE: If that was love, would to God you had hated me. But I give you this much. That I am what I am today is due to you.

ELIZA (*catching at the straw*): I am proud to hear you say it, John.

JUSTICE (*fingering his chain and rising*): The collar of gold, Eliza. I had to learn the old lesson: that gold and power are the only realities in this world. All the rest — love, friendship, goodness, kindness, faith, hope, charity, piety, bravery — pshaw! Illusions. (*Goes to the windows.*)

ELIZA: I don't know what's got into you, John Scott. You never used to be like this.

JUSTICE: As for your son —

ELIZA (*convulsed with sobs*): I never showed a line you wrote to anybody. Flossie had no right to say I did.

JUSTICE: Forget about Flossie. I hadn't thought of her for forty years until this came up. Now about Peter —

ELIZA: All lies lies. I never joked about you. (*Swinging around and looking earnestly at him.*) You must believe at least that. I never joked about you — never.

JUSTICE: It hardly matters now whether you did or not.

ELIZA: I know I've gone old and I've lost my figure.

The lord chief justice is touched. He goes over and lays his hands on her shoulders.

JUSTICE: You haven't, my dear. Not really. (*She begins to perk up.*) When you came in through that door I recognized you immediately. You have hardly changed at all.

ELIZA: I knew you too. But you looked so fierce in your red cloak.

JUSTICE: My armor.

ELIZA: Your what?

JUSTICE: My wig. My robe. (*Pulls off his wig and flings it aside.*)

ELIZA (*with a half giggle*): Oh John — what have you done with all your lovely hair? You that used to be as black as a crow, with that thick mop of lovely curly hair.

JUSTICE (*fingering the top of his head*): Damn it, Eliza, I'm nearly sixty. There's many a man completely bald at thirty nowadays.

ELIZA: I always knew you would grow stout. Even as a boy you were plump. Of course I know *I* shouldn't talk.

JUSTICE: Stand up there and let me see you.

ELIZA: No I won't. Don't be silly.

JUSTICE: Stand up, I said.

ELIZA: I don't want you to look at me.

He takes her hand and in spite of some resistance, hauls her to her feet. She is very confused.

ELIZA: Well — aren't you glad you didn't marry the like of that?

He walks around her, surveying her. She goes to sit down but he deftly moves the chair with one hand and saves her from flopping on the floor with the other. She is virtually in his embrace.

JUSTICE: Old times, eh?

ELIZA: My goodness, John Scott, but you haven't changed one bit.

JUSTICE (*both arms around her*): You always had a fine rump, my girl.

ELIZA: Now, John, behave yourself. Suppose someone came in.

JUSTICE: Well, suppose someone came in — ?

ELIZA: It's all very well for you. You never cared what anyone ever said about you —

JUSTICE: Oh didn't I?

ELIZA: But a woman can't afford to have people talk about her.

He unfastens the clasp of his robe and lets it fall to the ground. Eliza, startled, backs away with surprising agility.

ELIZA: Now John Scott, what are you up to?

JUSTICE: Come back here to me.

ELIZA (*sitting primly in her chair*): I'll do no such thing. Put your cloak back on you and sit down in your chair and behave yourself.

JUSTICE: I don't like behaving myself, Eliza. (*He defiantly unbuttons his waistcoat and throws it on the floor.*)

ELIZA: Take that up and put it back on you.

He begins to unfasten his braces.

ELIZA (*turning her back on him*): Oh — !

JUSTICE (*grinning*): Why don't you leave the room? Why don't you scream?

ELIZA: Because I know you're only trying to frighten me.

JUSTICE: Are you that easily frightened? (*He stoops to retrieve his waistcoat, wheezing loudly.*)

ELIZA (*swoops on the garment and holds it for him to get into*): That's what happened to my husband. Stooping down to get his pipe and burst a blood vessel. Of course he was even stouter than you.

JUSTICE: So you married a fat man after all. And you used tell me you liked only thin men.

ELIZA: He was nice and thin when I married him. (*Picks up the robe.*)

JUSTICE: Your son takes after *you*, though.

ELIZA: Maybe. But as stubborn as his father. My goodness, the weight of this thing. It must kill you in the hot weather.

JUSTICE: I'm used to it. (*Goes to his chair.*) Pull the bell. I'll have them fetch him in to us.

275

ELIZA (*pulling bellrope at mantelpiece*): Yes, get him in. And give him a good telling off. That'll teach him to listen to his mother in future.

JUSTICE (*gently*): Eliza, I cannot stop his being hanged — not now.

ELIZA: Nonsense. If you say he's to be hanged you can as easily say he's not to be hanged. (*He shakes his head.*) I think you should put on your wig. It makes you look fiercer.

JUSTICE: I've told you, the matter is out of my hands.

ELIZA: How can it be? Aren't you the lord chief justice? Just go out into your court and tell them you have changed your mind.

Milligan comes in.

JUSTICE: Bring in the prisoner Shanks.

Milligan bows and goes.

JUSTICE: If he were to turn informer — not that I think he will. I know his type. You could hang them ten times over and they still wouldn't do the sensible thing.

ELIZA: It'll be different when you speak to him. You see, he was only fourteen when his father died and boys need a man over them. He was a perfectly good child until he was sixteen but then something got into him. It was the books. Those accursed books. I got the vicar to talk to him but poor Mr. Benson might as well have been talking to the wall. Those books should be burned, and the men who wrote them burned along with them.

Milligan comes in, followed by two turnkeys escorting Peter Shanks, who is fettered hand and foot.

SHANKS (*surprised and angry*): What are you doing here, Mother?

TURNKEY: Quiet, until his lordship speaks to you.

JUSTICE: Get out, you hangdog curs. All of you.

Milligan and the turnkeys go.

SHANKS: Mother, it's no use.

ELIZA: This is what I've had to put up with for the past five years.

SHANKS: Why in God's name didn't you stay away?

JUSTICE: She came in God's name to rob you of your martyr's crown, my boy.

SHANKS: Mother, not only do you waste your time but you sacrifice your dignity — and mine.

ELIZA: Be respectful to his lordship.

SHANKS: Desist, Mother, desist. I command you. (*To lord chief justice.*) As for you, I know what you want of me. If I turn informer I shall have the means to start a new life in America.

JUSTICE: No, not America. We shall be more merciful than that. Australia.

SHANKS: You've got my answer, Copperfaced Jack.

ELIZA: Peter! How dare you speak to his lordship like that! He could have

276

you flogged for your impertinence and really I couldn't blame him if he did.

JUSTICE: You are very young to die.

SHANKS: A few years more or less — what does it matter when the cause is honorable?

JUSTICE: Death at the end of a rope — honorable?

SHANKS: More honorable than yours in a featherbed will be.

JUSTICE: We know there were other men in this conspiracy — men older than you, and more dangerous.

SHANKS: No use — no use. I shall not inform.

ELIZA: Peter, we are only trying to help you.

JUSTICE (*kindly*): Give us an excuse *not* to hang you, my boy.

SHANKS: Hang me and ten thousand swords shall spring from their scabbards to avenge my death. Hang me and every drop of my blood shall be a dragon's tooth to rend you and your attendant jackals limb from limb. Hang me and — and — and — be damned to you.

ELIZA: Go down on your knees and ask his pardon for saying the like of that. *Peter is about to refuse angrily when he pauses.*

SHANKS: Very well. (*Kneels, but without trace of fear or servility.*) I willingly ask your pardon, Copperfaced Jack — if — if — I have done you any wrong. (*He rises.*) Are you satisfied, Mother?

JUSTICE: I told you so, Eliza.

SHANKS (*starting*): How dare you address my mother in that familiar way? Keep your distance, Copperfaced Jack.

JUSTICE: Your mother and I are old friends.

Peter stares aghast at Eliza.

ELIZA (*uncomfortable*): I had the honor of knowing his lordship when I was young.

JUSTICE: Love, Peter. She loved me. Ask her.

ELIZA (*giggling*): My lord, I don't think we need —

SHANKS (*shattered*): Oh Mother — to think you could have done this to me!

JUSTICE: Such is life, Peter. C'est la vie.

SHANKS: This redfaced old clown, this bloated mashtub of drink and pigswill, this heap of offal — how could you have ever walked the same side of the street as him? Isn't my cup of bitterness full enough without your adding humiliation to it? Why have I been dragged here to be insulted by this swindler, this rogue, this lecher, this —

ELIZA: Peter! (*To lord chief justice.*) I am ashamed — utterly ashamed.

SHANKS: I take no favors from Copperfaced Jack. Let me be brought back to my cell.

JUSTICE: He's an amusing young devil. I'm just wondering could I by any chance have been his father?

With a yell Shanks raises his fettered fists and runs at the lord chief justice.
Eliza throws herself in front of him. Shanks lowers his fists and steps back.

JUSTICE: What, Peter! Strike an old man — old enough to be your father?

ELIZA: Don't be saying these things, John. He wouldn't understand that you're only joking.

SHANKS (*stung*): "John!"

JUSTICE (*putting his arm around Eliza*): Old friends. Old friends. (*Holds out his hand to Shanks.*) Give me your hand, Eliza's son.

SHANKS (*ignoring the gesture*): Mother, from this moment forth I do not know you.

ELIZA: A nice way to speak to your own mother. And in front of strangers.

SHANKS (*to the lord chief justice*): You can torture me with your tongue as much as you like, but another word out of me you will not get. I have only this to say to you: I see I am dealing with a madman.

ELIZA (*flouncing away to her chair*): Wouldn't he make you sick? I've a good mind to let them hang you. It's down on your knees you should be, thanking me and his lordship for what we're trying to do for you, if you'd only let us.

JUSTICE: I see his point, Eliza. Take the martyr's crown away from his otherwise not very distinguished brow — and what's left?

ELIZA: His father was the same. Would never listen to me. And then when he died there was all that trouble over the property. Men are such fools.

JUSTICE (*sardonic*): How true.

ELIZA: I don't mean men like you, my lord. After all, no fool could have got where you are.

SHANKS (*raising his clenched fists to his forehead*): Oh God, Mother, will you stop?

JUSTICE: Be as emotional as you like but don't rattle your chains so much.

SHANKS (*near tears*): Send me back to my prison cell.

ELIZA: If you'd only listened to your mother who knows what's good for you, you wouldn't be standing where you are today. (*Whimpers.*) Disgracing the family . . . chains . . . thank heaven your grandfather isn't alive to see it. (*Sobs.*) Oh my lord, you knew our family and how respectable we always were. And now . . . chains! A convict!

JUSTICE: Not a convict, dearest Eliza, the President of the new republic, the Lord of the new Earthly Paradise. Though admittedly under something of a cloud at present.

ELIZA: He had a private tutor after his father died, though God knows I could hardly afford it.

SHANKS: Great God, Mother, you'll drive me mad.

JUSTICE (*going to him*): Women always spoil our finest performances, Peter. Mothers particularly.

SHANKS (*shrinking*): Don't touch me.

A knock. The attorney-general opens the door.

WOLFE (*stiffly*): I am sorry to intrude but —

JUSTICE: Come in, Arthur, I was just about to send for you. Close the door. (*Sits.*) I am considering a new trial for Peter Shanks.

SHANKS (*with a vehemence that makes Wolfe jump*): I want no new trial.

WOLFE: This man has confessed.

JUSTICE: A new trial this afternoon.

WOLFE: Upon what grounds? I shall certainly not consent to a new trial except on proper grounds.

JUSTICE: Don't forget yourself, Mr. Attorney-General.

WOLFE: Let your lordship not forget the law.

JUSTICE (*pounding the chair*): I am the law, Mr. Attorney-General.

WOLFE: That contention shall be judged elsewhere.

JUSTICE (*bellowing*): No insolence, or by God you shall know who and what I am.

SHANKS (*with much rattling*): Cease your bickering. (*His intervention causes both men to stop and look at him.*) I refuse the offer of a new trial.

WOLFE (*hardly able to talk*): Chief Justice, if you are prepared to allow a condemned traitor to address you like that, I am not.

JUSTICE: Quack quack quack, Arthur. Sit down and be quiet.

Wolfe turns on his heel and walks out. The lord chief justice strides after him and bellows, "Arrest him! Arrest him!" Confused shouts outside. The lord chief justice returns to his chair. Wolfe is brought in by two turnkeys, with Milligan, betraying not the least surprise, following.

WOLFE (*to turnkeys*): You have dared lay hands on His Majesty's attorney-general.

JUSTICE: Contempt of court, Arthur. Now listen to me.

WOLFE: I refuse to listen. You have gone out of your mind.

SHANKS: You see what happens, Mother, when thieves fall out.

WOLFE: Mother?! Is she his mother?! Now I KNOW you have gone out of your mind.

JUSTICE (*to turnkeys*): Release Mr. Attorney-General. (*They do so.*) Take away the prisoner, but not beyond the precincts of my court. (*Rises.*) Madam, be so kind as to withdraw.

Eliza curtseys to the lord chief justice. All leave except Milligan, who has been motioned to stay.

JUSTICE: See that Mistress Shanks is allowed to remain with the prisoner, Milligan. Send to the tavern for wine and victuals for them.

Milligan bows and goes.

WOLFE: I respectfully request your lordship's permission to withdraw.

JUSTICE: I know I am a hasty man, Arthur, but by God I brook no threats from you or anyone else.

WOLFE: I did not threaten you. You threaten the law.

JUSTICE: This is a matter that we settle out of court, I think.

WOLFE: I am not falling into that trap.

The lord chief justice suddenly strikes him across the face. Wolfe reels, partly under the force of the blow, but chiefly from shock. He stares at the lord chief justice with mounting fury, and speaks in a choking voice.

WOLFE: You are only an old man.

JUSTICE: Still young enough to handle a pistol.

WOLFE: That may follow.

JUSTICE: I had forgotten. (*He takes off his chain of office and throws it into his chair.*) I am now a private gentleman, sir.

WOLFE: Very good, Lord Clonmell. A friend of mine shall call upon you.

JUSTICE (*pulling the bellrope*): I can dispense with ceremonial.

WOLFE: So can I.

JUSTICE: Then . . . here and now.

WOLFE: When I get a pistol I shall be at your service.

JUSTICE: I have pistols here.

Milligan comes in.

JUSTICE: The pistols, Milligan.

Milligan takes a case of pistols from the cupboard and places the weapons on the table. Meanwhile the lord chief justice has unfastened his robe and flung it on the chair.

JUSTICE: My coat, Arthur. It's somewhere over there.

Wolfe reluctantly goes to the corner and gets the coat. He has to hold it for the lord chief justice.

MILLIGAN: The pistols, m'lud — they've been loaded for a long time. The powder may be damp.

JUSTICE: Reload.

MILLIGAN (*reloading the pistols*): Shall your lordship be requiring the services of a friend?

JUSTICE: No.

WOLFE (*to the lord chief justice in an undertone*): I shall wait in the meadow two miles beyond the turnpike.

JUSTICE: Why walk yourself to death before I kill you? I shall have my court cleared. That place will be as good as any. A new kind of legal duel, eh?

WOLFE: If you have such little respect for your own court, I have nothing further to say.

JUSTICE: Profaning that temple of truth and eloquence — eh?

WOLFE: And justice.

MILLIGAN: The pistols are ready, m'lud.

JUSTICE: Take your choice, Arthur.

WOLFE: As your lordship is the person challenged, you have the right of choice.

JUSTICE: Pedant.

WOLFE: I insist, my lord.

JUSTICE: I waive the right as the pistols are mine.

The attorney-general takes up the pistol nearest his hand and hides it under his gown. The lord chief justice takes up his other pistol and thrusts it carelessly under his arm. The two men bow to each other and walk out of the room, the lord chief justice indicating that the attorney-general is to precede him.

JUSTICE (*as he goes through the door*): Remain here, Milligan. In case I should become indisposed, break the news to her ladyship as tactfully as you can.

MILLIGAN: Yes, m'lud.

The lord chief justice goes out, leaving the door open. Milligan quite calmly sits down in his chair and props his feet up on the table. He takes a toothpick from his pocket and begins to use it with gentlemanly elegance. There is dead silence. Then two shots reverberate through the building. Milligan, quite unperturbed, rises and addresses the audience.

MILLIGAN: My lords, ladies and gentlemen, and others, those shots need not cause you a moment's alarm. Gentlemen who fight duels like this never aim at each other. But that pair are such rotten shots they could have hit each other by accident. So I took the precaution of putting in only a little powder . . . and no bullets. (*He bows and retires as light vanishes and the curtain falls.*)

Act II

A large yard in Newgate jail, Dublin, where prisoners are herded together during the day, men and women alike, old and young, first offenders and hardened criminals. There is a wall of massive granite blocks at the back, with an arched gateway in the middle, and a smaller gate near it; at left is an open passage leading to another yard. Also to be seen is the front part of a ramshackle wooden shed, which serves as a privy. Some female prisoners, of varying ages, dirty and ragged, are sitting on wooden benches to the left of the main iron gate. They are Rosalind and Viola, a pair of slatterns; Bessie, who is young, buxom, and good-natured; and a couple of others who are no more than slightly animated bundles of rags. In the corner, right, Michael Fennessy, a carpenter, is putting the finishing touches to a black coffin on rough trestles. He is a tall, gaunt man of indeterminate age, of transparent simplicity, with a manner to match. In happier circumstances he might be jolly and good-humored, but his expression is now sad and lonely; even his rare smiles are sad. He works away, clearly oblivious of the chatter around him.

VIOLA (*holding her hands to her ears*): Gawd, Mr. Fennessy, will ye soon be finished hammering at that thing? You have me head splitting.

FENNESSY (*hammering in one more nail*): There, ma'am. I'm finished. There won't be any more hammering now for a bit.

BESSIE: This place'd get on your nerves.

VIOLA: Sometimes it's all the noise. Sometimes it's all the quietness. Things was never the same since poor oul' Billy-in-the-Bowl was hung.

BESSIE: It was a tragedy for a fine man like that to be hung, especially when you look at the dreeps they leave behind.

FENNESSY (*mournful*): I'll be out of your way in three days' time, ma'am.

BESSIE: Don't worry, Mr. Fennessy, it may never happen.

FENNESSY: It wouldn't be me luck, ma'am. If they was to do away with hanging it'd be the day *after* I was hung.

VIOLA: I sometimes wish I was going on the swing-swong myself. It'd be a bit of excitement after sitting here day after day, week after week, month after month. D'ye know what it is, ma'am, I've clean forgot what I'm in jail for?

BESSIE: I'll try to believe ye.

FENNESSY: Isn't Mr. Brian Borroo lively enough for you, ma'am?

VIOLA: He's too full of himself. Though he has a gorgeous voice.

BESSIE: The voice isn't bad. I love the way he sings "The Night Before Larry Was Stretched." Great humor he puts into it. But the filth that comes off his tongue — even when there's ladies present.

VIOLA: I blame his mother. What way did she rear him?

BESSIE: There's no control over childer nowadays. Dare ye open your mouth to your father and mother when I was a girl and you'd be knocked flying.

VIOLA: Me own father was a very nice man. He was hung for a rebel.

BESSIE: They don't hang half enough of them. Why don't them fellows go out and do an honest day's work instead of shooting from behind hedges at poor landlords and proper gentlemen? There was this lovely young gentleman I had, and he showed me where he'd been shot by them blackguards. No use he'll ever be now, ma'am, to any poor girl. I nearly cried. Such a gorgeous young gentleman he was too.

ROSALIND (*mournfully*): I love a man that gives you a bit of a laugh.

VIOLA: Oh Rosalind, I thought you was asleep.

ROSALIND: I was just thinking with me eyes shut.

282

BESSIE: That gorgeous young gentleman what was shot . . . skin like a baby he had.

ROSALIND: Aye, a laugh and a bit of an oul' song.

BESSIE: Lovely long thin legs and as straight as a pole.

ROSALIND: I mean to say, if ye couldn't have a bit of laugh you'd go mad.

VIOLA: Mr. Fennessy, would you ever trot down to the well and get us a jar of wather. I'm famished with the drooth.

FENNESSY: Very good, ma'am. (*He goes out.*)

ROSALIND: Gawd a'mighty, it's inhuman sticking the likes of him on top of us.

VIOLA: Do ye know how he spends the night? On his knees saying prayers for himself.

BESSIE: You'd be the same if you were going up on the swing-swong in three days.

VIOLA: I would not. God and me parted company many's the long year ago. It was friendly but final.

BESSIE: Don't be saying things like that. D'ye want us all to be struck dead?

Fennessy comes back with jug of water.

FENNESSY: There's wather for ye now, ma'am.

VIOLA (*taking the jug*): If you had the price of a pot of porter, Mr. Fennessy, you could have an hour of joy before you go on the swing-swong.

FENNESSY: In what way, ma'am?

VIOLA (*winking at the others*): Oh in any way that took your fancy, sir.

FENNESSY: I don't rightly follow ye, ma'am?

BESSIE: Ah leave the poor fella alone.

VIOLA: Gawd pity his poor wife, that's all I say.

FENNESSY: Why would you say that, ma'am?

BESSIE: Sing us a bit of an oul' song, Mr. Fennessy.

VIOLA: Jasus no, the only one he knows is "Faith of Our Fathers." (*Sighing.*) Ah Billy-in-the-Bowl, why aren't ye here with us now?

ROSALIND: Was Billy really in a bowl?

BESSIE: He had to be. Both his legs was cut off down to the stumps, so he sat in a little baskety bowl on wheels and begged from the quality.

VIOLA: He'd just about enough of himself left to sit on.

BESSIE: But he was all there, all the same. Ten children he had.

VIOLA: God love him.

BESSIE: And a perfect gentleman.

VIOLA: Even the oul' faggots he raped out in Ballybough had to admit that.

BESSIE: They said he took off his hat.

VIOLA: Which is more nor a certain viscount I used to know did. Wouldn't even take off his dirty boots.

ROSALIND: Was it for that they hung Billy? — for what he did out in Bally-bough?

BESSIE: A damn shame it was.

FENNESSY: Fancy hanging a poor man like that and he with no legs. Didn't that good God put enough affliction on him without men adding to it?

ROSALIND: Justice is justice, Mr. Fennessy.

FENNESSY: But listen, if Billy-in-the-Bowl had no legs, why didn't those ladies out in Ballybough run away when he went for to attack them?

VIOLA: Gawd, where were *you* brung up at all at all?

BESSIE: A nice gentleman like you wouldn't understand, Mr. Fennessy.

VIOLA: Some ladies goes outa their way to meet their fate.

ROSALIND: I wonder is he all that much of an innocent lamb? Hasn't he four childer? So he mustn't use it only for stirring his tay.

BESSIE: Leave him alone. I only wish there were more like him.

VIOLA: Gawd forbid.

FENNESSY: I wonder how did they hang a man with no legs? Sure he couldn't climb up the ladder.

VIOLA: He wasn't asked to. Mr. Galvin rolled him in his bowl up the plank.

BESSIE: A perfect jintleman is Mr. Galvin.

FENNESSY: Thou shalt not kill.

ROSALIND (*puzzled*): I beg your parsnips, Mr. Fennessy.

FENNESSY: Me last words to Mr. Galvin on Monday will be: "Fifth, thou shalt not kill."

VIOLA: Suppose he says back to you, "Seventh, thou shalt not steal — ?"

FENNESSY: I hadn't thought of that. (*Sighs.*) Seventh, thou shalt not steal.

BESSIE: Ach, you shouldn't have said that to the poor man, and he . . .

VIOLA: Isn't it the truth?

ROSALIND: The greater the truth the greater the libel, as me granddad used to say.

VIOLA (*haughty*): We're not here for robbing people.

ROSALIND: It was givin' people too much good value for their money has us here.

VIOLA: Ladies shouldn't be put in here for what they does be doin' in the privacy of their own room.

ROSALIND: *Where's* your private room?

VIOLA: Where's *yours*?

ROSALIND: Did I say I had one? It's anywhere outa the east wind for me.

VIOLA (*sneering*): Up ag'in the trees of the Royal Canal?

ROSALIND: Like yourself, darling.

BESSIE (*restoring the peace*): Sure them poor oul' trees is more sinned against than sinning.

A man is heard singing.

BESSIE: Oh here he comes.

Fennessy with a grimace goes back to his coffin-planing. Brian Borroo comes in from the left; he is young, and would be good-looking if he didn't carry a hundredweight of fat and his fine features weren't so often distorted by a sneer. He carries a bucket of whitewash and a brush. He stops in the middle of the room, takes a deep breath, and sings at the top of his voice.

BORROO (*singing*):

> Sez the daughter to the mother,
> "Yer talk is all in vain,
> For knights 'n' lords 'n' dukes 'n' earls
> Their efforts I disdain.
> I'd sooner live a humble life
> Where time I would employ
> Doing what comes natcherally
> Wid me bonny laborin' boy."

VIOLA: Go and do a dance for us, Mr. Borroo. Gawd knows the place needs a bit of livening up. I'll be the band.

Viola begins to troll an Irish jig, clapping her hands in rhythm. Borroo folds his arms and executes a step dance with peculiar elegance. While he is dancing a turnkey marches briskly across the room and in passing gives him a tap of the head with a huge key. Borroo immediately stops and throws himself into a fighting attitude. On seeing the turnkey he becomes respectful, giving him a little bow.

BORROO: God save your honor.

TURNKEY (*unlocking the little gate*): You get on with your work.

BORROO: Yes, your honor.

Borroo takes up the bucket and brush again, but the moment the turnkey is gone he puts them down.

BORROO: I'm damned if I will. (*Glowers after turnkey.*) My God, I hate them crawling sniveling sleeky snuffly bitch's bastards.

FENNESSY: Ladies present, Mr. Borroo.

BESSIE: Declare to Gawd, he's crying.

BORROO: I'm not crying. It's only water in me eyes. If you got a belt on the head with a great big goddam key, wouldn't *you* get water in your eyes? (*Angry and frustrated, he looks around to see whom he can vent his spleen on. He decides to bait Fennessy.*) Well, Fennessy?

FENNESSY (*mildly*): Yes, Mr. Borroo?

BORROO: Whose are ye making today?

FENNESSY: Me own, Mr. Borroo.

BORROO: You're the right eejit to be killing yourself making your own. Let them provide one for you. They can't leave you above ground.

285

FENNESSY: They're paying me a shilling for it, and that'll come in handy for me wife.

BORROO: Yer widda.

FENNESSY: Widda — ? That's true. God help me, I haven't much to leave the poor girl except the memory of me shortcomings and four children.

Peter Shanks, Doyle, Mahon, and Kehoe come through the gateway, guarded by a posse of turnkeys. Only two turnkeys come in with them. Borroo picks up his bucket and brush and stands respectfully to one side. The two turnkeys unlock the prisoner's chains and take the chains away as they go off to the left. When Borroo is sure that the turnkeys are out of earshot, he lays down his bucket and brush, and faces the prisoners, rubbing his hands.

BORROO: A hundred thousand welcomes to ye.

SHANKS (*with a slight bow*): Thank you. (*Bows to the women.*) Good afternoon, ladies. (*The women rise and give him a little curtsey. He turns to Fennessy.*) Good afternoon, friend.

BESSIE (*whispering*): Isn't he the gorgeous young gentleman?

FENNESSY: Me name's Jack Fennessy, sir, and I'm to be hanged a Monday on the stroke o' noon.

SHANKS: I grieve to hear it. I am (*momentous*) Peter Shanks.

FENNESSY: And what are you in for, sir?

SHANKS (*put out*): Don't you know? (*Recovering his dignity.*) Ah but of course. In prison you are held incommunicado. Nevertheless I thought that even in this place the echoes of my name would have sounded. We shall soon lay down our lives for our country.

VIOLA (*disgusted*): Rebels, me dear. It's a disgrace putting the likes of them in with respectable women.

Doyle has been cowering at the sight of the coffin.

DOYLE (*suddenly shrieking*): What's that thing in here for?

FENNESSY: It's only mine, sir.

DOYLE: My God — tormenting us like this.

SHANKS (*through his teeth*): Try to be a man, Captain Doyle.

DOYLE: It's all very well for you to talk, but I'm innocent.

SHANKS (*contemptuous*): Well, go and turn informer and save your neck.

DOYLE (*babbling*): What could I tell them? You never trusted me. You never told me a thing.

SHANKS: I was wiser than I knew.

FENNESSY: If the sight of me handiwork is upsetting the young gentleman, perhaps you'd consider taking him down to the yard. I can't go meself. I've been ordered to stay up this end.

SHANKS: Come along, Captain Doyle, we shall inspect the premises. Your pardon, ladies.

THE WOMEN: Not at all, sir. You're welcome. Don't mention it.

Shanks and his companions go out, left.

BORROO (*spitting*): Wouldn't it make ye throw up? If the rebellion had been a success them fellows would have been driving round in carriages with a string of lackeys tailing out behind them and decent people like me paying for it all.

VIOLA: There wasn't much spunk in the little fellow to be sure. But the youth of today is gone soft with fat living and easy money.

BESSIE (*dreamily*): And to think that gorgeous young gentleman is going to be hung.

A turnkey comes in briskly from the left. Borroo immediately bends down to pick up his bucket. The turnkey kicks him, nearly sending his head into the bucket. The women scream with laughter.

TURNKEY: Get on with your work, d'ye hear? (*He unlocks the gate, right.*) Well, what are ye waiting for?

BORROO: I was just waiting, yer honor, to see if the women were finished going to the jakes till I clean it out. Does any of youse ladies want to see a man about a dog?

The women close their eyes and turn away haughtily. The turnkey makes a threatening move toward Borroo.

TURNKEY: Move, d'ye hear me?

Borroo goes quickly into the shed with his bucket and brush, and closes the door. The turnkey stands watching the door quietly. After a moment Borroo thrusts out his head.

BORROO: Is that goddam bitch's bastard —

Borroo sees the turnkey and shoots in again, but the turnkey goes into the shed after him. A sound of blows and howls. The turnkey comes out, slamming the door. As he reaches the gate Jack Galvin, the hangman, comes in.

TURNKEY: Good day to you, Mr. Galvin.

Galvin is elderly, somewhat stooped, and as lean as a greyhound. His hands and feet seem to be disproportionately big and the sleeves of his ill-fitting coat are so short that about four inches of wrist are visible. He has small, narrow-set eyes, under bushy grey brows. He will not look people straight in the face, but restlessly and watchfully surveys them through the corner of his eyes. He wears a pair of rusty black gloves with the fingers out of them, which he removes with exaggerated elegance while talking.

GALVIN (*meaning*): Have they arrived yet, Mr. Smith?

TURNKEY (*nodding toward the left*): Down at the other end. Four of them.

GALVIN (*disappointed*): Only four?

TURNKEY: God almighty, if the whole country were given over to you to be hung, you still wouldn't be satisfied.

GALVIN (*without humor*): I'd need them all to make a decent living.

TURNKEY: Maybe you'd like me to go and start up another rebellion to provide you with customers.

GALVIN: If I didn't take the rough and tough ones off your hands, Mr. Smith, life would be hard for you and your brethren. (*Turns round and rubs his hands together slowly.*) Good day to ye, Mr. Fennessy. Good day to ye, ladies.

The women return his greeting with cheerful cordiality and more than a little respect. Galvin saunters slowly toward the left, and peers out at the condemned men. He scratches his ear thoughtfully.

ROSALIND (*sympathetic*): Ye have your hands full these days, Mr. Galvin, with all them rebels.

GALVIN (*with a sigh*): Hard work, ma'am. But amn't I keeping the country well pacificated and fit for ladies and genkilmen to live in? Though it's a pity the same ladies and genkilmen don't reckonize that the laborer is worthy of his hire.

Borroo, brush in hand, opens the door of the shed. As Galvin is behind the door he doesn't see him for a moment.

BORROO: Gawd, the stink in there'd choke ye. (*He draws in huge gulps of air. Then his eye falls on Galvin and he hurriedly goes back into the shed.*)

GALVIN (*scratching his chin*): I only hope I never have to attend to that young man. (*Shaking his head.*) He'd make a very unbecoming end. (*With a glance over his shoulder in the direction of the condemned men.*) Not like those genkilmen down there.

ROSALIND: That little downy fellow will give ye trouble, Mr. Galvin, with his howling and struggling.

GALVIN: Devil a bit. It's the likes of him are always the easy jobs. They're fruz stiff with the fright. But it'll be a pleasure to do that same young man. Don't ask me why because I daren't tell you. It's not fit for the ears of ladies to hear.

BESSIE (*knowing he intends to tell them*): If it's not fit for ladies' ears we better not hear it.

GALVIN: Too shockin' and scandalous it is.

The women say tsk tsk tsk and look meaningly at one another.

GALVIN: God knows I'm only too well tutored in the ways of the wicked. But when the major who arrested them told me, it rose me hair.

VIOLA (*holding her ears*): Don't tell us, Mr. Galvin — for Jasus sake don't tell us.

GALVIN: The four of them were in this room all be themselves.

The women shriek with horror.

GALVIN: And there was the little downy fella — oh don't ask me to say it.

BESSIE: Gawd love you, Mr. Galvin, having to hear these things. But I suppose it's yer jooty.

GALVIN: Me jooty it is. Oftentimes I have to soil me ears, I have to grovel in dirt, but it's me jooty. (*Lowering his voice.*) The little fella was bending forward over a table and don't ask me where his pantaloons was!

Women shriek and cover their faces.

GALVIN: I ax yer pardon for mentioning pantaloons in the presence of ladies —

ROSALIND: Spare us, Mr. Galvin, spare us.

GALVIN: Those articles — garments I might call them (*more shrieks*) — were hanging down around his ankles. There he was bending down as un- adorned as the day he was born. (*Shrieks.*) Not as much as a square inch of wool or cotton to cover that which should be hidden from the eyes of man and beast —

BESSIE: Don't tell us any more, Mr. Galvin, not another word out of ye.

GALVIN: Sez I to the major, major, sez I, it may be that he was short took. It may be that he had taken opening medicine.

BESSIE: 'Tis only a kind Christian jintleman'd think the like of that.

ROSALIND: The good Gawd'll reward ye for yer charitable mind, Mr. Galvin.

GALVIN: Short took?!!! sez the major. Opening medicine?!! sez the major. (*Earnest.*) Wasn't it only me jooty, ladies, to think the good thing? Ah no, sez the major. No, sez he. A pure mind like yours, Mr. Galvin, sir, would naturally think the good thing. (*Momentous.*) But this is just the Bishop of Clogher all over again.

The women shriek and squeal.

VIOLA: Say another word, Mr. Galvin, and I'll fall fainting to the ground.

GALVIN: The Bishop of Clogher all over again! Ladies — when those words crept in through the holes of me ears, me hair riz. (*Holds up extended fingers.*) Like that, ladies. Stiff as a —

ROSALIND: Don't tell us: we know only too well.

GALVIN: Mr. Galvin sir, sez the major, you'll be called upon to perform your painful jooty on these villains. And I'll tell you this, ladies, as long as the good God leaves me the strength of me arm I'll do me bit to stop them turning poor oul' Dublin into a Sodom and a Gomorrah.

Feeling he has reached his apotheosis, Galvin strolls over to Fennessy, whom he claps on the shoulder in a comradely manner.

GALVIN: A very mellingcholy occupation for you, Mr. Fennessy.

FENNESSY: Yessir.

GALVIN: If the ladies and genkilmen was only left to me and me alone, Mr. Fennessy, I'd be on the pig's back. But them that should be mine is being handed over to the millingtary.

BESSIE: Oh the millingtary's a disgrace, Mr. Galvin, a proper disgrace.

GALVIN: Not trained for the job, ma'am. Butchers. Many's the day since the rebellion started, I've had to stand and look at the millingtary, and shout

"Not that way, ye clown — will ye put the knot under the genkilman's ear, not his Adam's apple."

THE WOMEN: Disgraceful. Croolty, that's what it is. They should leave the job to the proper tradesman.

GALVIN: What's more, the millingtary only annoys the people. The people hates bad workmanship. And d'ye know? The govermint won't even pay me a livin' wage. D'ye know what me rate works out at? A penny an hour. How's that for a Christian country, Mr. Fennessy? (*Spits in disgust.*) And if you open yer mouth you're told the millingtary will do it for nothing. (*Confidential.*) What's this you're being done for, Mr. Fennessy? A little touch of forgery, eh?

FENNESSY (*shocked*): Oh no, sir, nothing like that. (*Shamefaced.*) To tell the truth, sir, I done away with a sheep on Lord Delville's estate.

GALVIN (*almost a screech*): A sheep!!!

FENNESSY (*humbly*): I couldn't stand seeing me poor childer go hungry, sir.

GALVIN (*with throbbing emotion*): Ah no, Mr. Fennessy, you still oughtn't to have done it. I have little ones of me own, but I'd sooner see them dropping down at me feet from the hunger before I'd steal another man's property.

FENNESSY: It's a hard and bitter world for the poor, sir.

GALVIN (*with a sigh*): Won't ye be as well off out of it?

FENNESSY (*almost unconsciously fingering his neck*): Does it hurt much, sir?

GALVIN (*airily*): It needn't.

Fennessy stares at him uncomprehending. Bessie goes over and whispers in his ear.

FENNESSY (*starting*): Oh I'm sorry, sir. I didn't understand. (*Reluctantly takes coin from his pocket and gives it to Galvin, who registers disgust.*) It's all I've left, sir.

GALVIN: Outa the sheep? (*Fennessy stands mutely miserable.*) Well, I won't do much damage to me liver drinking that.

FENNESSY (*piteous*): Sure ye wouldn't be after hurting me, sir?

GALVIN (*brusque*): If the millingtary was doin' ye it'd be pure hell. But with a proper tradesman looking after ye, you've nothing at all to worry about.

BESSIE: Give him an aisy drop, Mr. Galvin, and God'll reward ye.

GALVIN (*putting his arm around her*): As aisy and delicate as I'd give yerself me love. (*Pinches her.*)

A turnkey unlocks the gate and comes in dragging Mary Neale. He flings her amongst the women and goes over to other turnkey.

SECOND TURNKEY: See everything's all right down in the yard. Copperfaced Jack's on his way.

Some excitement among the women as they hear the name.

GALVIN: What's the oul' bastard coming for now? We're not doing any flogging today, are we?

FIRST TURNKEY: Devil a one.

GALVIN: Though I thought he was going off the flogging a bit, this while back. Just like her excellency's going off the hangings.

SECOND TURNKEY: Women never stick anything for long.

GALVIN: Her excellency always slips me a guinea for meself. Once she gave me two guineas . . . I was doing a great big bull of a young fellow. "Make it slow," she said. "Make it slow."

Borroo comes out of the shed.

BORROO: Gawd, I'm choking for a breath of air. The stink in there'd kill ye.

FIRST TURNKEY: Have you finished the whitewashing?

BORROO: Yes, your honor.

Borroo bows the turnkey into the shed, remaining outside himself, mouthing curses and cocking snoots. He seems to have forgotten about the second turnkey behind him, who raps him smartly on the head with a big key. The women again scream with laughter. The first turnkey comes out of the shed.

SECOND TURNKEY: Go on — do it to his face now.

FIRST TURNKEY: Oho — was he up to his little tricks again?

The turnkey grips Borroo's ear, twisting it with venomous cruelty, so that Borroo falls to his knees with a howl of anguish. The second turnkey kicks him in the groin. Borroo falls to the ground, writhing and gasping in agony. Mary covers her eyes and turns away. The other women huddle together in fear. Fennessy's eyes narrow and his grip on the chisel in his hand tightens ominously. The first turnkey, with a careless kick at the prostrate figure, goes out again with his companion. When they have gone, Fennessy and the women crowd sympathetically round Brian Borroo. Peter Shanks and his companions come back from the left.

SHANKS: What's wrong?

BESSIE: They're after beating him up something cruel.

With a cry of rage Shanks rushes to the gate, shakes the bars violently, and yells after the turnkeys.

SHANKS: You brutes, you brutes! You damned cowardly brutes! Hellhounds! By God, if we were free men you wouldn't do that.

Meanwhile Borroo has been helped up and has been placed sitting on one of the benches, where he huddles, moaning.

BORROO: Oh let me be, let me be. Don't move me — just let me be.

SHANKS (*shouting*): Get a physician! Where is the prison doctor? Send for the apothecary.

FIRST TURNKEY: Hold your tongue.

During the commotion Dr. Jacob Palmer has appeared at the gate. He is one of the very few men in a cleanshaven age who have let their beard grow; but he has close-shaved cheeks, and his iron grey goatee and moustaches are trimmed after the style of Charles I. The turnkey opens the gate and stands at a respectful distance from the doctor who, resting elegantly on his staff, bends a dignified gaze upon the group before him.

SHANKS: I know you — you're the viceroy's physician.

GALVIN (*going to Palmer*): Good day to yer honor.

SHANKS (*pointing to Borroo*): Attend that man.

PALMER: I am not the prison doctor.

SHANKS (*fiercely*): There's a man in agony. He has been kicked by a damned cowardly turnkey. Are you going to —

PALMER: I said I am not the prison doctor.

SECOND TURNKEY: Speak when you're spoken to, prisoner.

SHANKS: I shall see the governor about this. (*He marches out with his companions.*)

PALMER (*to Galvin*): I shall require two bodies this week. (*Takes pinch of snuff.*)

GALVIN: Your honor can have your pick of any of the four men that have just gone away.

PALMER: One must be female.

GALVIN: There aren't any females this week, yer honor. There'll be a couple next week, please Gawd.

PALMER (*looking after Shanks*): That impudent young fellow who spoke to me . . . he can be one.

GALVIN: Wouldn't you like that big bull of a fellow that was with him?

PALMER: Too fat. Fat makes dissection unnecessarily laborious.

GALVIN: Indeed it must, yer honor. I find that meself when I'm drawing and quartering a man. The carpenter won't be ready till Monday afternoon, but you could have the other fellow tomorrow morning. (*Snapping his fingers.*) Gawd blast it, I nearly forgot. The young fellow's a treason case. He'll have to be drawn and quartered. But I tell you what I'll do. I'll just go through the motions. I won't damage the carcass.

PALMER: I trust not. The last two subjects were very badly damaged.

GALVIN (*shaking his head mournfully*): They must have come from the millingtary, yer honor.

An excited turnkey runs to the gate.

THIRD TURNKEY: They're here. (*Rushes away to spread the news.*)

The other turnkeys look at each other. The second turnkey nods significantly towards Brian Borroo, who is surrounded by the women. The turnkeys push their way to him and take him gently by the arms.

FIRST TURNKEY: Come along with us, lad.

SECOND TURNKEY: Poor fella, are ye after hurting yerself?

FIRST TURNKEY: Aisy does it, aisy does it.

They have got the groaning Borroo to his feet when Shanks and his companions march back.

SHANKS: Where is the governor? I demand to see the governor.

SECOND TURNKEY: Hould yer tongue and get to hell out of our way.

SHANKS (*pointing to Palmer*): I shall denounce you for refusing to attend an injured man.

FIRST TURNKEY: We're taking him away to be attended.

SHANKS: I shall denounce you for your brutality.

SECOND TURNKEY: We'll look after you in a minute, me man. Get out of the way.

The lord chief justice appears at the gate with the governor. Milligan is in attendance. Silence. The gate is unlocked and the lord chief justice enters. The women curtsey. Palmer and Galvin and the turnkeys bow deeply. Kehoe, Doyle, and Mahon incline their heads in some show of respect. Only Shanks remains erect.

JUSTICE: What are *you* doing here, Palmer?

PALMER (*bowing again*): I am performing a small work of mercy, my lord. Every now and then I visit the prisons to tend the sick.

SHANKS: Liar and hypocrite.

The second turnkey rushes at Shanks.

JUSTICE (*shouting*): Do not touch him.

The second turnkey stops dead, falls back sheepishly.

SHANKS (*pointing to Borroo*): That man has been savaged by these brutes. (*Pointing to Palmer.*) He refused to attend him.

GOVERNOR: Be silent, prisoner. Do not presume to address his lordship.

JUSTICE: Be silent yourself, governor. (*To Borroo.*) Is this true? Were you assaulted?

GOVERNOR: Scandalous accusations, my lord. My officers are most kindly and humane men. I have distinctly laid down regulations — not indeed that they are really necessary —

JUSTICE (*to Borroo*): Is it true? What do you allege against the turnkeys?

BORROO (*gasping out the words*): Very good men, yer honor — noble, kind, and generous men — couldn't ask for better.

SHANKS: Tell the truth, you fool. Tell him you've been kicked.

JUSTICE: Let the witness speak for himself. Has a turnkey kicked you?

BORROO: The turnkeys is all very good men, yer honor. I wouldn't complain about them for the world.

JUSTICE: Answer my question — did a turnkey kick you?

BORROO: Yes, yer honor — but I'm not complaining.

JUSTICE: Examine him, Palmer. You, turnkey, what have you to say for yourself?

FIRST TURNKEY: If yer honor was to believe everything them scoundrels say, it'd be a poor lookout for us.

JUSTICE: Did you or did you not kick the prisoner?

FIRST TURNKEY: Yer honor, I —

JUSTICE: Answer me, yes or no.

FIRST TURNKEY: I may have brushed me ankle off his leg and I passing him, yer honor. The lazy devil was lying snoring in the sun instead of doing his work. I didn't notice him in me way.

JUSTICE: Well, Palmer?

PALMER: The prisoner would appear to have received a kick, my lord. A vicious one.

JUSTICE: You hear that, governor? The prisoner has been wantonly and viciously assaulted.

GOVERNOR: I cannot bring myself to believe it, my lord.

JUSTICE: I can. (*Governor shrugs.*) Do not shake your head at me, Mister Governor, or by God I'll give you good reason to shake it. (*Indicating first and second turnkeys.*) Let those two men be given fifty lashes. Are you in good form for work today, Mr. Galvin?

GALVIN (*bowing*): I'll do me best, your honor.

GOVERNOR: My lord, I must protest. I cannot permit my officers —

JUSTICE: I give you liberty to share as many of their lashes as you desire.

GALVIN (*sidling up to lord chief justice*): Does your honor wish to —

JUSTICE: No, I do not wish to attend their punishment. Now Mr. Governor, have the yard cleared of everyone except the prisoner Peter Shanks. And fetch a chair for me.

The governor passes the instruction to third turnkey. The lord chief justice, in glancing around at the prisoners, notices Mary Neale. He starts.

JUSTICE: What is that young woman doing here?

GOVERNOR: Which one, my lord? (*Mary identifies herself by shrinking back.*) Answer his lordship. What's your name?

MARY: Mary Neale.

JUSTICE: I discharged you this morning. Why are you here?

MARY: They said I stole the money you sent me. I told them to go and ask you.

GOVERNOR: I remember now, my lord. She is charged with receiving five guineas which were obviously stolen.

JUSTICE: The money was not stolen. Let her be released forthwith.

GOVERNOR: I shall need an official warrant —

JUSTICE (*flaring up*): My word is your warrant.

GOVERNOR: If your lordship will condescend to give me a scrap of paper for the attorney-general.

JUSTICE: To hell with the attorney-general. Now clear the place.

GOVERNOR: For safety's sake I'd better have the prisoner Shanks chained.

JUSTICE: I did not order the prisoner Shanks to be chained.

GOVERNOR: Your lordship is making it extremely difficult for me to preserve discipline.

JUSTICE: We have seen the kind of discipline you preserve.

GOVERNOR (*stung*): I am not accustomed to being addressed in such a tone before my own staff, my lord. (*The lord chief justice glowers.*) I apologize, my lord. (*To the turnkeys.*) Clear the place.

The turnkeys clear the prisoners away to the left. Galvin and Palmer take a conspicuous part in helping Borroo off. The third turnkey has returned with a chair for the lord chief justice.

JUSTICE (*to governor*): What are you waiting for?

GOVERNOR: My lord, it is customary for the governor to be present at all interviews with condemned persons.

JUSTICE: My patience is not unlimited.

After some hesitation, the governor bows stiffly and goes out.

JUSTICE (*sitting*): Peter Shanks —

SHANKS: Once and for all, Copperfaced Jack, it is no use.

JUSTICE: On reflection I felt that it would be pointless to order a new trial.

SHANKS: I do not want a new trial. I will not have life on your terms, Copperfaced Jack.

JUSTICE: Do you think it matters a farthing to me whether you live or die?

SHANKS: Why should it? You are not God, no matter what you may think. Oh I know all about you. I made my mother tell me.

JUSTICE: Tell you — everything?

SHANKS: She did not dare conceal anything from me.

JUSTICE: Refresh my memory.

SHANKS: You were born in a pigsty.

JUSTICE: A stable, Peter. There is a precedent.

SHANKS: Your father begged the fat from my grandfather's kitchenmaid to make candles.

JUSTICE: And married the kitchenmaid.

SHANKS: My mother didn't tell me that.

JUSTICE: The poor dear must have had her reasons for omitting that one.

SHANKS: So you can sit there in your satin and your velvet, and you do not impress me in the least.

The lord chief justice edges his chair into a shaft of sunlight, but without rising.

JUSTICE: You will of course forgive me for remaining seated while the president of the new republic has to stand. (*Stretching his legs.*) But I am only a poor old man, Peter, only a poor old man. Why don't you move out into the sun, my boy? It won't shine much longer on either of us.

SHANKS: I prefer to stand where I am.

JUSTICE: In the shade? Peter, I was nearly forty years of age before I plucked up enough courage to take my rightful place in the sun. I have always been too humble. Do you know that I once tried to sell my soul to the Devil?

SHANKS: Does it matter? He'll soon have it. For a little while honest men will spit upon your grave and then you'll be forgotten.

JUSTICE: And you won't be?

SHANKS: I shall live in the hearts of my countrymen.

JUSTICE: Why?

SHANKS: Because I gave my life for them.

JUSTICE: Did they ask you for it?

SHANKS: No man has the right to ask for another's life. But when that life is sacrificed for him, let him be grateful.

JUSTICE: And if he isn't grateful?

SHANKS: There is always the ungrateful wretch. But honest men remember to pay their debts.

JUSTICE: Provided they are aware of their debts. They may not think they owe you anything. (*Shanks is silent.*) Peter, you and I have many things in common.

SHANKS: God forbid.

JUSTICE: We share a craving for distinction. Let me tell you how I tried to sell my soul to the Devil.

SHANKS: It was characteristic of you to try to sell what you haven't got.

JUSTICE (*laughing*): And to someone who didn't exist. (*Enjoys the joke.*) Ah Peter, Peter, what I would sell my soul for today would be to be remembered tomorrow. These last few months I have tasted death so many times I have lost my dread of it. But I cannot lose my dread of being forgotten.

SHANKS: As the man who sentenced me to die you shall have a footnote in history.

JUSTICE: I'd prefer you to be the footnote in my history. But we could earn our page apiece, my boy. Let me persuade you to recant.

SHANKS: To recant would be to dishonor my country's cause for fifty years.

JUSTICE: Precisely.

SHANKS: Copperfaced Jack, I no longer hate you. I pity you. You never give up the fight, do you?

JUSTICE: While there's life there's hope.

SHANKS: You mean, while there's life for me there's hope for you.

JUSTICE: Death is *your* only hope, Peter. Die at the right time and a page of glory in the history books will be yours. Live to a ripe old age and you will be found out for what you are, and history will dismiss you in a contemptuous paragraph.

SHANKS: We shall see.

JUSTICE: We shan't, that's the pity of it. Listen, Peter. The only point in being a martyr is to be seen to be a martyr. Nine years ago in Paris there were hundreds of martyrs for the revolution, but now they're forgotten because there were too many of them. When everyone's a martyr no one's a martyr. The only martyrs we remember are those who make themselves memorable. Like that French fool who got himself stabbed in a bath by a pretty young girl — he is among the immortals.

SHANKS: There is no comparison between —

JUSTICE (*forceful*): There *is*, Peter, there is. History is shortsighted. You have to dance in front of her and wave your arms and shout to draw her attention. There are too many rebels being hanged just now. You won't be noticed in the crowd.

SHANKS: You are wrong.

JUSTICE: You must go on living for another couple of years, Peter, until there is peace. Then disturb it. You need only start a rebellion in a back street with a dozen drunken rascals. Do something ridiculous. March on a fortress at the head of your drunken troops and for generations your folly will be remembered — but not as folly. For you will have taken care to escape to the mountains. You will have left your drunken dozen to be flogged into sobriety, leaving only yourself to be caught. They will put a price on your head. You will let yourself be captured. You will have carefully rehearsed your speech from the dock and left several copies for posterity. Then you will have the gallows all to yourself. You will be the dream of all actors: the only figure on the stage, and the fool will become the hero.

SHANKS: Scoffer.

JUSTICE: The people will crowd to see you hang. They will dip their handkerchiefs in your martyr's blood, though not one will lift a finger to save you. Future rebels will canonize you and invoke your name, for the only glorious leaders are the leaders who died before they had the chance to lead. The people shall hang a flattering portrait of you on their walls that shall not bear the least resemblance to you, and twenty generations shall call you blessed. Then one day a rebellion will have an accidental success and you'll have a fine statue. And oh — I nearly forgot. Have a lady in the case. Don't marry her, because there is no romance in marriage. Leave her, a lonely figure at the foot of your cross, to weep not for Jerusalem but for you, and the sentimental bards will make us weep for you both.

SHANKS: You poor unhappy envious man. Not even you could reduce nobility to absurdity.

JUSTICE (*ironic*): Help me, Peter. A martyr's crown for you. A brief glory for me.

SHANKS: It's the lack of love has made you what you are.

JUSTICE: Then long live the lack of love.

SHANKS: I understand this because I know what love is.

JUSTICE: A mother's love? Now *there's* a blessing, my boy.

SHANKS: You can only sneer, God help you.

JUSTICE: And a wife's love — but only the married know what a blessing *that* is.

SHANKS: If only you knew how cruel Providence has been to you.

JUSTICE (*smiling*): I know.

SHANKS: You don't. You couldn't unless like me you had loved and had been beloved.

JUSTICE: So you had a girl in your drama after all. I underestimated you.

SHANKS: It is you I have to thank for saving her life.

JUSTICE: I have saved no ladies' lives recently that I can recall.

SHANKS: Mistress Mary Neale.

JUSTICE: Neale . . . Neale . . .

SHANKS: And a few moments ago you freed her after they had flung her in here again on a trumped up charge. (*Earnestly.*) I suppose there's a touch of good in you, Lord Clonmell. If so, I honor you for it.

JUSTICE (*slowly*): Are you mad enough to tell me a thing like this?

SHANKS: I can respect a good deed even in a foe.

JUSTICE (*grinning*): Oh you fool, you young fool. (*Shouting.*) Governor! Governor! (*To Shanks.*) Fool fool fool fool. (*Rises and walks about, rubbing his hands.*)

The governor runs in with drawn sword.

JUSTICE: That female prisoner whom I ordered you to discharge —

GOVERNOR (*confused*): What prisoner, my lord? (*Looking toward Shanks.*) I thought you were calling for help.

JUSTICE: Damn your cheek. Help against *him*?!! Where is that female prisoner? Is she discharged?

GOVERNOR: You didn't give me much time to do it, my lord. You ordered me to clear the yard and —

JUSTICE: Bring her here immediately.

The governor goes off angrily.

JUSTICE: Oh Peter Shanks Peter Shanks, I could have torn you with red-hot pincers and I wouldn't have got a word out of you. Then in your ridiculous vanity you put this weapon into my hands.

SHANKS (*moaning*): I might have known. I might have known.

JUSTICE: Do you love her?

SHANKS (*feebly defiant*): I do not know the girl. I was making a fool of you to amuse myself.

JUSTICE: Do you love her, Mr. President of the new republic?

SHANKS: I never set eyes on her until a few minutes ago.

JUSTICE: Was she to sit at your side in the earthly paradise you had planned for us all?

SHANKS: It was only a trick. I do not know her.

JUSTICE: Thrice have you denied her. Peter, you are well named.

The turnkey hauls Mary Neale in and slings her before the lord chief justice. He motions the turnkey to go away.

JUSTICE (*after sitting again and surveying them silently*): My child, the prisoner Peter Shanks has told me how things stand between you.

SHANKS (*violent*): I do not know her.

Mary Neale looks quickly at him, then lowers her eyes. At this moment the whipping of the turnkeys begins in the upper yard. The victim's shrieks are heard after each stroke.

JUSTICE (*after sitting in silence for a few moments*): Governor! Governor! *The governor comes in with deliberate slowness.*

JUSTICE: Tell them to stop the flogging till I'm gone. (*The governor hesitates.*) Look lively, man. (*The governor bows and turns to go.*) Send the hangman in to me.

The governor goes. Mary Neale fingers her dress nervously. The whipping stops. Galvin hurries in. He has taken off his coat and has rolled up his right shirtsleeve. He carries his cat-o'-nine-tails.

GALVIN (*bowing almost to the ground*): Yer honor — ?

JUSTICE: The female prisoner —

GALVIN: Certainly, yer honor. (*Goes eagerly toward her.*)

JUSTICE (*bellowing*): Stand back. (*Galvin, surprised and puzzled, does so. The lord chief justice rises slowly, goes to Mary, takes her arm, and gently pushes her against Peter Shanks. He then stands back and surveys them.*) A fool and his love. Peter, an intelligent man always comes to terms with his conscience. A little affectionate word to a conscience and it forgives you everything. Except yours. Your conscience is sickly and stubborn. The flesh is willing but the spirit is weak.

MARY (*breaking*): Tell him, Peter. Tell him what he wants to know and he'll let you go.

JUSTICE: Don't do that to him, child — not at the eleventh hour. Give him strength. It is at the eleventh hour that strength is needed most.

MARY (*hysterical*): Tell him, Peter, tell him. (*Kneels to lord chief justice.*) If I tell you will you let him go?

JUSTICE: Woman, do not filch away that poor man's crown of martyrdom.

MARY: It's William O'Sullivan is at the head of it all —

299

JUSTICE: Silence. I do not wish to hear anything. Stand up. (*She does so. He puts his arm around her.*) You would not wish the father of your children to be a coward. (*Puts his free hand on Shanks's shoulder.*) They all marry afterwards, Peter — and usually one of the hated oppressors if they're as pretty as she is. I tell you what. You must let me call my chaplain to marry the pair of ye.

SHANKS (*almost involuntarily*): No.

Mary shrinks. She half understands his refusal but is hurt by his vehemence.

JUSTICE (*who has noted her reaction*): Not even that little sacrifice, Peter. Well! And it's not that your death would save the others. Soon they will all stand where you stand.

SHANKS: You've got to catch them first. They walk in and out of the castle and his excellency smiles upon them, not knowing who they are.

JUSTICE: Oh there's many a man smiles upon his executioner without knowing it. But not in this case.

SHANKS: You will see.

JUSTICE (*takes slip of paper from pocket*): William O'Sullivan, innkeeper, Drumcondra Lane. Francis Browner, coachman, Church Street. James Rafter, bootmaker, Aungier Street . . . and so on and so forth.

SHANKS: Not that trap either. I neither confirm nor deny.

JUSTICE: You could tell me nothing I do not already know.

SHANKS: But I shall not recant.

The lord chief justice sits.

JUSTICE: Galvin.

Galvin cringes toward him.

JUSTICE: I have reason to believe that the female prisoner has hidden a knife under her petticoat. Search her.

Galvin pounces on her. She fights him off like a wildcat. He grips her waist, throws her down, and flings himself on her. She cries for help, for mercy. Shanks turns away and is compelled to cover his ears. Some of the prisoners creep back to watch, but do no more than mutter rebelliously to each other. The lord chief justice walks over to the struggling pair and kicks Galvin away. Mary runs to a corner where she huddles, a sobbing, quivering bundle of clothes.

GALVIN: I'm sure there's a knife there under her petticoat, yer honor. Will I try again?

JUSTICE: Get away. (*Galvin moves away but keeps staring at Mary.*) One word from you, Peter Shanks, would have stopped all that. Was she not worth it? (*Goes to Mary and puts his arm around her.*) In his place, my child, I would have died to save you. (*She accepts the protection of his arms and rests her head on his shoulder.*) Send the governor to me.

The governor steps forward from behind the little knot of prisoners.

GOVERNOR (*icy*): My lord — ?

JUSTICE: Let this female prisoner be discharged forthwith as I have ordered.

GOVERNOR (*with undisguised triumph*): My lord, Mr. Attorney-General desires to see you. I gather he has received certain commands from his excellency.

Mary Neale whispers in the lord chief justice's ear.

JUSTICE: No, my child. It would be better if you did not stay with me. (*He disengages himself from her and goes to his chair.*) She is free to go.

GOVERNOR: Mr. Attorney-General —

JUSTICE: Can go to the devil. I am finished with the prisoner Shanks.

SHANKS: I have a favor to ask.

JUSTICE: Have you, by God?

SHANKS: Will you be good enough to have me placed in a cell to myself?

JUSTICE: You are free to remain here if you wish. I am a humane man. Only the worst of the worst are put into solitary cells.

SHANKS: Am I not the worst of the worst?

JUSTICE: You cannot claim even that distinction.

SHANKS: It is my last request to you — my lord.

JUSTICE (*looking up sharply at the "my lord"*): Very well, Mr. President, a solitary cell if you wish it. (*To the governor.*) Let his mother have free access to him at all times. (*To Shanks.*) Though we shan't force maternal consolation on you if you'd prefer not to have it. Take him away.

The governor signs to the third turnkey, who takes Shanks by the arm. The attorney-general enters rather melodramatically.

WOLFE: Where is the prisoner Shanks going, m'lud?

JUSTICE (*ignoring Wolfe*): Take him away.

The governor whispers reassuringly to Wolfe, who nods. As he is brought to the small gate, Peter Shanks turns around.

SHANKS (*choking with emotion*): Mary . . . remember.

MARY (*sullen*): I shall never forget what you made me suffer. And in front of all those people too.

The turnkey has unlocked the gate. He takes Shanks out. The gate is locked again. Wolfe saunters insolently to lord chief justice.

WOLFE: As I happen to know of the unusual relationship between your lordship and the mother of a certain condemned felon, I took the precaution of procuring from his excellency a warrant for the immediate execution of the traitors you sentenced this morning.

JUSTICE: You are too clever by half, Arthur.

WOLFE (*handing the warrant to the governor with a flourish*): There's your warrant, Mr. Governor. I shall witness the executions myself.

JUSTICE: You shall have to wait a long time, Arthur.

WOLFE: No longer than it takes to procure four ropes, m'lud.

JUSTICE: The prisoners shall not be put to execution until the high sheriff of this city produces a warrant signed by me.

GOVERNOR (*insolently holding up warrant*): And this, my lord?

JUSTICE: Wipe your arse with it.

The prisoners titter but are silenced by a glare from the governor and Wolfe.

WOLFE: His excellency's orders must be obeyed.

JUSTICE (*holding out his hand for the warrant; the governor looks uneasily at Wolfe*): Give it to me. (*The governor hands it over. The lord chief justice glances carelessly at it and tears it up.*)

WOLFE: This is outrageous. Mr. Governor, you may proceed to execution. My personal order shall be your warrant.

JUSTICE: I have had occasion to observe to you before, Mr. Attorney-General, that my patience is not unlimited.

WOLFE: For what you have done you can be impeached ten times over.

JUSTICE (*springing up*): Arrest him.

WOLFE: The man who lays a finger on me will be charged with treason.

JUSTICE: I said arrest him. By God I'll teach you who and what I am. Have I to repeat my orders? Get the yeomanry. The military. Have the jail surrounded. This is contempt. This is — (*His voice falters: he begins to choke.*)

Palmer rushes forward and grabs the lord chief justice before he falls. Turnkeys and prisoners crowd around him, and he is helped to his chair. Only Wolfe and the governor remain unmoved.

GOVERNOR (*to Wolfe*): The problem seems to be solving itself.

JUSTICE (*slowly and thickly*): Leave this place, Mr. Attorney-General. I have decided that the prisoners shall have a new trial.

WOLFE: Not in this world, m'lud. Governor, proceed to execution immediately.

JUSTICE: Do not dare.

WOLFE: You have seen his excellency's orders.

The third turnkey appears at the gate, very excited.

THIRD TURNKEY: Yer honor, the prisoner Peter Shanks has done himself an injury.

General excitement. The third turnkey unlocks the gate and rushes in.

THIRD TURNKEY: Cut his throat, yer honor.

Shocked murmurs. Everyone instinctively looks toward the lord chief justice.

JUSTICE: What a very clever thing for that foolish young man to do.

WOLFE: Is he dead?

THIRD TURNKEY: No, yer honor — but nearly.

Mary bursts out crying.

JUSTICE: He took my advice after all. (*Shakes his head.*) But cutting his throat — no. Stabbing himself through the heart would read better on that page of history.

WOLFE: He can't be let escape like this. He must be hanged immediately.

GOVERNOR: My lord, will it be in order to hang him now?

JUSTICE: Master Palmer, you will report to me on the condition of the prisoner Shanks.

Palmer goes out.

GOVERNOR (*to third turnkey*): How in the devil's name did you let a thing like this happen? Why wasn't he under proper guard?

THIRD TURNKEY: He had a knife hidden somewhere on him, yer honor.

WOLFE: We needn't worry about all this now. The important thing is to have him hanged at once.

GOVERNOR: Galvin, are you ready in case his lordship permits us go ahead?

GALVIN: Well I'm ready, yer honor, and the little swing-swong is ready, but it's hard to do a proper job when a genkilman's in that condition.

WOLFE: I don't care what mutilation there is. You won't suffer by it.

GALVIN: The people won't like it, yer honor.

WOLFE: If you wish to hold your job you'd better *do* your job.

GALVIN: Ask the millingtary, yer honor. Them blackguards don't care what they does. They'd ate him for dinner if they was asked to.

Palmer hurries back.

PALMER: Dead, my lord.

A sympathetic murmur runs through the crowd. Mahon comforts the weeping Mary Neale.

JUSTICE: He is now the page of history. I am the footnote.

PALMER: I big your lordship's pardon — ?

JUSTICE: Nothing that you'd understand, Master Palmer.

WOLFE: Dead or alive he shall hang in public in accordance with his excellency's orders.

JUSTICE: He has glory enough, Mr. Attorney-General. Do not give him more. (*He collapses again. Palmer fusses around him.*)

WOLFE (*quietly to Milligan*): Is the old fox shamming?

MILLIGAN (*unmoved*): No, sir. I have seen him take many fits like this. During the last few weeks they have occurred almost every day.

WOLFE: Um — I see.

MILLIGAN: May I respectfully beg your kind consideration, sir, if you should be looking for a personal attendant, sir, when — h'm — when your honor is lord chief justice?

WOLFE (*with a faint smile*): I shall bear you in mind, Milligan.

MILLIGAN: Thank you, m'lud. (*Suavely.*) A slip of the tongue, sir, but pardonable I'm sure.

JUSTICE (*rasping tone*): Milligan.

PALMER: Please, my lord — don't put any further strain on yourself by talking. It is essential that your lordship should rest.

JUSTICE: It is essential, Master Palmer, that I get out of this fetid hole.

PALMER: I respectfully suggest that I attend your lordship to your home.

JUSTICE: No. Stay here. (*Milligan has taken up his old place behind the lord chief justice.*) Milligan, the purse. Master Palmer, take the body of the prisoner Shanks into your possession —

WOLFE: It shall hang in public.

JUSTICE: And deliver it to the crown coroner. (*Grinning at Wolfe.*) Little is the law that I know, Arthur, but you seem to know less. (*To Palmer.*) Let an inquest be held upon it. And Master Palmer —

PALMER: My lord — ?

JUSTICE: No dissection.

PALMER (*raising his hands*): Oh my lord, I never —

JUSTICE: Make the body as presentable as you can and see it is handed over to his mother with due decorum. Milligan, give him the purse. (*Milligan does so.*) Not a cheap coffin, Master Palmer. Let it have silver mountings. (*Hauls himself up.*) And let the inscription be, "Shanks, First President of the New —" No, don't put that. Just "Peter Shanks, died in youth, the 23rd of May, 1798. To be with Christ which is far better." (*He perks up.*) How pleasing it is to forgive one's enemies. Good Christians like you, Arthur, miss a lot of fun if only ye knew it.

PALMER: I respectfully suggest that your lordship permit yourself to be carried to your coach.

JUSTICE: Why?

PALMER: Merely a precaution, my lord.

JUSTICE: I have never taken precautions. What was the use? I was born unlucky. Here, lend me your stick. (*He begins to go toward the gate, feeble and rather tottery. The third turnkey opens the gate for him. He stops as he is passing Mary Neale, who is still standing with Mahon's protective arm about her.*) What's this he said to you? "Remember." Puh! You have already begun to forget him. Next week you'll find it hard to remember what color his eyes were. (*Thrusts his face close to hers.*) But you won't forget my face quite so easily, eh? (*He moves on, but half turns and winks at her.*) Goodbye, my child. Love me when I am dead.

MARY: Take me with you, your honor. (*The lord chief justice looks surprised. His face lights up with pleasure and hope. She adds an explanation.*) They won't let me out when you go.

JUSTICE (*his face goes blank*): Oh I see. (*He hides his disappointment under the familiar grin.*) I see . . .

MARY: Please . . . please. (*She would go and touch him if Mahon slackened his grip on her.*)

The lord chief justice motions her to go through the open gate. She breaks away from Mahon and scurries through the gate like a frightened animal. As the lord chief justice gazes after her, amused, Wolfe signals Milligan to his side and whispers. The lord chief justice drags himself toward the gate. He misses Milligan and turns. The sight of Milligan and Wolfe whispering rouses him. He draws himself up. His voice is as strong as ever.

JUSTICE: I am not dead yet, Milligan.

Milligan hurries over obsequiously and attends him as he goes through the gate. The turnkeys bow deeply. The prisoners and the others stare after him in silence.

THE young Irish playwright who in recent years has probably received the most opposition from critics and the most applause from audiences is John B. Keane (the "B" stands for Brendan, his confirmation name). He was born on July 21, 1928, in Listowel, the fourth in a family of five boys and four girls; his father was a schoolteacher. He went to primary and secondary schools in Listowel, and then became a fowl-buyer, a chemist's apprentice, and finally an emigrant to England. After two years there that were really a season in Hell, he made his way back first to Ireland and then to Listowel, where he and his newly-married wife managed to buy the pub that he still runs.

Pub hours are long, and Keane's writing is done after midnight when the pub is cleared. His first stage play, the immensely popular *Sive*, was begun one night after he had seen the Listowel Drama Group do Tomelty's *All Soul's Night*. "When I came home that night," he writes, "I was impatient and full of ideas. . . . I started to write and six hours later, or precisely at 6:30 a.m., I had written the first scene of *Sive*." In 1959, the Listowel Drama Group's production of the play won the Esso Award as the best production at the All-Ireland Drama Festival at Athlone, as well as quite a few other awards. The play was then produced and toured by the new Southern Theatre Group from Cork, going on to become the most popular play for amateur groups in the country.

Keane's other work includes the plays *Sharon's Grave*, first produced by the Southern Theatre Group in Cork on February 1, 1960; *The Highest House on the Mountain*, produced by Orion Productions at the 1960 Theatre Festival; *Many Young Men of Twenty*, produced early in 1961 by the Southern Theatre Group in Cork and later at the Olympia in Dublin; *No More in Dust*, produced by Orion during the 1961 Theatre Festival at the Gas Company Theatre in Dun Laoghaire; *The Man from Clare*, produced by the Southern Theatre Group in Cork on July 1, 1962; *Hut 42*, first produced by the Abbey on November 12, 1962; *The Year of the Hiker*, first produced by the Southern Theatre Group in Cork on July 17, 1963; *The Field*, first produced at the Olympia, Dublin, by Gemini Productions on November 1, 1965; and *The Roses of Tralee*, first produced in the autumn of 1965 in Cork by the Southern Theatre Group, and at the Gaiety, Dublin, on April 12, 1966. Keane has also written a short autobiography called *Self-Portrait*, a volume of poems called *The Street*, and a large number of informal essays for newspapers, some of which have been collected in the volume *Strong Tea*. He has also made a couple of phonograph records.

Although I am not sure how meaningful it is, Keane's plays might be divided into three groups. First are the folk or country plays, like *Sive, Sharon's Grave, The Highest House on the Mountain*, and *The Year of the Hiker*, which most show the influence of Molloy. Second, there are the plays of modern life, like *No More in Dust* about young working girls in Dublin, *Hut 42* about Irish laborers in England, *The Man from Clare* about a man's obsession with football, and the untitled play Keane is currently working on which is about menopause. And, finally, there are the musicals, *Many Young Men of Twenty* and *The Roses of Tralee*. This division may be more arbitrary than meaningful, for, despite his great productivity, Keane has not been writing long, and it is difficult to tell this early how his career may develop. Certainly, a recent piece like *The Field*, which was much admired even in Dublin, blends elements of both the folk and the modern plays and shows how the deeply ingrained Irish lust for land can still conquer modern law and justice even when those qualities are upheld by both police and the clergy.

In his modern plays, Keane seems really to be breaking new ground and finding themes in Irish life which earlier writers had not touched on. *The Man from Clare* and *No More in Dust*, for instance, while not major Keane, are very interesting, and part of their interest derives from their concern with issues central to Ireland but new for Irish drama. The obsession with sport seems actually a kind of sex substitute for the late-marrying Irish male; Keane's point is that it keeps him in an extended adolescence. The plight of young country girls sent up to Dublin by their parents to make a living has been treated by Edna O'Brien in a novel or two, but not dealt with, I believe, by any other playwright. Although one hardly thinks of Dublin as a "swinging" town, there is a segment of Dublin life, composed of the young, that is much closer to modern life in London or San Francisco or New York than it is to what Irish life has traditionally been. Probably in no other area of Irish life is the clash between traditional values and the values of the modern world quite so apparent.

The themes of Keane's earlier folk plays are rather less interesting because they are the traditional ones of Irish drama: the made marriage, the lust for land and money, emigration, pride in social position. Even as effective a play as *Sive* is really no more than a carbon copy of half a dozen earlier Irish plays. Compare its theme and story, for instance, with Louis D'Alton's *Lovers Meeting*. Yet what puts these early plays apart from a horde of similar ones by other playwrights is a highly individual blend of intense lyricism, sensual grotesquerie, and vivid theatricality.

Sharon's Grave, which had a brief off-Broadway production, is more original in its treatment than in its subject matter. It diverges from straight realism by many touches of heightened imagination which might loosely be described as poetic. But it is chiefly distinguished by a pervasive grotesquerie, strong enough to put one in mind of Grand Guignol. Though this is one of those plays the Dublin critics regard as overly melodramatic, it seems to me defensible in two ways. First, the quality of life in Kerry is a great deal different from the quality of life in Dublin. Dublin is quickly growing into a modern city not hugely different from Stuttgart or Zurich or Des Moines. But in out-of-the-way places like Kerry, there is still a broader, bigger spirit of the old savage Ireland in the life of the people, and *Sharon's Grave* reflects that spirit. Just the other day I read a newspaper account of a revival of pishoguery, or witchcraft, in parts of Kerry. It is in Kerry that the tinkers annually meet for Puck Fair, that strange survival of pagan days described so vividly in MacMahon's *The Honey Spike* and in Muriel Rukeyser's *The Orgy*.

Second, the bizarre characterization and heightened intensity of the action really dramatize, quite curiously for an Irish play, the urgency of the sexual drive. Indeed, the macabre Dinzie Conlee is so obsessed that he seems akin to some of the more fiendish characters from Jacobean tragedy. But if sex has made Dinzie almost demonic, it has just as strongly affected the curiously angelic Neelus. And even Trassie and Peadar, who apparently stand for healthy sexual love, have an intensity to their feelings that reminds one more of Tennessee Williams than of T. C. Murray.

Some of Michael Molloy's plays are pervaded by a gentle yearning for the sexual life and a melancholy regret about its loss. But in Keane we see more than that: we see passion driven to madness and urgently dramatized. This is probably the farthest the traditional material of the folk play has been pushed, and the old situations are given an exciting new vigor by it.

Much of the excellence of Keane's musicals can be seen from just reading *Many Young Men of Twenty*. Still, a musical has vivid theatrical and emotional values that are not apparent on the page. *Many Young Men of Twenty* is thicker on the page than Brendan Behan's *The Hostage*, but, like *The Hostage*, its true life is on the stage where the rich lines and situations are made doubly intense by the superb songs that Keane has composed. The Joan Littlewood production of *The Hostage* and the long-running off-Broadway production of Brecht's and Weill's *The Threepenny Opera* have given me probably more of a theatrical jolt than anything I have seen in the last ten years. But not far behind those brilliant productions I would rank the Southern Theatre Group's production of *Many Young Men of Twenty*. It was consummate theater.

There are many exciting young talents in the Irish theater today, and it is too early to say that any one of them will dominate the next twenty years of Irish drama. One can say that none works harder and that none is more basically talented than John B. Keane.

Sharon's Grave

DONAL CONLEE, an old farmer	PATS BO BWEE, a healer
TRASSIE CONLEE, his daughter	MAGUE, a neighbor
NEELUS CONLEE, his son	MOLL, a neighbor
DINZIE CONLEE, his nephew	TOM SHAWN, a neighbor
JACK CONLEE, his nephew	AN OLD WOMAN
PEADAR MINOGUE, a wandering thatcher	MISS DEE, the schoolteacher

Act I

SCENE I

The action takes place in a bedroom in a small farmhouse on an isolated headland on the southwestern seaboard of Ireland. From the window, and through the open door, can be seen a drear stretch of mountain falling down to a sea. Crooked thorn trees are everywhere along the mountainside and distant crags are evident also. The room is poorly furnished. A large iron bed faces the audience from center back wall. On right of bed, on back wall, is a door (front door). At left of bed on back wall, is a window. An old iron washstand, on which a basin and ewer are deposited, stands at left of window, in the corner. A small wooden table stands between the bed and the door. Over the bed hangs a large Saint Brigid's cross. On left wall of room, center, is another door (room door), partly open. An old man, emaciated, with scanty white hair, sits, propped by pillows, on the bed. He faces the audience. A bright quilt covers his lower body. In his hands a rosary beads rests. He would appear to be asleep.

© Copyright 1960, 1967 by John B. Keane. Address inquiries concerning performance or translation rights to Robert Hogan, Proscenium Press, Box 561, Dixon, California 95620. The play was first produced by the Southern Theatre Group in the Father Mathew Hall, Cork, on February 1, 1960, directed by Dan Donovan, with settings by Frank Sanquest.

The time is a late evening in March-ending, in the middle thirties of this century.

A knock is heard at the front door. The man on the bed inclines body barely, but does not otherwise heed knock. The knock occurs secondly, a little louder . . . no movement from the old man on the bed. The latch on the door lifts and the door opens. Enter Peadar Minogue. He is a well-made, youngish man, thirty-five or so, with a weatherbeaten copper-colored face. He wears an old felt hat on his head, an old three-quarter length leather jacket, and strong boots. His trousers ends are tucked inside his rough socks. He carries a large satchel on his back. For a while he looks at the form on the bed, and then peers closely at the old man. . . .

PEADAR (*tentatively, barely touching the old man*): In pardon to you, sir. Could I disturb you?

The old man does not move.

PEADAR: If you're asleep, sir, I won't wake you. Maybe you're only dozing and you might hear me. I'm looking for directions. (*Looks around the room.*) Maybe I'm in the right house, but I don't know. (*Doubtfully, to himself.*) I shouldn't be here if 'tis the wrong house, disturbing people in their privacy, stealing into a place and witnessing things not meant for me. (*Then, kindly, to the old man.*) Sleep your good sleep, old man.

The old man stirs but barely, and inclines his head to Peader, who bends near him. The old man moans a little, tries to convey something, fails, and is still again.

PEADAR (*reflectively*): Trying to tell me something? Would you be sick now, by any chance, and not be able to dress your thoughts in words? I don't know! (*Turns and surveys room again.*) If you're sick, there will be somebody attending to you before we're older. I hope it isn't sick you are, but asleep. I hope somebody comes in. I'll bide my time. They'll hardly turn me away. (*Takes off his satchel, places it on floor, tiptoes to window, peers out.*) No sign of a being or animal to be seen!

Peadar turns from window, goes to door, opens it and looks out, and stands a while in thought, looking into the distance. As he stands thus, a woman enters, silently, from the left. She is dressed in a dark frock, covered by a sacking apron, and wears strong boots. A cloth is tied tightly about her hair. She carries a bunch of daffodils in one hand and a short-stemmed earthenware vase in the other. She is slightly startled and looks in perplexity at Peadar, who does not see her. She harrumphs. Peadar wheels suddenly and looks at her, sweeping off his hat and clutching it in his hands. The woman is Trassie Conlee, thirtyish, of good carriage.

TRASSIE: Who are you?

PEADAR: My name is Peadar Minogue.

TRASSIE: Peadar Minogue! There are no Minogues in these parts.

PEADAR: I am not from these parts. Is this the townland of Baltavinn?

TRASSIE: It is!

PEADAR: Would this, by any chance, be the house of Donal Conlee?

TRASSIE: It is! That's Donal Conlee there in the bed.

PEADAR: Oh! (*Looks at Donal.*) It's a strange thing to see a door leading into a bedroom, a door any man might walk in from the road.

TRASSIE: There were two holdings here in time gone. There are two doors still. We often thought to close one.

PEADAR: Who are you?

TRASSIE: I am Trassie Conlee, his daughter (*indicating bed*). He isn't well.

PEADAR: I thought he might be sick.

TRASSIE: Would you sit down?

PEADAR: Thanks, I will. (*Closes door.*) There is a fall of ground the whole way from here to the sea, I saw from the door. A healthy place and a wholesome place to live in. There is no air like the sea air.

TRASSIE: You can hear the sea here all of the time while there is quietness; at night above all. The sea is all around you. We live on a headland here.

PEADAR: I saw that from the rise of ground. Not many houses hereabouts?

Peadar circles bed and sits on chair at left of bed. Trassie places flowers in vase and vase on table.

TRASSIE (*notices satchel*): Did you come far today?

PEADAR: From Carraig Head.

TRASSIE: A good journey. You must have business in these parts?

PEADAR: I'm a journeyman thatcher. I heard there were houses in the townland of Baltavinn that needed thatching.

TRASSIE: It's going late into the year now for thatching.

PEADAR: Work is hard to come by. No harm to try here for it. I saw the thatch of this house from the road. 'Tis rotting in every quarter. I heard in the next townland — Roseerin, I think they call it — that I would find a few days' work in the house of Donal Conlee. They never said a word about there being sickness in the house.

TRASSIE: They'll never say that! 'Twas a pity you came so far with a false account. Anyway, while you're here, you'll drink tea.

PEADAR: No . . . no . . . don't bother yourself! . . . You have enough to think of . . .

TRASSIE: I would be making it, anyway. I have a brother — Neelus; he is carting seaweed with the pony.

PEADAR: It's good to have somebody in the house with you, especially with sickness.

TRASSIE: Did they tell you in Roseerin about him?

PEADAR: Your brother?

TRASSIE: Yes, my brother!

PEADAR: No word of him. His name was not drawn down one way or the other.

TRASSIE: Did they say anything about me?

PEADAR: No! (*Significantly.*) Only that the house of Donal Conlee would fall if it wasn't thatched.

TRASSIE (*smiling*): Looking for custom you are?

PEADAR: Only what they said (*smiles*). A man in search of work will go by all roads to come by it.

TRASSIE: What did they say about my brother Neelus?

PEADAR (*smiles faintly*): There was no mention of him. Why do you ask the second time?

TRASSIE (*rearranging clothes on bed — hesitantly*): Neelus is strange. He is a good worker — a great worker, but he is a small bit strange. People here in Baltavinn are saying he thinks of nothing but women, day in, day out; nothing but women! They do not know he is kind and gentle and they do not know he will wash the ware for me after the meals and make the beds. All they say is that he is mad for women, which is a lie for them.

PEADAR: Are there no women in Baltavinn?

TRASSIE (*surprised*): There are no girls here, only myself.

PEADAR: Are there many men?

TRASSIE: Only a few, but all would marry if they could. There are no women of my age here.

PEADAR (*indicating the old man*): What sickness has he?

TRASSIE: The heart! Three different attacks he has put over him. He was anointed yesterday by the priest. The doctor said there was only a little life left in him.

PEADAR: What did the priest say?

TRASSIE: That he was not long for this world — to expect it any minute.

PEADAR: Death is worse than a curse. (*Sympathetically.*) He looks to be a good age. A life lived is no loss much!

TRASSIE: No loss to you!

PEADAR: True!

TRASSIE: Is there anything else you do but thatch?

PEADAR: I will do any work that will give me a good diet, a fire to warm by, and a bed to sleep in.

TRASSIE: Are you a married man?

PEADAR: No! Traveling from one parish to another — no woman wants a man who won't sit still.

TRASSIE (*listening attitude*): That's Neelus putting the pony in.

Peadar rises.

TRASSIE: Stay sitting, let you. There is no harm in him, only foolishness. Stay

314

sitting and don't be put astray by what he tells you. I'll put your bag out of the way.

Trassie takes the bag and exits left with it, Peadar surveys the man in the bed, rises, and looks out the window curiously. Enter Trassie.

TRASSIE: Why are you looking out?

PEADAR: No harm intended . . . (*Doubtfully.*) If I should go tell me!

TRASSIE: Wait and have tea. Sit down, or he will be asking questions about you. Surely you will have a mouthful of tea and a forkful of meat cold before you go. (*Suggestive.*) Or maybe 'tis how you're afraid of things you do not meet every day.

PEADAR: I'm not afraid, but I would hate to be the cause of upsetting the house by staying a while.

TRASSIE: There is no fear you will do that, but a sweet plate of bacon would give you heart for your journey.

PEADAR: You make me feel hungry. But this is a strange house.

TRASSIE: All people are strange in their own way.

PEADAR: True! . . . Does he know his father is bad?

TRASSIE: In his own way! A different way from ours, but he knows. He knows something is wrong. He is worried from that, too.

PEADAR (*nods his head in understanding*): Did he ever give you trouble?

TRASSIE: Not him! He is always helpful. Anything I tell him do, he will do. (*Worried.*) Not *him*, but others are always making trouble.

Peadar looks at her for a spell and returns to his chair.

TRASSIE (*change of tone*): Of a Sunday Neelus will go down to Carraig Head and go in hiding about the cliffs. He will spend his day watching the sea. If the sea is wild and making noise, he will come home deaf and you might as well be idle as to try and talk to him. If the sea is resting, he will come home saying things to himself . . . strange things. (*Awkwardly.*) He talks of the wind and the sea and Sharon's Grave and . . .

PEADAR (*solemnly*): Some men are like that from thinking too much about women.

Peadar stirs nervously in his chair. Enter Neelus Conlee from left. He is twentyish, dressed in tattered overalls and waders. He has a vacant look, yet is handsome and refined of face. He looks puzzled when he sees Peadar.

TRASSIE: This is Peadar Minogue, Neelus. He was passing the road and he called, asking the way . . .

NEELUS (*smiling*): Peadar Minogue . . . Trassie . . .

Trassie looks hopefully at Peadar.

PEADAR: Very happy to meet you.

NEELUS (*shakes hands with Peadar*): Pleased the same.

PEADAR (*tentatively*): I heard good things about you.

NEELUS (*suspicious*): Where did you hear them?

315

PEADAR: Oh, lots of places . . . Glounsharoon and Coilbwee and Kilbaha. Everywhere you could imagine.

NEELUS (*hurtfully*): What used they be saying about me?

PEADAR: Oh, you know the way people do be?

NEELUS: Used they be telling you about me and the women?

Peadar looks doubtfully at Trassie.

TRASSIE: I'll lay the table for the tea. (*Moves toward left, then loudly to Neelus.*) If he wakes, call me. (*Indicates man in bed.*)

Exit Trassie. Neelus moves closer to Peadar.

NEELUS: Go on about the women.

PEADAR (*doubtfully, delicately*): They were saying you were a gifted hand with the ladies.

NEELUS: Were they telling you about me and Sharon with her golden hair? (*Cautiously.*) And Shiofra, the little vixen, with her face like the storm?

PEADAR (*thoughtfully, weighing up Neelus*): It seems to come to me that I heard talks of you and these women you mention. (*Sureness.*) Yes, I heard tell of it in several places. Yes, I'm sure now I did.

NEELUS: They don't believe it, you know — a lot of them. They do be laughing at me, especially the girls in the mainland when we go to the chapel on a Sunday. I've seen them pointing me out (*cautiously*) and I've heard them giggling and whispering. Sharon has beautiful hair, red and golden like the sunset (*elaborates with his hands*) shining like the summer sea and her skin is as white as new milk and her voice is as rich and deep and sweeter than the voice of a thrush. You never saw her golden hair?

PEADAR: No, I never saw her golden hair but I have heard of it. But I know the way a girl's hair is and I can imagine what Sharon's would be like.

NEELUS (*shrewdly*): What did you hear about it?

PEADAR: I have forgotten most of it but I remember to hear it was brighter than gold.

Neelus studies him suspiciously, and is then apparently satisfied.

NEELUS: Shiofra is a little demon.

PEADAR: Shiofra?

NEELUS: Did you see Sharon's Grave when you were coming here?

PEADAR: No!

NEELUS (*looks about cautiously and confides to Peadar*): Did you not hear of it?

PEADAR (*interested*): What about it?

NEELUS (*withdrawing a little — astonished*): You never hears tell of Sharon's Grave?

NEELUS (*walks to window and looks out. He turns. There is a distant look about him and awe in his voice. Points to window suddenly*): It's a great deep hole over there on the cliffs. There is no bottom to it. It sinks down

316

into the middle of the earth and water is always wild and willful in it, even when the rest of the sea is calm.

PEADAR: Why is it called Sharon's Grave?

NEELUS (*suddenly brought back to reality, eager to relate his obsession*): Sharon was a young princess of ancient times. Her father was a powerful chieftain in the County of Tyrconnell in the north country. Sharon was gentler than a dog and sweeter than wild honey. Her wild hair fell down over her white shoulders like a golden cape. (*Looks out the window, sad note in his voice.*) Sharon was traveling on horseback to the rich country of the Maharees down the coast. She was being married to a handsome chieftain with far lands and a tall castle rising over the sea . . . (*He pauses.*)

PEADAR: But go on! What's the rest of the story?

NEELUS: Shiofra was the name of Sharon's handmaiden. She was swarthy and humped and ugly and jealous of Sharon because Sharon was so beautiful. She poisoned the warriors of Sharon's father and there was no one left to help poor Sharon (*reflective sadness*), poor beautiful Sharon, and the old people say that Shiofra whispered a spell in the horse's ear when they were passing the great hole down below and the animal reared and jumped into the hole with Sharon upon its back . . .

PEADAR: Shiofra was an evil creature! Did she wed the young chieftain herself?

NEELUS: Oh, no, indeed! (*Shakes his head.*) No — no, indeed, she did not, for, as the horse was about to fall into the hole, Sharon made one last attempt to save herself and her fingers seized on Shiofra's girdle and she carried the wicked woman with her.

PEADAR: And that is why they call it Sharon's Grave?

NEELUS: That is why! But there is more to the story. The old people say . . . (*Looks about him as if he found somebody were listening.*)

PEADAR: Go on, Neelus. What do the old people say?

NEELUS: The old people say that what you would think to be the wind crying is the sweet voice of lovely Sharon crying for her handsome young chieftain. They say that what you would think to be the wind blowing is the voice of Shiofra wailing and cursing in her misery.

PEADAR: It is a sad story.

NEELUS (*lonely*): It will be the same story always unless the bodies of two young men are cast into the hole. One will be small and ugly and wicked and the other will be tall and straight and pure like the noble chieftain.

PEADAR: Is that part of the legend?

NEELUS: 'Tis all in the story . . . (*Turns to his father.*) He's very bad . . . my poor father, my poor father!

PEADAR: With the fine days coming now, he'll improve. The fine weather is a great cure for all forms of sickness.

NEELUS (*looks at Peadar vaguely*): The Banshee was crying last night over Baltavinn. I know the cry of the Banshee because it makes you shiver as if the cry was inside in your ear. The last time the cry was heard, my mother died a few days after. God grant her a silver bed in Heaven, my poor mother. (*Looks at his father.*) He's that sick he doesn't know who are here and he doesn't know we are talking about him. That's very like death, that sickness.

PEADAR: He's a long ways from being dead, Neelus.

NEELUS: Did you ever hear the way Sharon cries in her grave in the quiet nights of summer?

PEADAR (*doubtfully*): No!

NEELUS (*cups his hands over his mouth*): Oooh! . . . Oooooh! . . . (*Long drawn out and eerie.*)

In the bed the old man stirs and moans faintly. In a panic, Neelus rushes to left exit and calls loudly.

NEELUS: He cried out, Trassie! He stirred himself. He gave a moan out of him.

Peadar rises and stands anxiously. Enter Trassie. She hurries to bed and bends over the old man. She takes his hand and feels his brow. Then she turns to Peadar.

TRASSIE: It was nothing. The same as always. He is very weak in himself. He calls from time to time.

PEADAR: Is he long ailing?

TRASSIE: This long time now. He got a fit a year ago. They said it was a stroke. He never rose from the bed since he took sick. This last week or so he is going from worse to worse. There isn't much a body can do.

PEADAR: Is there no hope for him?

TRASSIE: He is too old to fight now!

NEELUS (*draws near bed, places his hand on his father's hand*): 'Tis when we'll all be asleep he'll go, the Lord save us! with no one to be near him. He'll be alone when he'll be called away into the caves (*tone of awe*) and he'll be walking for ever and ever through the caves and he won't know where he's going and he'll be for ever and ever going deep down into the roundy caves and he'll never . . .

TRASSIE (*gently*): Don't talk like that, Neelus. You know what will happen if you'll be talking like that. You'll be crying again and you won't be able to sleep. Stop it now, Neelus!

NEELUS (*dejected tone*): 'Tis in the dark he'll come. Oh, he'll come like a fox and he'll sweep him away in a flash.

TRASSIE (*firmly, gently*): Neelus, stop will you? You'll make trouble for all of us. (*Puts her arm around his shoulders.*) Go down to the kitchen and wet the tea. The kettle is boiling. Go on now, Neelus a chroidhe. (*She gently maneuvers him toward left exit.*) You've a gift for making tea, Neelus. (*She exits Neelus.*)

TRASSIE (*to Peadar*): What was he saying to you?

PEADAR: Nothing you'd bother to carry with you.

TRASSIE: You needn't tell me. He talks of nothing else. He is a good-looking boy, a fine gradhbhar-looking young fellow and the girls *did* take to him and they used to go with him, but somehow they would run away from him. (*Hastily.*)

PEADAR: I understand.

TRASSIE: I'm not denying he's a bit odd now. But he was better than he is now.

PEADAR: It's all right. I know what is with him. No fault of his, the poor boy.

TRASSIE: Will you come to the kitchen and eat something now? You'll want something for the cold road.

PEADAR: If you like me to, I'll sit awhile and keep an eye on the old man. I won't mind. Many is the time I sat up with my own father when he was ailing . . . I could stay. I wouldn't mind.

TRASSIE (*quickly, fearfully*): No! . . . No! No need for you! Come to the kitchen. I'll stay here.

PEADAR: Sorry if I am making too free. I meant well.

TRASSIE: And sorry myself to think I refused your kindness. But his people will be here shortly. (*Hesitantly.*) They might take offense if they thought a stranger was sitting up.

PEADAR: You have somebody to relieve you, then?

TRASSIE: I have.

PEADAR: Are they the one drop of blood?

TRASSIE: His brother's two sons, my first cousins. They come here every night, about this time, to see him.

PEADAR: That's a pleasant thing to hear — that you have your own near you, when you want them.

Trassie frowns a little; Peadar, puzzled, looks at her.

PEADAR: When there is sickness in a house, your own will be the first to help you.

TRASSIE: You should be thinking of putting something in your stomach. Neelus forgets to keep the teapot warm.

PEADAR: There was no need to go to so much trouble for me. (*Rises.*) In pardon to you I'll go down, then.

Exit Peadar. Trassie seems to be about to call him back, but hesitates and folds her arms, worried. She tends to her father's comfort, leaves him and looks out window, biting her lips, clutching her waist with her arms, ponder-

ing. She looks out the window. She starts, and pats her father's forehead, waits a moment, and exits left, leaving door but barely open. She exits. There is a sound of movement outside front door. Very slowly the latch lifts and the door is pushed inward but nobody appears. After a few seconds what seems like a man with two heads appears in doorway. They are two people, one carrying the other on his back. The man on the back moves and looks craftily over the other's shoulder, watching for movement in the room. The other looks stupidly about. The man on the back is Dinzie Conlee. The man carrying him is his brother Jack Conlee. Dinzie Conlee is young, in his early twenties, with a shock of dark hair falling about his pale face. His face is gruesome, twisted, as he looks about. He is slightly humped. He is a wizened, small person. His legs seem paralyzed. Jack Conlee, on the other hand, is a well-cut, well-proportioned man of about twenty. He has a stupid face — stupid in the sense that his expressions contain perpetual worry. He is fairhaired and handsome in the Nordic sense.

DINZIE (*as he looks about*): Bring us in, Jack. Bring us in, boy! (*Gives Jack a prod in the back.*)

JACK (*wincing, worried*): Go aisy, Dinzie, can't you? . . . Go aisy! You're always hurting me.

DINZIE (*ignoring Jack's feelings, goads him to center of kitchen*): No one in, Jack! No one in! (*He surveys the old man.*)

JACK: Trassie is out, Dinzie.

DINZIE (*always careful to ignore Jack's feelings*): Take us a-near the bed. Jack boy. Take us a-near the bed.

Dutifully, Jack carries him to the bed. Dinzie leans over Jack's shoulder and surveys the old man.

DINZIE (*to old man*): Are you listening, Donal? . . . Are you listening? . . . (*Prods Jack.*) Straighten, Jack! Straighten! You'll have me inside in the bed with the next. Are you paying heed, Donal? Wouldn't you die for yourself, wouldn't you? (*In anger.*) Wouldn't you die, you old ropaire, and not be keeping God waiting? (*To Jack, chuckling.*) Maybe 'tis devils that's waiting for him.

JACK (*pleading*): Ah, don't, Dinzie, don't! Leave him alone. He's our uncle!

DINZIE: Put me down, Jack!

JACK: Where down, Dinzie?

DINZIE (*prods Jack on back, and slaps back of Jack's head so that Jack squirms*): On the table, Jack, boy. On the table. Or would you like to fly to the moon with me, and back? (*Chuckles.*) On the table, Jack. Steady the blood! Whoa, pony!

Jack backs Dinzie toward table and puts him sitting on it. Jack, relieved of the weight, exercises his shoulder muscles. Dinzie, by the use of his long

320

arms, swings his legs back and forth contentedly. Satisfied, Jack approaches the bed to survey his uncle.

JACK: Will he last long, Dinzie?

DINZIE (*shrewdly*): It can't be soon enough for me, Jack! Frightful blackguarding, keeping the whole country waiting. He's holding on for spite, Jack.

JACK (*pleads*): Ah, Dinzie, he's our uncle. 'Tisn't right to talk like that.

DINZIE (*shouts at man in bed*): Wouldn't you die for yourself and not be keeping us all dancing attendance on you?

Enter Trassie from left.

TRASSIE: I heard the voices. I knew who it was. I was getting the tea.

DINZIE: Wouldn't you have a word of welcome for us, anyway? We aren't soupers!

TRASSIE (*pleasantly*): I'm sorry if I sounded the way you said, especially when ye come here every evening to see him.

DINZIE (*sanctimoniously*): There's no harm in us. We praises everyone as we goes along. We keeps to ourselves. Don't we, Jack? . . . I say, don't we, Jack?

JACK: We do, Dinzie, we do.

TRASSIE (*indicating bed*): He's not good this evening.

DINZIE: We was praying all night for him. Jack said a pile of prayers, too. Didn't you, Jack? You should have heard Jack praying. His guts rumbles when he says his prayers. I say, didn't you, Jack?

JACK: Oh, I did! I did!

TRASSIE: Would you like a drop of tea?

DINZIE: You know it wasn't tea that brought us, Trassie! I'm the kind of man that if I wanted tea, I'd ask up. We're not oul' women, Trassie. We never drink tea, except for our breakfast and supper.

TRASSIE: That, what so?

DINZIE: Ah, now, Trassie, don't be trickin' with your own cousin. You know the thing we were talking about, don't you?

TRASSIE (*hotly*): I told you before, Dinzie Conlee, that I wouldn't even give ear to such a thing . . . Why should you have such a desire to do an awful thing like that?

DINZIE: Will I tell her, Jack?

JACK: I don't care!

DINZIE (*pleads mockingly*): Ah, will I tell her, Jack?

JACK: Go on, so!

DINZIE: When the old man here die, Trassie . . . when he die, I say, 'twould be the best thing if you moved yourself over into my father's house, where you'll be safe with your own people. (*Quickly.*) The country is crawling with villains and lads that do be watching lone women with a thought

321

for catching them. They'd put you down on a floor in a minute and go across you.

TRASSIE (*indignantly*): With Neelus in the house, who would bother me? Neelus will stay here as long as I'm here.

DINZIE (*mock sadness*): But, sure, you won't be here, Trassie, my little jewel. Won't you be over sitting down by my father's hearth and the whole houseful of them bringing you tea and leaving you in bed in the cold mornings.

TRASSIE: You'd better be going home now, Dinzie. This is my house and Neelus's house, and here we'll stay, and we want no one here but ourselves.

DINZIE (*as if he had not heard*): You'll be like a queen there with my father telling you stories and my mother tending to your every want and Jack here breaking the hasp of his behind to give you comfort. Tell her, Jack!

JACK: Yerra, Dinzie, I'm no good for explaining.

DINZIE: You don't know the life you'd have. Jack will be up early . . . (*Shouts at Jack.*) Jack!

JACK: That's right.

DINZIE (*soft voice*): Jack will be out of his bed with the first light of day to bring you in musharoons for your breakfast and when the water be low in the warm weather he'll be capturing white trout for you. We kills four pigs in the one year and think of the puddings and porksteak frying for you and your own cut off every flitch that hangs from the ceiling.

TRASSIE: If you don't go home and stop your cross talk, I'll call in the dogs out of the yard to scold you.

DINZIE (*unperturbed*): I wouldn't like to be you, Trassie, when the old man die, with no one . . .

TRASSIE (*resolute*): I'll have Neelus here with me and I want to hear no more about your house or about your father and mother or about Jack . . . (*Jack squirms.*) Oh, Jack, you're a man without a mind to let that little devil control you. Wouldn't you give a buckjump some day below near Carraig Head and fire him away out into the sea? Or wouldn't you find a nice girl and make a marriage bed for yourself?

JACK: The weather'll be getting too warm soon for marriage, Trassie.

DINZIE (*calmly*): Don't mind her, Jack! She's only trying to come between us, between two brothers . . . two out of the one litter.

TRASSIE: Wouldn't you go home, Dinzie? Jack, wouldn't you take him up on your back and let my father die in peace? Carry him with you, Jack, out of here!

DINZIE (*in a rage, strikes table with his fists*): I won't go out of here! . . . I won't go out of here! I have no legs to be traveling the country with. I must have my own place. (*Violent rage.*) I do be crying and cursing myself at night in bed because no woman will talk to me. I puts my nails to my flesh (*grits teeth with temper*) because no girl will ever look at me on account of my dead legs (*then indicates his back*) and this impostor here (*wrathfully tries to claw hump on back*), this hound of the devil, this curse o' God on my back.

JACK: You'll give yourself a fit, Dinzie. We'll go now.

DINZIE (*fiercely*): We won't go home. My father promised me this place would be mine, and it will be mine. *She'll* go home to our house. What do she want with a house of her own and land and cattle besides? What do she want with it, when she has no notion of marrying, herself?

TRASSIE: Close your mouth!

DINZIE (*beats upon table*): I will not close my mouth! (*Opens mouth pitifully, says sadly.*) When I was fourteen years of age I used to be thinking of girls . . . thinking I was then and thinking I am now . . . and thinking I'll be for the rest of my living days unless I have a house and land to draw women to me.

TRASSIE: Close up and go! Go now, Dinzie Conlee and leave us alone! (*Pathetically.*)

DINZIE (*absently*): Will I sing, Jack? I say, Jack, will I sing? (*To Trassie.*) I have black teeth, but I have beautiful gums. I can't sing, but I can hum like a honeybee.

TRASSIE: Are you going to take him, Jack, or will I call in the dogs?

JACK (*defensively, weakly*): Sure, if I'll put him up on my back now he'll kill me with the pucking he'll give me. Wouldn't you be said to him, Trassie, and stay over with us. Leave him here an' he'll get some oul' woman. 'Twill satisfy him.

DINZIE: Be said by Jack, Trass! Be said by him! Jack is as sound as the tar you'd be walking on. Jack looks like an ass, Trassie, but he's tricky. Aren't you, Jack?

JACK (*modestly*): Ah, Dinzie!

Enter Peadar Minogue, from left.

PEADAR (*politely salutes newcomers and addresses Trassie*): How is he now?

TRASSIE: No sign of a change in him. He's still the way he was.

DINZIE (*accusing*): Who's he? Who's he, I say? Who's he, Jack? — Threaten him, Jack! Ask him who he is, with his head bare in a strange house. Go on, Jack!

JACK (*draws himself up to his full dimensions*): What's your name?

PEADAR: My name is Peadar Minogue.

JACK (*reflects stupidly for a second*): Why so are you here?

PEADAR: I'm a journeyman thatcher.

DINZIE (*chuckles*): Could you put a thatch on a baldy head? What call have you to be here? Ask him what call he has to be here, Jack. Go on, Jack.

JACK: What call have you to be here?

PEADAR: Searching for work only. I was passing the road by and saw the thatch rotten on this house and I said to myself 'twould be as gay for me to call.

DINZIE: I never heard of the name Minogue in these parts!

PEADAR: I'm only going the road looking for work.

DINZIE: The best thing you could do would be to keep on going the road.

PEADAR: That's my intention. I said I only called looking for trade.

DINZIE: Fellows like you upset me, leaving the road, going into houses, looking for bread and meat.

PEADAR: I work for what I eat and I always did that same.

DINZIE: You have the look of a man who never had the full of his belly!

PEADAR: If 'tis insults you want to cast, cast them! I'm a black stranger here. I mean no harm.

DINZIE (*anger*): There was more thrown to dogs in our house than was eat in yours in the round of a year!

PEADAR: *We* were never hungry, and any man what struck the dinner in our house was never hungry.

DINZIE: Who's to say? Every fool will boast about his table. In my house when myself and Jack sat down facing each other there was that mound o' spuds between us that we couldn't see each other 'atin!!

TRASSIE (*to Peadar*): Maybe you'd be wanting to wash yourself before you go. You'll find a bucket of water on the small table near the dresser. There's a towel hanging about it.

PEADAR: A wash would do no harm.

Peadar exits left, looking curiously at the company in the room.

DINZIE: The house will be alive with fleas after him!

TRASSIE: He's as clean as you!

DINZIE: You could fill a bucket with the mud and grease of him.

TRASSIE: He doesn't look that way.

DINZIE: D'you hear that, Jack? D'you hear the way they're blackguarding your brother?

JACK (*halfhearted*): Ah, leave him alone, can't ye?

DINZIE (*points finger at sick man in bed*): He won't be long more in the world, Trassie. They're calling him now and he won't go. When he goes you'll be coming over to our house and we'll send Neelus off to the home . . . Will you let me talk, Trassie; will you let a poor oul' cripple talk; will you let your own cousin talk? Why do they be all plaguing me, Jack? Trassie, this is the way of it. When your father die, my father will give him a good wake and funeral — won't he, Jack?

JACK: My father said it all right, Trass! He said he'd buy four firkins of porter and a dozen of wine and whiskey and the dearest coffin in the town of Lenamore.

DINZIE (*quickly, as Trassie is about to interrupt*): I will come here then to this place, and I'll find some oul' woman to marry me. (*Pitifully.*) Sure, I sees the girls going to chapel every Sunday. They do be lovely with their long hair jumping up and down on their shoulders and their fleshy collops so dainty walking the road. (*Hits table again.*) I must have a girl to marry me.

JACK: Go aisy, Dinzie, or you'll upset yourself.

DINZIE (*shrieks loudly*): Stop telling me to go aisy! Stop will you, or I'll stick you! 'Tis fine for you that can walk into a dancehall and catch hold of a woman and dance with her. (*Challenge.*) Will you swap backs with me? Will you knock this villain of the devil's breed from between my shoulders?

JACK: Your turn will come, Dinzie. 'Twill come in time.

DINZIE: Don't be teasing, Jack, don't be teasing.

The old man stirs in the bed.

TRASSIE: Wouldn't the two of ye go away home or ye'll wake up my father?

DINZIE: What does he want waking up for? Wouldn't he stay the way he is?

TRASSIE: Take Dinzie home, Jack, or your uncle will wake.

JACK: Come on away, Dinzie. We'll come back again.

DINZIE: "Come on away, Dinzie." "Come home, Dinzie!" Ye're all ag'in me. Have I no feelings at all? Do I see or feel nothing? Which of ye knew what I feel? . . . I watches the lads with their girls over on the strand near Carraig Head in the height of summer. I sees the big mountainy farmers galloping like stud horses through the shallow water and they dragging their girls after them through the spray. Is it how you think I don't notice the way a drop o' water do be shining on the white milky flesh of a young woman?

JACK: Ah, Dinzie, 'tis only bringing tortures on yourself you are.

DINZIE: I sees the handsome young girls and they casting warm looks of longing over the young men and I know what they do be thinking, but none of them cares about giving an eye to Dinzie Conlee. (*Sincerely.*) What harm but I would be fonder of a girl than any one of 'em. I would mind her the same as a child and give over to every wish she'd put to me.

JACK: Ah, Dinzie, 'tis only yourself you're hurtin'!

DINZIE (*unaware*): I would leave no one say a single word to her in crossness. I would polish and shine her shoes for her like the black of a crow's wing. I would cut her toenails and wash her feet for her in the evening. Oh, I would give in to her no matter what she would say as long as she wor a woman, even if she wor a black woman or a yellow woman, so long as she would come into my bed at night and hear out the end of my troubles and we could be whispering to each other the small things of the day. (*Shakes fist at the old man in the bed.*) Wouldn't you give over, you oul' pizawn? Wouldn't you die and have done with it?

The old man stirs in bed, rises on elbow, and opens eyes. Trassie rushes to assist him. The old man, helped by Trassie, sits up in bed, looks at Dinzie and tries to speak. He stammers at Dinzie who recoils a little. He raises his right hand in threatening attitude toward Dinzie who recoils further. The old man then falls back against Trassie's hands. She lays him on the bed.

TRASSIE: Will you have no pity for a sick old man? Will you see my father dying and have no consideration for him?

She lays him gently again on the pillows.

DINZIE (*assured that the old man is helpless, lifts his fists toward the bed in fighting attitude and shouts*): Come on! . . . Come on, I say! . . . Come on, let you! If you want one of these . . . You might be older than me but I'm not afraid of you. (*Viciously points finger at old man.*) We'll beat him, Jack. Did you see him pointing at me, Jack?

TRASSIE (*tearfully*): 'Tis you that should be in the home, not Neelus. Are you taking leave of your senses altogether? My father is dying! Jack, take that brother you have and carry him home to his room and shut him in from all of us.

DINZIE (*indignantly*): D'you hear her, Jack? D'you hear what she's saying about your own brother? (*Gently.*) Put me up on your back, Jack. Put me up on your back, my own brother.

JACK (*hopefully*): Are we going home, Dinzie?

DINZIE (*shrieks*): We won't go home! We won't go home! Put me up on your back, Jack. Put me up on your back till I attack her. I'll kick, Jack. I say, Jack, I'll kick.

JACK: The last time you kicked a body was at Leanmore fair and I gave twenty-eight days in jail for you. If you kick Trassie, Dinzie, it might be worse . . . (*menace*) . . . if you kick the old man they'll have it that you killed him and 'tis me they'll hang, Dinzie. I'll take no more blame for you. I'd hate to hang from a rope for any man.

Dinzie thumps the table viciously and scowls.

JACK (*a little afraid*): I didn't mean that, Dinzie, 'pon my soul and conscience. But come on away home. Can't you come on? They'll be wondering what's holding us here all night.

DINZIE: All right, Jack, we'll go! (*Warningly to Trassie.*) No more of your nonsense now. I won't have it from you. The minute he's put into his hole I'll be making my way over here. Have your clothes bundled and ready. Put me up, Jack. Put me up and carry me home. (*Jack hoists him onto his back.*) I say, put me up, Jack.

JACK: Have you a grip? Get a good grip.

DINZIE (*putting his arms around Jack's neck*): Right, Jack! Right, Jack! Steady, boy! (*To Trassie.*) Send word over by Neelus if he takes a turn for the worse.

TRASSIE: Ye'll have word.

DINZIE: Go on, pony! Go on! (*Clicks his tongue.*)

JACK: I told you not to be calling me pony?

DINZIE: Right, Jack! Right, Jack! Right, boy! (*As if he were addressing a pony, clicks his tongue.*) Go on! Go on!

Jack opens door and exits with Dinzie hitting his back. Trassie stands perplexed after their departure. As she does so, Peadar enters from left.

TRASSIE: Did you eat enough?

PEADAR: I had plenty, thanks.

TRASSIE: Where will you go now?

PEADAR: To the West. The men will be busy now with the fishing and there's sure to be work.

TRASSIE: Have you people of your own anywhere?

PEADAR: I have a brother, married, with a small farm in the mountains. I spend the winters there. If you had my bag now, I'd be going.

Trassie exits and returns with bag. She places it on the floor.

TRASSIE: Where will you sleep the night?

PEADAR: I'll find a place — maybe a hayshed or an old stable.

TRASSIE: But how will you sleep without clothes over you? There is cold in the wind, and wet, too, in it from the sea. You would be frozen.

PEADAR: I'm well used to it. (*Sincerely.*) I was often frozen to the heart, sleeping without shelter.

TRASSIE: Have you been to the West before?

PEADAR: Not as far as this before.

TRASSIE: It is far different from the mountains where you will find shelter. There is no shade here, only the hard wind blowing into you. It would go through your clothes and sting you.

PEADAR (*stooping to pick up his bag*): I'll find some place.

TRASSIE: Wait . . . maybe . . . maybe you could sleep here if you weren't afraid to sleep with Neelus.

PEADAR: Why would I be afraid?

TRASSIE: Sometimes he goes out and might not come back till morning.

PEADAR: Where does he go?

TRASSIE: Down to Carraig Head to have a look at the sea. The full moon and the high tide is the worst time for him or when the peal salmon run in the first days of summer. He acts queerly then.

PEADAR: What harm is that?

TRASSIE: It is not right to be wandering around in the night. (*Then in a tone which has some appeal.*) Would you sleep with him and not notice him?

327

PEADAR: I wouldn't notice him. I sleep sound. I would be very thankful for the chance of a bed.

TRASSIE: You could start away with the first light tomorrow. We rise early here.

PEADAR: Do you keep milch cows?

TRASSIE: We have seven, three calving. We have a few head of sheep. They graze the open mountain that falls into the sea.

Enter Neelus from left. He surveys his father.

NEELUS: Did they go — Dinzie and Jack?

TRASSIE: They're gone.

NEELUS: Why don't you lock the door on them, Trassie? Lock the door and they can't come in.

TRASSIE: They're your cousins, Neelus. I couldn't do that.

NEELUS (*fearfully*): I know what they want to do with me. I hear them talking. They want to drive me away from here — away from Carraig Head and the salt water. Where you would see no seagull drifting against the black of the cliffs. Where you would never hear the cannon guns in the caves.

TRASSIE: No! No! No! Neelus . . . I won't let them do that! I would never see you sent away like that. I would never let them touch my boy — my own dear boy.

NEELUS (*looking around him fearfully, hands to sides*): I know Dinzie Conlee. He hates me. He hates you, Trassie. He'll hunt me away from Carraig Head and the tides. (*Fearfully.*) I won't see the fingers of silvery tide feeling the goldy sands before she throws her body down on it. I'll choke and smother in the black room. They'll hunt you, too, Trassie. Dinzie Conlee is the devil!

TRASSIE (*touches his hand consolingly*): We will always stay here, Neelus . . . the two of us.

NEELUS (*faraway look*): Dinzie and Jack will hunt you, too, Trassie. (*He looks helplessly at Trassie.*) What will I do, Trassie?

TRASSIE (*looks at Peadar*): He's trying to help me, but his mind is bothered. (*Neelus nods helplessly.*)

PEADAR: Why should you want help? Is there something wrong? Can I do anything to help?

TRASSIE: No! . . . Nothing! (*Hastily.*) You mustn't take notice of what he says. Talk to him a while. I'll go to fix your bed.

Trassie looks at her father and exits.

PEADAR: What did you mean when you said Dinzie and Jack would hunt your sister? (*Waits for reply. Receives none.*) Think, Neelus! Think, man! What did you mean when you said it? There must be something bad in store for the two of you. Think of Trassie, Neelus. You wouldn't want

to see Trassie hurted, would you? Think, Neelus, of what you were saying a while back. Think of Trassie.

NEELUS: Trassie . . . (*Vaguely.*) . . . Trassie . . . (*Gently.*) . . .
Trassie.

PEADAR: Yes, Trassie! You wouldn't like if she were hurted, Neelus.

NEELUS (*awestruck*): Below in Sharon's Grave where they do be crying
. . . below in the deep wet black of the cold rocks . . .

PEADAR (*touching Neelus's arm with his hand, says considerately*): No, Neelus! Think! (*Pause; reflects.*) We will follow each other with talk out
into the night. I will tell you about the singing finches in Glashnanaoan,
my country, and then, maybe, you'll tell me about yourself and Trassie
in your own time.

SCENE 2

*The action takes place in the same room as before. The time is late evening,
two days later. The room is changed, inasmuch as there are now several
plush-covered chairs in it. On the bed the old man lies dead. He is facing the
audience slightly propped up. He is dressed in a frilly brown habit and has the
inert sallowness of death on his face. The bed is made neatly underneath him.
The uppermost clothes are white. Six assorted brass candlesticks, holding
lighted candles, stand on a table. There is also a saucer filled with snuff on the
table. A new, white, embroidered curtain covers the window. A prayerbook
props the old man's head up. A rosary beads is entwined in his hands. Neelus
—dressed in a span-new suit of coarse quality, stiff collar and new brown
boots—stands near the closed door, hands behind back. He walks toward
bed, looks at the old man, and turns again to the door, standing impatiently,
hands behind back. He continually screws up his face and admires his new
clothes with his hands. After a few minutes of this, there is a subdued knock
at the door. Neelus is alert immediately. He lifts latch and stands aside. Enter
two women, one tall and one small. The tall one is a cadaverous, sad-looking
person; the other short and stout and of a nosy disposition—both in their
middle fifties. The tall woman is covered with a black shawl. The smaller one
wears a tight-fitting black coat and a small black straw hat. The tall woman
is Moll, the small woman Mague. Both shake hands with Neelus sympathetically.*

MAGUE: What time did he die, the poor man?

NEELUS: Last night late.

MAGUE: Had he a lot of pain?

NEELUS: No! No pain! He only left a little gasp out of him.

MAGUE (*to Moll*): Wasn't he lucky to have no pain?

MOLL (*reedy voice*): He was blessed.

MAGUE (*to Neelus*): Did he say anything an' he dyin'?

NEELUS: He did! He said, "God take me out of my misery!"

Both women sigh sympathetically.

MAGUE: Any more?

NEELUS: He said we'd get rain in the course of a few days . . . I have his watch. (*Takes silver watch from his pocket and fondles it.*) Trassie gave it to me. It loses three minutes in the day.

The women shake their heads sorrowfully and advance to the bed.

MOLL: Ah! God bless him, isn't he a handsome corpse!

MAGUE: He's lovely, the fine dacent man.

MOLL: That had a hard word for no one.

MAGUE: That would give you the bite he'd be eatin'.

Moll feels the quality of the cloth of the habit and says to Mague.

MOLL: The best of material.

Both take pinches of snuff, apply it to their noses, and survey room.

MOLL (*to Neelus*): Where's Trassie?

NEELUS: She's feeding the visitors in the kitchen.

MOLL: Is there many of them there?

MAGUE: Did your cousins from Luascawn come?

MOLL: What about your mother's people from Lenamore?

Neelus does not reply but goes forward and holds watch to ears of women.

NEELUS: D'you hear the little heart thumping inside?

Neelus returns to door. The two women exchange meaning glances. Both kneel, cross themselves, and commence to pray. Neelus holds watch to his ear, smiling. A knock at door. Neelus lifts the latch and stands aside. Enter a small old man, poorly dressed, strong boots and cap, moustached. He shakes hands with Neelus. Neelus, in return, holds watch to the old man's ear. The old man expresses great wonder. Both Moll and Mague rise and sit on chairs. The old man snatches his cap from his head and goes to bed where he stands looking down at the dead man. He kneels and prays, watched coldly by Moll and Mague who converse in whispers. Another knock at door. Neelus stands aside and an old bent woman, covered with a black shawl, enters. She carries a stick which helps her to walk. She shakes hands with Neelus. The old man rises from where he is kneeling.

OLD WOMAN (*to old man*): Is that you, Tom Shawn?

TOM SHAWN: 'Tis me!

OLD WOMAN: Did you come to keep a watch with your ould friend?

TOM SHAWN: That I did! Sit over here, let you.

Tom Shawn directs her to a chair near Moll and Mague. Tom and the old woman sit, Moll and Mague looking indignant. Tom takes pipe from his pocket and lights it.

MOLL (*loudly*): There's no respect for the dead in this part of the world.

MAGUE: True for you, Moll; true for you. Settin' up pipe smoke over a death-bed.

MOLL: Will you look at what they have at the door?

MAGUE: 'Tis terrible, girl; terrible!

Moll and Mague sit upright, righteously. Enter Trassie from left, dressed in black, followed by Peadar, who sits on chair.

TRASSIE: Will ye come down to the kitchen for a drop of wine or a mouthful of tea?

MOLL: Is there a big crowd below?

TRASSIE: Only a few of the neighbors.

MOLL: We'll sit here where 'tis quiet.

TRASSIE: I'll bring a drop o' wine up to ye, if ye would sooner stay here. (*To Tom and the old woman.*) A drop o' whiskey for my father's old friends?

TOM SHAWN: In honor of him that's dead!

OLD WOMAN: I would hardly be able for whiskey. It gives me a megrim.

TRASSIE: A tiny hint of it. 'Twill heat you up.

Trassie turns and exits. Moll and Mague whisper and watch Peadar closely.

NEELUS (*confidentially, yet loudly*): The two of them are looking at you, Peadar, wondering who you are and where you came from.

Peadar turns and looks calmly at the women.

NEELUS: That's Peadar Minogue, the thatcher. He sleeps in the one bed with me. (*Proudly.*) He hails from Glashnanaoan where the singing birds do be. He tells me all about the singing birds before we go to sleep.

TOM SHAWN: You're welcome to these parts, sir.

PEADAR: Thank you kindly.

The old woman nods welcome.

TOM SHAWN: Would you, by any chance, be anything to the Minogues of Tooreentubber that used to keep the boar?

PEADAR: I have heard tell of them but there's no relationship between us.

TOM SHAWN: The Minogue bonhams were as hardy as terriers. There was a piebald in every litter.

PEADAR: No, there's no relation.

Moll and Mague look disgusted at Peadar and Tom.

TOM SHAWN: There was a Minogue, now, a small block of a man, a thatcher, too, by the same token — Thomas Timmy Minogue they used to call him. He married into six cows in Glounsharoon. He used travel to Aonach-more Pattern in a common car. A jinnet he had and the white knight he used to call him. That same jinnet was a born gentleman.

PEADAR: I heard tell of him, too, but we're not connected.

TOM SHAWN (*brightly*): What would your mother's name be now? Is she alive or dead.

PEADAR: She's dead this long time, the Lord ha' mercy on her. From Errimore, a Hennessy.

TOM SHAWN (*reflectively*): Hennessys from Errimore, Hennessys from Errimore. Hennessys. There was a Timmineen Hennessy, a flamin' stepdancer, from the Errimore side. Would they be the one Hennessys?

PEADAR: Timmineen Hennessy was my granduncle.

TOM SHAWN: Glory be to us all, but isn't it a small world? (*Looks around for proof.*) And you tell me Timmineen Hennessy was your granduncle? Sure, his feet were like forks of lightning. He would dance on a threepenny bit for you. Have you any step yourself?

PEADAR: I can dance a hornpipe.

TOM SHAWN: Kind for you to be able! Kind for you! (*Reflectively in wonder.*) And Timmineen Hennessy to be your granduncle. Was there ever better than that?

Enter Trassie carrying a tray. Peadar rises and takes it from her. Trassie chooses drinks and hands them around. She also takes plate of biscuits. The women accept biscuits but Tom Shawn scorns them. Trassie takes tray and goes toward exit. She turns. All sip drinks.

TRASSIE (*to Neelus*): Will you come to the kitchen and have something to eat?

NEELUS: I want to stay here at the door.

TRASSIE: You can eat later on. (*To Peadar, who has seated himself again.*) Will I bring you something to drink?

PEADAR: Thank you . . . but I have no mind for it.

TRASSIE: You must be tired — up all night, with no sleep.

Moll and Mague nudge each other.

PEADAR: Glad to give a hand only.

TRASSIE: Maybe you would like to go out in the air. It would put new life into you.

PEADAR: I'll walk a little ways, so.

Peadar rises and goes toward door where Neelus is. Neelus opens the door for him. Exit Peadar. Trassie exits left.

MOLL (*to Mague, loudly*): There was a banshee heard calling over the inches last night.

MAGUE: Notice in plenty.

TOM SHAWN (*to old woman, loudly*): There was an ould bard of a tomcat with whiskers like needles by him, crying over the inches last night.

MOLL (*to Mague*): The banshee gave three long cries of torment every while.

TOM SHAWN (*to old woman*): This ould whiskery tomcat used to leave three lonesome cries out of him every while.

MOLL (*angrily*): For a finish there was one long terrible cry and then no more.

TOM SHAWN: For a wind up didn't this ould cat leave one long terrible cry out of him, that you would hear in the other world. Calling, he was, for his little pussy and she never came to him. You'd swear it was the banshee that was crying but it was only an oul' whiskery tomcat.

Moll gives Tom Shawn a withering look.

TOM SHAWN (*to ceiling*): People do be easily fooled.

There is a knock at the door. Neelus lifts latch and stands aside. Enter a well-dressed woman of fifty. She walks as if she owns the world. Her accent is precise, affected. She shakes hands with Neelus and kneels by the bed in prayer. She is the local schoolmistress, Miss Dee. There is respectful silence while she prays, broken only by Neelus who takes a pinch of snuff. Miss Dee rises and sits on a chair.

MISS DEE: Good evening, everybody!

MOLL & MAGUE (*ingratiatingly*): Good evening, Miss Dee.

MISS DEE: Must you smoke when a man is dead?

Tom quickly puts his pipe in his pocket. Neelus comes forward and holds watch to Miss Dee's ear. She strikes his hand violently. Frightened, Neelus returns to the door.

MISS DEE (*to Neelus*): Where is Trassie?

Neelus hangs his head.

MISS DEE (*firmly*): Don't try to fool me, my boy. I know what goes on in your head. You're not half as simple as people think. *Where* is your sister?

Neelus points finger toward kitchen.

MISS DEE: Do you mean she's in the kitchen?

Neelus nods.

MISS DEE: And why didn't you say so? Making signs as if you were dumb. I know you, my boy!

Moll and Mague nod in agreement.

TOM SHAWN (*meekly*): And how are all your scholars, Miss Dee?

MISS DEE: They are not my scholars, my good man. I merely teach them.

Moll and Mague nod in agreement.

MISS DEE (*turns to Moll and Mague*): What in heaven's name are you nodding at? If you have something to say, say it. I fancy if that poor man on his deathbed could say something, he would, and be very glad if he could.

NEELUS: I know who's coming now! (*Puts his ear to door.*) I know who's coming now!

MISS DEE: Whatever are you talking about?

NEELUS: My cousins, Jack and Dinzie.

MISS DEE (*a little anxiously*): How do you know?

NEELUS: Because I know the heavy fall of Jack's legs from carrying Dinzie.

333

Suddenly there is a loud knocking at door. Neelus stands well back. The latch lifts and the door opens.

DINZIE (*from without*) : Go on, Jack, boy! Go on, pony!

Enter Jack, carrying Dinzie on his back. Jack shakes hands with Neelus. Neelus puts watch to Jack's ear, then to Dinzie's. Dinzie snaps watch and puts it into his own pocket. Neelus stands cowed, hands covering his head.

DINZIE: Go on over to the bed, Jack. Go on.

Jack carries Dinzie to the bed.

DINZIE: Bend over him till we see is he dead.

Jack leans forward. Dinzie touches corpse lightly.

DINZIE (*to corpse*) : Are you dead, Donal? Are you dead, I say? Look at the face of him, Jack. Are you dead, Donal, I say? Will you have me talking to myself? Is he dead, Jack?

JACK (*placatingly*) : Oh, wisha, Dinzie, he's dead all right. Leave him alone and don't be tormenting him.

DINZIE: Go on, Jack. Go around till we see who's here.

Jack takes Dinzie around.

DINZIE (*to Moll and Mague*) : What business have ye here? A nice pair of oul' hags, snuffin' an' gossipin' an' drinkin' your little sups of wine an' cut- tin' an' backbitin' everybody.

Jack carries him to where Miss Dee sits.

DINZIE: Who left you in?

MISS DEE: I came to pay respect to the dead.

DINZIE: You came spyin' to see who was here. Why don't you get an oul' man for yourself an' get married?

MISS DEE: How dare you!

DINZIE (*mimicking her voice*): How dare you! How dare you!

MISS DEE: You should be on your knees, praying for your dead uncle.

DINZIE: Should I, now?

MISS DEE: Yes, you should, and show a little respect for the dead.

DINZIE (*in a rage*) : Give her a lick of the fist, Jack. Go on, Jack!

JACK: Ah, can't you go aisy, Dinzie! Isn't it in a wake room we're in?

DINZIE: Go on, give her a lick! She used to give me slaps at school long ago when I usen't know my tables. She used to give a poor oul' cripple slaps.

MISS DEE (*viciously*): And you richly deserved them. You were the wickedest boy in the school, pinching the infants, and tying the girls' hair into knots. I didn't slap you half enough, you wicked boy.

DINZIE: Oh, good God, Jack, are you going to let her talk to a poor defense- less cripple like that? Ketch her by the throat, Jack, and give her a squeeze.

JACK: But sure you well know I can't, Dinzie. We'd have the law down on top of us. I went to jail before for you, Dinzie. I know what 'tis like.

DINZIE: Only for a month! Only for a month, Jack; and wasn't it worth it?

JACK: Are you going to sit down at all?

DINZIE: You're mad to be rid of me. (*Shouts at Neelus.*) Who's below in the kitchen?

NEELUS (*fearfully*): A crowd of 'em drinkin' and 'ating.

DINZIE (*to Jack*): Come on down and we'll rise a row with some one.

JACK (*pleads*): Ah, can't you stop? Isn't it a wake night? Wait until we're going home.

DINZIE: Frightful scampin' coming to examine a dead man and spillin' porter all over the house. A wake house is worse than a publichouse. We'll ketch some fellow half drunk and we'll give him a most unmerciful pucking goin' home.

JACK: Will you sit down now for a while? My back is achin' with the pain.

DINZIE: Put me down, Jack, boy. Put me down, let you.

JACK: Where will you sit, Dinzie?

DINZIE: Put me down where I can keep an eye on all of 'em.

Jack places Dinzie on a chair where he commands a view of all. Jack goes through the motions of exercising his cramped muscles. Dinzie pulls his legs up under him in the chair.

DINZIE (*surveying crowd*): The quarest lookin' bart of weeds I ever witnessed. Wouldn't ye go away for yourselves and not be annoying the poor man in the bed?

MISS DEE: You'll answer for your sins yet.

DINZIE: What do you want me to do? Start screeching and roaring with sorrow an' pull the hair out of my head in lumps?

MISS DEE: You *are* to be pitied! Can't you at least keep silent in the presence of death?

DINZIE: Sit down, Jack! Sit down! You'll strain yourself.

Jack sits on a chair.

DINZIE: Jack, are you listening? I say, are you listening, Jack?

JACK: I am, Dinzie.

DINZIE: Do you know what I'm going to do when I die, Jack? Will I tell you?

JACK (*resignedly*): Go on, Dinzie! Tell me!

DINZIE: Well, Jack, when I be stretched out dead in my bed with a brown shirt on me like the lad here and my face like the color of limestone, I'll send orders beforehand to Coolnaleen townland for Nell Keown, the concertina player, and I'll get about fourteen fiddlers from all over the parish and I'll have all of 'em playin' at my wake. I'll have porter to swim in and whiskey in tanks and I'll poison half the parish with drink. (*Laughs.*) That'll be the sport, Jack. I'll have geese, Jack — roast geese, and male and rolled oats for this gang here. (*Points to Miss Dee.*) We'll get a ladder for her and put her sittin' on top of it where she can see all. (*To Miss*

Dee.) Will you come? Ah, you will! Ah, you will! You'll come all right. Sure, there'd be no sport at all without you. (*Plucky, violently mischievous*.) Ah, do, say you'll come. Say you'll come. 'Twould be no good being dead if your puss wasn't facing me. (*Changed tone*.) I swear I'd wake up and give a roar at you and carry you screechin' to the coffin with me.

MISS DEE: If it wasn't for the respect I have for the dead, I'd leave here this instant minute.

DINZIE: Do you know what you must do, Jack, when I'm dead. You must pull a thick ashplant and put it beside me in the coffin and when they're shoulderin' me to the churchyard, Jack, I'll hit the cover of the coffin a kick and knock it off . . . You are listening, Jack?

JACK: Ah, stop, Dinzie!

DINZIE: I say I'll knock off the cover, Jack, and sit up inside o' my coffin and flake the four polls of the livin' bastards that's carrying me to my grave.

MISS DEE: The curse of God attend you!

DINZIE: I told you, Jack, you should have given her a kick. (*Threat to Miss Dee*.) Would you give me a slap now for not knowing my tables? One and one is two. Two and two is two. Three and two is two. Two and one is nine. Come on, give me a slap! (*S-l-o-w-l-y*.) If you give me a slap now, I'd hang for you, woman!

Enter Trassie.

DINZIE: Will you be ready to go after the funeral tomorrow?

TRASSIE: Will you take something, Jack . . . a drop o' whiskey?

JACK: I'll chance it.

DINZIE: Don't give me the deaf ear, Trassie. I won't take it from you. By God! I won't. You can be ready to go tomorrow evening.

TRASSIE: I'll bring you a drop of whiskey, Jack. (*Notices Miss Dee*.) Oh, Miss Dee! I didn't see you. Will I bring you something?

DINZIE: Bring her a fist of oats and a gabhail of hay. She's braying there with hunger since she landed.

TRASSIE: A drop o' wine?

MISS DEE: Just a little drop, if you please.

DINZIE (*loudly, boastfully*): I'll have my heels up on the hob of this hearth tomorrow night and maybe a woman of my own after a while. Jack, you'll be the best man at my wedding. I'll be well catered for. I'll have good times presently. I say, Jack, I'll have good times.

JACK: You're fond of yourself, Dinzie.

DINZIE (*wonder*): Fond of myself! I like myself, Jack — every man likes himself, Jack, hump or no hump. I knew a fellow once going with a girl and he was fond of himself . . . (*Pauses reflectively*.) . . . he was so fond of himself that every time he'd give her a rub, usen't he to give himself a rub, too.

MISS DEE (*to Moll*): How's your husband keeping, these times?

MOLL (*delighted to be asked*): Oh, he's fine, thank you.

MISS DEE (*to Mague*): And you, Mrs. Hallissey! How's your son in America?

MAGUE: Oh, he's going great entirely. He sends home ten dollars every week.

MISS DEE: Isn't he a good boy to do that?

MAGUE (*proudly*): Every week of his life he sends it. I gets my envelope every single Monday morning from Jotty King, the postboy, with the ten dollars pasted inside to the letter and he sends a great bundle of money at Christmas, too.

DINZIE (*triumphantly, to nobody in particular*): Isn't that more of it an' they'd be bla-guardin' me for wanting a wife. Sure, isn't it well known that the postboy wasn't near her door in the space of five years since the shop-keepers got tired of sending her bills for the meal and flour she owes? (*Smiling at ceiling.*) God help us! They do be boasting about their sons and about the money they get. (*Tone of impeachment — to Mague.*) Wouldn't you tell the truth? "He sends you home ten dollars every week!" He sends you home nothing! Ye spend your days slaving for your sons and go into debt to send them to America. And what do they do when they land in America? Forget about ye. And aren't they right, too? Isn't it a blessing in itself to get away from ye?

MISS DEE: What a horrible unkind little person you are. Have you no consideration for the feelings of other people?

DINZIE: Give us a song, Jack! Go on, Jack, give us a song — a lonesome one. *Enter Trassie with drinks on tray. She hands same to Jack and Miss Dee. Jack swallows his in one gulp. Miss Dee sips genteelly.*

TRASSIE: Some biscuits, Miss Dee?

MISS DEE: No, thanks, Trassie. I don't care for sweet things.

DINZIE: Are you going to ask me have anything? Is it how you think I have no mouth? Firing drink into black strangers and leaving your own flesh and blood go dry!

TRASSIE: You know what happens to you when you take drink.

DINZIE: Nothing happens to me . . . nothing . . . nothing. Ye're all down on me.

TRASSIE: You're welcome to what we have in the house, but drink only sets you stone mad altogether. (*Exit Trassie.*)

DINZIE (*to Neelus*): Come over here!

Neelus advances timidly.

DINZIE (*taking watch from pocket*): Do you want your watch back?

NEELUS (*nods fervently*): I do! . . . I do! . . .

DINZIE: Right you are, so! . . . Down with you to the kitchen and the first bottle of whiskey you clap your eyes on, put it under your coat and bring it up to me. Mind you let no one catch you, or I'll dance on the top of your watch.

Neelus hurries to the kitchen.

MOLL (*rises*): 'Tis time we were going home, Mague, girl.

DINZIE: What's your hurry? Yerra, sit down a while and rest yourself. Sure, aren't you going all day? Go on, sit down awhile.

Doubtfully Moll sits; Neelus hurries in and produces a partly filled bottle of whiskey, triumphantly, from under his coat. He hands it to Dinzie and extends his hand for his watch. Dinzie shakes hands with him and drinks with relish from the bottle. After the first draught he gets excited.

DINZIE: Cock-a-doodle-doo!

He swallows lengthily again, places bottle on the ground and rubs his hands together with delight. He motions to Neelus as if he would whisper with him. He whispers something into Neelus's ear. Neelus nods understanding and hurries out by front door.

JACK: What did you put him up to now, Dinzie?

DINZIE (*drinking from bottle*): Cock-a-doodle-do! . . . Cock-a-doodle-do! . . .

JACK: Ah, what did you tell him do, Dinzie?

DINZIE: Soon enough we'll know, Jack.

JACK: Ah, can't you tell us, Dinzie?

DINZIE: 'Twill make a good year for hay . . . I say, 'twill make a good year for hay, Jack.

MISS DEE: I hope you haven't put the poor boy up to any mischief.

DINZIE: Out for a gallop I sent him, to loosen him out.

JACK: Ah, Dinzie, you're a fright, you are!

MISS DEE: If you put that poor simple boy up to anything bad, God will visit you for it.

DINZIE: We'll have the kettle on for Him when He comes!

All the women assume shocked expressions, sighs of horror, etc.

DINZIE (*drinks from bottle again*): Cock-a-doodle-doo! . . . Cock-a-doodle-doo . . . doo . . . doo . . . (*Shrieks of laughter.*)

Enter Neelus by front door. He goes immediately to Dinzie. He has something under his coat. First he extends hand to Dinzie for watch. Dinzie hands him watch and Neelus takes a leathern whip from under his coat and hands it to Dinzie. Dinzie accepts it and puts bottle aside.

JACK: What's that for, Dinzie?

DINZIE: Not for you, Jack! Did I ever use a whip on you, Jack?

JACK: No, but you often threatened me!

DINZIE: Yerra, wasn't I only coddin' you? Put me up on your back, Jack, like a good boy.

JACK: Sure you won't flake me with the whip?

DINZIE: No fear, Jack. Is it me whip my own little pony? Come on now, Jack. Give us a hoist up.

Reluctantly, wearily, Jack gets Dinzie up on his back. Dinzie cracks his whip.

DINZIE: D'you know what we'll have now, Jack? We'll have tables!

JACK: Tables, Dinzie?

DINZIE: Tables is right, Jack. Two and two is four. Tables, Jack. (*Contemplates.*) We'll start with Miss Dee. (*To Miss Dee.*) How much is the cost of seventeen quarts of porter, if blackberries were a guinea a bundle?

Miss Dee frowns irritably.

DINZIE (*clucking his tongue*): Should be four slaps by right, Jack, but we'll try her with another one. Hmm! Let me see now . . . How much is the price of nineteen canisters of nettles if hearts is trumps an' the ace is robbin'?

MISS DEE: Get away, you cheeky bla'guard!

DINZIE: She's very bad, Jack, very bad! I say, Jack, she's very bad. Four slaps I'd say now!

JACK: Ah, can't you stop, Dinzie? If you don't be quiet now I'll put you down again.

DINZIE (*menace*): If you do, I'll choke you.

JACK: Ah, sure, I was only mockin', Dinzie.

DINZIE: I'll give her one more question and if she doesn't answer it, I'll have to give her the slaps. Fair is fair, Jack. We can't have no favorites. Now, the last question. Supposin' you left water flowing into a bucket when would you have it filled? . . . (*Waits for an answer.*) . . . Ah, Jack, there's no meaning to this . . .

Dinzie suddenly leans sideways and gives Miss Dee a smack of the whip across the ankles. Miss Dee jumps up with a scream.

MISS DEE: Oh, you little hellion! I'll have the law on you! . . .

Miss Dee retreats backwards toward the kitchen.

DINZIE: After her, Jack! . . . After her! . . . After her, the wine-sucking gossiper!

Dinzie makes several attempts to whip Miss Dee again but she runs into kitchen. Dinzie guides Jack back triumphantly and confronts Moll and Mague.

DINZIE: Two lively scholars here, Jack!

JACK: Ah, Dinzie, 'tisn't right. There'll be trouble. What will happen if Miss Dee goes for the guards?

DINZIE: She'd be afraid to go for the guards. Doesn't she know what'd befall her after? We won't be in jail forever, Jack!

JACK: 'Tis me that'll go to jail, Dinzie. 'Tis me that always gets the blame for what you do.

DINZIE: Now, we'll test out the lassies here. (*He draws the whip downwards at Moll and Mague.*) Go on, ye thievin' hussies, gallivantin' around the country, spyin' on people an' backlashin' and cutting.

Dinzie whips Moll and Mague into the kitchen and Tom Shawn and the old woman follow. Neelus bolts out through the front door in terror. With the room empty, Dinzie raises the whip aloft.

DINZIE: Glory, Dinzie Conlee! Glory to the man who hunted the grabbers and snappers. Glory to his brother Jack who carried him up on his back. Glory to the bould Dinzie for a gaiscioch and a hayro and that scabs and scour descend on all the vagabonds and villains that come to people's wakes to gossip and spy like beggars for whiskey and porter.

JACK: Ah, go aisy, Dinzie. Go aisy, let you!

Dinzie gives Jack a vicious wallop in the back.

JACK: Jaminy, but you'll capsize me, Dinzie! You've hurted me, man!

DINZIE: Put me down, Jack. Put me down till I get a rest after that. We cleared the room, Jack — Dinzie Conlee and his brother Jack. (*Jack puts Dinzie on chair. Dinzie lifts bottle and hands it to Jack.*) Drink up, Jack. 'Tis great for the gizzard!

Jack swallows heartily from the bottle and shakes head after it.

JACK: 'Tis strong stuff!

DINZIE: Give us a song, Jack!

JACK: Ah, I wouldn't like to, Dinzie.

DINZIE: Glory to Jack Conlee, with the voice of a thrush. Go on Jack. (*Bawdily.*) Go on, Jack Conlee.

JACK (*doubtfully*): Would it be any harm, do you think?

DINZIE: No harm at all. Won't it shorten the road for him? (*Indicates corpse.*)

JACK: Will I give "The Boys of Ned's Mountain"? 'Tis an airy one.

Jack assumes a singing stance and clears his throat. Enter Trassie. She glares at Dinzie.

TRASSIE: Are you going out of your mind? . . . What right have you to drive all these people out of the room? Whipping Miss Dee and the women the same as if they were cattle. How dare you do that in this house where you have no right?

DINZIE: No right! . . . Isn't this *my* house now?

TRASSIE: It is not your house.

DINZIE (*shrilly, thumping chair*): 'Tis my house! 'Tis my house! You'll be comin' over to our house when we bury what's in the bed.

TRASSIE: I'm going down to the kitchen and tell the people you're sorry — that you didn't know what you were doing, you were so foolish with the drink.

DINZIE: Tell them nothing, or I'll use the whip again. I'll mark 'em this time. I swear I'll mark 'em. I'll file the skin off their bones.

TRASSIE (*menace*): Dinzie Conlee, I'm going down into the kitchen now, and

I'll be coming back to this room again in the space of a few minutes. If you aren't gone home, I'll call the dogs in from the yard.

DINZIE: Don't be upsetting me now! Don't be upsetting me. I have a plan in my head.

TRASSIE: A plan! . . . What plan?

DINZIE: We'll have Neelus examined.

TRASSIE: Examined! . . . By whom?

DINZIE: By the father of all doctors.

TRASSIE: He was examined before by doctors and they said there was nothing to be done. They said he was harmless.

DINZIE (*thumps table*): He isn't harmless, I tell you. Wait till he be examined by a proper doctor and we'll soon find out what's wrong with him.

TRASSIE: What are you talking about?

DINZIE (*pause*): Pats Bo Bwee!

TRASSIE (*wonder*): Pats Bo Bwee!

DINZIE: Pats Bo Bwee, the Cures, from the Wiry Glen. He has cures for all aches and pains, for every dis'ase you could put a name to.

TRASSIE: He's not a doctor!

DINZIE: He's better than any doctor.

TRASSIE: He's a quack!

DINZIE: D'you hear that, Jack? D'you hear her? D'you hear what she is calling Pats Bo Bwee, a man that could read your mind for you? She's calling Pats Bo Bwee a quack! If he heard you he'd turn the eyes around in your head, and give you a dose of the itch.

TRASSIE: Maybe he has cures, but he's not a doctor.

DINZIE: He'd lose what doctors are in the country. There was an old man, blind, beyond Lenamore, that never saw the sight of day or night in twenty years. Pats Bo Bwee gave him a black bottle and a clatter into the side of the poll with his brass hammer and didn't the sight come back to him?

TRASSIE: He knows nothing about Neelus.

DINZIE: What harm? What harm? 'Tis how you're afraid to bring him over. 'Tis how you're afraid of what he'll tell you for you know well in your heart and soul that Neelus is as cracked as the crows and worse he's getting.

TRASSIE: I am not afraid. Why should I be afraid?

DINZIE: Pats Bo Bwee will put his finger on the harm. You know he will and you don't want Neelus's trouble to be known.

TRASSIE: I know what Neelus's trouble is.

DINZIE: Ah . . . but do you know what his trouble is? If you're so sure why won't you let him be examined?

TRASSIE: Because he was examined by doctors.

DINZIE: But he wasn't examined by Pats Bo Bwee that's better than all doctors.

TRASSIE: I'm not afraid to have Pats Bo Bwee see him. Why would I when I know that Neelus is as harmless as a child in the crib.

DINZIE: I'll have Pats Bo Bwee here the day after the funeral. I'll tell him to bring his brass hammer and his bag of cures. Thanking me you should be that I'm doing this for Neelus. Wait till Pats Bo Bwee is finished with him and you'll soon know what the trouble is. . . . Put me up on your back, Jack, and carry me home . . . Carry me home, Jack!

JACK (*helping Dinzie onto his back*): Get a good grip, Dinzie. (*Hoists him on his back.*)

DINZIE: Don't be giving out wine and whiskey to them scroungers in the kitchen. That's all they're there for, for what they can get out of you. (*To Jack.*) Go on, pony . . . Go on up, there. (*Hits Jack on back.*)

JACK: Didn't I tell you not to be calling me pony? Do you want the people of Baltavinn to be calling me pony?

DINZIE: Yerra, 'tisn't a pony you are at all, Jack, but a horse. Sure, you're desperate strong. Open the door and we'll be going . . . I'll have Pats Bo Bwee over the day after tomorrow . . . Go on, Jack! Go on, Jack! Are you going to keep me here all night?

Jack opens door and exits, with Dinzie on his back. When they have gone, Trassie tidies the room and collects a few discarded empty glasses from the floor. After a few moments the latch lifts and Peadar Minogue enters.

TRASSIE: Did you go a long ways on your walk?

PEADAR: Just over the fields a piece, down to where there is the deep hole with the sea coming in under it — the hole they call Sharon's Grave.

TRASSIE: Oh, that is a dangerous place! Many is the fine cow that fell into it, never again to be seen. You know the story?

PEADAR: But that is a pagan story, surely, and not one you could believe?

TRASSIE: Oh, to be sure, it is a pagan story but the old people . . . many of them believe it to be true.

PEADAR: It was sad that Sharon should die in such a way.

TRASSIE: It is lonesome to think of her falling into the dark and sad to think of her young sweetheart waiting, never again to see her.

PEADAR: Thinking about it would be lonesome.

TRASSIE: Sometimes when the moon is a full moon over the sea, Neelus will go down and sing lullabies for Sharon, thinking to give her sleep.

PEADAR: No harm in it, surely, that he should want to help a soul in trouble?

TRASSIE: I shouldn't be talking like this with my father dead. Praying I should be!

PEADAR: A thing to talk about is good. I saw your cousins from the fields. I could see the small fellow, on his brother's back. The two of them were singing to wake the country! (*Hesitantly.*) Was there any trouble while I was out?

TRASSIE: Nothing to bother about.

PEADAR: If there was trouble, I could help, maybe!

TRASSIE (*looks at him as if she would tell, but changes her mind. They look at each other*): How could you help and you next to nothing to me and it would be no way fair to expect you to interfere? People like you are kind, but relatives are the very devil and a death in the house makes them ten times worse and turns life into a bedlam.

Act II

SCENE 1

The action takes place in the kitchen of Trassie Conlee's farmhouse. Since bedroom and kitchen are of identical design (apart from fireplace at left of kitchen) there is no need for change of walls. Where the bed was, there should now be a table. A number of sugawn chairs should be distributed convenient-ly. A dresser fitted with delph at right. A holy-water font hangs at left of front door. The time is two days later, midmorning. Trassie is cutting seed potatoes at the table. She wears a sack over her skirt. She uses a common kitchen knife for the cutting. While she is thus occupied Peadar Minogue enters by the front door.

TRASSIE: What is the day doing?

PEADAR: The day is holding up fine. There's a dry wind from the sea and there's no rain likely.

TRASSIE: Did you see Neelus?

PEADAR: I saw him. He has the drills opened for the potatoes. He was start-ing to draw manure.

TRASSIE: 'Twould be an ease to get the potatoes down. We could begin with the bog then. We have three sleens of turf to cut and make up. I suppose you'll be going your road now?

PEADAR: 'Tis time to go, I'd say! I am very thankful to you for keeping me these last days.

TRASSIE: 'Tis how I should be thanking you . . . the great help you were to us.

PEADAR: That was nothing.

TRASSIE: Will you go back to your brother's house now, or will you go west in search of work?

PEADAR: I think I'll chance the west — the Kerry Head direction. Few journeymen go that far. There should be work.

TRASSIE: What kind is your own home in the mountains?

PEADAR: Only a small place with the grass of a few cows.

TRASSIE: Is your brother the older of the two of you?

PEADAR: No, I'm a year older. My mother died after he was born.

TRASSIE: God rest her! . . . Shouldn't the place be yours, though, if you are the eldest?

PEADAR: It was willed to me by my father.

TRASSIE: And how is it then that your brother has it?

PEADAR: He married a girl he was fond of and he had no place to take her, so I gave the place over to him.

TRASSIE: And did you not think to marry yourself?

PEADAR: I thought about it often enough but there was no one I was fond of.

TRASSIE (*pause*): Wasn't it foolish to give away your house and land and cattle?

PEADAR: There is always a place for me there. My brother is a good brother and his wife is a kindly person.

TRASSIE: Would you think of working at anything else besides the thatching?

PEADAR: I am best at the thatching, but I wouldn't turn away from a day's work of any kind.

TRASSIE: There is work here for a few weeks, maybe longer, if you like to stay. We would pay what we could.

PEADAR: There is no need for payment. I would be very happy to work here for my keep.

TRASSIE: Why is that?

PEADAR (*awkwardly*): It is a nice place to be.

TRASSIE: There will be hard work in the bog, and then there are the crops and the corn.

PEADAR: No matter! I'll get used to it.

TRASSIE: What do they call the place you come from?

PEADAR: Glashnanaoan.

TRASSIE: That's a nice name — Glashnanaoan!

PEADAR: It means "the stream of the birds"!

TRASSIE: I know! Are there many birds there, then?

PEADAR: It is a great place for linnets. And you could hardly count the swarms of finches. 'Tis the first place you'll hear the cuckoo and the goureen roe is as quiet as a plow there.

TRASSIE: All you will hear in these parts is the seagull or maybe the curlew crying in the rain when 'tis dark and stormy. The curlews crying in the rain is lonely but it is nice to hear when you have a good bed to sleep in.

344

PEADAR: Maybe you will come visiting some time to my brother's house in Glashnanaoan. You could bring Neelus. He would like to see the finches.

TRASSIE: Maybe some Sunday when the weather is fine we would go visiting. It is nice, too, here in Carraig Head in the height of summer. You can sit on the trippols of finnaum over the cliff and you would see the ships passing down the coast, little ships only.

PEADAR: I imagine it would be nice of a fine day to sit and watch the ships passing. I hope there will be work enough to keep me through the summer. It would be nice.

TRASSIE: Maybe there will. We have three mountain meadows that have to be cut with a scythe. Plenty work in that. 'Tis settled then that you'll stay for a tamaill?

PEADAR: If you want me.

TRASSIE: It would be good to have you. There is money to be made in the pooleens of the stream that flows near the meadows. A man with a good net and a head on his shoulders wouldn't want for salmon. They fetch a fair price in Lenamore in the summer.

PEADAR: It wouldn't be my first time poaching salmon. Of course, a man alone . . . (*Shrugs.*)

TRASSIE: Neelus is afraid of the pooleens but I would pull a net as good as any man when the salmon are there.

There is a knock at the door, a long steady knock.

TRASSIE: Who could that be, at this early hour of the day?

PEADAR: Maybe Dinzie Conlee and his brother.

TRASSIE: They would never knock.

PEADAR: Who, then?

TRASSIE: Maybe a tinker man looking for the coloring of his tea or a stranger inquiring his way. You would never know at this time of day. (*She moves toward door and calls.*) Who is it that's out?

VOICE (*thunderous, yet refined, of most musical southwestern tone*): Pats Bo Bwee with his bag on his back. Pats Bo Bwee from the Wiry Glen.

TRASSIE (*excitedly*): Pats Bo Bwee! Oh! Dia linn! Looking for Neelus he is.

PEADAR: I heard tell of Pats Bo Bwee. That's the man with the great name out of him for cures.

Trassie, flustered, opens the door. Enter Pats Bo Bwee. He is sixtyish, florid, bearded, with a great advance guard of a stomach. He carries his leonine head thrown back. He wears a small coat tightly buttoned over his protuberance of stomach. He carries a bag on his back. He wears corduroy trousers, hobnailed boots, and shirt open at neck. He gives the impression of health and vigorous vitality belying his years. He surveys the kitchen indulgently.

PATS BO BWEE: The last time I put my foot inside this door was twenty-seven years ago. Kawtee Conlee, your grandmother, was alive at the time. She

345

was suffering from "the runs." It nearly killed her, but I cured her. 'Tis four walking miles from the Wiry Glen to Baltavinn and four more back.

TRASSIE (*arranges a chair for him near fireplace*): Will you sit down, and will I make tea for you? (*Anxiously.*)

PATS: It was a great sorrow with me that I wasn't here for your father's wake. I was beyond in Glounsharoon attending to the father of nine children. He got a swelling on his elbow and I gave the best part of a week curing him. By all accounts it was a wake to be remembered! I drinks tea but seldom. There is great boasting in Baltavinn about the whiskey that was brought to this house. A man was heard to say that 'twould take a week to drink it.

TRASSIE: There's whiskey left if you care for it. I should have asked you in the first place. You'll think very poorly of us in Baltavinn, the small respect we show you . . . I won't be long.

Exit Trassie. Pats Bo Bwee goes and sits on a chair previously proffered by Trassie. He places his bag between his legs and his stick across his knee.

PATS: What name have they for *you*?

PEADAR: My name is Peadar Minogue.

PATS: What keeps you here?

PEADAR: There was a death . . .

PATS: Death! What is death but a long sleep.

Peadar makes no answer but walks a little to and fro.

PATS (*authoritatively, pompous*): You say your name is Peadar Minogue. I say my name is Pats Bo Bwee. I am Pats Bo Bwee with my one cow and my cures. But who are *you*?

PEADAR: Peadar Minogue!

PATS (*stamps foot*): But what keeps you here?

PEADAR: I stay here only for Trassie Conlee.

PATS: And you tell me you stay here only for Trassie Conlee! Do you ever get pains?

PEADAR: Never! Do you get pains yourself?

PATS: Where is the boy of the house?

PEADAR: What boy? There are no boys here, or girls either — only two men and the one woman.

PATS (*looking into the fire*): I'm cursed with the flowers of genius. I'm damned from thinking nether thoughts. Where is the boy, Neelus? Where is Neelus Conlee that's gone simple?

PEADAR: Neelus Conlee is out working his day's work.

PATS: When is he due to arrive?

PEADAR: For his dinner.

PATS: Is there meat for the dinner?

PEADAR: I couldn't tell you that. I'm not boiling it.

346

PATS: You'll be eating it.

PEADAR: What's boiled must be eat.

PATS (*winningly, to Peadar*): What time is dinner?

PEADAR: It changes, day in, day out.

PATS: Did you travel, thatcher?

PEADAR: Some!

PATS: Ah, but did you travel the mind? . . . We were all at Aonachmore at the pattern and there's more went to America, but did you travel the mind . . . strange roads in that country, thatcher!

Enter Trassie, with two glasses in her hand, one filled with whiskey and the other partly filled. She hands the small quantity to Peadar and the large one to Pats Bo Bwee, who accepts the larger as his due.

PATS (*toasts*): God increase wakes. (*Taking a goodly swallow of whiskey — toasts.*) That we may never lose the tooth for it! (*Swallows drink in a gulp.*)

TRASSIE (*taking glass*): Would you have more of it?

PATS: Enough is enough! We mustn't make pigs of ourselves. 'Twould be as well to bring in the boy of the house. I have a call to make in Goildarrig to a stutterin' child and I have a woman calling to the Wiry Glen tonight with blisters on her behind. There's a heifer calf in Trieneragh with the white scour — all waiting to be cured.

TRASSIE: Was it Dinzie Conlee told you to call?

PATS (*surprised only slightly*): He told me that young Neelus Conlee was ailing with a troubled head. It should be aisy to cure for there is no dúchas. I never heard of a Conlee being soft in the head.

TRASSIE: There is nothing much the matter with Neelus. There were two doctors from Lenamore with him and they said he would always be the same. They said he would never be violent but that he was finished with words of sense.

PATS (*uplifts his head*): Doctors must account for their aisy lives. They always have some story for you. Mind you, I don't condemn. We must be on the one word. You'll never hear of a thrush eating another thrush.

TRASSIE: Peadar, will you call Neelus in from the fields?

PEADAR (*putting his glass on table*): I'll call him in.

PATS (*uplifts head*): I'll call out and call him in! (*Rises pompously. Points at bag.*) The curse of the crows on the hands that interfere with the work of Pats Bo Bwee or goes near his bag.

TRASSIE: What harm would it do if someone else called him?

PATS: Did you not ever hear of the devils in hell, the way they do have their ears cocked? Do ye know the misfortune that might befall your brother if one of ye called him? There's no devils at all in hell except a few tending their fires. The rest of 'em do be around tormentin' people and coaxin' them and working their best plans to fool people. (*Dramatic pause.*) God forbid that Pats Bo Bwee would ever say a word against the devils. We all have our faults and 'tis as well to be in with the two sides. 'Tis hard sayin' who we'll have to face — whether 'twill be the Man Above or the Man Below. 'Tis only a brave man like myself that would open his mouth against either of the two of them, with the grave staring me in the face.

TRASSIE: Let you call him yourself, so. Far be it from me to go putting obstacles in your way.

Pats Bo Bwee goes to front door, opens it, and looks out, standing with great dignity — stomach protruding.

PATS: What name was it that you said he should be called by?

TRASSIE: Neelus.

PATS: I'll go down a ways and call him.

TRASSIE: You might only frighten him. He might not come to the call of a strange voice.

PATS: He will answer to the call of Pats Bo Bwee. The devils in hell would rise to the sound of my voice. The lark in the sky would give over his singing. All things, good and bad, will die to silence when I call out. I will go out and call him and when he turns his head I will beckon on him to come in out of the fields. (*Tone of warning.*) Let ye put no hands to my bag or be for feeling it to find what's inside fearin' ye might come to harm.

Exit Pats Bo Bwee. After he has gone Trassie resumes her seed-cutting, slowly, abstractedly. Peadar walks nearer to her.

PEADAR: Trassie!

TRASSIE (*startled*): What is it?

PEADAR: Do you think that this Pats Bo Bwee or what's in his bag will cure a person or ease a troubled person? What I mean is that Neelus is what he is, 'tis delicate, the handling. A man should want to know him well.

TRASSIE: There is a great name out of him for curing.

PEADAR: It could be — but who is to cure a troubled mind?

TRASSIE: There is no harm in attempting it. I know, as well as I know my two hands, that Neelus is harmless.

PEADAR: Why so do you allow Pats Bo Bwee to examine him? Why should you let a man like that decide what thing is before your brother?

TRASSIE: Because I know there is nothing up with Neelus.

PEADAR (*deliberate tone*): I will be leaving Baltavinn tomorrow or after.

TRASSIE: I thought to hear you say you would be staying a while.

PEADAR: I don't hold with what's going on! I don't hold with Bo Bwee or your cousins Dinzie and Jack Conlee.

TRASSIE: I am doing the best thing I know.

PEADAR: There is nothing in that oul' bag excepting maybe bottles of water or cut rushes.

TRASSIE: They say he has great powers and by all accounts there's a bad curse out of him.

PEADAR: If he is so wise why is it he is the way he is? Why so should he be so full of draoidheact and mystery instead of saying his say openly. An honest man will give you his whole mind.

TRASSIE (*hurriedly*): You never gave your whole mind. How is one to know what's in a person's mind, anyway?

PEADAR (*stupidly*): How do you mean? Sure you couldn't know a person's whole mind?

TRASSIE: How do I mean, only that you were a stranger first and now I don't know what you are for sure.

PEADAR (*embarrassed, puzzled*): Just that I was a bit bothered about ye.

TRASSIE: Why should you be bothered about Neelus or about the cures of Pats Bo Bwee? (*Hurriedly.*) Why should you be troubled about the way things are in this house or why should you trouble yourself to stay at all when you are so well used to the roads, or what private thing of your own keeps you under the one roof so long? (*She cuts the seed quickly.*)

PEADAR (*throatily, huskily, muffled*): I stay here . . . (*looks away*) . . . I stay here because you were pleasant and not full of pride when I first put my foot inside your door.

TRASSIE: Was that what brought you then (*unexpectedly*), the chance of a bed with sheets, and the chance of keeping your feet under a table three times a day with no worry of the roads before you?

PEADAR: I was hungry often and many a night without a bed but many a man without a home to go to will find himself in the same tangle of trouble. It's nothing to a single man who has no one to worry about him.

TRASSIE: You have a free life. Fine for you to be so.

PEADAR: I traveled every road of the west coast but I never gave more than two nights under a roof in the same house. The urge not to remain was in me. I have given the best part of a week here, what I have never done. What ails me is — why should I do this?

TRASSIE: You mean, why should you give so much time here? Well right so. Answer it! Why do you give so much time here?

PEADAR: You!

Peadar turns to examine wall at rear. Trassie examines the fire in the hearth.

TRASSIE: It's time I looked after the dinner.

PEADAR: It's early yet.

Trassie returns to table and continues to cut potatoes.

PEADAR (*throatily*): There is a pile of things I could tell you, if you let me.

TRASSIE: What things?

PEADAR (*turning, uncertain tone*): I would say you are among the best girls
I have seen upon my rounds.

TRASSIE: Go on with you!

PEADAR: I would say things all day to you.

TRASSIE (*without raising head*): What things?

PEADAR: I would say that you have eyes in your head like the eyes distant of
a stormy evening; that you have calves to your legs like a pair of running
trout; that you have voice that would keep a man awake at night thinking; and, above all things, that you would be a lovely person to have near-
abouts to be telling things to. I would say I would like to have soft hold
of your two hands.

TRASSIE: You would say that?

PEADAR: I would say that. I would say likewise that I would love to sit and
watch you at your work. I would love to see you moving here and there
and be watching and admiring you. I would think things then to myself
about you.

TRASSIE: What things?

PEADAR: Things, maybe, you would not like.

TRASSIE: Only a miser would keep a nice thought.

PEADAR: If you want to hear, so, here it is. (*Bends head.*) I would think of
the beauty of you, of the way your eyes do be, and how I would give my
heart and soul to be lying down in your bed and to be holding you and
feeling your softness against me. (*Shakes head.*) It is too sweet and hurtful to think of it. To think of the lovely body under your clothes, and to
think of the wintry nights when I would be shielding the soft trembling
whiteness of you from the cold and we whispering together in a room
with nobody else in it.

TRASSIE: You should not say that!

PEADAR: I am a man, amn't I? . . . You are a girl of rare niceness with
pretty ways to you and a neat form by you. If I said another thing I would
be telling lies. I have a terrible longing for you, growing worse lately,
growing worse every time you will look my way.

TRASSIE: It is wrong of you to be saying this with my father only barely
buried.

PEADAR (*angrily*): The dead are dead and won't they be always dead? Will
you have them rise up again out of their graves and be changing the pattern of things that are alive and with us. (*Gently.*) I'm sorry, Trassie, to
give you hurt. I know the feelings you store for your dead father and
I am weak for your sorrow. (*Dramatic pause — Peadar is in real anger —
violent anger.*) But I swear by the Lord God that made me, I will have
the life of Dinzie Conlee if he comes here again before I leave; if he comes
here again (*gently*) frightening you. I've seen the look of worry and fear

in your eyes when they're here. (*Angrily.*) I will let no man frighten you!

TRASSIE: 'Tis temper now!

PEADAR (*calmly, slowly*): Temper *is* what it is! What else would I have except it was temper? I will! . . . I will! And I swear this by the Mother of God . . . I will tear the heart out of Jack Conlee, your cousin, if he lays a hand on you. (*Uplifts his finger.*) I will! . . . I warn you! . . . I will take the lifeblood from the two of them if they make a fool of your brother Neelus.

TRASSIE: Neelus!

PEADAR: Neelus, my good friend.

TRASSIE: It is a great change in you to see temper.

PEADAR: I have been on the highroad this many a day, falling in tune with every wind, taking my feet where the smallest notion inclined them. What I wanted to do, I did, and free was I to do it. It was not my place here to interfere but there is too much of thievery going on and I will not sing dumb when I see it.

TRASSIE: Pats Bo Bwee will have Neelus in from the fields any time at all. (*Looks toward window.*)

PEADAR: Surely you don't believe that old quack has any powers?

TRASSIE: Pats Bo Bwee is old in giving cures. Will you insult a man of practice and experience.

PEADAR (*slowly*): I tell you, Trassie. I will kill for you and for Neelus. (*Gently.*) I will have no man put hands to you or fling hard words at you. I would do anything for *you*.

TRASSIE (*coquettishly*): For me?

PEADAR: Stop, will you? Stop with your teasing?

TRASSIE: I never thought to see such temper in you! You're like a devil with temper.

PEADAR: I'm worse than a devil. I'm a man, born a man.

TRASSIE (*gently, seriously*): I would not like to tease you, Peadar.

Peadar goes and takes Trassie's hands suddenly in his, holding them roughly.

PEADAR: Now I have your hands and, God forgive me for a coward, I haven't the courage to see what's in your eyes.

He lets go of her hands and looks directly at her. Trassie closes her eyes. Peadar places his hands over each of her eyes, allowing them to play there. Trassie opens her eyes and inclines her head.

PEADAR: Now I have your head in my hands and your lovely face under my fingers, and I have to feel you . . . I have to feel you for the ease of my body and my mind. I have to feel your kind back within my hands and your lively breasts to my chest. (*He places hands upon her shoulders.*) I have to feel the ease of the woman that you are against me. (*Tras-*

351

sie inclines herself. Violently he draws her to him. She yields wholly to his embrace.) I have to hold you against me for I keep the picture of what is happening now with me. It is joy to hold you, Trassie — pure joy!

TRASSIE (*whispers — urgently*): Peadar!

Peadar holds her tightly and kisses her face and, finally, her lips. Suddenly the door opens and Neelus enters. He looks stupidly at Trassie and Peadar, who break apart. Trassie resumes her work and Peadar stands facing the fire. Neelus is followed by Pats Bo Bwee.

PATS: T'anam an deel, but this is a great wall of an idiot. Four times I called him and four times he hung his head. "Come up here, you gommalogue!" says I for a finish, but there wasn't a hum or a haw out of him, so I caught him by the sleeve of his coat and brought him here. Does he be like this always?

TRASSIE: There is no harm in him.

PATS: Doesn't he know I have people to cure in other parts? You will have to give me the use of the table there.

Trassie gathers the potatoes and puts them into a bag. Peadar turns to watch. Trassie places the bag at end of kitchen. Pats Bo Bwee takes his own bag and with ceremony places it on table. He directs Neelus to sit on a chair near table. Neelus sits in a frightened way.

TRASSIE: This is Pats Bo Bwee from the Wiry Glen, Neelus. He is only trying to help you.

PATS: He has the wild eyes of his grandfather.

PEADAR: What will you do for him?

PATS (*to ceiling — pompously*): Ye will all leave the kitchen now, a-barring myself and the boy. Too many times rogues and scoundrels have stolen my cures and made fortunes for themselves.

PEADAR: What would I want with your oul' cures?

PATS: Every spailpin in the country is aching for the knowledge I contain, and when they can't have it they will have curses pouring down on the top of me . . . (*Magnanimously.*) What harm, if it will make them content? I bear no hate . . . (*Distantly, slightly reproving.*) Ye will leave now! I have an hour's work before me. This is no place for common people.

Trassie takes Peadar by the hand and leads him through the side exit. He follows grudgingly.

PATS: Hide nothing from *me*, gearrcach. *I* have seen the minds of people like you before. The priest hearing sin in his box will forgive what he's told, but Pats Bo Bwee will find out hidden things.

Pats opens his bag delicately and produces a hammer with a head of brass. The head is highly burnished, the handle delicate and of tiny circumference. Pats lays hammer on table and explores further into the bag. He produces

352

several stalks of mature ragwort and lays them on table. He produces a number of eggshells, cup-shape as if the shells were neatly divided (these would be measures for medicines). He lays several of these on the table together with a handled clay container, gallon size, which he shakes and holds to his ear. Satisfied, he places container on table and takes his brass hammer in hand. He passes in front of Neelus and takes his stand at his side. He holds the hammer behind his back and surveys Neelus professionally.

PATS: Is it women that's troubling you, or is it the stars?

Neelus looks frightened.

PATS: I think a tap of the hammer is what you want.

Ceremoniously he brings hammer to front, fondles it, and suddenly taps Neelus on the head, with some force. He leans forward eagerly.

PATS: Did you feel that? Did you feel as if someone spoke to you? (*Neelus looks at him.*) Out with it!

NEELUS (*hesitant*): I remember to hear my father talking when I was small.

PATS: Aaah! . . . You did, did you! So well you might, you mad scut! So well you might. What more?

NEELUS (*with some ray of understanding*): I remember the bed, with my mother, and to see my father shaving and to be watching him (*Neelus pauses dejectedly*), and to be playing with Trassie in the meadows (*absently, lovingly*), and Trassie taking me by the hand to school and I remember Trassie with her white dress at confirmation. Trassie was sweet.

PATS: Go on! Go on, you folbo! Tell!

Enter Peadar angrily with Trassie clutching his hand. Peadar pauses and he hears Neelus.

NEELUS (*rubs head*): I remember my father . . . to sit on his lap . . . (*wanderingly, truthfully*). To sit on his lap and be warm, secure, like the pony in the stable . . . and to watch him smoking his pipe and he looking at me, laughing. They were all outside my father's lap. They were all outside. I saw the entire lot looking in at Trassie and me and they watching my father . . . my father . . . (*loneliness, abject*) . . . My father and he lifting me up into the air . . . the strength of my father . . . (*pathetically*) . . . Dada! Dada!

Pats taps Neelus viciously with the hammer.

PATS: Dada! Dada! Is your head that empty? When your father was buried you were laughing and talking to yourself. Is your memory as short or is it going altogether?

NEELUS (*childishly — to impress Pats — tone of awe*): The rain is belting the black rocks and the white horses are rearing in the sea. Sharon is ullangoning in her grave and Shiofra is screeching in the belly of the wind.

PATS (*stands back in amazement*): Oh, Lord God in your fine house above us with angels and saints attending to You, give me patience with this fool — who is seven different kinds of a fool. Come away from your angels and saints and give ear to the words of Pats Bo Bwee and tell me not to tamper with the mind of this bollav.

PEADAR: 'Tis a terrible wrong to see a man like you dealing in life and death.

PATS (*puzzled, pompous*): Life . . . death! What does a thatcher know about these things? You know what death is, thatcher? You will know a man and you'll hear he's after being left a fortune and you will say I was talking to him an hour ago, or you will know a man (*meaningly*) and you'll hear he's after dropping dead . . . (*pause*) . . . and you'll say I was talking to him an hour ago. That is Death!

PEADAR: Leave Neelus alone!

PATS: He is to be examined, and he will be examined. No man interferes with Pats Bo Bwee.

TRASSIE (*fearfully*): It might be better to leave him alone, Peadar.

PATS (*to Neelus*): We will go up to the room and bolt the door and I will work my cures in peace.

PEADAR (*snatches hammer from Pat's hand*): You will work your cures without this.

PATS (*draws himself to full height*): I will work my cures with nothing at all. (*To Neelus.*) Up to the room!

Neelus rises and goes to room quietly, followed by Pats Bo Bwee who turns and looks at Peadar.

PATS: Minogue, from the bogholes of Glashnanaoan, put my hammer from you or your hand will waste. They say that Glashnanaoan is a hive of thieves. They say that if a man stuck out his tongue there 'twould be stolen off him by the Glashnanaoan highwaymen.

Pats Bo Bwee turns and enters the room after Neelus. Peadar throws hammer onto table in disgust.

PEADAR: Trassie, there is no meaning to having that man in the house. You know as well as I do that he is as false as a fiend. You know well that he was sent here by Dinzie Conlee and that he was paid money by Dinzie Conlee to come here.

TRASSIE: Everyone sends for Pats Bo Bwee when all fruit fails.

PEADAR: Are you so much afraid of Dinzie Conlee, Trassie?

TRASSIE: Dinzie is dangerous! Jack is bad but you could fight with Jack and you could beat him but you couldn't beat Dinzie. Not Dinzie. Nobody could get the better of Dinzie Conlee.

PEADAR: I see nothing to fear in either of the pair of them.

TRASSIE: You don't know Dinzie, Peadar. Dinzie would do for you. Do you know he carries a long knife with him in hide where no one can see it. He can be sweet, too. He'd let on to be all about you and that's the time you couldn't trust him at all.

PEADAR: I wouldn't fear him. I'd watch him.

TRASSIE: No! No! Leave Dinzie alone! You don't know him. He's mad. Oh, he's madder than anything in this world. Great God, he has no faith in anything. You couldn't trick with Dinzie. He might be doing one thing but he would still be watching all things. You'll never know what he's watching or what he's thinking.

Enter Pats Bo Bwee, triumphant, followed by a dejected Neelus.

PATS (*in a rage — throws his hands; to Neelus*): Clear . . . there's a devil in you! Clear out, you devil you! The devil is 'ating away at your mind and soul and you're clear and clane mad altogether. There is no cure for that grows in the ground. God give me a silver bed in Heaven for the patience I have with you.

Frightened, Neelus flies before Pats' fury. Pats stands in the doorway calling.

PATS: Go on! Gallop away like the mountainy jackass that you are. Gallop away from the sight and sound of godfearing people. Gallop away into the wind and the wild air where demons are dwelling and sweeping around the bare windly roads of the sky! . . . Go! . . . Go!

TRASSIE: Is something wrong? What's wrong with him? Where is he going? (*Innocently.*) Did you send him on a journey?

Dignified, Pats returns his cures to his bag, takes his stick in hand, and slings his bag over his shoulder. He stands up with great hauteur.

PATS: I will cure warts, boils, and carbuncles. I will put hair growing on a man's palm. I'll put a woman by way of having child and I'll knit broken bones (*loudly*), but I vow, I vow to you, that I will have no truck with geowckacks.

TRASSIE: Geowckacks!

PATS: Geowckacks and fostooks like that savage of a brother you have, that would take my sacred life but for that he was afraid of my brassy hammer.

PEADAR: Your brassy hammer is on the table!

Pat quickly accepts hammer and conceals same on his person.

TRASSIE (*fearfully*): Where is he? Where did you send Neelus?

PATS: Where is he, you say? . . . (*Points stick at door.*) Where is he but gone as fast as his legs will take him to the gravelly slopes of the moon.

TRASSIE: But why . . . ?

PATS (*pointing his stick upwards*): Because he's mad! . . . mad! . . . mad! (*He opens door.*) He's as mad as a flea on a hot coal. I'll have no handling of him. He's as mad as the heidle fo peeb and the heidle fo peeb is as mad as the breeze. Dinzie Conlee instructed me well. Dinzie Conlee said he was mad all along. I should have taken the advice of sensible people and stayed away from this house where a common thatcher is the master.

Exit Pats Bo Bwee with dignity, closing the door behind him. Trassie stands

355

*and begins to pour potatoes onto table from bag. She allows bag to fall on
table and withdraws dejectedly from table and sits on chair nearest her and
buries her face in her hands and is seen to be crying. Peadar stands idly, helplessly, watching her.*

SCENE 2

*The action takes place in the kitchen as before. The time is a day later. It is
evening. Trassie sits near window, patching the sleeve of an old coat. While
she is thus engaged Neelus enters. He sits on a chair near the fire, looking into
the fire, clasping and unclasping his hands despondently. Trassie peers at him
carefully.*

TRASSIE: Where is Peadar?

NEELUS: You does be kissing with him and he does be holding you. (*Trassie
   holds her breath.*) There is a storm outside, Trassie, I see the two of ye
   holding together the day of Pats Bo Bwee.

TRASSIE (*nervously*): You did not!

NEELUS: I see him with his hands around you, givin' kisses onto you.

TRASSIE: What harm is there in kissing or holding?

NEELUS (*tearfully*): I have no girl. I have only Sharon a-blow in her grave
   and she crying the whole time and Shiofra do be scolding her.

TRASSIE: That is only an old bit of gossip for aging people. Why do you be
   going down there at night like an old fool, singing to them, leaving your
   warm bed behind you? . . . The day we take the calves to town, I will
   buy you a jew's harp.

NEELUS: And . . . a red concertina with a yellow belly?

TRASSIE: I will buy that same.

NEELUS: And a fiddle and a German flute for me, too?

TRASSIE: A fiddle and a German flute for sure and certain, the day we sell the
   calves.

NEELUS (*somewhat appeased*): What else will you buy for me?

TRASSIE (*motherly tone*): Oh, I will buy you a highfiddle for the Wren's Day
   at the year end. (*Stops sewing and looks upwards.*) I will buy you a gansey colored yellow and green with white cuffs and I will buy you books
   with pictures of ships in them and black shiny shoes with buckles on.

NEELUS (*childish, serious*): Did Sharon wear black, shiny shoes, Trassie?

TRASSIE (*reproach, mild*): Sharon is part of your head, Neelus!

NEELUS: What else will you buy for me?

TRASSIE (*dreamily*): Oh . . . I will buy currant tops that you like and a
   white collar for your stripy shirt and maybe a hat for you going to Mass
   and maybe togs for bathing, and we could go down to the tide, Peadar
   and myself and yourself.

NEELUS (*shakes head in wonder*): Did Sharon have a hat to her head, Trassie? (*Looks up dreamily.*) Or was it a ribbon she wore or a comb to gather the length of her golden hair? What was it she wore, Trass?

TRASSIE: Who's to know what she wore, Neelus, since 'tis years since she was drowned. Sure, nobody would take notice of Shiofra or Sharon or how is one to know they were there at all?

NEELUS (*mysteriously, confidentially*): They were there all right, Trass. I does often hear them when you does all be in bed, Trass. (*Wonder and fright mingled.*) Well, if you heard poor lovely little Sharon and she giving sighs and sobs to the wind and her little lively tears to the tide (*then hatefully*), and that other little thing, that Shiofra, is never done with screeching back at the wind, out of temper, Trassie.

TRASSIE (*resumes her stitching*): You were very good, Neelus, at our poor Dada's funeral . . . (*pauses*) . . . the mud on his boots and the sigh of him when he bended to take them off — my father. (*Sighs.*) The stories he used to tell us. (*Smiles sadly.*) The gay stories about cats that wore waistcoats and bonhams that wouldn't eat their dinner unless they were dressed in collars and ties and the crows that used to go to their own schools the same as ours.

NEELUS (*clasping and unclasping hands*): Poor Dada . . . Poor Dada . . . Poor Dada . . . Every small bird I see on a tree or hopping, I think to myself of my poor dead Dada.

Enter Peadar Minogue by way of the front.

PEADAR (*going toward fire*): There's a desperate storm rising on all sides. (*Heats himself.*) 'Twill make a wild night. I wouldn't wish to be in a boat on the sea tonight.

TRASSIE: The clouds were flying across the sky all day — always the sign of a storm.

NEELUS: Wait until you hear the wind tonight!

PEADAR: Awful screeching like the inside of a pig's bladder if you blew it up and left it off. The goureen roe was calling for the rain in the bog far in — all evening it was on.

TRASSIE: What about the sheep?

PEADAR: I counted them all near the house. They're safe enough. They know the storm is breaking. Sheep aren't as foolish as people think.

TRASSIE (*putting coat aside — rises*): Will ye have a game of cards to pass the long evening?

PEADAR: 'Twould give us something to do. What games do ye play in Baltavinn?

TRASSIE: "Beggar Thy Neighbor" or "A Hundred and Ten." I'll get the deck in the room.

Exit Trassie.

357

NEELUS: I see you with your hands around Trassie.

PEADAR: I am very fond of her.

NEELUS: Why are you fond of her?

PEADAR: I don't know why.

NEELUS: Is she fond of you?

PEADAR: I hope so, Neelus. I think maybe she might be a little bit fond of me; I hope she is.

NEELUS (*mournfully*): I have no one that's fond of me!

PEADAR: Trassie is fond of you, man; and I'm fond of you.

NEELUS: Dinzie Conlee isn't fond of me!

Enter Trassie with pack of cards.

TRASSIE: We will play "Hundred and Ten." Neelus can deal.

They draw chairs to table. Neelus sits at the head, Trassie at center, and Peadar at bottom. Neelus deals three hands of five cards each and five to the sides. They examine their cards.

TRASSIE: We will play for pennies. I'll chance twenty.

PEADAR: I pass!

NEELUS: I'll pass too.

Neelus takes the five other cards quickly and examines them and throws them down again.

TRASSIE: 'Tis hard to beat Neelus at a hundred and ten. He has a great brain for following cards.

Neelus deals cards secondly but drops cards halfway through and sits bolt upright.

TRASSIE: What's wrong, Neelus?

Neelus does not answer but sits listening. Trassie looks, bewilderedly, at Peadar.

PEADAR: What's wrong, Neelus?

NEELUS: It's them!

PEADAR: Them! Who?

NEELUS: 'Tis Dinzie and Jack. I hear Jack's feet.

TRASSIE: Oh, merciful God! And we having such peace.

The three sit silently watching the door.

DINZIE (*shouting loudly — outside*): Come up, I say, come up! I'll sell you at the next fair and buy a donkey. 'Pon my soul, but you'll fall me!

JACK (*complains*): Ah, sure, you'll kill me, Dinzie; you'll kill me; aren't we going all day?

DINZIE (*maliciously*): Ah, come on, my little pony! Ah, come on and I'll buy a quarter stone of oats for you. Open the door now till we go in.

The door opens and Jack enters carrying Dinzie on his back. Both men wear heavy overcoats and caps.

JACK: Will I put you down, Dinzie?

DINZIE (*thumps Jack on back*): Aren't you in a great hurry with the poor oul' cripple? Set back a bit, let you, till we see what's here. Go back, pony . . . back, boy . . . back!

Dinzie forces Jack to retreat while he surveys the occupants of the kitchen.

JACK (*retreating*): Don't call me pony any more, Dinzie!

DINZIE: D'you see them, Jack? . . . Ah, Jack, will you have a look at the faces of the craturs. Wouldn't you love to be like them? (*Loudly — pompously.*) There should be no gambling allowed where there was death! 'Tis flying in the face of God. 'Tis the end of the world when people show no respect to the dead. . . . Carry me up to the fire, Jack. I'm perished with the cold. . . . (*Jack carries him to fire and faces trio.*) Ye should be ashamed of your lives — gambling and arguing and cursing over money with your father roasting below in the halls of Hell. Ye'll have no luck for it.

JACK: Will I put you down, Dinzie?

DINZIE: Will you go aisy! You're like an oul' woman, grumbling.

JACK (*wearily, first trace of anger*): Amn't I after galloping to the Wiry Glen today to see Pats Bo Bwee, and into the town of Lenamore to Macky Flynn, the motor, and amn't I after coming here on top of it? You give me no peace or ease.

DINZIE (*to trio*): Do you know at all what I'm going to do for Jack? I'm going to buy a pony's harness with bells on it for him and a reins made out of light leather and I'll make silver shoes for his feet.

Dinzie gives Jack a thump in the small of the back. Jack winces and sets Dinzie down on a chair near fire. Jack goes to corner and begins to limber up and exercise his cramped muscles. He does this exaggeratedly. Then he takes off coat and cap and helps Dinzie off with his.

DINZIE (*perched on chair*): Ye'll be ready in the morning, Trassie.

All watch him.

TRASSIE: Ready for what?

DINZIE (*vicious*): Ready to put your feet under you and leave here!

TRASSIE: Are you mad?

DINZIE: Not mad but in earnest! Today, myself and Jack walked all the ways to the town of Lenamore. We were telling the civic guards about Neelus and they said 'twould be safer to have him locked away.

TRASSIE (*rises*): What lies did you tell the civic guards?

DINZIE: I told what was true.

TRASSIE: You told lies, I know.

Peadar rises and glowers at Dinzie.

PEADAR: Better to take no notice of him, Trassie.

Dinzie fumes and thumps his chair.

DINZIE (*hysterically*): Listen to the lying tramp of a thatcher. Put me up on your back, Jack, till we kick the stomach out of him. Put me up, Jack, and we'll dance on his guts.

Jack goes to Dinzie's side. Peadar advances a step, fists clenched.

TRASSIE (*command*): Peadar! (*Peadar stops.*) Go out, to the stall and see if the cows are all right, and pacify the pony, he's afraid of storms.

Peadar looks at her doubtfully and looks at Dinzie again, clenching his fists.

PEADAR: What about *him*?

TRASSIE: Go out now, Peadar. I'll be all right. I'll call if I want you.

Peadar exits casting threatening looks at Jack and Dinzie.

DINZIE: That's right! Take the side of wandering villains that would murder you in your sleep.

Dinzie scowls at Neelus. Neelus rises, looks fearfully at Dinzie, and exits.

TRASSIE: Why do you be always putting the heart crossways in Neelus when he has never done anything to you?

DINZIE: Because he's a blasted nuisance that should be under lock and key. We were at the Wiry Glen this morning, myself and Jack. Isn't that right, Jack.

JACK: That's right, Dinzie.

DINZIE: I say we were at the Wiry Glen this morning talking to Bo Bwee and he's not feeling well, the poor man, after his visit to this house. He swore on his oath that Neelus will smother us all some night in our sleep. He swore on his oath that there's no madder omadawn of a man from here to Donegal. Isn't that right, Jack?

JACK: He said it, all right, Trassie.

TRASSIE: And how much money did you give him?

DINZIE (*mystified*): Money! What money? Give him money for what? Explain to me, Jack, what she's saying. I never gave him money. That I might be as dead as my Auntie Noney that's in her grave and my Uncle Pat that was slaughtered by the Turkeys in Salonika if I gave him money. Money for what?

TRASSIE: How much did you pay Pats Bo Bwee for saying Neelus was dangerous?

DINZIE (*puzzled*): What ails her, Jack? What ails her now? Sure she don't know what she's saying at all, Jack. God forgive her, she's getting violent. 'Tis that rat's spawn of a thatcher that has this house upset. A man told me in a publichouse in Lenamore that you couldn't be up to the Minogues —that they were the greatest tribe of pratey-snapping mongrels from Goilldearg to the salt water.

TRASSIE: Go home, Dinzie. Take him home, Jack. He has no business here.

DINZIE (*thumps chair*): That's the respect she has for her uncle's sons, her own flesh and blood, that's for her good.

TRASSIE (*firmly*): Dinzie Conlee, you're going out of this house now and you'll never come inside the door of it again. Take him up, Jack, and carry him away.

DINZIE (*thumps chair, shouts*): I will not leave here! I will never leave here! My place is here! I want a little woman of my own to marry here! No one will have me if I haven't a house and land. What would you do if you had this millstone of mine on your back? What would you do if you had only dead branches of legs? What would you do if you were never to feel the grassy ground under your feet or never to vault a gate or a ditch and you passing through land? What would you do when the fiddles are tuning up for the sets and everyone tapping toes on the stone floor? What would you do when the lads are kicking ball and you have wild feeling to draw a kick for devilment? What would you do?

TRASSIE: 'Tis hard for you, I know, but it is no fault of mine. Go away from here — home!

DINZIE (*bitterly*): Aisy for you and for Jack here with your legs firm and strong and your straight backs. (*Shrieks.*) I have nothing at all to show for myself. I have twists and turns to my body like a mountainy stream. (*Roars.*) I'm no fool! Dinzie Conlee's no fool. I know my value but if I have this place I will have plenty single women thinking of settling with me. (*Pleading.*) Will you condemn me for that, Trassie? . . . for thinking the way I do? (*Pause.*) Everybody knows you yourself would have no trouble latching a man to you and I swear to God I will give you what few pounds I have to add to your fortune if you let me have this house (*pause*) . . . and a bit o' land . . . (*pause*) . . . and the few cows . . . and the pony. (*Placatingly.*) Won't we go visiting Neelus in his fine tall home when we get the fine day . . . and the roads dry?

TRASSIE (*sincerely*): 'Tis a pity for you, but . . . I have doubts about you — the way you made plans for Neelus as if he was mad.

DINZIE (*reverting to old, demoniacal self*): He is mad, I tell you! He's stone mad!

TRASSIE: How do you know but maybe 'tis yourself that's mad?

DINZIE (*thumps chair*): In what way would I be mad when I'm as sane as a man of ninety? Sure, you never heard anyone saying that I was mad?

TRASSIE: They'd be afraid to say it — afraid of yourself and Jack.

DINZIE: D'you hear that, Jack? Good almighty God, Jack, I say, did you hear that? I say, Jack, that's the last of all!

TRASSIE: You have some spatter of sense, Jack; take him away with you now.

JACK: Ah, faith, I will not take him away. 'Twould be a great aise to me to see him settled here. Sure, hasn't he my back nearly broken? Sure, aren't there hollows in my shoulders from his hands and my ribs are black and blue from the pucking he gives me?

DINZIE: Hush, Jack! Hush, pony!

361

JACK: Don't be calling me pony, Dinzie! The young lads going the road to school does be saying "Hup!" to me now and . . . (*clicks his tongue several times*), "Go on there, horsey!" 'Tis not fair, Dinzie.

DINZIE: Ah, sure, don't I only be coddin' you, Jack? Sure I wouldn't say a word to my own little pony. Sure, wouldn't I lick the ground under your feet, man dear, I'm so fond of you?

JACK: You have a quare way of showing it.

DINZIE: Be ready in the morning now, Trassie. Be ready with your coats and dresses and hats, and we will have the motor here in the daytime for Neelus. 'Twill be a happy day for him.

TRASSIE (*in real anger*): Get out of here, you demon!

DINZIE (*loudly*): I won't go home! I won't! There's nothing at home for me, God help us! Nothing but an empty bed and a corner out of the way. I'll be master here, with my own woman pampering me.

TRASSIE: I'll bring the gun down out of the room to you.

DINZIE: Bring what you like. Nothing will move me out of this seat. My place is here!

TRASSIE: I will call Peadar.

DINZIE (*shocked*): Ooooh . . . Ooooooh! . . . You will call in Peader! Did you ever see a paper bag blown up, full of wind. (*Puffs out his cheeks to show, then claps his hands violently.*) Jack will crack in his head like that and send his brains squirting all over the ceiling. (*Draws a large clasp knife from his pocket and displays blade.*) I'll rip him open with this, the same as you'd open a sheep's belly. Bring her over to me, Jack. Bring her over and when she'll be done with me, I promise you she'll be anxious to do what I say.

JACK: Ah, Dinzie, poor oul' Trassie is only a girl. Sure she'll go all right. Say you'll go, Trassie. Tell him you'll go an' he'll be quiet then. There's no knowledge what plan he'll think of if you don't give in to him.

TRASSIE: I will not give in to him. Why would I? This is my place and Neelus's place and nobody, not even Dinzie Conlee, will ever put us away from what's our own.

DINZIE (*loudly*): Ketch her, Jack, and bring her over to me.

JACK: Ah, Dinzie, don't ask me!

TRASSIE (*nervously*): Pay no heed to him, Jack. Don't be said by him, Jack. He'll get you in jail again, Jack, and this time they won't leave you out in a hurry.

DINZIE (*slowly, throatily, tightening his grip upon the knife*): Ketch her, Jack, and bring her over to me, till I get a grip of her. I say, Jack, to ketch her!

JACK (*afraid*): Ah, Dinzie . . .

DINZIE (*slowly*): "Don't mind Dinzie," she says. "Don't mind your own

362

brother." (*Hopelessly, in a wonderfully plausible vein.*) O holy, holy saints, Jack, she's putting mountains between us; mountains between us, boy. 'Tis a terrible sight to see a person coming between two borned brothers or does she know what she's saying at all, Jack? Does she know the trouble our mother had rearing us?

TRASSIE (*determinedly*): Stop your prattle. Stop trying to work Jack's will and all our wills and clear away out of here.

DINZIE (*sincerely*): For the last time, Jack, I'll ask you to ketch her by the hair of the head and bring her over to where I am.

JACK (*sincerely*): You don't mean it, Dinzie!

DINZIE (*fiercely*): I'll lob this knife between the breasts of her and stick her like a pig if you don't ketch her, Jack. You'll see the blade of this buried in her, and the handle standing out from her bosom like a paling stock in the depth of a hollow. (*Slowly.*)

JACK (*turns directly toward Trassie*): I'll have to ketch you, Trassie . . . (*Trassie eludes him.*) Stand aisy, Trassie!

DINZIE: Blast you, you oul' fool, make a drive at her and pull her hether.

JACK (*confident*): I'll ketch her!

Jack makes another advance toward Trassie but again she eludes him and succeeds in opening door and calling loudly.

TRASSIE: Neelus! . . . Neelus! (*Then quickly.*) Peadar! . . . Peadar!

As Jack advances toward door she suddenly avoids him by availing of table and they watch each other dartingly.

DINZIE (*excited*): Jump over the table at her and you have her.

JACK (*calmly*): She might only run from me again. Man, dear, if only I was quick on the feet I had her caught long ago. Wait, let you, and she can't escape us!

Jack outstretches both hands as if he were heading geese and tries to get Trassie into corner.

JACK: Cush! Cush!

Jack warily advances at one side of table. Trassie immediately avails of the other side.

DINZIE: Pull the table out of your way and you have her.

Jack lifts table and drops it suddenly to face Peadar Minogue who has entered quickly, through open door.

DINZIE (*yelling*): Aha, the thatcher is landed. (*Dramatic pause.*) Now Jack! Up on him, Jack! Rear up on him and we'll settle him for once and for all! (*Roar of encouragement.*) Rip, him, Jack. Tear him! Stick him! Go on, Jack!

Dinzie settles back on his chair to watch the fight. Jack draws himself up to his full height and uplifts clenched fists as a fighter will. Peadar advances immediately to Trassie and surveys her worriedly.

TRASSIE (*standing nearer to Peadar*): They were trying to catch me. He wants to hunt Neelus and myself out of the house.

PEADAR (*determinedly*): Well, they'll never do that while I'm here, Trassie.

DINZIE: Are you going to listen to Minogue the thatcher, Jack? Minogue the robber from Glashnanaoan. We heard all about you, Minogue, and the thieving breeding that's in you.

PEADAR (*menace*): There is no bad breeding in the Minogues. Three hundred years they farmed in Glashnanaoan and never a mean or cowardly act against them; never a poor man turned away from the door; never a neighbor in want of help; never a bad word thrown out against any man.

DINZIE: Your breeding is bad! Didn't you know that a foxy-haired tinker from Tipperary was the first Minogue to come to Glashnanaoan? Didn't you know that he gattled a loose woman under the blind eye of Glashnanaoan Bridge and that's how you came by your breeding?

PEADAR: It's a roaring lie! (*Anger.*) It's a holy lie, you humpbacked ferret from hell. If you were a full man, I'd break every lying bone in your body.

DINZIE (*thumps chair with fury*): Will you listen to him, Jack? Do you hear him? Attack him! Attack him, I say! Attack and trample the life out of him. At him, Jack.

JACK (*assuming fighting stance*): Come, on, boy!

PEADAR (*clenches his fists and looks calmly at Jack*): I never sought after fighting but I'll fight you and beat you if that's the way of it.

DINZIE: Go on, Jack! Give him the boot!

Jack dances around Peadar, who looks at him calmly.

PEADAR: We won't fight in here. We'll fight outside in the open.

DINZIE (*fingering knife*): Fight him here, you coward. Fight him here!

PEADAR: I'm no coward.

DINZIE: Fight him so!

PEADAR: And have a knife between my shoulders when my back is turned to you? Give the knife to Trassie and I'll fight him here.

DINZIE: And have her stick Jack and maybe myself, a poor oul' cripple.

PEADAR: Trassie wouldn't stick anybody.

TRASSIE: I'll stick him if he harms you, Peadar!

PEADAR (*to Jack*): Out here, if you're a man. (*Indicates door.*)

JACK (*fists up*): I'm not in dread of you, boy. I'm not in dread of you.

DINZIE (*impatiently*): Give him one, Jack, I tell you! Draw one kick at him, into the stomach, and you'll do for him.

Suddenly Jack draws a kick at Peadar but Peadar avoids it and walks toward door. He turns to Jack with upraised finger.

PEADAR: Out here, you awkward fostook, and I'll show you how to fight. (*Peadar exits.*)

DINZIE: After him, Jack. Give it to him hot and heavy, Jack boy. Put stones into your fists.

JACK: I'll bate him fair, Dinzie. He won't stand for long against Jack Conlee. I was never bested yet.

Jack struts out.

DINZIE: Jack will tear him to ribbons with his bare hands. We'll settle for you then.

TRASSIE: He'll never beat Peadar Minogue. Peadar would beat two men.

DINZIE: The Conlees were never beat. If he beats Jack I'll give him this where 'twill sink. (*Raises knife.*) I'll fool him.

TRASSIE (*advancing near Dinzie*): Would you ever think of being fair for once in your life? Have you no bit of goodness at all in you or is there nothing inside of you but evil and sin?

DINZIE (*violently*): Shut up! . . . Shut up, I say, or I'll bury this in you . . .

TRASSIE: I'm not afraid of you! I'll warn Peadar and he'll take the knife from you. 'Tis you they'll be taking away to the Home then and not Neelus. You should be in the madhouse years ago. I never in all my life saw anything as mad as you. You're the maddest little man in the whole of Ireland. Even the maddest of the birds and the beasts aren't half as mad as you.

DINZIE (*erupts, thumps chair, screams*): Shut up, I say! Shut up, or I'll dig my knife into you.

TRASSIE: You know 'tis the truth for me. You're a demon, a dirty sly demon and the mind is gone out of your head and there's nothing inside but sparks and flashes and frightful explosions and 'tis pity people should have for you and not fear.

DINZIE (*upraises his hands*): Stop! Stop! Stop! . . . I'll kill you if you don't stop! I'll kill you for sure if you won't stop!

Dinzie swings knife wildly at Trassie. He falls from chair to floor but comes to balance quickly and sits on floor. Trassie flees into corner.

DINZIE (*maliciously*): Come here to me! Come here, I say!

Trassie cowers in corner. Slowly Dinzie edges nearer — ludicrously.

TRASSIE: Keep away from me! (*Calls.*) Peadar! Peadar! Peadar!

DINZIE: He's getting his due from Jack! No one to help you now, my doxie. No one to save you now. Come here to me. Come here, I say. (*Edges closer.*)

TRASSIE (*in terror*): Don't come near me! Don't come near me!

DINZIE (*in triumph*): I'll give you something that'll put you screeching properly . . . something that'll do your heart good.

TRASSIE (*cornered, looks about her hopelessly*): Oh, holy God, help me. (*Calls loudly.*) Neelus! . . . Neelus! . . . Neelus! . . . Help me, someone!

DINZIE: I'll help you when I get my hands on you!

TRASSIE (*kicks as Dinzie tries to catch her by leg*): Go away from me!
Enter Neelus.

TRASSIE: Oh, thank God, Neelus. Thank God you're here!

NEELUS (*simply, without surprise of any kind*): What's Dinzie Conlee doing down on the floor, Trassie?
Dinzie slowly turns to look at Neelus for an instant, and turns to Trassie again.

TRASSIE: He's trying to cut me with his knife, Neelus. Don't let him, Neelus.

NEELUS (*advances, puzzled*): What's Peadar Minogue fighting with my cousin Jack for? You never saw such a fight, Trassie!

TRASSIE (*wearily*): Will you take the knife from Dinzie here. He has nothing in his head but killing people.
Neelus advances and looks down at Dinzie.

NEELUS: You can't kill Trassie!

DINZIE (*puzzled*): Kill Trassie? Who said anything about killing Trassie? A bit of sport I was having. What would make me kill my own dear cousin?

TRASSIE: Don't you believe him, Neelus. He's only fooling you. He wants to put you into the Home, Neelus, and he wants to hunt you away from me forever. You'll never be free again, Neelus.

NEELUS (*puzzled*): Do you want to put me into a Home, Dinzie?

DINZIE (*outraged*): Oh, good God almighty, them are the lies she's telling you. Sure, don't you know well I wouldn't put you into a Home, Neelus. I never heard such a story. Put me up on your back, Neelus. God bless you, boy bawn, sure if I had my way 'tis around with a circus I'd send you every day of the week where you could be watching clowns and ponies as small as greyhounds. Put me up now on your back, Neelus.

TRASSIE: Don't do it Neelus. He'll kill us all.

DINZIE (*coaxing*): Ah, Neelus, sure I wouldn't put a finger on one of my little cousins, if I got the use of my legs back again even. Amn't I mad about ye altogether? Yesterday week it was, I think, I said to Jack: Jack, says I, we must buy a pipe and tobacco for Neelus and train him how to smoke.

TRASSIE: Neelus, if you listen to him, he'll hunt you into the madhouse.

NEELUS (*looks for a long time at Trassie, then at Dinzie, then at ceiling*): Would you promise me you wouldn't stick Trassie, Dinzie, if I put you up on my back?

DINZIE: Oh! . . . I swear by all that's dead and buried belonging to me, I wouldn't do that!

TRASSIE (*hopelessly*): Oh! don't listen to his lying tongue, my poor Neelus.

NEELUS: I'll put you up so, Dinzie, if you promise.
Neelus goes on all fours on floor, Trassie runs out from corner and stands

with table between herself and Dinzie. Dinzie manages to get on Neelus's back. Neelus stands holding Dinzie tightly about his neck.

DINZIE: Get a good grip on me, Neelus boy. Get a good grip I say and we'll have sport in plenty. 'Pon my soul and conscience but you're every bit as good a pony as my brother Jack.

NEELUS: I'll give you a good gallop.

DINZIE: How? . . . Whah? . . . A good gallop? . . . Put me down, you thunderin' pothead! . . . Put me down, I say!

Suddenly Neelus twists Dinzie's hand with knife in it and knife falls. Dinzie struggles but his legs are dead and Neelus's grip is too strong to break with his hands.

DINZIE: Put me down, I say! (*Screeches.*) Put me down! Put me down! (*Agony.*) Oh, great God, take me off the back of this persecuted oma-dawn!

TRASSIE: Where will you take him, Neelus?

NEELUS: I'll take him for the finest gallop he ever had.

DINZIE (*prolonged wail*): Oooh! . . . Ooooooh! . . . God, take me off his back! (*Wheedling.*) Put me down, Neelus, and I'll give you a lovely gold watch I have under the mattress at home. I'll give you fifty golden sovereigns I have in hiding and I'll get a handsome girl out from Lena-more to marry you if you'll put me down.

NEELUS (*casual, vacant*): Sure I can't, Dinzie!

DINZIE (*threat*): Put me down!

NEELUS (*earnest vacancy, shakes head*): Japers, Dinzie, sure I'd put you down if I could but I can't.

TRASSIE (*firmly*): Don't put him down, Neelus. (*Pleading.*) But don't harm yourself for my sake, Neelus.

NEELUS (*shakes his head, casually, as he moves to the door*): Sharon is wait-ing for me, Trassie, and Shiofra is waiting for Dinzie.

DINZIE (*appalled*): Shiofra . . . Sharon . . . He's in the power of the devil. (*Appeals pitifully to Trassie. Screaming, struggles.*) Put me down to the ground, you madman. Put me down or I'll get Jack to kill you. Oh Lord God, put me down!

TRASSIE: Listen to me, Neelus! Listen to me! (*Helplessly.*) Oh, dear God, my poor Neelus!

Neelus goes toward door, carrying Dinzie.

DINZIE (*high-pitched, terrified*): He's going to kill me in the lonely seas . . . in the black hole . . . I'll be dead . . . (*Screams.*) Put me down! . . . I'll kill you! . . . Kill you . . . Kill you . . . !

Trassie stands motionless with horror.

DINZIE: Oh, sweet God, he'll drown me!

Neelus pulls Dinzie higher on his back and exits furiously. Trassie runs to door calling.

TRASSIE (*tearfully*): Oh, my poor foolish Neelus, come back! Come back, Neelus! (*She extends her hands.*) Neelus, come back to your *own* Trassie . . . Neelus . . . Neelus . . . come back . . .

Trassie turns, hands covering face. Enter Peadar, hair tossed, clothes disordered, pushing a badly beaten cowed Jack Conlee before him. Jack's face is blood-smeared and badly bruised. Peadar dashes him to one side, into a chair, where Jack sits, head hanging stupidly, fingers feeling wounds.

PEADAR (*as he pushes Jack aside*): There's one man be't! Where's the other fellow? Where's Dinzie?

TRASSIE: Oh, Peadar! . . . Peadar! . . . quick! It's Neelus . . . It's Neelus and Dinzie . . . !

PEADAR (*takes her hands in his*): Easy, Trassie, girl! . . . Easy! . . . Easy! . . . Tell me what's wrong? Take control of yourself.

TRASSIE: Oh, Peadar . . . (*Sobs.*) . . . Neelus ran away with Dinzie up on his back . . . (*Sobs.*) . . . Hurry, Peadar! Hurry, Peadar! Go after them!

Peadar exits. Jack rises stupidly and lurches toward door.

JACK: The thatcher be't me but he'll never beat Dinzie. (*As he lurches out the door he passes Peadar coming back in.*) You'll never beat Dinzie.

PEADAR: Neelus has beaten him this time. (*Pauses, then helplessly to Trassie.*) He took one mighty bound like a deer and the two of them disappeared into Sharon's Grave. Poor Neelus was doing his last service to us. The poor, innocent fellow, helping the only way he knew how.

Trassie shakes with tears. Peadar places his arm about her shoulders.

PEADAR: I will look after you, Trassie. I will stay here with you always and I'll mind you. Neelus did not know what he was doing. It was to happen the way it happened. Neelus is with his own now, in the hands of God. Don't cry now, Trassie. That is the way it was cut out for us. I'm here with you forever, Trass . . .

Trassie looks up at Peadar tenderly. Peadar takes her hand in his. She sobs and he takes her in his arms. Enter Pats Bo Bwee agitated and excited, dressed and equipped as before.

PATS BO BWEE (*delight*): We're free! We're free at last from Dinzie Conlee. Did you see the way he took him? Did you see the way Neelus ruz like a bird with him?

Peadar edges away a little from Trassie.

PATS BO BWEE: 'Twas always in Neelus's head to do what he did. He has his eternal reward by now. 'Tis a great thing to be free of Dinzie Conlee.

PEADAR (*anger*): You were as much at fault as any that Neelus is dead.

PATS BO BWEE (*palm upraised, measuring Peadar carefully*): There was no other way out of it . . . (*Conciliatory*.) You'll settle here and you'll be wanted here. There's fresh blood wanted in here sore.

PEADAR: You're a born rogue!

PATS: Mustn't we all live? What have I but the one yella cow? I couldn't be raising my hand ag'in my betters.

PEADAR: Get out of here!

PATS (*minor warning*): Ye might want me yet.

PEADAR: We'll manage well without you.

PATS (*head cocked aside*): Will ye though? Will ye for sure? Ye'll marry now, won't ye? Ye'll marry now and think to bring a big litter o' children into the world. Ye're well-blossomed the two of ye. Maybe a little too well-blossomed for children. Ye're far advanced beyond your prime.

PEADAR: We'll manage.

TRASSIE (*touches Peadar's arm*): Peadar . . .

PEADAR (*indignant*): Who's he to talk? A short while ago he was dead set against us. Anyway what counsel could he give that never had a child of his own?

PATS (*knowingly*): Ooooh! . . . Who's to tell? . . . No papers to show, maybe, but they're there! (*Conspiratorially*.) Ye'll want me, maybe, when ye find the days going past with no child to keep ye awake at night.

PEADAR: We'll manage.

TRASSIE: We're not getting younger, Peadar.

She links his hand. Peadar looks at her tenderly. Pats Bo Bwee seizes his chance.

PATS: After ye're wedded, wait for a news of a sickle moon in the sky. Ye must have the same soft will to ye for love. (*To Peadar*.) She must have a two o' wet lips and all of a softness to her. Go with her out of her warm bed at the first light of a day. Let ye be fond companions in the new light. Put you something woollen around her from airly cold. Lie her down on dewy ground with the soft wool to warm her. Face her then to the first foot's fall of a flowing tide and then let ye throw all thoughts of worries and woes away from ye. There must be a tide and ye must face the tide, a young silver tide with giddy antics. (*Turns to go*.) And I'll be calling within the space of a year maybe to cure a blockin' of wind in a young thing or to give advice about nursin'. (*Exiting, hand raised*.) The blessing of God attend ye. (*Exits*.)

Many Young Men of Twenty

PEG FINNERTY, a waitress in a village pub

DANGER MULALLY, a seller of holy pictures

TOM HANNIGAN, a publican

SEELIE HANNIGAN, his sister

MAURICE BROWNE, a village schoolteacher

DAWHEEN TIMMINEEN DIN, a mountainy farmer

MAYNAN, his wife

KEVIN, his son

DINNY, his son

MICKY, his son

MARY, his daughter

KITTY CURLEY, a fortuneteller

DOT, Dinny's Cockney wife

J. J. HOULIHAN, T.D., a member of the Irish parliament

JOHNNY, his son

ALOYSIUS, an early drinker

A MELODEON PLAYER

Act I

The action takes place in the back room of a village publichouse somewhere in southern Ireland. There are appropriate advertisements hanging from the walls. Two tables occupy the room, one large and one small. There are several chairs and a bench. A man and a woman sit at the larger table, a girl in her early twenties at the smaller one. They are completing breakfast, backs to each other. The man is Tom Hannigan. The woman is his sister Seelie. The girl is Peg Finnerty. Tom Hannigan is coatless, smoking a cigarette. He is fortyish. Seelie is slightly older and outwardly composed. Peg Finnerty is young, pretty, and dressed poorly. The time is the morning of a summer's day in the present.

SEELIE (*precise, correct*): What time is it?

TOM (*alerted*): Almost half-ten; nearly time to open.

SEELIE: Yes; there should be a few going to England.

TOM: Ah, well . . . (*Rises.*) . . . I'll open the front door. We should have a few before the train.

Tom opens front door. A tattered but respectable figure stands outside.

TOM: Oh, it's you, Aloysius. First to the door as always. The usual, I suppose?

Aloysius nods and sits.

SEELIE (*rising*): You brush and tidy up here, Peg. I'll take the ware to the back kitchen.

Seelie finds a basin under table and proceeds to fill it with the breakfast things. Peg rises and exits to left, briefly, returning with brush.

SEELIE: Watch what he's doing!

PEG: Who?

SEELIE: Who do you think . . . ?

PEG: I'll watch him.

Peg commences to brush floor toward fireplace at right.

SEELIE: You'll get a cloth, Peg, and shine the place up a bit and . . . (*meaningly*) you remember what I told you about himself . . . if you see him nippin' at the bottles, be sure and tell me.

PEG: Yes, Miss Seelie!

Exit Seelie by door near fireplace. Peg continues with her brushing and commences to sing.

PEG (*singing*):

> Many young men of twenty said goodbye,
> All that long day,
> From break of dawn until the sun was high.
> Many young men of twenty said goodbye.
> My boy Jimmy went that day
> On the big ship sailed away,
> Sailed away and left me here to die
> Many young men of twenty said goodbye.

Peg continues to hum the air. Tom enters cautiously.

TOM: Is she gone?

PEG: She's probably washin' the ware. She told me to keep an eye on you.

TOM: Good! (*He exits hastily.*)

PEG (*singing*):

> My Jimmy said he'd sail across the sea,
> He swore his oath
> He'd sail again, back home to marry me.
> My Jimmy said he'd sail across the sea
> But my Jimmy left me down.
> O, my Jimmy, please come back to me!
> O, my Jimmy, please come back to me!

Peg sings the song again. Tom enters, head craned forward first, hands be-

Many Young Men of Twenty

Mikey Houlihan

Black Puddin' Song

hind back. He walks toward fireplace and produces a tumbler of whiskey from behind his back.

TOM (*to Peg*): You won't say a word about this?

PEG: No!

TOM (*surveys whiskey*): 'Twas never needed more, Peg! (*Swallows whiskey — sighs contentedly.*) Ah, good God, there's a great rattle in that!

Tom shakes his shoulders. Enter Seelie suddenly. Tom just manages to get the glass into his trousers pocket.

SEELIE: Why aren't you in the bar?

TOM (*a little flustered*): Checkin' up! Just checkin' up!

SEELIE: Come here at once! (*Tom goes toward her.*) Come on, puff!

Tom extends his head and blows his breath onto her face. Immediately she slaps his face. She turns to Peg.

SEELIE: You . . . You . . . Don't you know what he's doin' to himself? I thought I told you to tell me? I should have known what to expect from you . . . a tramp!

TOM: Peg knew nothing about it. She didn't see me.

SEELIE: Taking sides against me! . . . Listen to me, Tom Hannigan. If you touch another drop of that bottle today, you can be ready to leave here . . . and I mean it, this time! (*Rousing herself.*) How long do you think I'm going to take it from you? Every night when you go to bed, you're drunk . . . stupid drunk. You think I don't hear you staggerin' against the sides of the stairs and missin' every other step?

TOM: 'Twas only a little drop to cure myself after the night. I'd a shake in my hand.

SEELIE: It's the same every morning. I'm not taking any more of it, Tom, and I'm not warnin' you any more either. (*She exits.*)

TOM: A wonderful start to the day. (*Takes the glass from his pocket.*) She knocked all the enjoyment out of it. How do you stick it here at all, Peg? Why don't you pack your traps and hit away for England?

PEG: I can't go.

TOM: If 'tis the money, Peg . . . I have some. I often thought to make a break of it myself, but sure she'd have no one to give out to if I went.

PEG: She's your sister, Tom. She doesn't like me. I'm only the servant girl here. All she has is you, Tom.

TOM: Forget about her! Do you want money?

PEG: 'Tisn't the money. Sure I couldn't go without the little fellow.

TOM: He'll be all right with your father and mother. You'll never do any good for yourself here. I see you there often, Peg, when lads walk into the bar outside, especially them travelers with motorcars, an' they all tryin' to get off with you . . .

From without the door on the wall facing audience, from a distance, can be heard the voice of a man singing. Aloysius rises and departs at the sound.

VOICE (*singing*):

> Oh, rise up, Mikey Houlihan, 'tis you're the dauntless man,
> When Ireland, she was in her woe, you was always in the van.
> Near to the town of Keelty, you were murdered in July;
> God rest you, Mikey Houlihan, the darlin' Irish boy.

PEG (*in the middle of the singing*): That's Danger Mullaly comin'!

TOM: With a sick head as usual, an' short fourpence for the price of a pint.

Enter Danger Mullaly. He is fiftyish, tattered, curious. His accent is semi-detached and varied and stentorian. He carries a timber box, painted red, in his hand. The box is a foot square and about three inches high. He enters by door on wall facing audience.

DANGER (*to no one in particular*): "Oh, rise up, Mikey Houlihan, that brave and dauntless boy . . ." Mikey Houlihan! Mikey boloney! Shot by accident for Ireland. Twenty-four of his relations drawing state pensions and twenty-four more in government jobs, and here am I, Danger Mullaly, with my box full of holy pictures an' short fourpence on the price o' the pint. (*Changes tone to intimacy.*) 'Tis frightful quiet, Peg Finnerty, for a mornin' before the train. 'Tis frightful quiet, Tom Hannigan. (*Puts his box on the table.*) That's the lookin' they have at me! You'd swear I was the solicitor that advised Pontius Pilate . . . (*Changes tone.*) Tom Hannigan, as sure as there's brown bastards in China, I'll pay you the extra fourpence . . . here's a shillin' on the table, a silver shillin', made an' manufactured by tradesmen that had a feelin' for beauty . . . proposed, passed, and seconded herewith . . . one pint of Guinness for a sick man . . . balance to be paid in due course on the word of Danger Mullaly, guilty but insane . . . (*Pause.*) . . . Guinness, a portermaker that had his face on a stamp the same as Parnell.

TOM: What'll we do with him, Peg?

PEG (*now dusting about room*): I'm not speakin' to him! Don't ask me!

TOM: It's lookin' bad, Danger!

DANGER (*dignity*): Peg Finnerty, I know you love me . . . so does many a young girl in this locality and away unto parts west. I can't marry ye all an' besides I had a letter yesterday from a doctor's daughter in Knocknagoshel that she might have an heir for the throne.

PEG (*laughing*): Give him the pint, Tom!

Exit Tom, shaking head. Danger sits, dignified, on chair. Peg continues to sing, pausing from her dusting when she reaches the line: "I knew I bore . . ." then she goes on.

PEG (*singing*):

> The dawn was fledged upon the mountain's rim
> The day he went.
> I knew I bore the livin' child of him;
> I knew I bore the livin' child of him;
> And the child was born to me.
> Jimmy's gone across the sea,
> The dawn is dead upon the mountain's rim.
> Here I wait for word of my love, Jim.

DANGER: Why do you be always singin' that oul' song? Where did you pick it up, anyway?

PEG (*absently*): The song suits me! Did you know I was called to a training college for teachers once, years ago? My father an' mother couldn't imagine that their daughter might be a teacher, an' they couldn't pay.

DANGER: Oh . . . so that's it! . . . because you had a bit o' misfortune, you're goin' to be chantin' like an ordained parish clerk for the rest of your life? (*Loudly.*) You had a baby . . . sure, you're not the first an' you won't be the last. What about it? You've a figure for fun an' frolickin', an' you're as handsome as ever stood or l'id. 'Tis hardly a monkey you'd have! Who in the parish o' Keelty is better designed an' molded for such things? Divil the one! Sure, there's no children at all be born here, only divils that carry stories an' the twins of spite an' bitterness, an' do you know who their fathers an' mothers are? You don't! . . . I'll tell you, Peg Finnerty. Mr. Jealous and Missus Ignorance, an' you're grumblin' with a fine bonny boy with limbs as supple as a cat an' a grin on his dial like a drake in the rain . . . (*Triumphant.*) Didn't you give birth?

PEG (*impulsively touches his arm*): Oh, you're a treasure, Danger! You always cheer me up! God bless you! (*Change.*) But I know you're lookin' for a pint and that you'd rise me up to the moon if you thought I'd stand one. My hard-bought experience says blow, blow, Danger!

DANGER (*jumps up, in false pride*): My one boast is that I'm the greatest liar an' the biggest sinner in the parish o' Keelty an' now you're tryin' to deprive me o' my natural rights by tellin' me that I'm a treasure.

Enter Tom with a pint of Guinness which he places on table. Danger surveys the pint from various angles.

DANGER: A very knowledgeable man, the man that filled that; a man that knows his oats. A very . . . very . . . (*Sings.*)

> Oh, rise up, Mikey Houlihan, the brave and dauntless man,
> For when you ate black puddings, sure you used no fryingpan.
> You fought for Ireland's glory, and there's no one can deny
> You filled up English factories with many an Irish boy.

Seizes pint and quaffs most of it, grins and relaxes.

I see a pony-load of mountainy cawbogues untacklin' in the yard when I was comin' in.

TOM: I suppose a few lads hittin' for England . . . Did you know 'em?

DANGER: I have no truck with that mountainy crew. They'd sell the britchin' o' Saint Joseph's ass.

TOM: I wonder who from the mountains is goin' across the water tonight?

PEG: Don't ask me! I'm in the other side o' Keelty.

Danger sups pint, replaces same, and surveys its diminishing content.

DANGER: Here they are now!

Door on wall facing audience opens and a procession of four enters: No. 1 is Dawheen Timmineen Din. No. 2 is his wife Maynan. No. 3 is his son Kevin. No. 4 is his son Dinny. Dinny and Kevin carry a heavy suitcase each. Dawheen Timmineen Din is a weary, crafty man of sixty with cap pulled down over shrewd eyes. Dressed in country fashion, he wears a gansey zipped to throat and carries a whip and trap cushions in his hand. He places these in the corner while the trio wait behind him.

D.T.D. (*to Tom — slow, tough speech, ingratiating yet domineering*): Would there be any chance you'd get some one to throw a quarter stone of oats to the pony?

PEG: I'll do it!

Peg exits. D.T.D. with a motion of his hand orders his people to occupy kitchen.

TOM: Sit down, let ye! Are the two lads for England? (*D.T.D. sits.*) You're Dawheen Timmineen Dinny, aren't you?

D.T.D. (*occupying seat — nasally*): That's right!

His wife Maynan wears shawl over blouse and skirt. She sits near her husband. Kevin and Dinny wear new suits. They deposit their suitcases out of the way and sit together awkwardly. Kevin is the older and taller. Dinny seems to lean toward Kevin for protection. They would be about twenty-five and eighteen.

TOM: What will I be gettin' for ye?

D.T.D.: Is your clock right?

TOM: Right by the church clock.

D.T.D.: What time is it now?

TOM (*looks through left door into bar*): Ten to eleven.

D.T.D.: What would that leave us for the train?

TOM: A half an hour with a few minutes to spare.

D.T.D. (*nudges wife*): What'll you sample?

MAYNAN: Have they port wine?

D.T.D.: Give us a port wine, a whiskey for myself and give the boys two bottles o' minerals.

KEVIN: Give me a pint o' stout . . . D'you want one, Dinny?

Dinny looks anxiously at his father.

376

D.T.D.: A half whiskey, a half o' port wine (*viciously*), a pint and a bottle o' minerals. (*Singing.*)

> When you go to London town, work like Maggie May,
> Like Mikey Joe, send home the dough
> Let no week pass without your father's fiver.
> Rise at first light, stay home at night,
> And never ate black puddings of a Friday.

KEVIN AND DINNY (*singing*):

> We'll do all the things you say:
> We'll work day and night.
> On each payday we'll kneel and pray,
> And send our poor old father home his fiver.
> And we declare, we hereby swear
> We'll never ate black puddin's of a Friday.

Tom, exiting, repeats order to himself. Danger husbands his pint and surveys newcomers arrogantly.

D.T.D. (*addressing his sons*): Ye know what's before ye over there. 'Twill be a great change for well-reared foolish young country lads. Ye'll see doxies with dyed heads cockin' their dresses high in the air, an' exposin' fair amounts o' thigh to entice the innocent young gorsoons; trickers an' twisters of all sorts persuadin' you the sun was the moon; whiskery looberas with silvery tongues speechmakin' from timber boxes . . .

MAYNAN: An' eatin' black puddin's on a Friday!

D.T.D.: Ye'll hear thunderin' black-hearted buckos at every street corner in the city o' London callin' God away from His sky, an' threatenin' people with the end o' the world.

MAYNAN: There's a frightful test before ye. Keep to yeerselves an' to your brothers an' sisters over. Call every stranger ye meet sir an' look as foolish as ye can, an' praises in all be to the Holy Mother o' God, ye'll be a credit to your father an' mother.

DANGER (*advances with his red box*): Will ye buy a picture of the sacred heart, threepence the piece, to be hung up, with a thumbtack thrown in. I sold four already this mornin' to four beautiful girls goin' over workin' in factories. (*He is ignored.*) Have I some class of a disease, or are ye gone deaf? (*Turns to Kevin and Dinny.*) What about the two of ye? Ye'll be wantin' a sacred heart to pin up over the bed when ye go across.

D.T.D.: 'Tis little enough money them two has!

DANGER (*piously, sanctimoniously, to ceiling*): O, Holy High Heaven! (*Latinish twist.*) O, Sanctimonii Gazulio! (*As if he were addressing a judge.*) How many sons is he sending to England today? . . . (*Counts.*) . . . One! . . . Two . . . (*To himself.*) Two! . . . How many has he there before? . . . Approximately seven with daughters included. A wise investment. (*To the two boys.*) Did he tell ye to send home a pound or two every week to your poor father and mother? Did he tell ye not to forget the starvin' couple at home, rearin' what's left of ye? (*Kevin and Dinny exchange glances.*) Did he tell ye the trouble he has to make ends meet an' how his bones are fettered with hunger from shortages of money an' the deadly struggle he had supportin' ye? Take a good look, boys, at yeer da and ma! Is there a tear on their faces? Is their hearts broke? Did ye ever in all the shortness of yeer lives see such a brace of dog-bucketin', cat-huntin', cantankerous curiosities? . . . (*Completely changes tone and addresses Kevin.*) Stand us an oul' pint, young fella!

KEVIN (*mildly*): Right! Wait till he comes in with the drinks.

Danger, his own self, quaffs remainder of pint and places glass in Kevin's hand.

D.T.D.: 'Tis little enough money you have without buyin' pints for bar bums in the village o' Keelty!

DANGER (*squarely addressing D.T.D.*): I know all about you!

D.T.D. (*nettled*): Me! You don't even know the name that I'm called by.

DANGER: Don't I? Not that it makes any odds! (*Screws his head upwards in thought; then in sparsely divided bursts.*) Mountainy farmer, chickens twenty, cows six, dogs two, wife one. Misery. (*Pause.*) Sons numerous. Daughters too. All departed. House of grumblin'. House of arguin'. Dawheen Timmineen Din!

D.T.D.: That's my name!

DANGER: An' your grandfather, Din, was no joke! The Blocker they called him on account of he blockin' a cross-eyed doxy on a gravemound in the churchyard o' Keelty.

D.T.D. fumes and engages his wife in furious whispers. Enter Tom Hannigan bearing tray with drinks.

TOM (*plausibly*): Now! A half a port . . . (*Hands it to Maynan.*) a half a whiskey. (*Hands it to D.T.D.*)

Tom hands pint to Kevin and orange juice to Dinny.

D.T.D.: What's goin' to you?

TOM: Five an' tuppence for the drinks.

Carefully D.T.D. extracts five shillings and two pence and hands it to Tom.

TOM: And two an' tuppence more for the oats.

D.T.D.: Oats! (*Regretfully finds additional money and hands same over.*) Oats are an awful price by you!

TOM: They're scarce! (*Accepts money.*)

KEVIN: Bring in a pint to this man. (*Indicating Danger.*)

Tom takes Danger's empty glass and exits.

DANGER: Danger Mullaly is the name, sir. "Danger" on account of my red box with my holy pictures. (*Impulsively thrusts pictures at Kevin and*

Dinny. Then, on a whim, gives one to D.T.D. and one to Maynan.) Fair
   due is my policy. (*To Kevin.*) What part of England are ye bound for?
KEVIN: London.
DANGER: A great spot! A fella was tellin' me he saw a five-acre garden of cab-
   bage from the train going into it. They must ate a sight of cabbage there.
   What sort o' work will ye be fallin' in to?
KEVIN: The brother is foreman in a factory there. He has jobs got for us.
DANGER: I hope ye'll have every day's good luck.
*Enter Tom with Danger's pint. Kevin pays him. Danger accepts pint and
Tom exits.*
DANGER: 'Tis a sin to drink it! (*Swallows deeply.*)
D.T.D. (*rises*): I can't be wastin' my day in a publichouse. 'Tis warm weath-
   er an' there's the milk o' six cows for the creamery. (*A little kindly.*) Ye
   know the way to the station? (*Kevin nods.*) Well, safe journey! (*Shakes
   hands with both sons, obviously embarrassed at the contact.*) Say good-
   bye to your mother. (*Goes toward street exit, having collected his be-
   longings.*) An don't be lookin' over the side o' the ship for fear one of ye
   might fall into the salt water.
*Exit Dawheen Timmineen Din, followed by the amazed stare of Danger
Mullaly.*
DANGER: If I hadn't seen and heard it with my own two eyes, I wouldn't believe it. That man has a flagstone for a heart.
Danger retreats a little as Maynan approaches her sons.
MAYNAN (*shakes Kevin's hand*): Don't forget yeer prayers an' the three Hail
   Marys for purity an' a happy death. Tell your brother Padna that Juleen
   is for confirmation next month, an' 'tis time he sent home a few pounds —
   that his father said it. (*Takes Dinny's hand.*) Mind yourself, Dinny, an'
   don't be wanderin' off on your own. Stand close to Kevin on the boat an'
   you'll come to no harm. The grace o' God an' His Blessed Mother go
   with ye. I have the holy water here with me. Katty Fitzgerald brought it
   from Knock.
*She produces small bottle filled with water and pours some on her fingers,
sprinkles it on her sons and crosses herself as the boys do. On second
thought she sprinkles some on Danger. Enter Peg Finnerty.*
PEG: Your husband said to hurry on, Mrs. Din, or the milk'd be gone sour in
   the tank at home!
*Maynan corks bottle and conceals it, gently touches the heads of both boys,
then turns to go.*
DINNY (*weakly*): Ma . . . !
MAYNAN (*turns briefly, quietly*): What, Dinny? (*He suddenly takes both her
   hands and begins to sob into them. She draws away after a second and, at
   door, turns.*) Mind him, Kevin! He's only a child!

379

Exit Maynan. Dinny continues to sob childishly. Kevin buries his head in his hands for a moment, then, realizing where he is, defensively sits upright, and puts his arm about Dinny.

KEVIN (*gently*): Don't cry, Dinny . . . Don't be lonely . . . we'll be home again soon and, sure, won't I be with you the whole time an' won't you be meetin' all the lads over? . . . Your own brothers an' sisters . . . they'll be all waitin' at Euston. We'll be home again for a holiday in a year. Sure a year is no length of time, man!

Dinny continues to cry.

KEVIN (*very gently*): Now, Dinny! 'Tisn't so bad. (*Near to tears himself, Danger turns away. Peg Finnerty occupies herself with dusting.*) Don't by cryin', Dinny, or you'll have me cryin' too an' 'twould never do to have the two of us be cryin'. Sure you won't be cryin', Dinny? Think o' the journey before us an' all the new things we'll see an' the gay time we'll have when we meet the lads. Do you know what we'll do, Dinny — the two of us'll get blithero on the boat goin' over an' join up with a singsong . . . Won't you stop cryin' now, Dinny . . . for me, Dinny?

Dinny sniffles and Kevin immediately gives him his handkerchief.

DINNY: I'm sorry, Kev . . . I'm ashamed o' myself!

KEVIN: Don't be sorry, Dinny. I understand. If you didn't cry I'd have started myself.

DINNY: I want to go out a minute, Kev . . . I don't want to go away at all, Kev.

KEVIN: I'll take you out.

DANGER: Stay as you are! I'll take him out! (*Danger assists Dinny to exit.*) That one there is makin' eyes at you all the time. I seen her.

PEG: Go on out, or I'll fire the pint at you! (*Exit Danger and Dinny.*) That oul' devil! He's always makin' up things.

KEVIN: He's a gay old man.

PEG: Your brother is awful lonesome goin'!

KEVIN: So would you be lonesome, too, if you were goin'!

PEG: Don't tell me that a big boy like you is goin' to be lonesome, too?

KEVIN: Everyone is lonesome at leavin' home.

PEG: Usen't I see you a few years back at the dances at Fahera Cross?

KEVIN: We used often go there. I used to take Dinny. I never remember seein' you, though!

PEG: Ah, I used be dressed up that time. Anyway, you'd be too young.

KEVIN (*laughs*): Sure, I'm away older than you!

PEG (*seriously*): I was too grown up, maybe. (*Changes tone.*) You're a nice fella, the way you minded Dinny.

KEVIN: Someone had to mind him.

PEG: Danger'll tell him a fistful o' lies now. He's a great warrant to cheer a person up.

KEVIN: 'Tis strange, I don't remember you at all at Fahera dancehall.

PEG: Sure, I told you I was all dressed up in them days.

KEVIN: Still I should remember you.

PEG: D'you remember Jimmy Farrelly, the teacher's son, that used play the football?

KEVIN: I do well! I often saw him playin'. He was goin' to the university. He ran away from home, or somethin'.

PEG: He ran away all right! D'you remember the lady he used have dancin' with him, the one with all the fancy steps?

KEVIN: I do, well! She was the best-lookin' girl in Fahera dancehall. I was often half tempted to ask her for a dance but I was afraid.

PEG (*knowledgeable*): Oh, he'd let no one dance with her!

KEVIN: I wasn't afraid of him! I was afraid of her! She'd knock you down with the good looks she had.

PEG: Would you know her if you saw her again?

KEVIN: I'd know her anywhere!

PEG: You would, would you? . . . Well — have a good look!

KEVIN (*looks at her curiously*): God in Heaven! . . . You don't look . . . Japers! . . . You are!

Peg places hand on hip, raises other over head, permitting her fingers to delicately touch head.

PEG: Remember now?

KEVIN: That's right! That's the way you used to dance all right. (*Stands up.*) Jimmy Farrelly would stand back from you and clap his hands, an' you'd swing away dancin' on your own around the floor.

Kevin commences to clap his hands while Peg commences a modern dance. When she completes a circle or two around the room, she throws herself backwards onto a chair.

KEVIN: You can still dance!

PEG: If Miss Seelie saw me now, I was sacked on the spot.

KEVIN: That was good dancin'. (*He sits down.*)

PEG: I don't know what made me do it. I couldn't help it. I suppose there's a kick in me yet in spite of all my misfortune.

KEVIN: God, you were great! It brought me back to Fahera dancehall and the innocent times I had. Myself an' Dinny! Myself an' Dinny, we'd have gay times there. We often saw a few ladies home. Where did your man Jimmy Farrelly go to?

PEG (*sadly*): I don't know . . . he disappeared one mornin'. That night we had a date for the pictures here in Keelty an' he never came. I waited for four hours. He knew there was somethin' wrong.

KEVIN: Did you ever hear from him since?

PEG: Never!

KEVIN: I supose you were in love with him?

PEG: I was.

KEVIN: How is it you never chanced to come out to the dancehall since?

PEG: Are you tryin' to grig me by any chance?

KEVIN: No, indeed!

PEG: You mean you don't know about me?

KEVIN: As God is my judge, I don't . . . (*Passionately.*) . . . An' I'm not griggin' you either.

PEG (*stands suddenly upright and looks into fireplace*): I had a baby!

KEVIN: Oh, you married since, so, did you?

PEG (*viciously but without intent*): No, I did not marry! I had a child out o' Jimmy Farrelly an' my own foolishness an' fancy steps. Don't look so sorry for me. I'm able to manage my affairs.

KEVIN (*regaining his composure*): I'm not sayin' a word to you.

PEG (*defensively*): An' you don't have to. I know what's in your head, the same as every other fella that comes in here half drunk. They know I made a mistake an' they think on that account I'm a bit of an ape an' they all want me to go to a dance or a picture, thinkin' to have a night's sport outside.

KEVIN: I'm not half drunk . . . an' I'm sorry for what happened to you. Where's the child?

PEG: At home with my father an' mother. (*Brusquely.*) I didn't mean to lose my temper with you. I couldn't help it. (*Pitifully.*) I made one mistake an' I'm supposed to remember it for the rest of my life!

KEVIN (*appealingly*): I'm awful sorry.

PEG: Here's in your brother, with Danger.

KEVIN: Would it be all right if I wrote to you when I got over?

PEG: Oh, don't be coddin' me, boy!

Enter Dinny, followed by Danger.

DANGER: By the jingoes! There was enough eggs in his belly to journey to the moon.

Dinny sits near Kevin, who takes his hand in his.

DANGER (*to pint*): Did you miss me, my little black sweetheart? (*Swallows some.*) My little black woman that I love! (*Suddenly, to Kevin and Dinny.*) A word of advice about London. Marry two black women if ye can.

Some laughter from Peg and Kevin.

DANGER: There's rumors that the sweat off a black woman would cure any class of an ache or disease. There's some kind of oil in 'em. And about holy water; don't ever ask an Englishman for holy water, because he'll say " 'Oly wot?"

382

Enter Tom, hands carrying glass of whiskey behind his back.

TOM (*customary ultimatum*): There's only a quarter of an hour left for the train. (*He walks forward to fire and puts his back to it.*)

DINNY: Time we were goin', Kevin!

DANGER: 'Tis only two minutes' walk. There's no use in ye standin' above with every hairy molly in the village o' Keelty watchin' ye.

TOM: Good luck!

Tom quaffs glass of whiskey and puts glass in his trousers pocket. Enter See-lie.

SEELIE (*to Tom — pointing at Danger*): I thought it was understood that he was barred here?

TOM (*falsetto — to Danger*): Come on! Come on! Finish that drink, an' out with you! We can't have this kind o' thing goin' on.

DANGER: Oh, but excuse me! (*To Seelie.*) These two boys contracted with me to bring up their bags to the train. This dacent boy here stood me a pint. Am I goin' to renege on my word?

SEELIE: When I think of the hardworkin' poor men with families an' watch your idleness, it makes my heart twist an' turn like a snipe. Every mornin' it's the same. You come in here on the bum. How can these poor boys afford to be buyin' you porter? What have they but the bare few shillings to spare? How is it always the poor people you fasten on?

DANGER: Hang the poor! Damn the poor! Blast the poor! Why should I give a dog-bucketin' damn about the poor? What good are they? When they have a bit o' money it burns holes in their pockets. Down with the poor! Dance on 'em! Keep them down! That's my policy. The poor, how are you? Sheepdogs — that's what the poor are — trained, tamed sheepdogs. I seen lads like these before in this very pub an' they hittin' the highroad for England, lonesome stinkin' sheepdogs. Then they come back with new suits an' fancy shirts, with tall tales about loose women in Piccadilly, boastin' an' braggin' about all the money they're earnin'. Fine mannerly accents like a country curate at his first sermon. Men o' the world, with stories about the wonderful sights o' Camden Town. They'll buy porter for me when they come back on their holidays. They'll buy porter for anyone. They'll buy porter for every smart man that'll believe their stories. I'm only an oul' bum! I know that! I'm only Danger Mullaly with my sacred hearts! I'll watch hundreds of 'em goin' back again till the summer's over — back to their nightshifts, an' filthy digs an' thievin' landladies. I'll be lookin' at them with their long faces leanin' out o' the carriage windows, with all their hard-earned money gone, an' their hearts broke with the thoughts of what's waitin' over. (*To Kevin and Dinny.*) 'Tisn't so bad this time. This time it's an adventure. But wait'll ye be goin' back the next time an' the time after that an' the time after that again. 'Twon't be an adventure then. (*Pitch of indictment.*) But I don't blame you two misfortunes . . . (*Indicates departed father and mother.*) I blame them — your fathers and your mothers. They take the easy way out. England is there or America is there. Ship 'em off an' we'll be rid of 'em.

SEELIE: Don't you dare raise your voice in this house!

DANGER (*courteously plausible*): Sure, I'm an oul' bum! No one takes any notice o' Danger Mullaly.

KEVIN (*suddenly*): We'll have to be goin' or we'll miss the train.

DANGER: I'll take the bags. (*He does so.*)

SEELIE (*exiting*): And don't come back! (*Exit Seelie.*)

KEVIN (*to Peg — extending hand*): Goodbye! (*She accepts his hand half-heartedly.*) I'll see you some time next year, please God!

Kevin hurries out door, followed by Dinny.

PEG: Good luck — Kevin!

DANGER (*holding bags — to Tom*): I often felt a strong an' willful desire for the companionship of a woman, an' I was often plagued by the thought of what I was missin'. What I say is — thanks be to God that it isn't me that's sending them two sons away from their natural country, this fine summer's mornin'. (*Exit Danger.*)

TOM: Danger is in a contrary mood this mornin'. And, look! he forgot his box of holy pictures.

PEG: He was tellin' the truth but he didn't tell it all. 'Tis stories about prostitutes an' easy money that carries half of 'em over there — that half doesn't be long comin' home again.

TOM: Not them two lads!

PEG: No — not them! You could see they were decent lads, especially the big fella — the way he put his hands around his brother. They're a pity, them two lads. No place to come home to, if they don't make out for themselves; no one wantin' them!

TOM: The big fella was on to you, Peg. Did you see him?

PEG: Everyone is on to me! What else does a man do when he comes into a pub an' sees a girl workin' there? (*Thoughtfully.*) Although he wasn't like the rest of them . . . was he, Tom? You could see that about him. You could see he was a lad that was lookin' for nothin' soft; a lad that was out to make his own way in the world. (*Musingly.*) He said he'd write to me! (*Laughs.*) Sure, he'll have me forgotten the first Saturday night he lays his eyes on a painted woman in the streets of London.

TOM: He seemed a likely lad. Did you never think of goin' to London, Peg?

PEG: I thought of it!

TOM: You could take the baby, get a job maybe, an' do better for yourself than you're doin' here.

PEG: I wouldn't give it to say to the sneakin' gossips o' Keelty that they put the wind up me.

TOM: You know, I have a few thousand in my own name, and a few hundred fiddled in case I'd be stuck for money some time. I often thought about boltin' off an' leavin' her to herself . . . but she's my own an' there's no goin' for me.

PEG: She's a good woman! Someone must have the reins. I don't want the money. Thanks all the same. (*Urgently.*) What time is it?

TOM (*looks out into bar*): Eleven — traintime.

Tom raises hand to command attention. In the distance the whistle of a train is heard.

PEG (*distantly*): I see the two of 'em sittin' down on their seats, an' their faces white an' the young fella cryin'. I can see their faces. I can see the train pullin' out o' the station. I can't help it, Tom. All them young boys an' girls, holdin' on tight to their bags, an' every minute feelin' their pockets in case their money was lost.

TOM (*a little hurt for her sake*): Don't be thinkin' too much about them things, Peg, for your own good.

Peg whistles the first bars of "Many Young Men of Twenty." She whistles with her breath forcefully. Then she sings it and in the distance (if that is feasible) a chorus of voices joins in.

PEG AND VOICES (*singing*):

> Many young men of twenty said goodbye.
> It breaks my heart
> To see the face of every girl and boy;
> It breaks my heart and now I'm fit to die.
> My boy Jimmy's gone from me
> Sailed away across the sea.
> My Jimmy's gone and here alone am I.
> Many young men of twenty said goodbye.

TOM: I could almost hear the voices of the boys an' girls goin' away.

PEG: I feel the same thing every mornin' I hear that oul' train whistlin'.

Tom clenches hand and lends an ear to the distance.

TOM: There's a quare voice comin' now!

DANGER (*outside — singing*):

> Haha, says Mikey Houlihan, I'll tackle up my ass,
> An' I'll put on my new brown suit, that I wears goin' to Mass
> O, I'll put on my new brown suit, an' I'll put on my vest,
> I'll die for mother Ireland, the land that I love best.

Enter Danger.

DANGER: Big crowd at the train this mornin'. I could have sold a dozen o' those only for forgettin' 'em. (*Looks severely at both Peg and Tom.*) Ye know me well enough, the two of ye. Well, I'm goin' to do somethin' now that'll shock the sugar out of your shaggin' skins. (*Begins a search in obscure pockets of coat.*) Excuse the language!

PEG: What way did the boys take it?

DANGER (*half to himself, still fumbling about obscure pockets*): I have a reserve here someplace.

TOM: Wouldn't you answer Peg, Danger, when she asks you a question?

DANGER: Who? The two boys! Sure, God dammit, 'tis them that has me the way I am. The youngest one of 'em started cryin' before he went on the train. (*Pauses in his search.*) An' what does Kevin do? He puts his hands on his head an' he says "I love you, Dinny, an' I'll mind you!" an' he kissed him then.

Pause.

PEG: What else?

DANGER: That was enough for Danger Mullaly! Sure, 'twould be the talk o' Keelty for two generations if I left a salt tear run down the side o' my face! (*Triumphantly.*) Aaah! I have her! (*Produces ten-shilling note and holds it on high.*) I always keep this in reserve for fear of emergency. I told ye I was goin' to shock ye. (*Command.*) Peg, bring us two large whiskies an' keep the change!

Peg looks at him anxiously.

DANGER: An' be quick about it!

Peg exits, taking ten-shilling note.

TOM: What notion possessed you to spend it?

DANGER: 'Twouldn't do your heart good to see them two young fellows goin'. I had to come away, man, I tell you. I couldn't be watchin' them cryin'. (*Plea.*) Fair play to me now, Tom. If it got known within Keelty that Danger Mullaly stood a drink, I could never walk down the street again.

TOM: I won't say a word.

Enter Peg with two whiskies. Danger and Tom accept same.

DANGER: Here's a safe journey to them two young lads. God go with them!

Danger finishes his drink in a swallow, seizes his red box and prepares to exit.

TOM: God go with them! . . . You're not going?

DANGER: I am!

TOM: I never in my life before saw you standin' a drink to any man. The least I can do is to stand a one back.

DANGER (*at door — sadly*): If you ever see me inclined to stand a round of drinks again, notify the civic guards and tell them that Danger Mullaly wants to be certified.

Act II

SCENE 1

Action takes place as before. The time is the late evening of a day one year later. Danger Mullaly sits in a half-drunken state and is bent over a table. On the table is a pint glass which is quarter filled with stout. Also on the table is his box of holy pictures. He addresses one of the pictures. Distant pipes or the sound of an oboe should introduce this soliloquy.

DANGER: You gave me a lot o' rope, an' You're still givin' it to me. What good are fellows like Danger Mullaly to the world — useless, drunken oul' fools that everyone makes a joke of? What did I ever do for You? Every one in the village of Keelty condemns me, but You never condemned me, and I'm sellin' Your picture every day to fellows an' girls that throw it away . . . No, that's not true . . . They don't throw it away. You were never thrown away, but they forgot about You, or You're left in the bottom of a suitcase or You fall to the floor an' You're brushed out o' the room by an English landlady. But I'll keep on sellin' Your pictures. (*Places his palms on the table and looks at picture thereon.*) Great God, if I was there the day they crucified You, I'd beat what soldiers was at the foot of Calvary. (*Stands erect — corrects himself.*) No! I wouldn't! I wouldn't! I'd go into some pub along the way an' meet a few fellows like myself or fellows like Kevin that went to England an' I'd say: "Lads, lads, here's a great chance for us — our last chance . . . They're bringin' Him up the road now an' they have a big cross on His back an' 'tis knockin' Him." I'd say then: "We'll be cute now, lads. We'll get a few sticks an' a few stones an' we'll find a handy gable end of a house an' we'll ambush 'em." Then we'd wait, wait, until the crowd that were followin' the procession were leapin' over us, to see the sight of Him an' He draggin' it after Him. An' I'd say then: "Now, men, now!" an' I'd jump out in front of 'em, an' the first soldier I'd see I'd catch him by the throat an' I'd squeeze with all my strength, an' I'd say, very slow, "Take that cross off His back, you reptile!" An' then the crowd would rise up in anger against the soldiers an' you'd hear their curses a mile away, an' the day would be won . . . But no! He'd keep His cross an' He'd say: "Thanks, Danger! Thanks, oul' son! But this is the way!" an' he'd lift up His hand 'an He'd say: "Peace! Peace! Peace!"

Danger finishes his pint and sings with feeling.

DANGER (*singing*):

> They crowned Your head with thorns, they brought you misery;
> You died upon a cross, high up in Calvary;
> There is no other love for me;

You will be mine through all eternity.
Round here they laugh an' call me "Drunken Danger!"
But I have you in spite of Keelty town;
The greatest pal that ever walked a roadway;
The only Man who never let me down.

Enter Peg from bar, humming theme song.

DANGER: That oul' song, again! They aren't all home yet from England, Peg. He might come!

PEG: He won't come! You know that, Danger!

DANGER: You never know!

PEG: I heard every word you said there, when you were talkin' to yourself.

DANGER: You did not!

PEG: I did! And, Danger, He won't be as hard on you as you think when you pass across. Sure, that's why He died, to be where the judgment is, so that we'll all be treated fair.

DANGER: I was drunk!

PEG: You were as sober as ever you'll be. Sure, aren't we all in the same boat? He'll allow for everything, Danger.

DANGER: Everything?

PEG: I think He will! I think He'll make special allowance for you, seein' that you love Him so much.

DANGER (*taking heart*): Do you know who's coming home tomorrow night?

PEG: There's always someone comin' home.

DANGER: D'you remember the two young fellas who left for England the mornin' last year? You remember the tall good-lookin' lad, surely, that stood me the pint? You remember him?

PEG: I remember the two boys an' their father an' mother.

DANGER: That's right! Dawheen Timmineen Din, that was the father's name, a pauperized crabjaw. I heard him boasting the other day in a pub how they were comin' back, his two sons. One of 'em is married.

PEG: Which one?

DANGER: You needn't worry — it's the small lad.

PEG: As if I cared.

DANGER: He was inquirin' what time the train came in.

PEG: Ten to seven.

DANGER: I have to earn my few bob, Peg, bringin' down bags. I told him 'twas ten to eight.

Enter Tom from kitchen.

TOM: Give us a ball o' raw malt on the spot, Peg.

PEG: What about your sister?

TOM: Do as I say! I'm not goin' to stick this much longer. I can't even look sideways with her. Bring in that drink!

Exit Peg.

TOM (*to Danger*): She says to me, before the tea: "Show me a smell o' your breath!" I put my foot down and said "My breath is my own!" She hit me a slap across the face.

DANGER: 'Tis bad to drink alone!

TOM: Now, now, now! I've enough problems!

DANGER: I'll tell you about the civil war and where I was wounded during an ambush.

TOM: You wounded?

DANGER: As bad as any of 'em; stabbed and stung and pierced . . .

TOM: By what?

DANGER: Nettles!

Enter Peg with a glass of whiskey. Tom accepts it.

DANGER: Very few men can drink alone and find contentment.

TOM: You'll miss the train!

DANGER: What time is it?

TOM: Traintime!

DANGER (*reluctantly goes to exit*): You won't stand?

TOM: I can't be standin' to you always.

DANGER: I'd stand back if you did.

TOM: With what?

DANGER: Out of this small Paddy of yours that you hid outside in the turf-shed. (*Exit Danger.*)

TOM: Any evening paper?

PEG: I'll get it.

Peg exits by door to bar. Tom sips whiskey cautiously. Enter Peg with paper. Tom accepts same and shrewdly conceals himself and whiskey behind paper.

PEG: I'm goin' in the back, to lock the store.

The paper nods. Exit Peg.

TOM (*reads aloud*): "Ballinacourtney Bridge Congress Declared Open" . . . (*Mutters.*) . . . "What's Wrong with Irish Jumpers?" . . . is it ganseys they mean, now, or horses? . . . "C.I.E. Buffet Burned over Closing of West Cork Railway" . . . "Ass an' Car Abandoned in Bandon" . . .

Enter a well-dressed man of thirty. Tom suddenly discards paper and furiously seeks to conceal whiskey. The entrant is Maurice Browne.

MAURICE: It's all right, Tom! It's only me!

TOM: Good God, man, you frightened the wits outa me! I thought 'twas Seelie.

Maurice sits wearily aside.

TOM: Well? How do you like Keelty?

MAURICE: Too early to judge.

389

TOM: How do you like your digs?

MAURICE: Tom, all digs are mediocre! If they were good they'd be hotels. All hotels are mediocre. If they were good they wouldn't be open to the public.

TOM: Will you join me in a drop of this?

MAURICE: I'll chance it. (*Tom rises.*)

TOM: Do you like the school?

MAURICE: All schools are the same, Tom — the same smell, the same sadness, the same teachers. Get them through the course but teach them nothing. That's all you have to do, Tom. I teach English. (*Bitterly.*) Do you know what I teach, Tom — twenty prescribed poems and ten prescribed essays and one prescribed play. I've taught in four different schools by prescription only. This is the age of the specialist.

TOM: I'll bring in the drink.

Exit Tom. Maurice rises and looks into the fireplace.

MAURICE (*to fireplace*): Withered broom and roses with cankerous appendages. (*Turns and shouts to Tom.*) Who is this Peg Finnerty, Tom?

TOM (*shouts from bar*): One minute and I'll be in to you with the drinks.

MAURICE (*shouts back*): Why I ask is because most of the young lads at the school come into the bar here on their way home from school and I know they're not coming to see you.

Enter Tom with two glasses of whiskey. He hands one to Maurice.

MAURICE: Am I to understand you're standing?

TOM: You can buy the next one if Seelie doesn't come in.

They both sit.

MAURICE: About Peg Finnerty?

TOM: If Seelie comes in, you can let on you insisted on I having a drink. You're well-spoken and educated. She won't mind, Maurice.

MAURICE: Tom, when I came here a week ago to teach in a school, yours was the first bar I entered. You were in the same predicament then. Being a stranger in the locality I suggested, improperly perhaps, that the barman have a drink with me. You readily acquiesced. We exchanged confidences, Tom. You told me about Seelie and I told you about the reason for my being dismissed from my last school and the school before that and the school before that, Tom. We became confidants. Now I have asked you a question and for some unknown reason, you balk me. (*At the end of his tether.*) Who is Peg Finnerty, Tom? And, Tom, I didn't come here to listen to your troubles. I have enough of my own.

TOM: Good luck! (*They quaff.*) As you know, she works here with me. She's only just gone out now to lock the store and she should be in.

MAURICE: Go on, Tom!

TOM: Her history you want, isn't it?

MAURICE: If I want to know why ten candidates for the Leaving Certificate stop at your bar, three out of six evenings, the answer is yes!

TOM (*comfortable*): She comes from a small farm a few miles from here. She used be doin' a line with a schoolmaster's son. He used play with the county team — maybe you heard of him — Jimmy Farrelly?

MAURICE: Never heard of him! Go on, Tom!

TOM: I'll put it in brief for you. She was in receipt of a child from him and he buzzed off like a wasp. (*Whiskies are supped.*)

MAURICE: All wasps fly after they sting. But why do my young English pupils stop off here on their way home?

TOM: Songs, Maurice! Songs! She's a great hand to sing songs and she can make them up as she goes along.

MAURICE: A rare quality! I'll have to hear her some time.

TOM: Do me a favor! When she comes in now, ask her to sing the song she made up about Kitty Curley.

MAURICE: Who the hell is Kitty Curley?

TOM: Another one of the clients that come in here. You didn't meet her yet?

MAURICE: Not yet! What's she like?

TOM: Oh, she has a shawl and she's oldish now, but she used be a great favorite when the British army was here. She tells fortunes. The same oul' scrawl — you'll meet a black man on your travels. Beware of a woman called M.O.C. . . . and that you'll cross water . . . you know, that sort of stuff . . . Don't say a word now; she's coming in. I'll introduce you nice and proper to her and you can form your own opinion, provided you ask her to sing.

MAURICE: Don't worry. I'll ask her. I like a song.

Peg is heard singing.

PEG (*singing*):

> The dawn is breaking now, where fields are wet with dew,
> And in my lonely heart are memories of you

Closing door behind her.

> There is no other love for me,
> You will be mine through all eternity.

Peg sees Maurice and stops suddenly.

MAURICE: Please, go on!

Peg looks at him for a moment and then goes on, looking at him in a hard-boiled way.

PEG (*singing*):

> You will be mine while stars of night are shining
> And we shall sleep until we meet again;
> The stars have fled and shades of night are pining;
> The dawn won't break, my love, until we meet again.

391

MAURICE: He must have been a considerate lover!

PEG: Who?

MAURICE: Jimmy Farrelly! (*Points at Tom immediately.*) He told me.

TOM: I told him, Peg, how you could sing and a few more things. Peg, this is Maurice Browne. He's a secondary teacher after coming to town here. I was tellin' you about him. This is Peg Finnerty, Maurice.

They exchange "How do you do's."

MAURICE: I've heard a lot about your singing.

PEG: Really?

MAURICE: The lads at the school never stop talking about you.

PEG: There's more than the lads at school talkin' about me!

TOM: It's a small town.

MAURICE: How about a song now?

PEG: Sorry! I'm not in the mood!

MAURICE: That's a pity. I heard you were good.

PEG: Oh, you did, did you? And what else did you hear . . . ?

MAURICE: Nothing! Why?

PEG: You're all the same, aren't you? (*To Tom.*) You're just as bad!

MAURICE: I didn't mean to offend! (*Tom exits to bar.*) Do you make up these songs yourself, or what?

PEG: Well, if you want to know . . . I do!

MAURICE: Strange!

PEG: Is it? I'm educated, if that's what you mean. I spent a few years with the nuns and learned how to play the piano but, of course, because I'm a servantgirl, it's strange. That's what makes it strange, isn't it, my being a servantgirl?

MAURICE: Well, why don't you leave? You could get a job in England.

PEG: And leave my baby?

MAURICE: Oh!

PEG (*mimics*): Oh!

MAURICE: Well, what's wrong with being a servantgirl?

PEG: Don't make me laugh! How much a week do you earn?

MAURICE: Well, with tax deducted, about twelve pounds.

PEG: Do you know how much I earn? Thirty bob a week. And do you know how long I work? From eight in the morning till eight at night, twelve hours a day with every second Sunday off and a half-day every week. Of course I'm the luckiest servantgirl alive in Keelty because I work with Tom Hannigan who is the best-off man in the town, but the other girls are shoved into work when they are fifteen. They're not human beings — they're beasts of burden. They start in the morning at eight. Do they get an hour for lunch? What a hope! Of course, to hear the ladies of fashion in Keelty talking, you'd swear they were doing the girls a favor. (*Apes a*

Keelty lady of fashion.) "I have to train her, you know! Couldn't let her near the cooker. Off to dances every chance she gets and jaded in the mornings." (*Reverts to herself.*) And then when she's trained, what does she get? Periodic raises until she has enough to dress like a decent girl? No bloody fear! If she goes to England, she's supposed to be ungrateful, or they'll say: "Oh! she'll get her senses there!" (*Viciously.*) Oh, to every little servantgirl, I say: "Clear to hell out of it — to England where you'll be treated like a human being, where the boys of your own class earn as much as the schoolteachers here, and where you'll have a chance of marrying and dressing decently and where, when you go into a dancehall, you'll meet nice boys, not like the farmers' and the shopkeepers' sons and the university students of Ireland who want nothing from you but a good night of pleasure and who'd be ashamed of their sacred lives to talk to you in the street the day after."

MAURICE: You're very hardboiled!

PEG: I was cooked all right!

MAURICE: Don't pick me up wrong now, but would you mind if I took you out some night?

PEG: Oh, I won't pick you up wrong! I know exactly what you mean. You have a car, naturally! We'll go in to the pictures in Cork some night. Early house. A few drinks after. And home then. But what a homecoming!

MAURICE: That's what I had in mind, but not the way you think. (*Seriously.*) We'd go to the pictures here in Keelty if you like and I'd be honored if you did no more than walk down the street with me.

PEG: I didn't mean to be so hard. Thanks for the offer.

MAURICE: You'll come, so?

PEG: No, I won't! Sorry!

Enter Danger.

DANGER: A half-one, quick, Peg!

Exit Peg. Danger sizes up Maurice, shakes his head and winks at him tentatively.

DANGER: Very weathery!

Silence.

DANGER: A draft o' low pressure on the wireless.

Enter Peg. Hands whiskey to Danger.

MAURICE: Put that down to me, Peg!

PEG: How's it going, Danger?

DANGER: Three bags for Moran's Hotel. Yanks.

Exit Peg.

DANGER: Who's that you are?

MAURICE: Maurice Browne. I'm the new teacher.

DANGER: I remember the fellow that was here before you. Pioneer! Never smoked! A terrible man for talking Irish. Good luck! (*Drinks his whiskey.*) If I score well out of these fellows, I'll stand back to you. The fellow before you used teach history. Always talkin' about Brian Boru and Finnbarr MacCool. Do you teach history, too?

MAURICE: I try to!

DANGER: D'you see the hotel I'm goin' to now? There's a great short history of Ireland there.

MAURICE (*interested*): Is there?

DANGER: All wrote down by an ordinary painter on the front door.

MAURICE (*puzzled*): What is it?

DANGER: A short history of modern Ireland — in one word — PULL! (*Exit Danger.*)

SCENE 2

Action takes place as before. The time is traintime (due in) of the following evening. Peg Finnerty is sweeping kitchen. Then she sits at table dejectedly, and commences to sing.

PEG (*singing*):

> I'll be waiting for you where the cockerel cries,
> Down here in Keelty where the heart in me dies;
> I'll be waiting for you till the heart in me sighs
> For the strength and love of you down here in Keelty.

Unnoticed, Maurice Browne enters and listens; unobserved Peg continues to sing.

PEG (*singing*):

> I'll be waiting for you where the small waters flow
> Down here in Keelty where the whitethorns grow
> The white fires of joy in your bosom will glow
> When you see your fine babe in my arms down here in Keelty.

After a moment, Maurice Browne claps and Peg turns, surprisedly, to see him.

PEG: You shouldn't do that!

MAURICE: What?

PEG: Sneak up on a person.

MAURICE: I asked you to sing several times and you refused. I availed of an opportunity.

PEG (*rises and commences to brush*): I like courtesy in people. You might have coughed. I wouldn't mind singing. I felt like singing and I sang but I don't like it when a man spies on a woman.

MAURICE: Unless the woman wants him to spy!

PEG: You must have known a lot of women?

MAURICE: A few!

PEG: In that case you're wasting your time with me.

MAURICE: Don't misunderstand me. I'm just a human being.

PEG: Oh, this human being baloney! I was a human being too, but I'm not any more.

MAURICE: I just want to take you out for a night.

PEG: Why don't you be completely honest and tell me what happens if I do?

MAURICE: That's up to you.

PEG: That's the standard answer.

MAURICE: I want to take you to a picture in Cork because there are hotels there. When the picture finishes, I would appreciate it if you had several drinks with me, and you can do what you like then.

PEG: After several drinks! Do what *I* like?

MAURICE: Yes! (*Peg laughs.*)

PEG: But I never took several drinks in my life.

MAURICE: We'll have a few drinks, then. One or two.

PEG: And if the night doesn't work out for you, you'll never talk to me again. Isn't that it?

MAURICE: No! — that's not true.

PEG: You're honest, Maurice, only when I prompt you. The rest of the honesty you leave up to me.

MAURICE: No! No! That's not true, Peg.

PEG: Look, Maurice, I've been honest with you. If you said to me: "Come to bed with me!" I'd be honored but I'd say "No!" If you said "Marry me!" I'd be honored but I'd also say "No!" Now listen carefully to me, Maurice. If you said: "Come out and get plastered drunk with me because I'm lost to the world and I have friends nowhere and I'll probably get sick when I go to bed" I would probably go with you because I'd feel sorry for you and I'd think it was my fault and you'd need me.

MAURICE: You're a very wise old woman!

PEG: A servantgirl has to be.

Enter Danger burdened with suitcases which he proceeds to deposit in a convenient corner.

DANGER: They're back!

Enter Kevin looking much the same as when he went. Peg shakes hands with him and welcomes him home and introduces him to Maurice Browne.

MAURICE: I have to be going. See you later, Peg. (*Exit Maurice Browne.*)

DANGER: I'd better give your brother a hand with the rest of the bags. (*Exit Danger.*)

PEG: Your brother married?

KEVIN: Oh! — you heard?

PEG: Danger heard your father talking in a pub.

KEVIN: I'm surprised my father wasn't there to meet us.

PEG: Danger gave him the wrong time for the train . . . Why didn't you marry, too?

KEVIN: Plenty time for that!

PEG: I suppose you know it all now — after a year in London?

KEVIN: No more than I did when I left. I worked hard.

PEG: Do you like your job?

KEVIN: I do. I'm a chargehand now.

PEG: Good!

KEVIN: Did you go dancing since I left?

PEG: No! Did you?

KEVIN: No.

PEG: Sit down now, Kevin. Your brother wasn't long finding himself a wife.

KEVIN: He was lonely and she was lonely. It isn't so bad over there when you have some one to go home to at night.

PEG: I suppose you'll be the next to marry?

KEVIN: Maybe! You never answered my letters.

PEG: I know. I'm sorry about that.

Enter Danger with additional suitcases which he deposits, followed by Dinny and Dinny's wife. Dinny is dressed elegantly, hair slicked, narrow trousers, etc. His wife is young, frail, and wears tight-fitting red trousers, tight-fitting yellow sweater, and hair in a ponytail. Dinny with a marked Cockney accent introduces his wife Dot to Peg.

DANGER: Here they are, an' wait till you see what he's after landin' home from London.

DINNY: Peg, this is Dot. Dot, this is Peg.

PEG: How do you do?

DINNY: Put it down over there, darling!

Dot sits at table, right.

KEVIN: How about a drink?

DOT: Gin and lime!

DINNY: Scotch!

DANGER: A pint!

KEVIN: And I'll have a pint.

PEG (*repeats*): Gin and lime, Scotch, and two pints. (*Exit Peg.*)

DANGER: Sit down, let ye!

They sit. Enter Tom.

TOM: Is Peg lookin' after ye?

KEVIN: She is, Tom.

Tom welcomes them home and is introduced to Dot.

TOM: Well, how do you like Ireland?

DOT: I 'aven't seen much of it yet, 'ave I? The sausages got a nice flavor.

Dawn in Keelty

Kitty Curley

X and Y Song

I Am a Servantgirl

TOM: Eh?

DOT: The sausages — they got a nice flavor.

TOM (*confused*): I'll give Peg a hand in the bar. (*Exit Tom.*)

DANGER: I expect your father will be here shortly. He'll be greatly surprised to meet (*to Dinny*) your missus.

DINNY: He'll get used to it.

DANGER: There's a big change in you from the day you left. You were stinkin' cryin' that mornin'!

DINNY: Wot?

KEVIN: It was the same at every station along the way, Danger. 'Twould make anybody cry. Young boys and girls leaving home for the first time. Fathers and mothers heartbroken, turnin' their heads away to hide the tears. 'Twould turn you against railway stations.

Enter Peg bearing tray of drinks which she distributes. Kevin pays her.

DANGER: Here's to Dail Eireann and the Irish language!

He quaffs. They all quaff. Dinny gulps his back.

DOT: Wot's Dail Eireann?

DANGER: Dail Eireann? The only place in Ireland where the civil war is still going on!

Enter Peg with Kevin's change.

DINNY (*to Peg, handing her his glass*): Fill that again and make it a double this time.

KEVIN: You'll be drunk.

DINNY: I want plenty of ammunition before I meet the old man.

Exit Peg with glass. She returns with glass of whiskey. Dinny snatches it and swallows it. He hands Peg money. Enter Kitty Curley followed by a man wearing a melodeon strapped about his shoulders. He has a shade over one eye and a hat far too large for him. Kitty goes straight to the English girl and takes her hand. Kitty wears a shawl about her shoulders, is fiftyish, grey, and wears Wellingtons.

KITTY: Tell your fortune, Miss?

Danger intercepts Kitty's hand.

DANGER: Tell my fortune, Kitty darling.

KITTY (*looks at his hand*): You'll go to the Gaeltacht and you'll be the first Gaelic-speakin' T.D. You'll open the West Cork Railway, and you'll pass water before the night is out — the way you're drinkin' porter.

Danger, holding her hand, kneels and commences to sing while others clap their hands.

DANGER (*singing*):

> When I land in dear Dail Eireann,
> Kitty, I will marry you!
> An ermine coat you will be wearin'

> The T.D.'s wives will all be rearin'
> I love pretty Kitty Curley,
> 'Deed I do! 'Deed I do!

Danger rises and dances about Kitty while the melodeon player plays. Peg comes upstage to sing.

PEG (*singing*):

> I love pretty Kitty Curley, 'deed I do! 'deed I do!
> Love her late, I love her early,
> Love her 'cause her teeth are pearly
> I love pretty Kitty Curley, 'deed I do, 'deed I do.

All join in while Danger still executes dance.

ALL (*singing*):

> I love pretty Kitty Curley, 'deed I do! 'deed I do;
> Love her late, I love her early;
> Love her 'cause her teeth are pearly
> I love pretty Kitty Curley, 'deed I do, 'deed I do.

Dinny calls Tom from the bar while Kevin exchanges conversation. Enter Tom. Dinny indicates crowd and Tom exits to bar.

DANGER: What about a song from the little Englishwoman?

All vent approval.

DINNY (*proudly*): She used to sing in a shebeen over!

DOT: It wasn't a shebeen. It was a night club. They called it a night club anyway.

DANGER: Come on and give us the song!

DOT (*singing, in a tinny Cockney voice*):

> Let X be equal to my love for you,
> It's as simple as ABC.
> Because I'm a mathematician in the very best tradition.
> So let X be equal to my love for you,
> Let Y be equal to your love for me,
> It's as simple as ABC.
> Put the X and the Y together and we'll soon discover
>   whether
> We will mingle mathematically.
> Take the square root of love and divide by the stars above,
> Take one quarter of a moon and a sweet romantic tune,
> Take a circle from a ring you're sure to see mathematically.
> Let Y be equal to your love for me
> It's as simple as ABC.
> Put the X and the Y together and we'll soon discover
>   whether
> We will mingle mathematically
> It's as simple as ABC.

All applaud politely.

DANGER: Imagine learning that in Irish?

Enter Peg with the drinks, followed by Tom who has a glass of whiskey for Kitty Curley and the melodeon player. Dinny pays Peg. Peg exits with money.

DANGER: You should hear Peg singing! (*To melodeon player.*) A waltz! The one Peg sings!

Melodeon player starts to play the waltz, "I Am a Servantgirl." Danger bows elaborately and asks Kitty Curley to dance. They lead the floor. Dinny and Dot follow them. Peg enters and Kevin waltzes with her. After a moment of waltzing Peg takes Kevin's hand and stands facing audience. She sings while the others dance in the background.

PEG (*singing*):

> I am a servantgirl, fair game to one and all;
> At thirty bob a week, I am the beck and call
> The golf club won't have me as you can plainly see,
> I am a servantgirl, the miss in misery.

Peg waltzes around again to the music and stops after a circuit.

PEG (*singing*):

> All this is very fine, the drinking and the song;
> It happens all the time, why must it happen wrong?
> How simple now for you to say that you'll be true?
> How simple now for me to whisper — I love you!

They waltz around again and the music suddenly stops. Tom disappears into bar and everybody is stock still under Miss Seelie's icy glare.

SEELIE (*calls loudly*): Tom! . . . Tom! . . . (*Dejectedly Tom returns.*) What's going on here? I just go down the street to the chapel and I find the scruff of the village here when I come back!

KITTY: Tell your fortune, Miss Seelie. (*She suddenly takes Seelie's hand.*)

SEELIE (*withdraws her hand in distaste. To Tom*): I'll be back in five minutes and I want to see him gone! (*Points to Danger.*) And her (*points to Kitty*) and him (*points to melodeon player*) gone! (*Exit Seelie.*)

DANGER: 'Tis oul' gazebos like her that has this country the way it is! There's hundreds of young wans wantin' to get married an' there's her an' her likes addlin' the priests. Sure the priests have no time for her! 'Tis oul' sinners like me the priests want. (*To Kitty.*) Bring on the melodeon player. I see a crowd of Yanks gettin' off the train. They'll be in the bar at Moran's Hotel now.

KITTY: I'll tell fortunes and you can sell holy pictures.

DANGER: 'Tenshun!

Melodeon player, Kitty, and Danger spring to attention and to the strains of "Kitty Curley" exit.

PEG (*to Dot*): Are you long married?

DINNY (*slips hand around Dot's waist*): Nearly a week!

DOT: It seems like yesterday! I found him on the street one night an' 'e couldn't foind 'is way 'ome. I been takin' 'im 'ome ever since.

DINNY: I'd be lost only for her.

Enter Danger in a furious hurry.

DANGER: They're comin'! They're comin'!

ALL: Who?

DANGER (*points at Kevin and Dinny*): Their father an' mother, Dawheen Timmineen Din and his missus. I wouldn't miss it for the world.

Dot whispers into Dinny's ear. Dinny in turn whispers into Danger's ear. Danger takes Dot by the arm and leads her to door which he opens. He points expansively.

DANGER: Up to the end of the yard an' you'll see a field an' it's the first furze bush you see after that.

Exit Dot.

DANGER (*to Kevin, indicating Peg*): She was all the time talkin' about you while you was away.

PEG: I was not, indeed! I had something else to be doin'.

DANGER (*to Kevin*): When are you goin' back?

KEVIN: A week's time.

DANGER: You'll nearly be married the next time you come.

KEVIN: Maybe.

Peg looks at him in some alarm. Enter Dawheen Timmineen Din, followed by his wife Maynan.

D.T.D. (*to Danger*): You're the lyin' impostor that told me the train wouldn't be in till eight o'clock.

Maynan meanwhile shakes hands with Kevin and Dinny.

DANGER (*dignity*): I never said anything of the kind!

D.T.D.: Liar! I've a mind to give you a crack of this whip!

Danger squares out, safely away from him, assumes a boxer's posture and does some fancy footwork. Dawheen ignores him and shakes hands with Kevin and Dinny.

D.T.D. (*to Dinny*): Where's the wife?

DINNY: She's out in the back. She'll be in shortly.

D.T.D.: Is she a Catholic?

DINNY: I don't know what she is, but she's a lovely singer.

D.T.D.: Had she a fortune?

DINNY: Oh, she had!

D.T.D.: How much?

DINNY: Thirty bob.

D.T.D.: What?

DINNY: That's a big fortune in England.

Enter Dot. D.T.D. and Maynan look appalled.

DINNY: This is her! Dot, this is my father and mother. Dad, this is Dot!

D.T.D. is too surprised to say anything.

DOT (*breezily*): Hello, Dad! (*Impulsively pecks Maynan on the cheek.*) When do we go?

DINNY: We'll have a drink first.

D.T.D.: No . . . No drink! (*Turns to Danger.*) I'm like a braddy cow above around the railway station all over him.

DANGER: Dawheen Timmineen Din, with his hands out for money. The more he has the more he wants.

DINNY: I must give you a present of a few pounds, Dad.

Dinny impulsively takes wallet from his pocket and extracts several pounds. D.T.D. advances eagerly to accept them but Dot snatches them and tucks them inside her sweater.

DOT: Silly clot! Wot's 'e want it for? . . . (*Takes D.T.D. by the hand.*) Come on, Dad . . . let's hit for the old mud cabin!

Danger and Dinny take the bags between them and exit together with D.T.D., Maynan, and Dot, singing "It's as Simple as ABC." Kevin stands abashed for a while. Peg begins to collect empty glasses.

KEVIN: Can I take you out walking tomorrow night?

PEG: Walking?

KEVIN: Well, the weather is fine and the evenings are long. We could go by the river where the swans are.

PEG: Sorry! I never go out on dates with boys now.

KEVIN: I think that's foolish. You're young and it's the summertime and why should you shut yourself away. You've every right to go walking — a better right than anybody in Keelty because you're prettier than anybody here.

PEG: It takes courage! I've left it go so long now that I can't face it.

KEVIN: I used always walk where the swans were before I went away. 'Twould be a thousand times nicer if you were with me.

PEG: Can't you get some girl who hadn't my trouble? You'll get plenty here to go with you.

KEVIN: You're the only girl I want with me. It would only be lonelier with any other girl.

PEG: I don't know! I wish you wouldn't be so nice about it. It makes it harder for me to have to say no.

KEVIN: Just this once!

PEG: But what would people say?

KEVIN: Well, if they're talking about us, they can't be talkin' about anybody else.

PEG: You're too persistent for me, but you don't understand.

Enter Danger.

DANGER (*to Kevin*): Your man is havin' canaries outside. You'd better come on.

Exit Danger.

KEVIN: Right! I'm comin'! (*Looks at Peg.*) I wouldn't ask you if I didn't mean it — there's no harm in my heart.

Kevin looks dejectedly at Peg. Kevin exits. After a moment's hesitation Peg goes to door and calls out.

PEG (*calls out*): Don't forget the swans . . . sometime . . .

She closes the door quickly and leans with back to it and sings the first verse of "Keelty."

Act III

Action takes place as before. The time is morning, one week later. In the back room Maurice Browne sits with a drink. Enter Peg from the bar.

PEG: I had no idea you were goin' by train this mornin'.

MAURICE (*sullen*): Well, the school is closed for holidays. You hardly expect me to spend them here.

PEG: Where will you go? Home?

MAURICE: No, I won't go home. I don't know, Peg; I don't know what I'll do.

Enter a heavily built middle-aged man with a youth of eighteen. They are father and son. The father is J. J. Houlihan, a local T.D. The son is Johnny Houlihan. The father wears a hat of the homburg variety.

PEG (*respectfully*): Good morning, J.J. — Johnny.

J.J.: Ah, Peg, how are you? And how's that young gorsoon o' yours?

PEG: Fine, J.J.! Fine!

J.J.: You've great guts, Peg. Great guts! And who's this man here? Do I know him?

PEG: Hardly, J.J. This is Maurice Browne, the new secondary teacher. Maurice, this is J. J. Houlihan, the T.D. and his son Johnny.

Nods of acceptance are exchanged.

MAURICE: Houlihan . . . ! (*Thoughtfully.*) Are you anything to Mikey Houlihan that Danger Mullaly sings about?

J.J. (*proudly*): Only his nephew! You know all about Mikey Houlihan, my uncle? One second . . . Peg, give us a drink. Whiskey for you, I see. A large whiskey for Mr. Browne, Peg, an orange for Johnny and — what will I have? (*Explains to Maurice.*) . . . I had a hard night last night — give me a drop of brandy, Peg.

PEG: Right, sir! (*Exit Peg.*)

402

J.J.: Sit down, Johnny. (*Both J.J. and Johnny sit. To Maurice.*) Mikey Houlihan's name is respected far and wide.

MAURICE (*finishing his drink*): I have an analytical mind, Mr. Houlihan. Forgive me! You probably won't buy me any more whiskies, but — how did your uncle die?

J.J.: Shot by an English officer. He was a marked man. They were out for his blood. (*Confidential.*) There was more than that to it, too.

MAURICE: The way I understand it from Danger Mullaly, he was shot by accident.

J.J. (*plausibly*): Don't mind that bum!

MAURICE (*accepting drink from Peg, who has entered*): Danger Mullaly says he was shot by accident while he was carrying tea to a mohill of men working.

J.J. and Johnny accept their drinks from Peg. J.J. hands her a pound note.

J.J.: Keep the change out of that, Peg and buy a pair of nylons for yourself. *Exit Peg.*

J.J. (*still plausible*): If I had time I'd explain to you fully about my uncle's history but my son and I are catching the train.

MAURICE (*finishing his drink*): So am I!

J.J. (*proudly*): Johnny here is starting off on his new job today in the north of the county.

MAURICE: What job?

J.J.: Rate collector.

MAURICE: I take it he has the qualifications?

J.J.: Oh?

MAURICE: Leaving Certificate or clerical experience; experience and trustworthiness in the handling of money.

J.J. (*dangerous*): I bought you a drink because you were here alone. That doesn't mean you can insult me and get away with it.

MAURICE (*calls*): Peg! The same again!

Maurice finishes his drink. So does Johnny. So does J.J., after consideration. Enter Peg. She collects their glasses and exits.

MAURICE (*rises and stands well apart from J.J.*): Tell me Mr. Houlihan, nephew of the exalted, the hidalgo-like, Hungarian-like guerilla, how many other candidates were there for the job your son has?

J.J.: You have a job in this town, sonny boy. Mind it!

JOHNNY: Six — three of them were lads with their Leaving and the other three were clerks in the County Council offices.

J.J. (*ferociously — to son*): Shut up!

MAURICE: And yet you get the job, and I take it you never went near a secondary school.

JOHNNY: Useless at books, but I can paint gorgeous pictures o' racehorses.

Enter Peg with drinks. Maurice pays her with a pound note.

MAURICE (*to Peg*): Keep the change out of that and stick it on to your Leaving Certificate.

Exit Peg. She returns partly to door leading in from the bar.

J.J.: See here, son — you'd better watch out!

MAURICE: Don't threaten me, you smug, ignorant cabóg! What about the other lads who were all better qualified than your son?

J.J.: You won't have any job here when you get back. I guarantee you that!

Enter Danger Mullaly. He is dressed respectably in a suit far too large for him. He carries a brown paper parcel in his hand.

DANGER: Good mornin', Maurice! Is that the great J. J. Houlihan himself I see? How'll they manage in the Dail without you at all?

J.J.: What are you all dressed up for today?

DANGER: I'm being received at Arus an Uachtaran by the chief. I hear they're building a monument to Mikey Houlihan, your uncle?

J.J.: That's right! The Taoiseach himself will be down for the unveiling.

DANGER (*sings*):

> God be with you, Mikey Houlihan, the pride of Keelty town,
> An anointed bloody idiot, and a born bloody clown.
> You never fired a rifle, and you never heard a drum,
> You died for dear old Ireland with a bullet in your bum.

J.J. (*jumps to his feet with fists clenched*): Take that back! Take it back! By jingoes, I didn't take that from the Tans not to mind you!

Danger retreats behind Maurice's back and raises his fists when he is safe.

DANGER: Twenty-two years in Dail Eireann and never opened his mouth, except to pick his teeth!

MAURICE (*to J.J.*): Simmer down!

J.J.: A bloody turncoat, that's what! I never changed my politics.

MAURICE: And you never will. You have the same politics as your father before you, and your sons after you will have the same politics. That's this damn country all over. You're all blinded by the past. You're still fighting the civil war. Well, we don't give a tinker's curse about the civil war or your damn politics, or the past. The future we have to think about. If there was any honest politician, he'd be damned. If our Lord walked down the main street of Keelty tomorrow morning, ye'd crucify him again. We're sick to death of hypocrisy and the glories of the past. Keep the Irish language and find jobs for the lads that have to go to England. Forget about the Six Counties and straighten out the twenty-six first.

DANGER: I'd give 'em six more if I had my way.

J.J. (*furious — to son*): You wait here! I'm not travelin' on a train with this bloody crew. I'll get a car and we'll drive up.

DANGER: Up Connolly!

J.J.: Communists, that's what ye are! Bloody Communists!

J.J. exits. Danger glowers at Johnny.

JOHNNY: Don't want that job at all! The man that should have got it is a married man with two kids. I've my fare for England and that's where I'm going.

DANGER: Good bloody man you are!

JOHNNY: Would you meet any Cork men in London?

DANGER: Oh, you would! Stop in the middle of London one night and shout "Echo!" and everyone that turns his head will be a Cork man.

PEG (*to Danger*): Did I hear you say you were goin' to England?

DANGER: That's right!

PEG: But how . . . why?

DANGER: Because I'm lonesome, that's why, an' because I have pride, too. Your man Kevin gave me the fare an' he's gettin' a job for me, too. I'll be treated fair there anyway.

PEG: I can hardly believe it. What's in the parcel?

DANGER (*retrieves parcel*): A couple of pounds of drisheen for the dook!

Enter Kitty Curley followed by melodeon player.

KITTY: Ah, Danger, me darlin', I heard it below in Moran's Hotel. You're off across the water. Didn't I always read it in your fortune. Show here! (*Takes his hand.*) You'll marry an elderly widow woman with money in the post office and a poodle dog. Ye'll have no family but ye'll adopt a black baby and he'll be the first black T.D. in Dail Eireann. (*She sees Johnny.*) Tell your fortune for a bob! (*She takes Johnny's hand.*) You'll marry a woman with blonde hair on her head and black hair under her oxter. You'll be lord mayor of Dagenham and you'll be chased by a Poll-Angus bull.

JOHNNY: Japers, tell me no more! That's my father! Here's your money.

DANGER: Bring us one last drink for the road, Peg. Bring me a ball o' raw malt. Bring us all malt.

Exit Peg.

DANGER (*to Kitty*): I'll send you a pair of false teeth from England, Kitty.

KITTY: I'll keep the ones I have. I'm not in the habit of dismissin' faithful servants. They were white an' pearly one time an' there's many a gay soldier could tell you the same. Give us one ould song, Danger, before you go!

DANGER (*singing*):

> I'd sooner join the Foreign Legion,
> What in hell am I to do?
> I've no wife or son or daughter,
> I've a chance across the water
> I love pretty Kitty Curley, 'deed I do, 'deed I do!

Peg enters with tray of drinks.

DANGER: Come on! All together!

They all sing together.

ALL (*singing*):

> I love pretty Kitty Curley, 'deed I do, 'deed I do
> Love her late, I love her early
> Love her cause her teeth are pearly
> I love pretty Kitty Curley, 'deed I do, 'deed I do!

KITTY (*singing*):

> Cross my palm or you're a goner
> I know what life holds for you
> I tells fortunes for a tanner
> Tells the truth, upon my honor.
> All the lads know Kitty Curley
> 'Deed they do! 'Deed they do!

All repeat chorus. Peg distributes the drinks and collects money from Danger.

DANGER: Ladies and gentlemen, a toast! To the emigration commission! (*They quaff.*) To the new licensing laws! They'll tell us what time to go to bed next. (*They quaff.*)

KITTY: To the West Cork Railway! (*They quaff.*)

MAURICE: To Danger Mullaly, the navigator! (*They cheer this.*) Speech! Suas ar an Ardan. (*They hoist Danger onto a chair.*)

DANGER (*gutturally*): A Chairde Ghael! O, Uh, Gu, Bo, Boola, Bo, Wo, Bow Wow! I always believe in a few words in Irish first. (*Applause.*) Men an' women o' Keelty, there's tears in my eyes an' an ache in my heart to be leavin' the country o' my birth this grand summer's mornin'. But I go proudly because I know that the T.D.'s and the ministers above in Dail Eireann will be cryin' their eyes out after I'm gone, an' the Holy Josies will be prayin' for me so that I won't stray from the path. I'll be a member of the I.B.N.A. next week an' forever more I'll be disgraced in the eyes of my schoolmasters who taught me for better things.

KITTY: What's the I.B.N.A., Danger?

DANGER: The Irish Buck Navvies Association!

Quotes poem

> When I was a young man my books I attended
> But a poor man's a poor man, I know to my grief.
> So I'll be a buck navvy, as God has intended
> And work with my hands for the cheat and the thief.

Cheers from listeners.

> We can't all be doctors, we can't all be teachers.
> To England I'll go, where there's money in sweat.

> So here's a farewell to the religious preachers
> From an Irish buck navvy who goes to his death.

Cheers from listeners.

> Oh, young men of twenty, I issue fair warning,
> There's no hope for me since I failed at my books;
> Stay here in old Ireland this fine summer's morning,
> And save her from politics, chancers, and crooks.

Cheers from listeners.

> The wild geese are gone, but the goslings are flying;
> The young men of twenty are leaving the land.
> The old men are old, and the old men are dying.
> Stay here in old Ireland and make a last stand.

Cheers from listeners.

DANGER: Take me down off this shaggin' table an' let me finish my drink.
They help him from table.

KITTY: Peg, give us one touch o' that oul' song o' yours!

PEG: 'Tis too early in the mornin' for singin'!

MAURICE: For me, Peg?

PEG (*humorously*): For you, Maurice. (*In her hardboiled way.*) Anything
for you, Maurice!

KITTY: D'you know the song you'll sing, me bonny barmaid? Sing that song
about goin' away. Fool I was I didn't go when I was young an' handsome
—I might have a husband now and be naggin' the nose off his face.

DANGER: Put her up on the table, the same as me. Peg is a coulogeous singer.
Peg is lifted up on the table.

KITTY: Give us our own song.

Approval is evident from the others on stage.

PEG (*sings*):

> Many young men of twenty said goodbye.
> I had a son,
> A healthy love child and a bonny boy.
> Many young men of twenty said goodbye.
> My boy Jimmy went away,
> Maurice Browne is here to stay,
> Maurice Browne is here, and here am I —
> Many young men of twenty said goodbye.

All join in the chorus.

ALL (*chorusing*):

> Many young men of twenty said goodbye,
> All that long day;
> From break of dawn until the sun was high
> Many young men of twenty said goodbye.
> My boy Jimmy went that day,

On the big ship sailed away,
Sailed away and left me here to die
Many young men of twenty said goodbye.

Peg is lifted from the table.

DANGER (*toasts*): To Elizabeth the Second of England and to the job she has waitin' for me!

Enter Kevin carrying suitcase. Danger immediately shakes his hand.

DANGER: Where's the rest of 'em?

KEVIN: They're on their way — I came on ahead. (*Looks for a moment at Peg. Hesitantly.*) I want to talk to you for a minute . . . alone!

All characters onstage move to remotest points and begin to converse. Kevin advances upstage and Peg goes to him.

KEVIN: I don't know how to begin . . . but I want you to come with me.

PEG (*slowly*): I see!

KEVIN: I've seen the best and the worst of life in England and I know what loneliness is in a big city. I want to marry you and make a home for you, if you'll have me.

PEG: Why me?

KEVIN: I think I know you! You remember the evening we went walking . . . It was only an hour with you but I know that you're honest and that you'd make a good wife. I have a good future over there and with you I could go a long way. That is why I came early this morning, before the others, to ask you.

PEG: And the baby . . . (*Kevin turns away.*) . . . But surely you don't expect me to leave my baby. I couldn't do that.

KEVIN: After a while . . . if things work out!

PEG: I see! . . . Surely you don't expect me to leave my baby. I couldn't do that!

KEVIN: Well, if you can't, we'll take the baby then. Will you?

PEG: No . . . I don't think so! You don't need me so badly. You'll work out fine.

KEVIN: But why? . . . It's a grand chance for you . . . you'll never do any good for yourself here.

PEG: I like you, Kevin. You're sensible and ambitious and you know where you're going. (*Shakes head.*) But you see, I'm not too keen on sensible men who know where they are going and anyway I made a vow that I'd never send a son of mine to England.

KEVIN (*indicates Maurice Browne*): Who is it? Your man over there? . . . He's an alcoholic!

PEG: No, I don't think he is, somehow. He could be. But he isn't one yet.

KEVIN: Is it because of him you won't come with me?

PEG (*looks askance at Maurice who is watching them*): No! You needn't worry. He doesn't think of me like that.

Maurice advances and joins them.

MAURICE: You can tell me clear out if you like, but I have something to say, too. I take it he asked you to go to England with him?

KEVIN: I don't see why you should interrupt a private conversation!

MAURICE: I'll tell you why! Because I have a claim to stake, too. (*Turns to Peg and takes her hands.*) I want you to come to England with me. I love you and I can't bear the thought of anybody else marrying you, and you're the only hope I have . . . so now!

PEG (*affected but hurt*): Oh, Maurice!

KEVIN: And the baby! What about the baby?

MAURICE: If she'll have me, I'll have her baby, her father and mother, or anything else she wants.

PEG: You're a fool to go to England, Maurice! You could do so much here. I heard you talking to the T.D. this morning. You only said what everyone is thinking. You have the guts, Maurice, and the education.

MAURICE: But I don't want to go! I'll stay here if that's what you want. I'll do anything you want me to do. I'll teach in Dublin, Cork, Limerick, or Waterford, if you'll marry me. What do you say?

PEG: I say — stick it out here in Keelty, come hell or high water T.D. or no T.D.

MAURICE: With you behind me, he'd have a job shiftin' me out of Keelty . . . You'll marry me, Peg?

PEG: Will I, Maurice?

MAURICE: Oh, God, I hope you will, Peg!

Enter Dawheen Timmineen Din followed by a procession of five, all carrying suitcases. They are his wife Maynan and Dinny and Dot and another son and daughter, Micky and Mary. Micky is approximately sixteen, Mary about fifteen. Micky and Mary are nervous and poorly dressed. D.T.D. orders his retinue to be seated.

D.T.D. (*to Peg*): A half whiskey, a half o' port wine, and two minerals. (*Nudges Dot.*) What's for you?

DOT: Gin and It!

D.T.D.: Wouldn't the It be enough for you? (*To Dinny.*) What's for you?

DINNY: I'll have a brandy.

D.T.D.: Brandy! Isn't that the last of all! A gin and It and a brandy. (*To Peg, who is absorbed in Maurice.*) A gin and It and a brandy.

Exit Peg. D.T.D. calls Micky and Mary aside.

D.T.D.: There's a frightful test before ye over there. Go to bed early at night and talk to no one with a strange accent. Don't forget to send home a few

409

pounds now and again and, above all, don't attempt to ate mate on a Friday.

MAYNAN: Keep yourselves to yourselves and your own brothers and sisters over. Call every stranger you meet sir and look as foolish as you can and don't forget the Hail Marys for a happy death and purity, and praise be all on high ye'll be a credit to your father an' mother.

D.T.D.: Don't go spendin' money foolish. Spare every halfpenny because there'll be a great scarcity o' money before the end o' the year. I saw it in *Old Moore's Almanac.*

DANGER: 'Twill ruin small farmers!

D.T.D.: No one talkin' to you!

DANGER: So you're sendin' another shipment this mornin'. 'Tis worse than the horse trade.

Enter Peg with drinks, which she distributes.

D.T.D. (*to Dinny*): Pay for that — you called for it!

Dinny does so.

D.T.D. (*to Maynan*): Drink that up. There's milk for the creamery.

DANGER (*to D.T.D.*): Promise me you won't cry. I couldn't stand it!

D.T.D.: Bum!

D.T.D. finishes his drink.

DANGER (*to no one in particular — vehemently*): We'll always be goin' from this miserable country. No one wants us. There's your Ireland for you, with grief and goodbyes and ullagoning at every railway station. (*Passionately.*) What honest-to-God politician with an ounce of guts in him would keep his mouth shut when he sees the father of a family goin' away alone with his heart broke, leavin' his poor children behind him? 'Tis the end of the world for them because their father is leavin' them behind. What man, with a drop o' honest blood in his veins, wouldn't rise up an' shout: "Stop! Stop it! Stop this cruelty. Stop tearin' the hearts out of innocent people! Stop sittin' down on yeer backsides an' do somethin'!"

D.T.D. (*to Maynan*): Come on! The milk will be sour in the tanks. (*To Mary and Micky.*) Say goodbye to your mother now!

Tremulously Mary says goodbye, as does Micky. So do Dot, Dinny, and Kevin.

D.T.D.: Have you the Knock water?

Maynan produces the Knock water, which she sprinkles over them. She then exits hurriedly.

D.T.D.: Don't forget the few pounds, an' God bless ye all!

KITTY (*loudly*): Boo!

She is joined by some of the people onstage. Enter Seelie.

SEELIE: What's all this racket? What's this bar turning into? (*To Danger.*) What are you doing here?

DANGER (*affected tone*): I'm goin' to England, but I knew you'd be disappointed if I went without sayin' goodbye to you.

SEELIE: Good riddance!

She notices Kitty and the melodeon player.

SEELIE: And you! What are you two doing here? (*To Peg.*) Where's Tom?

PEG: I didn't see him this morning.

SEELIE: You mean he hasn't shown up at all this morning?

PEG: That's right!

SEELIE: And why didn't you call me?

PEG: Well, you were gone to Mass, an' I was too busy.

Enter Tom, wearing mackintosh, looking spick and span, and carrying a suitcase. With an air of independence he places bag at Seelie's feet.

TOM (*loudly*): Peg! A ball o' malt! I have a train to catch.

Exit Peg.

SEELIE (*angrily*): What do you mean — you have a train to catch? Where do you think you're going?

TOM: England!

SEELIE: Now, listen to me, Tom Hannigan! You get that silly notion out of your head right away.

TOM: I see nothing silly about it. It might sound silly to yourself and that bunch of Holy Josies you hang around with, but it's a very serious thing to me.

SEELIE (*alarmed*): What's the matter with you, Tom? Are you feeling all right?

TOM: Never felt better in my life, except that I just copped onto myself. (*Peg enters and hands him glass of whiskey. He immediately swallows it.*) I'm getting old, Seelie. Do you understand that? In another ten years I'll be an old man and what have I done with my life? Damn all! And if I stay here I'll never do anything. I've been a mouse for thirty years. But this morning I copped onto myself. I'm going to England, Seelie, and nothing is going to stop me.

SEELIE: But why? What put this madness into your head so suddenly? You might have let me know!

TOM: I didn't know myself until this morning. I could never get married here.

SEELIE: You don't know what you're doing! It's the drink!

TOM: Oh, I know what I'm doing all right! I know at last.

SEELIE: But you have everything you want here.

TOM: No, Seelie, I haven't! You have! You have your Mass every morning and your devotions every evening. But I'm different, Seelie. I'm weak. I want flesh and blood. Maybe I'll meet a girl that'll take to me. Maybe

I'll turn out like other fellows and be married and have a wife to look after me. 'Tis only fair, Seelie. You'll probably tell me to go to Hell, but I can tell you — go to Heaven!

DANGER: 'Twon't be much fun up there if they're all like her.

SEELIE: Oh! . . . wait till I tell Father Madigan. (*Exit Seelie.*)

TOM: I knew she'd say exactly that!

DOT: Anybody got the time? My watch has stopped!

JOHNNY: We have thirteen minutes to be exact.

DANGER: We'd better be gettin' ready. I never thought I'd see the day I'd be leavin' Ireland. (*Assumes a stentorian tone, military-like.*) All right, my lads! Form a line here!

They form a line across the stage. The line consists of those who are going to England. Peg and Maurice Browne stand at one side. Kitty and melodeon player stand behind line.

DANGER (*loudly*): Number off! (*They number off.*) 'Tenshun! (*They stand to attention.*)

DANGER (*falsetto*): We are not the first and we will not be the last. God help us! Chins up an' let me see smiles on those faces. Don't blame poor oul' Ireland but blame the hypocrites that brought us to this pass. Come on, Kitty. Play us up to the station. Your song, Peg, before we go.

Peg comes forward.

PEG (*singing*):   Many young men of twenty said goodbye
                                All that long day,
                                From break of dawn until the sun was high,
                                Many young men of twenty said goodbye.
                                They left the mountain and the glen,
                                The lassies and the fine young men;
                                I saw the tears of every girl and boy
                                Many young men of twenty said goodbye.

DANGER: All together!

ALL (*singing*):   Many young men of twenty said goodbye
                                All that long day,
                                From break of dawn until the sun was high,
                                They left the mountain and the glen,
                                The lassies and the fine young men;
                                I saw the tears of every girl and boy.
                                Many young men of twenty said goodbye,
                                Many young men of twenty said goodbye.

KITTY: We'll play you up to the station. Start up the music Davy.

Singing the last verse over again they exit, led by Kitty and Davy, the melodeon player, who plays the tune on his melodeon. The last line of the song is repeated until it fades out, and on the stage Maurice Browne and Peg Finnerty embrace.

♣ *JAMES DOUGLAS* ♣

JAMES DOUGLAS is a difficult playwright to discuss because he still seems to be developing a style. His first two stage plays, *North City Traffic Straight Ahead* and *The Ice Goddess* have both a very definite and notable style, but it seems to be one that Douglas in his recent television work is growing away from. One of his strongest literary influences is the American writer Sherwood Anderson, who was noted for his simplicity of expression. This simplicity is the most obvious quality of the dialogue of Douglas's two produced stage plays. Indeed, it is a stylized hypersimplicity that puts one in mind of the dialogue of Steinbeck's *Of Mice and Men* or of Hemingway at his most Hemingwayish. On the page, such dialogue seems sometimes an irritating and affected mannerism. On the stage, however, these terse and simple repetitions build often to a devastating revelation of private anguish.

Douglas was born in Bray, a seaside resort a few miles south of Dublin, on July 4, 1929. After school, he became an apprentice electrician, and he still works as an electrician three days a week. His first produced play, *North City Traffic Straight Ahead*, was directed by Alan Simpson for the 1961 Theatre Festival. In the 1963 Theatre Festival, *Carrie*, a musical, was based upon a story of his. In the 1964 Festival, his *The Ice Goddess* was produced at the Gate. He has, since *North City Traffic*, done a good deal of television writing. He devised and spent twenty-six painful weeks writing the television serial *The Riordans*, and he has also written several original television plays, including *The Bomb, The Hollow Field*, an adaptation of *North City Traffic*, and the recent *Babbi Joe*. Currently, he

413

is working on a play called *The Savages* which treats of the effect of the Congo police action upon Dubliners.

His plays, probably more than those of any other writer in this book, reflect the new Ireland. It is not only that they are urban and could conceivably occur in London or Philadelphia almost as readily as in Dublin, but also that they reflect the modern sense of isolation, even of anguish. Harry Hopkins, the middle-aged hero of *North City Traffic*, is afflicted with the same spiritual malaise that has blighted the lives of Osborne's Jimmy Porter or of Donleavy's Sebastian Dangerfield. In one sense, his plight seems a bit more puerile because he is old enough to be more mature. However, his story, the circumstances of his life, which have given rise to his self-laceration, should not probably be taken as literal and realistic. More plausibly, the story seems a framework upon which Douglas may hang his real preoccupation in this play — the poignant isolation of Harry Hopkins, his inability to make any human contact. That moment at the climax of the play when it briefly seems that Harry and Emmy, both of them full of pain and anguish and suppressed love, will touch each other as human beings, is a moment of great pertinence for a modern audience. And their failure to make contact is not only intensely moving in the theater, but also a painfully appropriate comment upon the nature of modern life, in Ireland or anywhere else.

The Ice Goddess is in a narrow sense a coming-of-age story. It is also much more than that. Mrs. Fury's grand old house and Mrs. Gage's small modern villa are both obviously symbolic, and so also is Kevin's tree house. Really, the play might more properly be considered a realization story. Douglas's point here is rather more complex than that of *North City Traffic*, and certainly this play more baffled the rather easily baffled Dublin reviewers. He is saying that an ideal state is impossible to maintain. Everything is in a cycle of repetition, for that is the nature of human existence. Mrs. Fury, the Ice Goddess, has furiously attempted to maintain unchanged the house which embodied her dead husband's dream. But it, like Kevin's childish ideal symbolized by his tree house, is destroyed in the storm, and a new house embodying a totally different dream will be built in its place by Kevin's father. The Ice Goddess, Kevin learns, must thaw in the face of time and the necessity of things. So really Kevin has learned something basic about the human state — that it must change, but that in a larger sense it is changeless and repetitive and unimproving and probably unimprovable.

The play's story is less simple than that of *North City Traffic*, and the characters are more humanly arresting. Harry and Emmy of the earlier play, for all of their theatrical effect, were little more than poignantly meaningful cartoons. Here, Kevin and Mrs. Fury and the sensual Mrs. Gage are more fully drawn. And here also, from this story, arises a deeper and more meaningful compassion.

Douglas may be still hammering out an appropriate style for what he has to say, but what he has to say already comes across the footlights with tremendous effect. Perhaps more than any other of the young Irish dramatists is Douglas a man of his time. One winds up comparing him more with writers like John Arden or Harold Pinter or Edward Albee than with his Irish contemporaries. He is an Irishman speaking to the world more as a modern man than as an Irishman, and that perhaps is the direction in which the modern Irish drama is tending.

The Ice Goddess

MRS. FURY
KEVIN, her grandson
MELANIE, her daughter, Kevin's mother
LESLIE PHIBBS, Melanie's husband

MRS. GAGE
BERTIE GAGE, Mrs. Gage's husband
JOE SHIELDS, JEAN STRINGER, school-
mates of Kevin

The place is a small town in summertime in no particular period. The action takes place on a single day in summer and is more or less continuous. The house dominates the set. It is raised on a dais, back center, represented by its main room: opulent and grand in an old manner. There are two small sets of stairs, one right, one left of the dais. Those on the right give to the interior of the house; those left to the outside. Essential to the action here are back center a bay window, now covered in red velvet drapes with golden bobbins at the fringe; a seat in the window bay; rising left a stairway with four steps and then a small landing and more steps; another window is on the landing. There should be a good deal of heavy, handhewn furniture and a fireplace, large and pretentious, of stone, with huge fire irons. This room formed part of a man's Xanadu; it should reflect the ambience of the remainder of the house: over-large, a trifle ridiculous, somewhat vulgar, the product of a lot of love, drive, imagination, wrought when hope was highest and the fact of death full at bay, most disdainfully denied. The room should have a rocking chair, prominently placed, throne-like, for Mrs. Fury and also a stand with liqueur bottles.

The villa is forestage, left. It has no fixed reference. Its physical properties may be added to or subtracted from as the action demands. The villa is modern, clean and bright. Among the properties required will be a large window frame with venetian blinds, two doors on frames, one door with a hinged window above it, a modern sink unit, a set of tubular steel chairs and table to match.

The wood like the villa is impermanent, expanding and contracting to the demands of the play. It is forestage right. Its main and permanent feature is a huge beech tree.

Act I

SCENE 1

At curtain-rise, Kevin, a sixteen-year-old boy, dressed in sweatshirt and jeans, is crouched on the landing. He is looking out of the window down on the villa. It is early morning on what will be a long, hot summer's day. A chirping of birds is heard. This chirping starts off in a low key. At first it is hardly discernible. But it grows louder, reaching its climax at Mrs. Fury's entrance. The villa now is represented by a wide window frame with venetian blinds which are lowered. There is movement behind the blinds, and a quiet, dreamy, crooning. The blinds are raised by Mrs. Gage, a young pretty woman, short and heavy-fleshed. She looks out upon the morning. She is never aware of being watched. She waltzes round the room, in the act of dressing. She makes a ballad of this act of dressing. She plays with many garments, selecting and discarding each in turn. She seeks newness, craves the exotic. She comes to the window. She remains still for a moment, looking out. She inhales, exhales deeply. She, too, is aware of the starting day. The long, hot, lonely day to come. Being aware, she kneads her breasts in a subconscious gesture. She sighs. Kevin stares down at her. The sound of the birds is now growing in intensity. It is loud and shrill. There are footsteps and someone descends the stairs in the house. Kevin stands with his back to the window. Mrs. Fury comes down the stairs. She looks about as she moves, seeming to check a series of sights and sounds and smells against an inventory that she holds in her head. She is neither short nor tall. All of her movements are sharp and severe — free from cloyingness. Her grey hair is bobbed short in the back. She moves her head a good deal in a quick, fluid fashion.

MRS. FURY (*raising her voice above the sound of the birds*): Ah, Kevin! Good morning!

KEVIN: Grandmother. . . .

He is embarrassed at being caught. He goes to Mrs. Fury and kisses her.

MRS. FURY: Those birds! They are preparing for the day. Soon they will fly away. They lodge in the ivy. You are up early. It's not yet eight.

KEVIN: I couldn't sleep.

MRS. FURY: The heat. It will be another warm day.

She goes to the window to look out. As she does so, Mrs. Gage closes her window with a sigh and goes from it. She is gone when Mrs. Fury looks out. Kevin is afraid to turn. There is a flutter of wings. The bird sounds cease.

MRS. FURY: There. I've frightened the birds away.

KEVIN: Have they all gone? All the birds?

MRS. FURY: All gone. Everything is quiet again. The grass is still wilted.

KEVIN: Yesterday's sun.

MRS. FURY: Even under the dew. That odious villa down there. Where the Gages live. How ugly its red roof is.

KEVIN (*turns*): The Gages . . . ? Can you see?

MRS. FURY: The roof is crusty and red like a sore.

Kevin looks and sees that Mrs. Gage has gone. He is enormously relieved. He laughs and points.

KEVIN: But, see! The oak, Grandmother!

MRS. FURY: The first thing I looked at.

KEVIN: Grandfather's oak.

MRS. FURY: Fresh and green as ever.

KEVIN: Not wilted. Not wilted at all.

MRS. FURY: It would take more than the sun to wilt that oak.

She descends into the room. Kevin follows.

KEVIN: It's cool down here.

MRS. FURY: Because the drapes are drawn. We must leave them so.

KEVIN: They keep out the sun.

MRS. FURY: They don't let the sun destroy your grandfather's furniture.

KEVIN: It's hard to realize that he made all of this himself.

MRS. FURY: Oh, but he did.

KEVIN: I know.

MRS. FURY (*as an echo*): That he made himself . . . (*Slight pause.*) You are going into the wood, Kevin?

KEVIN: The house. It's nearly built.

MRS. FURY: Your house. Built in a tree.

KEVIN: Only the roof.

MRS. FURY: That's important.

KEVIN: I know.

MRS. FURY: More important than the walls.

KEVIN: The roof is shelter. The walls are protection.

MRS. FURY: One day you must take me.

KEVIN: But how could you climb?

Mrs. Fury laughs. Her laugh is a tinkle, a cascade of tinkling sounds. Kevin joins in.

MRS. FURY: Of course! Of course! How could I climb? Anyway you don't want to take me.

KEVIN: Oh. I do. (*He doesn't.*)

MRS. FURY: You don't. I don't blame you. I'm an old woman.

KEVIN: You're not! You're not!

MRS. FURY: A house in the woods is only for a young woman. A girl. I was such a girl once.

Kevin is embarrassed.

MRS. FURY: But it's cruel of me to tease you. (*She kisses his forehead.*) I must see to the food. Much too hot for heavy food. (*She goes down the steps, left, and exits.*)

Kevin looks about the room. He looks awesomely. He walks about. He touches some of the furniture. He rubs his hand on his shirt after the touching. Then, he suddenly parts the drapes, lifts the window, and leaves. The drapes fall back into place and the fierce sunlight is once more excluded.

SCENE 2

Leslie Phibbs comes down the stairs. He stands in the center of the room. He is tall and thin. He doesn't seem to have total command of his body. Against his will, at times, his pose crumbles. His body assumes a crooked stance. He fights against this, desperately. The results are at times comic to behold. His bones push out through his body and twitch. He clasps and un-clasps his sweaty, knuckly hands. He is dressed in funereal black. He carries a bowler hat. His long black hair is extravagantly pomaded and slicked back. He looks at his watch which he wears about his thin wrist. He taps his foot with impatience.

LESLIE: What can be keeping that woman? What can she be at? I am the one who will be seen. Not she. No one will look at her. (*He goes to the stair end and calls.*) Melanie! Melanie!

MELANIE (*off*): Coming, dear. I'm coming.

LESLIE: Hurry! Hurry!

He goes back center, and stands again tapping his foot with impatience. He does this with as much arrogance as he can muster. Mrs. Fury comes from the kitchen and ascends the steps, re-entering the room. She moves without noise, though not with stealth. Leslie is unaware of her coming. She stands beside him for a moment without speaking, looking at him.

MRS. FURY: You called, Mr. Phibbs?

Leslie starts when he hears her. He turns. His pose sags. He laughs to cover.

LESLIE: Melanie . . . It was Melanie . . . I called Melanie.

MRS. FURY: Oh. Your voice. It is so indistinct. (*She is being insulting — and knows it.*)

LESLIE (*laughing uneasily again*): The echoes . . . The echoes . . . In this house, you know. The echoes . . .

MRS. FURY (*in total command*): Ah, yes. The echoes, Mr. Phibbs.

Melanie comes down the stairs. She is small and fragile. Everything about her is pitched in a low key. She is rather washed out and wan. She is dressed to go out. Her dress is sober. She wears a hat.

MELANIE: Here I am, Leslie.

MRS. FURY (*enjoying this scene carnivorously*): Here she is, Mr. Phibbs.

MELANIE: Your black handkerchief. You forgot your —

MRS. FURY: How could you?

MELANIE: — Black handkerchief. (*She sees Mrs. Fury.*) Oh, Mother! Good morning!

MRS. FURY (*standing to be kissed*): Good morning, Melanie. You look tired. (*Glancing at Leslie.*) The echoes, Mr. Phibbs. The echoes.

MELANIE (*an embarrassed laugh*): Me? Why, I'm not. I — I — Leslie — forgot his black handkerchief — he has a funeral this morning.

MRS. FURY: So I heard you say. He wouldn't be dressed without it. Would you, Mr. Phibbs? And black so becomes him.

MELANIE: Shall I tuck it in for you, Leslie? I always tuck in his handkerchief.

Leslie is constricted with impatience. He tries to quell his impatience. He bends for Melanie, holding himself with difficulty.

MELANIE: Lower, dear. That's it. A little more. More, dear.

LESLIE: It is late, Melanie. I have no wish to be late. (*His words are a little above a whisper, but they come deeply charged.*)

MRS. FURY: It is extremely unlikely, I should say, Mr. Phibbs, that a move will be made without you.

LESLIE: This is an important occasion.

MRS. FURY: John Robertson's funeral.

LESLIE: He was a friend of yours, Mrs. Fury?

MRS. FURY: Yes. Yes, he was.

MELANIE: And of my father.

MRS. FURY: My husband and I were guests at John Robertson's wedding.

LESLIE (*looking directly at Mrs. Fury; not troubling to quell the viciousness*): And now he's dead.

MRS. FURY (*turning her whole body at Leslie in a regal gesture*): Yes. And now he is dead.

MELANIE: They both are. He and my father. My father's dead too . . .

They don't seem to hear Melanie's words. Beneath Mrs. Fury's eyes, Leslie is naked. He continues to battle.

LESLIE: And about to be buried.

MRS. FURY (*with glacial hardness*): Dead. And about to be buried. (*She seems to grow in stature.*) Of all the inevitables, Mr. Phibbs, death is the most inevitable, is it not?

Mrs. Fury laughs her tinkling silver laugh. Tableau. This is held for some time. Leslie capitulates.

LESLIE: If — if you'll excuse me, I must be about my business.

Mrs. Fury gives her head a short inclination, a frosty smile of triumph on her face. Leslie exits down the steps, left. Melanie follows him after a glance at her mother.

MELANIE: Yes. It is important. It is, Leslie. Very important. You mustn't be late. You mustn't . . .

Mrs. Fury looks after them a moment before the stage goes black.

SCENE 3

The stage is black for an instant. Then the forestage is brilliantly lit. The house is in the background, brooding in darkness. Mrs. Fury is gone. Forestage is a hidden clearing in the green heart of a June wood. Sunlight streams and spills and bounces off heavy long-stemmed grasses. Birds sing. A rope is fastened to the limb of the beech tree. Kevin uses it to get up and down. Fresh branches are strewn at the base of the tree. Joe comes into the clearing. He swings from the dangling rope, his foot through the noose at the end. He yodels. Joe, although he is Kevin's age, is bigger than Kevin, more brash, without Kevin's depth of feeling.

JOE (*calling*): Kevin? Kevin, where are you?

KEVIN (*in the tree*): Heaven. I'm in Heaven.

JOE: Yeah? Doesn't sound like it to me.

KEVIN: How'd you know?

JOE: I'd know. It finished yet?

KEVIN: Nearly.

JOE: "Ark of pine and willow boughs" . . . That's where you got the stupid idea in the first place. Out of the poetry book. Ark of pine and willow boughs . . . Crazy stuff! Mad!

Kevin comes out on the limb of the tree.

KEVIN: Why don't you go away?

JOE: Where could I go for a bigger laugh?

KEVIN: You've frightened it away.

JOE: Yeah? What?

KEVIN: The peace. It was all around. But you had to frighten it away. Shouting.

421

Joe sways on the rope.

JOE: Can see the Sugarloafs from here. Two of them. Little and Big.

KEVIN: Sometimes I think they talk to each other, across the valley.

JOE (*mocking*): Go on! What are they saying now?

KEVIN (*shouting*): Stop twisting on that rope! You're shaking the house.

JOE: Yeah? That up there? Leaves and branches. The wind'll blow it down.

KEVIN: You think so?

JOE: I know so. (*A definite statement.*) Yeah. The wind'll blow it down.

KEVIN: You're wrong.

JOE: Am I?

He laughs, an old, wise laugh.

KEVIN: Shut up and get off the rope. I'm getting down.

Joe gets off the rope. Kevin slides down.

JOE: I was thinking.

KEVIN: You?

JOE: I know where there're some terrific trees.

KEVIN: Yeah?

JOE: Be terrific for the house.

KEVIN: No.

JOE: I'll show you. We'll build it together. I know a lot about building —

KEVIN: No.

JOE: You're doing it all wrong.

KEVIN: I'm doing it the way I want it.

JOE: Want to do it all yourself?

KEVIN: That's it.

JOE: Bringing some bird here when it's finished?

KEVIN: Might.

JOE: Thought that. Who?

KEVIN: No one you know.

JOE: In this town, I know them all. The ones who lift it and the ones who like you to lift it.

KEVIN: Quit that kind of talk.

JOE: These trees I told you about. They're near the old quarry. Palms.

KEVIN: Palms?

JOE: What's wrong with palms?

KEVIN: Plumes. Black plumes that they put at a funeral horse's head. Palms.

JOE: You ought to know. Your old man in the racket.

He clasps his hands, imitates Leslie's smile, bows.

JOE: It comes to us all . . . The great leveler . . . Your father's really worth the money!

Kevin takes off his sweatshirt. Joe whoops like a redskin.

JOE: Hair. You've got no hair.

KEVIN (*after a look at his bare chest*): Who wants hair?

JOE (*poking Kevin's chest with a stick*): No! Wait! There's one. Definitely. A hair. A single hair!

Kevin snaps the stick from Joe and breaks it.

JOE: A single hair can be quite a menace! You could lash yourself to death with a single hair! Know that?

KEVIN: You're only a mouth!

JOE: Ever see Gage?

KEVIN: The gargoyle?

JOE: Gargoyle? That's good!

KEVIN: Read it in a book. He's a brute.

JOE: Such hair!

KEVIN: A brute.

Kevin prepares the loose branches for the tree house. He uses a long knife.

JOE: She's OK, though.

KEVIN: Who?

JOE: Her, his wife.

KEVIN: Yeah?

JOE: I wouldn't say no. Anytime she likes she can put her slippers under my bed.

Kevin comes close to Joe, menacing him with knife.

KEVIN: Why don't you shut up!

JOE: Gargoyle takes off his shirt when he mows his lawn. She comes out and puts stuff on his back.

KEVIN (*very anxious*): How do you know?

JOE: She's like something out of a book.

KEVIN (*cautiously*): What kind of book?

JOE: Not the kind that I read, you can bet your life on that.

KEVIN: What kind?

JOE: Ancient stuff. Damsels in distress. Knights in armor. Maiden in the tower. Unhand me, knave . . . !

KEVIN (*satisfied*): You're right. That's the kind.

JOE: Always looking out of windows. Over walls. Just like her place was a castle.

KEVIN: Most of the time she's there by herself. He's away in the country selling sugar.

JOE: Sugar?

KEVIN: That's what he does. Sells sugar.

JOE: A sugar merchant! You hear about people like that!

KEVIN: He's one.

Joe picks up a branch.

JOE: Let me help?

KEVIN: No.

JOE: I know a lot. We could turn it into something good.

KEVIN: Build one of your own.

JOE: I couldn't do that . . . She mows the grass herself sometimes.

KEVIN: I know.

JOE: It's long now. I saw it.

KEVIN: When he's away, she mows it herself. She borrows our machine.

JOE: Maybe you'll get a chance to talk to her.

KEVIN: What?

JOE: Talk to her. When she borrows your mower.

KEVIN: Yeah.

JOE: I'd put sods on the top of the branches for the roof. It needs that.

KEVIN: Wish that sun had a bit more of belt in it.

JOE: Hear me?

KEVIN: Yeah.

JOE: What do you think?

KEVIN: No.

JOE: You know Jean Stringer?

KEVIN: Everyone knows her.

JOE: Not everyone. Not the way I do. I know her. I know her real well.

KEVIN: Yeah?

JOE: She's — she's all right. Plenty of sods on the roof, I'd put. I'm seeing her today. I'd put grass on the floor. That soft green stuff. Lovely to lie on. I'm seeing her down by the old quarry. If she comes this way, tell her. It'd be good. Very good house, then.

KEVIN: Go away, you bother me.

JOE: I'll stay if you want me to.

KEVIN: I don't.

JOE: Remember what I said.

KEVIN: I'll remember.

JOE: It'll fall down.

KEVIN: It won't.

JOE: The wind'll blow it down.

KEVIN: No.

JOE: The branches'll wither.

KEVIN: I told you! Go! Beat it!

JOE: The leaves'll curl up, go brown! Go brown! Your ark! Your ark of pine and willow — !

Suddenly, Kevin charges at Joe, his head down. He strikes Joe in the stomach with his head. They fall and tussle on the ground. They roll over and over. It finishes with Kevin astraddle of Joe. Kevin jumps up and down on Joe, who groans.

KEVIN (*panting through his clenched teeth*): Now will you go away? Will you?

JOE (*winded*): OK. OK. Let's up. Let's up and I'll go.

Kevin lets him up.

JOE: Know what? You're mad.

KEVIN: Maybe.

JOE: Your whole family are mad! Candidates for cuckoo land! Everyone says it!

KEVIN: I don't care. Just let me build my house, that's all.

JOE (*walking away, he looks over his shoulder and laughs*): Remember what I said, boy. It'll blow down. But you get sun on your back. Get sun on your back for the damsel in distress. But watch the gargoyle. He bites. (*Joe goes.*)

Sure that he has gone, Kevin ties his shirt across his shoulders, knotting the sleeves under his chin. He turns to look at the round disc of the sun. He stands and beats his bare chest for a while. He goes off in search of more branches for the house in the tree. The stage goes black.

SCENE 4

The lights come up on the house. The brilliant forestage lights are gone. The house is as it was. The drapes are still drawn against the sun. Leslie, followed by Melanie, enters from the left. They are returning from the funeral of John Robertson.

LESLIE (*petulantly*): That town down there.

MELANIE: It gets worse. All the time.

LESLIE: That awful heat. So hard to maintain a manner proper to the occasion.

MELANIE: All eyes were on you.

LESLIE: I do have a certain flair. I can be solemn.

MELANIE: Very. (*She is wiping his brow with his black handkerchief.*)

LESLIE: Not many people can be solemn. She never can. Not really solemn. Your mother.

MELANIE: You never faltered, Leslie. Poetic, it was poetic.

LESLIE: Did you watch? All the time?

MELANIE: You made a truly beautiful occasion of it.

LESLIE: It does require that little touch. That extra little touch.

MELANIE: Undoubtedly.

LESLIE: Solemnity. Solemnity.

Melanie is unfastening his black tie and loosening the stern collar of his

*white shirt and his shirt front, wiping him with black handkerchief. There is
nothing solemn about this. It is comic.*

LESLIE: She doesn't think that death is important.

MELANIE: You mustn't mind her too much.

LESLIE: It is, Melanie. It is.

MELANIE: You mustn't mind her when she laughs.

LESLIE: No respect. She has no respect.

MELANIE: None.

LESLIE: You heard her laugh. She laughed. As if it wasn't important. As if I
wasn't important. It is important. I am important.

MELANIE: Very important.

LESLIE: I am. I am. (*He expands, looks about.*) This house. Draw those
drapes, Melanie. Draw them.

MELANIE (*unsure, afraid*): The drapes, Leslie?

LESLIE: Draw them across.

MELANIE: But, Leslie.

LESLIE: Draw them, Melanie.

Silence. They look at each other.

LESLIE: Do as I say, Melanie.

MELANIE: She has them drawn to protect the furniture.

LESLIE: Draw them. Are you afraid of her? Don't tell me you're afraid of
her?

MELANIE: She is my mother.

LESLIE: What can she do?

MELANIE: Nothing. She can do nothing. But —

LESLIE: Then?

MELANIE: No! We'd better not.

LESLIE: I am not afraid. She has no power. No power over me. I am Leslie
Phibbs. I am as good as she.

MELANIE: You draw them.

LESLIE: No.

MELANIE: See.

LESLIE: But I want you to do it.

MELANIE: Why?

LESLIE: As an act of obedience. Draw them.

*Melanie looks at him. He prods her with his eyes. She moves to the window
and pulls back the drapes. The room is lit up eagerly by the sun.*

LESLIE (*gleefully*): Ah, the sun. It's hot. Very hot.

MELANIE: What about the furniture, Leslie?

LESLIE: What about it?

MELANIE: It is precious.

LESLIE: Only to her. — The sun, how hot it is!

MELANIE: My father made it.

LESLIE: That is why. It is worthless. Has no value. None — it sears, the sun!

MELANIE: It is rare and beautiful. (*She touches a chairback reverently.*)

LESLIE: It took Leslie Phibbs to pull the business of making this rare and precious furniture out of bankruptcy.

MELANIE: My family owes you a great deal, Leslie.

LESLIE: She despises me.

MELANIE: She doesn't.

LESLIE: She does. But I don't care. I refuse to care. And you have paid, Melanie.

MELANIE (*head down*): I have paid.

LESLIE: You have. In full.

MELANIE: You mustn't blame her too much.

LESLIE: Never a word of gratitude.

MELANIE: It is her way.

LESLIE: She should be grateful.

MELANIE: Only her way.

LESLIE: A bob of her head. Just a bob of her head, that's all.

MELANIE: She is strange. Kevin is the only person to whom she talks. She tells him things.

LESLIE: You're her daughter. I am your husband. I am married to you for sixteen years.

Melanie looks up quickly, an appeal.

MELANIE: More than sixteen, Leslie. More. Seventeen, Leslie. Seventeen. Kevin — Kevin is sixteen.

LESLIE (*giggling*): Is it seventeen, Melanie? Time flies. Seventeen. Yes, perhaps it is. (*He hardens.*) But I'm still Mr. Phibbs to her. Mr. Phibbs and a bob of her head.

MELANIE: She has a high regard for you.

LESLIE: What?

He wants to believe this, wants very much to believe it.

MELANIE: She has.

LESLIE: What did she say?

MELANIE: She said it.

LESLIE: A high regard, she said?

MELANIE: Yes.

LESLIE: A high regard, she said?

MELANIE: Those were her words.

LESLIE: A high regard! (*He sounds it out.*) What were her words? Her exact words?

MELANIE: She said she had a high regard for your business ability.

Leslie jumps up in disgust.

427

MELANIE (*not understanding*) : Leslie, is something wrong?

LESLIE: Nothing's wrong!

MELANIE: When you jumped just now, I thought there was. A sudden cramp, I thought. You know you're liable to them. To cramps.

LESLIE: Don't think. No one asked you to think.

MELANIE (*head down*) : I'm sorry, Leslie.

LESLIE: That woman. Your mother. She has gone too far. Some day I knew she would. That is why I have my plan. My plan for her. For this house.

MELANIE: What plan, Leslie? What plan?

LESLIE: You'll know. You'll know and she'll know. Yes, she'll know.

Silence. Melanie's head is down. Leslie looks at her.

LESLIE (*with a lot of craft*) : It isn't your fault, Melanie.

MELANIE (*looking up; glad of the tone*) : It's the heat.

LESLIE: That's what it is.

MELANIE: It made you jump. The tension of it.

LESLIE: Awful heat.

MELANIE: One thing, Leslie. Mother loves Kevin.

Leslie hasn't heard fully. He turns rapidly.

LESLIE: What did you say, Melanie? What did you say about your mother and love?

MELANIE: She loves Kevin.

LESLIE: Too much is made of that boy!

MELANIE: Too much?

LESLIE: He is told too much. Has too much freedom. Where is he now?

MELANIE: In the woods.

LESLIE: The woods?

MELANIE: He's building a house.

LESLIE: Girls go into the woods. Do you know that girls go into the woods? He has too much freedom. Far too much free —

Mrs. Fury descends the stairs. The words dwindle on Leslie's lips. He gathers his opened shirtfront in his hands at the sound of her voice.

MRS. FURY: Ah, I thought I heard voices. And I did.

MELANIE (*after a fearful glance at the drapes*) : Hello, Mother.

LESLIE: Goodday, Mrs. Fury.

Mrs. Fury inclines her head to each in turn.

MRS. FURY: Melanie. Mr. Phibbs.

Silence. Mrs. Fury smiles. She is taking in the spectacle of Leslie.

MELANIE: We — we were talking of the heat.

MRS. FURY: Oh, yes. The heat.

LESLIE: Down in the town, Mrs. Fury, it is oppressively warm.

MRS. FURY (*playing with the words*) : Is it? Oppressively warm?

MELANIE: But Leslie was wonderful.

428

MRS. FURY: Wonderful?

MELANIE: Even in the heat.

MRS. FURY: I'm sure he was. (*Turning to Leslie.*) I'm sure you were, Mr. Phibbs.

Silence.

MELANIE: It was a large, well-attended funeral.

LESLIE: An important occasion. Many, many mourners.

MRS. FURY: I'm sure John Robertson didn't mind. I see the drapes are drawn. (*She has been aware of this all along.*)

MELANIE (*a guilty look at Leslie*): Yes, we —

LESLIE: Melanie drew them.

MELANIE (*quickly*): I'll put them back. (*She starts to do so.*)

MRS. FURY: No.

LESLIE: I think she should. The sun is strong. It will destroy the furniture.

MRS. FURY: Would you, Mr. Phibbs?

LESLIE: Me?

MRS. FURY: Replace the drapes? As you say: the sun is strong.

Silence.

MRS. FURY (*totally aware; repeating with a cold smile*): Would you, Mr. Phibbs? Be good enough?

Hold again. Leslie finally capitulates. He draws the drapes partly, and turns.

MRS. FURY: All the way, if you please, Mr. Phibbs. All the way.

Leslie draws the drapes all the way. The room isn't darkened; the strong sunlight is only softened. The room itself seems to welcome this softening of the light. It becomes more fully Mrs. Fury's room.

MRS. FURY: Ah, you are so good, Mr. Phibbs. So good. Isn't that better?

MELANIE: Much better, Mother.

MRS. FURY (*sweetly*): Don't you find it better, Mr. Phibbs?

LESLIE: Really, I —

MRS. FURY (*more sweetly still, prodding him with her tongue*): Yes, Mr. Phibbs?

LESLIE: It is much better. Much better.

MRS. FURY (*with her tinkling laugh*): Ah, yes. I thought it would. And we must mind the furniture. Mustn't we mind the furniture?

Tableau. Hold for a moment before the stage goes black.

SCENE 5

Bring up the brilliant forestage lights. The girl, Jean Stringer, walks into the clearing, looking about. She has lithe and graceful animal movements. She is dressed to show herself off in a drawstring blouse and silken skirt. Her feet are bare except for sandals. Her hair is in a pony tail. She appears as if she can take care of herself. Sometimes, though, this appearance doesn't come off. She sees the rope dangling from the beech tree. She is drawn to it. She plays with it, wonders what it is. Kevin enters. He has a load of branches on his back. There are flowers threaded through his hair. Jean sees him and laughs. It's a spontaneous laugh, unmarred by undertone.

JEAN: Flowers in your hair!

Kevin throws down the load of branches. He takes the flowers from his hair, laughs.

JEAN: Why've you got flowers in your hair?

KEVIN: I don't know. Just have.

JEAN: Looked nice. They looked nice. Looked different.

KEVIN: Yeah?

JEAN: Strange. Looked strange. Strange and wild. Made my heart beat. Looked different.

KEVIN: You wear them.

JEAN: Me?

KEVIN: I'll give them to you.

JEAN: They're all over the place.

KEVIN: I know. But it's not the same as someone giving them to you.

JEAN: No. It's not.

KEVIN: Here.

He gives over the flowers. She takes them.

KEVIN: Put them in your hair.

JEAN: Think I should?

KEVIN: Put them in your hair. And sit up on the branches.

She does. This is all very light and innocent. The laughter is innocent laughter.

JEAN: How do I look?

She is sitting atop the load of branches. The flowers are in her hair.

KEVIN: You're Queen of the Forest, Jean!

JEAN: Queen of the Forest! Queen of the Forest . . . ?

For a brief moment, she is Queen of the Forest. Then the laughter goes. She takes the flowers from her hair, slowly.

JEAN: I'm no queen.

KEVIN (*protesting*): Jean —!

JEAN: I'm not. No queen.

KEVIN: You are, if you want to be.

JEAN: No. — He kept me back at school today.

KEVIN: Who?

JEAN: Higgy. Mr. Higgins. "Hands."

KEVIN: "Hands"?

JEAN: You serious? You mean you don't know about "Hands"? (*She takes out a cigarette.*) All the rest were gone. Don't know why he picked on me. Why did he pick on me?

KEVIN: What happened? What did he do?

JEAN: He got a big book out of his drawer. About medicine. Bodies. Pictures in it. He showed me some of the pictures.

KEVIN: Why?

JEAN: He kept saying: "You made like that, Jean? Are you, Jean? Are you? Are you?" I threw ink in his face and ran away.

KEVIN: You're crying. Don't cry.

JEAN: Who's crying? (*Trying to quell her tears.*) I'm not! Not! Why did he choose me? You tell me. Why?

KEVIN: Joe — Joe said to tell you. He's down by the old quarry. Waiting for you.

JEAN: Did he see something? Did "Hands" see something? See something in my face? Can you see anything in my face? Look.

Kevin looks.

KEVIN: Freckles. Your face is full of freckles.

JEAN: It is not!

KEVIN: It is, Jean. It is. Don't be silly.

JEAN: Silly? Who's silly! Who had flowers stuck in his hair?

KEVIN: You said they were different.

JEAN: No one goes around with flowers in his hair.

KEVIN: Why? I felt like doing it. Not for any reason. But because I felt like doing it. Made me feel good.

JEAN: Doesn't take much, then, to make you feel good. And your shirt off! Why was that?

KEVIN: Jean, shut up!

JEAN: Didn't even know why Higgy was called "Hands." Didn't even know that. You'd know if you were a girl.

KEVIN: I'm tired talking now.

JEAN: Are you? Too bad.

KEVIN: What do you want here, Jean Stringer?

JEAN: Nothing.

KEVIN: Then take it and go.

JEAN: There's nothing that you could give me that I'd take. What'll you do if I don't go away?

KEVIN: Do?

JEAN: Yeah. Do.

KEVIN: You'll find out.

JEAN: Yeah?

KEVIN: I said you will!

JEAN: If you don't start being nice to me, I'll kiss you. How'd you like that?

KEVIN: Kiss me?

JEAN: Right on the lips.

KEVIN: Leave me alone!

JEAN: That's better.

KEVIN: Just leave me alone. Go away, please.

JEAN: That's a lot better. What're you doing here, anyway?

KEVIN: Nothing.

JEAN: Something. Flowers in your hair.

KEVIN: Building a house.

JEAN (*laughing wildly*): Out of branches!

KEVIN: You don't understand!

JEAN: Grow up!

KEVIN: I'm grown.

JEAN: You?

KEVIN: Me!

Jean shows herself off.

JEAN: Yeah?

KEVIN: I am.

JEAN: Only a boy. A little boy.

KEVIN: I'm a man! A man!

JEAN (*with colossal female impudence*): You're only a boy. You're not a man. A man'd be glad of a kiss from me.

KEVIN: Some men might.

JEAN: Some men?

KEVIN: Only some men.

Jean lifts her hand as if to slap him. Kevin stands still. Jean's hand wilts.

JEAN: Any man would. But you're only a boy. Joe likes to kiss me. Did you hear what I said? Did you hear?

KEVIN: I heard.

JEAN: I make him beg for kisses. A game. Like a dog.

KEVIN: Some game.

JEAN: When I'm kissing him, I feel like a queen. Know that? A queen!

KEVIN: Anyone can be anything they want to be, I told you that.

JEAN: You're laughing at me!

KEVIN: No; I'm not, Jean.

JEAN: Making fun of me!

KEVIN: Who's laughing?

JEAN: Men keep asking me for kisses. Lots of men. It's true! I'm telling you! It's true! True!

KEVIN: I believe you, Jean.

JEAN (*crying*): You rotten liar! Where is this house? In that tree? It's up in that tree over there! I'm going up. I'm going to climb up and get into your house.

She runs to the rope. She puts her foot through the stirrup.

JEAN: You can't keep me out.

KEVIN: Don't do it, Jean.

JEAN: Try and stop me.

Kevin is able to reach above her on the rope with one hand. The knife is in his other hand. Their faces are close. Kevin is ice-cold and determined.

KEVIN: Get down!

JEAN: No!

KEVIN: Get down, Jean Stringer!

JEAN: No! No!

KEVIN: Down. I'll cut the rope.

She stops. She is arrested by the new quality of his tone.

JEAN: Too good for this world.

KEVIN: Down.

JEAN: Like her. Too good for this world, that old lady. Live in the biggest house in town.

KEVIN: My grandfather built that house. Built it with his own hands. And brought her there.

JEAN: Highest-up house on Town Hill. She lives there like a goddess.

KEVIN: You don't know her.

JEAN: Everyone knows her. And everyone talks.

KEVIN: Talks?

JEAN: About her. About your grandfather. He built the great big house with his own bare hands.

KEVIN: He did! He did!

JEAN: Talks about how he died.

KEVIN: How did he die?

JEAN: Twisted up. All twisted up. Like a thorn tree.

KEVIN: He didn't! He did not!

JEAN: And your mother. The quiet one. They talk about her, as well. Will I tell you what they say about her? I could tell you!

Jean laughs.

KEVIN: I'm going to cut the rope.

JEAN: You haven't the guts.

KEVIN: I have.

JEAN: You're like your father. Pussy-foot Phibbs, the coffin-carrier! Always dry-washing his bony hands and showing his yellow teeth!

KEVIN: Shut up!

JEAN: Don't want to hear about him. About Pussy-foot.

KEVIN: No. I don't.

JEAN: Afraid of him? He gives me the creeps. Everyone's afraid of him. Everyone.

KEVIN: I'm counting. At ten, I cut the rope.

JEAN: If you don't stop that, I'll kiss you. Right on the lips. Your teeth aren't yellow . . . Then you won't be able to stop me from getting into your house.

KEVIN: Nobody goes up there.

JEAN: I'll change you with a kiss.

KEVIN: Your kisses couldn't change me.

JEAN: Who's could?

KEVIN: Nobody's you'd know.

JEAN: You'll bring her here?

KEVIN: It's my house. I built it. It's a sacred place.

JEAN: Sacred place!

KEVIN: It is. One! Two!

JEAN: Who is she? Tell me who she is.

KEVIN: No! Get down!

JEAN: I warned you, Flowery-head!

KEVIN: Three! Four!

JEAN: I made them beg! But not you. Not you!

KEVIN: Five!

JEAN: We're poor. My family doesn't live on Town Hill.

KEVIN: Six, Jean! Six!

JEAN: Bloody meat! My father delivers bloody meat with bloody hands!

KEVIN: Seven! Please, Jean!

JEAN: See! Like him! Like Pussy-foot! The whine! "Please, Jean!" Like him, the whine!

KEVIN: Get down!

JEAN: I dreamed of being different!

KEVIN: Eight!

JEAN: I had something somebody wanted. They came to me. Some from Town Hill. Even came to me from there, when the word went out!

KEVIN: Nine!

JEAN: But not you! You Pussy-foot Phibbs! You coffin-carrier!

She has grabbed his hair in one hand. She holds the rope with the other. He is about to shout the word "Ten!" when her lips stem it on his. Kevin assumes a frozen stance. She kisses him violently, many times. She gets no reaction. She stops and looks at him.

JEAN (*brokenly*): What am I? What am I?

They regard each other as the curtain comes down.

Act II

SCENE 1

The lights come up on the house. Everything is as last seen. Mrs. Fury and Melanie are in the room. Mrs. Fury is in her chair.

MELANIE: Mother, why are you like that to Leslie?

MRS. FURY (*sweetly, with mock incomprehension*): Like what, Melanie? Like what?

MELANIE: Unpleasant.

MRS. FURY: Unpleasant? (*The tinkling laugh.*) Dear me, was I unpleasant?

MELANIE: Unpleasant, brusque, cruel even.

MRS. FURY: I must say I hadn't noticed.

MELANIE: You never notice.

MRS. FURY: Mr. Phibbs made no comment. Perhaps he hadn't noticed either.

MELANIE: He *has* got feelings.

MRS. FURY: Yes; well, I'll accept your word for that.

MELANIE: The hurt was in his eyes.

MRS. FURY: I find them difficult to see. They are so far back in his head.

MELANIE: And in the way he left the room. We — should be grateful to Leslie, Mother.

MRS. FURY (*a rising inflection*): Grateful, Melanie? Grateful?

MELANIE: Yes; grateful. He saved the business.

MRS. FURY: Only weak people, Melanie, find it possible to be truly grateful. Soft and weak people. And then, mostly, it's for favors yet to come. Gratitude I find to be a most suspicious emotion.

MELANIE: And you're not weak, Mother.

MRS. FURY: No; I am not weak.

MELANIE: Nor soft.

MRS. FURY: Neither soft, nor weak.

MELANIE: Ice. You're ice.

MRS. FURY: Oh, there are those who cannot stand the coldness of strength. Who turn away.

MELANIE: The cold wasn't the only thing I could not stand.

MRS. FURY: Oh? Something else? There was something else, Melanie?

MELANIE: You still pretend. You always pretend, pretend.

MRS. FURY: Pretend?

MELANIE: Brush it aside. Cover it up.

MRS. FURY: My dear child —

MELANIE: That's what I never was: a dear child.

MRS. FURY: Oh, but you are, Melanie. You are. You've no idea just how dear a child you are. Shall I tell you? Would you like me to tell you what

435

a dear child you are? Begot with such groping, such sweaty, ineffectual groping?

MELANIE: Stop!

MRS. FURY: Such mumbled excuses?

MELANIE: I won't listen.

MRS. FURY: You'll have to listen.

MELANIE: No.

MRS. FURY: And the nightmares. When I'd touch him inadvertently in his sleep and he'd plead — plead, plead, plead — to be left alone.

Melanie picks up a vase and stands threateningly over Mrs. Fury.

MELANIE: Stop! My God, stop! Or I'll — I'll — tear your face to pieces!

Mrs. Fury laughs her silvery, tinkling laugh. Silence. Melanie replaces the vase.

MRS. FURY (*quietly*): It is over.

MELANIE: It is not over.

MRS. FURY: Please.

MELANIE: No.

MRS. FURY: We've both become unquiet.

Melanie stares at her, comes close to her and stares.

MELANIE: We are unquiet. Always unquiet.

MRS. FURY: No more talk.

MELANIE: Yes.

MRS. FURY: Leave it lie.

MELANIE: But you never do. Is it a game we play, Mother?

MRS. FURY: Isn't it all a game?

MELANIE: This time, I'm going to finish the game.

MRS. FURY: You are, Melanie? You are?

MELANIE: I am. Now you listen.

MRS. FURY: To you?

MELANIE: To me.

Silence. This is a naked moment. There can now be no pretense, no subterfuge.

MRS. FURY (*a hand playing at her throat*): What do you wish to say, Melanie? What?

MELANIE (*an accusation*): You know.

MRS. FURY (*a flaw coming in the ice*): Know? I know?

MELANIE (*with devastating simplicity*): Yes. You know.

Silence.

MRS. FURY (*an attempt at rationality*): Melanie, your father —

MELANIE (*the same matter-of-factness*): Don't you mention his name.

MRS. FURY: But, Melanie —

MELANIE: Don't do it, Mother. Don't. Listen. You listen.

436

MRS. FURY: I refuse to have —

MELANIE: He's dead.

MRS. FURY: Yes, he's dead. Frank Fury's dead.

MELANIE: We both know how he died.

MRS. FURY: Do we, Melanie? Do we?

MELANIE: What killed him. We know.

MRS. FURY: If you say so.

MELANIE: I do. I say so. Everything he did was an obeisance, a bow and a scrape to you. And you reveled in it. Reveled in it. Even to the end. The very, very end. In the town they still call you The Goddess.

MRS. FURY (*a wry bitter sound like laughter*): The Goddess . . .

MELANIE: The *Ice* Goddess.

MRS. FURY: The Ice Goddess . . . Funny . . . How funny . . .

Another attempt at laughter. Mrs. Fury rises, goes to the drink stand, lifts ice from a bowl with tongs into a glass, pours in wine.

MRS. FURY: Wine on ice . . . I adore wine on ice . . . Red wine on ice . . .

MELANIE: So, don't mention his name. Don't mention my father's name. I won't listen.

Silence. Mrs. Fury speaks after a time with a shrug, the hint of a sigh.

MRS. FURY: Very well then, Melanie. Very well. But your Mr. Phibbs. (*She is regaining herself.*) The person to whom you turned. He did not save your father's business.

MELANIE: He did. Leslie did. And I should be careful of Leslie, Mother. If I were you.

MRS. FURY: Careful?

MELANIE: Of how you treat him.

MRS. FURY: Oh?

MELANIE: You can go too far.

MRS. FURY: A lion? Is Mr. Phibbs a lion? I am quaking.

MELANIE: Lion enough. He can be. Leslie can be.

MRS. FURY: But how lucky you are! Who would have believed it!

MELANIE: Lucky?

MRS. FURY: Never mind. He changed the nature of your father's business, Mr. Phibbs.

MELANIE: He made a success of it.

MRS. FURY: Your father fashioned fine and delicate furniture. The wood was hard under his hand. And he had his way with it. The crude, rough slabs came alive under his hand. Took on strange and delicate shapes. But that, that was before your Mr. Phibbs turned it into (*with awful loathing*) into a coffin-making concern!

MELANIE: Father, Father was — was sick . . . Leslie had to do something.
He had —

MRS. FURY (*in ringing tones*): He did not have to seduce you! As well as
everything else, seduce you! His elbows! Does Leslie lean on his elbows?
A gentleman would lean on his elbows.

MELANIE: Why do you say such things to me? Hateful, horrible things!

MRS. FURY: And you? Are you small and submissive? Do you lie, small and
damp and submissive, for him to crawl all over you like some caterpillar?
Do you, Melanie? Do you? In your case, Melanie, conquest is uncalled
for. And, in any event, Mr. Phibbs would be incapable of it! Caterpillars!
Caterpillars!

*Mrs. Fury laughs her tinkling laugh. But now the laughter is wilder, less con-
trolled. A black silence. Each crawls up out of it in her own way. What follows is fast, commonplace, comforting — for as long as it can be — at any
rate, long enough for the binding of gaping wounds.*

MRS. FURY: Mrs. Gage called.

MELANIE: She did?

MRS. FURY: While you were at — at — while you were down in the town.

MELANIE: Oh.

MRS. FURY: Yes. The pushmower. She wished to borrow the pushmower.

MELANIE: She may have it?

MRS. FURY: Of course.

MELANIE: I pity her.

MRS. FURY: What on earth for?

MELANIE: Happy. I don't think Mrs. Gage is happy.

Mrs. Fury laughs at the notion of happiness.

MRS. FURY: Melanie! Well, now!

MELANIE: I mean it, Mother. I can tell. It's plain to see.

MRS. FURY: Why isn't she happy?

MELANIE: She's afraid.

MRS. FURY: Afraid? And that's strange? Fear is strange?

MELANIE: Of him.

MRS. FURY: Oh. Who?

MELANIE: Mr. Gage. I wouldn't call him a gentleman.

MRS. FURY: Last week he gave me a rose. One of his blood-red roses. A
strong smell . . . (*She inhales deeply.*)

MELANIE: Roses have such a heady —

MRS. FURY: I wasn't thinking of the rose. Gage. He smelled. Horse urine
drying in the sun. Strong and sweet.

MELANIE: Mother!

MRS. FURY: Male odor.

MELANIE: Leslie doesn't smell like that.

MRS. FURY: Musk? (*She laughs.*) Mr. Phibbs?

MELANIE: He gave you the flower because he knew it would please you.

MRS. FURY: Of course. I made no secret of my pleasure.

MELANIE: He's vulgar.

MRS. FURY: Oh, come, now, Melanie.

MELANIE: Vulgar and obscene.

MRS. FURY: If by that you mean he has no reticences and inhibitions, I agree.

MELANIE: You sound almost as if —

She stares at Mrs. Fury, not able to go on. Mrs. Fury laughs.

MRS. FURY: As if what, Melanie? As if what?

MELANIE: As if —

MRS. FURY: He is a man.

MELANIE: When he smiles, his tongue almost touches his chin.

MRS. FURY: Scimitar.

MELANIE: What?

MRS. FURY: The great beak he has. It's like a scimitar.

MELANIE: Strange word.

MRS. FURY: Old-fashioned. It's a sword. An Arabian sword.

MELANIE: Leslie has quite a good nose.

MRS. FURY: Nondescript.

MELANIE: What did you say?

MRS. FURY: Oh, but, then, you've actually been in contact with the thing. Been touched by it. Tell me, is it cold at the end? No, no. Don't tell me. I'd prefer not to know.

MELANIE: Mother, really, I —

MRS. FURY: And what do you think of Mr. Gage's moustache?

MELANIE: When he's in the garden, he ogles, touching his moustache.

MRS. FURY: Poor Melanie. Poor, timid Melanie.

MELANIE: He takes off his shirt to show his muscles.

MRS. FURY: All covered with hair.

MELANIE: He shows off.

MRS. FURY: He has something to show.

MELANIE: She doesn't like his doing that.

MRS. FURY: Selfish creature!

MELANIE: I'm serious, Mother.

MRS. FURY: You are never anything else.

MELANIE: Kevin can take the mower. It will give him something to do.

MRS. FURY: He has something to do. Kevin has something to do. He's building a house.

MELANIE: A house, Mother? Kevin? Don't be ridiculous.

MRS. FURY: In the woods. A tree house in the woods.

MELANIE: Some childish thing. It's time he stopped being a child.

MRS. FURY: Oh, but he has, Melanie. He has stopped.

MELANIE: But, Mother —

MRS. FURY: In his head, Melanie. In his head, Kevin has a vision.

MELANIE: He has? Kevin?

MRS. FURY: Your father once had a similar vision. It comes to all men. Even, I have no doubt, to such as Mr. Phibbs.

MELANIE: You mean — you mean this house?

MRS. FURY: Your father saw it, in his mind, and built what he saw. Built it strong and beautiful. Oh, I know. It is excessive. Vulgar. Ridiculous. But he saw it. He built it. He built it when hope was highest, and death — the fact of death — was held at bay. Denied. Most disdainfully denied.

Silence. Kevin has come through the window. He stands with his back to the drapes. He looks from one woman to the other. He has lilac in his hands. He comes forward.

KEVIN: Flowers. I've plucked you some flowers, Grandmother.

MRS. FURY: Lilac. I love lilac. (*She takes the flowers.*)

MELANIE: You came through the window. (*Melanie is resentful. She senses her exclusion.*)

MRS. FURY: I shall put these in water. (*She exits to do so.*)

MELANIE: You've been told many times that you mustn't come through the window. What are doors for?

KEVIN: Doors?

MELANIE (*pointing*): That is a door. Your father has told you many times.

KEVIN: I know. He keeps telling me.

MELANIE: And you keep disobeying him.

KEVIN: I forgot.

MELANIE: You'll want to waken up. Clean yourself. Then come to the kitchen.

KEVIN: I'm not hungry, Mother.

MELANIE: Not hungry? You'll eat.

KEVIN: I feel all full up.

MELANIE: What with?

KEVIN: I don't know.

MELANIE: I know.

KEVIN: You don't, do you? Do you, Mother? Tell me if you know. I don't know myself. It's a feeling I have. All full up. The feeling that always comes before something happens.

MELANIE: Nothing's going to happen.

KEVIN: No? I'm glad. I don't want anything to happen. Anything bad.

MELANIE: Come to the kitchen. I'll fill you up with food. And you'll eat. You'll eat it all, my lad. Every morsel. Then I'll know what's inside you.

KEVIN: Yes.

MELANIE: When you've eaten, take the pushmower over to Gage's. Stay and
mow the lawn. That'll be something for you to do. Mr. Gage is away in
the country.

*On Kevin's ear, Melanie's words sound as part of a dream. As he speaks, the
villa, still represented by the wide window, is suffused in blood-red light. Mrs.
Gage appears. She is held in the window. Again she is crooning and moving
in a dreamy way.*

KEVIN: . . . over to Mrs. Gage . . . away . . . away in the country . . .

*Neither Kevin nor Melanie is looking in the direction of the villa. As soon
as Melanie speaks, the blood-red light is gone.*

MELANIE: Mowing the Gage's grass'll give you something to do for a change.
Something useful.

KEVIN (*starts guiltily. He blushes. He tries to explain, excuse himself*):
Mother, Mother, I — I —

*Melanie exits without noticing. Mrs. Fury re-enters with the lilac in a vase,
which she sets down.*

MRS. FURY: Now, Kevin. Aren't they beautiful? Such a sweet smell.

KEVIN: They grow near my house.

MRS. FURY: And how goes the house, Kevin?

KEVIN: Today I put the roof on. It smells sweet under the leaves when the
sun shines on them.

MRS. FURY: When I first came here and this house was new, it smelled sweet.
An odor of bruised wood. Pine. I can even yet come upon it at times.
Very odd times. Like the lilies.

KEVIN: The lilies?

MRS. FURY: Come. I'll show you.

They go to the window and look out.

MRS. FURY (*pointing*): Over there beneath the tree, the oak tree, there was
a patch of lilies once.

KEVIN: They aren't there now.

MRS. FURY: When we came, they were in full bloom. The flowers were white
and heavy. They bent the stems with the weight of their heads. Their
heavy, pregnant heads.

Mrs. Fury has begun to recede from the boy; to talk over his head.

KEVIN: Where are they now?

MRS. FURY: We sat among the lilies. Then we lay. We trampled them. Made
them bleed with our threshing about. Our bodies were soaked in the
scent. We uprooted them.

KEVIN: And they died?

MRS. FURY: The roots dried in the sun. And in the autumn and the darker
days, the wind blew the dried roots. The black wind blew the dried roots

of the lilies against the shuttered windows of the house. The husks were like bubbles. Bubbles blowing on a black wind.

Silence.

KEVIN: Today, I climbed all the way to the top of the house tree. I could see this house. And the oak.

MRS. FURY (*coming back*) : Did you understand, Kevin?

KEVIN: Understand? What?

MRS. FURY: The things I've just said.

KEVIN: No.

MRS. FURY: Not a little?

KEVIN: Maybe a little. More a feeling than anything else.

MRS. FURY: Don't apologize.

KEVIN: I wasn't.

She takes his face in her hands.

MRS. FURY: You were. And that is the start.

KEVIN: Of what?

MRS. FURY: I hope you'll never know. (*She releases him.*) And you saw the oak? Your grandfather's oak?

KEVIN: I could see it. All the way over.

MRS. FURY: Your grandfather built this house beside the oak tree. It is the straightest, tallest oak I have ever seen. He was straight and tall, too. But — but that was before his sickness.

KEVIN: His sickness? What sickness?

MRS. FURY: He got very sick. But before his sickness, he was straight and proud and beautiful. I — I stared at him. I was a girl, then. He wore a blue serge suit and a soft felt hat. It was a Sunday afternoon. I had never seen the man before. My sister and I were walking through the town where we lived. A promenade. I, this girl, told her sister that she stared at the man because he wore brown boots with his blue serge suit. Imagine, she said, brown boots with a blue serge suit! You see, this girl was — was — that is, she prided — yes, prided! — herself on knowing so much — such a great deal — about Taste, Fashion, Food, Art.

Each of these four words as she sounds it has a hollow ring, an echo, a mocking, hollow echo. She laughs.

MRS. FURY: Empty-headed little bitch! So cruel! The ideas she had! But then, poor dear, she had been brought up that way. In her house, the chamber-pots had chintz covers and were called Miss White! Oh, it's true. But the brown-booted man knew nothing of that. When he saw the girl stare at him — he — he stared back. Right back. Burned her with his eyes. He had an awful, fluid, breathtaking quickness. After that, they met many times on the street. They began to smile to each other, slow smiles, at first. Then, the brown-booted man called at the house of the girl's father. He climbed the steps, the ten granite steps, shyly, but with pride, so that he didn't use the handrail. From behind the blinds, the girl watched the man, her heart beating. Safe behind the blinds, her wind broke with fright. She saw his being sent away. The man did not go in anger. He went sweetly, laughing, his pride not diminished. His pride no way diminished. Maybe he had heard her breaking wind. Who knows? The blithe spirit betrayed by its squelching guts. We all have guts, Kevin. Even the most spiritual. He said he'd come back. And he did. Many times. The last time he came back, the girl went with him. She could not be stopped. He took her away.

KEVIN: Where did he take her?

MRS. FURY: To a house. A house that he had built. Beside an oak tree.

KEVIN: We all want to build houses, don't we? Some kind of a house.

MRS. FURY: Who shall you take to yours?

KEVIN: Mine?

MRS. FURY: Your tree house. I know that there's someone you'll take.

KEVIN: You do? There is someone, if she'll come.

MRS. FURY: I knew. But then a funny thing happened. A terribly funny thing! (*She laughs.*)

KEVIN: What was it?

MRS. FURY: You must laugh, Kevin. Promise me you'll laugh. When I tell you to.

KEVIN: I'll laugh. Tell me when.

MRS. FURY: The woman took his boots away. His brown boots. Laugh now. *They both laugh.*

MRS. FURY: In the Palace of Varieties, they make jokes about such things! That was the first of the many terrible things that the woman did to the man, after they had trampled the lilies.

KEVIN: He became sick?

MRS. FURY: He became very sick. Slowly. By degrees.

KEVIN: What about doctors? Didn't he have doctors? And medicine?

MRS. FURY: He had doctors. They hemmed and hawed and cleared their throats and polished their spectacles and seemed very wise. They knew about the body. Had studied it in large, stone colleges.

KEVIN: But they didn't cure him?

MRS. FURY: They didn't cure him. They couldn't. But they used big words.

KEVIN: Doctors always do. Don't they always use big words?

MRS. FURY: Especially when they don't know.

KEVIN: Didn't anybody know?

MRS. FURY: Someone did.

KEVIN: Who? Who knew?

MRS. FURY: The woman. She knew. She knew all the time. And listened to the doctors as they cleared their throats and said their big words and polished up their spectacles and injected — yes, injected — his bending body.

KEVIN: Why didn't she say? Why didn't she tell it to the doctors?

MRS. FURY: Because knowing, knowing fully and completely, she knew that it would make no difference. No difference no matter what she did or said. No difference to Frank Fury. (*She laughs. Her tinkling laugh stops.*) No difference at all . . .

Kevin stares at her. She is silent a moment. Then she laughs, again her tinkling laugh, but now with a touch of bitterness that springs from self-hate. The lights go down.

SCENE 2

The house may be seen behind what now represents the villa. On left and right a door on a frame. The door left has a hinged window above it, and leads to the remainder of the house. The door right gives to the garden. There is a modern sink unit with cupboards around and beneath it. Tubular steel chairs with matching table are rendered in a red the color of dried blood. On the table, the remains of a lonely meal for one. The curtain comes up on a vacant set. A lawnmower is heard for a little while. Voices. The voices come nearer. Mrs. Gage and Kevin come in from the garden.

MRS. GAGE: I'd no idea the sun was so strong.

KEVIN: It's strong.

MRS. GAGE: To do that in such a little while.

KEVIN: Yeah. Funny. It's funny.

MRS. GAGE: Your back's a mass of blisters. That's not funny.

KEVIN: It is? Blisters?

MRS. GAGE: Big red blisters.

KEVIN: Don't know how it could have happened.

MRS. GAGE: I feel terrible.

KEVIN: Just took off my shirt for a little while as I mowed your lawn.

MRS. GAGE: And look at your poor back.

Kevin laughs.

MRS. GAGE: What's wrong?

KEVIN: Nothing! Nothing!

MRS. GAGE: Have I said something awful? I'm always saying awful things. Never realize what I've said till it's out. Then it's too late. Mostly, though, it doesn't matter what I say; nobody hears. I'm usually alone here. Usually say these things to myself. — What have I said?

KEVIN: My back. About my back.

MRS. GAGE: What?

KEVIN: You said "Look at your poor back."

MRS. GAGE: I did, didn't I? Or did I?

KEVIN: Nobody can look at his own back. Except in a mirror. And you didn't mean that. I wouldn't say you meant that. A mirror.

MRS. GAGE: Oh. (*The meaning dawns on her.*) Oh. Oh, I see! Nobody can see his own back!

They are both laughing. Their laughter is an overinvestment. It dwindles.

MRS. GAGE: — Put something on it.

KEVIN: Sorry. I didn't hear?

MRS. GAGE: We — we must put something on it.

KEVIN: That's an idea!

MRS. GAGE: Tomorrow it'll be sore if we don't.

KEVIN: Definitely.

MRS. GAGE: It'll be sore tomorrow. Anyway, that's why I brought you in here. That is why.

KEVIN (*with extravagant innocence*): I know. I know it is.

MRS. GAGE: No other reason.

KEVIN: What other reason?

MRS. GAGE: You've got big, believing eyes. Mr. Gage is a most jealous man.

KEVIN: He looks fierce.

MRS. GAGE: He is fierce.

KEVIN: Like a beast.

MRS. GAGE: What kind of beast? Never thought of that before.

KEVIN: A gargoyle. Guarding the princess in the tower.

Silence.

MRS. GAGE: What can we put on it? Your back?

KEVIN: Olive oil?

He doesn't want her to put olive oil on his back.

MRS. GAGE: I've got some. That what you want? It good?

KEVIN: No. No, it's not what I want.

MRS. GAGE: Then?

KEVIN: I don't know.

MRS. GAGE: Sit up on the table. You're easier to reach.

Kevin sits up.

KEVIN: What about —?

MRS. GAGE: You're a pretty boy. — Yes?

KEVIN: — About that stuff? Know that stuff?

MRS. GAGE: What stuff?

KEVIN: On Mr. Gage? The stuff you use on Mr. Gage?

The statement has come loose almost in spite of Kevin, although he wants it loose.

MRS. GAGE: Oh. That stuff. (*She chills.*)

445

KEVIN: Yeah. I thought that it'd be good.

MRS. GAGE: Good?

KEVIN: For sunburn. You know?

MRS. GAGE: It's not for sunburn.

KEVIN: No?

Mrs. Gage commences to laugh wildly. Kevin looks at her.

KEVIN: I feel foolish!

MRS. GAGE: Depends.

KEVIN: On what? Are you laughing at me?

MRS. GAGE: No.

KEVIN: You're laughing.

MRS. GAGE: Scent. Scent.

KEVIN: That you rub on him?

MRS. GAGE: He likes to smell nice. He sweats a lot. Then he smells like a herd of horses. I've never seen the funny side of it before!

She stops laughing. Silence. She looks suspiciously at Kevin.

MRS. GAGE: You knew. How did you know?

KEVIN: Saw you. I saw you.

MRS. GAGE: How?

KEVIN: From our window. One of our windows.

MRS. GAGE: And you watched?

Kevin nods.

MRS. GAGE: Oh. (*Then quietly.*) Anyway, it was good for a laugh. Now it was good for a laugh.

KEVIN (*not laughing*): Yeah, now. You weren't laughing at me?

MRS. GAGE: No.

KEVIN: I'm young.

MRS. GAGE: Why should I laugh at you?

KEVIN: You might laugh at me because I'm so young.

MRS. GAGE: I wouldn't do that. I'd never do that. It's no disgrace to be young.

KEVIN: No. It isn't.

MRS. GAGE: Young and fresh. Innocent. No wrinkles. Flesh gets ropy. Gooseberries grow on it. Bones come through. If that happens on the outside, what must be happening on the inside? No; it's no disgrace to be young. I know what we'll use.

KEVIN (*at a loss*): What?

MRS. GAGE: On your back.

KEVIN (*eagerly*): Ah, yeah.

MRS. GAGE: Butter.

KEVIN (*terribly let down*): Butter?

MRS. GAGE: What's wrong with butter?

KEVIN: I don't know.

MRS. GAGE: There!

KEVIN: Is butter good?

MRS. GAGE: Why? Isn't it?

KEVIN: You don't know, either.

MRS. GAGE: I'm a little lost.

KEVIN: Lost?

MRS. GAGE: I don't know what to do. It's — it's good. I've heard people say — I think I've heard people say — that butter was good for sunburn. Smear of butter. Two kinds. We've got two kinds.

KEVIN: Of butter?

MRS. GAGE: Salted and unsalted. Bertie — Mr. Gage — eats unsalted butter. He's got blood pressure.

KEVIN: Sick? He's sick?

MRS. GAGE: Blood pressure. Only blood pressure. It's something I don't wonder at. I really don't. But I can't eat it without salt. Which kind do you think you should have? The unsalted?

She is being extremely cruel and in a feminine way, phrasing the words to slant his choice.

KEVIN: I didn't think you'd use butter.

MRS. GAGE: No?

KEVIN: I didn't think that at all. It doesn't matter what kind.

MRS. GAGE: It does. (*She keeps on as before, now more fully deliberate.*) You thought of something exotic? Subtle and exotic. (*She laughs.*) The unsalted won't sting your back. Not if the blisters are broken. (*She picks up the platter from the table.*) But this could be painful.

KEVIN: I'll take that.

MRS. GAGE (*she has judged him exactly*): You sure? The salted? (*The perverse pleasure she feels comes through the words.*)

KEVIN (*shouting*): The salted stuff! The salted! I said the salted!

She commences to smear his back with butter. He winces. He tries to suppress the pain. It pains a good deal. He welcomes the hurt, delights in it.

MRS. GAGE: Around those castles they had moats.

KEVIN: Castles? Aw, yeah.

MRS. GAGE: And snakepits.

KEVIN: And drawbridges on chains. And gargoyles.

MRS. GAGE: And gargoyles. They had gargoyles, too.

KEVIN: Great beasts with fangs and claws.

MRS. GAGE: This is your first time. Isn't it?

KEVIN (*dumbly*): First time?

MRS. GAGE: To play here.

KEVIN: That's a game?

MRS. GAGE: Could be. You've never played here before? Never played and knew you were playing?

They look at each other. Mrs. Gage ceases to rub his back.

KEVIN: No. Never before.

MRS. GAGE: I'm sorry if it hurts.

KEVIN: It doesn't. Not now.

MRS. GAGE: I really am. At first, I wanted to hurt you. Know that?

KEVIN: Why? I haven't done anything. Not to you.

MRS. GAGE: For something that's happened to me. And that's a lot. Quite a lot. I could tell you.

KEVIN: Now. Do you want to hurt me now?

MRS. GAGE: Not now. (*She starts to rub again.*)

KEVIN: It's not so bad now. Your hands, they're more gentle. Why not now?

MRS. GAGE: Because you're young. And this is your first time to play here. Like me, you don't know how the game goes. How it really goes. But for you, this is the beginning. The very, very beginning. Did you see me often? From your window?

KEVIN: A lot. I kept looking for you.

MRS. GAGE: Did you?

She laughs. He nods. He laughs.

KEVIN: I'd see you looking out.

MRS. GAGE: Looking out?

The laughter goes.

KEVIN: And — and dressing sometimes. (*This is a confession.*)

MRS. GAGE (*not giving tone to the words*): Dressing? (*Then.*) Undressing?

KEVIN (*looking down*): Sometimes. That too.

MRS. GAGE: Oh.

Silence.

KEVIN: I own a house.

MRS. GAGE: You? A house?

KEVIN: In the woods.

MRS. GAGE: Each house is a different world, isn't it? People look into the windows of every house except their own.

KEVIN: Up a tree.

MRS. GAGE: What?

KEVIN: My house is up a tree. Made from branches. Up a beech tree.

MRS. GAGE (*gradually becoming excited with him, with his conception of the house*): Branches?

KEVIN: Big green branches!

MRS. GAGE: Like banners?

KEVIN: Yeah. Yeah. Like banners! Big, green banners in the wind.

MRS. GAGE: I've seen them too. Your skin glistens. Banners in the wind. Under the butter sheen. Your skin glistens in the sun. Soft green leaves. Tender.

KEVIN: No one else saw them like that, the branches. No one. Except you. I was afraid you'd laugh at that too. But you haven't.

He is embarrassed at this admission. She notes his embarrassment.

MRS. GAGE: You — you dreamed of making it?

KEVIN: For a long time.

MRS. GAGE: What else did you dream?

KEVIN: What else?

MRS. GAGE: You know.

KEVIN: No.

MRS. GAGE: And now you've made your house.

KEVIN: Now, I have.

MRS. GAGE: I dreamed of a house, too. When I was small. You know. From the time my mother died, and I lived with my father and my aunt in the granite house. It was called that: Granite House.

KEVIN: What kind of house did you dream of?

MRS. GAGE (*a laugh at herself*): One with roses round the door. (*Another laugh.*) Red roses!

KEVIN: You've got those.

MRS. GAGE: Gage gave them to me. He was a friend of my father's. My father was a very friendly man. He sold sugar. Those people he wanted to sell sugar to must have felt like lollipops. He could be that friendly. Gage was a sugar-seller, just like him. Do you know what it is to feel like a lollipop?

KEVIN: He gave you a house with roses round the door.

MRS. GAGE: Blood-red roses. But with the thorns on the stems. Long, sharp thorns. But it got me from the Granite House.

KEVIN: Our house is granite, too.

MRS. GAGE: Your grandfather built it.

KEVIN: For my grandmother.

MRS. GAGE: She doesn't like the other houses that have since come on the hill. Started to reach up to hers. I've seen her look at them. At mine. I mean at Gage's. It isn't mine. Never can be.

KEVIN: It's the way she feels about things.

MRS. GAGE: The way she has to feel. The way she must force herself to feel. I know. There isn't any freedom. The master just changes his clothes. And the master's name is fear. I know that now. And I worry about the compromise, the continual compromise that keeps fear down and loneliness away. Or, I did once. Believe this: once I bathed every day. Unhealthily clean! I was!

Kevin turns to look at her face.

449

KEVIN: Would — would you come to my house in the wood? It's nice there. No thorns.

MRS. GAGE: Seven days since I've had a bath . . . Your house in the woods?

KEVIN: Would you?

MRS. GAGE (*blowing the bubble*): You'd want me to? Really, I mean? *Kevin nods.*

KEVIN: Really.

MRS. GAGE: What way'll I wear my hair? Like this? Or, like this? (*She shows him. She is excited.*) And clothes? How about clothes? Something simple. Elegant but simple. Stupid! Elegance is simplicity! And I'll bathe. We must find an ass!

KEVIN: An ass? What for?

MRS. GAGE: Milk! I must bathe in ass's milk!

KEVIN: I've never milked an ass.

MRS. GAGE: Never mind. Eau de cologne. Strong! Very strong! Corrosive!

KEVIN: We wouldn't have to go together . . .

MRS. GAGE: Wouldn't? Wouldn't? Wouldn't?

KEVIN: I could meet you there.

The bubble bursts.

MRS. GAGE: Oh. Oh. (*Then.*) How old are you?

KEVIN: Old?

MRS. GAGE: That's what I said.

KEVIN: Sixteen. But I'm getting older every day. And I do chest exercises.

MRS. GAGE: Eighteen. I was eighteen when he came. When Gage came. Bertie. Now, I'm thirty. Married when I was twenty two. My aunt didn't want it. But I wouldn't listen. She was always so against everything. I thought at the time it was envy.

KEVIN: And your father?

MRS. GAGE: Did I tell you he sold sugar? That was his business. Know what he did for pleasure? Prayed!

KEVIN: Prayed? For pleasure?

MRS. GAGE: A lot of people do. On his knees. In his room. Before an enormous crucifix. Behind the crucifix, there was palm. Big branches of it.

KEVIN (*in an eerie voice*): Palm?

MRS. GAGE: Palm. When I say that word, I see the branches waving.

KEVIN: But not branches like banners. Plumes. Black plumes. Like at a funeral horse's head.

Silence.

MRS. GAGE: That crucifix . . .

KEVIN (*thankfully clutching at the word*): Crucifix? Crucifix?

MRS. GAGE: It had blood on it from the wounds. Whenever the blood on it got dull in color, my father would touch it up. As I say, he was a friendly

man. Prided himself on being ordinary. Over it again and again in scarlet. He always locked the door when he did this. And when he prayed.

KEVIN: Didn't he pray in church?

MRS. GAGE: Not after my mother died. I used to think it was the collections.
He never went to church. He prayed in his room. Prayed and reddened
up the wounds. Small and dry like a stick. He did all of this with an awful
passion. That was *his* compromise. He had found something to fasten
onto. To keep fear away. Gage came.

KEVIN: When he laughs, his nose touches his chin.

MRS. GAGE: Gage? When they were giving them out, he wasn't behind the
door.

KEVIN: A whopper!

MRS. GAGE: He slapped my father's back. My father's bony back. He rattled
the house with his talk. And looked at me. Kept looking at me. But I
wanted to get away. I thought that he could take me. That at last, I'd
be able to draw in a big deep breath. So silly of me!

She laughs, a wild mocking laugh. It ebbs away. Silence. She hangs her head,
sighs. Kevin looks at her. Compulsively, he stoops and kisses her on the lips.
His action surprises them both. It makes them afraid.

KEVIN (*drawing back*): — Sorry. I'm sorry.

She wipes her lips with the back of her hand.

MRS. GAGE: So am I.

KEVIN: I — I saw your lips.

MRS. GAGE: My lips?

KEVIN: They looked sad. A little bit sad.

MRS. GAGE: My lips looked sad?

KEVIN: They were smiling sadly.

MRS. GAGE: And you kissed them?

KEVIN: It happened. I don't know why it happened. I — I — I'm beginning to
apologize.

MRS. GAGE: Apologize?

KEVIN: I shouldn't apologize. My grandmother says never to apologize.

MRS. GAGE: No? It's all an apology. We apologize all the time for being alive.
And it's easier that way, to go with the wind.

KEVIN: Your lips, I kissed them. The sweetness . . .

MRS. GAGE (*anxious to know: a terrible anxiety*): Sweetness?

KEVIN: They're sweet.

MRS. GAGE: Not sugar-sweet? They're not sugar-sweet?

KEVIN: I don't know. But they're sweet. Soft and sweet. I've — I've never
kissed other lips.

MRS. GAGE: I know.

KEVIN: Don't laugh! Don't laugh!

MRS. GAGE: I wasn't.

KEVIN: Don't . . .

MRS. GAGE: I can tell. I can tell with Bertie too.

KEVIN: Bertie?

MRS. GAGE: Gage. When he comes back. Tell about the women he's been with.

KEVIN: Women?

MRS. GAGE: Bertie is a man of affairs —

KEVIN: What's that?

MRS. GAGE: I've kissed no other lips but Bertie's. And not then. I've never kissed Gage. Gage has kissed me. Always kissed me. And I let him. Because it's the price I pay. My compromise, my apology.

KEVIN: And me. I've kissed you.

MRS. GAGE: You sound so proud.

She laughs. The laugh turns to cries.

KEVIN: Don't do that. What do you want to do that for?

She continues to cry in gentle sobs.

MRS. GAGE: My eyes are sweating.

KEVIN: Is it the kiss? The kiss I tried to kiss you?

MRS. GAGE: It is the kiss. Your kiss.

KEVIN: I've got a strange effect on women.

MRS. GAGE: Very strange.

KEVIN: Sorry, I'm sorry. A towel. I'll get a towel.

He gets a towel from the towel rack on the door to the garden.

MRS. GAGE: I'll stop in a minute.

KEVIN: It'll make your eyes all red.

MRS. GAGE: You wouldn't like that?

KEVIN: No. No.

MRS. GAGE: Gage . . . It's a long time since I've cried. Not since the Granite House. (*She takes the towel then gives it back to him.*) Wet it. Will you wet it, please? I've never thought of tears. Didn't let myself think of tears.

He wets it at the cold tap. She takes it.

KEVIN: I've never seen tears so big.

MRS. GAGE: Think I'll drown you? As I tell you, it's a long time since I've cried.

KEVIN: Must be . . .

MRS. GAGE: Now I gave in. I've never given in since the Granite House. Wouldn't let myself give in.

KEVIN: You could wash the whole world in those big tears.

MRS. GAGE: I doubt it. They're only enough for me. Enough for me and no more. (*She moves the towel about her eyes and face.*) I can taste the salt.

452

KEVIN: In the tears? Like the butter salt?

MRS. GAGE: Nearly. Nearly like the butter salt.

KEVIN: Are you washing the kiss away?

MRS. GAGE: Your kiss? Your kiss?

KEVIN: My — my kiss?

MRS. GAGE: I'm washing away every kiss. All the kisses. To change the taste of my lips. To change the taste, that's why.

She has ceased to cry, but gently continues the washing motion with the towel, over and over, eye to lip, lip to eye. Finally finished, a smile smoulders on her face. It is a tentative smile, a terrible, tentative flicker; but it evokes an echo in Kevin. He smiles as well. She laughs.

KEVIN (*awed and delighted*): You're — you're laughing!

MRS. GAGE: Nearly. Nearly laughing. Let — let me wipe your face.

KEVIN: My face?

MRS. GAGE: With the towel.

KEVIN: That towel?

MRS. GAGE: I know it's wet. Wet with my tears. Do you mind?

KEVIN: Not — not if you want to.

MRS. GAGE: I want to. Bend.

He bends. She wipes his face and lips gently.

MRS. GAGE: The sun has freckled your face.

KEVIN: Little birds. Your hands are like a lot of little birds, hopping about.

MRS. GAGE: I'll wipe your lips. Wipe it all away.

KEVIN: All what away? All what?

MRS. GAGE: The sugar.

KEVIN: Aw, yeah.

MRS. GAGE: Is it all gone?

Kevin licks his lips. He can't make up his mind. He licks them again.

MRS. GAGE: Is it? Is it?

KEVIN: On my lips there's a salt taste now.

MRS. GAGE: A salt taste. Good!

KEVIN: Good?

MRS. GAGE: Now will you kiss me? Kiss me now!

KEVIN: Kiss you? Kiss you?

His voice thins and rises to mirror his terror.

MRS. GAGE: On the lips. Slowly on the lips. Kiss me, and maybe then I can draw that big, deep breath.

A deep silence. She burns him with her eyes.

KEVIN: This isn't a joke?

MRS. GAGE: No joke.

KEVIN: I — I can't. Not if you look at me.

MRS. GAGE: I'll close my eyes. On the lips. Slowly on the lips. My — my eyes are closed.

She waits blindly for his kiss, not striking any attitude. He looks at her. He is near to panic. He looks about. He sees that the door to the garden is still open.

KEVIN: The door. It's open. I'll close the door. I'll need to close the door.

He closes the door and comes back to her.

MRS. GAGE: Now.

KEVIN: All right, now.

MRS. GAGE: Kiss me. Kiss me.

He bends to kiss her. His lips are almost on hers when he wheels his whole body quickly away.

KEVIN (*in anguish*): I can't! I can't!

MRS. GAGE (*opening her eyes*): Can't? You can't?

KEVIN: I — I don't know how!

MRS. GAGE: It doesn't matter.

KEVIN (*enraged at himself*): It does! It does!

MRS. GAGE: I knew you wouldn't. Knew you couldn't. It seemed so simple. So easy.

KEVIN: It isn't easy at all, I can tell you. Nor simple, either.

MRS. GAGE: There has to be the compromise. I shouldn't have asked you.

KEVIN: You shouldn't have had to ask.

MRS. GAGE: I'm glad you didn't.

KEVIN: Glad?

MRS. GAGE: Now I'm glad. For a reason that I hope you'll never know. It's easier to go on and never know.

Kevin stares at her. A door bangs elsewhere in the house. She starts and runs to the door from the kitchen to the house. Kevin continues to stare at her.

MRS. GAGE: Go! Go home! Get out of here!

A booming, fruity voice is heard, off. It is Gage's voice.

GAGE: Surprise! Surprise, my little one! Home! I'm home and it's only Tuesday. Speed, that's my middle name.

Mrs. Gage has her back to the door. She has locked it now.

MRS. GAGE (*to Kevin in an angry whisper*): Get out! Go on!

Kevin can't move.

MRS. GAGE (*to Gage in a squeal of delight*): Oh, Bertie! Bertie! (*To Kevin.*) Didn't you hear what I said?

Gage is outside the door. He is a big man, going bald. He is richly dressed and wears jewelry.

GAGE: I'm home to do a deal with Dead-and-Alive Phibbs, who undertakes to undertake to undertake. Big deal. Involves the old lady. We've really

454

fixed her now. No more, my pet, her haughty look for you to endure. No more. We'll really rub her nose in it. But open the door, baby. Open it.

MRS. GAGE: My big man's home!

GAGE (*his hand on the doorknob*): I have plundered occidental cities for my love! I have carried off silks for her soft skin! And perfume! Perfume to anoint her!

Gage tries the door.

MRS. GAGE (*to Kevin*): Go! For God's sake!

GAGE: A game, my love? Another little game?

MRS. GAGE (*the same squeal of delight*): Bertie! You brute! My big brute!

Gage growls and barks like an animal. Mrs. Gage laughs. It is a simulated laugh for Gage. She looks at Kevin. Kevin looks at her. She makes a gesture with her hand, a drowning gesture, as if she would touch him just once more before the final wave.

GAGE: A small sample of the bounty that I bring!

He throws a black negligee through the fan sash. Mrs. Gage looks at Kevin. Kevin's eyes are on the garment, that now is like a gigantic black moth on the floor. He raises his eyes to meet hers. She shakes her head as if in denial. Kevin doesn't move. She sees that explanations can't be made. She shrugs, sighs. She picks up the garment. She changes, she changes utterly. To Kevin, her words come in a mean coarse tone, but to Gage her voice is silk.

MRS. GAGE (*to Kevin*): Now, will you get out? Get out or you'll see the reason! You'll see! You'll see! (*To Gage.*) It's beautiful, Bertie! Oh, it's beautiful!

GAGE (*intimately*): Open the door, little one. Open it.

MRS. GAGE: I will.

GAGE: I'll break it if you don't.

MRS. GAGE (*cooing*): You wouldn't do that, big man.

GAGE (*silken menace*): Wouldn't I? You know I would.

MRS. GAGE: I know you would.

Gage gives the door a couple of experimental pushes.

MRS. GAGE: You don't have to do that, Bertie! You know you don't! I'll open it!

She looks at Kevin, waits. Kevin picks up his shirt. Suddenly, he puts his shirt to his mouth, and a hand on his belly. He runs into the garden. Mrs. Gage opens the door. Gage comes in. He laughs. Mrs. Gage laughs with him. They tussle over the negligee. Gage pulls it from her. It tears. Gage has the greater piece. He puts it on her neck and knots it, halterwise. This play is accompanied by much laughter from both of them.

GAGE: Down! Down, my little one!

Mrs. Gage gets down on all fours.

GAGE: Neigh! Neigh, my little one!

Mrs. Gage neighs as if she were a horse. Gage flays her flanks with the torn strip of the negligee as she neighs and walks on all fours about the table as the curtain comes down.

Act III

SCENE 1

The lights come up on the house. Now the day has turned. It is thundery. All life wilts in the steamy air. Mrs. Fury reclines in her chair. Kevin, at Mrs. Fury's feet on a hassock, peels an orange and breaks up the peeled orange into segments. Melanie moves about the room in her tentative fashion. She touches various objects, straightens covers, puts newspapers and magazines into their proper places — and she lifts the drapes to look out the window. Her movements are short and sharp, and crackle with nervous energy.

MRS. FURY: Melanie, sit down. This heat. This awful heat. I feel like chicken in aspic.

MELANIE: Leslie . . . Leslie's late . . .

MRS. FURY (*knowingly*): It is the thunder.

MELANIE: Thunder . . . ?

MRS. FURY: Well, you do know he is afraid of it.

MELANIE: Leslie isn't afraid of anything.

MRS. FURY: Oh, yes; you did say he was a lion.

MELANIE: Lion enough, I said.

MRS. FURY: A thunderstorm is quick and violent. We all suffer by comparison. Even Mr. Phibbs, the lion.

KEVIN: It hasn't started yet.

MRS. FURY: It will. Before long. I can feel it.

KEVIN: Thunder doesn't frighten me.

MRS. FURY: Mr. Phibbs is waiting for the storm to pass.

KEVIN: It excites me. I get excited.

MRS. FURY: And when the storm is past, the air is a wonder. The softened air . . .

There is a lightning flash. It streaks the room. Melanie drops the drape and comes from the window.

MELANIE: Deliver us, O Lord! Deliver us!

MRS. FURY (*laughs*): In Heaven, too, if there be such a place, they are probably troubled by the heat. And this is by way of diversion. I can well imagine the guffaw you drew by your outburst, Melanie!

MELANIE: Mother, what makes you so cold? So like a lump of ice?

KEVIN: Your orange, Granny.

MRS. FURY: Exactly the way your grandfather always did it!

MELANIE (*a sharp, deep probe; sure of what she will find*): Exactly, Mother? Exactly?

The rumble of thunder is heard in the suddenly quieted room. Mrs. Fury selects an orange segment with far too much deliberation.

MRS. FURY: Yes, Melanie. Exactly.

MELANIE: It isn't. Mother, you know it isn't.

MRS. FURY (*an awful calm*): Oh. (*She bites the orange and wipes her hands. The whole act is nakedly carnivorous.*)

MELANIE: Your teeth, Mother . . .

MRS. FURY: You say that as if I were a horse.

MELANIE: . . . Sharp . . . Sinking into the soft flesh . . . Car — car —

MRS. FURY: — nivorous? And strong. Sharp and strong for such an old lady. Did — did your father peel my orange differently, Melanie?

MELANIE (*struggling to be defiant*): Mother, why is it so important for you to pretend?

MRS. FURY: Pretend?

MELANIE: I don't have to tell you. That's what you're doing. Pretending again. Starting up again.

MRS. FURY: Strange. I do not recall your father's doing it any dif —

MELANIE: I recall! I recall!

MRS. FURY (*the form of the word changed on her lips by Melanie's words, letting it come softly and easily*): — fer-ent-ly.

KEVIN (*uneasily*): Should I peel *you* an orange, Mother?

MELANIE (*not turning*): You have never seen me eat an orange!

MRS. FURY: Your mother has no taste for oranges, Kevin. No taste at all.

KEVIN: I thought —

MELANIE: Not since my fifteenth birthday.

MRS. FURY: But every day I eat an orange. I like them with lots of blood.

KEVIN: You let me peel them for you.

MRS. FURY: And you do it beautifully. You are a good boy.

MELANIE: *His* fingers aren't bent.

Lightning flash. Melanie cowers at the window, the drape down, her back to them.

MELANIE: Not bent! The orange juice doesn't drop from his fingers! He doesn't mash up the flesh and smile like a fool! Keep smiling like a fool!

MRS. FURY (*sternly, but with less invulnerability*): Melanie! Melanie!

MELANIE (*turning*): Well, does he, Mother? Does he?

MRS. FURY: Kevin, go see if Mr. Phibbs is coming. Go see.

Kevin makes as if to move, but doesn't. He is held.

MELANIE: You want him out of the way. You want him not to hear.

MRS. FURY (*an effort at evenness, almost succeeding*): Hear, Melanie? Hear what? What is there to hear? I am tired of this. So tired.

MELANIE: One thing I can always hear. Your voice.

MRS. FURY (*taken despite herself*): My voice? My voice, Melanie?

MELANIE: *That* voice!

MRS. FURY: It offends you?

MELANIE: Short and sharp. A day that I remember . . .

MRS. FURY: I remember many days . . .

MELANIE: This day, you carried him in on your back.

KEVIN: Who? Who was carried?

MELANIE: My father.

KEVIN: A game? Was it a game?

MELANIE: It wasn't a game. Or, maybe it was. Was it, Mother? A game?

MRS. FURY (*with great weariness*): Game . . . ? A most unusual game. *Silence.*

KEVIN (*almost to himself*): I've seen some games. Some most unusual games . . .

Both women look at him. They are unmindful of the blood-red light that as in Act I again suffuses the villa area. Gage and Mrs. Gage are seen as we last saw them. Mrs. Gage is on all fours. Gage beats her with the strip of cloth. Now the actions are extravagant, over-mimed. Terribly lewd and obscene. But, despite this, we sense the apartness of Mrs. Gage. Her eyes are not in phase with what is going on, with what she seems to be doing so wholeheartedly. Kevin screams, a wild, shattering scream. The blood-red light is shut off suddenly. The villa is gone. Both women are still looking at Kevin. His scream unfreezes them.

KEVIN (*his finger in his mouth*): My finger. I — I bit my finger! (*He is on the verge of tears.*)

MRS. FURY: What is it, Kevin? Are you all right?

MELANIE: What a stupid thing to do!

MRS. FURY: Is it bleeding?

MELANIE: Yes. He's brought blood.

KEVIN: It doesn't pain.

MELANIE: Stupid! Why did you do it?

MRS. FURY: Can we help what we do? Any of us? Show it me, Kevin.

Kevin shows her. It is a tiny wound.

MRS. FURY: You are not dead.

They smile at each other. She tousles his hair.

KEVIN: No. No, I'm not. (*He sits down again.*)

MELANIE: Can you help what you did, Mother?

MRS. FURY: What I did, Melanie?

MELANIE: What you did to him. To my father.

Lightning; great, multiple flashes; then the thunder. After the thunder, quiet — a shuddering quiet that Melanie shears with the thin flute of her voice.

MELANIE: *The day,* the day that I remember, you carried him in on your back from the bedroom. You had washed and dressed him and combed his hair, and done all the other things, all the other sickening things, for him in the bedroom. You did it all for him gently, as if he were a little boy.

MRS. FURY (*tenderly*): A very little boy. Very little boy . . .

MELANIE: He was thanking you all the time, moving his lips. The lapdog look was on his face. He — he couldn't keep the saliva in his mouth. It — it drooled out and over the stubble on his chin, as he thanked you, his head shaking.

MRS. FURY: Melanie, do you know what you are doing to me? I cannot believe that you know.

MELANIE: I know. I know.

MRS. FURY: Yes. I brought him into this room. On my back. His hands were locked under my chin, my hands holding his legs at the knees. He always liked this room.

MELANIE: And he liked the window bay seat.

KEVIN: There? Over there?

MRS. FURY: At first, when we came here we would sit there — just there — looking out at the twilight coming down. At the twilight and at the tree.

KEVIN: The oak? At the oak?

MELANIE: You let him down, gently — as always.

MRS. FURY: You want to keep on, Melanie.

MELANIE: You kept on.

MRS. FURY (*quietly, with self-cruelty*): Yes; I kept on. (*Simply.*) I loved him.

MELANIE: Loved him?

MRS. FURY: I did, Melanie. I did.

MELANIE: You? Love?

Melanie laughs. It is derisive laughter. Mrs. Fury laughs, but her laughter is self-directed. Kevin uneasily joins them, looking from one to the other.

MELANIE: Was it love that made you say it?

MRS. FURY: Say it? I don't know. Say what, Melanie?

MELANIE: He was happy sitting there in the sun. Then you said it. You told him about the house.

MRS. FURY: Ah, the house.

MELANIE: He was talking of it to you. He was slanting his words. He was hoping for praise. Hoping for praise from you. And then you told him.

MRS. FURY: Yes. I told him.

459

MELANIE: You told him what a vulgar place it was. How pretentious. And in what deplorable taste.

MRS. FURY: Is it not?

MELANIE: You showed your smooth white throat and sharp white teeth and you laughed your little laugh.

MRS. FURY: I laughed my little laugh . . . And when the words were coming out, they tore at my throat, pieces of sharp stone passing through . . .

Melanie comes close to her mother to accuse her.

MELANIE: Little silvery laugh. Why couldn't you let him go on being happy, sitting there? Why couldn't you?

MRS. FURY (*looking straight into Melanie's face*): Yes, why couldn't I? This house was wrought when hope was highest, when death — the fact of death — was fully at bay, when he was invincible. In telling him, I was being what he wanted me to be. Nothing else would do. Not for him. No, not for him. Anything else would have been pity. And he was too strong for pity. Melanie, it was he who made me the Goddess. And I couldn't bend down. Not to him.

MELANIE (*straightens up and moves away*): The next day, the day after my fifteenth birthday, Leslie Phibbs came to work for us.

MRS. FURY: He sidled in. Softly, very softly.

MELANIE: He changed everything. The business began to make money again.

MRS. FURY: Out of coffins.

KEVIN: Coffins?

MRS. FURY: He calls them caskets, if you please. As though they were to contain sweets. Or gold. Or precious things. And sells them for different prices. (*This strikes her as funny. She addresses herself to Kevin.*)

MELANIE: Naturally.

MRS. FURY: Naturally?

MELANIE: Well, some are satin-lined. Real satin. I mean —

MRS. FURY: You mean, Melanie?

MELANIE: It is a business. Isn't it a business?

MRS. FURY: Rows and rows of coffins . . .

MELANIE: And Leslie does have a flair for it.

MRS. FURY: As some have a flair for music.

MELANIE: You could call it a gift.

MRS. FURY: From whom? He also has a gift for intrigue.

MELANIE: How cruel!

MRS. FURY: How true! He intrigues against me, now. I feel it.

KEVIN: Against you?

MRS. FURY: His plan, Melanie? You did mention his plan for me.

MELANIE: Mother, you mustn't — (*A truth dawning on her.*) You're afraid, Mother! Afraid of Leslie!

MRS. FURY: One fights fire with fire. What does one use against Mr. Phibbs, Melanie? Mothballs and lavender bags? Whatever he does will be cheap and shabby, like his coffins. But satin-lined. Not real satin, of course.

MELANIE: Leslie has received many testimonials —

MRS. FURY: Unsolicited.

MELANIE: Unsolicited — from people who matter.

Mrs. Fury laughs.

MRS. FURY: But not from *the* people who matter. Hideous brown boxes with smiling scraps of brass. Even — even *that* coffin —

KEVIN: That coffin?

MRS. FURY: Was hideous and cheap. Not, of course, that it mattered. It did not matter. Mr. Phibbs told them how to bring it into the house, the empty coffin.

MELANIE: It sounded like a drum when they thumped it with their hands. They got it into the room, the room where he was, and shut the door.

MRS. FURY: I heard the door shut.

MELANIE: It was shut for a long time.

MRS. FURY: They opened it and called.

MELANIE: Leslie.

KEVIN: My father? They called my father?

MELANIE: He went.

MRS. FURY: The door was closed again.

MELANIE: It was quiet.

MRS. FURY: That awful, awful quiet before — before — before that short, sharp *snap!* (*Mrs. Fury is crying.*)

KEVIN: You're crying!

MELANIE (*in a strange voice*): Mother. Mother, I have never seen you cry before.

KEVIN: Three times today I have seen a woman cry . . .

MELANIE (*coming to her*): Don't, Mother. Don't cry.

MRS. FURY: It is easy to cry, Melanie. Very easy. What happened to your father, he did to himself. I was the Goddess, Melanie. And not merely in play. Always the Goddess. He would not let me be anything else. Did not want me to be anything else. The Goddess — even against myself. I tried to descend. Tried to come down. And he, he would never reach up and pull me down! Never! Not once! Not even once destroy me. And, God, how I ached to be destroyed! Trampled on!

KEVIN: You? Trampled on! By Grandfather!

MRS. FURY: Had he been able, had he once been able, Mr. Phibbs would never have had — never have had to — to — to break his back.

KEVIN: Break his back? My father — my father broke his back?

MELANIE: For the coffin. To fit him into the coffin.

461

MRS. FURY: The snap was short and sharp.

MELANIE: And then, the quiet.

KEVIN: The quiet . . . ?

MRS. FURY: The awful, awful quiet. It began when the girl — when the girl took away the brown boots. A subject for jokes and laughter. When he let the girl take the boots away. But that time the quiet was laughed at. Chased away with laughter. Only to come again. And again it was chased away. Only this time the laughter was less loud. And every time after that that the quiet came back there was less loud laughter to chase it away. Then there was no laughter. None at all . . . only quiet . . . But, still, the house was sick with sound . . . sick . . . sick . . . the silent house . . .

Silence. An enormous flash of light, a great roar of thunder. The room and people in it are wilted in the furious intensity of light and sound. Quiescence. No one moves; all are held in the dusty lifeless room as the lights go down.

SCENE 2

The lights come up on the clearing in the woods. The storm has passed. In its passage, it has wrecked the house in the tree. Branches are strewn about in a capricious, mocking aftermath. Joe Shields and Jean Stringer come in, hand in hand.

JOE (*looking at the wrecked house*): See, I told you. It's wrecked.

JEAN: You told me a lot of things.

JOE: You believed me.

JEAN: I was innocent.

JOE: Stop worrying. I'll take care of you.

JEAN: You will.

JOE: Didn't I? Just now? In the storm? Lucky thing I knew that cave.

JEAN: Yeah.

JOE: Well, wasn't it? He wouldn't know a thing like that.

JEAN: Who?

JOE: Kevin!

JEAN: He was building a house. He gave me flowers to wear in my hair. Said I was Queen of the Forest.

JOE: Crap! Still didn't know about the cave. I knew.

JEAN: His house reached up into the sky.

JOE: Yeah. Till the wind blew it out of it. I knew it would.

JEAN: Caves are holes in the ground.

JOE: Wasn't I right? Look. You can see. It's all down.

JEAN: Holes in the ground. Moles . . . rats . . . rabbits . . .

JOE: He wouldn't let me touch it. But I told him — What?

JEAN: What?

JOE: Moles, rats, rabbits — what?

JEAN: Live in holes in the ground . . .

The lights go down.

SCENE 3

The lights come up on the house. Mrs. Fury, Kevin, and Melanie are as we last saw them. Nothing is changed. Leslie enters. He carries a briefcase. He walks to Mrs. Fury and stands before her. His movements have a new firmness. He is pleased and excited. When he speaks the thrill of pleasure comes through.

LESLIE: Good evening, Mrs. Fury.

MRS. FURY: Ah, Mr. Phibbs. So, the storm is passed.

MELANIE: I wondered. You were late, Leslie.

MRS. FURY: I was doubted, Mr. Phibbs, when I suggested you had found some quiet place to await the storm's abatement.

KEVIN: Were you hiding, Father?

MELANIE: Kevin!

KEVIN: Some hole, Father? With your head down. That where you were? Hiding with your head down some hole?

MELANIE: How dare you!

LESLIE: I have been busy.

MRS. FURY: That, too, I have said.

LESLIE: Ah, but you do know the nature of my business, Mrs. Fury.

MRS. FURY: Only that it some way concerns me, Mr. Phibbs.

LESLIE: How very perceptive you are, Mrs. Fury!

Mrs. Fury inclines her head. She laughs.

MRS. FURY: Perhaps you would be so good as to enlighten me further?

LESLIE (*unzipping his case*): That I shall. With pleasure.

MRS. FURY: Yes. I had not supposed otherwise. There is a thrill in your voice.

MELANIE: Leslie, what have you done? What is it?

MRS. FURY: Savoring the sweetness of revenge, Mr. Phibbs?

MELANIE: Leslie — ?

LESLIE: Be quiet, Melanie!

MRS. FURY: Yes. Do be quiet, Melanie. I must attend on Mr. Phibbs.

Leslie is looking at his papers. His next speech is most calculated. It is delivered with utmost obliqueness.

LESLIE (*his head down, casually*): You know the tree is gone? Lightning.

KEVIN: The tree?

LESLIE: The one out there.

MRS. FURY: You mean the oak, Mr. Phibbs?

LESLIE: Yes. I do mean the oak.

KEVIN: Grandfather's tree . . .

LESLIE: I have had an eye on it for years.

MRS. FURY: Yes, Mr. Phibbs? No doubt you have had.

LESLIE: The timber is sound. Strange, that . . .

MELANIE: Leslie, you wouldn't!

LESLIE: Why not?

MELANIE: But, Leslie — !

LESLIE (*ignoring her*): It was that last great flash that felled it. The snap was very loud.

KEVIN: The snap?

LESLIE: Yes. The snap. That's what I said.

MRS. FURY: Was it short and sharp, Mr. Phibbs?

LESLIE: Yes. As a matter of fact, it — it — (*He realizes what she refers to.*)

MRS. FURY: As the snap when you broke Frank Fury's back? Was it? Do tell me.

Silence.

KEVIN (*going out*): Grandfather's tree! Grandfather's tree broken!

MELANIE: Kevin! Kevin, come back here!

MRS. FURY: Leave him go. He has gone to the woods, I know.

MELANIE: That boy!

MRS. FURY (*sweetly*): But you have news for me, Mr. Phibbs?

Leslie shuffles his papers. He puts them down and looks Mrs. Fury straight in the eye.

LESLIE: Yes. I have news. As you know, by virtue of my position I own the main interest in the business.

MRS. FURY: That is known to me. I also know the manner in which you acquired that interest, Mr. Phibbs.

LESLIE: You have, I believe, commented favorably on my business ability.

MRS. FURY: A neat combination of trickery and fraud.

LESLIE: There are times, Mrs. Fury —

MRS. FURY: When I go too far? Undoubtedly.

LESLIE: This house and lands adjoining are part of the business assets.

MELANIE (*fearful*): Leslie. Leslie.

MRS. FURY: I am listening, Mr. Phibbs.

LESLIE: You honor me.

MRS. FURY: As I would a serpent.

LESLIE: I have sold this house. I, Leslie Phibbs, have sold your fine house, Mrs. Fury. The house your husband built for you with his bare hands. Sold it, I, Leslie Phibbs.

He enunciates slowly, clearly. He laughs. It is a nervous, excited laugh, but of an inner tension.

MRS. FURY (*partly rising*) : Sold it? Sold it?

MELANIE: You can't. You mustn't! You mustn't, Leslie! You mustn't!

MRS. FURY (*subsiding*) : Sold the house?

LESLIE: To Gage. To Gage, the dealer in sugar who lives in the villa.

MRS. FURY: Gage? To Gage?

LESLIE: He wanted it. Always wanted it. For his wife. She has always had an eye on it. Always wanted to live here, the highest house on the hill. So she could look down, he says.

MRS. FURY: To look up is much the easier.

MELANIE: Leslie — Leslie, you've done a terrible thing.

LESLIE: I have plans.

MRS. FURY: Plans, Mr. Phibbs? You have more plans?

LESLIE: Many more.

MELANIE: Haven't you planned enough, Leslie? Done enough hurt?

LESLIE: I intend to build a new house.

MRS. FURY: Even you . . . ?

LESLIE: My own house. I can see it in my mind's eye.

MRS. FURY: No doubt you can, Mr. Phibbs.

LESLIE: Large. I want a large house. With wide walls.

Mrs. Fury begins to see the humor in Leslie's description of his house.

MRS. FURY: Wide walls, Mr. Phibbs?

LESLIE: Of stone!

MRS. FURY: Stone?

LESLIE: Built to last! I shall leave my mark! I shall! I shall!

MRS. FURY: To last? To last? Your mark? You shall? You shall?

LESLIE: Yes! Yes! And a tower! A square stone tower!

MRS. FURY: Up? or down, Mr. Phibbs? The tower?

LESLIE: — On which I shall put a telescope.

MRS. FURY: So that you can look at the stars?

LESLIE: It will be seen for miles, this tower! Miles . . . ! (*He reins in.*) How did you know? How did you know?

MRS. FURY: I knew. I knew. (*She looks about the room.*) And all this is no more. Frank Fury's house is gone. And the oak is gone. And I am free. You, Mr. Phibbs, have set me free. It's all over now. All over. Funny, is it not? Is it not funny?

Mrs. Fury exits; a tinkling laugh. A sudden silence settles on the room.

LESLIE (*quelled*) : She laughed at me. Your mother laughed at me.

MELANIE: No, she didn't.

LESLIE: You heard her.

MELANIE: She wasn't laughing at you.

LESLIE: No?

MELANIE: Not at you in particular.

The lights go down.

SCENE 4

The lights come up on the wood. Jean and Joe sit and watch as Kevin looks at what remains of his house in the tree.

JOE (*a little, uneasy laugh*): Well, I told you, Kevin. You've got to admit it. Didn't I tell you?

JEAN: Stop crowing.

KEVIN: It's down. My house is down.

JOE: That's what I said. Some wind! Didn't I say about the wind?

JEAN: The wind can't get into a cave. (*She says this sadly.*)

JOE: I know it can't! You watch: the sun: it'll make those leaves curl up. They'll all curl up and go brown. (*He breaks a branch.*) Dead already. The sap's all gone.

A little silence. Kevin walks about what's left of the house. Jean and Joe look at him.

JOE: Hear about me, Kevin?

KEVIN: Huh?

JOE: Jean and me?

JEAN: Don't tell him.

JOE: Why? It's all right.

JEAN (*not at all sure; a little lost*): Is it? Is it, Joe?

JOE: 'Course it is! Stop moaning!

JEAN: I wasn't moaning.

JOE: Sounded like it to me. Sounded very like it to me. What did it sound like to you, Kev?

KEVIN: Like you were married.

JOE: There! See!

JEAN: He's not far wrong, is he?

JOE (*flexing his muscles*): Hey Kev, look at me! I'm going to be a daddy!

KEVIN: Yeah?

JOE: Well, what do you think?

KEVIN: What's there to think?

JOE: It's something, isn't it?

JEAN: Yeah.

KEVIN: People are doing that all the time.

JOE (*lowering his arms*): Yeah, they are, aren't they?

466

KEVIN: All the time. People keep doing it. Children get born.

JEAN: Our baby'll be different.

KEVIN: Everyone says that.

JEAN: I believe it.

KEVIN: They believe it, too, Jean.

JEAN: Our baby'll be different from Joe, different from me. It'll be easy for him.

JOE: A boy already!

JEAN: We'll make it easy for him. We'll put him right.

JOE: Wise him up, like.

KEVIN: You will?

JOE: Yeah. Me. I'm his daddy, aren't I?

JEAN: And I'm his mammy.

JOE: We'll get a place to live.

JEAN: It doesn't have to be big. Not at the beginning. But we'll improve.

KEVIN: A place of your own? Your own house?

JEAN: Yeah.

JOE: Yeah. Yeah.

JEAN: I'm going. Come on, Joe.

Jean walks off. Kevin and Joe look at each other. Joe shrugs his shoulders and follows Jean off. Kevin walks about his house again. Finally, he sits down amid the ruins. Mrs. Fury's voice is heard calling, off.

MRS. FURY (*off*): Kevin? Kevin?

Kevin stands up. Mrs. Fury comes into the clearing.

MRS. FURY: Ah, here you are. I have been searching for a long time. I am quite out of breath.

KEVIN: It's down.

MRS. FURY: Your house?

KEVIN: Yes. It's true, isn't it?

MRS. FURY: What is, Kevin?

KEVIN: Everything falls.

MRS. FURY: Everything.

KEVIN: Falls down and dies. Nothing lasts.

MRS. FURY: Oh, things last, Kevin. They last — but not for long. Therein lies their beauty.

KEVIN: Like us, they die.

MRS. FURY: Like us. And we are beautiful — *can* be most beautiful. But we must look up. Keep looking up. Never down. We cannot afford to look down, Kevin.

KEVIN: It's always there, isn't it? Death, dying?

MRS. FURY: Always. People give to it too much importance.

KEVIN: They do?

MRS. FURY: Some people. Because of it — to deny the fact of it — houses are built, battles are fought, trophies are raised, love is made. Even love is made . . . Remember, Kevin. Do not apologize. You must never apologize for being. You did not ask to come. You are here. And here is now.

GLOSSARY

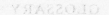

♣ *GLOSSARY* ♣

A Chairde Ghael! O, Uh, Gu, Bo, Boola, Bo, Wo, Bow, Bow: Keane is satirizing drill in basic Irish
amach mo chroi istigh: with all my heart
amadan: fool
asthore: my treasure
Árus an Uachtarán: House of the President
avic: my son
blithero: rotten drunk
bodhrán: a shallow drum or tambourine, struck with the knuckles or a short two-headed stick
bollav: dumb
bonav: a little pig
bone-tapper: a man who taps time on the rib-bones of a cow
boyo: lad
cabóg: a sexless person
china: pal, buddy
civic guard: an Irish policeman
coulogeous: terrific
cully: pal, friend
currach: a coracle or little wicker boat
dawny: small, delicate, pale
dekko: look
Dia linn: God help us!
dixie: a small, lidded can used for tea, stew, etc.
draoidheact: magic
drisheen: black pudding

duchas: human nature
folbo: a bold person
fostooks: a thick fellow
gadhail: a reaping hook
gaisceach: a brave man
gansey: a seaman's jersey
gearrcach: a young bird, a fledgling
geowckacks: silly people
gob: mouth
gommalogue: a fool
Gogaí ó gog: the beginning of an Irish poem in which a bird asks something like this: "Eggie, o egg, where shall I build my nest?" The phrase itself is a nonsense jingle reminding one of eggs but incapable of translation.
Gold Flake: a popular cigarette
gombeen: usurer
gorsoon: a pronunciation of "gossoon" or boy
grig: kidding, joking
halk: a clever person in his own estimation
heggins, by: an exclamation similar to "by gosh!"
jewked: defrauded
Leopardstown: site of a popular race course
leppin': leaping
looberas: twisted men
mohill: a body of workmen

napoo: finished, dead, nothing doing

naygerly: niggardly

Paddy, this small: a wee bottle of whiskey

pizawn: a bitter little fellow

plank: put or set down

pooleen: a little pool

pritchel: a sharp pointed instrument used for punching the nail holes in horseshoes

puck: hit, smack

rawser: uncomplimentary Dublinese for "policeman"

ropaire: a plunderer

ruskey: fleecy

segotia: a term of endearment, as in the expression "my old segotia" (or "segocia")

short-taken: he should have been better employed

slean: a spade used for turf cutting

slingeing: slinking

spancelling: fettering

stimless: blind

sugawn: a straw rope

Suas ar an Ardan: up on the platform

tamaill: a little while

T'anam an deel: In the name of God

Taoiseach: Prime Minister

tape: to size up, to detect

Tilley lamp: a very bright oil lamp in which the oil burned is vaporized

trippols of finnaun: clumps of rough grass by the sea

ullagoning: crying

yoke: apparatus, gadget, gun